MH & xmh

E-mail for Users and Programmers

MH & xmh Road Map

What to Read

Don't be intimidated by the size of this book: MH and *xmh* are easy to learn and use. You can use MH or *xmh* right away by reading the quick-start tutorials. The rest of the book is here to help you do much more, but you don't need to read it all!

Need to Get Started in a Hurry?

The quick-start tutorials have the basics of reading and sending mail. You'll be using MH or *xmh* right away.

First, do the short setup in Chapter 3. Then:

- To get started with MH, read Chapter 4.
- To get started with *xmh*, read Chapter 14.

If you find that you need more e-mail basics, refer to Chapter 1.

Finding the Good Stuff

Some questions come up again and again: "How can I do ...?" You'll find a list of commonly-asked questions, with a reference to the part of the book that explains them, at the end of each quick-start tutorial.

Have More Time?

This road map suggests what you should read, depending on your background and your needs.

If you aren't using the X window system:

- To get a complete understanding of MH, read Chapters 1 through 11. Browse through the programs in Chapter 13 to see if any look useful to you. Get familiar with the manual pages in Appendix I and the MH Reference Guide at the end of this book. Read Appendices A and E; glance at Appendix D.

- Wizards-to-be should read all of Parts I through III. Read your online manual pages and notice the obscure information that this book doesn't cover. Read Appendices A, C, E, and F; browse Appendix D.

For X window system users:

- If you'd like to get familiar with all of the features of *xmh*, read all of Parts I and IV. In Appendix I, read the *xmh* manual page and the first *mh* manual page. Glance at Appendix D and the xmh Reference Guide.

- To be a real *xmh* wizard—to understand how *xmh* works with MH and how to extend and customize it—first read Parts I and IV. Then read Parts II and III and also Appendices A, F, and G. Pay particular attention to the sections with X in their headings. Read through all of your online MH and xmh manual pages.

MH & xmh

E-mail for Users and Programmers

Jerry D. Peek

O'Reilly & Associates, Inc.
103 Morris Street, Suite A
Sebastopol, CA 95472

MH & xmh: E-mail for Users and Programmers ⁕

by Jerry D. Peek

Editor: Tim O'Reilly

Printing History:

January 1991:	First Edition.
August 1991:	Minor corrections.
September 1992:	Second Edition.
November 1992:	Minor corrections.
August 1993:	Minor corrections.

ISBN: 1-56592-027-9

Table of Contents

Figures

Examples

Tables

Preface

The MH Message Handling System is a set of electronic mail programs in the public domain. If your computer runs UNIX, it can probably run MH. MH is free, powerful, flexible—and the basics are easy to learn. This book starts with an introduction to electronic mail; if you've never used e-mail, that's a good place to start. Next is an overview of MH and then a tour of MH 6.7. You can start sending and reading mail with MH right away, by following the examples and step by step instructions in the tour. In just a few pages, you'll have the flavor of the system and a hint of the advanced features.

This book also covers *xmh*, a way to use MH from the X Window System Version 11 Release 5. (*xmh* under X11 Release 3 is fairly different, but you shouldn't have much trouble using it with the instructions for Release 4. For a user, *xmh* with Release 4 is almost the same as the Release 5 version.) *xmh* runs MH commands with an X interface using windows, buttons, and a mouse. Again, there's a step-by-step tour that will have you sending and reading mail within a few pages.

The tour through MH is for anyone who understands the basics of UNIX (how to log in, type command lines, and use a text editor like *vi* or GNU *emacs*). You don't need to be a UNIX expert to read and send mail with MH. The tour for X users assumes you know the basics of X and of your window manager. Other chapters build on these tours to show you more features and help you customize the programs if you want to. Chapter 12, *Introduction to Shell Programming for MH*, explains how to program with MH and the UNIX shell—to get the most out of it, you should have done some computer programming. Chapter 13, *MH Shell Programs*, shows some useful shell programs that use MH. But even if you've never programmed, you should be able to get most of these programs running with just a little help from a friend. The programs are explained in detail. This book's index will point you to explanations of the concepts.

Why Choose MH?

The big difference between MH and most other mail user agents is that you can use MH from a UNIX shell prompt. In MH, each command is a separate program, and the shell is used as an interpreter. So all the features of UNIX shells (pipes, redirection, history, aliases, and so on) work with MH—you don't have to learn a new interface. Other mail agents have their own command interpreter for their individual mail commands (although the *mush* mail agent simulates a UNIX shell). For more information and examples, see Chapter 1, *MH and xmh*, and Chapter 4, *Tour Through MH*.

If you use X, you'll be comfortable with *xmh* right away. *xmh* lets you use the most common MH commands without typing them. The *xmh* interface also makes complex MH commands like *pick* easier to use. But if you need to do something more, you can just open an *xterm* window and type MH commands. The description of *xmh* is in Chapter 14, *Tour Through xmh*.

Why Read This Book?

The set of documents that comes with MH 6.7.2 (the latest version, as of this writing) is more complete than what you get with a lot of programs in the public domain. But the documentation is big and is organized by command name, not by task. The tutorials in it are okay for getting started, but harder to use if you want to learn more than the basics. The *xmh* manual pages are fairly complete but don't have many examples; they also assume that you have other X documentation.

This book summarizes what I've learned in ten years of using MH as a user, an instructor, a programmer, and a system administrator. It has the basics you'll need to get started. Then, it leads you through more advanced features, topic by topic. Here's where you'll learn the real power in this mail system. I'll explain the documented and undocumented features, point out some of the bugs, show you how to configure MH (MH is *very* configurable), and share tricks that I've learned for doing things faster and better.

What's in This Book

The book is divided into five parts. The *MH & xmh Road Map* on the first page past the front cover suggests the chapters you might want to read, depending on your background and needs. The following list describes each chapter and appendix.

This book is organized so that beginners don't have to read all the chapters to get the information they need. Therefore, information on some commands is spread across several chapters. Extensive cross-references point to other related information. The index lists topics and concepts.

Part I has overall information about both MH and *xmh*.

Chapter 1, *MH and xmh*, provides a quick overview.

Chapter 2, *MH and the UNIX Filesystem*, shows how MH and *xmh* use the UNIX filesystem.

Chapter 3, *Setting Up for MH and xmh*, makes sure that your account is set up for MH and gets you ready for Chapter 4, *Tour Through MH*, and Chapter 14, *Tour Through xmh*.

Part II has detailed explanations and examples of MH commands. Because *xmh* actually runs MH commands, *xmh* users will get insight into the program here.

Chapter 4, *Tour Through MH*, gives a guided tour of basic MH. This is all you need to start using MH.

Chapter 5, *Reading Your Mail with MH*, covers commands that read messages.

Chapter 6, *Sending Mail with MH*, covers commands that send messages.

Chapter 7, *Finding and Organizing Mail with MH*, contains lots of information and tips about MH folders, sequences, and commands that help you organize and find messages.

Part III describes customizing and programming MH. *xmh* users can take advantage of this, too, in customizing xmh. There's an introduction to UNIX Bourne shell programming.

Chapter 8, *Making MH and xmh Work Your Way*, explains how to customize MH and *xmh* with MH configuration files.

Chapter 9, *New Versions of MH Commands*, shows how to make new versions of existing MH commands easily. The chapter has lots of useful examples.

Chapter 10, *MH Formatting*, explains the mysterious MH formatting syntax that lets you display messages and message summaries exactly as you want them.

Chapter 11, *Processing New Mail Automatically*, gives lots of detail and examples on the tersely-documented features in the *mhook*(1) and *rcvstore*(1) manual pages.

Chapter 12, *Introduction to Shell Programming for MH*, introduces UNIX Bourne shell programming, plus tips on shell programming with MH. It has the techniques you'll need for understanding the next chapter.

Chapter 13, *MH Shell Programs*, digs in and shows how to extend the MH system to make some new and useful mail programs with the Bourne shell. Several of the programs work with *xmh*. This chapter should give you plenty of examples to use yourself—and to go from if you want to program with MH.

Part IV is about *xmh*.

Chapter 14, *Tour Through xmh*, gives a guided tour through *xmh*—all you need to start using it.

Chapter 15, *Using xmh*, describes buttons, windows, and other interactive features of *xmh* in detail.

Chapter 16, *Customizing xmh*, shows how you can customize *xmh* to change the way it looks and works.

Part V, the Appendices, have related information.

Appendix A, *Where Can You Go from Here?*, suggests ways to do more with MH.

Appendix B, *Early History of MH*, was written by two of the people involved with MH at the start.

Appendix C, *Reference List*, gives a list of reference books, articles, and other documents.

Appendix D, *Converting Messages to MH*, shows techniques and programs for converting from other mail systems to MH/*xmh*.

Appendix E, *Copies of Files Over the Network*, shows how to use *ftp*, *uucp*, and electronic mail to get copies of many of the files and shell programs in this book.

Appendix F, *The execit Programs*, has *execit*, a way to run MH programs with new names.

Appendix G, *Customizing xmh: Configuration Files*, contains copies of *xmh* configuration files.

Appendix H, *Glossary*, defines UNIX, e-mail, *xmh*, and MH terms.

Appendix I, *Manual Pages*, has selected MH and *xmh* user manual pages.

The *Reference Guide* is a chart that lists the MH and *xmh* commands and features covered in this book.

How to Read This Book

MH is a rich, sophisticated set of programs which let you do an incredible number of things with e-mail. *xmh* is versatile and customizable. You might not want to learn all the features now, though. There's a "road map" for this book inside the front cover. The road map has some suggestions on what you should read, depending on your background and your needs.

New in the Second Edition

This second edition has been updated for X Release 5 and MH 6.7.2. Other changes include:

- A new Chapter 11, *Processing New Mail Automatically*, on the powerful *mhook* features.

- There's a new *xmh* Reference Guide in the purple pages. The existing MH Reference Guide has been expanded.

- Chapter 13, *MH Shell Programs*, has three new programs. *edprofile* lets *xmh* users change the way that commands work by clicking a button. *mysend* is an MH *sendproc* that edits your messages as you send them—it's configured to add a "signature" to the ends of messages, but you can edit it to do almost anything else. *autoinc* handles a batch of incoming mail automatically.

  Many programs from the first edition have been improved. The *rmmer* message-removing script is more efficient; it will also prompt for confirmation before removing messages from certain folders. The *replf* and *fixsubj* shell programs have been replaced (though they're still in the book's online archive; see Appendix E).

- The index has been expanded.

- The *xmh* file *.xmhcheck*, for incorporating mail from many mailboxes, is covered.

- Chapter 10, *MH Formatting*, has more examples. It also explains new *mh-format* features introduced in MH 6.7.2.

- The Release 5 *xmh* is much more flexible with its optional external editor and the *XmhShellCommand* for running any UNIX shell command. See Chapter 16, *Customizing xmh*.

- New sections tell how to handle packed mail files with *packf* (Section 7.10) and use the MH-like "mail shell" *msh* (Section 7.11).

- There are even more tips for using MH and *xmh* in real applications, including new time-saving aliases, buttons, and command versions. Several new sections show how to use UNIX links to organize your mail.

- Appendix B, *Early History of MH*, should give you some insight into why MH is the way it is.

- I've incorporated lots of reader comments and suggestions. (If you have more, please send them! The address is in the section called "Request for Comments" below.)

What Isn't in This Book

This book doesn't cover the MH front ends like GNU *emacs mh-rmail*, *plum*, and *mhe* or *mh-e*. There's just a brief explanation of the POP (Post Office Protocol) features. UCI BBoards aren't covered.

This is a book for MH users. It doesn't explain how to install or maintain the MH software. That could take another book to explain.

Conventions Used in This Book

Italic   is used for the names of all UNIX utilities, switches, directories, and filenames and to emphasize new terms and concepts when they are first introduced.

Bold   is used occasionally within text to make words easy to find. For example, it is used with line numbers in the descriptions of files and programs—just like movie stars' names in the People section of your local newspaper . . .

`Constant`   is used for sample code fragments and examples. A reference in
`Width`   text to a word or item used in an example or code fragment is also shown in constant width font.

`Constant`   is used in examples to show commands or text that would be typed
`Bold`   in literally by the user.

`Constant`   is used in code fragments and examples to show variables for
`Italic`   which a context-specific substitution should be made. (The variable `filename`, for example, would be replaced by some actual filename.) Constant italic is also used to highlight line numbers in examples (like `12>`). These line numbers are not part of the file; they are for reference only.

function(n)   is a reference to a manual page in Section *n* of the UNIX programmer's manual. For example, *mh-format*(5) refers to a page called *mh-format* in Section 5.

☒   marks a section or chapter containing information about *xmh*. This makes it easy to find *xmh*-related information in the MH sections.

%   is the C shell prompt.

$ is the Bourne shell prompt.

. . .   stands for text (usually computer output) that's been omitted for clarity or to save space.

:-)   is an "electronic smiley face", a convention in electronic communication. It means "don't take that seriously."

CTRL   stands for a control character. To create $\boxed{\text{CTRL-D}}$, for example, hold down the "control" key and press the "d" key. Control characters are not case sensitive; "d" refers to both the uppercase and lowercase letter. Control characters are also shown with a caret (^) and the letter, as in ^D.

META   stands for a Meta character. Meta characters are written as follows: if the character is a lowercase letter, the meta character will appear as $\boxed{\text{META-C}}$. If the character is an uppercase letter, the meta character will appear as $\boxed{\text{META-}\uparrow\text{C}}$. To create $\boxed{\text{META-C}}$, for example, hold down the "Meta" key and press the "c" key. To make the $\boxed{\text{META-}\uparrow\text{C}}$ character, hold down both the "Meta" key and the $\boxed{\uparrow}$ (shift) key and press the "c" key.

The Meta key isn't always labeled "Meta". Some keyboards don't have Meta keys, in which case you'll have to use another command to do what you need.

Request for Comments

Please tell us about any errors you find in this book or ways you think it could be improved. Our U.S. mail address, phone numbers, and e-mail addresses are:

O'Reilly and Associates, Inc.
103 Morris Street, Suite A
Sebastopol, CA 95472
in U.S. and Canada 1-800-998-9938,
international +1-707-829-0515.
FAX 1-707-829-0104

Internet: bookquestions@ora.com   UUCP: uunet!ora!bookquestions

Acknowledgments

You wouldn't be reading this book without all the help I got from people and organizations.

The RAND Corporation placed MH in the public domain; The University of California at Irvine maintains it. A lot of the popularity of MH (and development of *xmh*) are probably due to this—also, of course, to the efforts of authors, maintainers and the many other people who've helped with MH and *xmh*.

Two employees of RAND, Phyllis Kantar and Isaac Salzman (who is now at Sun Microsystems, Inc.), reviewed this book and gave me other helpful information. Bruce Borden, who did much of the early MH work at RAND, gave me perceptive and useful comments about the first edition.

Terry Weissman of Silicon Graphics, Inc. reviewed the book and wrote the history of *xmh*. Donna Converse of the MIT X Consortium reviewed the *xmh* chapters, sent an example I used, and more, on a tight schedule. Big thanks to Einar A. Stefferud at the University of California, Irvine, his colleagues and students, including James McHugh, Jerry N. Sweet, Nanette Lee, Selina Wan, Steven Chou, Wai-Hung David Lee, Simi Dhaliwal, Jimmy Man—and Frances J. Tong, who read the book several times. John L. Romine of U.C. Irvine put me in touch with Stef and helped in other ways, too. Edward Levinson of Accurate Information Systems reviewed this and more. Some *xmh* customizations came from Michael J. Edelman of Sequent Computer Systems, who also reviewed this book. Eli Charne reviewed the book and told me about using *burst* to extract returned mail messages. Edward Vielmetti of MSEN, Inc., sent the nice *folder @.* trick. Eric Koldinger of the University of Washington Department of Computer Science and Engineering sent material used here about the "Send and Close" *xmh* button. My father, H. Milton Peek, read the first edition and did a superb proofreading job.

Thanks to several people and departments at Syracuse University: Paul M. Jackson, who read much of the draft; Academic Computing Services for laser printing and my manager at ACS, John Holt, for flexibility in my work schedule.

Of course, you wouldn't be reading this without the great people at O'Reilly & Associates—including Tim O'Reilly, who gave me the chance to write my first book and took time to help me along the way.

Finally, my wife Robin encouraged me, had faith in me and kept her sense of humor through the very, very busy months before the first edition. I couldn't have done this without her.

Part I:

Introduction to MH
and xmh

Part I has a general overview of electronic mail that emphasizes MH and xmh. It explains how MH works with UNIX. It also explains how to set up for using MH and xmh.

MH and xmh $\boxed{\text{X}}$

What is E-mail?
How UNIX E-mail Works
Addressing E-mail
MH Profile
What Computers Support MH?
History
Obtaining MH and xmh

This chapter starts with an introduction to electronic mail: we'll take a quick look at how e-mail is sent and how UNIX handles it. There's a brief comparison of MH, *xmh*, and other UNIX mail agents. Whether you've used other mail agents or not, this chapter should help you understand why (and how) MH is special. Next are some guidelines for addressing e-mail. Following that is an overview of the important file called the MH profile. The chapter ends with a brief history of MH and *xmh* and tells you about the latest versions.

For a quick overview of the important parts of this book, see the *MH & xmh Road Map* just past the front cover.

1.1 What is E-mail?

Electronic mail, often called "e-mail," is a way to communicate with people as close as your office or as far away as the other side of the world. You type a message and put addresses on it; e-mail programs use your computer and a network such as the Internet to deliver the message. E-mail programs run everywhere from microcomputers to supercomputers (of course, this book covers MH and *xmh* e-mail programs, which run under UNIX). The people who read your messages don't have to use the same mail system as you do; their computers don't even need to run UNIX. Many computer networks are connected to each other, and there are more connections made every week.

Messages usually arrive anywhere from a few seconds to a few hours after they're sent. (They're held at computers along the way if a connection can't be made; also, some computers send mail in batches periodically.) The recipient can read your message, print it, send a reply to you and other people who were copied, file it, remove it...right away or whenever it's convenient.

E-mail is getting to be a part of life. It connects people on all kinds of computers, handles an uncountable number of messages every day, and lets you stay in contact when you're not in your office. E-mail provides a handy way to get information to and from busy people without playing telephone tag or interrupting them with a phone call. You can use e-mail to announce or arrange meetings, discuss problems, share opinions among members of a group, and much more. Of course, e-mail isn't the answer for everything. You usually can't e-mail graphics (nontext files) or very large text files without special handling. Sometimes a phone call or a FAX is easier and quicker.

1.2 How UNIX E-mail Works

In general, each UNIX computer has two kinds of programs that handle mail:

- A *user agent* is a mail program that humans use. It collects the mail messages you send and shows messages you receive. (MH and *xmh* are user agents.) The user agent is an interface to the second kind of program: the *transport agent*.

- A *transport agent* is a "system" program that you usually don't run directly. It accepts messages from the user agent and routes them to their destinations. A transport agent usually also delivers mail into each user's *system mailbox*, a file where the user agent can get the new messages that other people send you. But a *mail hook* program can intercept and process the message before your mailbox—see Chapter 11, *Processing New Mail Automatically*.

There are lots of user agent programs and there are several common transport agents. Figure 1-1 is a diagram that shows what happens when you send a message. Your user agent collects the message and gives it to your computer's transport agent. Your transport agent either delivers the message if you're sending it to someone on your computer or sends the message across a network to another computer's transport agent. Then the person you sent the message to runs a user agent to bring in the message from the system mailbox, read it, and (maybe) to print it, reply to it, delete it, etc.

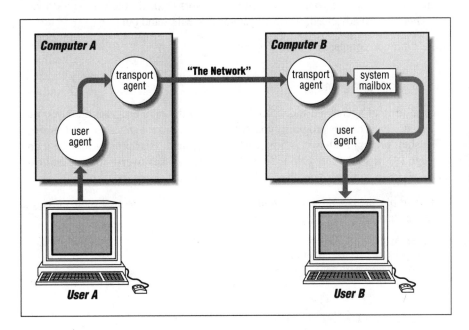

Figure 1-1. How a mail message gets from A to B

1.2.1 E-mail Transport Agents

Mail transport agents (MTAs) are complicated programs. They have to understand all kinds of nasty details about message addressing, networks, error handling, and other functions. Some typical MTAs are *sendmail* and MMDF. This book doesn't cover transport agents.

1.2.2 E-mail User Agents

If you send and receive only a few e-mail messages, you probably don't need to learn much about it. Almost any user agent will do (and there are a lot of them). MH and *xmh* are fine for beginners: there are just a few basic concepts and commands to learn.

But when you start to do more with e-mail, you'll want a user agent that saves you time, lets you organize messages the way you want to, and helps you find messages you've stored. You'll probably want to automate routine work. You might even customize your e-mail setup so it works exactly the way you'd like it to. This is when advanced, flexible systems like MH stand out.

Here's a quick comparison of user agents.

Monolithic Mail Agents

Most user mail agents are monolithic: you're in the mail program until you quit out of it. To start the program, you type its name, like *mail*, at a shell prompt. (The shell prompt is shown as a percent sign (%) here; your prompt may be a dollar sign ($) or something else.) Then that program takes over—it reads and executes all the commands you type until you use its *quit* command.

For example, here's how you would read, print, and delete two mail messages with the standard UNIX program named *mail*:

```
% mail
Date:  Mon, 07 Dec 92 07:53:55 EST
From:  nancyo (Nancy O'Leary)
To:  jdpeek
Subject:  meeting

I'm free at 3 today.  Is that okay?

? s toprint
Date: Mon, 07 Dec 92 08:54:22 EST
From: biffj (Biff Jameson)
To: jdpeek
Subject: the meeting

I can be there at 11 or 3 today.

? s toprint
% lpr toprint
% rm toprint
```

You show the first message on the screen. At the first prompt (which is a question mark (?) in this program), you give the command to save the message in a file named *toprint*, which also automatically deletes the message. (You're saving to a file because you can't print directly from this particular *mail* program.) You read and save the next message in the same file *toprint*. The mail agent automatically quits because it's given you all the messages. Then you print the messages you saved and delete the *toprint* file.

Some mail agents have more commands built in. For instance, many have a command for printing a message directly. A lot can send a reply to or a copy of a message. Some let you organize messages into groups. Most also let you type a single UNIX command without leaving the mail agent: that's called a *shell escape*.

Monolithic mail agents keep all of the messages in your system mailbox or a file in your account named something like *mbox*. These are single files which hold all mail messages together. The messages are separated in one of several ways. The mail agent knows how to parse (split) them into separate messages, but this format makes it harder to do complex things like rearranging the order of the messages.

MH

Here's the same example using MH. Because MH commands aren't part of a monolithic mail agent, you type all the commands at the shell prompt:

```
% inc
Incorporating new mail into inbox...
   1+ 12/07 Nancy O'Leary     Meeting<<I'm free at 3 today.  Is that
    2  12/07 Biff Jameson      the meeting<<I can be there at 11 or 3
% show
(Message inbox:1)
Date: Mon, 07 Dec 92 07:53:55 EST
From: nancyo (Nancy O'Leary)
To: jdpeek
Subject: meeting

I'm free at 3 today.  Is that okay?
% next
(Message inbox:2)
Date: Mon, 07 Dec 92 08:54:22 EST
From: biffj (Biff Jameson)
To: jdpeek
Subject: the meeting

I can be there at 11 or 3 today.
% show 1 2 | lpr
% rmm 1 2
```

Because MH commands aren't part of a monolithic mail system, you can use them at any time; you don't have to start or quit the mail agent. It's fine to mix other UNIX commands between your MH commands, to leave your mail for a while and do something else, and to work at several terminals at the same time. Because you use MH commands from a shell prompt, you can use all the power of the shell. For instance, I used a pipe to send the output of the *show* command to the printer directly. I removed the two messages after sending them to the printer.

If your shell has time-saving aliases or functions (and most do), you'll be able to use them with MH. And because MH isn't a monolithic mail agent, you can use MH commands in UNIX shell scripts or call them from programs in languages like C or *perl*.

Unlike most mail agents, MH keeps each message in a separate file. The filename is the message number. To rearrange the messages, MH just changes the filenames. MH can use standard UNIX filesystem operations such as removing, copying, and linking on its messages. The message files are grouped into one or more *folders*, which are actually UNIX directories.

The MH setup has a lot of advantages. A significant disadvantage is that it takes more filesystem space to store the messages. See Chapter 2, *MH and the UNIX Filesystem*, for an overview.

xmh and Other Front Ends to MH

The *xmh* program is something like a monolithic mail agent; it has its own familiar window/button/mouse interface in the X Window System. But *xmh* actually runs MH commands for you; if you need to do something that you can't do in *xmh*, you can always use the MH command instead. *xmh* is an example of what I call a *front end*. A front end is a program or set of programs that is an interface to MH commands. They let you do some of the most common things you need from MH, usually by pressing a single key, clicking a button, or using a menu. Examples of front ends include *xmh* and *emacs mh-rmail*, which runs under the GNU *emacs* text editor. In fact, if you know how to write a UNIX shell program ("shell script"), you can write a front end to MH. Chapter 12 has an introduction to shell programming.

Figure 1-2 is a typical *xmh* window. To read the message, the user highlighted a message in the middle window with the mouse, then pulled down the `Message` menu and selected a command to read the message. The same menu has commands to print the message and mark it for deletion. Many menu commands can also be run from the keyboard.

If you decide that a front end to MH (like *xmh*) is right for you, it's still a good idea to get familiar with the rest of the MH commands and features. That's because there's a lot in MH that you might need—to make your e-mail use easier or more efficient—that your front end may not let you do easily, if at all.

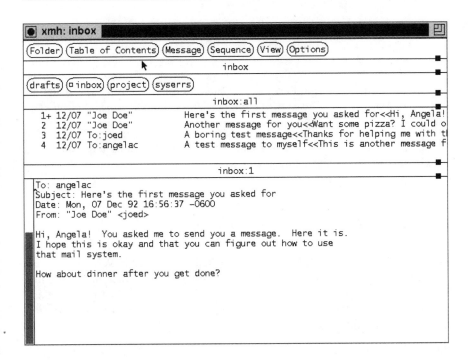

Figure 1-2. Typical xmh window

1.3 Addressing E-mail

E-mail addressing varies. How you do it on your computer and your network might be different than what I show here. Basically, though, there are two kinds of e-mail addresses:

- If you're sending a message to someone who has an account on your computer, address it to that person's username (login name). For instance, if Marty Waters logs on to his account with the username *mwaters*, you can address his mail to mwaters.

- If you're sending a message to someone who reads mail on another computer, you'll usually need to include that computer's name in your address. Two forms of addresses are pretty common:

  - Internet addresses have a username, followed by an at sign (@) and the other computer's hostname. For example, if Edie Nisbaum's username is *edie* and her computer is named *giraffe.zoo.utx.edu* you'd address Internet mail to her as *edie@giraffe.zoo.utx.edu*.*

- UUCP addresses have the other computer's name, followed by an exclamation point (!) and then the username. If Sandi Shore is *sandis* and her computer is named *beach*, you might address her mail as *beach!sandis*.

Those address guidelines won't be right for everyone. If you have questions, ask your system postmaster or administrator.

1.4 MH Profile

MH uses a file called the *MH profile*. By default, it's stored in your home directory and named *.mh_profile* (its name starts with a period, which makes it a hidden file that you won't see in an *ls* listing unless you use the *–A* or *–a* option). The MH profile defines your personal configuration for MH. The *mh-profile*(5) manual page in Appendix I has details.

Because *xmh* uses MH commands, a lot of your MH profile settings affect *xmh*.

When you first use an MH command like *inc*, if your account doesn't already have an *.mh_profile*, the command will make one for you. The most basic MH profile has just one line: the Path: component. You can add to or edit the file any time—in fact, as you learn more about MH, you'll probably want to make a few changes.

Example 1-1 is a fairly short MH profile.

Example 1-1. Short MH profile

```
Path: Mail
Folder-protect: 750
Msg-protect: 640
Signature: "Emma H. User"
repl: -annotate
scan: -form scan.time
```

That MH profile says that your MH directory is named *Mail* and stored in your home directory. It sets the default file access modes for folders and messages.

---

*On systems that use the at sign (@) as the line-delete character, type a backslash followed by an at sign (\ @) instead.

The fourth component tells MH how your name should look in the From: component of messages you send. The last two components make –*annotate* a default switch for the *repl* command and change the display format of the *scan* command.

Your MH profile can't have blank lines in it. Section 8.3 has detailed information and a longer example.

1.5 What Computers Support MH?

If you have a computer running UNIX, you can probably run MH. If you don't have MH, it can be copied from lots of places around the world by anonymous *ftp* or on tape. Someone who has a fair amount of experience installing UNIX software can probably get MH running on your system. The latest version (which this book covers) is numbered 6.7.2. MH 6.7 runs under Berkeley UNIX, System V, SunOS, and other versions of UNIX.

The *xmh* program is part of the standard X distribution from MIT. The latest version runs under X Version 11 Release 5.

Finally, MH runs across networks. The Post Office Protocol server (the "POP daemon") is a program that runs on a UNIX computer. Computers on a network (other UNIX machines, workstations, personal computers, and so on) can receive mail from the central machine running POP. MH itself can also get mail from another machine with POP.

1.6 History

Here's a quick look back at the interesting histories of MH and *xmh*. There's more about MH in Appendix B, *Early History of MH*.

1.6.1 MH

Early in 1977, R. Stockton Gaines and Norman Z. Shapiro of the RAND Corporation laid out the MH principles in a way that's been followed amazingly well since. At that time RAND had an electronic mail system called MS. MS worked the way most mail software still does today: it was a monolithic system which didn't take advantage of the UNIX file and directory structure. Among the ideas laid out in the MH memo were: storing messages in a directory as normal text files, which could then be read by other UNIX programs as well as MH; deleting a message by changing its name (moving it to another directory); and having a "user environment" file that keeps track of what the user did last. The MH

Part I
Introduction

commands were a lot like MS commands except that they became individual programs, one for each task, executed with a UNIX shell.

By 1979, Bruce S. Borden had developed MH; it has remained conceptually the
same ever since. Of course, some changes and a fair number of additions have
been made to MH since it was created. Since 1982, Marshall T. Rose,* aided by
John L. Romine, with some help from Einar Stefferud, Jerry Sweet and others at
the University of California, Irvine (UCI), have extended and maintained MH.
Performance enhancements were also made at the University of California,
Berkeley, and MH has been included with later versions of Berkeley UNIX
(4BSD). Versions of MH also come with Digital's ULTRIX, IBM's AIX, and others. People at UCI, along with help from contributors, are still updating MH.

1.6.2 xmh

xmh was born in the summer of 1986, at the Western Software Labs (WSL) of
Digital Equipment Corporation in Palo Alto, California. Smokey Wallace, the
head of WSL, was working on the early ancestor of the Xt toolkit and the Athena
Widgets that are part of X11R5. He was assisted by Terry Weissman, a Stanford
graduate student working at WSL for the summer. X11 was still being designed
and implemented; all development took place on X10.

The toolkit needed to have its design proven by using it to develop a significant
application. At the same time, people at WSL were unhappy with the tools they
had for reading mail. The solution to both problems was to have Terry create a
toolkit-based mail application.

To prove that the toolkit was useful for developing user interfaces and not merely
for building a new mail system, the *xmh* application was built on top of the MH
mail system. Terry also had considerable help on the design of the user interface
from Phil Karlton, who (in a previous life at Xerox) had developed a windowing
mail user interface named Hardy.† By the end of the summer, a usable but limited prototype was finished. Terry became a full-time WSL employee and continued working on *xmh* for about a year. It was ported many times to improved
versions of the toolkit. It continued to prove an important test case for the toolkit
and later the original X11 sample server.

Since then, Donna Converse of the MIT X Consortium has updated *xmh* further.

---

* Marshall Rose has since left UCI.

† Hardy, of course, was based on an earlier program named Laurel, whose authors never forgave him
for naming it "Hardy."

1.7 Obtaining MH and xmh

The MH programs are in the public domain. You can get them for free by using *anonymous ftp* from the sites *ftp.ics.uci.edu* and *louie.udel.edu* on the Internet network (see Appendix E, *Copies of Files Over the Network*, for help). You can also buy a 6250 BPI 9-track tape of MH, with a printed set of manuals, from the University of California, Irvine. Send a check for $75 U.S. currency (as of this printing), payable to Regents of University of California, to: University of California at Irvine, Office of Academic Computing, 360 Computer Science, Irvine, CA 92717 USA. Their phone number is +1-714-856-5153.

xmh is a standard client in the X Window System distribution.

2

MH and the UNIX Filesystem X

MH and *xmh* take advantage of the UNIX filesystem structure for storing folders, messages, and other files. As a new user, you really don't need to understand this because MH effectively hides the filesystem from you. You may want to skip this chapter.

If you're going very far with MH, though (especially if you're programming with it), you'll want to understand how MH stores messages and folders. You'll also need to know where other MH files are kept.

The chapter starts with a diagram of some directories and files that are important to MH. As you read about MH, you might want to refer to this diagram. Next are explanations of specific MH files. Finally, there's a warning about the format of some MH files.

To read this chapter, you'll need to know the basics of UNIX filesystems: path-names, directories, and subdirectories, as shown in Figure 2-1.

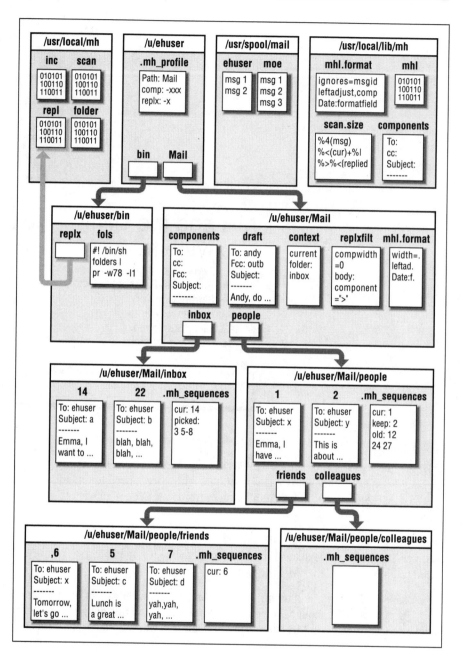

Figure 2-1. Important parts of a UNIX filesystem

2.1 An Overview of the UNIX Filesystem

MH is different from other UNIX mail user agents because it takes special advantage of the UNIX filesystem. Figure 2-1 is a diagram of typical files and directories that MH and *xmh* use. Here's an explanation of each of the filesystem parts:

- The gray boxes are *directories*. The full pathname of each directory is at the top. Most of the directories belong to the *ehuser* account, but three in the top row are "system" directories.

- Inside the directories are *files* and *subdirectories* (and one *symbolic link*)—each of these are shown as a white box. Each white subdirectory box has an arrow pointing out and down to another gray box, which shows what's in that subdirectory. The gray line represents a symbolic link.*

- There are two kinds of files here. *Text files* are shown with some readable (if cryptic) words in them. *Binary files* (directly executable programs) are shown in boxes full of 0s and 1s.

To keep things simple, the diagram omits a lot of directories. It also omits some (or many) of the files in each directory.

2.2 MH Programs (Binaries) Directory

The person who installs MH can choose where the executable MH programs like *inc* are installed. In Figure 2-1, this directory is */usr/local/mh*. You should put this directory in your shell's command-search path.

---

*Symbolic links, also called *soft links*, aren't available on all versions of UNIX.

2.3 MH Library Directory

The library directory (in Figure 2-1, */usr/local/lib/mh*) is usually separate from the MH binaries directory. Again, the location is system-dependent—but the pathname usually has *mh* and *lib* someplace in it. The directory has text files like *scan.size* and *scan.timely*, standard template files for draft messages such as *components*, and a few special executable programs like *mhl*.

2.4 System Mailboxes

Often, a directory like */usr/spool/mail* or */usr/mail* holds incoming messages for all users. This is the place where the *inc* and *msgchk* commands look. For instance, a user named *ehuser* would have a system mailbox named */usr/spool/mail/ehuser* or */usr/mail/ehuser*. Some system administrators install these mailboxes in each user's home directory and give them a name like *.mailbox*.

2.5 A User's Directories

Much of Figure 2-1 shows the directories for a user named *ehuser*. The home directory */u/ehuser* holds the MH profile (see Section 1.4). The *Mail* directory and its subdirectories are for MH. If the user wants any shell scripts or other programs, *bin* holds them.

2.5.1 bin Directory

The gray arrow pointing out of the *bin* directory is a symbolic link named *replx*. It points to the executable *repl* program in the MH binaries directory. See Section 9.4.1. *ehuser* also has a shell program named *fols* in her *bin*. It's shown in Section 13.5.

2.5.2 The MH Directory and Subdirectories

The MH directory (named *Mail* in this example) has two subdirectories. MH uses these directories as mail folders; there might be many more of them. The MH directory also has several files; some are explained here and others are covered in later chapters.

Drafts

When you make a new draft message, MH stores the draft in a file in the MH directory. The draft file is named (logically enough) *draft*. Alternatively, MH can make a folder for holding many draft messages. This folder is called (are you ready?) a *draft folder*. Section 6.5 covers that in detail.

Library Files

The *Mail* directory has *ehuser*'s private version of the *components* and *mhl.format* files, which MH will use instead of the corresponding file in the MH library directory. There's also a *replxfilt* filter file for the *replx* command (which is in her *bin*).

Context File

Each user's MH directory has its own *context* file. This file keeps track of your current folder and private sequences. If you've used any read-only folders (another user's folders, for instance), all information about them is stored here.

Folders

A folder (such as the *people* folder in Figure 2-1) has one text file for each message in the folder. The name of the message file is the message number. So the *people* folder has two messages in it, numbers 1 and 2. (There can be other messages, but they aren't shown in the diagram.)

The files whose names start with commas are "deleted" messages. File *,6* in the *people/friends* folder is an example. The *rmm* command prepends a comma to the filename (some systems use other characters). This "hides" the message from MH commands, but gives you a chance to recover the deleted message. At some later time, a system program normally removes the "deleted" messages. This is covered in Section 7.5.

.mh_sequences

In each folder (and subfolder), an *.mh_sequences* file keeps track of the sequences in the folder. (More exactly, *public* sequences are stored in *.mh_sequences*. *Private* sequences are kept in the *context* file.) Sequences are the lists of message numbers that you set with commands like *mark* and *pick*. There's a sequence called *cur* that holds the current message number, an *unseen* sequence that lists unread messages, and more. See Section 7.3 for more about sequences.

Subfolders
The *people* folder has two subfolders named *friends* and *colleagues*. Each of these subfolders has the same structure as *people*. They both have *.mh_sequences* files for themselves. They can even have subfolders (and sub-sub-subfolders...).* The only difference between a folder and subfolder is the name. See Section 7.1.5, "Subfolders," and Section 7.1.6, "Relative Folder Names," for more information.

2.6 Special Files for xmh

The *xmh* program is usually installed with other X clients. Because it also uses some MH commands, it needs access to MH files and commands.

xmh uses a few special files (for simplicity, Figure 2-1 doesn't show them). *xmh* makes a file called *.xmhcache* in each folder that you select. The file keeps a *scan* listing of the messages in the folder.

xmh uses the draft folder, too. It also makes temporary draft messages in files named *xmhdraft0* through *xmhdraft9* in each user's MH directory.

2.7 Links

If you keep a lot of mail in a lot of folders, you may want to file the same message in more than one folder. Because MH stores its messages in separate UNIX files, it can take advantage of a UNIX feature called a *link*. (To keep everything simple, Figure 2-1 doesn't show them. But Figure 2-2 does.)

**xmh under X11 Release 5 only recognizes one level of subfolders. If you have sub-sub...folders, *xmh* will ignore them. The X11 Release 3 version doesn't handle subfolders at all.

2.7.1   What's a Link?

Basically, a link is a name for a file. UNIX lets you have many links to the same file. In other words, the same file can have a lot of names.

Even when you have several links to a file, there's only one copy of the file stored on the computer's disk—that file has several names. If you add another link (another name), the new link doesn't take any more disk space.*

When you use the MH *refile –link* command, it links a message from one folder into another. In other words, it creates a second name for the same file without removing the original name. Section 7.1.4 explains how.

2.7.2   Technical Stuff About Links

When UNIX stores a file on the disk, the file's name (or, in the case of MH, the file's message number) is just a convenience for users. To find the file, UNIX actually uses its *i-number*. An i-number identifies the file to UNIX.

A file can have as many links (as many names), in as many directories, as you want to give it. UNIX just relates the name to the file's i-number. In fact, a directory is basically just a list of filenames and their i-numbers.

Figure 2-2 shows an example of a message with two links. One link is in the *friends* folder: message number 5. The other link is in the *meals* folder: message number 1. Both links have the same i-number (6241), so they both "point to" the same file on the disk. (If you know about "pointers" in programming, a link is a lot like a pointer to a memory location.)

Links can't span filesystems. Many newer UNIX filesystems have *symbolic links*. Symbolic links can span filesystems, but they take disk space to store.

----

*The directory file which holds the entry for the link will use a few characters to store the link itself, but that's usually insignificant.

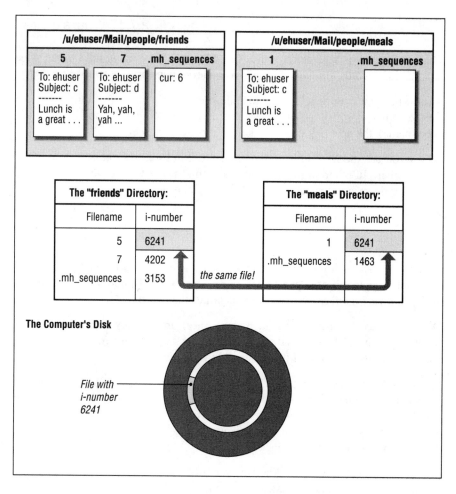

Figure 2-2. Two linked messages

2.8 Caution About MH Files and Newline Characters

MH commands expect their files, like the MH profile, to end with a newline character. (In general, you get a newline when you're using a text editor and press
RETURN.) The *vi* editor will automatically terminate the last line with a newline

character. Some other editors, including GNU *emacs*, may not always put a newline at the end. When you edit an MH file, be careful about this.

A file that doesn't end with a newline can put MH commands like *inc* into an endless loop. If your MH commands "freeze," be sure that your MH files end with a newline. You can use a UNIX command such as:

```
% tail -1 file | od -c
000000   s   h   o   w   p   r   o   c   :       m   h   l  \n
000016
```

to see exactly how a file ends—the last character should be \n.

Setting Up for MH and xmh [x]

Getting Mail Ready to Read
Setting Up MH

This short chapter shows how to set up to use MH and *xmh*. After this setup, you'll be ready for Chapter 4, *Tour Through MH*, and Chapter 14, *Tour Through xmh*.

If your site doesn't have these versions, the setup will probably be the same. The basics of MH haven't changed very much in years. After you follow these steps, you should never need to set up your account again.

By the way, if you decide that you want to switch from another mail system to MH or *xmh*, look at Appendix D, *Converting Messages to MH*, after you read this chapter. It explains how to convert existing messages.

3.1 Getting Mail Ready to Read

Chapter 2, *MH and the UNIX Filesystem*, explained how MH stores your messages: instead of keeping them all in the system mailbox or a big message file, MH keeps each message in a separate file. Once you start using MH, it takes a little work to move MH messages back to your old system. So if you've been reading electronic mail on your UNIX account before now and you're not sure that you want to use MH or *xmh* permanently, you may want to save your current e-mail messages in a place where your current e-mail system can find them.

3.2 Setting Up MH

Before you use MH, your UNIX account needs to be set up. Log in and get a shell prompt (which I'll show as a percent sign (%); yours might be different). If you're using the X Window System, open an *xterm* window (a terminal or command window) where you get a shell prompt.

Type the following command at the prompt:

```
% folder +inbox
```

If the answer is something like `folder: Command not found.` then the MH commands aren't in your shell search path or they haven't been installed on your system. Section 9.2.1 will help you set your search path. Your system administrator can help you find the MH commands—or install them.

- If you haven't used MH before, it will make an *.mh_profile* setup file (see Section 1.4). Then, it will ask you two questions; answer y (for "yes") to both questions:

  ```
  % folder +inbox
  Your MH-directory "/xxx/Mail" doesn't exist; Create it? y
  Create folder "/xxx/Mail/inbox"? y
              inbox+ has   no messages.
  ```

  Now, if you go to your home directory and type *ls –a*, you should see a directory named *Mail* and a file named *.mh_profile*. You're all set.

- If you've used MH before or if the system administrator already set up your account for MH, something like this will happen:

  ```
  % folder +inbox
              inbox+ has  5 messages (   1-  5); cur=  5.
  ```

At this point, it's a good idea to be sure that your *.mh_profile* file isn't left over from MH before Version 5. (Except, of course, if your computer is still running an old MH version. If you aren't sure, see Section 4.9, "The –help Switches.")

Look through the file with a UNIX command like *cat*, *more* or *pg*:

```
% cat .mh_profile
Path: Mail
Folder-protect: 700
Msg-protect: 600
   ...
Current-folder: xxx
   ...
```

If you see a `Current-folder:` component, like the one above, use a text editor (*vi*, *emacs*, and so on) to delete it from the *.mh_profile*. That component is left over from MH before Version 5,* and it can cause some warning messages when you run newer MH commands.

If there are components besides `Path:`, `Folder-protect:` and `Msg-Pro-tect:` in your *.mh_profile* and you didn't put them there, you may want to "comment out" those extra lines so that MH will ignore them. That way, when you use MH, you won't be confused by commands that work differently than you expect. An easy way to "comment out" a component is by putting a few capital X's before it, like this:

```
XXXrepl: -annotate
```

Later, after you have more experience with MH, you may want to delete the X's.

Now you're ready for the tours. Chapter 4 covers MH and Chapter 14 is about *xmh*.

Part I Introduction

---

*MH used to keep track of the current folder name in the *.mh_profile* file. Now it uses a file named *context* in the MH directory instead.

Part II:

Using MH

Part II is about using MH version 6.7.

Although xmh is powerful, the standard MH commands are much more powerful and flexible. To understand xmh in depth, the information here will help you—especially the sections and subsections with an ⊠ in their headings.

You should read Part III if you want to customize MH or program with it.

4

Tour Through MH

Getting Started
Sending Some Mail: comp, send
Reading New Mail: inc, show, next, prev
Replying to Messages: repl
Command-line Switches (Options)
Forwarding Messages: forw
Find and Specify with scan, pick, Ranges,
    Sequences
Cleanup: rmm
The –help Switches
Other MH Features

This chapter takes you on a tour through MH Version 6.7.2. You'll use basic functions to send and receive mail, organize it, and do most of the basic things you'd do with MH. Along the way are some brief looks at advanced features that are covered in the next few chapters.

Want A Fast Overview?

The *mh* manual page in Appendix I is a high-level summary of MH. In just a few pages, it covers the basics from setting up to reporting bugs. There are no examples, no information on some advanced features, and only one-line summaries of advanced commands. If you're good with UNIX, though, that manual page can get you started with MH in record time.

If your site doesn't have MH 6.7.2, try the tour anyhow. The basics of MH haven't changed very much in years. If a feature works differently on your version, ask someone who knows MH, look at the online manual page for your version of MH—or just try the next feature.

After you do the quick tutorial in this chapter, you'll have enough experience to handle your day-to-day mail with MH. If you're using a workstation or terminal that runs the X Window System, you can probably use *xmh*. *xmh* opens windows with buttons, scrollbars, and other familiar X features. You might want to start with the *xmh* tour in Chapter 14. Then, if you're curious, open an *xterm* window and try the MH tour. You can use both *xmh* and MH, though running both at the same moment can cause problems if you aren't careful.

For everyone else, you're in the right place.

4.1 Getting Started

Before you start the tour, be sure that you've read Chapter 3, *Setting Up for MH and xmh*.

Ask someone to send you two or three short mail messages. The messages don't have to be sent with MH. Almost any mail agent will work, although it should be able to put a `Subject:` on the message. You'll use these as test messages later in the tour. They don't have to make sense—any old garbage will do.

By now, you should have the MH configuration file, *.mh_profile*, in your home directory—whether MH created it or the file was already there. If you decided not to follow the suggestion at the end of Section 3.2 about commenting out extra components, here's another suggestion: as you do the tour, if your commands seem to work differently than the book shows, remember that your MH profile settings may have changed how MH works by default; make a mental note of the words at the start of each component (words like `comp:` and `Editor:`).

4.2 Sending Some Mail: comp, send

First, let's try the *comp* command, the usual way to compose a message in MH. If you'd like, look ahead to Example 4-1; it shows how your screen will look when you finish typing.

Start by typing the command at a shell prompt. When you do, you'll be prompted for the addresses where you want to send the message, as the following example shows:

```
% comp
To:
```

NOTE

If someone has changed the configuration of MH on your computer or your account, your *comp* may be a little different. For example, it might put you into a full-screen editor.

Pick someone to send the message to and type that person's address at the prompt (see Section 1.3, "Addressing E-mail"). Type a comma, and then put your username next on the line. This means the message will be sent to your friend and to you. Press RETURN .

Next, you'll be asked who should get a "carbon" copy (cc:) of this message. Leave it blank—let's not send a cc: of this message. Just press RETURN .

You'll get a Subject: prompt next. The people who receive your message can get a quick idea about your message from the subject. It's a good idea to spend a moment and think of a descriptive subject. For this message, you might type something like "Test message from Joe and the MH system." Or, for now, just type something fun . . . .

When you press RETURN , you'll see a row of dashes, and your cursor will be on the next line below them. Your screen should look something like this:

```
% comp
To: yourfriend, you
cc:
Subject: Thoroughly trivial experimentation
---------
```

Messages have two parts. One is the *header*—you just filled that in. The other part is the *body*—the contents of the message.

Now you can type the body. In MH, unless your MH profile is set up differently, *comp* uses a "text collector" program called *prompter* to collect the message header and body from you. *prompter* is a simple-minded program, and it doesn't understand how to do things like word wrap. You'll need to press RETURN at the end of every line of the body. (If you can't wait, Section 4.4 shows how to start a standard text editor like *vi* that has built-in word wrapping. (Also see Section 6.1.3, "What Now?—and the whatnow Program," and Section 6.2, "Changing Default Editors.")

After you've typed the short message, you should press RETURN so that the cursor is at the start of a new line. Press CTRL-D * to end the body.

---

*Actually, you use the *end-of-input* character. On some systems, this might not be CTRL-D . If you're not sure, ask a local expert. Also, with MH Version 6.7 or later, you can set *prompter* to end input with a single dot (.) at the start of a line—see Section 6.1.2.

Next comes the What now? prompt, which is where you tell MH what to do with the draft message you just typed:

- If you want to send the message, type send and press RETURN. Some text may be displayed while your mail is sent. After a few moments, you should get another shell prompt (%).

  ```
  What now? send
  %
  ```

- If you want to throw away the draft message, type:

  ```
  What now? quit -delete
  %
  ```

The draft will be deleted without sending it, and you'll get a shell prompt (%).

Example 4-1 shows what all that should look like.

Example 4-1. Using the comp command

```
% comp
To: yourfriend, you
cc:
Subject: Thoroughly trivial experimentation
---------
In the interest of furthering the educational
objectives and enlightenment of the above-stated
personage, the current electronic communication has
been rendered.  May I obtain a response?

John

P.S.  Yow!!
CTRL-D
---------
What now? send
%
```

Now, send a mail message to yourself—put your username on the To: line. Make the subject A long message. This one should be at least three screens long, though your individual lines don't need to be very wide. (Later, you'll use this to find out how MH displays long messages.) The words don't have to make sense, so practice typing or turn your four-year-old loose at the keyboard. (Just remember to press RETURN at the end of each line.)

4.3 Reading New Mail: inc, show, next, prev

With the messages that you and your friend sent, you should have at least five new messages waiting by now. You can't read the messages until you *incorporate* them from your system mailbox into your account. To do this, type *inc* at the shell prompt (%). For example:

```
% inc
Incorporating new mail into inbox...

    1+ 12/07 Joe Doe          Here's the first message you asked
    2  12/07 Joe Doe          Another test<<Well, this is another
    3  12/07 To:Joe Doe       What's happening--did you send the
    4  12/07 To:angelac       A long message<<sdfafdajur oru9 52
    5  12/07 To:Joe Doe       Thanks for helping!<<You said that
%
```

Okay—what's all that? Here's an explanation of the output from *inc*:

- The *inc* command got all your new mail from your system mailbox (the place that new mail waits for you) and moved it into your *inbox* folder.

- There were five new messages, which *inc* numbered 1 through 5. (If there were already some messages in your *inbox*, then *inc* would have started numbering the new messages one higher than the last message in the folder.)

- There's a one-line summary of each message called a *scan listing*. It shows the message number, the date when the message was sent, who sent it, and the Subject: component, if any. If there's room, you'll see the first few words of the message body (with the two left angle brackets (<<) first).

- One message has a plus sign (+) next to the number. In a scan listing, the + marks the *current message*. The + isn't part of the message number; *inc* just puts it in the *scan* line.

To read the first message, type show and press RETURN. You'll see the current message (in this case, message number 1) on your screen. Your screen will look something like this:

```
% show
(Message inbox:1)
Return-Path: joed
Received: by mysun.xyz.edu (5.54/ACS)
        id AA08581; Mon, 07 Dec 92 16:56:39 EST
Message-Id: <9001192156.AA08581@mysun.xyz.edu>
To: angelac
Subject: Here's the first message you asked for
```

```
Date: Mon, 07 Dec 92 16:56:37 -0600
From: "Joe Doe" <joed>

Hi, Angela!  You asked me to send you a message.  Here it is.
I hope this is okay and that you can figure out how to use
that mail system.

How about dinner after you get done?
```

The first part of the message, the *header*, has information (components such as Received:) that you can usually ignore. Your message may have more, fewer, or other header components. You can configure *show* to skip header components you don't want; see Section 5.1.6, "Using the mhl showproc."

If the message is longer than one screen, most users just see the first screenful. (What happens depends on your version of UNIX and how your MH package was set up.) Then, until all of the message has been shown, and depending on how your account is set up:

- There may be a prompt like --More--, or a single colon (:), at the bottom of your screen.

- Your terminal may beep.

- The screen may just sit still.

No matter what happens, if your screen pauses before the end of the message, try pressing the space bar or RETURN to get the next screenful of the message. When you've seen the message, you should get another shell prompt (%) on the screen.*

Now, to look at the next message, type next at the shell prompt. The display will be just like the one you got with the *show* command, but you'll see the next message (in this case, message number 2). Message 2 becomes the new current message.

When you're done reading message 2, type prev. This shows the previous message (if you've just seen message 2, *prev* will show message 1).

Because MH commands are used at a shell prompt (%), you can use all the other standard UNIX commands with them, too. For example, assuming your system's

---

*In some setups, you may need to type q (for "quit") first.

printer command is named *lpr*, you can print the current message by sending *show*'s output to the printer, like this:

```
% show | lpr
```

You can copy the current message to a file with:

```
% show > filename
```

and so on—output redirection works with other MH commands, too.

The current message is number 1 again. Let's skip over message 2 and go straight to message 3. Do that by giving the message number to the *show* command:

```
% show 3
```

Use *next* or *show* to read the rest of your messages.

4.4 Replying to Messages: repl

To answer a message, you could use *comp* and fill in the To:, cc:, and Subject: components yourself. But MH has a command for sending replies that fills in the header automatically.

To start, pick a message that you want to reply to. If it's the message you just read (with *show*, *next*, or *prev*) you can reply to it by typing:

```
% repl
```

without the message number. That's because it's the current message and, as with most MH commands, if you don't type a message number, the current message is used. If you want to reply to a message besides the current one, type a space and the message number—for example, to reply to message 1, type:

```
% repl 1
```

Take a look back at message 1. Compare its heading to the heading you get when you reply to it:

```
% repl 1
To: "Joe Doe" <joed>
cc: angelac
Subject: Re: Here's the first message you asked for
In-reply-to: Your message of "Mon, 07 Dec 92 16:56:37 -0600."
        <9001192156.AA08581@mysun.xyz.edu>
-------
```

MH automatically addressed the reply with a cc: to you. It used the original Subject: component with Re: in front of it. Finally, it added a two-line

In-reply-to: component that shows when the original message was sent and its Message-Id. (Of course, this can all be changed. See Section 6.7.

From here on, *repl* works the same as *comp*. The cursor sits under the row of dashed lines. You can type the body of the reply here. Remember to press RETURN at the end of each line. When you're done with the body of the reply, you should press CTRL-D at the start of a new line to get the What now? prompt.

Now, instead of sending the reply, look at it on your screen by typing list and pressing RETURN:

```
What now? list

To: "Joe Doe" <joed>
cc: angelac
    . . .

What now?
```

After the message has been shown, you'll get another What now? prompt.

You've got lots of choices here; Section 6.1.3 explains them all. For now, though, if you want to edit the draft reply (and if you know how to use a UNIX text editor—such as *vi*)—you can. Just type edit followed by the name of your favorite editor, like this:

```
What now? edit vi
```

When you press RETURN, MH will start the editor on the draft message. You can change anything you want—fix spelling, neaten the lines, add or delete words, read a copy of a file from your directory, whatever. You can even change the message header (addresses and so on)—but be sure not to put any blank lines in the header or add any nonstandard components besides To:, Subject:, etc., unless you know what you're doing with mail headers. Also, don't delete the row of dashes between the header and body.

When you're done editing, save your changes and exit the editor (in *vi*, for example, type ZZ).

You'll be back at the What now? prompt. Go ahead and send your reply. If there were problems with the message, MH will show error messages and give another What now? prompt. If everything's fine, though, you'll get a shell prompt (%).

4.5 Command-line Switches (Options)

Each MH command has some optional *switches* you can type on its command line. These switches are in the form of English words. They're called switches because most of them have two settings: on and off. For instance, *repl* (also the *forw* and *dist* commands, covered later) have a *–annotate* switch. This tells MH to mark the original message with the date and time you replied to (or forwarded or redistributed) the message. To get the "off" setting, you use the word "no" before the switch. For instance, the *–noannotate* switch tells *repl* not to annotate a message.

Most switches have default settings (if you don't tell a command whether the switch should be on or off, the default is used). For example, the default for *repl* is *–noannotate*.

Unlike many UNIX commands, which have options like *–a* or *–F*, the switches for MH commands are longer than a single letter (though you can abbreviate many of them).

Let's try *–annotate*. Pick another message and send a quick reply to it. For instance, to reply to message 2 and annotate it, you would type:

```
% repl -annotate 2
```

Because the order usually doesn't matter, you could also use:

```
% repl 2 -annotate
```

Section 6.7.7 has more about annotation.

If you want to go into your favorite editor (like *emacs*) directly, add the editor name, too. You can abbreviate MH switches. For instance, to reply to message 2, annotate it, and use the *emacs* editor, type one of these commands:

```
% repl -annotate -editor emacs 2
% repl -a -e emacs 2
```

By the way, if you want to use switches like *–annotate* and *–editor xxx* every time you reply, without having to type them, you can put them in a `repl:` component in your MH profile. Each command's switches are listed in the MH Reference Guide at the end of this book—and in the command's online manual page.

After you've typed your quick reply, you'll be back at the `What now?` prompt. Type `send` to send the reply. Then show the original message—by now, it's the current message, so you can just type `show` at a percent sign (%) prompt.

Because you used *–annotate* when you replied to this message, there should be a
`Replied:` component in the message header:

```
% show
(Message inbox:2)
Replied: Mon, 07 Dec 92 17:09:43 -0600
    ...
Subject: Another test
Date: Mon, 07 Dec 92 16:58:22 -0600
From: "Joe Doe" <joed>
    ...
```

And, when you *scan* the message, you'll see a dash (–). See the *scan* line for
message 2 in Section 4.7. Section 6.7 has much more information about replying
to mail with *repl*.

4.6 Forwarding Messages: forw

If you need to send a copy of a mail message to someone, you can forward it. To
forward the current message, just type:

```
% forw
```

To forward other messages, use the message numbers too. For example, to forward messages 3 and 5:

```
% forw 3 5
To: somebody
cc: somebodyelse
Subject: Messages I got about meeting tomorrow
--------

----- Enter initial text

Dear somebody, here's some mail I got.  I think you might
want a copy of these.  The second message is the most
important, blah blah blah...

CTRL-D

----- Forwarded messages

    ...Contents of message 3 is here...
```

```
----- Message 2

    ...Contents of message 5 is here...

----- End of Forwarded Messages

What now? push
%
```

Before it copies the messages you're forwarding, *forw* will prompt you on the screen (this doesn't go into the message) to enter any text ("initial text") you want to send along. You can type it here, and then press CTRL-D at the start of a new line. Or, type CTRL-D right away to go straight to the What now? prompt, where you'll have the usual choices.*

I've shown another way to send a message: the *push* command. The message is sent "in the background." You'll get another prompt right away so you can do something else while MH is sending the message. That has a lot of advantages, but a few disadvantages. The part of Section 6.1.3 called "push (or p)" is worth reading before you use *push* again.

As most MH commands do, *forw* has several other features. Like *repl*, you can annotate the messages you forward (with *–annotate*). Section 6.8.1 explains how to reformat the forwarded messages to delete useless components in the headers or neaten the body.

4.7 Find and Specify with scan, pick, Ranges, Sequences

MH gives you a lot of ways to find particular messages—and to specify one or more messages without giving the message numbers. Here are a few examples.

If you type scan at a shell prompt, you'll get a list of all the messages in your folder. The list looks like the one you get with *inc*, but it shows all your messages:

```
% scan
    1  12/07 Joe Doe          Here's the first message you asked
    2 -12/07 Joe Doe          Another test<<Well, this is another
    3  12/07 To:Joe Doe       What's happening--did you send the
    4+ 12/07 To:angelac        A long message<<sdfafdajur oru9 52
    5  12/07 To:Joe Doe       Thanks for helping!<<You said that
```

---

*If you want to add a note *after* the forwarded messages, or edit the forwarded messages themselves, use the *edit* command to go into the draft message with your favorite editor. You can also configure MH to let you put the note after the forwarded messages, without going into an editor, with the *prompter –noprepend* switch. Section 9.7 shows an easy way to do this.

The dash (–) next to message 2 means that you've replied to it with the *repl –annotate* command. The plus sign (+) next to message 4 means that it's the current message. If you sent a particular message, *scan* shows To: *recipient* as demonstrated in messages 3-5 (to make this work even better see Section 8.6, "Defining Alternate Mailboxes").

If you have a lot of messages, you don't have to scan all of them. You can specify message numbers, ranges, and MH *sequences*. For example, to scan the range of messages number 2 through 5, inclusive, type:

```
% scan 2-5
```

To scan the current message and the last three messages, type:

```
% scan cur last:3
```

Many MH commands let you give more than one message number at a time. There are quite a few ways to do this. Here are some examples. Compare them to the explanations that follow:

```
% show 3 7 22
% show 3-7 22
% scan last:20
% scan first-cur
```

The first *show* command shows message numbers 3, 7, and 22. The second *show* command shows messages in the range 3 through 7 (like 3, 4, 5, 6, and 7, though not all of them have to exist), also message 22. The first *scan* command scans the last 20 messages in the folder. The second *scan* command scans starting at the first message in the folder (which isn't necessarily message 1) through the current message. For more information, see the *mh-sequence*(5) manual page in Appendix I.

(Of course, this is most useful when you have more than five messages in your folder.)

The MH *pick* command lets you search for messages by what's in their header components or body. If you wanted to find all messages which have the word "oyster" in the header or body:

```
% pick -search oyster
1
4
%
```

Messages 1 and 4 contain that word.

Of course, the message numbers usually aren't enough. You'll usually want to *scan* the messages or read them or something—and retyping the message numbers is a pain, especially if there are a lot of them. MH has *sequences*, stored lists of message numbers with a name. MH commands that accept message numbers will accept sequences—just type the sequence name. You can tell *pick* to store matching message numbers in a sequence, too. For instance, the next example shows how to pick all messages you sent to the user *freddie* and save the numbers in a sequence called *picked*. I use the stored sequence twice—first, to scan the messages; then, to forward them:*

```
% pick -to freddie -sequence picked
3 hits
% scan picked
   6  12/08 To:freddie        Plans for the new project, part 1
  12  12/08 To:freddie        Plans for the new project, part 2
  14  12/09 To:freddie        Oops -- read this<<Freddie, I mad
% forw picked
To: ehuser
cc:
Subject: Messages I sent to Fred F.
    ...
```

There's much more about *pick* in Section 7.2. Also, if the online manual pages are available on your system, you can read the one for *pick*(1) by typing:

```
% man pick
```

And, as with all MH commands, you can get a quick list of all *pick* switches by typing:

```
% pick -help
```

See Section 4.9 for more about *–help*.

4.8 Cleanup: rmm

MH keeps messages until you tell it to delete them. The command for removing messages is *rmm*. If you don't give message numbers, *rmm* removes the current message. That's handy when you're reading new mail that you don't want to keep. A typical mail-reading session might look like this:

```
% inc
    ...
% show
    ...
```

---

*Time savers: You can abbreviate most MH switches; for example, you can type -seq instead of -sequence. Also, as with other MH commands, you can save typing by storing default switches like *–sequence picked* in your MH profile.

```
% rmm
% next
    ...
```

The command *rmm 3 5* would remove messages 3 and 5. MH sequences (like *rmm picked*) and message ranges (like *rmm last:3*) will work, too.

By default, *rmm* doesn't actually remove a message; it just changes the message filename to "hide" it from MH. Later, a system program should delete the "removed" messages. If you accidentally use *rmm*, read the explanation in Section 7.5, "Removing Messages (and Getting Them Back)" or ask an MH expert to help you.

4.9 The –help Switches

Any time you need a quick reminder of an MH command's switches, use the *–help* switch. For example, here's a list for *scan*:

```
% scan -help
syntax: scan [+folder] [msgs] [switches]
  switches are:
  -[no]clear
  -form formatfile
  -(forma)t string
  -[no]header
  -width columns
  -[no]reverse
  -(file) file
  -(help)

version: MH 6.7.2 #1[UCI] (ora) of Mon Apr 20 17:13:08 EDT 1992
options: [BIND] [BSD42] [BSD43] [DBM] [DUMB] [FOLDPROT='"0750"']
         [ISI] [MHRC] [MSGPROT='"0640"'] [POP] [POP2]
         [POPSERVICE='"pop3"'] [SENDMTS] [SUN40] [SUN41]
         [TYPESIG='void'] [ZONEINFO]
```

The `syntax:` shows what kinds of things you can type on the command line. Some parts of some switches are shown in parentheses—this is the shortest abbreviation you can use—for example, you can type *–forma* instead of *–format*. But it doesn't show all abbreviations; for example, you can use *–w* instead of *–width*.

The `version:` and `options:` information is important when you're asking questions or reporting bugs to someone who's not at your computer site. There are several versions of MH and lots of configuration options—an expert may need to know how your MH is set up, and this information will explain it. The `#1` means this was the first build of MH 6.7.2 on your computer. Local changes and rebuilds will change this to #2, #3, etc. The `options:` are explained in your online *mh-gen*(8) manual page.

4.10 Other MH Features

Some questions come up again and again: "How can I do ...?" There are too many features to cover in an introductory tutorial. (That's what the rest of this book is for.) Here's a list of answers to commonly-asked questions about MH. (Of course, there are many, many others.)

- Organize messages into folders and subfolders; "link" messages into multiple folders without taking more disk space. (Section 7.1, Section 7.8.)

- If you accidentally remove a message, get it back. (Section 7.5.)

- When showing messages, don't display header components you don't want; format the body. (Section 5.1.6, Section 10.1.)

- Read only the messages you haven't read before. (Section 5.1.2.)

- Read messages by typing just the message number(s). (Section 12.15.)

- Reorder messages in a folder many different ways. (Section 7.4.)

- Print your messages. (Section 5.1.5, Section 13.11.)

- Store long mail address(es) in an alias. (Section 6.3.)

- Handle many draft messages at a time with a draft folder. (Section 6.5.2.)

- Add your standard "signature" text to the ends of messages automatically. (Section 8.9.6, Section 13.13.)

- Customize and change the headers of mail you send. (Section 6.4.1, Section 8.9.)

- Include the text of an original message in a reply. (Section 6.7.4, Section 6.7.5, Section 9.4.1.)

- Make *repl* ask whether it should send your reply to each of the people who got the original message. (Section 6.7.1.)

- Mark the messages you've replied to with the date, time, and recipients. (Section 6.7.7.)

- Access mail in other users' accounts and let them access yours (if you give each other permission). (Section 8.5 through Section 8.7.)

- Check the spelling in your mail messages before you send them. (Section 6.1.3.)

- Make *scan* give more and different information. (Section 5.2.1, Section 10.2.1.)

- Search for messages, store the lists automatically for reuse any time later. (Section 7.2.1, Section 7.2.4.)

- Search many folders at once. (Section 7.2.9, Section 7.2.10.)

- Handle incoming mail automatically. (Chapter 11.)

By learning the principles behind MH and learning a little bit about UNIX shell programming, you can make MH do almost anything you need a mail system to do.

5

Reading Your Mail with MH

Showing and Printing Messages
More About scan
Checking for Mail Waiting: msgchk
Other Features of inc

If you're tired of screenfuls of header components like Received: *xxx*, and you want to display messages in a certain format, this chapter shows you the basics of the *mhl* message-formatting command. Just as you can change message formatting, you can also change the information that the *scan* command gives you. Both of those topics are covered in depth in Chapter 10, *MH Formatting*; this chapter shows easy ways to get started. We'll also look at features of *inc* such as keeping a log of incoming mail.

5.1 Showing and Printing Messages

By default, the *show* command puts all of your message, including "boring" header components like Received: *xxx*, onto your screen.

You can change the way that your message is shown by deleting these header components, folding lines that are too long for your terminal, and so on. You can print your messages with neat margins and a header line at the top of the page. Here's more about that.

5.1.1 The Current Message

When you show a message with *show*, it becomes the current message. When you show a message with *next* or *prev*, MH actually runs the commands *show next* and *show prev*, respectively — which also reset the current message. If you show a group of messages by typing, for example:

```
% show 1 3 5
   ...
```

the last message (5) becomes the current message.

5.1.2 Messages You Haven't Read

MH can track which messages you haven't read yet. When you *inc*orporate new mail, the message numbers are added to a sequence automatically. As you read the messages (with *show*, *next*, and *prev*), the message numbers are taken out of the sequence. See Section 7.3.

To set this up, pick a name for the unseen sequence (I call mine *unseen*).* Put a line in your MH profile:

```
Unseen-Sequence: unseen
```

Remember that in MH, you can use a sequence name any place you can use message numbers. For example, to get a list of the messages you haven't read, you can use:

```
% scan unseen
```

Would you like an automatic list of your unread messages as you log in? Use lines like the ones in Example 5-1 to your *.login* or *.profile* file. If there are messages in your *unseen* sequence, you'll get a *scan* listing.

Example 5-1. Automatic scan of unread messages

C shell:

```
mhpath unseen +inbox >& /dev/null
if ($status == 0) then
    echo "Unseen mail in inbox:"
    scan +inbox unseen
endif
```

Bourne and Korn shells:

```
if mhpath unseen +inbox >/dev/null 2>&1
then
    echo "Unseen mail in inbox:"
    scan +inbox unseen
fi
```

---

*MH will keep more than one unseen sequence, if you need that. Add other sequence names to the Unseen-Sequence: component, separated with spaces. All the unseen sequences will have the same message lists in them. You can use the *mark* program to modify one or more of them, though.

Each folder keeps its own unseen sequence, but it's mostly useful in the *inbox*. As of this writing, no version of *xmh* supports the unseen sequence.

5.1.3 Weeding Out Before You Read

Do you get a group of messages you don't want—system status reports that usually aren't worth reading, test messages to yourself, and so on? You might want to remove all of them with a *.maildelivery* file, as explained in Chapter 11, *Processing New Mail Automatically*. Example 5-2 shows how you can decide, though, before removing some or all of the batch. (The same trick works for refiling, printing, and so on—not just for removing.)

Our system manager and I get status reports from *uucp*. I ignore them unless he's out of the office. Example 5-2 shows how I delete them quickly.

Example 5-2. Finding and handling a group of messages quickly

```
% inc
Incorporating new mail into inbox...
  155+ 12/07 uucp            uu-status<<LCK..cuZ2: 23283 LCK..cuZ3
   ...
  189  12/07 Tim O'Reilly    New edition of MH & xmh<<How are the
% pick -from uucp -seq temp cur-last
12 hits
% scan temp
  155+ 12/07 uucp            uu-status<<LCK..cuZ2: 23283 LCK..cuZ3
   ...11 more messages from uucp...
% rmm temp
```

First I find the messages with *pick* and store them in the *temp* sequence. (I use `pick cur-last` because that'll be all the messages *inc* brought in. As Section 5.1.2 explains, I also could have used `pick unseen`.) A quick review with *scan* (and maybe *show* on a few) makes sure there's nothing I need to see. So, I remove the messages. There's more about this in Sections 4.7 and 7.2.3.

What if I decide not to remove one of the messages in that *temp* sequence? I can use *mark –delete* to take the message out of the sequence before I run *rmm*. See Section 7.3.2.

5.1.4 Where's the Next Message?

In Example 5-2, I removed a group of messages without paying much attention to the message numbers. How could I read the first message that I didn't delete?

- If I had deleted the current message, it'd be easy: type `next`. (This works because *rmm* doesn't change the current message. Neither does *refile*, by the way.)

- But maybe I didn't delete the current message. Then *next* would be the wrong command; it would skip the current message.

Here's the trick:

```
% show cur:1
```

In MH, *cur* has the current message number, even if it's been deleted. The `:1` is a range with one message in it—the *mh-sequence* manual page in Appendix H has details. Of course, ranges usually have more than one message—such as `first:10`, the first ten message numbers in the folder. But there's nothing wrong with `cur:1`—it means "up to one message in the range beginning with the current message." If the current message doesn't exist, MH automatically finds the next message number in the folder.

If that's too cryptic to remember, you might want to stick it in a shell alias. Then you can use *nx* to read the current or next message, whichever:

```
alias nx 'show cur:1'
```

5.1.5 Changing showproc for Viewing, Printing, and Editing

By default, *show* uses a screen-by-screen file viewer like *more*(1) to display the message on your terminal. To use a different viewer, like the program called *less* (which comes in the MH distribution), use the *–showproc* switch (or put it in your MH profile):

```
% show -showproc less
```

If you like the *less* viewer, or any other file viewer, you can make that the default for all messages you read. Put a component like this in your MH profile:

```
showproc: less
```

Before *show* starts the *showproc*, it prints a header line with the folder name and message number:

```
(Message inbox:24)
```

Usually, that's convenient. Sometimes, it isn't. For example, when you're printing a message that fits onto a page exactly, the extra header line can make the page too long. The UNIX *pr*(1) program does that kind of message formatting. It formats a file for printing, with a header and page number, one message per page. By default, *pr* output goes to the terminal, not the printer. But you can use a standard UNIX pipe to send output to your printer program (often called *lp* or *lpr*). For example, here's how to print the last three messages, formatted with *pr*, on the *lpr* printer:

```
% show -noheader -showproc pr last:3 | lpr
```

The *–noheader* switch stops the extra header line from *show*. Of course, that command line is pretty long. A shell alias or function can shorten it to something like:

```
% msgpr last:3
```

Section 8.2.1 explains aliases and functions. Section 13.11 shows a shell program called *showpr* that does even more.

If you need to edit a message you've received from someone else, the *show* command can do that too! Just set your *showproc* to be ... a text editor. The *mhedit* command version in Section 9.6 makes this convenient.

5.1.6 Using the mhl showproc

A very useful *showproc* for viewing on the terminal is called *mhl*. It's an MH program that's designed for formatting mail messages. Section 10.1 explains how to customize *mhl* output, but a lot of people just use the default *mhl* settings. Try it yourself—compare plain *show* in Example 5-3 to *show –showproc mhl* in Example 5-4.

Example 5-3. Showing a message without mhl

```
% show
(Message inbox:14)
Received: by mysun.xyz.edu (5.54/ACS)
        id AA22457; Mon, 07 Dec 92 10:32:37 EST
Received: from cliff.xyz.edu by asun.xyz.edu (4.1/CNS)
        id AA00488; Mon, 07 Dec 92 10:24:44 EST
Message-Id: <9002091524.AA00488@asun.xyz.edu>
Received: by cliff.xyz.edu (4.1/SMI-4.0)
        id AA00220; Mon, 07 Dec 92 10:24:42 EST
```

Example 5-3. Showing a message without mhl (continued)

```
To: jdpeek@mysun.xyz.edu, nancyp@hersun.xyz.edu
To: ed@hissun.xyz.edu
Subject: X Terminal Presentation/Demonstration next week; be there, please
Date: Mon, 07 Dec 92 10:24:39 -0500
From: "Wilbur, Orville" <owilbur@asun.xyz.edu>

Vince Molino from NAC Corp. will give a short presentation
    ...
```

Example 5-4. Showing a message with default mhl formatting

```
% show -showproc mhl
(Message inbox:14)
  -- using template mhl.format --
Date:    Mon, 07 Dec 92 10:24:39 EST
To:      jdpeek@mysun.xyz.edu, nancyp@hersun.xyz.edu,
         ed@hissun.xyz.edu

From:    "Wilbur, Orville" <owilbur@asun.xyz.edu>
Subject: X Terminal Presentation/Demonstration next week; be
    ***there, please
    ...
```

Unless your system has a different default or you customize it, *mhl* will do what you saw in Example 5-4:

- Omit header components like `Received:` and `Message-Id:`.

- Line up the header components neatly.

- Wrap long lines and put three asterisks (`* * *`) at the start of continuations.

- Change the date into a standard format.

- Run a file-paging program like *more*(1) or *less*(1) or use its built-in paginator.

To use *mhl* on a single message, give it as the *showproc* on a command line:

```
% show -showproc mhl
```

If you like *mhl*, you can use it to show all messages by putting this component in your MH profile:

```
showproc: mhl
```

Or you can add separate components for individual mail-showing programs:

```
show: -showproc mhl
next: -showproc mhl
prev: -showproc mhl
```

If you've set *mhl* as the default, you can override that default temporarily by typing the name of a different *showproc* on the command line:

```
% show -showproc more
% show -showproc pr 3-7 | lpr
```

mhl reads a *format file* that sets the appearance of your messages. The default format file is called *mhl.format* and is in the system MH library directory (like */usr/local/lib/mh*). You can copy the system *mhl.format* file into your MH directory and customize it. For example, to copy it and edit it with *vi*:

```
% cd Mail
% cp /usr/local/lib/mh/mhl.format .
% vi mhl.format
```

Example 5-5 shows the message above with my customized *mhl.format* file and showproc: mhl in my MH profile:

Example 5-5. Showing a message with customized mhl formatting

```
% show
(Message inbox:14)
 -- using Jerry's mhl.format template --
Date:    Mon, 07 Dec 92 10:24:39 EST
From:    "Wilbur, Orville" <owilbur@asun.xyz.edu>
To:      jdpeek@mysun.xyz.edu, nancyp@hersun.xyz.edu,
         ed@hissun.xyz.edu
Subject: X Terminal Presentation/Demonstration next week; be
     ***there, please

Vince Molino from NAC Corp. will be giving a short presentation
   ...
```

To make your own *mhl.format* file, see Section 10.1.3.

5.1.7 Without a showproc

To display a message exactly as it was received, with no formatting or pagination, use the *–noshowproc* switch. MH will display the message with *cat*(1).

5.2 More About scan

If you thought that *scan* couldn't do much, read on. It can show your messages in different formats, scan in reverse order (handy for reviewing your most recent messages first), and scan a file full of messages (like your system mailbox).

5.2.1 scan Format Files⊠

You can change *scan*'s output with a *format file*. This is something like an *mhl* format file. MH comes with a few standard *scan* format files named *scan.time*, *scan.timely*, *scan.size*, and *scan.mailx*. They're stored in the MH library directory.

To use format files, type the file's name after the *–form* switch. Section 10.2 explains how to write your own *scan* format files. You can show any component in the header, change the appearance of the output depending on the message you're scanning, get multiline output, and much more. For now, here are examples of the standard format files:

```
% scan 1-4
    1  04/24*mary@hahvahd.edu   rcvtty -- how do I use it?<<I've been
    2  11/23 Al Bok             Query about "repl -query"<<I have a q
    3 -02/09 "Wilbur, Orville"  X Terminal Presentation/Demonstration
    4+ 02/11 To:"Wilbur, Orvil  Re: X Terminal Presentation/Demonstra
% scan -form scan.time 1-4
    1  04/24 23:12CST*mary@hahvahd.edu   rcvtty -- how do I use it?<<
    2  11/23 05:13GMT Al Bok             Query about "repl -query"<<I
    3 -02/09 10:24EST "Wilbur, Orville"  X Terminal Presentation/Demo
    4+ 02/11 22:03EST To:"Wilbur, Orvil  Re: X Terminal Presentation/
% scan -form scan.timely 1-4
    1  Apr86*mary@hahvahd.edu   rcvtty -- how do I use it?<<I've been
    2  23Nov Al Bok             Query about "repl -query"<<I have a q
    3 - Fri  "Wilbur, Orville"  X Terminal Presentation/Demonstration
    4+ 22:03 To:"Wilbur, Orvil  Re: X Terminal Presentation/Demonstra
% scan -form scan.size 1-4
    1  04/24* 1119 mary@hahvahd.edu   rcvtty -- how do I use it?<<I'v
    2  11/23 15326 Al Bok             Query about "repl -query"<<I ha
    3 -02/09   739 "Wilbur, Orville"  X Terminal Presentation/Demonst
    4+ 02/11   530 To:"Wilbur, Orvil  Re: X Terminal Presentation/Dem
% scan -form scan.mailx 1-4
   N    1 mary@hahvahd.edu  Thu Apr 24 23:12 rcvtty -- how do I use it
   N    2 Al Bok            Thu Nov 23 05:13 Query about "repl -query"
   NR   3 "Wilbur, Orville" Fri Feb 09 10:24 X Terminal Presentation
  >N    4 To:"Wilbur, Orvil Sun Feb 11 22:03 Re: X Terminal Presentati
```

Here are some notes about the previous examples:

- Message 1 doesn't have a recognizable Date: component in its header. When that happens, the first four forms tell you by putting an asterisk (*) next to the date, and *scan* shows the last-modification time of the file that the message is stored in.

- The dash (–) next to message 3 in the first four forms means that it's been replied to with *repl –annotate*. The last format file, *scan.mailx*, uses R instead.

- The first four forms show a plus sign (+) next to the current message number. *scan.mailx* uses the right angle bracket (>).

- The *scan.timely* format file shows month and year for messages more than 26 weeks old (as in message 1), date and month for messages more than 7 days old (as in message 2), day name for messages more than 24 hours old (as in message 3); otherwise it shows the time of day it was sent (as in message 4).

- The *scan.size* format file shows message size in characters. If the size is over 99999, it starts with a question mark (?). For example, 103173 characters is shown as ?3173.

- The *scan.mailx* format file gives a format like the Berkeley UNIX *mail*(1) command. That program is called *mailx*(1) on UNIX System V.

If you want to use one of those format files every time you *scan*, add a line such as this to your MH profile:

```
scan: -form scan.timely
```

5.2.2 Scanning Backward

The *–reverse* switch scans from the highest message number to the lowest.

NOTE

In MH Version 6.6 and before, *scan –reverse* worked only on hosts configured with the MH [BERK] option. As of MH 6.7, the *–reverse* switch
works in all MH configurations.

Let's try it on the messages in the folder above:

```
% scan -reverse 1-4
    4+ 02/11 To:"Wilbur, Orvil  Re: X Terminal Presentation/Demonstra
    3 -02/09 "Wilbur, Orville"  X Terminal Presentation/Demonstration
    2  11/23 Al Bok             Query about "repl -query"<<I have a q
    1  04/24*mary@hahvahd.edu   rcvtty -- how do I use it?<<I've been
```

As usual, you can put *–reverse* in your MH profile if you want it to be the default. It works with *scan* format files, too.

CAUTION

If you use *xmh*, don't use *–reverse* in your MH profile. See Section 16.5, "Conflicts Between xmh and MH Customization," for a workaround.

5.2.3 Scanning a Mailbox File

Version 6.7 of MH of *scan* added a *–file* switch that lets you scan a mail file in "maildrop format." This is the format of the file where your new mail waits for you—for instance, the kind of file that *inc* reads messages from. The MH *packf* command, explained in Section 7.10, also makes files in this format.

For example, here's how *ehuser* could scan her system mailbox:*

```
% scan -file /usr/spool/mail/ehuser
   1  07/16 To:al@phlabs.ph.co New MH feature<<Al, scan has a new
   2  07/16 Al Bok            Re: New MH feature<<I saw that and
```

The command version called *msgscan*, in Section 9.9.3, makes that command line easier to type.

5.3 Checking for Mail Waiting: msgchk

The *msgchk* command will tell you whether there's mail waiting for you.

5.3.1 On Your Local Host

Here's an example:

```
% msgchk
You have new mail waiting; last read on Mon, 07 Dec 92 14:37:09
```

---

*There's a bug in MH 6.7 thru (at least) 6.7.2: *scan –file* looks in your current folder without saying so, then it scans the file you asked for. This isn't a problem unless your current folder is empty—if it is, *scan* will quit with a message `scan: no messages in current folder`. If that happens, you can keep *scan* quiet by giving it the name of any folder that isn't empty.

5.3.2 Across the Network with POP

msgchk is especially nice if you use the Post Office Protocol (POP) server to get mail across the network from other hosts. That's because you don't have to type *inc* and bring the mail into your inbox first (which can take some time across a slow network connection). Your host may be configured to use POP automatically—in that case, you'll never have to learn this POP business. But you also might be using POP to grab mail from other machines, as well as your own—in that case, this information should help. Here's an example using the ARPA POP protocol (the *–norpop* switch), which makes you type your password for the remote host. It shows that you have 508 characters of mail waiting:

```
% msgchk -norpop -host mailsrvr.cmp.xyz.edu
Name (mailsrvr.cmp.xyz.edu:ehuser):
Password (mailsrvr.cmp.xyz.edu:ehuser):
You have 1 message (508 bytes) on mailsrvr.cmp.xyz.edu
```

Typing all that stuff is a pain. This is a good time to add components like these to your MH profile:

```
msgchk: -norpop -host mailsrvr.cmp.xyz.edu -user ehuser
inc: -norpop -host mailsrvr.cmp.xyz.edu -user ehuser
```

Then, it's a lot easier to check your mail:

```
% msgchk
Password (mailsrvr.cmp.xyz.edu:ehuser):
You have 2 messages (12924 bytes) on mailsrvr.cmp.xyz.edu
```

For more information on *msgchk*, see your online manual page.

5.4 Other Features of inc

By now, you've used *inc*. It has some useful switches that we haven't covered, though.

If you need to keep track of the mail you get, *inc –audit* will make a log file. The *–silent* switch prevents the usual scan of messages incorporated. Use *–nochangecur* when you don't want the current message reset. Your new messages don't have to go in the *inbox* folder—you can give *inc* another folder name. Finally, there's a look at using *inc* with POP.

Part II
Using MH

5.4.1 Logging New Mail with –audit⊠

inc can keep an audit file of all the mail you incorporate. By default, it's kept in your MH directory. The log shows when you typed *inc* as well as *scan* lines for each message that's incorporated. Here's a piece of an audit file named *inc_log*. It shows two *incs*—the first brought in two messages, and the second brought one more:

```
% cd Mail
% cat inc_log
<<inc>> Mon, 07 Dec 92 08:22:45 -0600
   45+ 12/07 root              <<The job you submitted to at,
   46  12/07 Jim Bob Smith     Re: Encapsulation destroying go
<<inc>> Mon, 07 Dec 92 10:53:38 -0600
   47+ 12/07 Al Bok            Printer<<I am on the VAX system
```

To get more information, you can use a *scan* format file with *inc*. There are a few standard files (see Section 5.2.1) or you can make your own format file that will log just the information you want (see Section 10.2). For example, here's a line of the audit file made by the standard *scan.time* format file. Compare it to the lines in the previous example:

```
<<inc>> Mon, 07 Dec 92 17:48:10 -0600
   48+ 12/07 17:23EST Samantha Singer   Test<<This is a test m
```

To use an audit file, put the name of the file—and, if you want one, the *scan* format file—in your MH profile:

```
inc: -audit inc_log -form scan.time
```

5.4.2 Less-Used inc Features: –silent, –nochangecur, +folder

Although these features aren't used often, they'll help people with specialized needs.

Keeping inc Quiet

The *–silent* switch tells *inc* to bring in any new mail without showing the *scan* listing. If there's no mail, it will tell you; otherwise, *inc* won't display anything.

But if you have an audit file set up, *–silent* also prevents logging the individual messages in that file. All you'll get is the single time-stamp line:

```
<<inc>> Mon, 07 Dec 92 18:04:37 -0600
```

If you want *inc* to be silent on the terminal but also to write a complete audit file, try this command line (assuming you have the `inc: -audit` component set in your MH profile):

```
% inc >/dev/null
```

That throws the scan lines which would be on your screen into the UNIX "garbage can" named */dev/null*. It still shows the message `inc: No mail to incorporate` on your screen if there's no mail. You can't put `>/dev/null` in your MH profile, but you can add a shell alias so that it happens each time you use *inc*. In *csh*, for instance:

```
alias inc '\inc >/dev/null'
```

inc –nochangecur

Normally, *inc* changes the current message to be the first one you incorporate. The *–nochangecur* switch stops that—*inc* will still add the new mail to your *inbox* folder, but it'll leave the current message as it was.

Not Using inbox

Most users use *inbox* as a place to sort out new mail and, often, refile it to other folders. If you want *inc* to drop the new mail into another folder, put the folder name on the command line:

```
% inc +project
Incorporating new mail into project...
    ...
```

To use another folder every time you run *inc*, you can add `+foldername` to the `inc:` component in your MH profile. But then you won't be able to choose another folder on the command line; you'll get the error `inc: only one folder at a time!`. That's because, like most MH commands, *inc* gets all the arguments from both the MH profile and the command line. If you have that problem, try using shell aliases for *inc*.

5.4.3 Using inc with POP⊠

Just as *msgchk* works across the network to a mail server which runs POP, so does *inc*. It takes the same switches as *msgchk*. You'll usually want to put the switches in your MH profile. Of course, *inc –rpop* and *inc –norpop* drop mail into your folder on the host where you run *inc*, not on the mail server host.

Here's an example of a user, logged onto the local host as *ehuser*, who brings mail from the mailbox for *rschproj* on the remote server *mailsrvr.cmp.xyz.edu*:

```
% inc -norpop -host mailsrvr.cmp.xyz.edu
Name (mailsrvr.cmp.xyz.edu:ehuser): rschproj
Password (mailsrvr.cmp.xyz.edu:rschproj):
Incorporating new mail into inbox...

  8+ 12/07 biggrant@bucks.nih  You got $$<<We'll send champagne
```

Now the mail is in *ehuser*'s local *inbox*, so she can use *show* to read it, *rmm* to remove it, etc. ...

NOTE

xmh Release 4 may not work correctly with POP. If you have that problem, try this workaround. Set the following resources. The first (which is empty) is required. You'll probably need the other two, as well:

```
Xmh.InitialIncFile:
Xmh.CheckFrequency: 0
Xmh.CheckNewMail: true
```

That has been fixed in *xmh* with Release 5.

5.4.4 If New Messages Arrive ⊠

If your system is busy or you're incorporating a lot of messages, this may happen:

```
% inc
Incorporating new mail into inbox...
 143+ 12/07 To:al@phlabs.ph.co New MH feature<<Al, scan has
     ...
 450  12/11 mom@home.org       Where are you?<<I've sent yo
inc: new messages have arrived!
%
```

The new messages have arrived! means that, while *inc* was reading from your system mailbox and writing into your *inbox* folder, your system mailbox was modified somehow. Usually, that's because the system mail transport agent has written new messages into the system mailbox.

Normally, *inc* truncates ("zeroes") the system mailbox when it's done. Because *inc* doesn't want to miss a message, it won't truncate the system mailbox if new messages have arrived. If this happens, make a note of the first and last messages you just incorporated. Run *inc* again; the same messages—and the messages that just arrived—will be incorporated again. To delete the duplicates, remove the messages you incorporated first:

```
% inc
Incorporating new mail into inbox...
 451+ 12/07 To:al@phlabs.ph.co New MH feature<<Al, scan has
      ...
 757  12/11 mom@home.org       Where are you?<<I've sent yo
 758  12/11 Al Bok             More new MH features<<Now I
% rmm 143-450
```

6

Sending Mail with MH

Part II
Using MH

This chapter is about the specific programs that compose mail—like *comp* and *repl*. There's also information that applies to all the mail-composition programs—how to use mail aliases, what you can do at the What now? prompt, and so on. It starts with a step-by-step explanation of how mail messages are created.

If you want to use a new text editor or programs like a spelling or diction checker, Section 6.1.3 shows you how.

Section 6.3, "MH Aliases," describes a way to save time, to shorten long addresses, or to give an easy-to-remember name to a group of addresses.

MH gives you a lot of flexibility with draft messages, especially if you make a *draft folder*.

The chapter ends with tips about individual commands like *repl*—for example, how to include the original message in your reply . . . and how to mail files.

6.1 Sending an MH Message: An Overall View

Each of the four MH programs that are used to compose a mail message—*comp*, *repl*, *forw*, and *dist*—does some things differently from the others. For example, *comp* composes an original message and *forw* forwards existing ones. *repl* can build its header automatically; you fill in headers for the other three programs. But the programs have a lot in common. They all build a draft file in the same way, they all use *prompter* (unless you choose another editor), and they all have a What now? prompt. This section is about those similarities.

See Section 8.9.1 for more about how the draft message is built.

6.1.1 Making the Draft from the Template File ⊠

Each of the four mail-creating programs has its own *template draft* file. This file helps to form the draft message. For instance, the default template file for *comp* is named *components*. The *components* file looks like this (unless someone on your system has changed it):

```
To:
cc:
Subject:
-------
```

The row of dashes separates the message header from the body. It's automatically replaced with an empty line when you send the message.

When you start *comp*, it copies *components* into the draft file. The template file for *repl* is different—it's not just copied. Instead, the file, called *replcomps*, has MH formatting commands that automatically fill in the header of the draft file for you. *forw* and *dist* have their own twists, too. Figure 6-1 shows how they all work.

If you want to change the order of the headings—or add new ones—in all the messages you send with an MH command, read Section 8.9, "Draft Message Template Files."

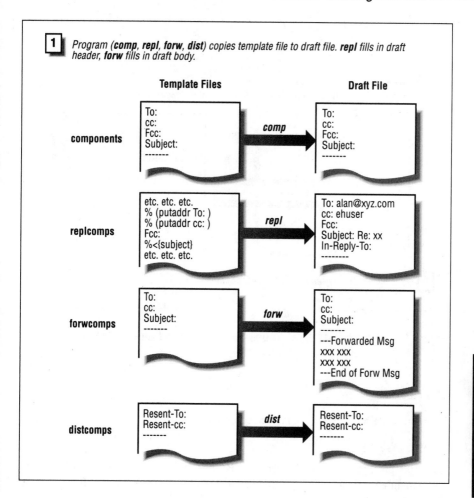

Figure 6-1. Sending a message. Step 1: Making draft from template

6.1.2 Editing the Draft with prompter

After the *comp*, *repl*, *forw*, and *dist* commands make the draft file in their own ways, they all start a program called *whatnow*. The first thing *whatnow* does is start an editor. The default editor is named *prompter*. (Section 6.2 explains more.)

prompter reads and edits the draft file, line by line. First it handles the header (up to the line of dashes). Next it handles the body. Figure 6-2 has an example.

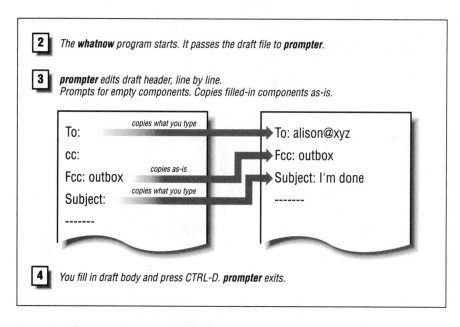

2 The **whatnow** program starts. It passes the draft file to **prompter**.

3 **prompter** edits draft header, line by line.
Prompts for empty components. Copies filled-in components as-is.

To: *copies what you type*   To: alison@xyz

cc: Fcc: outbox

Fcc: outbox *copies as-is*   Subject: I'm done

Subject: *copies what you type*   -------

----

4 You fill in draft body and press CTRL-D. **prompter** exits.

Figure 6-2. Steps 2-4: Draft message, before and after prompter edits it

The Header

If the draft file has any empty header components such as:

```
To:
```

prompter prompts you to fill them in. By now you know that if you leave the component empty, *prompter* just deletes that component from the draft.

Normally, after you fill in a header and press RETURN, *prompter* reads the next header component and shows it on your screen. But if you type a backslash (\) at the end of a line just before you press RETURN, *prompter* will keep collecting the same header component. That lets you put long lists of addresses in, say, the cc: component:

```
% comp
To: uunet!somewhere!somebody
cc: jjensen@bigcorp.se, lvalois@somecorp.fr, myboss,\
   phogan@auscorp.au
Subject:
```

You must start each of the continuation lines with a space or tab. The inset entitled "When is a Backslash Not a Backslash?" has more about this often-used character.

When is a Backslash Not a Backslash?

UNIX uses the backslash character (\) in a lot of places, which can be confusing for beginners. Here's a guide to backslashes:

- When you're typing a line of input on a terminal and you want to tell UNIX that "this next RETURN I'm going to type is not the end of the line," you'll often type a backslash just before the RETURN. That happened in the previous example, where you wanted to tell *prompter* that the next RETURN key you pressed would not be the end of the component. Backslashes are often typed before a RETURN, **to continue a line**.

- Backslashes are also used when you're **typing special characters**. For instance, some versions of UNIX use the at sign (@) character as the "line kill" character. That means, when you type an @ on your terminal, you're telling UNIX to forget everything you've typed so far on that line and start over.

  Sometimes—when you're typing a mail address like `vicki@squidbait`, for example, you want a literal @ character. You don't want the @ to erase the word "vicki." On those UNIX systems, you'd type `vicki\@squidbait` to tell UNIX "Treat this next @ literally."

- When some UNIX programs **display on a terminal** and a line is too long to fit on the screen, they split the line into pieces and show a backslash (\) at the end of each piece of the line except the last. One example is the GNU *emacs* editor. GNU *emacs* will display a very long line this way:

  ```
  This is the first part of the very long line etc. etc. \
  and... this is the second part blah blah blah etc. etc.\
  and now this is finally the end of the line.
  ```

  In that case, the backslash is not really in the file that *emacs* is showing; it's just a signal to you that the line continues.

To add or change the components in a header, you can either edit the header after *prompter* is finished or make your own private template files (see Section 8.9).

The Body

After the row of dashes in the draft file, *prompter* starts collecting the body of the message from your terminal exactly as you type it. Remember that *prompter* doesn't wrap lines; you should press RETURN at the end of every line. It reads until you press CTRL-D at the start of a line.* MH 6.7 added a new *–doteof* switch for *prompter*. If you set this switch (usually in your MH profile), then *prompter* will accept a single dot (.) at the start of a line, by itself, as the end of the draft message.

Next, if there was text in the message body when you started *prompter* (you're forwarding a message, re-editing an existing draft, and so on), *prompter* will scroll that text across your screen. With big messages or slow terminals, this can take time. If you don't want to see the included text, add the *–rapid* switch to the prompter: line in your MH profile. (If you have *–rapid* set and you want to see the included text, just type list at a What now? prompt.)

If your message had included text, there's one more pair of switches you might want to know about: *–prepend* and *–noprepend*. Because most users like to "set and forget" about these, the explanation is in Section 8.9.1.

6.1.3 What now?—and the whatnow Program

After you end the body of the message by typing (usually) CTRL-D, *prompter* quits and the draft message is handled by the *whatnow* program. It gives you a list of choices for your draft message. To see the list, just press RETURN at the What now? prompt. That list covers only the most common things you can do at the What now? prompt. Most commands accept other switches to change their operation. For instance, *send –width 60* tells *send* to fold header address components that are more than 60 characters wide. Or *list afile* will display the file named *afile* in your current directory, then give you another What now? prompt. For a quick list of switches, you can add *–help* to most commands, as in the following example:

```
What now? send -help
syntax: send [file] [switches]
  switches are:
     ...
What now?
```

Here's more information about each choice, with abbreviations in parentheses:

---

prompter reads what you type until it gets the *end-of-input* character. There's a chance that your account is set up to use something besides CTRL-D as end-of-input.

`list` (or the letter `l`)

Shows the draft message you just typed. On most systems, this shows the draft screen by screen (like the *show* program does)—to see the next screen, press either the space bar or RETURN (depending on the program that *list* uses). When *list* is done, you'll get another What now? prompt.

`display` (or `d`)

Works only with the *repl* and *dist** programs. It shows the message that you're replying to or distributing; otherwise *display* is just like *list*.

`edit` (or `e`)

Uses the default editor (usually *prompter*, or whatever editor you were using) to edit the draft. When you leave the editor, you'll get another What now? prompt.

You can set a different default editor in your MH profile. See Section 6.2.1, "Editor-next."

`edit` *editor* (or `e` *editor*)

Edits the draft with the editor named *editor* (example: `edit vi`). When you leave the editor, you'll get another What now? prompt. Then, you can use yet another editor program or any of the other *whatnow* commands.

The "editor" program doesn't really have to be an editor. Any UNIX program that accepts a filename argument will work—including shell programs that you write. For example, you can type `edit append` *filename* to append a file to your draft—see Section 13.2.

As long as the "editor" program doesn't modify the draft file, you can use the *edit* command to do anything else you can do with a standard UNIX program and a file. Here are some ideas:

`edit spell`   Runs the draft through the UNIX speller and shows you the misspelled words.

`edit diction`   Uses the UNIX diction checker to list wordy sentences to your screen.

---

*See Section 6.9, "Distributing Messages with dist."

`edit head`	Runs *head*(1) to read the first ten lines of your draft. That usually shows the header pretty well.
`edit wc`	Counts the number of lines, words, and characters in your draft (including the header).
`edit lpr`	(or `edit lp`, depending on your print command) Sends the draft to the printer.

`quit` (or q)

Leaves the draft message file where it is and takes you back to the shell prompt (%). You use this if you want to do something else and come back to your draft message later. To find out how, see Section 6.5.

`quit -delete` (or q -d)

Deletes the draft message you've been working on and takes you to a shell prompt. Use this if you decide not to send the message. The dash (–) in *–delete* isn't required, but that's undocumented and may be changed. Section 6.5.3, "Deleted Draft Messages," explains what happens when the draft is deleted — and how to change your mind after you delete a draft.

`refile +folder` (or r +folder)

Moves the draft message into the folder you name. The draft won't be sent. You'll get another shell prompt. See Section 7.1, "Folders."

`refile -link +folder` (or r -l +folder)

Links a copy of the draft message into the folder you name, but leaves the draft there to be sent. Now, no matter what command you type at the next What now? prompt, a copy of the draft will stay in the folder named *folder*. You'll get another shell prompt. Section 7.1.4 has more information.

whom (or w)

Lists the addresses that the message will go to. This is useful with aliases (Section 6.3). When *whom* is done, you'll get another What now? prompt.

whom −check (or w −check)

Lists the addresses that the message will go to and tells you if the address looks "deliverable."* Unfortunately, this doesn't mean that the mail will really get there. Depending on how the message is sent, an Address OK message from *whom* means something like "the remote hostname looks okay" or "the network is available."

Many electronic mail systems still can't tell you whether your mail addresses are correct—you have to wait to see if the message is returned to you. This may or may not be the situation on your host. But *whom −check* will try to tell you if addresses are "deliverable" and show you something about them.

Although you can use *whom* from a shell prompt (like %), you'll usually use it at the What now? prompt. Here's an example, with the middle left out:

```
% comp
To: gurus
    ...
What now? whom
danro... deliverable
rada... deliverable
rbwilbur@mysun.xyz.edu... deliverable
"| /usr/local/lib/mh/slocal −user ahof"... deliverable
```

Here, *whom* shows that the gurus mail alias has four members. The first two of them look like addresses on the local computer. The third has mail forwarded to another computer, and the fourth has mail forwarded to a mail-handling program (*slocal*—see Chapter 11, *Processing New Mail Automatically*).

My computer uses the *sendmail* transport agent, so *whom* calls *sendmail* to check the addresses. If your computer uses a different transport agent, your *whom* output may look different. Again, *whom* can't guarantee that your message will get through. But you can be fairly sure that if *whom* tells you there's a problem, you should check into it. Be sure your addresses are written correctly—if that doesn't help, ask an expert who knows your computer's transport agent.

---

*On some versions of MH, *whom −check* just prints the cryptic error whom: Only one message at a time!... even when there *is* only one message. Plain *whom*, without the −check switch, doesn't have the problem.

send (or s)

Sends the message as shown in Figure 6-3. Depending on how your system's transport agent is set up and where your message is going, the message may not be delivered for a few minutes, or even a couple of days. All "send" really means is "deliver the message to the transport agent." The rest is up to that transport agent.* If the message was sent (to the transport agent!) successfully, you'll get another shell prompt. If there were problems, you may see the error on your screen or you may get a mail message that explains what went wrong. Again, it all depends on your computer's setup.

You can add a *sendproc* processing program that does any handling you want before the message is given to MH for delivery. Section 13.13 shows a *sendproc* shell program named *mysend*.

send -watch -verbose (or s -wa -v)

Gives you an idea of what's happening as MH delivers your message to the transport agent.† How much you see depends on several things.

If your system is set up to do it, you'll see the message being delivered to the remote machine across the network. Here's an example of a message going from a user *georgeb* on a local machine named *fubar.gov* to a user named *gorby* on the remote machine *kremvax*.

```
% comp
To: gorby@kremvax.kgb.su
Fcc: outbox
    ...
What now? s -wa -v
Fcc: outbox
gorby@kremvax.kgb.su... Connecting to kremvax.kgb.su.tcp...
220 kremvax.kgb.su Sendmail 4.0/2.1CCCP- ready at Sun,\
 28 Jan 90 07:31:52 MST gripes to boris@kremvax.kgb.su
>>> HELLO fubar.gov
250 kremvax.kgb.su Hello fubar.gov, pleased to meet you
>>> MAIL From:<georgeb@fubar.gov>
250 <georgeb@fubar.gov>... Sender ok
>>> RCPT To:<gorby@kremvax.kgb.su>
250 <gorby@kremvax.kgb.su>... Recipient ok
>>> DATA
354 Enter mail, end with "." on a line by itself
>>> .
```

---

* *send* actually gives the message to the MH program called *post*, which in turn gives it to the transport agent.

† The undocumented –*snoop* switch on some versions of MH gives more information.

```
250 Mail accepted
>> QUIT
221 kremvax.kgb.su delivering mail
gorby@kremvax... Sent
%
```

(Well ... I admit that I made up those addresses, and that the example is dated these days, but *kremvax* was a network joke for years. Mailers really do "introduce themselves" to each other.)

push (or p)

Runs *send* with its *–push* switch, which sends your message "in the background." In other words, you'll get another shell prompt right away.

Using *push* has good and bad points. You can do something else while MH sends the message; that can be good, especially on a slow system or when it takes time to deliver the message.

But the draft file will stay there until it's been processed. That can be bad:

* If you're using annotation with *forw*, *dist*, or *repl* (Section 4.5), the message won't be annotated until it's sent. That means you'd better not remove or re-file the message until it's been annotated! (On systems with long delays, try refiling the message before you reply and annotate it. A script named *replf* is handy for that. It's in this book's online archive—see Appendix E—also in the *mtrenv* directory of the MH distribution.)

  To see if the message has been annotated, *scan* the original message* and look for the dash (–) before the date. Section 4.7 has an example.

* If you aren't using a draft folder (Section 6.5) and you try to start a new draft message before the first one has been sent in the background, here's what will happen:

  ```
  Draft '/yourMHdir/draft' exists; disposition? quit
  ```

  You should quit and wait for the draft to be sent. While you're waiting, think about setting up a draft folder. It avoids this problem.

Figure 6-3 is a diagram that shows what *send* (and *send –push*) do with the finished draft.

---

*If your *scan* can't find the message, try again. The message "disappears" for a moment as it's annotated.

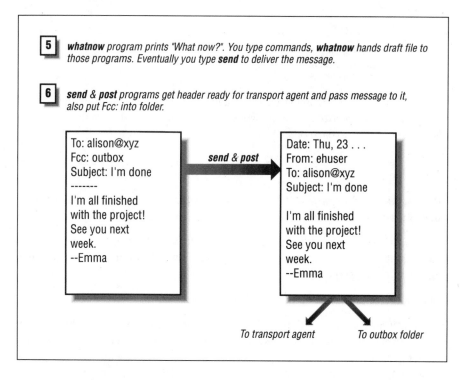

Figure 6-3. Steps 5-6: After composing the draft

6.2 Changing Default Editors

As Section 6.1.2 explained, after the *comp, repl, forw*, and *dist* commands create the draft message, they start the *prompter* editor. And, as you saw in Section 6.1.3, typing What now? **edit** gives you a default editor. The following sections explain how to change these defaults.

6.2.1 Editor-next

When *whatnow* runs an editor program (a program you name at a What now? **edit** prompt, or with an *–editor* switch in the MH profile), it keeps track of the editor's name. Then, after the editor (like *prompter*, *vi*, or any other editor) exits, it can have a new default editor ready to run.

You set the default editor with entries in your MH profile. For example, let's say that you have these three components in your MH profile:

```
prompter-next: vi
vi-next: spell
spell-next: vi
```

These tell MH that after you run *prompter* the default editor is *vi* and that after *vi* the default editor is *spell*. Finally, after you run *spell* the default editor is *vi* again. So when you use *comp* (which runs *prompter* for you, unless you've changed that), you can go into *vi* directly by just typing `edit` (or just `e`) at the `What now?` prompt. At the next `What now?` prompt, the default editor will be *spell*. Here's a demonstration:

```
% comp
To: someone
cc:
Subject: something
-------
blah blah blah...
CTRL-D
-------
What now? e

        ...vi starts...

What now? e

        ...spell puts a list of words on the screen...

What now? e

        ...vi starts...

What now? e

        ...spell checks the just-edited message...

What now? s
```

Of course, you don't have to use the default editor. You can use any other editor by typing its name after the *edit* (*e*) command.

6.2.2 Replacing the prompter Editor

If you don't like the way that *prompter* works, you can use any other UNIX text editor.*

If you never want *comp, repl, forw,* and *dist* to use the *prompter* editor, put a component like this in your MH profile:

```
Editor: whatever
```

where `whatever` is the editor you want—*vi*, for example. Then, when you start *comp, repl, forw,* or *dist*, they will put you straight into *vi*. When you save the message and exit the editor (in *vi*, type ZZ), you'll be at the What now? prompt.

But *prompter* can be pretty handy for entering message headers when you use *comp* and *dist*, for example. To choose different editors for different commands, use their *–editor* switches.

Let's assume that your default editor is *prompter* (if you have not added an Editor: component to your MH profile, as shown above). Then you can set the *repl* and *forw* entries in your MH profile to use *emacs*—and leave *prompter* as the other programs' default:

```
repl: -editor emacs
forw: -editor emacs
```

Or, let's say that you want to use *vi* as the default editor for everything except *dist* (which really doesn't need a sophisticated editor). Put these two components in your MH profile:

```
Editor: vi
dist: -editor prompter
```

Section 13.10 has an editor script named *distprompter* designed to be used with *dist*.

By the way, if you set *vi* as the default editor, here's a handy key map command for *vi*:

```
map! ^N ^[/: $^[A
```

---

* ...well, *almost* any editor. The editor must be able to read the draft message file, then write the edited text back to the same file. For example, the *sed*(1) editor wouldn't work unless you incorporate it into a shell program that replaces the original file.

The key map sets *vi* so that typing $\boxed{\text{CTRL-N}}$ from text-input mode will move you to the end of the next empty component.* For example, after you enter a component like To: fred, you can stay in text-input mode, press $\boxed{\text{CTRL-N}}$ to move to the end of the next empty component (usually cc:), and be in text-input mode, ready to fill in the next address.

6.3 MH Aliases ⊠

When you address a message, *aliases* can shorten the address and make it easier to remember.

Here's an example. You're working on a project with three other people, and you stay in touch by e-mail. If you didn't use mail aliases, you might address a message to all of them like this:

```
To: alissa@ketneg.com, uunet!abo!pxu341i, abd@mvus.bitnet
```

What a pain to type those addresses each time you want to send mail!

Instead, pick a name (an *alias*) for that group of addresses. Store that alias name and the addresses in an *alias file*, then tell the MH commands where your alias file is. After that, when you send mail, all you have to type is the alias name—for example:

```
To: project
```

6.3.1 Making MH Aliases

Let's go on with the example. You decide to name your alias file *aliases* and store it in your MH directory. To store those three addresses in an alias called *project*, you'd change to your MH directory (which is usually named *Mail*), then use an editor like *vi* to make the file:

```
% cd Mail
% vi aliases
```

---

*The map starts with an ESCAPE (^[) to go to command mode. Then, it searches for the next empty component—that is, the next line ending with a colon and a space (/: $^[). The A command resumes text input at the end of this empty component. For more information about *vi* key maps, see the Nutshell Handbook *Learning the vi Editor*.

You'd put this line into the file:

```
project: alissa@ketneg.com, uunet!abo!pxu341i, abd@mvus.bitnet
```

Tell MH commands where your alias file is:

- On MH Version 6.6 and before, you have to give the alias filename to each MH command which uses aliases. To do that, add these three components to your MH profile:

  ```
  ali: -alias aliases
  send: -alias aliases
  whom: -alias aliases
  ```

- On MH Version 6.7 and after, you can use this one component instead:

  ```
  Aliasfile: aliases
  ```

Now, when you use any MH mail-sending command you can send mail to *project* and it'll be delivered to those three addresses. (Actually, *mhmail*, which is covered in Section 6.10 and Section 12.17.2, can't use aliases directly. You can work around that problem with *ali* and command substitution, though, as the example in Section 6.10 shows.)

Your *aliases* file (or whatever you name it) can have as many lines as you need. Put one alias on each line. If an alias has lots of addresses in it, you can continue it on other lines by ending each line with a backslash (\), like this:

```
project: alissa@ketneg.com, uunet!abo!pxu341i, \
     abd@mvus.bitnet, moe%stooge@guys.org, \
     lizv@geknichon.xyz.edu
```

You don't need to indent the continuation lines, but I think it makes the meaning clearer.

Long alias files can be hard to maintain. ("Who is *k38d4@kumquat.usnd.edu*, anyway, and why is that person in my alias file?") Adding comment lines and names can identify aliases and the addresses on them. Example 6-1 shows how. A line that starts with a semicolon (;) is a comment. Legal RFC822 syntax works for addresses, in most cases, so you can include names. As above, indent continuation lines and end all but the last line of the alias with a backslash (\).

Example 6-1. An MH alias file with comments and real names

```
;
;  BOOK REVIEWERS:
;
rvwrs:  Freida Kumzickle <kumzy@hoople.usnd.edu>,\
        Ethel Michaelman <ethel@edsel.org>,\
```

Example 6-1. An MH alias file with comments and real names (continued)

```
"Dr. Mary Tallman" <tallman@lab.army.mil>,\
Harry Wielstrom <weilstrm@world.tsd.com>
```

Aliases can include other aliases. The other aliases must be listed *later* in the alias file. For example, the *allgroups* alias in this alias file would send to all the groups listed below it:

```
allgroups: mkt, sls, mgt
mkt: randy, xandra
sls: paula, nathan, will
mgt: gilligan, ozzie, harriet
```

But in the following alias file, the *allgroups* alias would not work because *mkt*, *sls*, and *mgt* are listed before it:

```
mkt: randy, xandra
sls: paula, nathan, will
mgt: gilligan, ozzie, harriet
allgroups: mkt, sls, mgt
```

So, always list an alias before the other aliases it references.

You can share alias files—say, between members of your group or students in a class. For this to work, the alias file has to be readable by everyone (one way to find out is to try to read the other user's alias file from your account with *cat*). You can put the alias file anywhere on the filesystem—it doesn't have to be in an MH mail directory. Just add a *–alias* entry to your MH profile—for example, in MH Version 6.6 and before:

```
ali: -alias aliases -alias /usr/groupproj/mh_aliases
send: -alias aliases -alias /usr/groupproj/mh_aliases
whom: -alias aliases -alias /usr/groupproj/mh_aliases
```

If there's an alias with the same name in more than one file, MH will use the first alias it finds—and it reads alias filenames left to right.

In MH 6.7 and after, you can only put one alias filename in the MH profile `Aliasfile:` entry. Other aliases have to be listed on the individual command lines. So in MH 6.7 the example above could look like:

```
Aliasfile: aliases
ali: -alias /usr/groupproj/mh_aliases
send: -alias /usr/groupproj/mh_aliases
whom: -alias /usr/groupproj/mh_aliases
```

Note that there may be a system-wide alias file with a name such as */usr/local/lib/mh/MailAliases*. Where it is and what aliases it has depends on your system postmaster or system administrator. If MH is trying to find an alias, and the alias isn't in any of your *–alias* files, it will search the system-wide file (if that file exists).

Some mail transport agents, such as *sendmail*, also have their own alias files (*sendmail* uses a file like */usr/lib/aliases* or */etc/aliases*). Section 6.3.3 introduces MTA aliases.

You can also use your personal or group alias files to send mail to users who are members of UNIX groups. (*Primary* group members are usually listed in the system */etc/passwd* file. *Secondary* group members are listed in */etc/group*.) For example, let's say that *joeb*, *amyl*, and *edwina* are primary members of the UNIX group named *staff*. If you put entries like these in your alias file:

```
gurus: +staff
everyone: *
```

and you addressed a message to *gurus*, it would be sent to everyone who is listed in the system */etc/passwd* file as being a member of the UNIX *staff* group ... that's *joeb*, *amyl*, and *edwina*.

If you sent mail to the alias *everyone*, it would go to every user who has an account on your computer.

These special alias entries depend on your operating system, local computer, and more ... there are too many possibilities to explain thoroughly here. If you have questions and you understand UNIX pretty well, start with the *mh–alias*(5) manual page on your system—it's terse, but it has examples. Otherwise, show this book to an expert on your computer for help—or grab a manual that explains the user and group setup on your version of UNIX.

Finally, you can take a list of addresses from a file by using a left angle bracket (<) and a filename. Here's an example of a file named */usr/ourgroup/staff* and how you could use its addresses in an alias named *mygroup*:

```
% cat /usr/ourgroup/staff
berthab
sherryo
vickiz
bigboss@gold-plated.bigcorp.com
% cat aliases
mygroup: < /usr/ourgroup/staff
```

Always be sure to use an absolute pathname, starting with a slash (/), no matter where the address file is stored.

Also see Section 6.3.2 on the *ali* command, which is good for testing your alias file. Section 6.1.3 has a section on the *whom* command, another way to test aliases.

6.3.2 Showing MH Aliases with ali

If you have set up MH aliases, you can see who belongs to an alias with the *ali* command. For example, to see who's in the *gurus* alias:

```
% ali gurus
danro, rada, rbwilbur, ahof
```

If you don't give it an alias name to list, *ali* will list all the MH aliases you can use.

The *–user* switch makes *ali* work in the opposite way: you give *ali* the address and it finds the aliases which contain that address.

The *–list* switch gives output in a column. It's used in shell programming and with commands like *mhmail* (see Section 6.10). Here's the previous example using *–list*:

```
% ali -list gurus
danro
rada
rbwilbur
ahof
```

After it searches your alias file(s), the *ali* command automatically searches the system MH alias file if there is one. If you don't want it to do this, use the *–noalias* switch. You can type that on the command line or add it to your MH profile.

6.3.3 Aliases in Your Transport Agent

Your system transport agent may have its own alias file. For instance, *sendmail*'s file is usually named */usr/lib/aliases* or */etc/aliases*.

Your transport agent's aliasing probably works about the same as MH alias files, though its syntax might be different. Also, the *ali* command won't show aliases in a system alias file (but *whom –check* might, depending on your transport agent—see Section 6.1.3).

If everyone on your system uses MH, you can put system-wide aliases in the MH alias file. But if some people run other user agents, system-wide aliases should go in the transport agent's alias file. Also, if you have an alias with many members, you might want to put it in the system alias file. That's because MH replaces the alias name with the expanded list of addresses, which can lead to some very large mail headers.

Finally, aliases that are set by the transport agent will probably be "visible" to users on other computers. For example, if the site *foo.xxx.com* put an alias called *staff* in its *sendmail aliases* file, then anyone in the world could mail to *staff@foo.xxx.com* and have it delivered to the addresses in that alias. MH aliases can't be used that way.

6.4 Headers and Addresses ⊠

The first part of a mail message—the To:, Subject:, and so on—is called the message *header*. The gory details of mail headers are listed in the *mh–mail*(5) manual page in Appendix I.

MH lets you customize the mail message header completely—to do some worthwhile and time-saving things. This section covers some common changes that you might want to make to your headers.

6.4.1 Components You Add to a Header

Here are some useful components you can add to the header of a draft.

To add one or more of them to your draft message, use an editor like *vi*. At the What now? prompt, if you type a command like *edit vi*, you can add components to the header of your draft message.

You can also put these components in template draft files. Then, the components will go in all the draft messages you compose with a particular MH command. *prompter* will prompt you for these new components, like it does for To:, Subject:, and so on. Or, you can fill in values for these components so that they'll *always* be included in mail headers and you never need to fill them in. For details on that, see Section 8.9, "Draft Message Template Files."

Bcc: Blind Carbon Copies

A header with a Bcc: component, like this:

```
To: bigboss
Bcc: curly, larry, moe
Subject: I recommend you promote Curly, Larry, and Moe
------
```

would send a *blind copy* of the message to those three users. People listed in the To: and cc: components will not know that the Bcc: users got a copy because the Bcc: component is removed from the header when the message is sent. This is like forwarding a copy of the message to someone else after sending it—except that a blind copy lets you do it as you send the original message.

The blind copies can take a couple of different forms, depending on your system configuration. In some cases, the user who gets the blind copy will get a copy dropped in his or her mailbox—without his or her mail address anywhere in the header or any indication that the message is a blind copy.

Other times, the message will be marked, much like a forwarded message. Here's an example of that—a message sent by *ehuser* to *bigboss*, with a blind copy to the three people she's writing about. Each of the "blind recipients" will get a message like this:

```
Received: by bigsun.ncs.xyz.edu (5.54/ACS)
        id AA14322; Mon, 07 Dec 92 08:24:05 EST
Message-Id: <9003131224.AB09482@bigsun.ncs.xyz.edu>
Date: Mon, 07 Dec 92 08:24:15 -0500
From: ehuser@bigsun.ncs.xyz.edu (Emma H. User)
Subject: I recommend you promote Curly, Larry, and Moe
Apparently-To: <curly@bigsun.ncs.xyz.edu>

------- Blind-Carbon-Copy

To: bigboss@bigsun.ncs.xyz.edu
Subject: I recommend you promote Curly, Larry, and Moe
Date: Mon, 07 Dec 92 08:24:15 -0500
From: ehuser@bigsun.ncs.xyz.edu (Emma H. User)

Dear Boss, you may think those three guys are stooges but
I think they're incredibly talented.  I believe that
you should promote them right away.

                        Emma

------- End of Blind-Carbon-Copy
```

If the message has no "sighted" recipients (in other words, if all the recipients are "blind"), the Bcc: recipients will all see the following:

```
Bcc: Blind Distribution List: ;
```

NOTE

If you send a blind copy to two or more addresses *on the same host*, both users may see each others' names in Apparently-To: components. If that would be a problem, you might save a copy of your message and use *forw* or *dist* to send separate copies to each of those addresses.

Dcc: Distribution Carbon Copies

The almost-undocumented Dcc: header* sends a message to each address listed after it. It's similar to Bcc:, but there's no ------- Blind-Carbon-Copy wrapper around the message. It's probably best for sending copies to an address which would never reply—for instance, an automatic archiver or printer. (See Chapter 11, _Processing New Mail Automatically_, for examples.)

Because Dcc: isn't documented, don't depend on it staying in MH forever.

Fcc: Folder Copies

This book doesn't cover folders in detail until Section 7.1. But here's a useful feature of MH that belongs with mail-sending commands: a _folder copy_. A component like this in your message header:

```
Fcc: project
```

would save a copy of the message in your folder named _project_ as you send it. If the folder doesn't exist yet, you'll be asked for confirmation when you send the message with _send_—or, if you send with _push_ (see Section 6.1.3) the folder will be created automatically.

If you put more than one folder name here, separated by commas, the message copy will go to all of those folders. Some versions of MH will put a separate copy in each folder; others will use links. If you care whether you get links or copies, see Section 7.8.2 or check with a local expert. If your version gives copies, you can get links by using Fcc: to a single folder, then using _refile –link_ on that message after the mail has been sent.

Reply–to: Give a Different Address for Replies

If you're sending a message from some computer but you don't read mail on that same computer, you can add a component to the header of your message that tells where reply messages should be sent. There are quite a few other reasons to do this. For example, if you send mail to a distribution list which has many addresses, you can use this to request that replies automatically to go to you or some other address.

Not all mail agents pay attention to this, but a lot (like MH _repl_) do—they'll see this special component in the header and automatically address replies to it

---

*It's mentioned in "The RAND MH Message Handling System: Administrator's Guide, UCI Version."

instead of the From: address. Carbon copies (cc:'s) are replied to as always. Put a line like this in the message header:

```
Reply-to: yourname@yourmachine.xxx.yyy.zzz
```

Make the address as complete as you can; it needs to be valid from computers outside your organization, as well as inside.

X-: Your Own Headers

The RFC822 transport standard, and others since it, carefully specify what headers are legal in mail messages. You can use any header name you want, though, if it starts with the characters X- (the letter X followed by a dash). For example:

```
X-fortune: Too much of a good thing is WONDERFUL.  -- Mae West
```

There are more serious examples in Sections 7.2.6, 11.10.2, and 9.5.

6.4.2   Signature and From:

When you send a mail message, the From: component looks something like:

```
From: ehuser@bigmachine.xxx.yyy.zzz (E. User)
```

depending on how your system and your MH programs are set up. You can change this component to something else in (at least) two ways.

Signature

If you define your *signature*, it replaces the text in the From: component (although your system may add more text at the end of your signature).

For example, you can put the following line in your MH profile:

```
Signature: "Emma H. User"
```

and your mail messages will have a From: component something like this:

```
From: "Emma H. User" <ehuser@bigmachine.xxx.yyy.zzz>
```

This signature needs double quotes (") around it because of the period (.).*
When in doubt, use the double quotes. If your account uses the C shell, you can
also set a *SIGNATURE* environment variable in your *.login* file:

```
setenv SIGNATURE '"Emma H. User"'
```

or, for Bourne shell users, in your *.profile* file:

```
SIGNATURE='"Emma H. User"'; export SIGNATURE
```

The single quotes (') protect the double quotes from the shell. The single quotes
won't appear in your From: components.

Some people like to add a standard signature, one or more lines, to the end of
their messages. An easy way to do that is by editing your draft template file. For
more ideas, see Section 8.9.6, "Automatic Signature on End of Messages," Section 13.13, "Add Signature (or Anything) to Drafts: mysend," and Section 13.2,
"Add Files to Your Draft Messages: append."

From:

Instead of defining your signature, you can use a completely different From:
header. I do that on my job. I'm one of the people at O'Reilly & Associates who
gets mail from system aliases like *bookquestions* (technical questions about
books) and *book–info–request* (to join our mailing list). When I reply to messages, I want the reply to have the same address in the header. I add a header like
this:

```
From: Jerry Peek <bookquestions@ora.com>
```

Any legal RFC822-style address is okay. When the message is sent, a separate
Sender: header will automatically be added with my "official" address:

```
Sender: jerry@ora.com
```

The big advantage of setting From: instead of the signature is that, if you put a
fully-qualified address in From:, many system mailers will leave it exactly as
you wrote it.

I make my From: header with a special command version called *replb*; see Section 9.4.4. It's simpler to just add it to your draft message template files (Section 8.9) or edit the message header.

---

*This is for the RFC822 mail transport standard, not for MH.

6.5 Working with Draft Messages

If you use the *quit* command at a What now? prompt, it leaves the draft message for you to work on later.

MH also has a very useful feature called *draft folders* that lets you keep many draft messages, work on them, and send them "in the background" while you do something else. This section explains how to work with draft messages in MH.

6.5.1 Single Draft Messages

If you started using MH from scratch, your account probably uses just a single draft message. (It has to be set up especially to use an MH draft folder instead of the draft message.) A "single draft message" means that whenever you start to send a message with *comp*, *repl*, *forw*, or *dist*, the draft is always written to a file named *draft* in your MH directory. If you start one of those programs and the draft file already exists, you'll see this message:

```
Draft '/yourMHdir/draft' exists; disposition?
```

Press RETURN for a list of what you can do. Here are the choices:

list (or l)   Shows you the existing draft.

quit (or q)   Exits from MH and leaves the draft alone.

replace (or rep)

> Deletes the draft and replaces it with a new, empty form. You start fresh, as if the old draft were never there.

use (or u)   Starts up your draft editor (usually, *prompter*) to keep working on the existing draft. You only have this choice if you're running *comp*. Note that if you start *repl*, *forw*, or *dist* before you get the disposition? prompt, they won't let you *use* an existing draft—you'll need to *quit* and run *comp*.

> You can also get here directly, and skip the disposition? prompt, by starting with the command:

> ```
> % comp -use
> ```

> That's the normal way to re-edit an existing draft message.

NOTE

If you're re-editing a draft that you started with *repl*, *forw*, or *dist*, and their *–annotate* switch, the original message won't be annotated. That's because there's no way for MH to find the original message number just by looking at the leftover draft.

You can annotate the message yourself with *anno*—see Section 7.7.

`refile +folder`

Moves the draft message into the folder you name. The draft won't be sent. Instead, the draft is moved and replaced with a new, empty form; you start over with a new draft. There's more about folders in Section 7.1.

6.5.2 Draft Folder⊠

Instead of using a single draft file, you can set up an MH folder that holds many drafts. This has some great advantages:

- You don't have to finish and send a draft before you start on another.

- If you use job control, shell layers, or window systems, or if you're just logging on to your account from more than one place at the same time, you can work on several draft messages at once.

- If you use:

  `What now? `**`push`**

  to send your messages, you don't have to wait to start a new message until the previous draft has been sent. This is because *push* doesn't process the draft right away—it takes a few seconds, especially on a busy computer. Without a draft folder, with only one draft file, the draft exists until it's been sent. A draft folder avoids this problem by letting *push* take its time sending a draft while you work on a new draft.

- If several users share the same account, each one can work on a separate message.

The disadvantage of a draft folder is that it can be easier for you to forget about an old draft message.

To set up a draft folder, you may want to skip ahead to Section 7.1 and read about folders. Once you've set up a draft folder, though, you don't need to think about folders much. Here's how you do it:

1. Pick a name for the draft folder (*xmh* uses the name *drafts*; that might be a good choice even if you don't use *xmh*).

2. Create the folder from a shell prompt, like this:

   ```
   % folder -push +drafts
   Folder /yourMHdir/drafts doesn't exist; create? y
           drafts+ has no messages.
   % folder -pop
   [previousfolder+ now current.]
   ```

3. Add this component to your MH profile:

   ```
   Draft-folder: drafts
   ```

Try using your draft folder. Type comp (or repl or...). When you get to the What now? prompt, type quit. You'll get a message that tells you where the draft message was left:

```
What now? q
whatnow: draft left on /yourMHdir/drafts/1
```

That shows that the draft message is number 1. Then start another draft (with *comp* or *repl* or...). Instead of the old prompt:

```
Draft '/yourMHdir/draft' exists; disposition?
```

MH will give you a fresh draft. Then, if you type quit again, you'll see that this new draft has the next higher message number in the draft folder:

```
What now? q
whatnow: draft left on /yourMHdir/drafts/2
```

How do you finish a draft that you've left in the draft folder? An easy way is with the following command:

```
% comp -use n
```

where n is the draft message number that you want to resume. Easier: if you want to re-edit the draft you started most recently, that draft should still be the current message in the draft folder... in that case, you can omit the message number n.

If you're not sure which message you want, you can scan the draft folder:

```
% scan +drafts
```

to get a summary of your draft messages. The shell script in Section 13.8 is probably the easiest way of all.

As explained in Section 6.5.1, if you're re-editing a draft that you started with *repl*, *forw*, or *dist*, and their *–annotate* switches, the original message won't be annotated.

6.5.3 Deleted Draft Messages

After you send a draft, MH renames it with a leading comma (,) or hash mark (#). For instance, without a draft folder, your draft file could be renamed *,draft*. In a draft folder, draft number 3 would be "deleted" by changing its name to *,3*. If you need to recover a draft message, just rename it without the comma or hash mark. The techniques are in Section 7.5, "Removing Messages (and Getting Them Back)."

If you type quit –delete at a What now? prompt—or, if your editor program returns a non-zero exit status to *whatnow* (see Section 12.17.8)—*whatnow* will delete your draft as explained above. When that happened, versions of MH before 6.7.2 just said that the draft was "deleted." MH 6.7.2 changed the message to a user-friendly:

```
whatnow: problems with edit--draft left in /yourMHdir/drafts/,2
```

Here's one editing feature that isn't user-friendly. Some editors return a non-zero exit status when the file they were editing is perfectly fine. (Recent versions of *vi* from AT&T and Sun have this "feature.") *whatnow* will think that the editor failed—and delete your draft.

If you use an editor like that, find out whether your version of MH can be compiled with the [ATTVIBUG] configuration option. (Section 4.9 shows how to check configuration options.) If you can't use [ATTVIBUG], you can make a shell script called something like *myvi* that edits the draft and always returns a zero exit status. See Example 6-2.

Example 6-2. Workaround for vi Editor Problem: myvi

```
#! /bin/sh
# myvi - workaround for "vi" that returns non-zero exit status
# and makes MH "whatnow" delete draft message.
# Usage (in MH profile)    Editor: myvi
vi $*
exit 0
```

To install *myvi*, see Section 12.2, "Writing a Simple Shell Program," and Section 6.2, "Changing Default Editors."

6.6 The comp Command

The previous explanation of generic mail-sending commands, along with Section 4.2, covers *comp* pretty well.

Besides starting new mail messages, the main use of *comp* is editing existing draft messages with the *comp –use* command. For details, see Section 6.5.1.

6.7 Replying to Mail with repl

The *repl* command is flexible—there are a lot of great features that weren't covered in the introduction, Section 4.4.

You don't have to reply to everyone who got the original message, and *repl –query* makes it easy to choose who gets your reply. The *–nocc* and *–cc* switches give you another way to choose. This section covers several different ways to include the original message in your reply. The original message can be marked automatically when you reply to it. And there's more.

6.7.1 Selective Replies with –query

By default, when you reply to a message, *repl* will send a copy of your reply to everyone who got the original message—that includes the author, you, and all addresses in the To: and cc: components. If you don't want that to happen all the time, *repl* can ask you. Just start *repl* with its *–query* switch. You can type it on the command line, just for particular messages:

```
% repl -query
```

Or, if you like *–query* enough to use it most of the time, you can add it to your MH profile—then, whenever you don't want *–query*, you can use *–noquery* on the command line:

```
% repl -noquery
```

Now, for a demonstration of *–query*. First, show part of the message. Then, start
`repl –query` and send copies of the reply only to a couple of people. Compare the addresses in the original message with the header of the reply:

```
% show last
(Message mh-users:8)
Date:  13 Nov 89 00:28:18 GMT
From:  Al Bok <al@phlabs.ph.com>
To: mh-users@ics.uci.edu
cc: auser@quack.phlabs.ph.com, aguru@mt.top.ph.com
Subject:  Query about "repl -query"

I have a question about repl -query...
   ...
% repl -query
Reply to Al Bok <al@phlabs.ph.com>? y
Reply to mh-users@ics.uci.edu? n
Reply to auser@quack.phlabs.ph.com? n
Reply to aguru@mt.top.ph.com? y
Reply to auser? n

To: Al Bok <al@phlabs.ph.com>
cc: aguru@mt.top.ph.com
Subject: Re: Query about "repl -query"
In-reply-to: Your message of "13 Nov 89 00:28:18 +0000."
---------
Al, I think this is the answer.  Guru, am I right?
   ...
```

If you hadn't used *–query*, your reply would have been addressed to all the original recipients.*

6.7.2 Selective Replies with –nocc and –cc⊠

You can also tell *repl* to ignore certain components in the message you're replying to—that is, not to send copies to anyone in those component(s). Here are examples:

1. If you started with message 8 in the previous section again, the command:

```
% repl -nocc to -nocc cc
```

---

*Notice the last query `Reply to auser?`. This happened because *repl* will automatically send a
copy to you (*auser*) at your local address. Even though *auser*'s complete address
(*auser@quack.phlabs.ph.com*) was already in the header, *repl* couldn't tell the difference, so it asked
again. There are ways around these problems besides *–query*. See Section 6.7.2, Section 6.7.3, and
Section 8.6.

would have sent the reply only to Al Bok and you. You might ask: why you? (Let's assume you're *auser*.) Didn't you use –nocc cc to ignore the cc: component? Yes, but *repl* always sends a copy to you, by default—unless, that is, you use the *–nocc me* switch.

2. To send a reply to only the From: component, you could type:

```
% repl -nocc to -nocc cc -nocc me
```

That's getting pretty long. Using *–nocc all* or *–cc all* lets you exclude or include cc:'s to everyone listed in the original message. You could do the same thing as the command above with:

```
% repl -nocc all
```

3. You can use the *–nocc* and *–cc* switches together. The order of the switches on the command line matters. The last switch on the command line takes precedence. So to send a reply to only the To: addresses (not cc: or me), the first command below would work—but the second one would not work:

```
% repl -nocc all -cc to
% repl -cc to -nocc all
```

The first one works (sends a copy to the To: addresses) because –cc to comes last on the command line and thus un-does part of the –nocc all.

4. You can also put your *–nocc* switches in your MH profile like this:

```
repl: -nocc cc -nocc me
```

Then, for example, you can use the *–cc* switch when you want to include one of the header components (overriding the *–nocc* switches in your MH profile):

```
% repl -cc cc
```

6.7.3 Changing the Message Header with replcomps☒

As you've seen, *comp* has a *components* file to control the header and *repl* has its *replcomps* file. The *replcomps* file is different, though, because it not only controls which lines are included in the header of the reply but also controls what is filled into each component and how it's formatted. This is good to understand because the default *replcomps* ignores some of the addresses that you might want to reply to!

For more information, see Section 8.9.3, "The replcomps File."

Part II
Using MH

6.7.4 Reading the Original Message Through Your Editor

When you reply to a message, you may want to include parts of the original message in your reply. That's especially true if someone besides the original readers gets a copy of your reply or if there's something controversial or important that should be seen exactly as written.

One way to do that is by editing your reply with a text editor like *vi* which can read other files. *repl* lets you read the original message file through a link named @ (at sign).* For example, with *vi*, just move to the bottom of the draft reply and type:

```
:read @
```

If it doesn't work, check to see whether you started *repl* from a read-only directory or if your current directory is on a different filesystem than the original message. In those cases, UNIX can't make a link to the original message.

Depending on your editor, you may also be able to read the original message by using the *editalt* environment variable. In *vi*, for instance, type:

```
:read $editalt
```

If neither of those work, the *mhpath* command can find the pathname for you. For example, you can always read the original message by typing the command in backquotes (`). For example, in *vi*, enter:

```
:read `mhpath cur`
```

Section 12.7 covers backquoting. Section 12.17.3 is about the *mhpath* command.

Another way to add the original message is with a program like *append*—you use it at the What now? prompt. The script is in Section 13.2.

Finally, Section 6.7.5, below, has what might be the best way of all.

6.7.5 Including the Original Message with –filter⊠

Another way to include the original message in your reply is by using a *filter file* and the *repl –filter* command. A filter file uses *mhl* message-formatting instructions to control which lines of the original message are included in the reply and how they're formatted.

---

*On systems that use an at sign (@) as the line-delete character, type \ @.

This isn't the place to explain *mhl* in depth. If you're interested, look at Section 10.1. Otherwise, here's some "cookbook" help.

For instance: to make a filter file that includes the original message in your reply, indented by a tabstop (eight characters), put the following two lines into a file named something like *replfilt* (the exact name doesn't matter) in your MH *Mail* directory:

```
:
body:nocomponent,compwidth=9,offset=9
```

Be sure that there's no space between `body:` and `nocomponent`. Then, reply to the message this way (use the original message number and other switches, as well, if you need to):

```
% repl -filter replfilt
```

A lot of people like to include the original message with the right angle bracket (>) and a space before every line of the original, like this:

```
% repl -filter replfilt
To: Al Bok <al@phlabs.ph.com>
cc: aguru@mt.top.ph.com
Subject: Re: Query about "repl -query"
In-reply-to: Your message of "13 Nov 89 00:28:18 +0000."
--------
> I have a question about repl -query.
> Why does it ask twice if I want a copy of my reply?

Al, that's because repl automatically sends a copy
    ...
```

To do that, make your *replfilt* file look like this:

```
body:component="> ",compwidth=0
```

Note that the right angle bracket (>) has a space (blank) after the >. The blank(s) are optional; depending on how you want the original message indented, you can use one, none, or several blanks. Also note that some earlier versions of MH would either put the right angle bracket (>) only before the *first* line of the included reply or insert a > in the middle of some lines of text. If yours does that, you'll need a newer version of MH, such as MH 6.7.

You can make that the default by adding *–filter replfilt* to a `repl:` component in your MH profile. There's a problem with adding that line to your MH profile, though: after you do that, it will be hard to reply to a message without that *replfilt* formatting. (*repl* doesn't have a *–nofilter* switch.) Section 9.4, "Versions of repl," shows some ways to make all of this easier. For instance, you can fix your own mail environment so you type *replx* to use your filter file or *repl* to reply without including the original message. To add text to the end of each reply, see Section 8.9.6, "Automatic Signature on End of Messages."

6.7.6 Displaying the Original Message

At a What now? prompt, you can type display or just d to show the original message on your screen. (This is different than list, which shows the draft reply.)

6.7.7 Annotating the Original Message

If you use the *–annotate* switch—on the *repl* command line or in your MH profile—the message you reply to will have components like these added to its header:

```
Replied: Mon, 07 Dec 92 18:28:46 -0500
Replied: Al Bok <al@phlabs.ph.com>
Replied: aguru@mt.top.ph.com
```

This lets you know that you've sent a reply—a useful feature for busy or absentminded people.

By default, *scan* looks for these Replied: components in messages. It marks these messages with a dash (–) in the listing. For example, here are two messages; you've replied to the second one:

```
 5  12/07 Al Bok         The next project...<<...is g
11 -12/08 Donna Lewis    About the next project...<<A
```

6.8 Forwarding Copies of Messages: forw

The *forw* command lets you send copies of one or more messages to other people. For an introduction, see Section 4.6.

6.8.1 Formatting Forwarded Messages

By default, every line of the message(s) you're forwarding is sent. If a message header is full of "junk" components like Received: *xxx*, you can save space on the copy you forward by telling *forw* to omit those components. You can also control the formatting of the rest of the header and/or body—line up header components neatly or rearrange them into a standard order, shorten lines in the body that are too long, and so on.

It's easy to get the most common formatting. If you use the *–format* switch, *forw* will process the message(s) you're forwarding with an *mhl* filter file. Your system should have a standard file called *mhl.forward* that:

- Omits all header components except From:, To:, cc:, Subject:, and Date:.

- Cleans up the Date: component.

- Lines up the header components neatly.

To use it, just type:

```
% forw -format
```

If you want to use this filtering on most of the messages you forward, you may want to add this line to your MH profile:

```
forw: -format
```

Before it checks the MH library directory for an *mhl.forward* file, *forw* looks in your MH *Mail* directory. If you don't like the system *mhl.forward* file, you can copy the system *mhl.forward* file into your directory and then edit it:

```
% cd Mail
% cp /usr/local/lib/mh/mhl.forward .
% vi mhl.forward
```

(You'll need to change the */usr/local/lib/mh* if your system's MH library directory is someplace else.)

forw gives you another choice: using a different filter file than *mhl.forward*. That can be handy if you forward different kinds of messages. You might have a second filter file that includes Resent: components from the original message, a third filter file that reformats the message body for a friend who has a 40-character-wide display, and so on. Section 10.1.4 explains how to make your own filter file.

If you set *–format* or *–filter* as a default in your MH profile, you can override either one of those switches by using *–noformat* as you type the *forw* command line.

Part II
Using MH

6.8.2 Adding Text to the Draft

By default, *forw* will prompt you for the header components—then it prompts you to:

```
--------Enter initial text
```

After you enter the initial text, *forw* will scroll the body of the forwarded message(s) across your screen. The "initial text" gives you a chance to type some extra text—for instance, you could write a note to the people who you're forwarding this to.

But you may not like the way that works. If you want the note you write to go *after* the forwarded message(s), add the *–noprepend* switch to the `prompter:` line in your MH profile. Unfortunately, though, that changes the way *prompter* works for all message-sending commands, not just *forw*. Section 9.7 has a solution.

6.8.3 Leave My Dashes Alone

Another thing some people don't like about *forw* is the way that it adds an extra dash (–) before any line which starts with a dash. For example, text that looks like this in the original message:

```
- Add one cup water.
  Stir.
- Cook for 25 minutes.
```

will be forwarded this way:

```
- - Add one cup water.
  Stir.
- - Cook for 25 minutes.
```

That's special formatting called "bit stuffing" that helps the MH *burst* command split forwarded messages back into separate message files.* If you don't like the extra dash (–) at the beginning of dashed lines, you can use the almost-undocumented *–nodashmunging* switch.† Of course, you should not use *–nodashmunging* if the person you send the message to will want to *burst* it. And, because it isn't documented, don't depend on *–nodashmunging* staying in MH forever.

---

*There's a detailed description in RFC934; see Appendix C, *Reference List.*

† Jef Poskanzer added *–nodashmunging* to *forw* and wrote about it in the *mh-users* mailing list in 1987. It's mentioned in "The RAND MH Message Handling System: Administrator's Guide, UCI Version."

The *–nodashmunging* switch only works in combination with *–format* or *–filter* and a filter file:

```
% forw -nodash -format
```

If you don't want any formatting, you can't use both *–noformat* and *–nodashmunging* to get it. The best answer for that is probably a filter file that does no formatting. Here's one that I call *mhl.noformat*; you can put it your MH directory:

```
width=10000
extras:nocomponent
:
body:nocomponent
```

If you want long body lines wrapped after the 79th character, add `,width=80` (with no space before it) to the end of the last line.

You use *mhl.noformat* by typing its name on the command line (which overrides any default *mhl.forward*), like this:

```
% forw -filter mhl.noformat -nodashmunging
```

mhl.noformat doesn't delete any header lines, and it leaves long lines as they are in the original message. For more information, see Section 10.1.4, "forw Filter Files."

6.8.4 Make Your Messages burst-able

It's always a good idea to leave a blank line between the initial text you type (if any) and the starting line (`------- Forwarded Messages`). That's because the message encapsulation guidelines in the document RFC934 (see Appendix C, *Reference List*) say that there must be a blank line before the forwarded messages. This lets message-bursting programs like *burst* (Section 7.9) separate the header of the total message from the header of the first forwarded message. If you enter initial text, be sure to press RETURN at least one extra time after you finish.

6.8.5 No Need for forwcomps

When *forw* prompts you for To:, cc:, and Subject:, it reads a default header file called *forwcomps* from the MH library directory. You can make your own *forwcomps* file—in your MH directory. But *forwcomps* has the same syntax as the *components* file that *comp* uses. Because I want the same default headers for both *forw* and *comp*, I tell *forw* to use my *components* file instead. So if I ever change my *components* file, I won't have to remember to change *forwcomps*, too. This component in your MH profile does the job:

```
forw: -form components
```

6.8.6 Annotating the Original Message

If you use the *–annotate* switch on the *forw* command line or in your MH profile, the message you forward will have components like this added to its header:

```
Forwarded: Mon, 07 Dec 92 09:13:52 -0500
Forwarded: al@phlabs.ph.com
```

These let you know that you forwarded the message to *al@phlabs* on July 19. There will be one `Forwarded: user@host` component for each address you forward the message to.

By default, *scan* looks for `Replied:` components in messages, but it doesn't look for `Forwarded:` components. If you want to, you can add that yourself, though: see Section 10.2.5, "Adapting the Default scan Format File: scan.hdr."

6.8.7 Creating Digests

The *forw* command can create message digests. Digests combine one or more messages in a format similar to an MH forwarded message. Digests are usually sent periodically to a list of users (a *mailing list*). Each digest message has its own volume and issue numbers; MH can keep track of these for you* and increment them automatically.

There's not space for a complete explanation of maintaining mailing lists. Here's a brief example, though. You're taking over as moderator of the *octopus–people* mailing list. Before the first issue, you store the recipients' addresses in an alias named *dist–octopus–people*. You ask your system postmaster to create a system alias named *octopus–people–request* with your name; this is where people send mail if they want to be added to or deleted from the mailing list. The first issue you're sending is volume 1, issue 26. To send messages 25-34:

```
% forw -digest octopus-people -volume 1 -issue 26 25-34
From:      octopus-people-Request
To:        octopus-people Distribution: dist-octopus-people;
Subject:   octopus-people Digest V1 #26
Reply-To: octopus-people
```

---

*MH tracks volume and issue numbers in your *context* file.

```
--------Enter initial text

Hi.  I'm Emma H. User, the new moderator of octopus-people.
Send submissions to: octopus-people@bigcorp.com.
CTRL-D
octopus-people Digest    Thursday, 25 Jul 1991
                    Volume 1 : Issue 26

Today's Topics:

        ...Messages appear...

End of octopus-people Digest [Volume 1 Issue 26]
**************************************************
--------

What now?
```

The header setup can be stored in your MH directory in a *replcomps*-style file named, by default, *digestcomps*. If you run more than one digest, you'll want to customize that file and create some versions of *forw* as well. See Chapter 8, *Making MH and xmh Work Your Way*, and Chapter 9, *New Versions of MH Commands*, for suggestions.

For the next issue, just type forw –digest octopus-people. MH will automatically assign volume 1, issue 27 unless you override it.

6.9 Distributing Messages with dist

The *forw* and *dist* commands do similar things. But *dist* is designed for resending (distributing) messages without any changes or extra text in the body. This means that the people who receive a *dist*'ed message from you will see it as:

```
From: whoever-sent-it-to-you
Date: whenever-original-was-sent
```

instead of:

```
From: you
Date: whenever-you-forwarded-the-copy
```

For example, let's say that Norm sent a message to Mary on May 13. Then, on June 24, Mary sent two copies of the message to Mike as a test—the first copy was with *dist*, and the second copy was with *forw*. Here's what Mike would see in his *scan* listing of the two copies of the same message:

```
1755+ 05/13 Norman Schwartzko  Summary of the Zeta project<<This is
1756  06/24 Mary Shepley-Hunt  Zeta info<<----- Forwarded Messages
```

You can *dist* only one message at a time (*forw* lets you forward several messages as a unit). Here's an example:

```
% dist 23
Resent-To: bigboss
Resent-cc:
---------
CTRL-D
---------

What now? send
```

If you try to add extra text (besides the Resent- headers), *send* will ask you to please re-edit draft to consist of headers only! The *dist-prompter* shell script shown in Section 13.10 will prevent this error and make *dist* easier to use.

The people you distribute the message to will get the original message with these three components added (or four, if you filled in Resent-cc:):

```
% inc
   ...
% show
   ...
Resent-To: bigboss
Resent-Date: Mon, 07 Dec 92 07:33:22 -0600
Resent-From: ehuser (Emma H. User)
   ...
```

Otherwise, the recipients' copies of the message will be identical to yours.

NOTE

dist (actually, the *send* command) can't distribute a message from a read-only folder (explained in Section 8.7, "Sharing Other Users' Folders"). When you try to send the message, it gives you an error like:

```
send: unable to link xx/yy/zz/83 to /xx/yy/zz/send012817:
Permission denied.
```

The *forw* command works, though.

6.9.1   A distcomps File

You can add a few other lines to the header besides the default `Resent-To:` and `Resent-cc:` by editing the draft header or putting a *distcomps* template file in your MH directory. See Section 8.9.5.

6.9.2   Annotating the Original Message

If you use the *–annotate* switch on the *dist* command line or in your MH profile, the message you forward will have components like this added to its header:

```
Resent: Mon, 07 Dec 92 09:13:52 -0500
Resent: al@phlabs.ph.com
```

Otherwise, this works just like *forw –annotate*; see Section 6.8.6.

6.10   Sending Files; The mhmail Command

Most users use *comp* to send mail interactively. MH also comes with a command called *mhmail*. Instead of having a *components* file, *mhmail* has switches called *–subject*, *–cc*, and so on. If you have a text file that you want to send in a mail message, there are a few ways to do it:*

- The *mhmail* command will read text from its standard input, such as a pipe (|) or left angle bracket (<). It also has a *–body* switch. Here are four examples:

```
% mhmail joe avax\!lynn -cc al -subject "My report" < report
% mhmail alice -body "See you at noon for lunch" -from Hungry
% myprg | mhmail teacher -cc ehuser -subject "My program output" &
% mhmail `ali -list gurus` joe jane -subject 'Help\!' < problem
```

The first command line mails a file named *report* to *joe* and *avax!lynn*; it also sends a `cc:` to *al*. (You can put spaces or commas between the addresses.) Be sure to use a left angle bracket (<) before the filename, *not* a right angle bracket (>)! The `To:` address(es) always comes first. Unless you understand how your shell handles characters such as parentheses and the ampersand sign (&), it's safest to put single or double quotes (' or ") around the subject. If

---

*The file should have just text—usually, that's letters, digits, and punctuation—unless you're using a multimedia mail standard like MIME. You shouldn't mail nontext files without special processing such as *uuencode*(1).

*Part II
Using MH*

you use the C shell (which displays a percent sign (%) prompt), you should also put backslashes (\) before any exclamation points (!), as I did here.

The second command line sends a short message about lunch to *alice*. The *–from* switch makes the message From: Hungry, but the mail system will add your real e-mail address, too, in a Sender: component. Again, you should use quotes around the body.

The third command line runs your program called *myprg* (although you could use most any UNIX program instead). The output is piped into *mhmail*, which collects all the output while the program is running, then sends the output to your teacher with a copy to you. The ampersand (&) on the end runs the commands in the background, so you can do something else while they work.

The fourth command line runs the MH *ali* command with its *–list* switch (Section 6.3.2) to get the addresses from the MH mail alias called *gurus*. This uses backquoting (explained in Section 12.7). Besides the addresses from the alias, this fourth message also goes to *joe* and *jane*.

• Another way to send a file is by starting *comp*, filling in the message header, leaving the message body blank (just use CTRL-D). Then, at the What now? prompt, go into an editor like *vi* and use the file-reading command (in *vi*, it's :read *filename*) to read in the file. You can edit it before you exit the editor and send.

• Finally, see Section 13.2 for a handy shell script that lets you append file(s) to your draft from a What now? prompt.

Section 12.17.2 has more *mhmail* techniques.

7

Finding and Organizing Mail with MH

*Part II
Using MH*

This chapter shows how to use MH commands to organize and find your messages. It starts with lots of details about versatile MH folders and subfolders. Just as the UNIX filesystem has directories and subdirectories, MH lets you split messages into groups and subgroups. You don't need to understand the UNIX filesystem to use basic MH, though; in fact, this chapter ignores the standard filesystem wherever it can and concentrates on how to use MH.

MH has commands for moving messages between folders, putting them into more than one folder, and splitting folders into subfolders. You can get summaries of one or more folders. There are shortcuts for referring to folders. You can move between a set of folders easily and quickly with an MH folder stack.

Next, there's a look at the powerful *pick* command. It lets you search for messages in all kinds of ways. This can be very useful for people who want to use their e-mail as a database of information—or just to find an old message by its contents, such as the name of the person who sent it and a word in the message body.

Another way to organize messages is with an MH *sequence*. This is a list of message numbers that MH "remembers" for you. Each folder can have up to ten of these. The *pick* command can make or add to sequences.

MH can sort messages by the date they were sent and remove "holes" in the message numbering. Those features are useful after you've done a lot of rearranging. MH Version 6.7 added a more flexible sorting program.

You'll see how to recover messages that you've deleted accidentally and how to remove folders.

You'll learn how to add components to message headers, which is useful for record-keeping. The book shows how this might be used in a group's problem-tracking system.

Then, the *burst* command is explained. It splits groups of messages into single messages. Finally, there are sections about the *packf* command, which packs messages into a single file, and *msh*, which uses MH-like commands on packed mailbox files.

7.1 Folders

If you don't send or receive many mail messages, you may not need to know about MH folders. But if you get a lot of mail, or if you want to organize messages into groups (like folders in a file cabinet), read on.

By default, MH keeps all your messages in a single folder called *inbox*. Each message in the folder has a unique message number. You can make other folders and move one or more messages into them.

7.1.1 Your Current Folder: folder

First, here's how to get a summary of your *current folder*. That's the folder MH uses until you tell it to change folders. Until now, your current folder has probably been *inbox*, the folder where new mail is put. To get the summary of your current folder, use the *folder* command:

```
% folder
      inbox+ has  46 messages (   1-  46); cur=  17.
```

If you want a heading that explains each part, add *–header*:

```
% folder -header
      Folder     # of messages (  range  ); cur  msg  (other files)
      inbox+ has  46 messages (   1-  46); cur=  17.
```

The two commands above show that:

- Your current folder is named *inbox*. The plus sign (+) means that it's the current folder.

- There are 46 mail messages in this folder. The first message is number 1, and the last message is number 46. (If some of the messages had been deleted or moved, the numbering might be different.)

- Message number 17 is the current (most recently referenced) message.

To get more information, use the *scan* command. It shows a listing of messages in the current folder, one line per message:

```
% scan
    1  12/07 Joe Doe           Test message<<Hi!>>
    ...
   17+ 12/09 To:Joe Doe        Re: Something that you should know
    ...
   46  12/11 someone@somewhere. Did we meet at USENIX?<<I think th
%
```

If there are lots of messages to scan, they can scroll off the screen faster than you can read them. Because MH runs from the shell, it's easy to use a pipe and UNIX paging commands like *more* or *pg* which let you see one screen at a time:

```
% scan | more
```

Or, if you don't really need to see all of your messages, you can scan a range of messages:

```
% scan last:20
```

Section 4.7 shows other choices.

7.1.2 Using the folder Command to Create and Change Folders

The *folder* command can also make new folders. To make one named *test*, type:

```
% folder +test
Create folder "/yourMHdir/test"? y
            test+ has   no messages.
```

After that, you wouldn't be in the *inbox* folder anymore. Your current folder would be *test*. You haven't put any messages there yet, so the folder is empty. For example:

```
% scan
scan: no messages in test
```

Your current folder will be *test* until you change it to something else or until you incorporate new mail (*inc* will change your current folder to *inbox*).

To change your current folder back to *inbox*, type:

```
% folder +inbox
            inbox+ has  46 messages  (   1-  46); cur=  17.
```

7.1.3 Changing to Another Folder

Section 7.1.2 showed that the *folder* command can change your current folder. But you don't have to use *folder*. When you give a folder name to most MH commands, they change the current folder. For instance, *show +junk* changes the current folder to *junk* and shows the current message there.

There are two MH commands which don't change the current folder:

- The *refile* command (unless you use its *−src* switch, as explained in Section 7.1.4).

- The *mhpath* command (covered in Section 12.17.3).

That is, the following command moves messages 45 and 47 to the *junk* folder, but it doesn't change the current folder:

```
% refile +junk 45 47
```

The relative folder operator @ (Section 7.1.6) can be used to change folders, too.

CAUTION

If you ask an MH command to change the current folder and the command doesn't work for some reason, the current folder won't be changed. For example, the following *scan* command fails because there are no messages in the *bar* folder (the folder is empty). As you can tell from the second *folder* command, the current folder wasn't changed:

```
% folder
                foo+ has    5 messages (   7- 22); cur=  9.
% scan +bar
scan: no messages in bar
% folder
                foo+ has    5 messages (   7- 22); cur=  9.
```

If you've just tried to change the current folder and you get a warning or error—you might use *folder* to check the current folder before using a command like *rmm* that's hard to undo.

Plus signs can be confusing when you start with MH. If you're a little confused, the inset below might help.

The Pluses of MH

Here are two ways plus signs (+) are used in MH:

1. When you give the name of a folder to an MH command, you type a + *before* the folder name, with no space between them. An example is:

   ```
   % folder +test
   ```

2. When an MH command tells you the current folder, it puts a + *after* the folder name. For example:

   ```
   test+ has    no messages.
   ```

   In both cases, + is not part of the folder name.

7.1.4 Moving and Linking Messages: refile

The *refile* command moves or links messages between folders. By default, the message is moved out of one folder into another folder. The *–link* switch leaves the message where it is and makes a link into another folder.

Moving

To move messages out of your current folder into another folder, use refile +*foldername*, where *foldername* is the destination folder. If you don't give message number(s), *refile* will default to the current message.

Here's an example. Find a message you want to refile by using *scan* and *show*. Then, move it to the *test* folder. To be sure it's gone, *scan* the same messages or try to *show* the current message:

```
% scan 1-4
   1  12/07 Joe Doe        Test message<<Hi!>>
   2  12/07 Joe Doe        Another test<<Well, this is another
   3+ 12/07 To:angelac     A message from MH mail<<Did this wo
   4  12/07 To:Joe Doe     What's happening--did you send the
% show
(Message inbox:3)
To: angelac
   ...
% refile +test
% scan 1-4
   1  12/07 Joe Doe        Test message<<Hi!>>
   2  12/07 Joe Doe        Another test<<Well, this is another
   4  12/07 To:Joe Doe     What's happening--did you send the
% show
show: no cur message
```

You refiled the current message into *test*. So the second *scan* and *show* tell you that there's no current message. (By the way, your current folder is still *inbox*.)

Did the message really get to the *test* folder? Here's a shortcut to find out. You can change the current folder *and* scan it by giving a folder name to the *scan* command as shown in the following example:

```
% scan +test
   1  12/07 To:angelac     A message from MH mail<<Did this
% folder
            test+ has   1 message (   1-   1).
```

Notice that:

- The message didn't keep the same number (3) that it had in the *inbox* folder. To choose a new message number, *refile* always uses one greater than the highest message number in the folder. In this case, the destination folder was empty, so the new message was renumbered to 1 automatically.*

- Your current folder is *test* (the *folder* command shows that).

- There's no current message yet in the *test* folder.

Linking Messages into More than One Folder

Let's say that you want to store a message in more than one folder. You might do this if you had a folder for each project you were working on, and one message had information about two different projects. You would do this by *linking* rather than moving the message. When a message is linked to another folder or folders, you can find it in the folder where it started and also in the other folders. On UNIX, linking a message into multiple folders takes no more disk space than keeping the message in just one folder. One gotcha: as Section 2.7 explains, the hard links MH uses can't cross filesystems (there's a workaround in Section 7.8.5).

For example, let's link our message from *test* into another folder named *junk*. Then, compare the *test* and *junk* folders:

```
% refile -link +junk 1
Create folder "/yourMHdir/junk"? y
% folder
             test+ has   1 message  (   1-   1); cur=  1.
% scan
   1+ 12/07 To:angelac       A message from MH mail<<Did this wo
% scan +junk
   1  12/07 To:angelac       A message from MH mail<<Did this wo
```

If you want to refile a message into two or more folders, you can do it all in one step—just type all the folder names at once. This works whether you're moving

Part II
Using MH

---

*If you want to keep the same message number, you can use *refile –preserve* ... but this only works if there's not a message with that number in the destination folder. Here's an example of trying to move message 1 (the current message) from *inbox* to *test* and preserve the message number. There's already a message 1 in *test*, so *refile* complains and won't move the message:

```
% folder
            inbox+ has  45 messages (   1-  45); cur=  1.
% refile -preserve +test
refile: message xxx/test/1 already exists
```

or linking. Let's try it. Scan the first four messages in your *inbox*. You can use the folder name and message numbers together, like this:

```
% scan +inbox first:4
   1  12/07 Joe Doe              Test message<<Hi!>>
   2  12/07 Joe Doe              Another test<<Well, this is anothe
   4  12/07 To:Joe Doe           What's happening--did you send t
   5  12/07 To:Joe Doe           Thanks for helping!<<You said that
```

To link message 1 from *inbox* into both the *junk* and *test* folders, use:

```
% refile -link +test +junk 1
```

Now the message should be linked into all three folders. (Check it if you want to.) Figure 7-1 shows what this might look like if MH stored messages on paper instead of a computer disk.

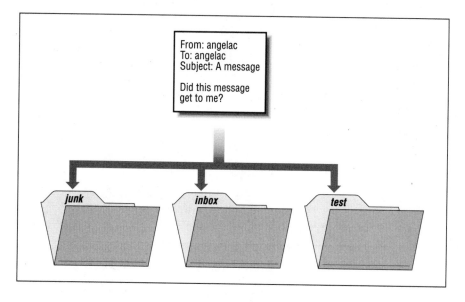

Figure 7-1. Message linked into three folders

If you hadn't used its *–link* switch, *refile* would have linked the message into *junk* and *test*, but removed it from the current folder (*inbox*).

Section 7.2.10 shows a nice way to use links: a single folder with links to many other folders. Section 7.8 explains more about links.

Refiling from Another Folder with refile –src

As you've seen above, *refile* moves or links messages from the current folder. You can tell *refile* to take messages from a different folder by using its *–src* switch and a folder name. For example, to move messages 1, 3, and 5 from the *project* folder into the *done* folder, you could do it in one step this way:

```
% refile 1 3 5 -src +project +done
```

The same thing done in two steps would look like this:

```
% folder -fast +project
project
% refile 1 3 5 +done
```

Either way you do it, after *refile* finishes, your current folder will be *project*. Unlike plain *refile*, the *refile –src* switch changes the current folder.

7.1.5 Subfolders

Okay, so you say that you're one of those people with thousands of mail messages, and you need to subdivide your folders? MH lets you do that: you can make *subfolders*—folders inside your folders. (In case you're wondering, you can make sub-subfolders, and sub-sub-subfolders, and ... I've made folders ten levels deep to see if it works. It does.)

Figure 7-2 shows a folder that has four messages and a subfolder in it. The subfolder has three messages in it.

To name a subfolder, type the top-level folder name, a slash (/), and the subfolder name—with no space between them. For example, if you have a folder named *reports*, and you wanted a subfolder called *jan*, the complete subfolder name would be *reports/jan.**

---

*Remember that in UNIX uppercase and lowercase letters are distinct. A subfolder named *reports/Jan* is different than a subfolder named *reports/jan*. Using all lowercase letters may be easier to type and less confusing in the long run; that choice is up to you.

To create a subfolder in MH 6.6* and previous versions, you first have to create
the folder levels above it. For example, if you want a folder named *reports/jan*,
you have to make the *reports* folder first:

```
% folder +reports
Create folder "/yourMHdir/reports"? y
          reports+ has    no messages.
% folder +reports/jan
Create folder "/yourMHdir/reports/jan"? y
          reports/jan+ has    no messages.
```

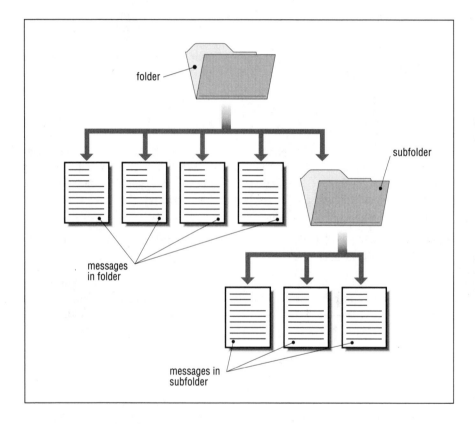

Figure 7-2. A subfolder

The MH 6.7 and later versions of *folder* will make the top-level folder and its
subfolder(s) for you. Just type the command:

---

*In January 1990, a patch (code change) was sent out for MH 6.6 that fixed this problem. MH 6.7 and later versions
also have this fix. If it's been installed on your computer, then you'll be able to make subfolders without making the
top-level folders first. But remember that not everyone will have this in their version of MH.

```
% folder +reports/jan
Create folder "/yourMHdir/reports/jan"? y
         reports/jan+ has    no messages.
```

To move (or link) messages into a subfolder, use the name with a plus sign (+) before it. (You can also use the relative-folder operator @ (at sign), explained in Section 7.1.6.) In this next example, we'll move message 6 from *inbox* into the *reports/feb* subfolder (in this case, *reports/feb* doesn't exist yet, so *refile* asks if you want to create it):

```
% show 6 +inbox
(Message inbox:6)
    ...
% refile +reports/feb
Create folder "/yourMHdir/reports/feb"? y
```

You can tell if a folder has subfolders by looking at the output of the *folder* command. For instance, by now the *reports* folder has two subfolders:

```
% folder +reports
         reports+ has    no messages              ;    (others).
```

The (others) at the end means "there's something besides messages in the folder." Those could be subfolders or non-MH files. An easier way to tell what's there is to ask *folder* for a "recursive" listing; that is, the folder and all the subfolders. That's what *folder –recurse* is for, as shown below:

```
% folder -recurse
         reports+ has    no messages         ;         (others).
    reports/jan has    1 message  ( 1- 1).
    reports/feb has    1 message  ( 1- 1).
```

Your current folder is *reports*; it has two subfolders named for two months.

A nice way to get a summary of your current folder and its subfolders is:

```
% folders @.
         Folder      # of messages ( range ); cur msg  (other files)
         reports+ has    no messages         ;         (others).
    reports/feb has    1 message  ( 1- 1).
    reports/jan has    1 message  ( 1- 1).

         TOTAL=    2 messages in 3 folders.
```

The @. means "the current folder"; see the next section.

7.1.6 Relative Folder Names

As you've seen, a complete (full) subfolder name always starts with the top-level folder name. Typing all of the name can be a waste of keystrokes, especially when you're already in the top-level folder. For instance, let's say that you have a lot of letters from friends in a folder named *friends*. If you decide to reorganize the mail into subfolders named for each friend, typing the complete subfolder name can get to be a pain:

```
% folder +friends
        friends+ has 124 messages (  12- 198); cur= 19.
% scan 12
   12  02/15 To: zebra!ellen    What Joseph and Annie are doing
% refile 12 +friends/Joseph +friends/Annie
Create folder "/yourMHdir/friends/Joseph"? y
Create folder "/yourMHdir/friends/Annie"? y
% scan next
   14  02/15 "Ellen K. Grimm"   Re: What Joseph and Annie are d
% refile 14 +friends/Joseph +friends/Annie
```

Because you're already in the *friends* folder (your current folder), it would be nice not to have to type its name. You can do that with *relative folder names*. To say "the subfolder called *xxx* in my current folder," you use an at sign (@) instead of a plus sign (+). If your current folder is *friends*, you can refer to the subfolder *Joseph* by typing @Joseph. Let's go on with the example above, but use relative folder names this time:

```
% folder
        friends+ has 122 messages (  15- 198).
% scan 15
   15  02/16 To: zebra!ellen    Joseph Annie & Carl(!)<<Guess w
% refile 15 @Joseph @Annie @Carl_B
Create folder "/yourMHdir/friends/Carl_B"? y
% scan next
   17  02/16 "Ellen K. Grimm"   Re: Joseph Annie & Carl(!)<<I d
```

Compare the two examples. Think how much more typing you'd need without the short folder names ...

NOTE

Remember, these relative folder names work only for subfolders *of your current folder*. If you're in the *reports* folder and you type @Annie, MH will think you mean the folder named *reports/Annie* (not the folder named *friends/Annie*). In this case, you want to use a plus sign (+) and the complete folder name: +friends/Annie.

You can use relative folder names almost anyplace, not just with *refile* (except with *rmm*—for some reason, *rmm* doesn't accept relative folder names). For example, here's how to change your current folder from *friends* to *friends/Joseph* and *scan* it:

```
% scan @Joseph
    1  02/15 To: zebra!ellen    What Joseph and Annie are doing
    2  02/15 "Ellen K. Grimm"   Re: What Joseph and Annie are d
    3  02/16 To: zebra!ellen    Joseph Annie & Carl(!)<<Guess w
% folder
  friends/Joseph+ has   3 messages (  1-   3).
```

The next obvious question is: how can you get back to the folder above (called the *parent folder*)? There are two ways:

1. Type the complete folder name (+friends).

2. Type the relative folder name (@..—that's an at sign with two dots after it).

If you've ever used .. in the UNIX filesystem (for example, cd ..), you'll see that this @.. in MH works the same way. Continuing the example above, from the *friends/Joseph* folder:

```
% folder @..
          friends+ has 121 messages (  17- 198).
```

Because you were in the *friends/Joseph* folder, typing folder @.. took you to the parent folder, *friends*. If this relative-name business seems too confusing, remember that you don't have to use it. But if you do a lot of work with subfolders, relative folder names can save you a lot of typing.

7.1.7 folder –fast

As you've seen, if you don't give the *folder* command any switches, it will summarize the folder's contents. This can take time on busy computers.

If you just want the current folder name without the summary, you can use the *–fast* switch, as shown in the following example:

```
% folder -fast
friends
```

The *–fast* switch won't save much time when you use *folder –recurse*. Although it won't print folder summaries, it still has to search every folder for subfolders—that takes more time.

```
% folder -fast -recurse
friends
friends/Annie
friends/Carl_B
friends/Joseph
```

As with other MH commands, you can abbreviate the switch names. Type just enough letters to make the name unambiguous. For instance, you can shorten *folder –fast –recurse* to *folder –f –r*. A quick way to see all the switches so you can figure out the shortest unique abbreviation is with the *folder –help* command.

To change your current folder quickly, nothing beats *folder –f*. For example, *folder –f +inbox* makes *inbox* current, without the folder summary. It just changes the folder and shows the name.

CAUTION

In early versions of MH, `folder -fast +foldername` would *not* change your current folder to `foldername`! Back then, the *folder –fast* command was just for showing the name of the current folder, *not* for changing folders. When you typed `folder -fast +newfolder`, the *folder* command would answer *newfolder* as if it had changed the current folder—but it hadn't.

If you're not sure what your MH version does, try to change to another folder with `folder -fast +foldername`. Then check the current folder name by typing `folder`. If the current folder isn't `foldername`, you're probably running an old version of MH.

7.1.8 List of All Folders: The folders Command

The *folder* command gives a summary of one of your folders. For a summary of all your top-level folders, use the command *folders* (plural) or *folder –all*. If you have subfolders, you can add *–recurse*. All of these commands put a header before the folder list and a summary at the end. Finally, if you just want the total number of messages and folders, use *folders –total*, with or without the *–recurse*. It's time for an example (and remember—you can abbreviate most switches):

```
% folders -recurse
            Folder      # of messages (  range  ); cur  msg   (other files)
             inbox has    45 messages (  1-  45); cur=  1.
           friends+ has   121 messages (  17- 198);           (others).
      friends/Annie has     3 messages (  1-   3).
     friends/Carl_B has     1 message  (  1-   1).
     friends/Joseph has     3 messages (  1-   3).
            reports has    no messages           ;            (others).
        reports/jan has     2 messages (  1-   2); cur=  2.
        reports/feb has     1 message  (  1-   1).

            TOTAL=  176 messages in 8 folders.
% folders -total
TOTAL=  166 messages in 3 folders.
% folders -t -r
TOTAL=  176 messages in 8 folders.
```

NOTE

Using *–recurse* will slow down *folders* quite a bit. Don't use *–recurse* unless you want to see your subfolders.

The *fols* shell script in Section 13.5 gives you a list of folder names in columns, with long names shortened.

7.1.9 Folder Stacks

If you're changing your current folder between two or more folders, over and over, you might want to use a *folder stack*. A folder stack is a set of folder names that MH saves for you. You arrange the stack with the *folder* command and its *–push* and *–pop* switches. Folder stacks work a lot like the C shell's directory stacks. (There are some handy aliases for folder stacks in Section 8.2.1.)

Overall Description of a Folder Stack

First, I'll describe a folder stack. Think of a desk top. On the desk are your current folder and a stack of other folders from a file cabinet. In Figure 7-3, the current folder is *reports/jan*. To check which folder you're in, use *folder*:

```
% folder
      reports/jan+ has    2 messages (  1-   2); cur=  2.
```

On the stack, there are three other folders; the *reports/feb* folder is on the top.

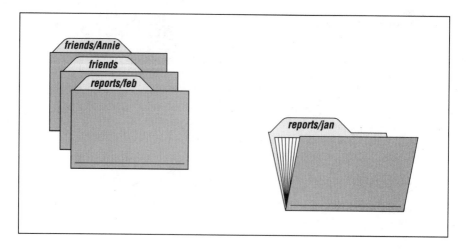

Figure 7-3. Current folder and folder stack

To get a list of the current folder and the stack, type:

```
% folder -list
reports/jan reports/feb friends friends/Annie
```

As you can see when you compare the *–list* output to Figure 7-3, the first folder listed is the current folder. The rest of the list is the folder stack, top folder first.

How did the stack get there? MH "remembers" the list of folders on the stack the same way it remembers the current folder.* You can keep the same stack as long as you want and change it at any time. You can add or remove folders from the stack (see the following example). So there's no one answer for "how" the stack got this way. But, assuming that the stack was empty when you started, these commands would have created it in the shortest time:

```
% folder -fast
friends/Annie
% folder -push +friends
% folder -push +reports/feb
% folder -push +reports/jan
```

The first command showed that the current folder is *friends/Annie*. The last three commands pushed three more folders on the stack and left *reports/jan* as the current folder. In real life, a folder stack usually grows more slowly.

If you use folder stacks a lot, typing *folder –push* and *folder –pop* over and over can get tiresome. This is a good place to use shell aliases or functions. Section 8.2.1 shows some useful aliases for folder stacks.

---

*In the *context* file.

Pushing a Folder onto the Stack

If you want to move the current folder to the top of the stack and get a new current folder, use `folder -push +foldername`. For instance, the command that would make the desktop look like Figure 7-4 (making *inbox* current and moving *reports/jan* to the top of the stack) is:

```
% folder -push +inbox
inbox reports/jan reports/feb friends friends/Annie
```

folder automatically does a *–list*, which displays the current folder followed by the other folders on the stack.

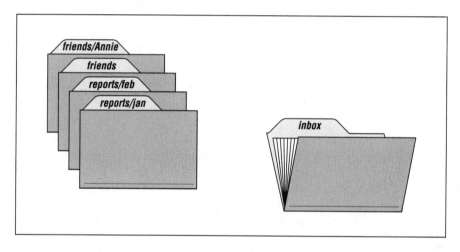

Figure 7-4. After pushing reports/jan onto the top of the stack

Going to Previous Folder

To swap the current folder with the top of the stack, use *folder –push* by itself. As Figure 7-5 shows, this puts *inbox* on the stack and makes *reports/jan* current:

```
% folder -push
reports/jan inbox reports/feb friends friends/Annie
```

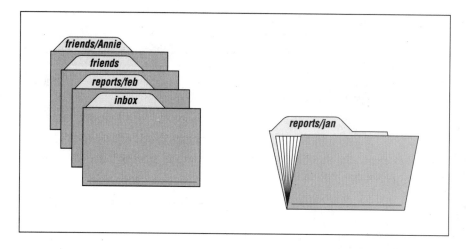

Figure 7-5. After swapping current folder with top of stack

Popping a Folder Off the Stack

To replace the current folder with the top of the stack (and not push the current folder onto the stack), use the *–pop* switch. If your shell has a "repeat-last-command" feature, you can use it to pop another folder. For example, here we pop *inbox* off the stack. Then we pop *reports/feb* off, too, using the C shell's history operator ! ! (you could also just type `folder –pop` again). Watch the folder list change:

```
% folder -pop
inbox reports/feb friends friends/Annie
% !!
folder -pop
reports/feb friends friends/Annie
```

NOTE

The *folder* command can change the current message. For example, the command *folder +junque 23* will change the current folder to *junque* and the current message in *junque* to 23.

But *folder –push* will ignore message numbers and won't change the current message unless you also use the *–print* switch. This might be considered a bug.

7.1.10 Renumbering Messages in a Folder

After removing and rearranging messages in a folder, there can be gaps in the numbering. For instance, if your *inbox* folder has messages 1-25 and you remove any ten messages, the other message numbers won't change. To renumber the messages 1, 2, 3 ..., use the command:

```
% folder -pack
          inbox+ has  15 messages (   1-  15); cur=  1.
```

7.2 Finding Messages with pick

Let's say that you've used MH for a few months and you've got a lot of messages. Somewhere in your *misc* (miscellaneous) folder, buried in a message from someone (you can't remember who), is a recipe for pickled herring. (Yuck.) How can you find it? Well, you could *scan* the folder and *show* some likely messages, then read through them until you find the one with the recipe. Or you could make MH search by typing:

```
% pick -search herring +misc
324
```

That tells *pick* to search through every line of every message in the *misc* folder and show you the message numbers that have the word "herring" in them. *pick* found that word in message 324. If you type show 324, voilà! (Then, if I were you, I'd type rmm...)

7.2.1 pick Switches

pick can do more than just *–search* entire messages. It will work more quickly if you only search each message *header*—say, the Subject: or the From: component. *pick* can search for messages *–to* a certain user (or host). *pick* can find messages sent on a certain *–date* or all messages sent *–before* or *–after* a date. You can use several different date formats.

For example, *pick –to jtq@orange* would hunt for any message which contained the string *jtq@orange* anywhere in its To: component. The message doesn't have to be one that you sent (though you can tell *pick* to do that—see Section 7.2.5, "Combining pick Switches"). As long as *jtq@orange* is somewhere in the To: component, *pick* will find the message(s) and return the message number(s). And unless you know a *jtq* on more than one computer, just try pick –to jtq.

To find messages from *zelda*, use:

```
% pick -from zelda
12
23
```

Another example:

```
% pick -subject 'research project'
```

would find messages with the phrase "research project" (uppercase or lowercase letters) anywhere in its Subject: component. (When you search for a phrase with spaces or other special characters in it, put quotes around the string you're searching for.)

pick can search for messages that were sent before or after a certain date. The syntax for date entry is in the order *day*, then *month*, then *year*. You can use special day names like *today* and *yesterday*—also *saturday*, *monday*, and so on—and you can give dates "*n* days ago." Here are some examples:

- To find messages sent before (but not including) April 7, 1989, use either *pick –before 7–apr–89* or *pick –before 7/4/89*.

- To find messages sent on or after April 7, 1989, use either *pick –after 7–apr–89* or *pick –after 7/4/89*.

- You can find messages sent before (but not including) the most recent Sunday with *pick –before sunday*. (For instance, if today is Tuesday, then the "sunday" MH looks for is the date two days ago.)

- Use *pick –after yesterday* to find messages sent yesterday or today.

- The command *pick –after –2* finds messages sent within the last two days as well as today. For example, if today is April 10, that command would find messages sent on April 8, 9, or 10.

- The command *pick –before –7* finds messages sent more than seven days ago.

NOTE

Remember, *–after* searches include the date you give, but *–before* searches do not.

When you're looking for messages sent on a certain date, *pick* makes you type the date exactly as it's shown in the Date: component, in the message header (but you don't have to capitalize the month). For instance, a typical date component in a message header looks like this:

```
Date: Sat, 23 Dec 89 05:51:20 PST
```

To find messages sent on December 23, 1989, use:

```
% pick -date '23 dec 89'
```

(Remember: when you search for something with spaces in it, put quotes around the search pattern.) Because *pick* is doing a textual search, you can search for any part of the `Date:` component. For example, a quick-and-dirty way to find all messages sent in December 1989 is:

```
% pick -date 'dec 89'
```

That won't match `Date:` components like `23-dec-1989`, of course. And that brings up another important point. With the year 2000 coming soon, many mailers are converting to four-digit years.* That adds more complication to the *–date* switch. Either of the next two searches would find a message sent in June 1993:

```
% pick -date 'jun 93' -or -date 'jun 1993'
% pick -date 'jun.*93'
```

The first one uses the *–or* switch, explained in Section 7.2.5, "Combining pick Switches." The second uses a UNIX regular expression to match `dec`, followed by any number of characters, followed by `93`. That second one would also match a date with dashes between its parts, like `23-jun-93` or `23-jun-1993`. The part of Section 7.2.7 called "Using Regular Expressions" has more information.

If you aren't careful, regular expressions can match lines you don't expect. Unless you know exactly how each message's `Date:` component is written, it may be easier to use a search like the following

```
% pick -after 1-dec-1989 -and -before 1-jan-1990
```

Part II
Using MH

---

*I've heard that MH will do this soon. MH 6.7.2 still uses two-digit years.

Getting Picky About Date Searches

If you need to be precise, here's something useful that isn't in the standard *pick*(1) manual page.

With date specifications like *yesterday*, *monday*, or *–2* ("two days ago"), *pick* actually counts *hours*, not days. Each day is counted as 24 hours in the past. This 24 hours even includes time zones.

For instance, *pick –before –1* would search for messages sent more than 24 hours ago. If it's 9:30 a.m. on January 17 now, that command would find messages sent before 9:30 a.m. on January 16—but not messages sent after 9:30 a.m. on the 16th. The command *pick –after yesterday* would find messages sent after 9:30 a.m. on January 16 (after 24 hours ago).

If the message is from someone in another time zone, *pick* counts that, too. If it's 9:30 a.m. EST (U.S. Eastern Standard Time) on January 17 now, the command *pick –before –1* would find messages sent before 9:30 a.m. EST on January 16—also messages sent before 8:30 a.m. CST (Central), 7:30 a.m. MST (Mountain), and 6:30 a.m. PST (Pacific). Whew.

For a cutoff at midnight on a certain day, ignoring the time zone, you have to use the *date*, *month*, and *year* format. For instance, if it's now 9:30 a.m. on January 17, 1990, you could find messages sent any time before midnight yesterday with *pick –before 16–jan–90* (this would find a message sent at 11:59 p.m. on January 15, but not a message sent any time on January 16 or 17).

Let's summarize. The *–date* switch does a textual (string) search through the messages. The *–before* and *–after* switches parse the date field and do a numeric comparison.

7.2.2 Passing picked Message Numbers with Backquotes

So far, you've seen *pick* output lists of message numbers, which isn't too useful. There are better things to do. You can use backquotes (`` ` ``) so the UNIX shell will collect this list of messages and pass it to another command.

Here's an example. The first command gives a list of messages. The second command passes the message numbers to the *scan* command, which scans them:

```
% pick -from joed
1
2
113
227
```

```
% scan `pick -from joed`
    1  12/07  Joe Doe            Test message<<Hi!>>
    2  12/07  Joe Doe            Another test<<Well, this is anot
  113+ 12/09  Joe Doe            The latest on my project<<It's g
  227  12/11  Joe Doe            <<I can't get MH to work so I'm
```

If you get an error like scan: bad message list pick -from joed, you probably used the wrong kind of quotation marks. Be sure to use backquotes (`), not single quotes (') or double quotes (").

Backquotes work with any MH command—not just *scan*. For instance,

```
% refile `pick -before -365` +old
```

would run *pick –before –365* to get a list of all messages more than 365 days old, and then use *refile* to move them into the *old* folder.

If *pick* doesn't find any messages, it prints an error for you. It also outputs the illegal message number 0 (zero) for other MH commands so they'll print their own error message and quit:

```
% scan `pick -subject xyzxyzxyz`
pick: no messages match specification
scan: no messages match specification
```

7.2.3 Storing picked Message Numbers in MH Sequences

The previous section explained how to use the shell's backquoting feature to pass message numbers from *pick* to another MH command. There's another way to pass message numbers from *pick* to other MH commands—with MH *sequences*. If you want to use the list of messages more than once, sequences are more efficient than backquotes.

A *sequence* is a named list of message numbers. This section only covers them enough for use with *pick*. See Section 7.3.

Before you tell *pick* to store the message numbers in a sequence, choose the sequence name. (I usually choose the name *picked* because it's easy to remember.) After you run *pick*, MH will keep track of the message numbers in the sequence. The list of message numbers in the sequence won't change* until you run *pick* again with the same sequence name.

---

*If you sort or pack the folder or remove or refile messages, the sequence will stay up to date.

In the following example, the first command makes a list of message numbers, as the examples with backquotes did. Because I type −sequence picked, *pick* stores the message numbers in a sequence named *picked* and prints 4 hits to tell me it found four messages. In the second command, I give the sequence name to *scan*, which reads the message numbers from the sequence and scans them. Finally, I use the sequence again—this time, to remove the four messages with *rmm*.

```
% pick -from joed -sequence picked
4 hits
% scan picked
    1  12/07 Joe Doe            Test message<<Hi!>>
    2  12/07 Joe Doe            Another test<<Well, this is anot
  113+ 12/09 Joe Doe            The latest on my project<<It's g
  227  12/11 Joe Doe            <<I can't get MH to work so I'm
% rmm picked
```

The advantage of sequences over backquoting is that you only have to run *pick* once; MH remembers the message numbers.

Notice that when you use the *−sequence* switch, *pick* automatically sets its *−nolist* switch too. Instead of a list of message numbers, you get something like 4 hits. If you want the message numbers instead, type −list on the command line or put it in your MH profile.

By default, *pick* replaces the list of messages in an existing sequence with the new list it finds. The *−nozero* switch tells *pick* to combine the new messages with ones already in the sequence. For example, you could keep a sequence called *problems* and add new messages to it over time. To start the sequence, you would *not* use *−nozero* (you could use *−zero* if you wanted to, but that's the default):

```
% pick -search 'needs maintenance' -sequence problems
24 hits
```

Later, to add other messages to the sequence, use *−nozero*:

```
% pick -search 'needs maintenance' -nozero -sequence problems
27 hits
```

That would merge any new messages containing the words "needs maintenance" into the sequence with the messages it kept before. Message numbers won't be duplicated; in other words, if a message is already in the sequence, it won't appear twice after doing *pick −nozero*.

7.2.4 Storing Sequence Name in Your MH Profile

If you like having *pick* store the messages it finds in a sequence, you can have
that happen automatically. Remember that your MH profile (usually, the file
named *.mh_profile* in your home directory) holds default switches for MH
commands, among other things. Choose a sequence name you want to use (like
picked), then edit your MH profile and add this component to it:

```
pick: -sequence picked
```

Now, whenever you use *pick*, it will automatically store the message numbers in
the *picked* sequence.

But what if you want to use backquotes with *pick* sometimes? You'll need a list
of message numbers, and the *–sequence* switch prevents that. The answer: use
the *–list* switch, too; it tells *pick* to list the message numbers (they'll be stored in
the sequence as well). You can add *–list* to the end of the `pick:` component in
your MH profile so that *pick* will always list the message numbers—or you can
use *–list* on the command line whenever you need it.

7.2.5 Combining pick Switches

You can pick messages based on more than one criterion. For instance, to find all
messages to *xavierq* or to *jpk*, use *–or*:

```
% pick -to xavierq -or -to jpk
```

(Notice that you need to use *–to* before *each* addressee.) Finding all messages
from *perryp* sent more than seven days ago needs the *–and* switch because you
want messages that meet both of those criteria:

```
% pick -from perryp -and -before -7
```

Use *–not* to find messages which do not match. For instance, to find all messages
that are not from you (assuming your username is *joannaq*), type:

```
% pick -not -from joannaq
```

If you've done much searching before (in databases, computer science courses,
and so on), you probably know what *operator precedence* means. If you don't
know, and you want to do much searching using *–and* or *–or*, it's good to get
some practice first. The next example shows a typical precedence problem:

```
% pick -to annk -or -to ronb -and -before sunday
```

Does that command:

- Find all messages sent before *sunday* to either *annk* or *ronb*?

- Find any message sent to *annk* on *any* day, or any message sent to *ronb* before *sunday*?

Table 7-1 lists the *pick* operator precedence.

Table 7-1. pick Operator Precedence

Precedence	Operator
high	*–lbrace, –rbrace* matching primitives (*–from, –to, –search*, etc.) *–not* *–and*
low	*–or*

If you're new to the idea of operator precedence, your best bet is to use the grouping switches *–lbrace* and *–rbrace*. Their names stand for "left brace" and "right brace." Use them to group other operators, as you'd use parentheses in algebra. Let's make the example above unambiguous:

```
% pick -lbrace -to annk -or -to ronb -rbrace -and -before sunday
```

Now it says you want messages sent to *annk* or to *ronb* before Sunday. With real braces (which don't work with *pick*, unfortunately), that would look like:

pick { to annk or to ronb } before sunday

The braces tell *pick* exactly which two terms you want the *–or* applied to.

And remember—you can abbreviate those switches:

```
% pick -lb -t annk -o -t ronb -rb -an -b sunday
```

7.2.6 picking Miscellaneous Components

You've seen how to search for messages by Subject:, To:, and From:. (You can also search the cc: component with *–cc*.) You can search for any other component—like Reply-To:, Return-Path:, and so on. Use the *--component–name* switch (with *two* dashes before the switch name). For example, to search for any message which had the component Sender: xandra@xyz.com, you would type:

```
% pick --sender xandra@xyz.com
```

repl –annotate and *forw –annotate* add Replied: and Forwarded: components to message headers (see Sections 6.7.7 and 6.8.3, respectively). So you could search for all messages which had been forwarded by typing:

```
pick --forwarded .
```

The dot (.) means "match any character." You need the dot because *pick* requires something to search for. Section 7.2.7 describes how searches find messages.

Here's one place I've used this. I was one of several consultants in a computer center. We got a lot of questions by e-mail. When we answered a message, we put a component in the reply header with the initials of the consultant who answered it (we all answered from the *consult* account). For example, the header of a message I sent would start like this:

```
From: consult
To: auser
X-By: jdp
cc:
```

(You can make up arbitrary components if the name starts with X-. We named ours X-by:.) To search for the messages that I (*jdp*) sent, we typed:

```
% pick --x-by jdp
```

You can set up your message headers this way before you send the messages or after you receive them. For help, see the parts of this book about customizing message headers like Section 8.9, "Draft Message Template Files," and Section 7.7, "Annotating Message Headers: anno."

7.2.7 How Searches Find Messages

When you use *pick* switches that search text—like *–subject*, *–to*, *–search*, and others—you may find messages you didn't expect. This section explains why and explains how to make your search more accurate. It also shows examples of searching with *regular expressions*, which let you match ranges of text without typing all the text exactly. (This section doesn't apply to switches like *–before* and *–after* that search for messages by date.)

Messages You Don't Want

pick searches *all* of a component. For example, if you type:

```
% pick -to ed
```

it will find all of these messages:

```
To: ed
To: ed@someplace.xxx
To: FRATED@UCI
To: kelly@bigcorp.com, mongo@medfly.com
```

because each of those components has an uppercase or lowercase "ed" *somewhere* in it.

After you know *pick* works that way, you can take advantage of it. For example, to find all messages from *any* user at *temptron.com*, you could use a search like:

```
% pick -from temptron.com
```

assuming that all of their mail has *temptron.com* in its From: components.

Now, back to the first example. What if you want to find mail to Ed, not to *frated* or *mongo@medfly.com*? Give Ed's address as exactly as you can. For example:

```
% pick -to ed@someplace.xxx
```

would do the trick, assuming that Ed's address looks *exactly* like that in the To: component. In other words, if Ed's address looked like this in some messages:

```
ed%somewhere@someplace.xxx
```

then you'd have to type a search line like this:

```
% pick -to ed@someplace.xxx -or -to ed%somewhere@someplace.xxx
```

As explained in the section below called "Using Regular Expressions," you could also use an expression to match any number of characters between the parts of the address:

```
% pick -to "ed.*@someplace.xxx"
```


Uppercase vs. Lowercase

If you type your search in lowercase letters, *pick* will match either lowercase or uppercase letters. As an example, if you want to find messages with the name "Sam" anywhere, the search:

```
% pick -search sam
```

would also find messages that have the word "flotsam" or a component such as To: kenny@samron.com.

If you type an uppercase letter, *pick* will match it exactly. So a much better search (that still finds the words "Samuel" and "Samantha", by the way) is:

```
% pick -search Sam
```

Watch Out for the Shell

"Aha," you think, "I could find Sam by typing his whole name, Sam Spade. Then 'Samuel' or 'Samantha' wouldn't match." Try it, if you'd like:

```
% pick -search Sam Spade
pick: bad message list Spade
```

You'll get an error. Why? Because the UNIX shell splits the words at the space, and *pick* thinks that the second word is a list of messages (like a sequence). The answer: put single quotes around the string you're searching for. Be sure to use two single quotes (*' '*), *not* the backquotes (*` `*), as shown in the following example:

```
% pick -search 'Sam Spade'
```

That won't match messages with "Sam" at the end of one line and "Spade" at the start of the following line, but it's progress . . .

Using Regular Expressions

pick can do more sophisticated searches with UNIX *regular expressions*. A regular expression uses special pattern-matching characters like these:

```
[ ] . *
```

to find arbitrary combinations of text.

pick uses the same regular expressions as UNIX utilities like *grep*(1) or editors like *vi*(1) and *ed*(1). Here are two quick examples:

1. You can write a regular expression to find a message with a subject that has the word "report" followed by the word "1989", any place after it on the line. Some of the subjects we want look like this:

    ```
    Subject: status report for May, 1989
    Subject: Report on the month of August, 1989
    ```

    The *pick* command you'd type is:

    ```
    % pick -subject 'report.*1989'
    ```

    The dot followed by an asterisk (. *) means "zero or more of any character."

2. You'd like to find messages with information about your company's product
    with model numbers of AB1234x, AB1234y, or AB1234z. Without regular
    expressions, you'd have to type:

    ```
    % pick -search AB1234x -or -search AB1234y -or -search AB1234z
    ```

    But with a regular expression that matches the three different last characters
    in those numbers, you could type:

    ```
    % pick -search 'AB1234[xyz]'
    ```

Even More Details...

This section, adapted from the MH 6.7 *pick*(1) manual page, has more precise
information about *pick* searches. If you don't want this much detail, feel free to
skip ahead.

pick searches messages within a folder for the specified contents, and then identifies those messages. Two types of search primitives are available: pattern matching and date constraint operations.

A modified *grep*(1) is used to perform the matching, so the full regular expression
(see *ed*(1)) facility is available for the search pattern. With *–search*, the pattern is
used directly; with the others, the *grep* pattern constructed is:

```
component[ \t]*:.*pattern
```

(where \t is a tab character). This means that the pattern specified for a *–search*
will be found everywhere in the message, including the header and the body,
while the other pattern-matching requests are limited to the single specified component. The expression:

```
--component pattern
```

is a shorthand for specifying:

```
-search 'component[ \t]*:.*pattern'
```

Pattern matching is performed on a per-line basis. Within the header of the message, each component is treated as one long line, but in the body, each line is separate. Lowercase letters in the search pattern will match either lowercase or
uppercase in the message, while uppercase will match only uppercase.

Independent of any pattern-matching operations requested, the switches
–after date or *–before date* may also be used to introduce date/time constraints on
all of the messages. By default, the Date: field is consulted, but if another date
yielding field (such as BB-Posted: or Delivery-Date:) should be used,
the *–datefield field* switch may be used. *pick* will actually parse the date fields in
each of the messages specified (unlike the *–date* switch which does a

pattern-matching operation) and compare them to the date/time specified by use of the *–after* and *–before* switches. If *–after* is given, then only those messages whose Date: field value is chronologically after the date specified will be considered. The *–before* switch specifies the complementary action.

Both the *–after* and *–before* switches take legal RFC822-style date specifications as arguments. *pick* will default certain missing fields so that the entire date need not be specified. These fields are (in order of defaulting): time zone, time and time zone, date, and date and time zone. All defaults are taken from the current date, time, and time zone. In addition to RFC822-style dates, *pick* will also recognize any of the days of the week (*sunday*, *monday*, and so on) and the special dates *today*, *yesterday*, and *tomorrow*. All days of the week are judged to refer to a day in the past (e.g., telling *pick saturday* on a Tuesday means *last* Saturday not *this* Saturday). Finally, in addition to these special specifications, *pick* will also honor a specification of the form *–dd*, which means "*dd* days ago."

7.2.8 Searching a Message Range or Sequence

If your mail folders are full of messages, each *pick* you run can take quite a bit of time. I like to limit my search to a range of messages.

For example, if I know the message I want is in the last 200 messages, I can type:

```
% pick -to auser last:200
```

Without the last:200, *pick* would search all 4000 messages in the folder. This way is much faster.

The string last:200 is an example of the predefined MH message number ranges. You can also use message ranges, like *pick –to auser 25–150*, to search only message numbers 25 through 150 (see Section 4.7 for details).

Or you can define a sequence of messages, then use it as a starting place for other sequences. For example, let's say that you manage a group of people. You have a folder with 600 messages from your employees. You want to find the 20 or 30 messages with a subject of "status report," and split those messages into folders by employee name. The inefficient way to do that would be to search all 600 messages, for each of your ten employees, like this:

```
% refile `pick -from pwb -and -subj "status report"` +paul_b
% refile `pick -from jsp -and -subj "status report"` +joan_p
% refile `pick -from dac -and -subj "status report"` +don_c
% ...
```

pick would have to search almost 600 messages each time (that's slow). Instead, tell *pick* to search all 600 messages just once to find all the status reports and store those 20 or 30 message numbers in a sequence. Then, to find an employee's individual status report, have *pick* search the sequence of 20 or 30 messages (that's fast). Notice that we only use the *–sequence* switch once to store the sequence:

```
% pick -subject "status report" -sequence picked
% refile `pick picked -from pwb` +paul_b
% refile `pick picked -from jsp` +joan_p
% ...
```

and so on.*

Prehistoric pick-ing

In the late 1970s, the *pick* command was pretty different. So was *folder*.

MH didn't exactly have subfolders back then. When you ran *pick* with its *–keep* switch, it would create a subfolder named *select*. The messages that *pick* found were linked into that *select* subfolder, and your current folder was set there.

To get in and out of the *select* subfolder, you used the commands *folder –down* and *folder –up*.

If you didn't use the *pick –keep* switch, you used a switch like *–scan* to *scan* the messages that *pick* found and/or *–show* to read them. Command lines could look like:

```
$ pick -subject ned -scan -show
```

(Section B.1 in Appendix B, *Early History of MH*, has a note about this.) The MH developers eventually decided to change *pick* and add MH sequences (see Section 7.3). This was a major enhancement; I think MH is the better for it.

7.2.9 Searching More Than One Folder

If you don't know what folder a message is in, use a shell loop to run *pick* on several folders. You can use backquotes (Section 12.7) and the *folders –fast* command (Section 7.1.7) to give the loop a list of all your top-level folders. Adding *–recurse* to *folders* will search your subfolders, too—but it can also be a lot slower. Use the *–sequence* switch (Section 7.2.3) to store a list of the messages *pick* finds in a sequence in each folder. Then you can go to *folders* and check the messages in that sequence.

---

*This example assumes that the MH profile does *not* have `pick: -sequence picked` in it. If it did, each of those *pick* commands would overwrite the previous contents; we'd need to use a different sequence name instead.

Example 7-1 shows two loops. The first runs *pick* on all my top-level folders and stores messages it finds in the *picked* sequence. Let's say I notice three likely folders where *pick* found matches ("hits"). In the second loop, I run *scan* on those three folders.

Example 7-1. Searching all top-level folders

C shell:

```
% foreach f (`folders -f`)
? echo "Checking $f"
? pick pick switches +$f
? end
Checking apple
pick: no messages match ...

     ...
Checking zebra
12 hits
% foreach f (chk memos zebra)
? scan picked +$f
? end
...Messages found in chk folder...
...Messages found in memos folder...
...Messages found in zebra folder...
```

Bourne and Korn shells:

```
$ for f in `folders -f`
> do echo "Checking $f"
> pick pick switches +$f
> done
Checking apple
pick: no messages match ...

     ...
Checking zebra
12 hits
$ for f in chk memos zebra
> do scan picked +$f
> done
...Messages found in chk folder...
...Messages found in memos folder...
...Messages found in zebra folder...
```

Instead of doing a separate loop to *scan*, you can use the shell's && operator to run *scan* only when *pick* returns a "true" exit status in a folder. (Section 12.8 explains exit status.) Change the *pick* line in the first loop of Example 7-1 to look like this:

```
pick pick switches +$f && scan picked
```

You can get fancier, storing folder names with a match in a shell variable and so on. But that's probably the place to write a little shell script. Chapter 12, *Introduction to Shell Programming for MH*, should help.

7.2.10 Easier Searches with an 'All Messages' Folder

Running *pick* across a bunch of folders, as you saw in Section 7.2.9 above, can still be inconvenient. You might want to operate on messages from several folders at the same time. Or, you might just be sick of typing shell loops. Section 7.8.3 has an idea: a folder full of links to messages in other folders. When you want to search for messages and you know what folder to look in, search that folder. Otherwise, search the folder with links to many other folders—it'll take more time because there are more messages to search, but it sure is easier.

7.3 More About Sequences

As you saw in the previous sections, an MH sequence is a list of message numbers. You choose names for the sequences. When you want to use the messages in the sequence, you can type the sequence name instead of typing all the numbers. Each folder can have up to ten sequences—and each sequence can have hundreds of messages. A sequence name can be made of letters only; it can't be one of the reserved message names like *first*, *last*, and so on (see Section 4.7). The new *mh-sequence*(5) manual page in Appendix I has a complete description. This section has examples.

Sequences are great for keeping track of certain messages—temporarily or for weeks or months. In my user-consulting job, for instance, we kept a sequence named *common* in each folder—a list of messages which answer common questions that we might want to reuse:

```
% scan common +file_xfr
    3  03/23 To:ann@suxpr.mar.   Re: FTP in the background<<> Is
   19  06/02 To:xvhang           Re: UUEncode<<> Can Quark handle
   61  11/13 To:carolo           Re: .arc unpacking<<> A while ba
   63  11/17 To:danr             Re: shar type file packager<<Tha
   85  01/15 To:Rudy Valleyfor   Re: 7 & 8 bit switches<<> It is
```

You've seen that the *pick* command can create or add to sequences. The other MH command for working with sequences is *mark*. With *mark*, you can create, add messages to, delete messages from, or remove sequences.

7.3.1 Adding Messages to a Sequence

You can add messages to a sequence with *mark –add*. There are two ways to add messages to a sequence: *–zero* and *–nozero*.

If the sequence already exists and you want to change it completely, the *–zero* switch deletes any old message numbers from the list before adding the new ones. Or, to merge messages to an existing sequence without deleting existing message numbers, use *–nozero*. By default, *mark* uses *–nozero*. (The *pick* default is *–zero*.)

Here's an example. First *pick* creates or replaces a sequence named *picked*; it stores the message numbers from *alison*. Second, *pick* adds the message from *steven* to the same sequence. Third, the *mark* command adds the current message to the sequence. (If you don't tell *mark* which one to add, it adds the current message.) Fourth, I use *scan* to see what's in the sequence. Finally, I start *forw* to

forward copies of the messages (4, 21, 23, 44) to *allan@mukluk.bitnet*, as shown
in the following example:

```
% pick -from alison -sequence picked
2 hits
% pick -from steven -sequence picked -nozero
1 hit
% mark -add -sequence picked
% scan picked
    4  03/21 Alison Cosgreave    What's happening here at UMass<<
   21  04/01 Steven Dommer       Re: meeting minutes<<> A while ba
   23  04/02 Alison Cosgreave    Re: What's happening at Tek<<Not
   44+ 04/29 To:jbq@animals.sc   What we talked about at lunch<<Jo
% forw picked
To: allan@mukluk.bitnet
cc:
Subject: Messages from Alison, Steven, and me
      ...
```

If you give *mark* the *–sequence* option, the default action is *–add*. (Otherwise,
the default is *–list*.) So, to add messages 12–25 to the *foo* sequence, you can type:

```
% mark -seq foo 12-25
```

7.3.2 Deleting Messages from a Sequence

A message is automatically deleted from a sequence when you use commands
like *rmm* or *refile* on the message—if the message is removed from the folder, the
sequence is updated for you.*

To take messages out of a sequence yourself, use *mark –delete*. To remove one or
a few messages, just give their message numbers—the first command below
removes message numbers 1 and 3 from the sequence called *info*. To remove a
sequence completely, use the message range *all*—as in the second command
below, which removes the *temp* sequence from your current folder. Remember
that you can abbreviate MH switches (in fact, you can abbreviate most *mark*
switches to single letters, though I haven't here):

```
% mark -del -seq info 1 3
% mark -del -seq temp all
```

There's a weird twist that you should know about. If you use *–zero* with *–delete*,
it will *add* all messages from the folder to the sequence *except* the messages you

---

*The current message number (explained in Section 7.3.6) won't be deleted.

name. An example will help here. Let's say that your current folder has messages numbered 1 through 10. The command:

```
% mark -delete -zero -sequence most 1
```

would put messages 2 through 10 in the sequence called *most*. Even more surprising, that command will create the sequence if it doesn't exist!

You can delete from (or add to) more than one sequence at a time. For example, to remove all messages from the sequences *march* and *april* (and thereby remove the sequences too), type the following:

```
% mark -del all -seq march -seq april
```

7.3.3 Listing Sequences

The switch *–list* shows you what's in one or more sequences. If you don't give a sequence name, it shows all sequences in your current folder:

```
% mark -list
cur: 2
info: 4 6
myinfo: 12-18 20 25-36
% mark -list -sequence info
info: 4 6
```

In fact, if you don't give a *–sequence* switch, the default is *–list*. So, to get a list of all sequences, just type mark.

The *mark –list* command lists message numbers two ways: in ranges like 12-18, and in single message numbers like 6. For example, the *info* sequence above has messages 4 and 6 in it. The *myinfo* sequence has messages 12, 13, 14, 15, 16, 17, and 18; message 20; and messages 25 through 36, inclusive.

The message ranges in *mark –list* output always contain exactly those messages, with no gaps. For instance, if your folder has messages 12, 14, and 16 in it, *mark –list* will always list those as:

```
seqname: 12 14 16
```

and never as:

```
seqname: 12-16
```

The special sequence named *cur* holds the current message number for the folder.

7.3.4 Previous–Sequence, Sequence–Negation

Here are two handy components you can add to your MH profile.

If you edit your MH profile and add a line like this:

```
Previous-Sequence: pseq
```

MH will save the message numbers from the previous MH command in a sequence named *pseq* (you can use any legal sequence name; I just like *pseq*). For example, if you *scan* four messages, you can show all of them on the next command line without typing their numbers—just use *pseq*:

```
% scan 1 2 113 227
    1  12/07 Joe Doe          Test message<<Hi!>>
    2  12/07 Joe Doe          Another test<<Well, this is anot
  113+ 12/09 Joe Doe          The latest on my project<<It's g
  227  12/11 Joe Doe          <<I can't get MH to work so I'm
% show pseq
   ...Messages 1, 2, 113, 227 appear...
% mark -list -seq pseq
pseq: 1-2 113 227
```

NOTE

A `Previous-Sequence:` entry can cause trouble if your folders have hundreds or thousands of messages with gaps in the numbering. If you run a command like *scan* or *refile all* in those folders, MH tries to put a complete listing of all the folder's message numbers on a single line in the *.mh_sequences* file. If the line gets too long, you'll see the error message *xxx*/.mh_sequences is poorly formatted.

To prevent this, keep big folders packed with *folder –pack*.*

---

*If it happens anyway, use the following five commands to delete the long line from the *.mh_sequences* file and pack the folder (these commands assume that your previous sequence is named *pseq*):

```
% cd `mhpath`
% mv .mh_sequences temp_sequences
% sed /pseq:/d temp_sequences > .mh_sequences
% folder -pack
% rm temp_sequences
```

(If you aren't confident about this, check with an expert first.) I used the command sed /pseq:/d instead of grep -v pseq: because some versions of *grep* truncate long lines.

Here's the other useful component. If you put something like this in your MH profile:

```
Sequence-Negation: not
```

and put `not` before the name of a sequence, MH will use all messages from the current folder that are not in the sequence. For example, if your folder has messages numbered 1 through 10 and the sequence named *important* has messages 1, 3, 5, 7, and 9 in it, then typing the following line:

```
% refile notimportant +junk
```

would move messages 2, 4, 6, 8, and 10 into the *junk* folder.

The sequence-negation shouldn't be part of a sequence name you already use. For example, a sequence named *notes* starts with the characters *not*, so *not* would be a bad sequence-negation. You can use nonalphabetic sequence-negation characters, like the exclamation point (!) and the tilde (~), but your shell may treat those as special characters and force you to type a backslash (\) before them.* One compromise is a colon (:) character:

```
Sequence-Negation: :
```

In the previous example, you could have typed the following cryptic-looking command:

```
% refile :important +junk
```

If you never start your folder names with an uppercase X, you might use that letter for a sequence-negation, so a negated sequence could look like `Ximportant`.

7.3.5 The unseen Sequence

The *inc* command—together with the *show*, *next*, and *prev* commands—can cooperate to keep a sequence of all the messages which have never been read in a folder. For instance, this is a good way to be sure that you've read every message in your *inbox*. Read about the *unseen* sequence in Section 5.1.2.

---

*For example, if you set this line in your MH profile:

```
Sequence-Negation: !
```

the C shell makes you type \! before a sequence name, like this:

```
% scan \!important
```

7.3.6 The cur Sequence⊠

The current message number in each folder is kept in a sequence called *cur*. Each folder has its own *cur* sequence—a single message number. MH commands update this sequence automatically.

A folder doesn't always have a *cur* sequence. For instance, when you first make a new folder, it won't have a current message.

If you remove or refile the current message, the *cur* sequence will *not* be deleted, though. That's so commands like *next* and *prev* will still be able to find the next or previous message.

7.3.7 Public and Private Sequences

Section 8.7, "Sharing Other Users' Folders," explains that useful MH capability. If anyone is sharing your mail folders and you make a sequence, the other person will be able to use the sequence too. This is called a *public* sequence. (If you've set your *Mail* directory and/or folders so that no one can access them, don't be concerned—the name "public" doesn't mean that other users can override your security.)* When you define a sequence, or add to one, you can use the switch –*nopublic* to make it private. If the sequence was public before, now it'll be private.

Here's an example that shows the user of *mark –nopublic* changing a sequence from public to private. Compare the listings for the *myinfo* sequence in the two *mark –list* outputs:

```
% mark -list
cur: 2
info: 4 6
myinfo: 4-6
% mark -add -seq myinfo -nopublic 8
% mark -list
cur: 2
info: 4 6
myinfo (private): 4-6 8
```

There is a bug in MH 6.6 and MH 6.7 (and maybe others). If you give *mark –list* the name of a private sequence, it won't show you that it's (private).

---

*Public sequences are stored in a file named *.mh_sequences* in the folder directory. The *.mh_sequences* is mode 644, but users won't be able to read it unless they have access to the top-level mail directory and the folder. Private sequences are stored in the file named *context* in the user's MH directory. The *context* file is mode 600, and each user has his/her own *context* file; other users' *context* files are never used. For more information, see the filesystem diagram in Figure 2-1.

Compare the listings of the previous *myinfo* sequence to the following:

```
% mark -list -seq myinfo
myinfo: 4-6 8
```

To make all sequences private, add the empty component:

```
mh-sequences:
```

to your MH profile. See Section 8.4 for an example of where this is useful.

7.4 Sorting Messages: sortm

After a lot of refiling and rearranging, the messages in your folders won't be in order by date anymore. If you want to sort a folder, use the *sortm* command.

MH now has two versions of *sortm*:

- In MH 6.6 and before, *sortm* sorts messages by the date and time they were sent* and renumbers the messages starting at 1.

- For MH 6.7, *sortm* was rewritten to sort on almost any header component—including the subject. This new version does not automatically renumber the messages. Instead, see the *folder –pack* command in Section 7.1.10.

Here's a short example of a folder before and after sorting with MH 6.6:

```
% scan +money
   3  07/14 yourfriend       Would you loan me $1,000,000?<<Dear
   6  06/28 To:mom@home      Your rich son<<Dear Mom, I just won
  7+  06/28 vannaw@wheel.for A prize!!!<<Hi!!!!!  Guess what????
% sortm
% scan
  1+  06/28 vannaw@wheel.for A prize!!!<<Hi!!!!!  Guess what????
   2  06/28 To:mom@home      Your rich son<<Dear Mom, I just won
   3  07/14 yourfriend       Would you loan me $1,000,000?<<Dear
```

In that example, *sortm* swapped messages 6 and 7 because message 7 was sent earlier the same day. It preserved the current message.

Here's the same folder under MH 6.7, sorted by subject with the *–textfield* switch and also with the *–verbose* switch, to show you how that looks. Section 7.4.1 explains the *–textfield* switch. Section 7.4.2 explains *–limit*.

---

*If *sortm* can't find a `Date:` component, it tries to keep the message in the same relative position. This doesn't always work.

```
% scan +money                   .
   3  07/14 yourfriend        Would you loan me $1,000,000?<<Dear
   6  06/28 To:mom@home       Your rich son<<Dear Mom, I just won
   7+ 06/28 vannaw@wheel.for A prize!!!<<Hi!!!!!  Guess what????
% sortm -limit 0 -verbose -textfield subject
sorting by subject-major date-minor
renaming message chain from 7 to 3
message 6 becomes message 7
message 3 becomes message 6
% scan
   3  06/28 vannaw@wheel.for A prize!!!<<Hi!!!!!  Guess what????
   6  07/14 yourfriend        Would you loan me $1,000,000?<<Dear
   7  06/28 To:mom@home       Your rich son<<Dear Mom, I just won
```

If you have a lot of folders and you want to sort all of them, you can type one of the loops in Example 7-2 on your terminal. They get a list of folders from the *folder –fast –recurse* command (if you don't have any subfolders, leaving out the *–r* will make this faster). Then they display the name of the folder on your terminal and sort with *sortm*.

Two notes for people who've never entered a loop like this:

1. Be sure to use backquotes (`), not single quotes (').

2. Don't type the question mark (?) or the right angle bracket (>) characters—they are "secondary prompts" from the shells, and you should see them as soon as you type the first line and press RETURN .

Example 7-2 compares the C shell with the Bourne and Korn shell syntax.

Example 7-2. Using shell loops to sort all folders

C shell:	**Bourne and Korn shells:**

```
% foreach f (`folders -f -r`)    $ for f in `folders -f -r`
? echo sorting folder $f         > do echo sorting folder $f
? sortm +$f                      > sortm +$f
? end                            > done
sorting folder apple             sorting folder apple
    . . .                            . . .
sorting folder zoo/zebra         sorting folder zoo/zebra
%                                $
```

If you haven't seen shell variables and loops, look at Chapter 12, *Introduction to Shell Programming for MH*. By the way, sorting all your folders can keep your computer busy for a while. If there are many other users, you'll make them happier by using the command *nice sortm* instead of plain *sortm*; your *sortm* commands will run at a lower priority. See your online manual page for *nice*(1) or your shell.

7.4.1 New Feature in MH 6.7 sortm: Sort by Any Component

The MH 6.7 version of *sortm* is more flexible than older versions. The *–textfield* and *–datefield* components will sort on any text or special date component in the message header.

For instance, the command *sortm –textfield subject* would sort messages by their subjects. When you sort by subject, *sortm* will ignore any Re: at the start of a subject. That groups replies with the original message.

Note that *sortm* sorts by the entire component (except the label, like From:). But *scan* may show only part of a component, like the person's real name in a From: header—and make you think that the sort didn't work.

7.4.2 New Feature in MH 6.7 sortm: Date Limit

When you sort messages on a text field with the *–textfield* switch, you can also group messages by the dates they were sent. The new *–limit* switch does this.

The easiest way to learn about *–limit* is with some examples. To start, here's a folder with messages from two different users. First, I'll use the *scan.time* format file to show the time that each message was sent (Section 5.2.1 has information about this). A lot of the messages were sent around the start of July, and a couple were sent later:

```
% scan -form scan.time
    1   07/02 17:34CDT Al Bok              Results are in, and
    2   07/02 13:43CDT Dave Lamphear       Status report<<Hi,
    4   07/03 09:43CDT Al Bok              More results<<Thing
    5   07/03 11:09CDT Dave Lamphear       Have a great Fourth
    7   07/05 08:11CDT Al Bok              Finished<<That's it
    9   07/12 13:13CDT Al Bok              The next project...
   11   07/13 11:58CDT Dave Lamphear       Re: The next projec
```

Group Messages Sent Within 1 Day of Each Other: –limit 1

Let's sort the folder by the From: component. If you use *–limit 1* on the command line (that's a digit 1, not the letter "l"), it tells *sortm* to group messages sent within one day of each other, with the same From: component. Now, *sort* and *scan*:

```
% sortm -textfield from -limit 1
% scan -form scan.time
    1   07/02 13:43CDT Dave Lamphear       Status report<<Hi,
    2   07/03 11:09CDT Dave Lamphear       Have a great Fourth
    4   07/02 17:34CDT Al Bok              Results are in, and
```

```
  5  07/03 09:43CDT Al Bok            More results<<Thing
  7  07/05 08:11CDT Al Bok            Finished<<That's it
  9  07/12 13:13CDT Al Bok            The next project...
 11  07/13 11:58CDT Dave Lamphear     Re: The next projec
```

That *sort* put the two messages from Dave together, first in the list, because the earliest message in the folder was from Dave. (Look at the time-of-day field.) Why didn't it put the third message from Dave (sent 07/13) together with the first two of his (sent 07/02 and 07/03)? That's because the third message was sent more than one day after the other two—and the −limit 1 told *sortm* to do that.

The first two messages from Al were sent within a day of each other, so they come out next to each other. Two more messages of his come next, strictly in date order.

Group All Messages with Same Component: –nolimit

Let's resort the folder, this time with –*nolimit*.

NOTE

The –*nolimit* switch is the default for *sortm*. You don't have to type it.

The –*nolimit* switch means that messages with the same component (here, the From: component) are grouped together, no matter how many days difference between the times they were sent:

```
% sortm -textfield from -nolimit
% scan -form scan.time
  1  07/02 13:43CDT Dave Lamphear     Status report<<Hi,
  2  07/03 11:09CDT Dave Lamphear     Have a great Fourth
  4  07/13 11:58CDT Dave Lamphear     Re: The next projec
  5  07/02 17:34CDT Al Bok            Results are in, and
  7  07/03 09:43CDT Al Bok            More results<<Thing
  9  07/05 08:11CDT Al Bok            Finished<<That's it
 11  07/12 13:13CDT Al Bok            The next project...
```

In this example, all of Dave's messages are grouped together. They came before Al's messages because Dave sent his first message before Al.

Part II
Using MH

Group Messages by Component Then Date: –limit 0

Use *–limit 0* (that's the digit 0, not the letter "O") to sort by the component first, then by the date. If you know sorting terminology, this sort is "component-major, date-minor":

```
% sortm -textfield from -limit 0
% scan -form scan.time
    1   07/02 17:34CDT Al Bok            Results are in, and
    2   07/03 09:43CDT Al Bok            More results<<Thing
    4   07/05 08:11CDT Al Bok            Finished<<That's it
    5   07/12 13:13CDT Al Bok            The next project...
    7   07/02 13:43CDT Dave Lamphear     Status report<<Hi,
    9   07/03 11:09CDT Dave Lamphear     Have a great Fourth
   11   07/13 11:58CDT Dave Lamphear     Re: The next projec
```

Because *sortm* sorted by the component `From:` before the date, the messages from Al came first (because "a" comes before "d" in the alphabet).

7.5 Removing Messages (and Getting Them Back) ☒

The *rmm* command removes one or more messages. Like most MH commands, if you don't give a message number, *rmm* acts on the current message.

7.5.1 How rmm Removes Messages

As explained in Chapter 2, *MH and the UNIX Filesystem*, MH messages are stored as files in UNIX directories—one message per file. By default, *rmm* adds a comma (,) or a hash mark (#) to the start of a message filename. The extra character hides the message from other MH commands and flags the message for a system program to remove later. (You or your system administrator have to set up an automatic procedure for actually removing these "removed" messages. It will probably use the UNIX commands *at*(1) or *cron*(8) with *find*(1)—most likely, just a one-line command.) This method of removing messages can give you a grace period to recover messages you've deleted accidentally.

7.5.2 Recovering a Removed Message

Recovering an accidentally removed message takes a little work. This section explains how to recover a message that you've just deleted. At the end, there's an easier method.

Let's start this example by removing message 10:

```
% rmm 10 +somefolder
% scan 10
scan: message 10 doesn't exist
```

Use these steps to get the message back:

1. Change your current directory into the mail folder where your message was. The `mhpath +somefolder` gets the pathname of the folder. (See Section 12.17.3, "The mhpath Command." Section 12.7 explains backquotes.) Use backquotes (`` ` ``), not single quotes ('):

   ```
   % cd `mhpath +somefolder`
   ```

2. If you know the old message number, use *ls* to look for a filename that's the same number with a comma or hash mark before it. For example, the removed message 10 would be named *,10* or *#10* so you'd type `ls ,10` or `ls \#10.*`

   If you don't know the message number, search through the deleted messages with *grep* for lines that start with the word `Subject:`. (You can also search for messages by `From:`, `To:`, and so on.) Use a wildcard file-matching pattern: `\#*` if your deleted messages have a hash mark before them, or `,*` if they have commas. Also, be sure to use single quotes ('), not backquotes (`` ` ``):

   ```
   % grep '^Subject:' ,*
       ...
   ,13:Subject: How to attain nirvana
   ,15:Subject: How to get to Newark
       ...
   ```

3. When you find the file, you can restore the message by taking away the extra character at the start of the name—use the *mv* command to rename the file. Let's say that the message you want to restore is *,13*. First, use *ls* to be sure that there's no other file (message) named *13*.

   - If there isn't a file named *13*, just rename the file. Finally, use *scan* to see the recovered message:

     ```
     % ls 13
     ls: 13: No such file or directory
     % mv ,13 13
     % scan 13 +somefolder
         13  11/25 yourfriend        How to attain nirvana<<Take I-90 to
     ```

---

*The backslash (\) tells the shell not to treat the hash mark (#) as a comment character. This isn't needed on all shells.

- If there is a file named *13*, it's probably a new message that was put in the folder since the original *13* was deleted. You'll need to use a new message number. You can use *ls* to list the folder and find a "hole" with no message. But it's probably safer to use the *mhpath new* command to find a new unused message number at the end of the folder. When you use *mhpath*, be sure to use backquotes (`), not single quotes ('):

```
% ls 13
13
% mv ,13 `mhpath new +somefolder`
% scan last +somefolder
   94  11/25 yourfriend     How to attain nirvana<<Take I-90 to
```

4. Whew. You're done. Now, think about using an *rmmproc* like *rmmer* (see below)!

7.5.3 Changing Your rmmproc

You can change the way that *rmm* works by specifying a message removing program in your MH profile. For instance, you can tell *rmm* to use the standard system file removing command, *rm*. That will actually remove your message permanently, right away, with no grace period. If that's what you want, put the following line in your MH profile:

```
rmmproc: /bin/rm
```

You can also set *rmm* to "remove" messages by moving them to a subfolder named *DELETE*, where a program can find them and remove them later. This is more convenient for most people because you can *scan* your removed messages and *refile* them back into the parent folder (where they came from). To find out about that, see Section 13.6. Then put this component in your MH profile:

```
rmmproc: rmmer
```

For instance, if you install *rmmer* and accidentally *rmm* a message, you'd just type:

```
% scan @DELETE
   ...
   24  11/25 yourfriend     How to reach nirvana<<Take I-90 to
   25  11/26 someone@xxx.yy How to get to Newark<<I wouldn't go
   ...
% refile 24 @..
```

Relative folder operators like @ . . are explained in Section 7.1.6.

7.6 Removing Folders: rmf

The *rmf* command removes a folder and all the messages in it. If you don't give a folder name, the current folder is removed.

CAUTION

When you use the *rmf* command, your messages are completely removed—you can't get them back.

rmf does not use the `rmmproc:`, if any, in your MH profile. Be careful.

In the following cases, *rmf* will remove a folder and all messages and will not ask for confirmation:

- If you give the folder name explicitly (`rmf +foldername` or `rmf @foldername`).

- If you use the *–nointeractive* switch.

    Please notice that because of a bug in MH 6.6 and 6.7 (and maybe others), you have to misspell this switch *–nointerative* (without the *c*) or abbreviate it to *–noint*. This bug was fixed in MH 6.7.1.

At other times, *rmf* is supposed to ask for confirmation before it removes a folder.

NOTE

I recommend that you put this component in your MH profile:

```
rmf: -interactive
```

That should help to ensure that *rmf* always shows you the folder name and asks for confirmation before deleting it. (You should spell *–interactive* correctly; it doesn't have the spelling bug mentioned above.)

After you remove a top-level folder, *rmf* will set the current folder to *inbox*. After you remove a subfolder, *rmf* will set the current folder to that folder's parent. This is shown in the following example:

```
% folder
        do/re/mi+ has    8 messages (    1- 15); cur=  7.
% rmf
Remove folder "do/re/mi"? y
[+do/re now current]
```

If you try to remove a folder which has subfolders or any other non-MH files in it, *rmf* won't remove them—it will complain and abort without removing the folder. But, before it aborts, it can remove the messages in the folder! Again, be careful with *rmf*.

The *rmf* command is also used to remove your reference to a read-only folder. See Section 8.7.

7.7 Annotating Message Headers: anno

You can add new header components to a message in your folder. Here's an example of where this could be useful.

Imagine that you're part of a group of people who maintain some products. When people in your group or in other parts of your company find a problem, they send mail to your group manager. Your group uses MH for a product problem-tracking system. The manager could use *anno* to add (or annotate) components like X-found: and X-fixed: to the message headers.

NOTE

To be sure that your component name is legal, it's a good idea to put the characters X- before it. The name should have only letters, digits, and dashes in it.*

Look at the following example commands. Here, I'll use *anno* to add the following component to the current message header:

```
X-fixed: Linda Farpel
```

Next, I display the message with *show*—notice the other X-fixed: component, which *anno* added with the current time. Also see the X-found: component that shows who found the problem. The annotation text has a space in it, so quotes are required when you type the following commands:

```
% date
Tue Feb 02 13:14:05 CST 1993
% anno -component X-fixed -text 'Linda Farpel'
% show
```

---

*For regulations about mail headers, see the document "RFC822 – Standard for the Format of ARPA Internet Text Messages." (RFC is short for *request for comment.*) You can get it by anonymous FTP from sites around the Internet. Or, ask your computer's Postmaster for help.

```
(Message server:234)
X-fixed: Tue, 02 Feb 93 13:14:29 -0600
X-fixed: Linda Farpel
X-found: Mon, 01 Feb 93 09:25:44 -0600
X-found: Jody Hammersmith
From: andyb@field.bigcorp.com (Andy Bowman)
To: bugtrack@sw.bigcorp.com
    ...
```

Besides being able to keep the history of a problem report in the header, you can use *pick* to search for messages by the dates in any of the annotated fields. For example, if someone wanted to find all the problems fixed in January 1993:

```
% pick -datefield X-fixed -after 1-Jan-93 -and -before 1-Feb-93
```

The *–datefield* switch tells *pick* to search X-fixed: component for its dates. (Without *–datefield*, *pick* would search the Date: component.) Be sure to put the *–datefield* switch before (to the left of) the *–before* and *–after* switches.

This kind of setup would be a good one for a read-only folder with bug reports that all the maintenance workers could read and only the manager (the user who owned the folder) could modify. Section 8.7 explains folder sharing.

Here are five miscellaneous points about annotation:

1. By default, *anno* uses its *–noinplace* switch. This breaks any existing links to the message. If you want to preserve the links, use *anno –inplace*.

2. If you don't use the *–component* switch, *anno* will ask for it:

   ```
   % anno -text 'Linda Farpel'
   Enter component name: X-fixed
   ```

3. As you've seen, *anno* usually adds two components, one with the date and the other with the text field. To make *anno* omit the text component, leave off the *–text* switch. To omit the date, use the *–nodate* switch.

   ```
   % anno -component xyz
   % anno -component xyz -text 'blah blah' -nodate
   ```

4. When you search for an annotation with *pick* or scan for it with a *scan* format file (as explained in Section 10.2), the commands will only pay attention to the first annotation with a particular name. The order of the annotations is important. By default, as the previous bugtracking examples above, each date

annotation comes before its corresponding text annotation. If you want to reverse the order of the annotations, use two *anno* commands this way:

```
% anno -comp X-fixed
% anno -comp X-fixed -text 'Linda Farpel' -nodate
% show
(Message server:234)
X-fixed: Linda Farpel
X-fixed: Tue, 02 Feb 93 13:14:29 -0600
    . . .
```

The most recent annotation will be found first. In this case, *pick* and *scan* would find the text field instead of the date.

You might also decide to give the date and text components different names.

5. The *repl, forw*, and *dist* commands can annotate your messages automatically. See Sections 6.7.7, 6.8.6, and 6.9.2, respectively, for information.

7.8 Using Links

Because MH stores messages in UNIX files, it can take advantage of UNIX *links*, introduced in Section 2.7. They let you have more than one name for the same file. The following list presents an overview of using links:

* When you tell MH to make links to a message, the same message can be stored in more than one folder without taking extra disk space. (Figure 2-2 has a diagram.)

* If you make changes to a message (for instance, annotating it with *anno* *–inplace*—or editing it, as in Section 9.6 on *mhedit*), the changes will appear in all the linked messages.

* If you remove a link, the other links will still be there. The message file isn't actually removed from the disk until *all* the links have been removed.*

* Other users can link to messages in your folders (if you give them permission, and if their MH mail directories are on the same filesystem as yours). You can link to their messages in the same way. Basically, if you can read the other user's message (even if it's in a read-only folder), you can probably link to it. See Section 7.8.4, "Links Between Users.:

---

*The delayed removal features of MH can keep links around for some time longer. Section 7.5 has details.

7.8.1 Making Links

To link messages, use the *refile –link* command, as explained in Section 7.1.4. Remember that MH makes standard ("hard") links, not symbolic ("soft") links. If you need to link between filesystems, see Section 7.8.5.

7.8.2 Are These Two Messages Linked?☒

(*xmh* users: instead of *scan*, check your table of contents. Instead of *rmm*, use `Delete`.)

To find out whether two messages are linked, first *scan* them both. The format file called *scan.size* will show the number of characters in each message (for examples of this see Section 5.2.1):

```
% scan -form scan.size 13 +reports
  13  12/14   892 Vicki Thomas     Progress Report<<I'm out o
% scan -form scan.size 22 +vicki
  22  12/14   892 Vicki Thomas     Progress Report<<I'm out o
```

The messages look identical: each one has 892 characters. But, to be sure that the messages are linked (and not just identical copies of each other), compare the files' *i-numbers*.* (See Section 2.7.2, "Technical Stuff About Links.") To compare the i-numbers, list the two message files with *ls –li*. Be sure to use backquotes (`` ` ``), not single quotes (`'`). Fill in the message number and folder name:

```
% ls -li `mhpath 13 +reports`
 20930 -rw-------  1 eds    892 Feb  1 04:32 /u1/eds/Mail/reports/13
% ls -li `mhpath 22 +vicki`
  2508 -rw-------  2 eds    892 Dec 14 17:31 /u1/eds/Mail/vicki/22
```

The first number in the *ls –li* output is the i-number of the file (your version of *ls* might be different—if you aren't sure, ask a local expert). These two files have different i-numbers (20930 and 2508), so they are not linked. The third item in each line is the *link count*—it tells how many links that file has. Here, the first file has one link (itself) and the second has two. If the files were linked, both link counts would be the same.

---

*To be completely sure, you need to compare the *device names*, too. But it's very unlikely that two message files which *scan* the same and have the same i-numbers would not be linked.

If you want to replace the "non-linked" message in the *reports* folder with a link to the message in the *vicki* folder, here's how:

1. Remove the message you don't want:

   ```
   % rmm +reports 13
   ```

2. Link to the other copy. You can do it in one step with *refile* and its *–src* switch (see Section 7.1.4):

   ```
   % refile -link +reports -src +vicki 22
   ```

   That might be easier to see in two steps:

   ```
   % folder +vicki
              vicki+ has    32 messages (   1- 32); cur=   4.
   % refile -link 22 +reports
   ```

The new link in the *reports* folder will have a new message number—the last message in the folder.

7.8.3 A Folder Full of Links⊠

(*xmh* users: instead of *refile*, use `Copy as Link`.)

Have you ever asked yourself "What folder did I put that message in?" You can use *pick* and a loop to search lots of folders, as in Section 7.2.9. This section explains a setup you might like better: a link folder. (That's not official MH terminology. I made up the name.)

When you want to save a message, you can link the message into two folders: the folder where you'd usually store it, and a special folder that has links to all (or many of) your messages. Because the link doesn't take any more disk space, why not do it? The *refile* command can link messages into more than one folder. (See Section 7.1.4.)

To find a message, search the link folder.

One Folder, Many Folders, Subfolders . . .

There are a lot of ways to set up a link folder, depending on your mail configuration and your wants. Find something that's simple enough to manage but capable enough to help you find your messages. Some ideas to get you started:

- The simplest way is to make all the links into one folder. I call mine *a* (I type +a).

- You could make a few top-level folders by subject, sender, date, whatever. Decide where to make the link when you refile the message.

- Do you use subfolders? You might make a link folder for each group of subfolders. For example, along with your *memos* subfolders called *memos/jan*, *memos/feb*, *memos/mar*, and so on—make a link folder named *memos/a*.

- Hard to remember where the link folders are? Group them all in a set of subfolders called *a/people*, *a/places*, etc.

- You could also link messages into more than one link folder: maybe a top-level *a* folder and a more specialized link folder.

  If you have MH 6.7 or later, a very handy trick is to link a message into several folders—and sort those folders different ways. For example, link a message into folders named *date*, *from*, and *subject*. Use the commands *sortm*, *sortm –textfield from*, and *sortm -textfield subject*, respectively.

Whatever you do, I think I've given you enough ideas to get you started! Why not try one—and take advantage of the flexibility that MH gives you?

Making the Links

To refile a message into your *recipes* folder with a link to the link folder *a*, type:

```
% refile +recipes +a
```

If you already have folders full of messages, you can use *refile –link* to link existing messages into your link folder. Use a command like:

```
% refile -link all +a
```

Or, use a shell loop like the one in Example 7-3. In the example, I give the loop a list of a few folders; it links all those into a folder called *ln*.

Example 7-3. Linking existing messages into new all-message folder

C shell:

```
% foreach f (rpts memos ...)
? refile -src +$f -link all +ln
? end
```

Bourne and Korn shells:

```
$ for f in rpts memos ...
> do refile -src +$f -link all +ln
> done
```

To link all messages in all folders, instead, you could replace the first line of Example 7-3 with the line:

```
% foreach f (`folders -f | fgrep -v -x ln`)
```

or:

```
$ for f in `folders -f | fgrep -v -x ln`
```

The command `fgrep -v -x ln` avoids trouble by omitting the *ln* folder in the list of folders to link from.

Finding Stuff in a Link Folder☒

After making that setup, you might want to sort the link folder by date once in a while (see Section 7.4). That makes it easier for *pick* to find messages, because the folder can get really huge. If you're looking for a message from the last month, and your *a* folder has a year's worth of messages, you can give *pick* a shorter range of messages to search. For example, if you guess that there aren't more than 100 messages from the last month, you can save a lot of time with:

```
% pick last:100 ...
```

Don't Break Links Accidentally☒

If you make links to many of your messages, you'll probably want to give the *–inplace* switch to commands that edit messages. It makes sure that annotations won't break one of your links. Do it in your MH profile for the *anno* command. Also, if you use *–annotate* with *repl, forw,* or *dist,* add *–inplace* there, too.

Removing Messages☒

There's one gotcha about linked messages. When you want to remove the message, if you don't remove all the links, the message isn't taken off the disk. There's no MH command that does the whole job. But, with help from a couple of UNIX commands, it's a pretty easy job to do. (Reading Chapter 2, *MH and the UNIX Filesystem,* should help you understand the steps below.) If you do this a lot, it's worth writing a little shell script to find the links for you—and maybe even to remove them.

Let's say you want to remove message 234 in your *reports* folder and its link in the *a* folder:

1. *cd* to your MH directory by typing `cd Mail`—or, more generally:

   ```
   % cd `mhpath +`
   ```

2. Find the i-number of the message. Do that by listing it in its folder with *ls –i*:

   ```
   % ls -i reports/234
   37023 reports/234
   ```

3. Use *find* to search the link folder for a message with the same i-number (in this case, it's 37023):

   ```
   % find a -inum 37023 -print
   a/1708
   ```

4. The message is number 1708 in your *a* folder. Remove it and its other link. Then you're done:

   ```
   % rmm 234 +reports
   % rmm 1708 +a
   ```

If you aren't sure what folder the links are in, have *find* search all folders for the message. Use the pathname . (dot) instead of the folder name:

```
% find . -inum 37023 -print
./reports/234
./done/23
./a/1708
```

There, we found the link in the *a* folder and another link too: message 23 in the *done* folder.

7.8.4 Links Between Users ⊠

It's as easy to link to another user's messages as it is to link to your own. This is especially useful when a group needs to share certain messages from folder(s), but doesn't want to wade through the unimportant messages in another user's folder—each user can link to only the messages he or she needs.

For example, a group of software maintenance people might want to link to certain messages in certain folders on a central problem-tracking account. Each maintenance person could have a folder in his or her MH directory, with a list of messages for the problems that were assigned to him or her. When a new problem is assigned, the maintainer could make a new link. When the problem is solved, the maintainer could *rmm* his or her personal link to the message. The group's manager could use a command like *anno –inplace* to update the messages in the central problem-tracking folders, and all the maintainers would see the changes in their linked messages instantly.

In the right situation, with some planning and forethought, a system like that can be effective. Here are some things to watch out for:

- Links only work between users on the same filesystem. (If you're not sure whether another user is on the same filesystem, ask your system administrator or just try to make a link and see what happens.) On UNIX systems with symbolic links, you can use them—carefully, as explained in Section 7.8.5. Where links won't work, you can still access folders of other users who give you permission—even across a networked filesystem. That can be safer than symbolic links because there's no danger of loops. For more information, see Section 8.7.

- Access permissions can be confusing unless you understand the UNIX filesystem. If you're not comfortable with this, it's good to have an expert around until you are (it's not *that* tough!).

- Once a user has linked to a message in someone else's folder, if the owner shuts off access to the folder, users with links to the messages will usually still be able to read them. The owner will also need to make the individual messages unreadable.

- If the original owner of a message removes it, other users who had a link to the message will still have their links and be able to access the message. (UNIX doesn't remove a file until all links to it have been removed.)

Here's an example. The user *ehuser* wants to link to message 2 in *jdpeek*'s folder named *tester*. She makes that folder her current folder, finds the message, then links it to her *test* folder:

```
% folder +/u3/jdpeek/Mail/tester
/u3/jdpeek/Mail/tester+ has      5 messages (  1-  5); cur=  4.
% scan
    1  04/06 mary@hahvahd.edu   rcvtty -- how do I use it?<<I've
    2  11/13 well!pokey@phlabs  Re: Encapsulation destroying goo
    3  03/09 Barbara Zimmerman  Confused over mh-format files<<O
scan: unable to open message 4: Permission denied, continuing...
scan: unable to open message 5: Permission denied, continuing...
% refile -link 2 +test
% scan +test
   1+ 12/14 jdpeek@rodan.acs.  I'm out of town<<I'm out of town
    2  01/28*To:               <<--Jerry Peek; Syracuse Univers
    3  02/03*To:jerryp         sdaff<<dfkjdf --Jerry Peek; Syra
    4  12/14 jdpeek@rodan.acs.  I'm out of town<<I'm out of town
    5  11/13 well!pokey@phlabs  Re: Encapsulation destroying goo
```

Notice that no matter what your current folder is you always refer to your own folders with their normal name (like *+test*). You refer to other users' folders by using a full pathname with a plus sign (+) before it, like *+/u3/jdpeek/Mail/tester*.*
Also notice the `Permission denied` warnings. The warnings tell *ehuser* that *jdpeek* hasn't given her permission to read those two messages. Section 8.7 explains more.

7.8.5 Using Symbolic Links⊠

(*xmh* users: do this with standard UNIX commands in an *xterm* window. I don't recommend symbolic links to folders for *xmh*; the NOTE in Section 16.2.1 tells why.)

As Section 2.7 explains, the hard links that MH uses can't cross filesystems. MH can't link to a message in a folder on another filesystem or across a network. (Not yet, at least.) Instead of bothering with the complications of links, MH (but not *xmh*) users can access any folder on any filesystem by typing its path-name—see Section 8.7.

Still need to make a link? Does your UNIX have symlinks (symbolic links, the *ln −s* command)? It's possible to make symlinks to folders, but that can be tricky. Symlinks will also work for individual messages. I recommend that you don't use symlinks unless you need them. Unlike hard links, each symlink takes a block of disk space. Also, because MH doesn't support them (not yet, anyway) using symlinks with MH seems like a "hack" to me ... but not enough of a hack to keep me from explaining how to use them. : −)

I'll use my setup as an example. I have a workstation with a local disk that has a */mhdir* directory; I store most of my mail there. But I need to share some of my mail with other people in the company. That mail is in my home directory, */u/jerry/Mail*, which is part of a filesystem mounted across the network to all of our computers. On my workstation, my MH profile has `Path: /mhdir` in it.†

Part II
Using MH

---

*But you can still use relative folder operators. For instance, let's say your current folder is */u3/jdpeek/Mail/tester*. You could get to its subfolder *sub* with `@sub` as well as with `+/u3/jdpeek/Mail/tester/sub`. See Section 7.1.6 for more information.

†On other computers, I set the *MH* environment variable to point to an MH profile with the other `Path:`. But that's not important in this example.

Symlinks to Messages

To make a new symlink from my *stuff* folder on my local filesystem that points to message 822 in the *bookq* folder on the other filesystem:

```
% scan 822 +/u/jerry/Mail/bookq
 822 -07/10 Jeffrey Smith    Vol 8 of X Windows set<<Hi! Is Vol 8
% ln -s `mhpath 822` `mhpath new +stuff`
% scan last +stuff
   2 -07/10 Jeffrey Smith    Vol 8 of X Windows set<<Hi! Is Vol 8
% ls -l `mhpath 2`
lrwxrwxrwx  1 jerry        23 Jul 14 09:20 /mhdir/stuff/2 -> \
                              /u/jerry/Mail/bookq/822
```

NOTE

Don't use *sortm* or *folder –pack* on the folder where a symbolic link points (in this example, the *bookq* folder). If you do, the link may end up pointing to a different message—or no message at all.

Hard links (the kind that MH makes) don't have this problem.

If you remove or refile the message that a link points to, remember to remove the link too. Otherwise you'll see strange errors like:

```
% scan +stuff
   1  01/26 To:jerry        Messages to handle in inbox, bookq
scan: unable to open message 2: No such file or directory, continuing...
```

In general, you can just use *rmm* to remove the link. If that doesn't work, remove it with the UNIX *rm* command:

```
% rm `mhpath 2`
```

Symlinks to Folders

You can also make a symbolic link from your top-level MH directory to another folder in a different MH directory or vice versa.

CAUTION

If you link to folders—especially to subfolders—be sure you know what you're doing. If you link to a folder, and there's also a symlink from a folder underneath it pointing back to your folder, you can get an infinite loop. MH commands like *folder –recurse* will not catch this.

Also, be sure to remove the link with *rm*, not *rmf*. See the CAUTION at the end of this section.

The other problem you can have with symlinks to folders comes when you use *folders* for a summary of your folders (or, worse, in a loop run by some script to do something to all your folders). If one of the folders is a read-only folder (Section 8.7), it can appear twice. Say I've made a symlink named *project* in my local MH directory that points to the read-only folder */u/barb/Mail/zeta*. Unless I remember to *rmf* the reference to */u/barb/Mail/zeta* (explained in Section 7.6), the *folders* output will look like Example 7-4.

Example 7-4. Symlink causes double listing of read-only folder

```
             Folder       # of messages (  range  ); cur  msg ...
/u/barb/Mail/zeta  has    52 messages (   1-  64).
              ...
          project  has    52 messages (   1-  64).
```

And, of course, the relative folder operator @ (Section 7.1.6) won't do what you expect it to after you change your current folder through a symlink.

"Okay, okay," you say, "tell me how to do it anyway!" It's easy. Just *cd* to the directory above where you want the folder to appear, then use *ln –s*. For instance, I'll make the link to Barb's *zeta* folder shown in Example 7-4 above. In this case, to make the top-level "folder" (symlink), I'll need to go to the top-level MH directory:

```
% cd `mhpath +`
% ln -s /u/barb/Mail/zeta project
```

The next example shows how to make a "subfolder" (symlink) called *work/zeta* to Barb's *zeta* folder. When the symlink has the same name as what it points to, you don't need to type the name twice:

```
% cd `mhpath +work`
% ln -s /u/barb/Mail/zeta
```

If you remove the folder that a symlink points to, remember to remove the symlink too. To remove the symlink, be *sure* to use the UNIX *rm* command, *not* the MH *rmf* command! For example, to remove a symlink named *tmp*, type:

```
% rm `mhpath +tmp`
```

CAUTION

Do not use the MH *rmf* command to remove a symbolic link to a folder. If you do (on my version of MH 6.7.2, at least), *rmf* will not remove the symlink. Instead, if it can, *rmf* will remove all messages from the folder that the link points to! The damage looks like this:

```
% folder +tmp
                 tmp+ has    8 messages (   1-   8).
% ls -l `mhpath`
lrwxrwxrwx  1 jerry        18 Jul 14 09:25 /mhdir/tmp -> \
                                           /u/jerry/Mail/test
% rmf
Remove folder "tmp"? y
rmf: unable to remove directory /mhdir/tmp:\
                           Not a directory, continuing...
rmf: folder +tmp not removed
% folder
                 tmp+ has   no messages.
% ls -l `mhpath` /u/jerry/Mail/test
lrwxrwxrwx  1 jerry        18 Jul 14 09:25 /mhdir/tmp -> \
                                           /u/jerry/Mail/test
/u/jerry/Mail/test:
total 0
```

That's another reason why I think you should avoid symbolic links to folders.

7.9 Bursting Forwarded Messages and Digests

When MH forwards message(s) with *forw* or makes a digest with *forw –digest*, it uses a special format called *bit stuffing*. That format makes it easy for the recipient to extract the "encapsulated" messages, one by one. The MH *burst* command does this; it splits (bursts) the group into separate messages.

This example shows the basics of *burst*. First, there's a forwarded message which contains three other messages (to save space, the middle of each message isn't shown). Notice that the original message has two lines of text after the last forwarded message. Next, the message is burst with the *–verbose* switch (which tells you what's happening but isn't required). Finally, a *scan* shows that the folder now has the three burst messages, as well as the original:

```
% scan
   1+ 12/11 To:daved            Mail questions I told you about
% show
(Message inbox:1)
To: daved
Subject: Mail questions I told you about
Date: Fri, 11 Dec 92 20:13:46 -0400
From: ehuser
```

Dave, here are the questions we were discussing.
Hope they're what you wanted.

------- Forwarded Messages

Date: Mon, 07 Dec 92 00:28:18 +0000
From: Al Bok <al@phlabs.ph.com>
To: mh-users@ics.uci.edu
cc: ehuser@quack.phlabs.ph.com, aguru@mt.top.ph.com
Subject: Query about "repl -query"

I have a query about repl -query...

Actually, this switch may already be in the message, just not
    ...
Thanks, all of you.   --Al Bok

------- Message 2

Date: Tue, 08 Dec 92 17:06:04 -0500
From: "Terry Y. Kritel" <tykritel@bigsun.ncs.syr.edu>
To: ehuser@animals.ncs.syr.edu (Emma H. User)
Subject: Re: Fast Find

Emma,

We never did get the fast find working in the NFS environment.
    ...
Terry

------- Message 3

Date: Wed, 09 Dec 92 11:24:45 -0500
From: "Terry Y. Kritel" <tykritel@bigsun.ncs.syr.edu>
To: ehuser@animals.ncs.syr.edu (Emma H. User)
Subject: Re: Mail problems... plus copy of my original question

Emma,

That's happened before. There's a problem with the name server,
and the request times out. We're checking into it.

------- End of Forwarded Messages

That's all for now, Dave.

% burst -verbose
4 messages exploded from digest 1
message 4 of digest 1 becomes message 4
message 3 of digest 1 becomes message 3
message 2 of digest 1 becomes message 2
% scan

```
1  12/11 To:daved            Mail questions I told you about
2+ 12/07 Al Bok              Query about "repl -query"<<I ha
3  12/08 "Terry Y. Kritel"  Re: Fast Find<<Emma, We never d
4  12/09 "Terry Y. Kritel"  Re: Mail problems... plus copy
```

NOTE

The *burst* command doesn't always work. The message format is important. Once you experiment and find a consistent setup, you'll probably
have little trouble. The *–noinplace* switch is safest. See your online
burst(1) manual page for more information.

Here's an unusual and interesting way to use *burst*. When you get a message that
was returned as undeliverable, you may be able to use *burst* to extract the original
message from the error mail. It may or may not work on your system, depending
on how returned mail messages are formatted. Briefly, here are the steps:

```
% show
    ...Returned message appears...
% burst
    ...Extracts original message, if format is right...
% comp -use -draftfolder @. -draftmessage next
    ...Original message appears as a draft; the @. means "the current folder"...
What now? send
```

Again, whether that works will depend on whether the returned message is in a
burst-able format. The *resend* program in Section 13.9 is more general and easier
to use for resending messages. Still, this example shows where an encapsulation
standard and *burst* can be useful.

7.10 Pack Messages into a File with packf

Normally, MH stores one message per file (see Chapter 2, *MH and the UNIX
Filesystem*). The *packf* command "packs" messages into a single file. As
Example 7-5 shows, the messages are separated by lines of four CTRL-A
characters. (This is the same way the MMDF transport agent formats its system
mailboxes).

Example 7-5. packf file format

```
% cat -v packedfile
^A^A^A^A
Header: xxx
Header: xxx
    ...
```

Example 7-5. packf file format (continued)

```
Body...
^A^A^A^A
^A^A^A^A
Header: xxx
Header: xxx
    ...
Body...
^A^A^A^A
```

Why use *packf*?

• It's an easy way to transport a group of messages to another computer.

• It can save disk space. That's because each standard MH message uses at least one block of disk space. Depending on the size of the messages, *packf* can pack several messages into a block.

    Packing a big folder that you don't use much can save a lot of room.

• You can handle the messages in file with *msh* (Section 7.11) and its MH commands *scan*, *show*, *rmm*, etc.

• Compressing the file with a UNIX utility like *compress* saves even more disk space. You'll have to *uncompress* the file to use it, though.

To get messages out of a *packf*'d file, use the command:

```
% inc -file packedfile
```

The messages will be read into your *inbox* unless you give a folder name (with a +, as usual) too. The messages will not be removed from the packed file unless you use *inc*'s *–truncate* switch. The default packed file name is *msgbox*.

7.11 MH Shell on a Mailbox File: msh

The files written by *packf* (Section 7.10) and *rcvpack* (Section 11.8) can be handled by the MH mail shell, *msh*. *msh* can read your system mailbox, too.

7.11.1 Overview of msh

msh is a monolithic user agent—the kind of program you thought you got away from when you decided to use MH! : -) Seriously, besides reading packed files, *msh* can be a good place for beginners to learn MH. That's because the only commands *msh* understands are MH commands.

The commands your *msh* supports depend on your *msh* version. Some of the commands don't have all the features the corresponding MH command does. Check your online manual page, type ? for help at an *msh* prompt, or just try the command—if what you want won't work, *msh* will tell you.*

Here's a sample short *msh* session:

```
% msh
Reading ./msgbox, currently at message 1 of 4
(msh) scan
   1+ 04/24 mary@hahvahd.edu   rcvtty -- how do I use it?<<I've been
   2  11/23 Al Bok             Query about "repl -query"<<I have a q
   3  02/09 "Wilbur, Orville"  X Terminal Presentation/Demonstration
   4  02/11 To:"Wilbur, Orvil  Re: X Terminal Presentation/Demonstra
(msh) show
(Message 1)
   ...Message 1 appears...
(msh) rmm
(msh) refile 2 +questions
Create folder /yourMHdir/questions? y
(msh) quit
Update file "./msgbox"? y
%
```

By default, *msh* reads a file named *msgbox* in your current directory. You can use a different filename by typing `-file packedfile` on the *msh* command line. One thing you might not expect is that *refile* does not write another *packf* format file. Instead, it writes to a standard MH folder. This is a nice way to move some messages out of a packed message file. To leave, type q or quit. *msh* will ask whether changes you've made, with commands like *rmm* and *refile*, should be made permanent. If you answer n, your packed message file won't be modified.

7.11.2 Handling New Mail with msh

If your system uses the MMDF transport agent, *msh* can read incoming mail without a problem. On systems with *sendmail*, though, your system mailbox will look like one long message to *msh*. You can always *inc* your mail into a normal MH folder from outside *msh*, then use *packf* to bundle the messages for *msh*. Or, to get a mailbox file in the format *msh* wants, automatically, set up a *.maildelivery* file like Example 7-6.

---

*I like the error messages—they start with **say what:**.

Example 7-6. .maildelivery file to convert incoming mail for msh

```
# Put all incoming mail into a msgbox file for msh:
* - ^ ? "/usr/local/lib/mh/rcvpack msgbox"
```

Chapter 11, *Processing New Mail Automatically*, explains how to set up
.*maildelivery* files.

7.11.3 msh and Your MH Profile

If you've done some customization in your MH profile, it can affect *msh* in
unusual ways. If your MH profile is as complicated as mine, you should probably
set the *MH* environment variable before you run *msh*. Make *MH* point to an alternate simple MH profile. Something like the *xmh* setup in Section 16.5 should be
fine.

*Part II
Using MH*

Part III:

Customizing MH

Part III is about changes you can make to your MH 6.7 setup.
Some of these are supported by MH directly. Others—aliases and
shell scripts—take advantage of the way that MH interacts with
UNIX.

Although *xmh* is powerful, your changes to MH can improve *xmh*
too. To understand *xmh* in depth, the information here will help
you—especially the sections and subsections with an ⓍΧ in their
headings.

You should read Part II first.

8

Making MH and xmh Work Your Way

Running an MH Command ⊠
MH and the Shell
An MH Profile, in General ⊠
Changing MH Directory Name ⊠
Setting Access Permissions for Other Accounts
Defining Alternate Mailboxes ⊠
Sharing Other Users' Folders
MH Library Directory ⊠
Draft Message Template Files

Whether you use MH or *xmh*, some part of it might not work exactly the way you want it to. For a lot of the work, you don't have to be a programmer—just follow the instructions here. Usually, you'll be making a change to your MH profile.

This chapter and Chapter 9, *New Versions of MH Commands*, show you how to extend MH itself. Chapter 12, *Introduction to Shell Programming for MH*, and Chapter 13, *MH Shell Programs*, explain how to write more complex shell programs that build completely new functionality around MH. Chapter 16 is about customizing *xmh*, but the information in these earlier chapters will help you adapt the parts of MH that *xmh* uses.

This chapter starts with overall information about how MH commands work. You'll see how to use different MH directories—including other users'. You'll read about how draft messages are built. Here are some ways to customize MH and *xmh*:

- Make your default mail headers just the way you want, so you don't have to make the same changes to the header by hand each time.

- Set default options in the MH profile.

- Rename, move, or "hide" your MH directory almost anywhere.

- For *xmh* users, here's information about the MH commands that *xmh* runs and how you can change what the buttons and menus do.

Up to now, this book has covered switches for specific MH commands. There are other overall configuration lines you can put in your MH profile. Many of these affect both MH and *xmh*.

8.1 Running an MH Command ⊠

This section explains what happens when you run an MH command, step by step. (This also applies when *xmh* runs an MH command for you.)

To help with the explanation, assume that you type the command:

```
% scan -noheader picked +inbox
```

and that your MH profile has the component:

```
scan: -form scan.size -header
```

The steps are:

1. UNIX searches for the *scan* program file and starts it running.

2. One of the first things *scan* does is to find the MH profile file. The `Path:` component in the MH profile has the name of your MH directory. (The MH directory is usually named *Mail*. Section 8.4, "Changing MH Directory Name," has more information.)

3. The command checks your MH profile for components with the exact command name. The settings in this component override the default *scan* settings.

   In this example, for instance, the `-form scan.size` overrides *scan*'s default format. Also, *scan* defaults to *-noheader*, but the `-header` in your MH profile overrides that default. So now, by default, *scan* will print a header over the listing.

4. Command-line parameters (−noheader picked +inbox) are read. Any switches override the corresponding default and MH profile switches. So in this example, *−noheader* wins the "battle of the switches" and will be used when *scan* runs.

Some arguments can't be used more than once. For instance, if you store this line in your MH profile:

```
inc: +somefolder
```

and also give a folder name on the command line, this happens:

```
% inc +otherfolder
inc: only one folder at a time!
```

5. The command looks in your MH directory for the file named *context*. This is where your current folder name and some other information are stored (see the *mh–profile*(5) manual page in Appendix I).

6. The command looks in your folder for the *.mh_sequences* file. This file holds the message number sequences like *cur* (the current message number) and, in this example, *picked*.

7. The command scans and displays your folder.

8. If the command succeeds, it changes the current folder and current message (if needed). Commands like:

```
% show 1234 +inbox
```

usually won't change the current folder to *inbox*, or the current message to 1234, if there isn't a message number 1234 in the *inbox*.

8.2 MH and the Shell

Unlike most other e-mail user agents, MH is used from the UNIX shell. This section lists two shell features that can make MH easier to use: aliases or functions, and shell variables.

8.2.1 Using Shell Aliases and Functions with MH

Most UNIX shells (except earlier Bourne shells) have aliases, functions, or both. Aliases let you execute complicated command lines by typing a short alias name. In general, functions can handle more complicated problems than aliases—but

Part III
Customizing MH

let's ignore that for now. Let's look at how aliases and functions can save time with MH.

Making Aliases and Functions

When I'm reading mail, I usually type rmm to read a message, then next to read the next one. An alias or function named something like *n* can do both. In the C shell, for example, you can type the following alias at a prompt or into your *.cshrc* file. The semicolon (;) is a command separator:

```
alias n 'rmm; next'
```

Now, for the Bourne shell—on the command line or in your *.profile* file:

```
$ n()
> {
> rmm
> next
> }
```

Lots of times, you'll need to pass arguments to an alias or function. That is, you need to give the name of a folder, some message numbers, some switches, or a combination of those. In the C shell, the most general way is to use the sequence \ ! * at the place you want the arguments inserted.* The next alias and function, *scap*, will run *scan* with the arguments you give it, if any. It pipes *scan*'s output to a pager program, to show one screen at a time. So, all three of the following command lines will work fine:

```
% scap
% scap +outbox
% scap +outbox -form scan.timely last:20
```

First, for the C shell:

```
alias scap 'scan \!* | more'
```

In a Bourne shell function, use $* to pass arguments. Here's *scap* written as a function, and with the System V *pg* pager:

```
scap()
{
scan $* | pg
}
```

As you saw above, the semicolon (;) is a command separator—after the first command finishes, the second command is executed. Sometimes, you only want

---

*You can "sprinkle" the arguments at different places in the alias, too. But there's not room here to handle specialized cases like that.

the second command to run if the first command succeeded. For example, a cleanup alias or function might run *pick* to find certain messages, then *rmm* to remove them. You only want *rmm* to run if *pick* found some messages! (For an example, see *cleandrafts* in the next section, "Some Handy Aliases.") That's where the && (two ampersands) operator is handy. The && means "if the first command returned a zero exit status, run the second command." As Section 12.8 explains, most MH commands return a zero status when they succeed. (If you're going to do something that's hard to undo, like removing folders, don't depend on a useful exit status from the previous command until you check its manual page or test it.)

Here's an example of the && operator. Most modern pagers can move backward or forward through a file. But they may not be able to back up when they're reading from a pipe. (The *less* pager, supplied with MH, can do both. So can modern versions of *more*.) Let's fix the *scap* alias from above to write its *scan* output to a temporary file. Then, if *scan* succeeds, run *more* to read the file. Finally, remove the temporary file. I'll call this alias *scap2*:

```
alias scap2 'scan \!* > /tmp/s$$ && more /tmp/s$$; rm -f /tmp/s$$'
```

That says "if *scan* succeeded and wrote lines to the temporary file, run *more* to read the file." (If you haven't seen */tmp/s$$* before, Section 12.11.2 will explain.) The semicolon doesn't test for success. So, whether *scan* succeeded or not, the temporary file will be removed next. In the Bourne shell, *scap2* looks like this:

```
scap2()
{
scan $* > /tmp/s$$ && pg /tmp/s$$
rm /tmp/s$$
}
```

Some Handy Aliases

You can write the commands in this section as aliases or functions. I'll show them as aliases. If you need functions:

- Change the alias **x** ' ... ' to **x**() { ... }.

- Change the \!* to $*.

The *fls* alias only works on shells with a *history* command:

Example 8-1. Shell aliases for MH

```
# Handle folder stacks:
alias puf 'folder -push \!*'
```

Example 8-1. Shell aliases for MH (continued)

```
alias pof 'folder -pop'
alias lsf 'folder -list'
# Search history list for folders I've worked on  (not for Bourne shell):
alias fls 'history >/tmp/f$$; grep "+[A-Za-z0-9/]" /tmp/f$$; rm /tmp/f$$'
# Handle draft folder (uses stack aliases above):
alias scandrafts 'puf +drafts; scan; pof'
alias cleandrafts 'puf +drafts; pick -before -14 -seq temp && rmm temp; pof'
# List unseen messages; show first message, if any (MH 6.7.2 only):
alias unseen 'scan unseen && show unseen:1'
```

A lot of the command versions in Chapter 9 can be written as aliases and functions.

They Won't Always Work

Aliases and functions generally only work when you're using a shell. Programs executed directly by the UNIX kernel can't use them. For example, the MH *refile* command calls an *rmmproc* to remove the message after it's been refiled. If you make a *myrmm* alias or function, you can use it from the shell prompt—but *refile* can't use it:

```
% alias myrmm 'something'
% refile -rmmproc myrmm +somewhere
refile: unable to exec myrmm: No such file or directory
```

MH also lets you make what I call *versions* of MH commands. (Chapter 9 explains them.) Those can be executed directly by other programs. On many UNIX systems, shell scripts (Chapters 12 and 13) can also be executed directly.

8.2.2 Using Shell Variables with MH

Before the shell executes a command line, it expands the values stored in any shell variables you use. You can store folder names (especially long names) in shell variables. MH has other ways to handle options you use often (see Chapter 9, *New Versions of MH Commands*) and lists of message numbers (sequences, see Section 7.3)—but variables can be used there, too.

Here's an example with folder names. I use a couple of folders with long names, +*mh–book/revisions* and +*/u/jerry/Mail/bookquestions*. I store those names in shell variables. I type a short shell variable name; the shell expands it into the long folder name before it starts the MH command.

As a general rule: when you define a shell variable, use single quotes (*'*), not backquotes (*`*), around the folder name. In the C shell, the *set* command stores a shell variable. The following commands, typed at a prompt or in my *.cshrc* file, set the variables:

```
set revs='+mh-book/revisions'
set bookq='+/u/jerry/Mail/bookquestions'
```

To set the variables in the Bourne shell, you don't need the set. Again, type the commands at a $ prompt or put them in your *.profile* file:

```
revs='+mh-book/revisions'
bookq='+/u/jerry/Mail/bookquestions'
```

When you use the variables, put a $ before the variable name. The $ works in both shells. For example, to change my current folder, I type:

```
% folder $bookq
/u/jerry/Mail/bookquestions+ has  774 messages (  1- 823); cur= 823
% show last $revs
    ...Last message in +mh-book/revisions appears...
```

8.3 An MH Profile, in General ☒

Section 1.4 gave an overview and showed a short MH profile. Here's more information and a bigger MH profile.

There are several kinds of components in your MH profile:

1. Components for individual MH commands, such as *repl* and *inc*. These lines start with the name of the command and a colon. The other part of each component is one or more command-line parameters that you'd like the command to use by default. For example, the line below tells *repl* to ask you who should get copies of your reply, then to start the *emacs* editor:

    ```
    repl: -query -editor emacs
    ```

    You use the same syntax for other MH commands, including the command versions explained in Chapter 9. Lines 19-30 and lines 31-56 of Example 8-2 are this kind.

2. Other components apply to (in general) more than one MH command. For example, the following component tells MH commands that you want to use the *vi* editor wherever possible:

    ```
    Editor: vi
    ```

    The *mh-profile*(5) manual page in Appendix I has a list of these. See lines 1-18 of Example 8-2.

*Part III
Customizing MH*

In most cases, those general settings are overriden by settings you make for individual MH commands. For instance, `repl: -editor emacs` would override a setting like `Editor: vi` when you use *repl*.

3. You can make comments in the MH profile by typing an "impossible" command name, followed by a colon. For instance, if you don't have an MH command named *comment* (which you won't, unless you followed the steps in Chapter 9, *New Versions of MH Commands*)—you can use that as a label for comments. You can also add other characters, like XXX, to "comment out" an existing component. Here's one way you might make a comment, and comment out a line:

```
comment: this isn't working now; figure out why!
XXXrepl: -querry
```

Lines 1-3, 24, and others in Example 8-2 show another way to make comments.

4. Don't leave blank (empty) lines in the MH profile.

Example 8-2 is an example of the MH profile from a heavy MH user. The line numbers to the left of each line (like *12>*) are not part of the file; they are for reference only. Any line that doesn't start with a line number is a continuation of the line above; we split it to fit the book page but you should type it on one line.

Example 8-2. A big MH profile

```
 1> #:
 2> #: First section: Overall setup for MH
 3> #:
 4> Aliasfile: aliases
 5> Alternate-Mailboxes: ehuser@*.xxx.yyy.zzz, emma@animals*,
 6>     ehuser@quack.phl.ph.com, *uucpit!ehuser
 7> Draft-Folder: drafts
 8> Folder-protect: 750
 9> Msg-protect: 640
10> Path: .Mail
11> Previous-Sequence: pseq
12> prompter-next: vi
13> rmmproc: /home/ehuser/.bin/rmmer
14> Sequence-Negation: not
15> showproc: mhl
16> Signature: "Emma H. User"
17> Unseen-Sequence: unseen
18> vi-next: spel
19> #:
20> #: Lines for specific standard MH programs:
21> #:
22> anno: -inplace
```

Example 8-2. A big MH profile (continued)

```
23> dist: -annotate -inplace -editor distprompter
24> #: -nodashmunging only works if you give -filter or -format:
25> forw: -anno -inpl -form components -format -nodashmunging
26> inc: -form scan.time
27> mhl: -nobell
28> pick: -seq picked -list
29> repl: -query -nocc me -annotate -inplace -editor prompter.nopre
30> rmf: -interactive
31> #:
32> #: Stuff for new versions of MH programs and shell scripts:
33> #:
34> auto_forw_send: -draftfolder +drafts
35> bomb: -form bombcomps -anno -inpl -editor head -query -nocc me -nocc cc
36> checkm: -file /usr/spool/mail/ehuser -form scan.checkm -width 150
37> cur: cur -form scan.more -width 235
38> curlast: cur-last
39> fo: -fast
40> foll: -form follcomps
41> follx: -form follcomps -filter follxfilt -editor vi
42> l10: last:10
43> l20: last:20
44> l5: last:5
45> l: last
46> msgnums: -format %(msg)
47> prompter.nopre: -noprepend -rapid
48> push: -push -draftfolder +drafts -forward -verbose
49> rapid: -rapid -prepend
50> replx: -filter replxfilt -query -nocc me -anno -inpl -editor
        prompter.nopre
51> resend: -editor resend.fixmsg
52> #: for 'rn' replies... there's gotta be a better way!:
53> rn-ans: -editor rn-ans.fixmsg
54> showpr: -format 'Message %(msg)' -mhl
55> showv: -showproc more
56> thanks: -form thankscomps -anno -inpl -editor cat -nocc all -whatnow
        push
```

Let's take a look at some of the lines in Example 8-2. The file is divided arbitrarily into three parts. (See the list above for the two general kinds of lines.)

- **Lines 5-6** list other addresses where this user, *ehuser*, gets mail. It lets MH
  find all messages which are actually from the user. See Section 8.6.

- **Lines 8-9** set the default UNIX filesystem protections that MH will use for
  new folders and messages. This particular protection scheme sets folders
  (mode 750) so that people in *ehuser*'s group can *scan* them. All the messages
  (mode 640) will also be readable by her group. See Section 8.7.

*Part III
Customizing MH*

181

- The signature in **line 16** doesn't go at the end of mail messages; it's put in the
From: component. See Section 6.4.2.

- **Line 24** is a comment for the line below it, a reminder of why the line is written the way it is. This is a good thing to do, especially in long MH profile files.

- **Line 35** is a version of *repl* that sends a picture of a bomb with its fuse burning. (Chapter 9, *New Versions of MH Commands*, explains how to make command versions.) The idea and the *bombcomps* component file came from the *miscellany/mtrenv* directory in the MH distribution. The −editor head doesn't actually edit the message; it uses the UNIX *head*(1) command to show the first ten lines of the draft on the screen. After that comes a What now? prompt, where you can choose a *real* editor if you want to.

- **Lines 37-38** and **lines 42-46** are all versions of *scan* that scan different ranges of messages. For example, 110: scans the last 10 messages, and 120: scans the last 20. See Section 9.9.

- **Line 47** is a workaround for a common MH problem: needing to give different switches to *prompter* for different mail-composing commands. It's used in **line 29** and **line 50**. See Section 9.7.

- The rmmproc: entry in **line 13** uses the full pathname of a shell script that's used for removing messages. You don't always need to give full pathnames to commands—for instance, **line 51** calls a program named *resend.fixmsg* with only its name; in this case, MH will search your shell's search path for the command you specify. But during jobs run by "background" processes like *cron*, the search path can be short. If a background process gives an error like unable to exec rn-ans.fixmsg: No such file or directory, a full pathname can help.

- **Line 54** is for a shell script (program). Your shell scripts can read the MH profile. See the *mhprofile* shell script in Section 13.4.

8.4 Changing MH Directory Name ☒

By default, MH names your mail directory *Mail* (note the capital M) and puts it under your home directory. You can actually name this directory anything and put it anywhere on the filesystem.* For instance, you can "hide" the MH mail

---

*It doesn't have to be in or under your home directory, but it should be someplace that you have permission to create new files and write.

directory by putting a period (.) before its name. This means it won't clutter an *ls* listing of your home directory (unless you use *ls –a*, of course).

To change the name, change the `Path:` component in your MH profile. By default, your MH directory name is *Mail*. So you should have this single `Path:` line:

```
Path: Mail
```

If your MH directory doesn't exist yet, MH will see your `Path:` and create it in the right place when you run your first MH command. If the directory already exists and you change the `Path:`, you'll need to move your directory. (If you're changing the directory name but not the location in the filesystem, you can use a command like mv `oldname newname`. If you want to move the directory someplace else, such as a subdirectory, you may need a command like *tar* to move your directory and preserve any links you've made.)

Here are rules for locating your MH directory. For this example, let's see what a user named Walt could do. His home directory is */u/walt*.

- If the MH directory name does not start with a slash (/), like *.Mail*, it must be in the home directory:

  ```
  Path: .Mail
  ```

  In this example, the exact location of Walt's directory would be */u/walt/.Mail*.

- The directory can be put someplace underneath the home directory (in a sub-subdirectory of the home directory) by using slashes (/) to separate the levels. For instance, Walt could put his MH directory in */u/walt/files/mh* with the following `Path:` line:

  ```
  Path: files/mh
  ```

- To put the directory someplace completely different (not under the home directory), use a full pathname starting with a slash (/). For example, let's say that Walt has several different accounts on the same computer* and has set up his */u/walt* account to allow writing by his other accounts. The home directories might be called */u/walt*, */u/project*, and */u/share/walter*. If Walt

---

*Or on different computers, with a networked filesystem that's shared by all the computers.

wants to keep all his mail in the */u/walt/Mail* directory, he would put this
Path: line in his */u/project/.mh_profile* and */u/share/walter/.mh_profile*
files:

```
Path: /u/walt/Mail
```

and this line in his */u/walt/.mh_profile* file:

```
Path: Mail
```

No matter what account he's logged on to, if he types a command like:

```
% folder +inbox
        inbox+ has 124 messages (  12- 198); cur= 19.
```

it will use the *inbox* folder in his */u/walt/Mail* directory. When he types inc,
the mail will go from his current account into that same *inbox*.* If there's a
chance that more than one of the accounts will be used at the same time, Walt
should think about putting the following two lines in each account's *.mh_pro-
file* file:

```
context: context.username
mh-sequences:
```

The first line sets a different MH context file for each username. (Those
filenames aren't required. Files named *context.1*, *context.2*,... would be
fine.) The empty second component means that all sequences will be private—that is, stored in the user's context file instead of in the folder. Both of
those will make conflicts between accounts less likely, though they will add
some overhead.

8.5 Setting Access Permissions for Other Accounts

Because MH uses the UNIX filesystem (directories and files) to store its messages,
UNIX filesystem security affects it. If no other users need to access your MH
messages, you can set any level of protection on your home directory and MH
directory, anywhere from completely accessible for all users to totally shut off
from all users. If other users are sharing your messages, though, you should be

---

*Each individual mail message file will still be owned by the account which created it. The group
ownership will be set to the group which owns the folder. But, if the access permissions are set correctly (in the Msg-protect: entry in *.mh_profile*), this shouldn't be a problem. If Walt's machine
has disk quotas, though, Walt should be sure that the other accounts will be allowed to make files on
the filesystem which holds */u/walt*.

sure that they have enough access but not too much. Because MH messages are usually stored under your home directory, giving other users access to some or all of your MH mail means that they could have access to your other files, too. With the information in Chapter 2, *MH and the UNIX Filesystem*, and good knowledge of the UNIX filesystem, you can figure out how to set access permissions yourself.

NOTE

xmh is designed more for single users than for sharing other users' mail. Section 16.2.1 has the gory details.

To help you share mail (just reading, or both reading and writing), your system administrator can create UNIX *groups*: lists of users who are allowed to share files with each other.

CAUTION

If you're really concerned about security and you're not experienced with UNIX filesystem security, ask an expert (like your system administrator) for help.

Here's an example to get you started. If all the members of a UNIX group want to share their mail with each other (reading each others' messages but not being able to modify any):

1. Everyone should put these entries in their MH profile files:

   ```
   Folder-protect: 750
   Msg-protect: 640
   ```

2. If anyone has existing folders or messages, they should reset the access permissions by using the *chmod* command. The UNIX *find* command below is an easy way to do this. Please type it carefully (the syntax is weird, but it works):

   ```
   % cd Mail
   % find . \( -type f -exec chmod 640 {} \; \) -o \
       \( -exec chmod 750 {} \; \)
   ```

If a user has thousands of messages and your system is slow, the following shell loop will probably be more efficient. (Section 7.4 has another shell loop example with an explanation of the loops.)* Be sure to use backquotes (`` ` ``), not single quotes (`'`):

C shell:	Bourne and Korn shells:

```
% foreach f (`folders -f -r`)       $ for f in `folders -f -r`
? echo fixing +$f                    > do echo fixing +$f
? set fp="`mhpath +$f`"              > fp="`mhpath +$f`"
? chmod 750 $fp                      > chmod 750 $fp
? cd $fp                             > cd $fp
? chmod 640 *                        > chmod 640 *
? end                               > done
fixing +apple                        fixing +apple
    ...                                  ...
fixing +zoo/zebra                    fixing +zoo/zebra
%                                    $
```

3. If any folders should stay private, the user should reprotect them. For instance, to make the folders *job_hunting* and *hate_mail* private:

```
% chmod 700 `mhpath +job_hunting +hate_mail`
```

Here are three other ways to set protection. Use the examples above but change the permission modes from 750 and 640, respectively, as shown below:

- To give everyone in your group permission to modify the folders' contents (*refile*, *rmm*, and so on) use modes 770 and 660.

- To give read access to everyone on your computer, use modes 755 and 644.

- To give your group permission to modify the folder contents and give everyone on your computer permission to read, use modes 775 and 664.

8.6 Defining Alternate Mailboxes ⊠

If you get mail at more than one "mailbox," you'll probably want to tell MH about your alternate mailboxes. In other words, if you receive mail at more than

---

*Careful readers will notice that, in every folder, the loop sets the mode of all messages and any subfolder directories to 640. A subfolder with mode 640 can't be accessed. But, because *folders −r* always gives the name of a folder before any of its subfolders, the subfolder permission will be set correctly in the next pass of the loop.

one address, on one or more computers—but all the mail is put into a single set of mail folders—then the other addresses are your "alternate mailboxes."

This can happen with a setup like the one in Section 8.4, where Walt is getting mail from three accounts that all *inc* into the same set of folders. It can also happen when mail is forwarded from other accounts—for example, with a *.forward* file under UNIX Sendmail, a SET FORWARD command under VMS Mail, etc.

Some good reasons to tell MH the addresses of these alternate mailboxes:

- The command *repl –nocc me* will know which other mailboxes should not get extra copies of a message.

- When you *scan* your folder, messages that you sent from any of those accounts will be marked `To: recipient` instead of shown as `From:` your other account.

Let's go on with the example of Walt, above. People can send mail to him at *walt*, *project*, and *walter*. But he receives and answers it all on the *walt* account. He should put this component in the *.mh_profile* file on his *walt* account:

```
Alternate-Mailboxes: project, walter
```

That component may not be enough to catch all of the mail, though; the `Alternate-Mailboxes:` component has to match the `From:` address exactly. Depending on Walter's computer, some of the mail he sends may have his full network address (like `walt@xxx.yyy.zzz`) in the `From:` component. An asterisk (*) means "match all." So Walt may want to use this component instead:

```
Alternate-Mailboxes: project@*, walter@*
```

That matches any addresses that start with *project@* ... or *walter@* ... Unfortunately, it also includes addresses which start with those words on other computers—even if they're not his accounts. The following component with his fully qualified hostname might be best of all:

```
Alternate-Mailboxes: project, project@xxx.yyy.zzz,
     walter, walter@xxx.yyy.zzz
```

(You can continue a component on another line by ending a line with a comma and indenting the next line with space or a tab.) Finally, if Walt reads mail while logged on to either of his *walter* or *project* accounts, he should put `Alternate-Mailboxes:` components in the *.mh_profile* files on those accounts.

8.7 Sharing Other Users' Folders

The sections above explain how a user can access one set of MH folders from several different accounts. You can also do the opposite: access many other users' folders from your account.

NOTE

> If you use *xmh*, you may not want to try this. Although *xmh* can share other users' folders, like MH does, it can get pretty confusing. See Section 16.2.1.

The other user can grant you permission to read and write the messages with a setup like Walt's, above. Or you can get permission only to read the messages—maybe to read only one or a few folders.

If you access a folder that's not under the Path: listed in your MH profile, MH makes special arrangements to keep track of that folder. This is usually called a *read-only folder*.*

As long as the access permissions let you, you can make any folder your current folder. Just type its full pathname (starting with a slash (/)) and add a plus sign (+) before it. Here are two examples: one shows how to access another user's MH folder and the next shows how a person might be able to read the USENET *mysys.general* newsgroup with MH commands.

```
% scan +/usr3/joe/Mail/share
    3  12/14 "Frank A. Man I'm going to a meeting<<In Pittsburgh
scan: unable to open message 4: Permission denied, continuing...
    5  12/17 Belinda Carli Plans for the holiday<<I'll be in Los
% show 3
(Message /usr3/joe/Mail/share:3)
    ...
% pick -from ehuser +/usr/spool/news/mysys/general
6 hits
% show picked
    ...
```

The other user can control which folders and/or messages you're allowed to read by setting the UNIX filesystem permissions. Joe did this to his message 4, above.

---

*In this case, instead of keeping folder sequences in the *.mh_sequences* file of the folder being accessed, MH keeps folder information in the file named *context* in the user's own MH directory. This happens whenever a folder (directory) does not belong to the user who is *scan*ning it. Even if a folder is writable, a user can't change its *.mh_sequences* file unless the folder belongs to that user.

The easiest way is with the *mhpath* command and backquotes (`` ` ``)—don't use single quotes ('). You can control access to whole folders, or only to some messages, by using commands like the following:

- To make one of your folders private (so no one else can read messages in it):

  ```
  % chmod go-rwx `mhpath +foldername`
  ```

- To make some of your messages in a folder private, give *mhpath* the message numbers or ranges:

  ```
  % scan +foldername
      ...Message list appears...
  % chmod go-rw `mhpath 1 3-7 10`
  ```

If you're not familiar with the UNIX filesystem, explaining all the protection schemes you could use would take too much space here. If you need help, ask someone who understands the UNIX filesystem well.

By the way, any read-only folders you access will stay in your list of folders (the *folders* command) until you remove them with *rmf*. For example:

```
% rmf +/usr/spool/news/mysys/general
[+/usr/spool/news/mysys/general de-referenced]
[+inbox now current]
```

8.8 MH Library Directory ⊠

Each computer that runs MH should have a publicly readable directory with some MH files. The directory will have a name like */usr/local/lib/mh* (yours might be different). The directory has programs like *slocal* and *mhl*. It also has some draft template files that commands like *repl*, *scan*, and *mhl* read. For more information, see those sections below. Figure 2-1 is a diagram of a typical UNIX filesystem, including the files and directories on a user's account.

8.9 Draft Message Template Files

When you start to compose a mail message with MH, the MH command (*comp*, *repl*, etc.) reads a template file for the draft message. Because *xmh* calls MH commands to build its draft file, these same template files also set the message headers in *xmh*.

*Part III
Customizing MH*

189

8.9.1 How the Draft Message is Built⊠

This section explains how commands like *comp* and *forw* create a draft message from their template files. Sections 8.9.2 through 8.9.5 explain how each individual template file is used.

Each mail composition command has its own template file, as shown in Table 8-1.

Table 8-1. Draft Message Template Filenames

Program	Filename
comp	*components*
repl	*replcomps*
forw	*forwcomps*
dist	*distcomps*

For instance, the default template file for *comp*, named *components*, looks like this (unless someone on your system has changed it):

```
To:
cc:
Subject:
--------
```

When you start a mail-composition program like *comp*, the program reads its template file and builds a draft file. For *comp* and *dist*, this is easy—just copy the template file into the draft file. The *forw* command copies the template file and the forwarded message(s) into the draft file. The *repl* command has to read formatting rules (*mh-format* strings) from the template file. For instance, here's a line from the default *replcomps* file:

```
%<{subject}Subject: Re: %{subject}\n%>\
```

That line says "If the original message had a `Subject:` component, output `Subject: Re:` followed by the original subject text and a newline character." (See Section 8.9.3, "The replcomps File," and Section 10.2, "MH Format Strings.")

After the MH program has built a draft file, it starts *whatnow* (*xmh* doesn't do this). Then, *whatnow* starts your message editor—by default, it's *prompter* (it may be different at your site).

Let's look at what *prompter* does with the draft file. (If you'd like to see some sample draft files while you read this description, look back at Figures 6-1 and 6-2. For an overview of the whole process of sending messages, see Section 6.1.)

1. When it reads a draft header line which has an empty component—a line that ends with a colon (:)—*prompter* prints that and a space to the screen and leaves the cursor after the space. For example, when *prompter* reads the line:

   ```
   To:
   ```

   it prompts you with To : and leaves the cursor there. Then:

   - If you type something and press |RETURN|, *prompter* copies the line you typed into the draft message file.

   - If you type something and end the line with a backslash (\) just before you press |RETURN|, *prompter* keeps reading what you typed. This is how you can type components that are wider than the screen. *prompter* copies what you type until you end a line with something besides a backslash. Start each of the continuation lines with a space or tab.

   - If you don't type anything and just press |RETURN|, *prompter* doesn't copy any line to the draft message. For instance, if you're at the empty cc: component and you just press |RETURN|, there won't be a cc: component in the message you send.

2. Each time you press |RETURN|, *prompter* reads the next component from the draft file. If the component is empty, it works like step 1 above. If a line in the draft file already has something after the colon, like this:

   ```
   Reply-to: ehuser@bigmachine.xxx.yyy.zzz
   ```

   then *prompter* won't stop or prompt you. It'll just leave the component in the draft message.

3. When *prompter* sees a *separator line* (a blank line or a line with only dashes) as it's reading the header from the draft file, it assumes that the separator line is the start of the message body. From here, *prompter* changes its behavior—instead of looking for header components and prompting you, it starts processing the message body. One of three things will happen as *prompter* processes the body:

   - The simplest case is when the separator line is the last line in the draft file. (This happens, for instance, when you're using the *comp* command.) *prompter* just copies what you type into the draft message body until you type end-of-input (usually, |CTRL-D|) at the start of a line.

   - The next case is when there's more text after the separator line (for instance, text from *comp –use*, *forw*, or *repl –filter*) and if you have not used the *–noprepend* switch. In this case, *prompter* will print on the screen (but not in the draft message):

```
--------Enter initial text
```

You can type any message that you want *prompter* to add before the text from the draft file. As always, *prompter* will read your message until you press CTRL-D at the start of a line. Then, *prompter* copies in the rest of the draft file and exits. The *whatnow* program, which started *prompter*, prints What now?.

• Finally, if you use its *–noprepend* switch, *prompter* treats existing text in the draft body differently. First, it rolls the existing text by on your screen. Then, it prompts you on the screen (but not in the draft):

```
--------Enter additional text
```

You can type a message to go at the end of the existing text. As before, after you press CTRL-D at the start of a line, *prompter* exits. The *whatnow* program, which started *prompter*, prints What now?.

To add or change the components in a header, you can edit the header (by starting an editor from the What now? prompt) when you compose the message. Or you can make your own private template files, as the next four sections explain.

8.9.2 The components File ⊠

The *comp* command uses this file. It's a pretty basic file; Section 8.9.1 explains it.

My *components* file (in my MH directory) looks like this:

```
Reply-to: jerry@ora.com
X-Mailer: MH 6.7.2
To:
cc:
Bcc:
Fcc: outbox
Subject:
-------
```

Section 6.4.1 explains Fcc:, Bcc:, Reply-to:, and X-. The X-Mailer: helps me identify messages I've sent with MH and does a little bragging, too. :-)

8.9.3 The replcomps File

The *repl* command builds the header of your draft reply automatically. The default reply header looks like this* (the *italicized* text comes from those components of the message you're replying to):

```
To: Reply-To or From
cc: cc, To, and yourself
Fcc: from -fcc switch, if any
Subject: Re: Subject
In-reply-to: Your message of "Date."
        Message-Id
```

That's set up in the system *replcomps* file. You can customize the heading and the way that components are filled in by making your own *replcomps* file. To do this well, you'll need to study Chapter 10, *MH Formatting*. But you can do a lot by imitating the changes I show you here and by experimenting. Ready? Let's dig in. Example 8-3 is a copy of the default *replcomps* file in MH 6.7.2. Example 8-4, at the end of this section, shows a copy of the updated *replcomps* file.

Example 8-3. Default MH replcomps file

```
 1>  %(lit)%(formataddr
        %<{reply-to}%|%<{from}%|%<{sender}%|%<{return-path}%>%>%>%>)\
 2>  %<(nonnull)%(void(width))%(putaddr To: )\n%>\
 3>  %(lit)%(formataddr{to})%(formataddr{cc})%(formataddr(me)))\
 4>  %<(nonnull)%(void(width))%(putaddr cc: )\n%>\
 5>  %<{fcc}Fcc: %{fcc}\n%>\
 6>  %<{subject}Subject: Re: %{subject}\n%>\
 7>  %<{date}In-reply-to: Your message of "\
 8>  %<(nodate{date})%{date}%|%(pretty{date})%>."%<{message-id}
 9>              %{message-id}%>\n%>\
10>  --------
```

Okay. One step at a time. I'll show you the important part of each line and how you might change it.

1. **Lines 1-2** build a `To:` address component for the draft. Line 1 is broken onto two lines here:

```
%(lit)%(formataddr
    %<{reply-to}%|%<{from}%|%<{sender}%|%<{return-path}%>%>%>%>)\
%<(nonnull)%(void(width))%(putaddr To: )\n%>\
```

---

* Adapted from the *repl*(1) manual page.

Those lines look for the best address in the original message. The %(lit) erases a storage register that'll hold the address. The %(formataddr . . .) formats an address and stores it in the register. The rest of line 1, the argument to *formataddr*, chooses the address:

```
%<{reply-to}%|%<{from}%|%<{sender}%|%<{return-path}%>%>%>%>
```

It's several nested *if-else* tests. It means:

- If (%<) the original message has a Reply-to: component in the header ({reply-to}), take that address.

- Else (%|), start another test:

  - If (%<) the original message has a From: component ({from}), take that address.

  - If that's not true, start yet another nested test for a Sender: component and use it if it exists.

  - Finally, there's one last check for a Return-Path: component.

- A test always ends with %>. So, four nested tests will end with %>%>%>%>. (MH 6.7.2 introduced a new *else-if* operator that avoids all the nesting. Section 10.2.9 shows an example.)

If none of those tests found the address they needed, we don't have a To: address for the reply.

On **line 2**, the %(putaddr To:)\n uses a function named *putaddr*. It gets the address field that was saved by *formataddr* in line 1 and prints To: followed by the address and a newline character (\n). We've got the address (whew).

2. **Lines 3-4** build a cc: address component:

```
%(lit)%(formataddr{to})%(formataddr{cc})%(formataddr(me))\
%<(nonnull)%(void(width))%(putaddr cc: )\n%>\
```

It's something like the To: component, but it doesn't have the *if-else* tests. Instead, it grabs all the To: and cc: addresses from the original message. It also includes your address (with formataddr(me)).

Notice that the first line has three separate calls to *formataddr*—there are no %<if%|else%> tests. That's why it takes *all* of the addresses from the original message, not just the first one it finds.

I get mail from hosts that run other operating systems and other mailers. The messages can have headers, like the ones below, that list addresses where the message was delivered:

```
X-Vmsmail-Cc: lonie%ahost@englvax.xyz.edu
X-To: nelson@mvus.bitnet
```

Because those addresses aren't in the To: or cc: headers on the message I get, *repl* won't let me reply there. I usually want my reply to go to those addresses, too. To fix that, I changed **line 3** to include those headers and more. My fix made it pretty long, so I also split it onto three lines. In my edited *replcomps*, the lines are:

```
%(lit)%(formataddr{to})%(formataddr{cc})\
%(formataddr{x-vmsmail-to})%(formataddr{x-vmsmail-cc})\
%(formataddr{x-to})%(formataddr{x-cc})%(formataddr(me))\
```

The *repl –query* switch (Section 6.7.1) helps me wade through this bunch of addresses.

3. **Lines 5-6** work about the same way—they make the Fcc: and Subject: components:

```
%<{fcc}Fcc: %{fcc}\n%>\
%<{subject}Subject: Re: %{subject}\n%>\
```

Let's look at **line 5**. The %< tells *repl* to test for a *–fcc* switch ({fcc}) on the command line or in the MH profile—if there is one, it outputs Fcc: with the folder name (%{fcc}) and a newline (\n) after it.

I like to be able to add another Fcc: component to my draft because I usually don't remember to use *–fcc* on the command line; I want to be prompted. So I put another line in my *replcomps* file, right after **line 5**:

```
Fcc:
```

When I start *repl*, it fills in the To:, cc: and the first Fcc: component (if any) automatically, as explained above. Then *repl* copies the empty Fcc: component into the draft. As *prompter* reads the draft, it skips right past those complete components. But *prompter* stops at this second Fcc: component and prompts for a folder name. If I don't want to send any other Fcc:'s, I just press RETURN; *prompter* will delete the empty component.

4. These three lines of the *replcomps* file make the one In-reply-to: component of the reply header:

```
7>   %<{date}In-reply-to: Your message of "\
8>   %<(nodate{date})%{date}%|%(pretty{date})%>."%<{message-id}
9>             %{message-id}%>\n%>\
```

Because there's no newline (\n) until the end of this, *repl* will format it to fit the header neatly.

One thing I don't like about this format is that the component says: "In–reply–to: *Your* message of ... " Sometimes—like when I'm replying to a list of people—the word "your" is wrong. I've changed my *replcomps* so it uses the From: address of the original message, instead of the word "your." For example, when I'm replying to a message like this:

```
Date:    Mon, 07 Dec 92 09:47:42 -0500
From:    "Keith E Smith" <KES@MVUS.BITNET>
Sender:  Help Squad <HELPOUT@MVUS.BITNET>
To:      Jerry Peek <jdpeek@asun.acs.syr.edu>
Subject: HELP!
```

the heading of my reply message says:

```
   ...
Subject: Re: HELP!
In-reply-to: Message from  "Keith E Smith" <KES@MVUS.BITNET>
    of "Mon, 07 Dec 92 09:47:42 -0500."
```

Here's how I do that—replace **lines 7-9** of the default *replcomps* with the following:

```
In-reply-to: Message from %<{from}%{from}%|%{sender}%>\n\
    of "%<(nodate{date})%{date}%|%(pretty{date})%>."\
%<{message-id} %{message-id}%>\n\
```

That format string outputs In-reply-to: Message from, followed by the From: address if there is one—otherwise, the Sender:. Then it outputs a newline (\n). If it can't parse the date in the message, it prints the Date: component as is; but if it can, it prints a "user-friendly" version of the date. Finally, if there was a Message-Id:, that's printed, too. Notice that even though the second and third lines are separated, that doesn't mean that the draft header will always have two lines. That's because there's no embedded \n here. The leading space before the second line is printed, though. The third line isn't indented because I don't want any space printed before the Message-Id: number.

This isn't perfect, but it's usually just fine.

5. **Line 10** is a row of separator dashes. When *prompter* sees this, it knows that the rest of the file (if any) is the message body.

You can do a lot more customizing. See Chapter 10, *MH Formatting*, and read the *mh–format*(5) manual page in Appendix I.

Example 8-4 is a copy of the updated *replcomps* file.

Example 8-4. Updated MH replcomps file

```
%(lit)%(formataddr
%<{reply-to}%|%<{from}%|%<{sender}%|%<{return-path}%>%>%>%>)\
%<(nonnull)%(void(width))%(putaddr To: )\n%>\
%(lit)%(formataddr{to})%(formataddr{cc})\
%(formataddr{x-vmsmail-to})%(formataddr{x-vmsmail-cc})\
%(formataddr{x-to})%(formataddr{x-cc})%(formataddr(me))\
%<{fcc}Fcc: %{fcc}\n%>\
Fcc:
%<{subject}Subject: Re: %{subject}\n%>\
In-reply-to: Message from %<{from}%{from}%|%{sender}%>\n\
    of "%<(nodate{date})%{date}%|%(pretty{date})%>."\
%<{message-id} %{message-id}%>\n\
--------
```

8.9.4 The forwcomps File⊠

The *forwcomps* file for the *forw* command looks like the *components* file. I won't explain it here.

In fact, I don't even have a *forwcomps* file. I use my *components* file for *forw*, as well as for *comp*, by adding this line to my MH profile:

```
forw: -form components
```

I could have done the same thing by using the UNIX *ln* command to make a link called *forwcomps* to my *components* file. If you want a separate *forwcomps* file, though, be my guest. Just look at Section 8.9.2.

8.9.5 The distcomps File

Don't put anything in the *distcomps* file except the header components and a row of dashes. That's because *dist* distributes messages as is. If you want to add text along with the message body, use the *forw* command instead.

You can add extra components to the message header, though. For instance, your *distcomps* could be:

```
Resent-To:
Resent-cc:
Resent-Bcc:
Resent-Fcc:
```

```
Resent-Comments:
Resent-Comments:
-------
```

The header names that end in To:, cc:, Bcc:, and Fcc: work just like the corresponding components in, say, *components*. The Resent-Comments: components give you a place to type a one or two-line message.* I have two Resent-Comments headers in case I want to write more than one line of comments. Of course, you can leave any of these empty when you *dist* your message; *prompter* will delete the headers you leave empty.

8.9.6 Automatic Signature on End of Messages

Some users like to have a few lines added automatically at the bottom of each message they send.

This is easy to do with *comp*. Put the line(s) at the end of your *components* file, and they'll be copied into the draft automatically. Unless you use its *–noprepend* switch, *prompter* will prompt you with:

```
--------Enter initial text
```

and wait for you to type CTRL-D before it copies the rest of the *components* file into the draft. Here's a typical *components* file with a signature at the end:

```
To:
cc:
Fcc: outbox
Subject:
--------

-- Emma H. User, ehuser@bigcorp.xxx.yyy, phone +1 301 456-7890
```

You can't add a signature to the template files for the *forw* or *repl –filter* commands, though. That's because they add their text (the forwarded message or copy of the original message) *after* the contents of the *forwcomps* or *replcomps* file, respectively. So your signature would be at the *start* of the draft message.

---

*Resent-Comments: isn't mentioned explicitly in the RFC822 mail guidelines, though it's apparently not illegal. Some people say that it violates the idea of redistributing messages exactly as they were. I think it's really handy.

In *repl*, you can handle that by adding the signature to the end of your *–filter* file. (Section 6.7.5 explains filter files.) *mhl* reads the filter file, so use a colon (:) before each line of the signature, as shown in the following example:

```
: -- Emma H. User, ehuser@bigcorp.xxx.yyy, phone +1 301 456-7890
```

It's hard to use one of these methods on forwarded messages because the signature goes in the wrong place whether you *prepend* or *noprepend*. Some answers are:

- Add the signature manually.

- Write an *–editor* shell script that adds it automatically (see Section 12.17.8).

- Use the *append* shell script from Section 13.2.

- Use a *sendproc* program like *mysend* in Section 13.13.

9

New Versions of MH Commands

This chapter is about MH. But if you use *xmh*, you might want to read this chapter anyway because there are some useful programs here—you can always exit *xmh* for a while, open an *xterm* window, run these programs, and then restart *xmh*.

The chapter takes you through the process of making a new MH command version step by step. The initial setup and the first new command or two can be a little tough for someone who's not particularly familiar with UNIX. After that, though, you'll be thinking of and creating new command versions of your own.

For instance, if you want to let someone know that you got their message, here's a version of *repl* that automatically sends a "thank you." Receptionists can send telephone messages through e-mail with a version that prompts them for the parts of the message. There are versions of *scan* that give you extra information without lots of extra typing.

As much as anything, this chapter should give you ideas for changes that will make MH work your way.

9.1 What's a New Version of a Command?

In UNIX, you can give the same command more than one name. For instance, typing the command *view* will run the *vi* program—but the program will notice that you've run it with the name *view*, so it automatically sets its read-only mode. You can do the same thing with MH programs.* An MH command will run the same way, no matter what name you give it—but it will look for a component in your MH profile with the name you use to run it. For example, you can set a second name for the *repl* command called *replx* (see the directions below). Then, add a component with the new name to your MH profile.

```
repl: -query
replx: -query -filter filter_file
```

Then, if you type:

```
% replx 23
```

the program will actually run as `repl -query -filter filter_file 23` and read a copy of your original message into your draft reply.

New versions are easy to make—almost as easy as shell aliases. Usually, you don't even have to be a programmer. (It might help to have a guru "on call" when you do the first setup.) Section 9.2 explains how to make them.

Unlike shell aliases or functions (Section 8.2.1), MH command versions can be run by any other MH or UNIX command. You can use MH command versions in *at* or *cron* jobs, from inside a shell script, from another MH command, from a C or *perl* program, and so on. Sometimes, though, an alias or function is all you need. Section 9.3 tells how to write these versions as an alias or function.

9.2 Making a New Command Version

This section explains the steps you'll use to make a new MH command version. Some of the steps need to be done only once before making the first new command version.

---

*There are some good examples in the *miscellany/mtrenv* directory of the MH distribution.

For example, you can make a new version of the *scan* command called *tscan*. After this, if you type the command *scan*, it will work the way it always has. But if you use *tscan*, it will automatically use the *–form scan.timely* switch to show the date in a different style, as shown in the following example:

```
% scan 3-5
   3  02/04*To:vicki@maxa.nap  Problems with maxa<<Vicki, I thi
   4  12/14 To:uunet!xyz!pamb  Holiday Greetings<<Pam, I just w
   5  04/06 mary@hahvahd.edu   rcvtty -- how do I use it?<<I've
% tscan 3-5
   3  Sun  *To:vicki@maxa.nap  Problems with maxa<<Vicki, I thi
   4  14Dec To:uunet!xyz!pamb  Holiday Greetings<<Pam, I just w
   5  Apr86 mary@hahvahd.edu   rcvtty -- how do I use it?<<I've
```

Let's start with a summary of the steps. Do these steps only once before making the first version (Section 9.2.1 explains how to do that):

1. Make a *bin* directory if you need one.

2. Choose the best way to make new versions on your host.

Do these steps for making each new version (see Section 9.2.2):

1. Pick a new name for the version. Be sure it's not already in use.

2. Add a component for the version to your MH profile.

3. Find the pathname of the MH command you're making a version of.

4. Make the version, the way it was chosen in Section 9.2.1.

5. If you use the C shell, run its *rehash* command.

Chapter 2, *MH and the UNIX Filesystem*, will help, too.

9.2.1 Setup Before You Make First New Version

This section has overall setup that you'll only need to do once.

Making a bin Directory

You need a place to put your new MH programs. This can be a directory on your account. Or, if several people want to use these programs, you could pick any other directory—as long as you have write access to it. Usually, the directory's name is something like *bin*. Here are the steps:

1. If you haven't set up a directory for programs, make one. For instance, to make a *bin* under your home directory, type:

   ```
   % cd
   % mkdir bin
   ```

2. If you have the directory for storing programs, be sure that the programs in it are accessible. Type the command `echo $PATH` and look for the directory's pathname. For instance, if your directory is called */u/walt/bin*, you should see:

   ```
   % echo $PATH
   ...:/u/walt/bin:...
   ```

   If the directory isn't in your *PATH*, add it. Do that by editing the `PATH= . . .` line in your *.profile* file or the `set path=( . . . )` line in your *.cshrc* or *.login* file.* Add the full pathname of the directory to the end of the *PATH*. Then, for the Bourne and Korn shells, type the command:

   ```
   $ . .profile
   ```

   For the C shell, type one of these commands, depending on which file you changed:

   ```
   % source .cshrc
   % source .login
   ```

   Finally, if other people are sharing the directory, use a command like *chmod go+rx bin* to give them access.

Finding the Best Way to Make New Versions

The first time you make a new command version, you'll need to figure out how to do it on your particular account and computer. There are a few different ways. Here's how to decide which one is best for you:

1. If your version of UNIX has *symbolic links*, this is usually the easiest way. (If you aren't sure, type `man ln` and look for the *–s* option.) Some people call these *soft links*.

---

*For help with this, see the Nutshell Handbook *Learning the UNIX Operating System*, by Grace Todino and John Strang, or just ask around your office.

For example, to make the version of *scan* called *tscan*, you first find where the *scan* program is stored. (There are instructions for doing that below.) Then, you *cd* to your *bin* directory and type commands like:

```
% ln -s /usr/local/mh/scan tscan
% ls -l tscan
lrwxrwxrwx  1 eds          16 Jul  1 14:32 tscan -> /usr/local/mh/scan
% ls -L tscan
-rwxr-xr-x  1 root      81920 May 26 19:04 tscan
```

The `ls -l` command shows the link itself and the `ls -L` command shows the file that the link "points to."

There's one thing to watch out for: each symbolic link takes a block of disk space. If you're short on disk space and you plan to make a lot of symbolic links, you may want to use one of the three other methods below.

2. If you won't be using symbolic links, you may be able to use standard links (I'll call them *hard links*). These are the same kind of links that MH makes between linked messages.

Hard links are good because they take virtually no filesystem space. But they won't work if the programs you want to link to are on a different filesystem.*

Another problem with hard links can happen when the system administrator installs a new version of the program you're linked to. Unless the administrator is careful, you could end up with a link to the *old* version of the program, instead of the new one! (There's one workaround here: the system administrator could make a system directory and put the hard links there for everyone on the system to use.) The bottom line: if you want to make hard links, talk to your system administrator.

Here's how to make a hard link. For example, to make the version of *scan* called *tscan*, you'd first find where the *scan* program is stored. Then, you'd *cd* to your *bin* directory and type commands like:

```
% ln /usr/local/mh/scan tscan
% ls -li /usr/local/mh/scan tscan
13256 -rwxr-xr-x  2 root  81920  May 26 19:04 /usr/local/mh/scan
13256 -rwxr-xr-x  2 root  81920  May 26 19:04 tscan
```

If you make hard links, it's a good idea to use *ls -li* every so often, to compare the original program with your link. If the two listings are different (except for the names), your link to the system version was broken.

---

*If you're not sure whether the program is on a different filesystem, try to make the link and see if it works, or ask a local expert.

3. If symbolic links and hard links don't appeal to you, a small program called *execit*, written in the C language, might be what you want. *execit* will run an MH command under any name you choose. If your UNIX system has a C compiler (usually named *cc* or *gcc*), that and the *ln* command are all you need to use *execit*. See Appendix F, *The execit Programs*.

To set up *execit*, edit a simple table of renamed commands in a file called *execit.include*. Then compile the *execit.c* file with one command. Finally, run a shell script named *execit.link* to make the links for you:

```
% vi execit.include
    ...Add a line for tscan to the table...
% cc -o execit execit.c
% execit.link
```

The *execit.link* script makes as many hard links to the *execit* program as you need, one link per version. If you're making many command versions, this can save disk space as compared to symbolic links.

4. Finally, you can write a shell script. It overcomes most of the disadvantages of a shell alias or function. But starting a shell to run just one MH command line in a script file is inefficient. Also, the switches are hard-coded into your script file; users who share your script can't customize it through entries in their MH profile files. To find out more about shell scripts, see Chapter 12, *Introduction to Shell Programming for MH*.

9.2.2 What to Do for Each New Version

After you've done the first-time setup in Section 9.2.1 (which you only need to do once), you're ready for this section. Here are the overall steps to do each time you make a new version of an MH command:

1. Pick a new name for your MH version. For instance, you might call it *tscan*. Make sure that it doesn't conflict with any other commands on the system by typing one of the commands in the following example. If you get output (besides an error) from one of them, there's probably already a command with the same name. (The *whence* command works on the Korn shell; I've shown it with the *ksh* dollar sign ($) prompt.)

```
% man 1 tscan
No manual entry for tscan in section 1.
% which tscan
no tscan in . /xxx/ehuser/bin /usr/bin/X11 /usr/local/bin ...
% whereis tscan
tscan:

$ whence tscan
```

2. Once you find an unused name, add a component for the command to your MH profile. The component line starts with the name of your command, then has a colon, and finally shows the command-line switches you want to use with the program. For instance, the line for *tscan* could be:

```
tscan: -form scan.timely
```

Be sure not to leave any blank lines in the file.

3. Find out where the actual MH command is located by typing each of the following commands until you get an answer:

```
% which scan
% whereis scan
$ whence scan
```

The answer should be a pathname, something like */usr/local/mh/scan*.

If you still can't find it, type `ls` in the MH binary directory or ask an expert for help.

4. Make the symbolic link or hard link or use *execit* as explained in Section 9.2.1.

5. If you're using the C shell, type the following command to reset the shell's command search table:

```
% rehash
```

That's it. Try your new version. If you want to change the switches you chose, you just need to edit your MH profile. If you get an error such as the following:

```
tscan: command not found
```

there's a problem with your shell's search path, your link, or your *execit.include* file. Reread these instructions carefully—if that doesn't help, it's time to get your guru. Once you get the hang of these steps, it only takes a minute to add a new command version.

9.3 Writing Command Versions as Aliases or Functions

As you saw in the part of Section 8.2.1 called "They Won't Always Work," aliases and shell functions can't be used everywhere that command versions can. Sometimes, though—especially for commands that you'll never use from anywhere except a shell prompt—an alias or function is all you really need.

Part III
Customizing MH

To write a command version from this chapter as an alias or function:

1. Use the version name (like *tscan*) as the name of the alias.

2. Use the MH command name (like *scan*) as the command run by the alias.

3. Put the MH profile arguments after the MH command.

As an example, the *tscan* command version from Section 9.2 would become this C shell alias:

```
alias tscan 'scan -form scan.timely'
```

When you run a C shell alias, the shell will use any arguments you type after the alias name as arguments to the command in the alias. What I mean is, if you use the *tscan* alias above and type:

```
% tscan +reports last:20
```

the shell will run:

```
scan -form scan.timely +reports last:20
```

That alias trick will work with all the command versions in this chapter that can be done as an alias. When you write a shell function, though, you need to include the arguments with $ *. Here's *tscan* as a Bourne shell function:

```
tscan()
{
scan -form scan.timely $*
}
```

Most command versions in this chapter can be written as an alias or function. The *prompter* version in Section 9.7 and the *send* version in Section 9.8 can't because they're run directly by other MH commands.

9.4 Versions of repl

Here are some new versions of the *repl* command. One lets you include the original message in your reply. Another shows how to send a standard answer without typing any text. A third lets you follow up to a message you've already sent. The fourth is for replies to messages that were sent to me at another address.

9.4.1   Including Original Message in Your Reply: replx

You may want to include the text from the original message in your reply. I have a version of *repl* called *replx*. It acts like *repl*, but extracts the original text and puts a right angle bracket (>) and space before every line, like this:

```
% replx
To: joeb@xyz.edu (Joe Blom)
Cc: mh-users@ics.uci.edu
Subject: Re: whatever
In-reply-to: <9003140757.AA02588@xyz.edu>
-------
On Tue, 08 Dec 92 09:51:06 EST  Joe Blom wrote:
> Blah blah blah
> Blah blah blah

Joe, I think that's right.  But...
```

NOTE

replx may not work on early versions of MH.

To install *replx*, use these steps:

1. To make *replx* as a version of *repl*, see Section 9.2. To make a *repl* alias or function named *replx*, see Section 9.3.

   Add the following component to your MH profile, or add the arguments to your alias or function. The –editor vi and –query are optional:

   ```
   replx: -filter replxfilt -form replxcomps -editor vi -query
   ```

2. Put a *repl* filter file named *replxfilt* in your MH directory. The first line, a comment, starts with a semicolon:

   ```
   ; filter file for replx command
   body:component="> "
   ```

3. This step simplifies the In-reply-to: component and adds the message date and originator, as shown at the start of this section. If you don't want this change, skip this step and leave the –form replxcomps out of your MH profile entry.

Put a draft template file named *replxcomps* in the MH directory. To make it, copy the default system *replcomps* file. Then delete the the last four lines, shown below (which may be a little different on your version):

```
%<{date}In-reply-to: Your message of "\
%<(nodate{date})%{date}%|%(pretty{date})%>."%<{message-id}\
         %{message-id}%>\n%>\
--------
```

and replace them by these three lines:

```
%<{message-id}In-reply-to: %{message-id}\n%>\
--------\n\
On %{date} %(friendly{from}) wrote:
```

Chapter 10, *MH Formatting*, explains how to modify this.

When you want to include the original message, use *replx*; for a standard reply, use *repl* instead. If you don't want to include all of the original message, just fix the reply body with an editor like *vi*.

9.4.2 Standard Replies: thanks

Sometimes, instead of typing a full reply, you just want to thank a person for something. Or you'd like to send some quick messages that say "OK," or "Request Approved," and so on. You can make versions of *repl* that send standard replies. For example, one called *thanks* looks like this. It fills in everything—you just answer y or n and type s at the What now? prompt:

```
% show
      ...Message appears...
% thanks
Reply to cathyw? y
Reply to bigboss? n
To: cathyw
Subject: Re: Your report is ready at the copy center
In-reply-to: ...
--------
Thanks!

--Jerry

What now? s
%
```

The following steps explain how to set up *repl* versions to send standard replies:

1. Make a file in your MH directory named *thankscomps* (the name is your choice, but this is a typical MH name). To make it, start with a copy of the usual *replcomps* file. Make the end of the file look like this (you can use any text, of course):

   > ...*These lines omitted*...
   >
   > _____
   >
   > Thanks!
   >
   > --Jerry

2. To make *thanks* (or *okay* or *approved* ...) as a version of *repl*, see Section 9.2. To make an alias or function, see Section 9.3.

   Add this component to your MH profile, or add the arguments to your alias or function:*

   > thanks: -form thankscomps -editor cat -query

The -editor cat shows you the draft, but doesn't prompt you to enter any text (if you want to, you can start an editor from the What now? prompt). The -query may be a good idea because you generally won't want to send a copy of your thank you to everyone who got the original message—or, if you *never* want other people to get copies, you might want to use -nocc all instead of -query.

9.4.3 Followup Mail Messages: foll, follx

After you send a mail message do you ever wish that you'd said one more thing? Here are two versions of *repl* to make that easier. The *foll* command sends a followup mail message with the same message header in your followup as in the original message—plus an X-followup-to: component that references the original. *follx* works like *foll*, but it also uses a filter file that extracts (reads in) a copy of your original message and starts a text editor for you. (Of course, you must have a copy of your original message—for instance, if your original had an Fcc: component in it, or if you cc: 'ed yourself.)

*If you write the *push* version which is explained in Section 9.8, you can add -whatnowproc push to that component, too. Then, you won't need to wait for the What now? prompt either. Wow, is that fast!

For example:

```
% comp
To: belle@vogue.com
cc: charles@ritz.fr
Fcc: outbox
Subject: I loved that show!
------
It was simply maaaahvelous.
You MUST invite me again.
CTRL-D

What now? send
% follx last +outbox
To: belle@vogue.com
cc: charles@ritz.fr
Subject: Re: I loved that show!
X-followup-to: My message of "Tue, 08 Dec 92 02:07:09 -0500."
          <9002110707.AA28207@mysun.xxx.yyy.zzz>
------
In my message, I wrote:
    It was simply maaaahvelous.
    You MUST invite me again.

I forgot to mention the lovely caviar!
Blah, blah, blah...
CTRL-D

What now? send
%
```

If you don't want to include all of the original text, just edit the followup at the What now? prompt (with *vi*, etc.) before you send it.

Here's how to add *foll* and *follx*:

1. Make a file named *follcomps* in your MH directory:

```
%(lit)%(formataddr{to})%<(nonnull)%(void(width))%(putaddr To: )\n%>\
%(lit)%(formataddr{cc})%<(nonnull)%(void(width))%(putaddr cc: )\n%>\
%<{fcc}Fcc: %{fcc}\n%>\
Fcc:
%<{subject}Subject: Re: %{subject}\n%>\
%<{date}X-followup-to: My message of "\
%<(nodate{date})%{date}%|%(tws{date})%>."%<{message-id}
          %{message-id}%>\n%>\
--------
```

If you never use folder copies, get rid of the Fcc: component. If you'd rather, you can send a cc: to yourself automatically by adding %(formataddr(me)) next to the %(formataddr{cc}).

2. Put a file named *follxfilt* in your MH directory. Here are two choices. This first one is basic; it's what you see in the previous example:

```
; filter file for follx
:In my message, I wrote:
body:nocomponent,offset=3
```

This second one puts the date of the original message in the heading (for help with it, see Chapter 10, *MH Formatting*):

```
; filter file for follx
date:nocomponent,formatfield="On %{text} I wrote:"
body:component="< ",overflowtext="< "
```

3. To make *foll* and *follx* as versions of *repl*, see Section 9.2. Or, to make an alias or function, see Section 9.3.

Add these components to your MH profile, or add the arguments to your alias or function:

```
foll: -form follcomps
follx: -form follcomps -filter follxfilt -editor vi
```

By the way, you can do the same thing in a simpler way with a command like:

```
% comp +inbox 12
```

where +inbox 12 is the message you want to follow up on. The *comp* command will make a new draft with a copy of that message. Then you can edit the draft copy and send it.

That's not as handy as the *foll* command version, though, because the draft header will have components (like Date:, Received:, Message-Id:, and so on) that you'll have to delete before you send the draft.

9.4.4 Reply from Another Address: replb

As Section 6.4.2 explains, I get mail from a few system aliases. When I do, and I want to reply, I'd like to use the alias address as the From: header of my reply. I usually also include some of the text from the original message in my reply. I have a version of *repl* called *replb*. Like *replx* (Section 9.4.1), *replb* includes text from the original message. It also changes the address in the header to match the alias. After I finish answering *repl* −*query* about the header, it puts me into the *vidraft* script to edit the message. *vidraft*, shown in Section 12.6, starts *vi* with the cursor at the first line of the message body. Of course, you can use any editor you want with *replb*.

NOTE

replb may not work on early versions of MH.

Here are the steps for installing *replb*:

1. To make *replb* as a version of *repl*, see Section 9.2. To make it as an alias or function, see Section 9.3.

   Add the following component to your MH profile, or add the arguments to your alias or function. The -ed vidraft and -query are optional:

   ```
   replb: -filter replbfilt -query -nocc me -ed vidraft -form replbcomps
   ```

2. If you want to use the *vidraft* editor from Section 12.6, put it in your *bin* directory. There are directions in Section 12.2, "Writing a Simple Shell Program."

3. Put a *repl* filter file named *replbfilt* in your MH directory. The body: line includes the body of the message you're replying to. You'll want to change my signature; it's made by the lines that start with colons (:):

   ```
   ; filter file for replb command
   body:component="> "
   :
   :--Jerry Peek, technical questions: bookquestions@ora.com
   :Orders FAX: +1 707 829-0104, technical questions FAX: +1 617 661-1116
   :Information or questions about orders: nuts@ora.com
   :phone US/Canada toll-free, (800)998-9938; international: +1 707 829-0515
   ```

4. This step adds the From: component and a cc: bookquestions, too, as shown at the start of this section. Of course, you'll want to change this in your version. The From: address might have a different syntax. You might use an Fcc: instead of a cc:.

   Put a draft template file named *replbcomps* in the MH directory. To make it, copy the default system *replcomps* file. Add the following two lines to the top of the file:

   ```
   From: "Your Name" <aliasname@host.xxx.yyy>
   cc: aliasname
   ```

When you want to reply to a message from the alias, use *replb*; for a standard reply, use *repl* instead.

9.5 msg: 'While You Were Out' Messages with comp

The messages you send with *comp* don't need to have components like cc: and
Subject: in the headers. As long as you have To:, your message should get
there.* For instance, here's a program that receptionists might want. It uses
prompter to take phone and other messages, then sends them via e-mail. This
version of *comp* is called *msg*.

The date, time, and person who took the message are added automatically by MH.
The draft template file uses Fcc: to automatically keep a copy of all messages
sent. *msg* is nice for messages to busy people who aren't at their desks but are
close to terminals—or who can't check their mailboxes for slips of paper—or
who want to track their messages electronically.

The messages look something like this:

```
% show
    ...
Date: Mon, 07 Dec 92 12:34:56 PST
From: receptionist's username
To: loisl
Subject: While You Were Out...
X-Person: Betty Smith
X-Of: Kumquat Associates
X-Phone: (619)234-5678
X-Called: x
X-Please_call: x
---------
About your new cheese straightener.
```

To make *msg*, follow these steps:

1. Make a file named *msgcomps* in your MH directory, like this:

```
To:
Fcc: msgs
Subject: While You Were Out...
X-URGENT:
X-Person:
X-Of:
X-Phone:
X-Called:
X-Came_to_see_you:
X-Wants_to_see_you:
X-Please_call:
```

---

*The other header components should follow rules in RFC822.

```
X-Will_call:
X-Returned_your_call:
---------
```

As *prompter* shows each empty component from that file, the receptionist either fill it in with a name or number, type x after it (to just include the component in the message), or leave it blank (and *prompter* will delete the component). This is a handy way to use *prompter*.

2. To make *msg* as a version of *comp*, see Section 9.2. Or, to make an alias or function, see Section 9.3.

   Add this component to your MH profile, or add the arguments to your alias or function:

   ```
   msg: -form msgcomps -editor prompter
   ```

3. If you want to use the Fcc: msgs component to keep copies of messages, as shown above, you might also want to add an *at*(1) job to clean up old messages.

It could remove copies from the receptionist's *msgs* folder which are more than, say, one week old. To do that:

1. Create a file named *msgs_clean.at*. Put the following lines in it, making sure to use backquotes (`), not single quotes ('):

   ```
   rmm `pick -before -7 -list +msgs`
   sleep 60
   at 0300 msgs_clean.at
   ```

2. Start it running tonight at 3 a.m. by typing:

   ```
   % at 0300 msgs_clean.at
   ```

   If your system has personal *crontab* files, they'll be better for this than *at*(1). For help, ask a local expert.

Some users don't want their phone messages mixed in with their other e-mail. If that's true, try one of these ideas:

1. Write a short shell script called *getmsgs* that uses *pick* to find messages with the subject "While You Were Out ...", puts them in a sequence, shows them, and then either refiles or removes them. (See Chapter 12, *Introduction to Shell Programming for MH*, and Chapter 13, *MH Shell Programs*, for help with shell programming. Section 12.9.2 has a small script that might give you a start on *getmsgs*.)

2. Ask the system administrator to add the user to the system transport agent's alias file with a different address. For instance, make an alias named *joeb_msgs* for the user *joeb*. When people send him messages to *joeb_msgs*, they'll be delivered to his usual address (*joeb*), but the message header will say:

```
To: joeb_msgs
```

Other users can send Joe's phone messages to his special address, even if they don't use the *msg* program. Then it will be easy for Joe to find his messages with MH tools like *pick*:*

```
% pick -to joeb_msgs ...
```

3. Your system administrator might make separate small accounts for users who get messages this way. Use a simple *.login* or *.profile* file that automatically shows the messages, if any, then asks the user what to do with each message. (A shell script with a loop would do it; see Chapter 12 and Chapter 13 for ideas.)

9.6 Edit Messages with show: mhedit

Edit messages with the *show* command? It sounds strange, but it works just fine. When you run *show* or a version of it, it first changes its current directory to your MH directory. Then *show* gets relative pathnames to the messages in the folders. Finally, it gives the pathnames to its *showproc* command. You can use any *showproc* command—including a text editor, as long as the editor can handle more than one filename on its command line. In this example, I'll use *vi*.

The time I usually edit messages is before I archive them in a folder: a message might include a long chunk of another message that I want to delete. When I get programs in the mail, in *shar* files, I start an editor on the message, write the program to a separate file, and save the rest in the message.

To make *mhedit* as a version of *show*, see Section 9.2. To make an alias or function, see Section 9.3.

---

* You could make a little shell alias or shell program named something like *showmsgs* that does this:
```
show `pick -to ${USER}_msgs -list`
```
See Section 7.2.2 and Chapter 12 for hints.

Add the following component to your MH profile, or add the arguments to your alias or function. Replace vi with another editor if you want to:

```
mhedit: -noheader -showproc vi
```

9.7 Version of prompter: prompter.nopre

MH message sending programs use *prompter* for filling in the header and collecting text for the body of the draft (unless you specify another editor). It's hard to change the way that *prompter* works, though, unless you make versions of it.

For example, there's no way to tell a command like *forw* which *prompter* switches you want to use. If you want *forw* to edit your draft with *prompter* *–noprepend*, commands like this do not work:

```
% forw -noprepend
forw: -noprepend unknown
% forw -editor "prompter -noprepend"
unable to exec prompter -noprepend: Permission denied
```

Just as bad, if you put the following component in your MH profile, it will *always* be used for *comp*, *repl*, and *dist*, as well as *forw*:

```
prompter: -noprepend
```

Here's a version of *prompter* named *prompter.nopre*. It's nothing more than *prompter* *–noprepend*. But you can use this as an editor for some MH commands without affecting others. For example, after you set up *prompter.nopre*, the following component in your MH profile will let you type a note *after* the message you're forwarding (instead of the default, *before*):

```
forw: -editor prompter.nopre
```

To set it up:

1. Make a new version of *prompter* named *prompter.nopre* (see Section 9.2).

2. Put the following component in your MH profile. (I also add *–rapid* to the end of this component. That tells *prompter* to let you add text immediately, without showing the rest of the draft. It saves time, especially on slow dialup lines, but it may confuse people who are used to seeing the whole draft shown

before the What now? prompt. The *–rapid* switch is documented in your online *prompter*(1) manual page.)

```
prompter.nopre: -noprepend
```

3. Decide which MH mail-sending commands should use *prompter.nopre* as an editor. (For instance, you probably want *replx* and *follx* to use it; you may not want *forw* to use it.) Fix the MH profile entries for those commands to include *–editor prompter.pre*.

9.8 Version of send: push

The command that sends your messages is called *send*. When you type s or send at a What now? prompt, the *send* program is executed. If you type p or push at the What now? prompt, *send –push* is run instead.

Here's a version of *send* called *push*.* If you replace the *whatnow* program with *push*, it will send your draft message as soon as the interface you're using (like *repl*) starts the *whatnowproc*. This means that *prompter*, or any other editor, won't run at all. So you can't use *push* with commands like *comp* which need an editor to fill in the draft. It's useful, however, for programs like *thanks* (see Section 9.4.2) that send "canned" messages, because you won't have to wait for a What now? prompt: your message is sent right away.

By the way, if you don't have a draft folder set up, you might do that before you use *push*. For more information, see Section 6.5.2.

*   Make a version of *send* called *push* (for help, see Section 9.2).

*   Add a component like the following to your MH profile (on MH 6.7 or after, if you use an Aliasfile: profile entry, you may not want the –alias *aliasfile*):

    ```
    push: -push -alias aliasfile draft_option_here
    ```

    The *send* command will ask you questions like this:

    ```
    Use "/yourMHdir/draft"?
    ```

    unless you add a *–draft* switch ahead of time, which will keep it quiet. If you are using a draft folder, replace *draft_option_here* with

---

*This idea came from the Marshall Rose examples in the MH distribution, the *miscellany/mtrenv* directory.

-draftfolder +*drafts* (where *drafts* is the name of your draft folder). Otherwise, replace it with -draft.

- Add -whatnowproc push to the MH profile component for those nonin- teractive commands (like *thanks*), which should bypass the What now? prompt.

```
thanks: -form thankscomps -editor cat -query -whatnowproc push
```

Using a different *–whatnowproc* than the default *whatnow* does more than just skip the What now? prompt. The *thanks* command (which, remember, is really a version of *repl*) first builds the draft message. Then, instead of pass- ing the draft to *whatnow*, the *thanks* program passes the draft to *push*.

Finally, try it and be sure that your messages are really sent. (Somehow, this *push* command made me uneasy for a while because I was so accustomed to seeing the What now? prompt ...)

9.9 Versions of scan

Format files and message ranges make the *scan* command really flexible, and the next two examples should get you started on custom versions that do just what you want. Beginning with MH 6.7, *scan* lets you scan files such as your system mailbox. This section shows you how to scan your new (unincorporated) mail.

9.9.1 Scanning a Range of Messages: cur, c10, l5, etc.

I have some folders with a lot of mail in them. Two of the commands I use the most are *scan cur:–10 cur:10* (scan the current message, the previous nine and the next nine—handy when I'm looking through new mail) and *scan –reverse last:5* (scan the last five messages in reverse order—great for finding my newest mail and Fcc:'s of messages I just sent). These are perfect for versions of *scan*—they have short names because I use them so much.

For example, to scan the current message (and change folder to *project*):

```
% cur +project
   24+ SENT: 19Jan  CHARS: 1068
     FROM: Raymond LaPlante <ray@phobos.spacey.com>
       TO: Al Bok <al@phl.ph.com>, zot!ant@uunet.uu.net
     SUBJ: Update on my research
```

To make *c10*, *cur*, *l5*, or whatever you choose as versions of *cur*, see Section 9.2. To make aliases or functions, see Section 9.3.

Then, add components like the following to your MH profile—or add the arguments to your alias or function. Of course, you don't have to use the same names or switches shown here:

```
c10: cur:+10
cur: cur -form scan.more -width 235
15: -reverse last:5
n20: cur:-10 cur:10
```

For cur:, I used the *scan.more* file shown in Section 10.2.8.

9.9.2   Scan and Show Size of Message

One of the standard *scan* format files is *scan.size*. Here's a version of *scan* called *sscan* that uses the format file every time. (You can do the same kind of thing with other format files.) For example:

```
% sscan 2 3
   2  11/23 15326 Al Bok              Query about "repl -query"<<I ha
   3 -02/09   739 "Wilbur, Orville"   X Terminal Presentation/Demonst
```

To make *sscan* as a version of *scan*, see Section 9.2. To make an alias or function, see Section 9.3.

Add the following component to your MH profile, or add the arguments to your alias or function:

```
sscan: -form scan.size
```

Section 10.2 shows how to make custom *scan* formats. These format files are perfect to use in a new *scan* version.

9.9.3   Scan Messages Waiting: msgscan

msgscan is like *msgchk* (see Section 5.3), but it does more than tell you that you have mail waiting. It *scan*s the new mail so you can decide whether to run *inc* now or wait. *msgscan* can use the *scan.time* format file (explained in Section 5.2.1) to show you what time of day each message was sent. Or, you can use a *scan.msgscan* file, shown below, to get more of the From: (or Sender: or Apparently-From:) header, as well as the Subject:.

*Part III
Customizing MH*

NOTE

msgscan only works with the new *scan –file* switch in MH 6.7—earlier versions of *scan* don't have it.

Here's an example—with a couple of *msgchk* commands:

```
% msgchk
You have new mail waiting; last read on Mon, 07 Dec 92 20:49:54 EST
% msgscan
   1  12/08 21:54EST To:al@phlabs.ph.co New MH feature<<Al, scan is
   2  12/08 21:13CST Al Bok            Re: New MH feature<<I scann
% msgchk
You have old mail waiting; last read on Tue, 08 Dec 92 09:00:05 EST
```

The first *msgchk* shows that there's mail to read. Running *msgscan* tells that there are two messages waiting; one is a message you sent last night, the other is a reply. Another *msgchk* calls your mail "old" and says that you've "read" the mail. That's because *msgscan* reads your system mailbox directly. But the mail is still there, like before; *msgscan* just changes the mailbox file's last-access time when it reads for new mail.

With the *scan.msgscan* file, the output looks like this:

```
% msgscan
From: "Emma H. User" <ehuser@phlabs
Subject: New MH feature
-------------------
From: Al Bok <al@phlabs.ph.com>
Subject: Re: New MH feature
-------------------
```

My *scan.msgscan* file cuts off the first line at 35 characters. Your version doesn't have to.

The steps to make your own *msgscan* are:

1. Make *msgscan* as a version of *scan* (see Section 9.2) or as an alias or function (see Section 9.3).

   Add a component like one of the two below to your MH profile—or add the arguments to your alias or function. Be sure to replace *username* with your own username and fix the pathname for your system mailbox:

   ```
   msgscan: -file /usr/spool/mail/username -form scan.time
   msgscan: -file /usr/spool/username -form scan.msgscan -width 120
   ```

2. If you're using the *msgscan* that uses the *scan.msgscan* format file, put this file in your MH directory:

```
%<{from}From: %35{from}%|%<{sender}Sender: %35{sender}%|\
Apparently-From: %35{apparently-from}%>%>\n\
%<{subject}Subject: %{subject}\n%>\
-------------------
```

9.10 Version of folder: Fast Folder Change

This version of *folder* called *fo* just does *folder –fast*. You can also add parameters on the *fo* command line to:

- Check the name of your current folder.

- Change the current message number.

- Change to a new folder.

- A combination of the above.

Here's how to make the last message current and see the folder name:

```
% fo last
inbox
```

To make *fo* as a version of *folder*, see Section 9.2. To make an alias or function, see Section 9.3.

Add this component to your MH profile, or add the arguments to your alias or function:

```
fo: –fast
```

NOTE

This won't work on early versions of MH. See the CAUTION in Section 7.1.7.

10

MH Formatting

mhl
MH Format Strings

MH commands like *mhl* (which *show* can use to format messages), *repl –filter*, *forw –filter*, and *scan* read special MH formatting instructions. These let you change the appearance of messages—including which components from the header you see and in what order, how long the lines will be, and more. If you're customizing MH, you'll want to understand MH formatting.

This chapter won't tell you everything about MH formatting. The *mhl*(1) and *mh–format*(5) pages in Appendix I have all the details and a complete list of MH formatting instructions. But, except for the examples in the back, those manual pages are so detailed that they're not an easy way to get started with MH formatting.

This chapter takes you through many ways that you can use MH formatting. It will help you learn the principles with lots of examples. The later examples go into depth. Many of the examples show practical formatting that you might want to use every day.

10.1 mhl

Let's start with the *mhl* message-formatting command. Section 5.1.6 explains
how to use it when you read messages. (Later in this chapter, you'll see how to
use it with *repl* and *forw*.) If you're not already using *mhl* when you read your
messages, add a component to your MH profile that sets *mhl* as the default:

```
showproc: mhl
```

(If you want to, you can delete that line after you're done with this section.)
Now, when you use *show*, *next*, and *prev*, they will format messages with *mhl*.

Before you go on, get familiar with the *mhl*(1) manual page, especially the table
of *mhl* variables and the sections that explain the format file lines.

In the following examples, I'll show how to format a test message that has lots of
components in the header and some long, messy lines in the body.* The test message is shown in Example 10-1. (I've used the *–noshowproc* switch, which tells
show to display the message as is, without *mhl*—so that you can see it exactly.)
The head −23 shows the first 23 lines (if your UNIX doesn't have *head*, you
can use the command sed 23q instead).

Example 10-1. Unformatted message with long lines in its body

```
% show -noshowproc | head -23
(Message test:21)
Forwarded: Sun, 04 Feb 90 03:41:35 -0500
Replied: Sat, 16 Dec 89 10:25:45 -0500
Return-Path: <al@phl.ph.com>
Date: Mon, 31 Jul 89 09:49:08 -0400
Received: by asun.phl.ph.com (5.54/PHL)
        id AA27070; Mon, 31 Jul 89 10:10:27 EDT
Received: by quack.phl.ph.com id AA26696
        Mon, 31 Jul 89 09:49:08 EDT
Message-Id: <8907311349.AA26696@quack.phl.ph.com>
From:  Al Bok <al@phl.ph.com>
Reply-to: Joe Doe <joe@foobar.ph.com>
```

---

*The text comes from the file */usr/dict/words*. If your UNIX system has the file, it's a handy place to
get text for testing. I used the UNIX *head* command to get the first 800 words from the file. The long
(250-character) lines in the message body came from the UNIX *fmt* command. I read that into my
message by using the *vi* editor's command *:r !*, which runs a UNIX command line and inserts its output. The whole command I used (from inside *vi*) was:

```
:r !head -800 /usr/dict/words | fmt -250
```

For normal length lines of words, I would have left off the −250.

Example 10-1. Unformatted message with long lines in its body (continued)

```
To:    ehuser@asun.phl.ph.com,
         bob@phl.ph.com
cc: liz@phl.ph.com
Subject:  A wordy message

Here's a message with some useless words and long
lines for your tests.

10th 1st 2nd 3rd 4th 5th 6th 7th 8th 9th a Aaron ABA Ababa a
back abalone abandon abase abash abate abbas abbe abbey abbo
t Abbott abbreviate abc abdicate abdomen abdominal abduct Ab
e abed Abel Abelian Abelson Aberdeen Abernathy aberrant aber
```

Example 10-1 doesn't show all of the body. The body has some very long lines of words, as if the person who sent it forgot to press RETURN where he should have. The long lines were folded on my terminal screen, so I've shown them that way here, but they might have just "run off the right-hand edge" of your screen.

mhl reads a *format file* that tells how your messages should look. In these examples, you'll be making your own format files and storing them in your MH directory.

10.1.1 Formatting the Message Header

Now that you've told *show* to use *mhl*, you're ready to make your own simple format file named *mhl.test1*. Change to your MH directory and use an editor (like *vi*):

```
% cd Mail
% vi mhl.test1
```

Put these three lines into the file. Start each line in column 1 (the left-hand edge of your screen):

```
: -- test mhl format file #1 --
To:
Subject:
```

When you use *mhl* and this format file to show a message, the line that starts with a colon will be displayed as is—that's a helpful reminder that you're using an *mhl* format file. The other two lines will display any components that match.

Tell *mhl* to use your own format file with the *show –form* switch. For example, here's how to show the message in Example 10-1 with the format file called *mhl.test1*:

```
% show -form mhl.test1
-- test mhl format file #1 --
To:     ehuser@asun.phl.ph.com,
        bob@phl.ph.com
Subject:    A wordy message
```

You didn't ask to see the body of the message, so *mhl* didn't show it (we'll fix that). *mhl* did show the comment line and the two components you asked for.

Here's the next generation. Put this in a file named *mhl.test2*:

```
: -- test mhl format file #2 --
leftadjust,compwidth=4
To:
Cc:
compwidth=10
ignores=message-id,received,forwarded,return-path
Extras:nocomponent
```

NOTE

Be sure that there aren't any spaces (blanks) in the lines which have `compwidth=`, `ignores=`, or `Extras:`. These lines, which set *mhl* variables, are sensitive about extra spaces.

Here's how that same message from Example 10-1 looks with this new format file:

```
% show -form mhl.test2
-- test mhl format file #2 --
To: ehuser@asun.phl.ph.com,
    bob@phl.ph.com
cc: liz@phl.ph.com
Replied:    Sat, 16 Dec 89 10:25:45 -0500
Date:       Mon, 31 Jul 89 09:49:08 EDT
From:       Al Bok <al@phl.ph.com>
Reply-to: Joe Doe <joe@foobar.ph.com>
Subject:    A wordy message
```

Some explanation of *mhl.test2*:

• The line `leftadjust,compwidth=4` sets two *mhl variables*. Variables affect the way that a message is displayed. Find these variables in the list in the *mhl*(1) manual page. You'll see that *leftadjust* removes blanks and tabs at the left-hand side of each word—compare the `To:` lines displayed with this format file to the lines from format file 1, and you'll see how *leftadjust* tidies up the message.

The *leftadjust* variable is on a line which doesn't start with a component name. That makes *leftadjust* a *global* variable, which affects all the components below it in the format file.

The `compwidth=4` sets another variable (which is global, for the same reason *leftadjust* is). A *compwidth* setting of 4 means that the component text should be indented by four spaces—in other words, it should start in the fifth output column. The `To:` and `cc:` components are formatted that way and they line up neatly under each other.

- After the `To:` and `cc:` lines in the format file, the *compwidth* variable is reset to 10. From there on, the text of each component is indented by 10 (starts in column 11)—the rest of the header components start in column 11.

- In the last two lines, the global *ignores* variable and the `Extras:` "component" work together. The *ignores* variable holds a list of components from the message that you don't want displayed. The usual components you want to ignore are `Message-Id:` and `Received:`, though I've added two more to the list. You can type the *ignores* list in lowercase letters; it matches any combination of uppercase and lowercase in the message header. If there are too many headers for one line, you can split the lists onto more than one *ignores* lines.

The `Extras:` looks like a component, but it's a special case. It means "output any component here if it hasn't been mentioned before." This format file has mentioned `To:`, `cc:`, `Message-Id:`, `Received:`, `Forwarded:`, and `Return-Path:`—any component in the message header which isn't in that list will be output here at the `Extras:`.

I don't want to see the literal string `Extras:` displayed on the screen when I show the message. Therefore, I've used the `nocomponent` variable on the same line. Putting the variable on the same line makes the variable *local*—it only affects this one component.

The `Extras:` is a special case, remember. Here, *nocomponent* means "don't print the string `Extras:`". As you can see, the "extra" component names are still printed.

Before we start working with the message body, here's one more. Format file 3 uses the *offset* global variable and the *component* local variable:

```
: -- test mhl format file #3 --
compress,leftadjust
Date:
```

```
From:
offset=2
To:
Cc:
offset=0
Subject:component="Subj"
```

This is how the message from Example 10-1 looks with format file 3:

```
-- test mhl format file #3 --
Date: Mon, 31 Jul 89 09:49:08 EDT
From: Al Bok <al@phl.ph.com>
  To: ehuser@asun.phl.ph.com,
      bob@phl.ph.com
  cc: liz@phl.ph.com
Subj: A wordy message
```

See how neatly the components are lined up? Look at the Subject: too, and compare it to the format file. To get some experience with the *mhl*(1) manual page in Appendix I, use it to find out how format file 3 works.

10.1.2 Formatting the Message Body

As demonstrated in the previous section, *mhl* won't show the message body unless you ask for it. The *mhl* command treats the body a lot like any other component. To show the message body, put Body: in your format file. Format file 4 is simple, more for demonstration than to be useful:

```
: -- test mhl format file #4 --
To:
Subject:
Body:
```

Here's the first ten lines of the result:

```
% show -form mhl.test4 | head
-- test mhl format file #4 --
To:    ehuser@asun.phl.ph.com,
       bob@phl.ph.com
Subject:   A wordy message
BodyHere's a message with some useless words and long lines
 for your tests.
Body10th 1st 2nd 3rd 4th 5th 6th 7th 8th 9th a Aaron ABA Ab
aba aback abalone abandon abase abash abate abbas abbe abbe
y abbot Abbott abbreviate abc abdicate abdomen abdominal ab
```

Notice that the message body starts just below the Subject: component, without a blank line to separate them. Also, because I didn't use the *nocomponent* variable, *mhl* has printed the word Body at the start of each line of the body.*

The *mhl* command has automatically folded the body lines. That makes sure that I'll see all of each line, even if my terminal hadn't wrapped the long lines.

Let's clean up the body. Here's format file 5:†

```
Messagename:nocomponent
: -- test mhl format file #5 --
To:
Subject:
:
body:nocomponent,overflowtext="+++",overflowoffset=2
```

And here are the first 13 lines of the *show* output—on Example 10-1 again:

```
% show -form mhl.test5 | head -13
(Message test:21)
 -- test mhl format file #5 --
To:     ehuser@asun.phl.ph.com,
        bob@phl.ph.com
Subject:   A wordy message

Here's a message with some useless words and long lines for
   +++ your tests.

10th 1st 2nd 3rd 4th 5th 6th 7th 8th 9th a Aaron ABA Ababa
   +++aback abalone abandon abase abash abate abbas abbe abb
   +++ey abbot Abbott abbreviate abc abdicate abdomen abdomi
   +++nal abduct Abe abed Abel Abelian Abelson Aberdeen Aber
```

In the format file, the colon (:) makes the blank line before the body. The local variables after body: tell it not to print the "component" name, what characters to mark the folded text with (+++), and how many spaces to put before the folded parts of the lines (two). The Messagename: component prints a string with the folder name and message number—again, you need the *nocomponent* variable to stop the component name from being printed.

---

*The lines of the actual message body were longer than the screen. The *mhl* command adds the "component name" Body before it folds the long lines.

†Be careful when typing in three plus signs (+++) if you're using a modem; that's the escape sequence for many modems. You might type the first +, then press the space bar and BACKSPACE, and then the last ++. Other ideas are typing two plus signs (++) or trying other characters (MH uses ***).

Of course, most messages don't have lines that are too long. A message with normal-length lines wouldn't have all those plus signs (++) in it. If you never want long lines flagged, you can leave out the *overflowtext* and *overflowoffset* variables so that *mhl* will fold long lines without telling you about it.

10.1.3 Default mhl format file for show, next, prev: mhl.format

mhl reads a *format file* that tells how your messages should look. The default format file for *show* is called *mhl.format*. The default format file for *forw* is called *mhl.forward*. The *repl* command will also use an *mhl* format file with the *repl* *–filter* switch, but there's no default filename. You can copy the system *mhl.format* and *mhl.forward* files from the MH library directory into your MH directory and customize them. If files with those names exist in your MH directory, *mhl* and *forw* will use them instead of the system default files.

Let's take a quick look at the default *mhl.format* file shown in Example 10-2. Then we'll explore how you can customize yours.

Example 10-2. Default mhl.format file and message formatted with it

```
% cat mhl.format
: -- using template mhl.format --
overflowtext="***",overflowoffset=5
leftadjust,compwidth=9
ignores=msgid,message-id,received
Date:formatfield="%<(nodate{text})%{text}%|%(pretty{text})%>"
To:
cc:
:
From:
Subject:
:
extras:nocomponent
:
body:nocomponent,overflowtext=,overflowoffset=0,noleftadjust
% show -showproc mhl
 -- using template mhl.format --
Date:    Mon, 31 Jul 89 09:49:08 EDT

To:      ehuser@asun.phl.ph.com, bob@phl.ph.com
cc:      liz@phl.ph.com

From:    Al Bok <al@phl.ph.com>
Subject: A wordy message

Forwarded: Sun, 04 Feb 90 03:41:35 -0500
Replied: Sat, 16 Dec 89 10:25:45 -0500
```

Example 10-2. Default mhl.format file and message formatted with it (continued)

```
Return-Path: <al@phl.ph.com>
Reply-to: Joe Doe <joe@foobar.ph.com>

Here's a message with some useless words and long lines for
your tests.

10th 1st 2nd 3rd 4th 5th 6th 7th 8th 9th a Aaron ABA Ababa
aback abalone abandon abase abash abate abbas abbe abbey ab
bot Abbott abbreviate abc abdicate abdomen abdominal abduct
 Abe abed Abel Abelian Abelson Aberdeen Aberdeen Abernathy
    ...
```

We haven't looked at the *formatfield* variable in the Date: component. It uses MH format strings to give you more control of the way a component is displayed. Section 10.2 covers MH format strings (they're not as tough as they look!). Briefly, the format string in Example 10-2 says that if MH doesn't recognize the format of the date in the Date: component, the component should be output as is; otherwise, it should be reformatted into an easy-to-read date style.

I'd do five things to change that default format file:

1. Change the first line to show that it's not the system default *mhl.format* file.

2. Put the From: line before the To: line.

3. Add *compress* to the Date: line to remove the newline character that's there on some MH setups. This takes out the blank line after the Date:.

4. Add more components to the ignores: line (or add another; you can use more than one ignores= line). For example, I'm never interested in seeing the Return-Path: or Reply-to: components (because *repl* will use them when I need them).

5. I don't like all the blank lines that the *mhl.format* file adds, especially when there are no extras:. I'd get rid of a couple of colons.

My *mhl.format* and the previous message formatted with it are in Example 10-3. If you don't like the default *mhl.format*, maybe this (and the test format files from previous sections) will help you fix yours.

Example 10-3. Revised mhl.format file and same message reformatted

```
% cat mhl.format

: -- using Nutshell mhl.format template --
overflowtext="***",overflowoffset=5
leftadjust,compwidth=9
ignores=msgid,message-id,received,return-path,reply-to,forwarded
```

Part III
Customizing MH

Example 10-3. Revised mhl.format file and same message reformatted (continued)

```
Date:compress,formatfield="%<(nodate{text})%{text}%|%(pretty{text})%>"
From:
To:
cc:
Subject:
extras:nocomponent
    :
body:nocomponent,overflowtext=,overflowoffset=0,noleftadjust
% show -showproc mhl
   -- using Nutshell mhl.format template --
Date:    Mon, 31 Jul 89 09:49:08 EDT
From:    Al Bok <al@phl.ph.com>
To:      ehuser@asun.phl.ph.com, bob@phl.ph.com
cc:      liz@phl.ph.com
Subject: A wordy message
Replied: Sat, 16 Dec 89 10:25:45 -0500

Here's a message with some useless words and long lines for
your tests.

10th 1st 2nd 3rd 4th 5th 6th 7th 8th 9th a Aaron ABA Ababa
aback abalone abandon abase abash abate abbas abbe abbey ab
bot Abbott abbreviate abc abdicate abdomen abdominal abduct
 Abe abed Abel Abelian Abelson Aberdeen Aberdeen Abernathy
    ...
```

Why not try it? Make your own *mhl.format* format file for *show* now. Use the information in the early parts of this chapter to display your messages just the way you'd like to.

10.1.4 forw Filter Files⊠

Section 6.8.1 explains how you can use *mhl* to filter messages you send with the *forw* command. The default *forw* filter file is named *mhl.forward*. Filter files for forwarded messages are almost the same as format files for displaying messages. This section looks at the default filter file and shows another filter file used for a special application.

NOTE

At first, it's easy to get confused about what formats the header of the forwarded message itself, and what formats the messages you're forwarding. It might help you to think of a paper envelope with some paper messages inside. The format of the envelope (the forwarded message header) is set by the template draft file (like *forwcomps*). The format of the messages inside the envelope is controlled by a filter file (like *mhl.forward*).

Let's start with *mhl.forward*, as shown in Example 10-4. Messages you forward with this filter file will have the Date:, From:, To:, cc:, and Subject: components from the original message. Other components will be skipped. The body will be broken into lines less than 80 characters wide.

Example 10-4. mhl.forward: Default forw format file

```
width=80,overflowtext=,overflowoffset=10
leftadjust,compress,compwidth=9
Date:formatfield="%<(nodate{text})%{text}%|%(tws{text})%>"
From:
To:
cc:
Subject:
:
body:nocomponent,overflowoffset=0,noleftadjust,nocompress
```

The *formatfield* variable uses an MH format string, which is covered in Section 10.2. Briefly, though, the format string in Example 10-4 says that if MH doesn't recognize the format of the date in Date: component, the component should be output as is; otherwise, it should be reformatted into an official RFC822 date style. If you haven't used a *forw* filter file yet, this is a good time to experiment with *mhl.forward*.

Example 10-6 is a filter file for a company that tracks its product bug reports with MH mail. A series of messages about a particular bug are forwarded together with this special formatting. You probably won't want to format your forwarded messages this way, but this is a simple example of the sort of customizing you can do. For example, the messages about the company's VMX2244 product might be forwarded as Example 10-5 shows.

Example 10-5. Four messages forwarded with mhl.prodsumry

```
% scan +vmx2244
  1+ 06/19 Ed Bledsoe        Kimzit broken in VMX2244<<Our
  3  06/20 To:Field Service  bug fix: VMX2244 Kimzit<<Ed B
  4  06/26 Ed Bledsoe        Kimzit fix for VMX2244<<Jane
% forw all -filter mhl.prodsumry
To: bugboss@bigcorp.com
cc: imah, edb
Subject: Bug Summary: VMX2244 Kimzit
--------

------- Forwarded Messages
```

Example 10-5. Four messages forwarded with mhl.prodsumry (continued)

```
Date:    Tuesday 6/19/90 13:35 MDT
Msgid:   <FCC5C552B13F201F9E@mysun.bigcorp.com>
From:    Ed Bledsoe <edb@bigcorp.com>
To:      bugtrack@bigcorp.com
Subject: Kimzit broken in VMX2244


Our customer Jane Bluenose in Snow Flow, Alaska reported the
   ...


------- Message 2

Date:    Wednesday 6/20/90 10:45 MDT
Msgid:   <900620100423@avax.bigcorp.com>
From:    Ima Hacker <imah>
To:      Field Service <fse@bigcorp.com>
Subject: ******** bug fix: VMX2244 Kimzit ********


Ed Bledsoe wrote in <FCC5C552B13F201F9E@mysun.bigcorp.com>:
   ...
```

The forwarded messages have some special formatting:

- The Date: components are in a new format.

- The Message-Id: components are included and labeled Msgid:.

- The cc: component, if there was one, isn't included.

- The Subject: component in the second message has asterisks around it.

That's all done by the _mhl.prodsumry_ filter file in Example 10-6. Line numbers to the left of each line (like _12>_) are not part of the file; they are for reference only.

Example 10-6. mhl.prodsumry: forw filter file

```
1> width=80,overflowtext=,overflowoffset=10
2> leftadjust,compress,compwidth=9
3> ; Reformat date into company standard:
4> Date:formatfield="%<(nodate{text})%{text}%|\
5>     %(weekday{text}) %(mon{text})/%(mday{text})/%(year{text})\
6>     %(hour{text}):%02(min{text}) %(tzone{text})%>"
7> Message-Id:component=Msgid
8> From:
9> To:
10> ; If subject contains "bug fix", put stars around it:
11> Subject:formatfield="%(void{text})\
12>     %<(match bug fix)******** %{text} ********%|%{text}%>"
13> :
14> body:nocomponent,overflowoffset=0,noleftadjust,nocompress
```

Let's look at the filter file:

- **Lines 1-2** came from *mhl.forward*. They set global variables that control the overall formatting.

- Because **line 3** starts with a semicolon (;), it's a comment. **Lines 4-6** format the `Date:` component. MH format strings like the one in this *formatfield* variable are explained in Section 10.2. As you read this description, you might compare lines 4-6 of Example 10-6 to the `Date:` components shown in Example 10-5.

  The *formatfield* variable uses MH format strings to control the format of a particular component. The text from that component is available in the *{text}* escape — look for `{text}` in the format string.

  There's an overall *if-then-else* test starting on line 4 that checks the format of the message `Date:` component. If MH can't parse the date, it's output as is by the end of line 4. If MH can parse the date, the format on lines 5 and 6 is used. This format outputs the day name; the month, date, and year separated by slashes (/); the hour and minute; and the time zone name. The `02` before the *(min)* function formats the minutes to have two digits with a leading zero if needed. MH date parsing is a powerful feature; Section 10.2.7 explains it.

  To continue a format line, end it with a backslash (\).

- **Line 7** outputs the original `Message-Id:` component with a different name.

- **Lines 11-12** use another *formatfield* variable. This one tests the message `Subject:` component. It stores the subject string in an internal register, then tests its contents with `(match bug fix)`. If the string contains the phrase `bug fix`, it's output with asterisks around it. Otherwise, the subject is output as is.

That's a quick example of what you can do with *forw* filter files. Remember that you won't always need MH format strings. When you do, read Section 10.2.

10.1.5 Screen Size and moreproc

The *mhl* command tries to find the width and length of your screen.

Unless you tell it differently, *mhl* will fold lines just before the end of the screen. For instance, if your screen is 80 columns wide (most are), *mhl* will make message lines 79 characters wide. On these screens, any line with more than 79 characters will be folded.

Part III Customizing MH

As long as your UNIX system "knows" about your screen (through the *termcap* or *terminfo* entries, for example), then *mhl* should be able to find your screen size.

The −width *nn* switch and the width=*nn* global variable both tell *mhl* to ignore the screen width information it gets from UNIX. For example, −width 40 on the command line or width=40 in a format file set the screen width to 40—and *mhl* will make lines no more than 39 characters wide.

By default, the screen length (number of lines top to bottom) doesn't matter to *mhl*. That's because *mhl* uses a *moreproc* program to show your messages—and the *moreproc* decides your screen size by itself, with no help from *mhl*. The default *moreproc* is the UNIX *more* program. This is the same program that *show* uses to display your messages, page by page, when it's not using *mhl*.

If you put the following component in your MH profile, then *mhl* won't use the *moreproc* program:

```
mhl: −nomoreproc
```

Instead, *mhl* will do its own paging. Then the screen length will matter—and you can change that, along with other *mhl* paging parameters. More on that in a minute.

First, though, here's a list that shows what MH does when you display a message in several different ways. This should help to clear up any *mhl/moreproc* confusion.

- The command *show*, without any *mhl* formatting, will give the message directly to the *moreproc* command. On Berkeley-type UNIX systems, the *moreproc* is usually the *more* program. If you're reading message 21 in *inbox*, the command executed is:

  ```
  more inbox/21
  ```

- The command *show −showproc mhl* or a component like one of these in your MH profile:

  ```
  showproc: mhl
  show: −showproc mhl
  ```

will give the message directly to *mhl*. Then *mhl* output is piped to the *moreproc*. The resulting command looks like:*

```
mhl inbox/21 | more
```

- If *show* is using *mhl*, but your MH profile has the component:

```
mhl: -nomoreproc
```

then the command executed will be:

```
mhl inbox/21
```

and *mhl* will use its own internal paging routines.

If you want to experiment with *mhl*'s internal pager, you'll need these two components in your MH profile:

```
showproc: mhl
mhl: -nomoreproc
```

mhl has several command-line switches and global variables for its format files that control its built-in pager:

- The *–clear* switch and the *clearscreen* global variable both clear the screen before showing each page of a message. The *–noclear* switch and the *noclearscreen* global variable tell *mhl* not to clear the screen. The default is *–noclear*.

- The *–bell* switch and the *bell* global variable both ring the terminal bell after showing each page of a message. The *–nobell* switch and the *nobell* global variable don't ring the bell. The default is *–bell*.

- The `-length` *nn* switch and the `length=nn` global variable both tell *mhl* to ignore the UNIX screen length information. For example, `-length 10` on the command line or `length=10` in a format file sets the screen length to 10—and *mhl* will stop after every ten lines.

When you're using *mhl*'s built-in pager and the display pauses, press the [RETURN] key to see the next screenful. Other keys do other things—see the *mhl*(1) manual page in Appendix I.

---

* Actually, the *show* program has its own built-in version of *mhl*. The real command executed is simply `more`, with *more*'s standard input coming from the *show* program. But I think the effect is easier to understand when shown as `mhl | more`. You can actually run this yourself with the real *mhl* program without running *show* at all.

10.2 MH Format Strings

The second paragraph of the MH 6.7 *mh–format*(5) manual page says: "Format strings are designed to be efficiently parsed by MH which means they are not necessarily simple to write and understand. This means that . . . users of MH should not have to deal with them."

The MH 6.6 page said just the opposite: format strings " . . . represent an integral part of MH. This means that . . . users of MH should deal with them."

I tend to agree with the MH 6.6 wording. Unless you're doing something very complex, MH format strings really aren't that tough to figure out. And they're very useful—if you thought *mhl* was impressive, you ain't seen nothin' yet! MH format strings let you:

- Parse components, especially dates and addresses.

- Build strings from other strings, including addresses.

- Do *if-then-else* tests.

- Do simple integer arithmetic.

You can use format strings to build message headers, or entire messages, from other messages. That's how the *replcomps* file works, by the way. The *scan* command can also use format strings to customize its output. And format strings are great for shell programming—you can use them to parse message headers, a real time saver. For more information, see Chapter 12, *Introduction to Shell Programming for MH*.

Until recently, the *mh–format*(5) manual page was fairly brief; it didn't document all of *mh–format*. The most recent version of the manual page, released with MH 6.7, has quite a bit of information. There's a copy of it in Appendix I. If your online version isn't up to date, you'll appreciate the one in this book.

One term you'll need to know is *escape*. An escape is a lot like a variable in programming or mathematics: it stands for (and is usually replaced with) something else. There are three kinds of escapes in MH format strings.

The easiest escapes to define are *component escapes*. These are replaced with the components' values from your message header. Here's an example. To get the subject of a message into your MH format string, you use the subject component escape. Write it this way:

```
%{subject}
```

There are two other kinds of escapes: *function* and *control*. You'll see examples of those below, and the *mh–format*(5) manual page defines them.

In fact, this is a good time to spend a few minutes with the manual page. You don't need to read it word for word, but you should see what sections are there and what topics they cover. See Appendix I.

This section will take you through MH format strings by example, like the *mhl* section did. An easy way to get started with MH format strings is the *scan* command.

10.2.1   scan Format Strings

A *scan* format string is an *mh–format* string. It tells *scan* how to format the output for each message it scans.

It's time for a few examples. I have a folder with two messages in it. In Example 10-7, I'll use *show* to display the header of the first message for reference. Then I'll scan both messages with the normal *scan* command. Because there's no *–form* or *–format* string, *scan* uses its default format.

Example 10-7. Sample folder with two messages

```
% show 1
(Message scantest:1)
Forwarded: Sun, 04 Feb 90 03:41:35 -0500
Replied: Sat, 16 Dec 89 10:25:45 -0500
Date: Thu, 14 Dec 89 17:31:21 EST
Received: by asun.phl.ph.com (5.54/PHL)
          id AA29237; Thu, 14 Dec 89 17:31:34 EST
Message-Id: <8912142231.AA29237@phl.ph.com>
From:  Al Bok <al@phl.ph.com>
Reply-to: Joe Doe <joe@foobar.ph.com>
To:  hquimby@asun.phl.ph.com
cc: ehuser@quack.phl.ph.com, aguru@mt.top.ph.com
Subject:  Query about "repl -query"

I have a question about repl -query...

% scan
   1+-12/14 Al Bok          Query about "repl -query"<<I have
   2  12/16 To:Joe Doe      Re: Query about "repl -query"<<Jo
```

Now let's give *scan* a format string. Either you can put format strings in a format file and use *scan*'s *–form* switch or you can type them on the command line with the *–format* switch. I'll start with *–format*.

A simple format string that prints a hash mark followed by the message number and a colon, then the subject, works like this:

```
% scan -format "#%(msg): %{subject}"
#1: Query about "repl -query"
#2: Re: Query about "repl -query"
```

(If you're not sitting at your keyboard, I think you should get up, go to the computer, and try typing that command line right now. Experiment a little with your messages.) Here are some points about that last example:

- That format string has double quotes (") around it. They tell the UNIX shell not to interpret most of the special characters in the string.

- In the format string, the %(msg) prints the value of the *(msg)* function escape. The %{subject} prints the component escape called *{subject}*.

- The hash mark (#), colon (:), and space are printed literally.

- The command *scan* uses the same format string on each message.

- I didn't give *scan* a message number list, so it scanned each message in the folder.

This is a good place to compare component escapes with function escapes. A component escape gets the contents of a component. A function escape performs some sort of calculation, operation, or other function. For example, the component escape *{to}* gets the contents of the To: component from a message. The *(size)* function escape counts the number of characters in a message.

If you don't use the percent sign (%) characters, MH won't treat what comes next as an escape. Look what happens without the % characters:

```
% scan -format "#(msg): {subject}"
#(msg): {subject}
#(msg): {subject}
```

You've already seen examples of two of the three types of escapes: component and function escapes. The third type, a control escape, does an *if-then-else-endif* operation. The parts are:

%< = *if*   (*then* is understood)   %| = *else*   %> = *endif*

NOTE

MH 6.7.2 added a fourth *else-if* operator, `%?`, to that list. To keep things simple, I won't cover `%?` here. There's an example in Section 10.2.9.

Let's add a control escape to this example. It will test to see who each message is from. If a message was sent by me, this control escape will display the words FROM ME (with a space before). Otherwise, it'll display who sent the message by printing the `%{from}` component escape. The control escape looks like this:

```
%<(mymbox{from})FROM ME%|%{from}%>
```

That's not as hard as it might look—we'll dissect it in a minute. Let's try it first, then explain.

I'll split the following command line onto two lines by using backslashes (\), but you can probably fit it onto one line on your terminal. Don't type the backslash(es) unless you split the line too. First, here's how this looks if you use the C shell:

```
% scan -format "#%(msg): \\
%<(mymbox{from})FROM ME%|%{from}%> %{subject}"
#1: Al Bok <al@phl.ph.com> Query about "repl -query"
#2: FROM ME Re: Query about "repl -query"
```

If you use the Bourne or Korn shells, you'll need only one backslash (if you don't split the line, you won't need a backslash). The opening quote tells the shell to keep reading, and it will prompt for more lines with a right angle bracket (>) until you type the closing quote:

```
$ scan -format "#%(msg): \
> %<(mymbox{from})FROM ME%|%{from}%> %{subject}"
#1: Al Bok <al@phl.ph.com> Query about "repl -query"
#2: FROM ME Re: Query about "repl -query"
```

The first message is from someone else, so *scan* prints his address. The second message is from me, so FROM ME is printed instead.

Let's dig into that control escape. Here's a diagram of the *if-then-else* parts:

```
%< (mymbox{from})  FROM ME%|  %{from}  %>
    if                then      else
   this is true      do this   do this
```

Actually, that's a nested set of all three kinds of escapes—control, function, and component.

The `%<` is the start of the control escape. It tests the return value of (in other words, the "answer" from) `(mymbox{from})`. The *(mymbox)* function escape tests whether an address belongs to the person who's running the MH command.

The *{from}* component escape is the address to test. Note the following:

- If the return value of (mymbox{from}) is 1 ("true"), then the message is from me. The control escape evaluates the first part (in other words, the *then* part) of the rest of the escape. Here that's the words FROM ME. Because those words aren't an escape, they're just printed as is. Then evaluation continues at the %> symbol.

- Otherwise, the return value of (mymbox{from}) must be 0 ("false"). Interpretation jumps to the %| symbol, which is the *else* part of the control escape. Just after this is a component escape, %{from}, that holds the address the message is from—so, the address is printed. Then evaluation continues at the %>.

Look back at the result of running that command. When the first message was scanned, it was not from me, the test failed, and the From: address was printed. When the second message was scanned, it was from me, the test was true and FROM ME was printed.

An escape returns one of two kinds of values, either *numeric* (integer) or *string*. The return values of escapes are put into registers (holding places) named *num* and *str*, respectively.

For simple format files, you don't need to know about registers. That's because the return value of an escape is always printed, unless the escape is nested in another escape. The outermost escape should always start with a percent sign (%); inner (nested) escapes shouldn't.

For instance, in the previous format string, the %(msg) and %{subject} escapes are not nested in others—so their values are just printed. But the nested set of escapes (mymbox{from}) is itself nested in a control escape. There the return value of {from} is passed to (mymbox), and the return value of (mymbox) is passed to the control escape. What's printed is the value of the control escape (which starts with a percent sign (%); that's a clue that it'll be printed).

It's a good idea to test yourself as you look at the other *mh–format* strings in this section. Experiment to be sure how they work, what will be printed, and so on. The *mh–format*(5) manual page in Appendix I has more precise information.

NOTE

Most address-parsing function escapes won't work if your MH is configured with [BERK]. *scan –help* lists your configuration.

Table 10-1 summarizes the three kinds of escapes.

Table 10-1. MH Format Escapes

Component Escape

Syntax	Example	Result
{component-name}	%{from}	What's in the From: component.

Function Escape

Syntax	Example	Result
(function-name)	%(mymbox{from})	True if the result of {from} is my address.

Control Escape

Syntax	Example	Result
%<if-then-else>	%<(mymbox{from})FROM ME\ %|To: %{to}%>	If(mymbox{from}) is true, value is the string FROM ME. Else, value is the string To: %{to}.

If you're still not exactly sure how this works, this is a good time to practice. To help you get started if you haven't done much programming before, you might want to lure a computer guru from down the hall somewhere.*

10.2.2 scan Format Files

Because the format strings in the example are getting pretty long to type, I'll start using format files in the examples.

A format file has the same syntax as the format strings we used above, but you type the format string into the file without quotes around it. (Use a text editor like *vi* or *emacs*.) You give the filename to *scan* with its *–form* switch—if the file is in your MH directory, you don't need to type a pathname. For example, here's what the above format string would look like in a format file named *scan.from* in your

---

*Hint: all computer gurus like pizza.

MH directory (I've left in the backslash at the end of the short first line, so you can see how to continue lines if you need to):

```
% cat scan.from

#%(msg): \
%<(mymbox{from})FROM ME%|%{from}%> %{subject}
% scan -format scan.from
#1: Al Bok <al@phl.ph.com> Query about "repl -query"
#2: FROM ME Re: Query about "repl -query"
```

Another note about these example format files: if you don't want to type them in yourself, you can get them electronically. For instructions, see Appendix E, *Copies of Files Over the Network*.

10.2.3 The scan.answer Format File

Let's turn the simple *scan.from* format file into one that's more useful:

- It shows the message number. If you've replied to the message with *repl –annotate*, an R is printed next.

- It gives the address you'd use to answer each message. In most cases, the address you want is the From: address—unless the message has a Reply-to: component. And, if the message is from you, you want FROM ME to remind you that it doesn't need a reply.

- It gives the subject of each message.

- It lines up text in columns—that is, each part of the line is the same width as lines above and below.

Here's the output and the format file:

```
% scan -form scan.answer
   1R Al Bok <al@phl.ph.co Query about "repl -query"
   2 ****** FROM ME ***** Re: Query about "repl -query"
% cat scan.answer

%4(msg)%<{replied}R%| %> \
%<(mymbox{from})****** FROM ME *****%|\
%<{reply-to}%20{reply-to}%|%20{from}%>%> \
%{subject}
```

Okay; let's take this step by step again:

1. The `%4(msg)` prints the message number in a field that's four characters wide.

2. `%<{replied}R%| %>` tests the value of the *{replied}* component escape. If there is a `Replied:` component in this message header, the test is true and the R is printed. If the message header doesn't have a `Replied:` component, the test will fail and a space is printed instead (to keep the columns neat).

3. `%<(mymbox{from})******` FROM ME `*****` is the same test as in the *scan.from* format file: if the message is from me, it prints FROM ME. There are enough asterisks to make the output exactly 20 characters wide.

4. `%|%<{reply-to}%20{reply-to}%|%20{from}%>` is the *else* part of the previous *if* (the `(mymbox{from})` escape). This *else* is actually made up of another complete *if-then-else*, as shown below:

   • `%<{reply-to}%20{reply-to}` says that if the message has a `Reply-To:` component, print that component with a width of 20.

   • `%|%20{from}%>` is the *else*—if the message didn't have a `Reply-To:`, then we use the `From:` component instead. Again, we use only the first 20 characters. `%>` is the end of this inner control escape.

5. And finally, the rest of the file:

   • `%>` \ is the end of the outer control escape. There's a space before the backslash; this makes the space between the address and the subject.

   • `%{subject}` prints the subject with no width limit except the screen size (see Section 10.2.6 for more information).

10.2.4 The Default scan Format File

When you use *scan* without a format file or format string, you get the default format. Here's an example of the default format:*

```
436+-06/28 Al Bok           <<I have a very complicated ques
441  06/29 To:              That complicated message Al sent
443  06/30*To:ehuser,emmab   More about lunch<<The meeting is
```

The default *scan* format isn't in the MH library directory; it's defined in the file *h/scansbr.c* in the MH source tree. There are two versions. If your MH is configured without the [UK] option (see Section 4.9 to find out), look at Example 10-8. In the [UK] configuration, the day of the month is printed before the month. That file is shown in Example 10-9.

You can also get a copy of those files from this book's on-line archives. See Appendix E, *Copies of Files Over the Network*. The files are called *scan.default* and *scan.default.uk*.

The only place that the default *scan* format is documented is the *mh–format*(5) manual page. Read through the description. As we work through the following examples, you might keep the *mh–format*(5) manual page close by and refer to it as we go.

Example 10-8. Default scan format file: scan.default

```
%4(msg)%<(cur)+%| %>%<{replied}-%|%<{encrypted}E%| %>%>\
%02(mon{date})/%02(mday{date})%<{date} %|*%>\
%<(mymbox{from})To:%14(friendly{to})%|%17(friendly{from})%> \
%{subject}%<{body}<<%{body}>>%>
```

Example 10-9. Default UK scan format file: scan.default.uk

```
%4(msg)%<(cur)+%| %>%<{replied}-%|%<{encrypted}E%| %>%>\
%02(mday{date})/%02(mon{date})%<{date} %|*%>\
%<(mymbox{from})To:%14(friendly{to})%|%17(friendly{from})%> \
%{subject}%<{body}<<%{body}>>%>
```

---

*Message 441 shows a problem in the default format: if a message is from you and its header doesn't have a To: component, *scan* will show an empty field. This particular message is a reply sent with *repl –query*, where I didn't send a copy to the person who wrote the original message. If you want a short exercise when you look at the default format file, try to find out why this happens.

10.2.5   Adapting the Default scan Format File: scan.hdr

Next, let's try a small change to the default (non-UK) format file. This new format file, *scan.hdr*, shows more information about the message header. The file, or one that you adapt from it, might be useful for you. Its output looks like this:

```
435+     05/20 root              <<The job you submitted to a
436 C  R 06/28 Al Bok           <<I have a very complicated
441 C    06/29 To:              That complicated message Al
443  DF  06/30*To:ehuser,emmab  More about lunch<<The meetin
```

This new version has four "header letters" between the message number and date:

C   The message header has a cc: component in it. This is useful for figuring out messages like number 441, which doesn't have a To: address (but, as you can tell, does have a cc: component).

D   The message has been distributed (either distributed from someone else to you or sent by you with the *dist –annotate* command). So message 443 has at least one Resent-To:, Resent-cc:, or Resent: header.

F   The message has been forwarded to someone. Message 443 has been forwarded with *forw –annotate*, and it has a Forwarded: header.

R   The message has been replied to with *repl –annotate*. (The default format file uses a dash (–), instead of an R, for this.) Example 10-10 shows the format file.

Example 10-10. scan.hdr format file

```
1> %4(msg)%<(cur)+%| %>%<{cc}C%| %>\
2> %<{resent-to}D%|%<{resent-cc}D%|%<{resent}D%| %>%>%>\
3> %<{forwarded}F%| %>%<{replied}R%| %>\
4>  %02(mon{date})/%02(mday{date})\
5> %<{date} %|*%>\
6> %<(mymbox{from})To:%14(friendly{to})\
7> %|%17(friendly{from})%>\
8>    %{subject}%<{body}<<%{body}%>>>
```

The differences between *scan.default* and *scan.hdr* are in the first three lines of Example 10-10. Compare those to the first lines of Example 10-8.

Most of the changes are the new control escapes to make the header letters. For example:

```
%<{cc}C%| %>
```

tests for a cc: header. If there is one, it prints a C; otherwise it prints a space.

The three-part control escape on the second line prints a D or a space. Here is the line with its three matching parts labeled:

```
%<{resent-to}D%|%<{resent-cc}D%|%<{resent}D%| %>%>%>
1111111111111122222222222222222333333333333333332211
```

1. If there's a `Resent-To:` header, part 1 of the test matches and a D is printed—then control goes to the matching `%>` at the end of the line, skipping parts 2 and 3.

2. If part 1 didn't match, control goes to the first `%|` and part 2 of this line tests for a `Resent-cc:` component. If there's a match, it prints its own D and goes to the matching `%>` at the end.

3. Finally, part 3 does the test for `Resent:` and prints a D if the test succeeds. Otherwise, the space (before the matching `%>`) is printed.

You might try adding another column for, say, a `Sender:` component. To test your new format file, use a text editor to add a `Sender:` component to a couple of mail messages. Under MH 6.7, you can also use a command like the following to add a dummy `Sender:` component:

```
% anno -nodate -component Sender -text someone@somewhere
```

In MH 6.6 and before, *anno* doesn't have a *–nodate* switch.

10.2.6 scan Widths

When *scan* writes to your screen, it tries to determine the width and fill it (if your format gives it that much text). For instance, the standard format string (stored internally in *scan*) will fill an 80-column screen to column 79. The same format string will fill a 40-column screen to column 39; the right-hand end will be cut off. For instance, here's the output of the same standard format string at three different screen widths:

```
18+ 02/13 To:omderose@mvus    Lunch<<Let's eat now. OK? >>
18+ 02/13 To:omderose@mvus    Lunch<<Let's
18+ 02/13 To:omderose@m
```

As another example, notice that adding the four status letters in Section 10.2.5 didn't make the *scan.hdr* output any wider than the *scan.default* output.

As an output line is printed, you can get the amount of space left by using the function escape *(charleft)*. The *(width)* function escape gives the total output width.

10.2.7 The scan.dateparse Format File

Let's try another example: the format file *scan.dateparse*. It uses date parsing functions to show the dates of messages. The output changes to fit the width available.

scan.dateparse isn't a format file you'd want to use every day, but it's a good demonstration of some important things:

- How date parsing works.

- How to compare two numbers (in this case, a "greater-than" test).

- The effect of line and data width, and how your format file can adjust automatically when text width or output width vary.

- Word wrapping and embedded newlines (\n).

- More examples of *if-then-else* branching (control escapes).

Let's see what the file does and then dig into a line-by-line explanation. First, here's a normal *scan* of a folder with four messages. The messages were sent from different systems in different time zones. Message 3 has an illegal Date:.

```
% scan
    1+-12/14 Al Bok           Query about "repl -query"<<I hav
    2  12/16 To:Joe Doe       Re: Query about "repl -query"<<J
    3  01/00 randy@atlantic.or Meeting is on!<<Be sure to get y
    4  08/16 randy@atlantic.or Meeting is on!<<Be sure to get y
```

The *scan.dateparse* format file (in Example 10-11) makes about 320 characters of output for each message. The amount depends on the length of the Date: component in the message. Here's an example of scanning the same folder with *scan.dateparse*:

```
% scan -form scan.dateparse -width 320
MESSAGE 1: Thu 14-Dec-89 17:31:21 est (STANDARD time)
 Official: Thu, 14 Dec 89 17:31:21 -0500
 "Pretty": Thu, 14 Dec 89 17:31:21 EST
629677881 seconds since UNIX, 8700976 seconds before now
DAY|WEEKDAY  |WDAY|SDAY|MONTH|LMONTH    |MON|YEAR|HOUR|MIN|SEC
Thu|Thursday |   4|yes |Dec  |December  | 12|  89|  17|  31| 21

MESSAGE 2: Sat, 16 Dec 89 10:25:45 -0500 (STANDARD time)
 Official: Sat, 16 Dec 89 10:25:45 -0500
 "Pretty": Sat, 16 Dec 89 10:25:45 EST
629825145 seconds since UNIX, 8553712 seconds before now
DAY|WEEKDAY  |WDAY|SDAY|MONTH|LMONTH    |MON|YEAR|HOUR|MIN|SEC
```

```
Sat|Saturday |    6|yes |Dec   |December | 12|  89|  10| 25| 45

MESSAGE 3: -0400 16 Aug 89 16:54:59 CAN'T PARSE DATE

MESSAGE 4: 16 Aug 89 16:54:59 -0400 (DAYLIGHT time)
 Official: 16 Aug 89 16:54:59 -0400
 "Pretty": 16 Aug 89 16:54:59 EDT
619304099 seconds since UNIX, 19074758 seconds before now
DAY|WEEKDAY   |WDAY|SDAY|MONTH|LMONTH   |MON|YEAR|HOUR|MIN|SEC
Wed|Wednesday|    3|no  |Aug  |August   |  8|  89|  16| 54| 59
```

Notice (on the first line of the listings) that each message has a different date format, but *scan* can parse all of them—except the one in message 3.

Format files you've seen up to now just let *scan* truncate their output when the width limit is reached. But *scan.dateparse* checks the available width. It prints the last two lines that show the parsed date only if there is enough room for all of both lines. In this next example, the width isn't quite enough, so the last two lines for each message aren't displayed:

```
% scan -form scan.dateparse -width 300
    ...These lines omitted...
629825145 seconds since UNIX, 8553736 seconds before now

MESSAGE 3: -0400 16 Aug 89 16:54:59 CAN'T PARSE DATE

MESSAGE 4: 16 Aug 89 16:54:59 -0400 (DAYLIGHT time)
 Official: 16 Aug 89 16:54:59 -0400
 "Pretty": 16 Aug 89 16:54:59 EDT
619304099 seconds since UNIX, 19074782 seconds before now
```

If you were going to use a format file like that a lot, you'd probably want to make a new version of *scan* called something like *scandp*. For help, see Section 9.9. When you make the new version, you'd put this component in your MH profile:

```
scandp: -form scan.dateparse -width 320
```

Then, you could just type *scandp* to use *scan.dateparse* without having to remember the width.

Example 10-11 shows *scan.dateparse*.

Example 10-11. Date parsing demonstration: scan.dateparse

```
1> MESSAGE %(msg): %{date} \
2> %<(nodate{date})CAN'T PARSE DATE%|\
3> (%<(dst{date})DAYLIGHT%|STANDARD%> time)\n\
4>  Official: %(tws{date})\n\
5>  "Pretty": %(pretty{date})\n\
6> %(clock{date}) seconds since UNIX, %(rclock{date}) seconds before now\
7> %(void(charleft))%<(gt 125)\n\
```

Example 10-11. Date parsing demonstration: scan.dateparse (continued)

```
 8>  DAY|WEEKDAY   |WDAY|SDAY|MONTH|LMONTH    |MON|YEAR|HOUR|MIN|SEC\n\
 9>  %(day{date})|%9(weekday{date})|%4(wday{date})|\
10>  %<(sday{date})yes %|no  %>|\
11>  %5(month{date})|%9(lmonth{date})|%3(mon{date})|%4(year{date})|\
12>  %4(hour{date})|%3(min{date})|%3(sec{date})%>%>\n
```

Next, a line-by-line explanation of how *scan.dateparse* works:

- Lines 1-3 produce the first line of output for each message. **Line 1** prints the message number and the actual unparsed date field from the message. The backslash at the end of the line is a continuation character.

  Line 2 starts with a control escape that tests the *(nodate)* function escape. If the test (nodate{date}) is true, the Date: line is missing or can't be parsed. Then, the words CAN'T PARSE DATE are output—and *scan* jumps ahead to the matching %>, which is at the end of line 12. For messages with unparseable dates (like message 3 here), only one line is output. On the other hand, if the test in line 2 fails (if (nodate{date}) returned zero), then the date is parseable—and interpretation goes to line 3, where the multiline output starts.

  Line 3 completes the first line of *scan* output with a string in parentheses that tells whether the message was sent during daylight savings time or standard time. Line 3 starts with a parenthesis that is output literally. Next is a control escape that tests the value of (dst{date})—if the value is nonzero, then the date is during daylight savings time and the control escape outputs DAYLIGHT. Otherwise, it outputs STANDARD. After the end of the control escape, a space and time) are output, followed by a newline (\n) which ends the first output line.

- Lines 4 and 5 print the Date: in two different formats. **Line 4** prints the official RFC822 version, and **line 5** prints a format with the time zone shown in letters instead of numerically.*

- **Line 6** prints two numbers that can be useful in UNIX programming: the number of seconds since January 1, 1970 *(clock)*, and the number of seconds since the message was sent *(rclock)*. Of course, these values will change each time you scan the same message.

---

*A numeric time zone tells the difference, at the sending site, before or after Coordinated Universal (Greenwich Mean) Time. For instance, the U.S. West Coast is eight hours behind Greenwich Mean Time in the winter; that's written −0800. In the summer, during Daylight Savings Time, the difference is seven hours, or −0700. Sites east of Greenwich have times starting with a plus sign (+). For example, +0030 means 30 minutes after Greenwich Mean Time.

- **Line 7** starts the part of this format file which won't be output unless there's room (as mentioned above). It starts by putting the number of output characters remaining (the output of the *(charleft)* function escape) into the *num* register. The *(void)* escape keeps the *(charleft)* output from being displayed on the terminal.

  Next, the *(gt)* escape compares the output of *(charleft)* (in the *num* register) to the constant 125, which is the number of characters that the next two lines of output require. If the test succeeds, then there's enough space, and we do lines 8-12 (starting with a newline from the end of line 7). Otherwise, we branch to the next-to-last %> on line 12, which is the end of this control escape.

- **Line 8** prints a title line with a newline at the end. **Line 9** prints the DAY, WEEKDAY, and WDAY fields with vertical bars between them (the vertical bars aren't part of a control escape because there's no % before them).

  Lines 10-12 use quite a few function escapes; they're all in the *mh–format*(5) manual page. Without the control escape, the (sday{date}) on **line 10** would print a number 0 or 1—but this way, it prints yes or no. **Line 11** and **line 12** fill in the rest of the fields. Line 12 ends with \n, which means each message will have a blank line after it. Because \n is after the last %>, it will always be used, even for messages with unparseable dates like number 3.

10.2.8 The scan.more Format File

The *scan.more* format file is a "do-it-all" format file that gives you a lot of information about messages in a short space. The output changes depending on which headers the message has. For example, here are four messages scanned with *scan.more* (by the way, if you were going to use this file a lot, you'd probably store the *–form* and *–width* switches in your MH profile):

```
% scan 435-443 -form scan.more -width 230
  435  SENT: 20 May   CHARS: 383
        FROM: root (Super User)
      APP-TO: jdpeek
      <<BODY: The job you submitted to at, "/u3/acs/jdpeek/.1
  436  SENT: Thursday   CHARS: 29387   REPLIED: Friday
        FROM: Al Bok <al@phl.ph.com>
          TO: ehuser@asun.phl.ph.com
      <<BODY: I have a very complicated question about the ph
  441+ SENT: Friday   CHARS: 499
          CC: ehuser@quack.phl.ph.com, jdpeek
        SUBJ: That complicated message Al Bok sent us
  443 FILED: 16:44   CHARS: 52
          TO: ehuser, emmab
        SUBJ: More about lunch
```

If you compare the four messages, you'll see how the output changes:

1. Message 435 was sent more than seven days ago, so its DATE: field shows the date and month that the message was sent. (*scan.more* uses the same date-formatting as the standard *scan.timely* format file—see Section 5.2.1.) This message has 383 characters. It doesn't have a TO: component, but it does have an APP-TO: component. There's no SUBJ:, so the first part of the message body is shown.

2. Message 436 was sent within the last week, so the day name is shown. I replied the next day (Friday) with *repl –annotate*.

3. Message 441 is the current message—the plus sign (+) shows that. I sent it on Friday. There's no TO: component (this can happen when you use the *repl –query* command and don't send your reply to the person who sent you the original message). Here, *scan.more* shows the CC: addresses instead. Finally, when a message is one that I sent (like this one), *scan.more* saves space by not showing a FROM: *me* line.

4. Message 443 doesn't have a DATE: component so *scan.more* shows the time that the message file itself was last modified. This message is a draft that was refiled from the What now? prompt.

The *scan.more* command is also used with the version of *scan* called *cur* (in Section 9.9.1). To save lines on the screen when you scan several messages, the format file hangs the message numbers into the left margin instead of putting blank lines between messages.

Example 10-12 shows the format file.

Example 10-12. Lots of information: The scan.more format file

```
 1> %4(msg)%<(cur)+%| %>\
 2> %<{date} SENT%|FILED%>: \
 3> %(void(rclock{date}))\
 4> %<(gt 15768000)%03(month{date})%02(year{date})%|\
 5> %<(gt 604800)%02(mday{date}) %03(month{date})%|\
 6> %<(gt 86400)%(weekday{date}) %|\
 7> %02(hour{date}):%02(min{date})%>%>%>  \
 8> CHARS: %(size) \
 9> %<{forwarded} (FORWARDED)%>\
10> %<{resent} (RESENT)%>\
11> %<{encrypted} (ENCRYPTED)%>\
12> %<{replied} REPLIED: \
13> %(void(rclock{replied}))\
14> %<(gt 15768000)%03(month{replied})%02(year{replied})%|\
15> %<(gt 604800)%02(mday{replied}) %03(month{replied})%|\
16> %<(gt 86400)%(weekday{replied}) %|\
```

Example 10-12. Lots of information: The scan.more format file (continued)

```
17>  %02(hour{replied}):%02(min{replied})%>%>%>%>\n\
18>  %<{apparently-from}  APP-FROM: %{apparently-from}\n%|\
19>  %<(mymbox{from})%|        FROM: %{from}\n%>%>\
20>  %<{to}          TO: %{to}%|\
21>  %<{apparently-to}    APP-TO: %{apparently-to}%|\
22>          CC: %{cc}%>%>\
23>  %<{subject}\n      SUBJ: %60{subject}%|\
24>  %<{body}\n    <<BODY: %60{body}%>%>
```

Most of *scan.more* uses the same techniques and escapes as other format files in this chapter. The parts of *scan.more* that print the DATE: and REPLIED: components are new, though. They were adapted from the MH *scan.timely* format file. Here's a look at one of the "date" section: **lines 3-7.** (The REPLIED: section, **lines 11-15**, is almost identical.)

- **Line 3** uses the *(rclock)* function escape to find how long ago (in seconds) the message was sent. The result from *(rclock)* goes into the *num* register.

  That number would also be shown on the screen, but the *(void)* function prevents that. *(void)* is useful where you want to store an intermediate result in the *num* or *str* registers without printing it.

- Next, a series of nested control escapes starting on line 4 uses the *(gt)* function to print a different date format, depending on how long ago the message was sent.

  For example, if the number from *(rclock)* is 100000, that means the message was sent 100,000 seconds ago. That's 27.8 hours, which is yesterday (or before). The control escape in **line 4** tests to see if the time is more than a month ago—it isn't. (Here, as with the *pick* command, "one day ago" means 24 hours ago instead of the previous midnight.)

  So control goes to the first % | —and the control escape on **line 5** is evaluated to see if the message was sent more than 604,800 seconds (one week) ago. It wasn't. Notice that the same number from (rclock{date}) is still stored in the *num* register.

  The number in *num* does match at the test in **line 6**—because 100,000 is greater than 86,400. The date is printed with the *(weekday)* function escape, which prints a time as a weekday name.

This format file needs an output width of about 230 characters. The exact amount depends on how wide each component is. *scan.more* limits the width of the subject and body to 60 characters each. But if the text of the address component (like TO:) is long, it can "steal" width from the subject or body. That almost never happens to me—if it's a problem for you, you should be able to fix it by now ...

10.2.9   The replcomps.addrfix Format File and the %? Operator

This section, and the rest of the sections in this chapter, show format files used by programs other than *scan*.

NOTE

The "*else-if*" operator %? (a percent sign and a question mark) was introduced in MH Version 6.7.2. If your version doesn't have %?, use nested tests, as shown in Section 10.2.5.

Example 10-13 shows a *replcomps*-like format file for the *repl* command. (Section 8.9.3 introduces *replcomps*.) This one handles an addressing problem I have with some of the e-mail I get. I can't reply directly to the From: addresses on those messages; I have to edit the To: address in my reply before I send it. Like *replcomps*, the *replcomps.fixaddr* format file gets the best reply address from the message headers. Then it uses a series of *(match)* escapes to decide whether the address is one I can't reply to. If a bad address matches, the file outputs To: *good-address*.

To make the series of tests, I used the new "*else-if*" operator %?. Any line in Example 10-13 that doesn't start with a line number is a continuation of the line above; we split it to fit the book page but you should type it on one line.

Example 10-13. The replcomps.addrfix format file

```
 1> %(lit)\
 2> %(formataddr %<{reply-to}%?{from}%?{sender}%?{return-path}%>)\
 3> %<(nonnull)%(void(width))\
 4> %<(match isla!tim)To: tim\
 5> %?(match djkortz@apl23r)To: djkortz@apl23r.zipcom.com\
 6> %?(match !sparc2gx!vanes@uunet)To: vanes@email.imelda.ac.uk\
 7> %|%(putaddr To: )%>\n%>\
 8> %<{fcc}Fcc: %{fcc}\n%>\
 9> %(lit)%(formataddr{to})%(formataddr{cc})%(formataddr(me)))\
10> %<(nonnull)%(void(width))%(putaddr cc: )\n%>\
11> %<{subject}Subject: Re: %{subject}\n%>\
12> In-reply-to: Message from %<{from}%{from}\
13> %?{sender}%{sender}%|%{apparently-from}%>\n\
14>    of "%<(nodate{date})%{date}%|%(tws{date})%>."%<{message-id}
        %{message-id}%>\n\
15> --------
```

After lines 1-3 store an address in the *str* register and test for it, lines 4-6 see if the address is one of the three that needs to be rewritten.

*For instance, if the original message was From: isla!tim, **line 4** would match it. The string To: tim would be output. The *else-if* operator $?, at the start of **line 5**, would see that the previous test succeeded; control would go to the matching *end-if* which is the first %> on **line 7**.

Here's another example. If the message had a Return-Path: header with the address *...!frobozz!sparc2gx!vanes@uunet.uu.net*, it wouldn't match at line 4 or line 5. The %? operator would keep executing tests until the matching test in **line 6** was found. You could add many more of these *else-if* tests.

If none of the %? operators match, the final *else* (after the %| operator) is executed. Here, the address is printed with no changes.

There's one more %? operator used. It picks an address for the In-reply-to: component in **lines 12-13**.

10.2.10 The rcvtty.format File

rcvtty will read an MH format file, as explained in the part of Section 11.5.2 called "Changing the Output Format." My *rcvtty.format* file is in Example 10-14.

Example 10-14. The rcvtty.format file

```
1>  ^[[7m\
2>  * MAIL: %(size)ch @ %(hour{dtimenow}):%02(min{dtimenow}) *\n\r\
3>  ^[[m\
4>  %<(mymbox{from})To:%14(friendly{to})%|%17(friendly{from})%>\n\r\
5>     %{subject}%<{body}<<%{body}>>%>
```

That file uses a few tricks worth explaining:

- The first line is written in standout mode. The escape sequence in **line 1** starts standout mode on VT100 terminals; **line 3** ends standout mode. (The ^[is the character made by an Escape key. The other characters are literal.)

  "Hard-coding" an escape sequence this way isn't very portable. VT100-style sequences work on a lot of terminals and window systems, though. If those escape sequences don't work on your terminal, check your terminal manual.

- *rcvtty* has a special component escape called *{dtimenow}*. It holds the date and time from the Delivery-Date: component. You can parse it with date function escapes like *(hour)* and *(minute)*.

- Have you had a program running in the background that writes to your terminal—and, at the same time, the foreground program (like a text editor) has put the terminal in raw mode? The lines from the background program

```
jump down
          the screen
                    like this
```

The same thing happens, by default, with multi-line *rcvtty* messages like this file creates. To fix it, I've added carriage -return characters (\r) at the end of **lines 2 and 4**. They move the cursor back to the left margin, something UNIX doesn't do by default in raw mode. When the terminal isn't in raw mode, these extra carriage returns don't hurt a thing.

10.2.11   The rcvdistcomps File

When a message is redistributed with the *rcvdist* command (Section 11.7), the formatting of the Resent-*xxx*: header components is controlled by an *rcvdistcomps* file. The default file is shown in Example 10-15:

Example 10-15. The rcvdistcomps file

```
%(lit)%(formataddr{addresses})\
%<(nonnull)%(void(width))%(putaddr Resent-To: )\n%>\
Resent-Fcc: outbox
```

Addresses you use on the *rcvdist* command line are available in the *{addresses}* component escape. By default, *rcvdistcomps* puts a copy of every message into your *outbox* folder. You can change all of this by making your own *rcvdistcomps* in your MH directory.

*Part III
Customizing MH*

11

Processing New Mail Automatically [X]

This chapter describes a set of MH programs that handle new mail for you. Here are some of the reasons you might want to use these *mhook* (mail hook) features:

- Do you get a lot of mail? Is some of it from mailing lists or system programs that you want to file and handle later, some of it that you want to leave in your system mailbox, and some that's an emergency (like mail from a system-monitoring program) that you want to see right away?

- Does your mail need handling while you're out of the office?

- When new messages come in, do you want to find out right away?

The *mhook* utilities can do those things, and many others, automatically. The *mhook*(1), *maildelivery*(5), and *rcvstore*(1) manual pages have some details. This chapter has much more about setting up and using these programs. (*xmh* users can use these features as well as a special *.xmhcheck* file, explained in Section 15.4.1.)

The *mhook* utilities are set up with a file named *.maildelivery* in your home directory. Each new message is checked against the lines in *.maildelivery*. Each line of the file describes the kinds of mail messages it will match—and the name of a program to run or a file to write when a message matches. Section 11.1 has an introduction and Section 11.2 has details about *.maildelivery*.

On systems with the *Sendmail* MTA (mail transport agent), you run a special MH program named *slocal* from the *.forward* file in your home directory—and *slocal* will read your *.maildelivery*. The *slocal* program adds some extra complication and its own quirks to the process. There are several sections of this chapter that are only about *slocal*, not about the *.maildelivery* file in general. Life is a little easier on systems running the MMDF II transport agent. They don't need *slocal* because MMDF II will read your *.maildelivery* file automatically. There are a couple of other variations. Section 11.3 has the details.

Section 11.4 has techniques to keep you from losing mail while you experiment. Next are sections about four MH programs run from your *.maildelivery* file:

- Section 11.5 on *rcvtty*, to notify you about new messages.

- Section 11.6 about *rcvstore*, to store messages in folders.

- Section 11.7 covers *rcvdist*, for redistributing messages to other addresses.

- Section 11.8 explains *rcvpack*, which saves messages in files.

Those programs won't be enough for everybody, so Section 11.9 discusses other ways to handle your mail automatically. Section 11.10 is a lot of fun: a bag of tricks for combining these programs with the shell and other utilities. Finally, Section 11.11 has tips for debugging.

CAUTION

Most people depend on getting e-mail reliably. Remember that you can lose some or all of your incoming mail if your automatic mail handling isn't working right.

If mail to your account fails and "bounces" back to the people who send it, they can be confused. If you're on a mailing list, and the list's messages to you bounce back, the list's owner may take you off the list.

Don't worry! Just be careful. If you have a second account, where you can experiment without losing important mail, test this setup there before putting it on your own account. Otherwise, while you're setting up and debugging your new setup, make duplicate copies of all your incoming mail—Section 11.4 explains how.

11.1 How .maildelivery Works: The Basics

Without a *.maildelivery* file, when new mail arrives, your computer's MTA drops it in your system mailbox. The lines you put in your *.maildelivery* file will control what happens instead. This section gives an overview. Section 11.2 has the details.

NOTE

You should not perform the steps in this section, to set up your *.maildelivery* file, yet. Instead, give the file another name. When you're ready to use the file, follow the instructions in Section 11.3 for enabling the file. Rename your temporary version to *.maildelivery* then.

When a new message comes in, the *.maildelivery* file is read line by line, from top to bottom. If a line matches the incoming message, an *action* on the line stores the message in a file or passes the message to a command listed on that line. Then, in most cases, the message will be flagged as "delivered." Following lines of *.maildelivery* can test whether the message has been delivered by a previous line.

The system is fairly easy to understand and set up. It's not as flexible as you might want it to be, but you can work around most of the problems.

Let's look at the simple *.maildelivery* file in Example 11-1. The line numbers to the left of each line (like *2>*) are not part of the file; they are for reference only. Lines starting with a hash mark (#) are comments that explain the following line. Comments aren't required, but they're a good idea!

Part III
Customizing MH

Example 11-1. Simple .maildelivery file

```
1> # Throw away all mail from this guy:
2> from      flamer@xyz.abc  destroy A  -
3> # File VAX mailing list in +vax folder; I read it later:
4> subject  "vax digest"    qpipe   A  "/x/y/rcvstore +vax"
5> # Put the rest into my maildrop:
6> default  -                file   ?  /usr/spool/mail/jerry
```

In general:

- **Line 2** will match if the message has the From: address *flamer@xyz.abc*. That message will be "destroyed"—in other words, unless another line in the *.maildelivery* file delivers it, the message will never be delivered.

- **Line 4** will match any message that contains the expression "vax digest" somewhere in its Subject: header. This will match a longer subject, in uppercase or lowercase, like "Info-VAX Digest, issue 23". There are double quotes (") around the argument because of the space in it. These messages are added to my MH folder named *vax*.

  The /x/y is the absolute pathname of the directory that holds the *rcvstore* program. See the NOTE in Section 11.2.

- If neither line above succeeded, **line 6** will append the message to my system mailbox, */usr/spool/mail/jerry*.

You can do a lot more than that simple example shows. Section 11.2 explains the syntax of *.maildelivery*. Sections after it cover *rcvstore* and other programs.

11.2 The .maildelivery File in Detail

Each line of *.maildelivery* has five arguments (except with the undocumented *slocal* select feature explained in Section 11.2.6). There's either a comma or one or more spaces between each argument. If an argument has space or a comma in it, put double quotes (") around the argument. To include a literal double quote, type \ " (put a backslash first).

This chapter uses eight normal words precisely, with an exact meaning. Because those words are used so often, I decided not to italicize them anywhere except where they're defined. The words are: *argument, field, pattern, action, result, string, succeed,* and *delivered*. The definitions are below.

The five arguments on a *.maildelivery* line, explained in the following five sections, are:

```
field pattern action result string
```

There are a few other things to mention first:

- When an action writes to a file, the action succeeds if the file is written successfully. When an action runs a command, the action succeeds if the command returns a zero (normal) exit status.

- If an action succeeds, the message will usually be marked as delivered. The next item explains what I mean by "usually."

- Lines in *.maildelivery* can test to see whether a message was delivered by previous lines. For instance, the ? on line 6 of Example 11-1 tests for delivery. If either line 2 or line 4 delivered the message, line 6 won't add the message to my system mailbox.

  But—just because an action succeeds, that does *not* mean the message has been marked "delivered." For instance, I could add a new line 5 to Example 11-1. The line would run *rcvtty* to tell me about new messages that come in. I wouldn't want this action to "deliver" the message; if it did, the messages I'd been notified about would never get into my system mailbox. As you'll see later in this section, using an *R* result on a line means that even a successful action won't mark a message delivered.

- The versions of *slocal* I've used have some rough edges. Some things don't work quite the way the manual page says they will. Others are undocumented. There are some small differences in the way that *.maildelivery* files are handled by MMDF and by *slocal*. If that matters to you, compare the *maildelivery–mmdfii* and *maildelivery–slocal* manual pages in Appendix I.

  Simple *.maildelivery* files usually work just fine. If yours doesn't work the way you think it should, the tips in Section 11.11 may help.

NOTE

Many pathnames in these examples start with */x/y*. That pathname is system-dependent. Yours might be something like */usr/local/lib/mh*. Type `ls /usr/local/lib/mh` to check. If you can't find *rcvstore* and other commands in this chapter, ask your system administrator.

Now, let's look at the five arguments in each line.

*Part III
Customizing MH*

11.2.1 First .maildelivery Argument: Field

The first argument, *field*, refers to a header component in the message. In line 2 of Example 11-1, for instance, the field argument `from` will match the `From:` header in a message. You can specify any component that might be in a message header, including ones you make up arbitrarily (like `X-auto-m-p:` in Section 11.10.2).

You can't always do what you need to by matching headers, though. Maybe you get mail from several addresses or aliases, and you want to match any of those messages with one line. Or, you might want to match all messages. So, the field can also have one of these four special values:

addr　　　Matches the address that was used to cause delivery to the recipient. It's typically your username (mine is *jerry*). This is explained in Section 11.10.4.

source　　Matches the *out-of-band sender information*. This is an address, supplied by the system's mail transport agent. You'll usually see it as the first line of a message header starting with `From somewhere`, or the `source` information may be stored in a `Return-Path:` message header.

　　　　　The `source` is handy for matching mail from mailing lists. This doesn't work for all mailing lists, but it works for many. I'll use the *mh-users* list (see Section A.2.3) as an example. Message headers in *mh-users* have header lines like these:

```
From mh-users-request@ics.uci.edu  Mon Dec 07 23:43:16 1992
Date: Mon, 07 Dec 92 23:43:16 GMT
From: Some Person <someperson@somewhere.org>
Subject: Some random subject
```

　　　　　You can't count on finding the address *mh-users* in any particular header (though it's usually somewhere on `To:`, `Cc:`, or `Sender:`). But you can bet that the out-of-band sender information, shown in the first line above, will have the address *mh-users-request@ics.uci.edu*—because that's the distribution point for the mailing list.

　　　　　So, a line in *.maildelivery* that begins with the following two arguments will catch mail from the *mh-users* list:

```
source  mh-users-request@ics.uci.edu  ...
```

default   Matches any message that hasn't been delivered by previous lines.
           For instance, look back at Example 11-1: If either line 2 or line 4
           delivers the message, line 6 won't. Otherwise, the message will
           always go into my mailbox.

*   An asterisk as the first argument matches every message, whether it's
           been delivered by other lines of *.maildelivery* or not.

           If the first argument has an * (asterisk), the action will always hap-
           pen when the *result* (in the fourth argument) is A or R. A result of N
           or ? can cause the line to be skipped when those conditions are met.
           Section 11.2.4 explains the result argument.

11.2.2   Second .maildelivery Argument: Pattern

The second argument, *pattern*, is the expression you want to match in the header
selected by the field argument. For instance, line 4 of Example 11-1 searched for
the expression "vax digest", in any combination of uppercase and lowercase, anywhere in the message Subject: header.

If the first argument is default or *, this second argument should be a dash
(-).

The pattern argument is not a regular expression like the UNIX *grep* command
uses; it's just a sequence of characters to match literally (such as the UNIX command *fgrep*).

You can take advantage of the "substring matching" in the second argument. You
might be looking for mail from *root* on any computer. Using root as a second
argument will match mail from *root* with or without a hostname. You can also
match mail from all users at a certain hostname (say, anyone at *xyz.com*).

The downside is that you can match some messages you weren't planning on. For
instance, a search for mail from *root* might catch mail from Joe G*root*enheimer.

One helpful trick takes advantage of the order that your *.maildelivery* file is read:
from first line to last. If you're trying to match more than one similar name, like
joebob and *joe*, put the longest name first. The first line that matches marks the
message "delivered," so the lines below it won't deliver the message too:

```
from  joebob  destroy  A  -
from  joeb       ^     A  "/x/y/rcvstore +read_now"
from  joe        ^     A  "/x/y/rcvstore +read_later"
```

Depending how your mail comes in, you may be able to add @ or ! to mark the
start or end of the address. For example, to match mail from *joe* on a particular

host and joebob@*anyhost*, use lines like the ones below. The joebob@ will never match mail from *joe* on any host:

```
from  joe@foo.unsd.edu   >  ?  somefile
from  joebob@            >  ?  otherfile
```

Of course, that first line would also match *moejoe@foo.unsd.edu*, but it's a start.

Whenever I use a *destroy* action (see Section 11.2.3), I'm always very careful about what I match. The part of Section 11.2.3 about *destroy* shows a safer way with a temporary folder.

11.2.3 Third .maildelivery Argument: Action

The third argument is the *action*: how to deliver the message. There are four different actions. Each action can be written in two ways, as a word or as a symbol. The actions are:

file or > (right angle bracket) Action

The *file* or > action appends the message to a file. (That's usually a file on the mail server computer; it may not be the same computer where you do most of your work. You might write the message into a filesystem that's shared between the two computers.) Put the filename in the fifth argument. Without a pathname, the file will be in your home directory. Typical mailbox names are /usr/mail/*yourname* or /usr/spool/mail/*yourname*.

The message is appended in "mailbox format." It's separated from the previous message in the file by either:

- Two rows of CTRL-A characters. This is an MMDF-style separator:

    ...End of previous message...
    ^A^A^A^A
    ^A^A^A^A
    ...New message...

- A blank line followed by a standard From separator line. This is what the standard UNIX *mail* command expects:

    ...End of previous message...

    From mh-users-request@ics.uci.edu Fri Jun 26 19:55:43 1992
    ...New message...

In some cases, until MH 6.7.1, the *slocal* From separator didn't work right. Sometimes, a group of messages stored this way would come in as a single long message when people ran *inc*. If you have that problem, upgrade MH to

Version 6.7.1 or later if you can. Otherwise, try using *rcvstore* (Section 11.6) to deliver your messages.

qpipe or ^ (caret) Action

This starts a program (*rcvstore*, other *mhook* programs, or almost any UNIX program). The program reads the incoming message from its standard input. If the program succeeds and returns a zero exit status (Section 12.8), then the action has succeeded. For example, to tell you when new mail comes in, set *.maildelivery* to pipe the message to *rcvtty* (Section 11.5), like this:

```
*    -    ^    R    /x/y/rcvtty
```

Here's the difference between the *qpipe* or ^ action and the *pipe* or | action: using the *pipe* or | action doesn't execute a program directly—it starts a Bourne shell; the shell runs the program.

Are you using a simple command string, one that has no special characters like a semicolon (;) or ampersand (&) for a Bourne shell to interpret? Then it's more efficient to use *qpipe* or ^ instead of *pipe* or |. That efficiency can be helpful on busy mail server computers.

There's no command-search path set, so be sure to give the pathname for any command you list. For instance, this command probably won't work:

```
*    -    ^    R    rcvtty
```

There are special variables that you can use in the fifth argument, the string, with the *qpipe* or ^ action. The easiest place to find typical settings of these variables is to run *slocal –debug* and look for the lines starting with `vars[n]:`, as shown in Example 11-6. The variables are listed in Table 11-1.

Table 11-1. Variables Set for pipe and qpipe

Variable	Typical Value	Explanation
$(sender)	xandra@x.y	The "return address" for the message. This is usually supplied by the system mail transport agent. Can be set as third argument on *slocal* command line. The address where you'll want to send replies, instead, is probably $(reply-to).

Table 11-1. Variables Set for pipe and qpipe (continued)

Variable	Typical Value	Explanation
$(address)	jerry	The address that was used to deliver the message to you. That's usually your username. Can be set as first argument on *slocal* command line.
$(size)	12345	The size of the message, in bytes.
$(reply-to)	"J. Doe" <jd@x.y>	The address where you should send replies. If the incoming message has a Reply-To: header, that address is used. Otherwise, this variable will contain the From: header.
$(info)		Miscellaneous out-of-band information. What you get depends on your system and the situation. Can be set as second argument on *slocal* command line.

For example, to make *rcvtty* print the message Mail: *nnn* bytes each time new mail comes in, use:

```
*,-,^,R,"/x/y/rcvtty -format \"Mail: $(size) bytes\""
```

The message size is filled in before *rcvtty* is invoked. The escaped double quotes (\") group the words between them into a single argument. With the quotes, *rcvtty* prints a message like Mail: 1232 bytes on the terminal. Without them, it would print just Mail: and drop the rest—that's because there has to be just a single argument after the –*format* option.

Single quotes (') won't work inside double quotes. They will work inside double quotes with the *pipe* or | action, though.

Also watch out for variables like $(reply-to) that might have quotes buried in their values—they can cause real trouble here. There's more about quoting in the *pipe* section below.

pipe or | (vertical bar) Action

The *pipe* or | action starts a Bourne shell to execute the command(s) in the fifth argument, *string*. The message is piped as standard input to the shell (and the command it runs). If you're running just one command, you may be able to save some execution time by using the *qpipe* or ^ action (explained above). But if you really need a shell, use *pipe* or | .

For example, I wanted to add a timestamp to a log file each time a message came in. I used the following line in my *.maildelivery* file:

```
From,uucp,|,A,"/bin/date >> uucp.msglog; /x/y/rcvstore +uucp_logs"
```

What is that fifth argument? The argument has two commands. The first one, `/bin/date`, appends a line with the current date and time (when a message is delivered) to the file *uucp.msglog* in my home directory. There's a shell semi-colon (`;`) operator to separate the commands. The first command doesn't read its standard input, but the second command does—so *rcvstore* reads the message that is piped to the shell. You can chain a series of commands with semicolons, as long as only one command reads the message from its standard input. (If more than one command needs to read the message, use a temporary file as shown in Section 11.9.4.)

Table 11-1 lists special variables that are set for the *qpipe* or ^ action. Those variables are also set for *pipe* and | . Here's an example. To send an automatic reply when I get mail from a user (sent to my system's *gripe* alias), I can add the following long line to my *.maildelivery* file (shown on three lines here). This has two commands, separated by a semicolon:

```
To,gripe,|,A,"/bin/echo \"Thanks for your $(size)-character message.
    I'll handle it ASAP.  --Jerry\" | /bin/mail '$(reply-to)';
    /x/y/rcvpack gripes"
```

- The first command runs */bin/echo* (with its full pathname because *echo* isn't built into my Bourne shell) and pipes a reply message to the standard input of the */bin/mail* command.

  The quoting (single quotes (') around the $(`reply-to`) address) is very important here. Let's say my command is building a reply to a message with the following header:

  ```
  From: "Ruth A. Lee" <ruthl@fcpe.ie>
  ```

  The shell will execute the command:

  ```
  echo "Thanks ... --Jerry" | /bin/mail '"Ruth A. Lee" <ruthf@fcpe.ie>'
  ```

In this case, the single quotes (which aren't very common in mail addresses) surrounded the double quotes (which are common) and things were fine. If the address had single quotes in it, though, the reply would have failed. What would happen if I had used double quotes (") instead of single quotes, like `"$(reply-to)"`? Or worse, what if I hadn't used quotes? Part or all of the address would have been unquoted and the shell could have been very confused. For more reliable automatic replies (and simpler command strings in your *.maildelivery* file, too), use a separate shell script; see Section 11.9.3. (For more about quoting, find a good shell programming book in Appendix C, *Reference List*—or see Section 12.6.)

NOTE

Some mail-sending commands, like */usr/ucb/mail*, will break correctly-quoted addresses into single words at the spaces. Don't use commands like UCB Mail or *mailx* here. The versions of */bin/mail* I've seen are okay. The *mhmail* command (see Section 12.17.2) is fine, too—but it runs more slowly than */bin/mail* (on my system, at least).

- The first command line didn't read standard input from the shell (*/bin/mail* read its *stdin* from */bin/echo*). So the second command, *rcvpack*, can read the new message from its standard input—and store it in the *gripes* file in my home directory.

This chapter shows lots of ways to use the *pipe* or | action; browse through the examples below. For more gory details, read the *maildelivery* manual pages in Appendix I.

destroy Action

(Before you read this section, take a look back at the definitions of *succeeds* and *delivered* at the start of Section 11.2.)

The *destroy* action does nothing with the message, and always succeeds. This action only makes sense with the result argument *A* that marks the message as "delivered." (See Section 11.2.4.) That's the whole point of *destroy*: to mark the message as delivered without actually delivering it to a file or program.

If this is the only line in your *.maildelivery* file that matches the message, the text of the message will go nowhere. But if another line has an * (asterisk) field, the message can still be given to a command or stored in a file.

Instead of using *destroy*, you might use *rcvstore* or *rcvpack* to write the message to a temporary folder or file instead. Clean out the temporary storage every so often, checking to be sure no messages were "destroyed" that shouldn't have been. Section 11.4 has more about making backup copies of mail.

Want an example? Here's a short *.maildelivery* file with an example of *destroy*:

```
From      uucp  destroy  A  -
default   -     >        ?  /usr/spool/mail/jerry
*         -     |        R  /x/y/rcvtty
```

If the message is from *uucp*, the first line matches it and "delivers" the message (to nowhere). The result argument, A, is important here: it means that if the *destroy* action succeeds (and it always does), the message is marked "delivered." The first line works with the second line and its ? result argument. The second line only writes to my system mailbox file if the message has not been delivered yet. Any message from *uucp* will have been delivered (to nowhere) already, so it won't go into my system mailbox.

The third line has an * (asterisk) field, which matches all messages. The R result means that *rcvtty* always runs to tell me about the message, whether the message has been delivered or not. So, even though messages from *uucp* have been "destroyed" and aren't delivered to my system mailbox, *rcvtty* will notify me about them anyway.

11.2.4 Fourth .maildelivery Argument: Result

The fourth argument in a *.maildelivery* line is a single-character *result*. (As before, the definitions at the start of Section 11.2 are important.) These *results* are:

A Result

This result argument is probably the most common. If the field and pattern are matched, an *A* performs the action. If the action succeeds, the message is marked "delivered."

You'll usually use *A* actions toward the start of your *.maildelivery* file to match certain messages. Toward the bottom, you'll use ? to match messages that *A* didn't match (and "deliver").

R Result

Like the *A* result, an *R* will perform the action if the field and pattern on a line match a message. But *R* never marks a message as "delivered."

If any line above an *R* result marks the message delivered, using *R* can't undo that delivery. In fact, nothing can undo a "delivered" mark. The *R* is probably most useful at the start of *.maildelivery* for actions you want to run on some or all messages—and not mark the message delivered, so that other lines can act on it.

? Result

The *?* (question mark) will perform an action only if the message hasn't been delivered by some previous line in *.maildelivery*. If the *?* delivers a message, the message is marked "delivered."

Use *?* in places where you've got a series of lines that might deliver a message—you want the line with the *?* to deliver only if lines above didn't deliver.

N Result

The N result was added to *slocal* in MH 6.7.2. The *N* result is a little harder to explain. According to the MH 6.7.2 *mhook* manual page, using an *N* result performs the action only if both of these things are true:

- The message hasn't been delivered yet, and

- The previous action succeeded.

If this action (with an *N* result) succeeds, then the message is marked delivered.

That's not quite the way *N* works for me. I looked at the source code (the *usr_delivery( )* function in the file *uip/slocal.c*) and came up with this more accurate (I hope!) description:

The *N* result performs the action only if:

- The message hasn't been delivered yet, and

- The previous action:

  - Succeeded, and

  - That previous action didn't have an * (asterisk) field.

Of course, I could have missed something.* Also, that description could change in other versions of MH. For MH 6.7.2, at least, I think you should be careful if you use the *N* result. Test your *.maildelivery* file to be sure it does what you expect.

11.2.5 Fifth .maildelivery Argument: String

The fifth argument, *string*, is a filename (for the *file* or > action) or a command line (for the *qpipe* or ^ and *pipe* or | actions). As for other arguments, if the filename or command line have any spaces or commas (,), surround the argument with double quotes (").

Because there are example *string*s all through this chapter, I won't give another example here.

11.2.6 Undocumented .maildelivery Arguments 6-8: select

The *slocal* command with MH 6.7.2 (and possibly other versions) has an undocumented feature that lets you control actions by the time of day and whether you're logged in. The three undocumented arguments (which must be used together) are:

```
select starttime endtime
```

Type the word `select` literally. `starttime` and `endtime` are two times in the format *hh*:*mm*, where *hh* is hours on a 24-hour clock (0 to 23) and *mm* is minutes.

If you use these optional arguments, the action will *not* happen if:

- The current time is between `starttime` and `endtime`, or

- You are logged on to the host that runs *slocal*.

So, for example:

```
# if I'm not logged on and it's not between 8 AM and 5 PM,
# send my mail to dan:
*   -   |  R  "/x/y/rcvdist dan" select 8:00 17:00
```

---

*The C code is fairly complex. It's a collection of C *switch* structures that fall through from *case* to *case*, several flags that test and store information about previous actions and delivery, *continue* commands that suddenly skip to the next line of *.maildelivery*, and so on. I've tried to summarize what the code does; see Section 11.11.1.

To ignore the time restrictions, set both times to something like 0 : 0 0 (midnight); then the action will happen whenever you aren't logged in.

11.3 Running Your .maildelivery File

In most cases, your computer's MTA (see Section 1.2) also has to be told to read your *.maildelivery* file. The list below explains what to do for common transport agents. If you aren't sure what MTA is running on your system, ask your postmaster—or read your system's online *mhook*(1) manual page; it should have been customized for your system's configuration.

- If your computer uses the *sendmail* or *smail* MTAs, make a file named *.forward* in your home directory (note the dot (.)). Put the line below, *including the double quotes* ("), in the file:

  ```
  "| /x/y/lib/mh/slocal -user username"
  ```

  where / x / y is the start of the path to the MH library directory where *slocal* is stored on your computer and username is your username. This command sends all your incoming mail through the *slocal* program.

  Your *.forward* file should be owned and writable only by you. (Use the command *chmod 644* or *chmod 600*.)

- If your system runs MMDF II, or (this is unusual!) uses the MH transport agent, your *.maildelivery* file will be run automatically. Think about creating *.maildelivery* with a different name, then renaming it to *.maildelivery* after you've finished editing it.

- On systems with MMDF, use these two steps:

  1. If you don't have a *bin* directory in your search path, add it. (Section 9.2.1 explains how.)

  2. Use the UNIX *ln* command to make a link named *rcvmail* to the system *slocal* command. For example:

     ```
     % ln /x/y/lib/slocal rcvmail
     ```

     If *slocal* and your *bin* directory are on different filsystems, a standard hard link won't work. You'll need to make a symbolic link (the *ln –s* option).

Your *.maildelivery* file, and the *.forward* file or link explained above, have to be in your home directory on the computer where your system mailbox file is written. If your own computer gets its mail from another host with POP (see Section 5.4.3) or by a networked filesystem, check to be sure your setup is on the right computer. If you don't have access to that machine, you can still automate your mail processing with scripts. See Section 13.14, "Process New Mail in a Batch: autoinc" and Section 11.9.5, "Processing with at or cron or by Hand."

11.4 Experimenting? Make Backup Copies of Mail

While you're setting up *mhook* programs, as you're changing the setup later, or any time you aren't sure that things are working right, it's a good idea to make backup copies of all your incoming mail. Periodically, check your backup mail to be sure you've gotten all the messages you should. Then remove the backup.

If you have access to a second account, forward a copy of all your mail to it. My main account is *jerry*, but I also have a *jerrytst* account. My system runs *sendmail*, so I make a *.forward* file like this on my *jerry* account:

```
jerrytst, "| /x/y/slocal -user jerry"
```

If you don't have a second account, you can use a *.forward* file that makes a copy in a file somewhere on your account. The file may need to be world-writable (mode 666 or 622), though, and that can be a security hole. The following *.forward* file copies all incoming mail to a file named *mail.bak* in my home directory:

```
/home/jerry/mail.bak, "| /x/y/slocal -user jerry"
```

A third choice: have *sendmail* drop a copy of the message into your system mailbox before (or after) it runs *slocal*. It's simple to set up but it's also a little messy because your mailbox may get two copies of a lot of messages. Put a backslash before your username to prevent reforwarding of the copy:

```
\jerry, "| /x/y/slocal -user jerry"
```

An easy way to clean out your backup mail file is by copying the system "empty file" onto it. For example, on the *jerrytst* account, I type:

```
% scan -file /usr/spool/mail/jerrytst
   ...Check scan listing of my backup mail...
% cp /dev/null /usr/spool/mail/jerrytst
```

Are you sure that *slocal* is working but uncomfortable that your *.maildelivery* file may be losing messages? If you aren't sure, add a line to file a copy of all messages into a folder:

```
*   -   ^   R   "/x/y/rcvstore +DELETE"
```

scan through your *DELETE* folder whenever you're looking for missing mail. Remember to clean it out with *rmm* or an automated script (see Section 13.6.3 or Section 13.6.4).

11.5 New Message Notification: rcvtty

(*xmh* users: This *rcvtty* section applies to you if you have an *xterm* window open onto the host where your system mailbox is located. Otherwise, look at the *rcvxterm* shell script in Section 11.9.4.)

The *rcvtty* program sends *scan*-like information to your terminal about new messages. UNIX comes with other ways to tell you about new mail, such as *biff*(1) or the shells' mail-checking variables. But *rcvtty* has a big advantage over other notification setups: you can set *.maildelivery* to run *rcvtty* only for certain messages. Also, *rcvtty* uses MH formats (explained in Chapter 10, *MH Formatting*) so it can notify you in almost any format or formats you want.

Here's a sample line for your *.maildelivery* file:

```
*      -     ^    R    /x/y/rcvtty
```

That example sends a one-line summary of all new messages. If a 456-character message comes from Emma H. User at 5:52 p.m., you'd see a line like this on your screen:

```
17:52:    456 Emma H User    Lo-cal pizza<<Do you have a recipe
```

The following sections explain how to change the places *rcvtty* notifies you, how to change what the notices look like, and how to make *rcvtty* run a separate command that shows you just what you want about your message.

11.5.1 Where rcvtty Notifies You

rcvtty can send the same notification to many places. By default, it writes to all the places you're logged in to* on the host where your mail is actually delivered. So, at companies with a central mail server computer (where users' computers run POP or mount their system mailbox filesystem over the network), *rcvtty* probably won't help. (In those cases, the shell's mail-notification variable or a program like *xbiff* would be better.)

---

* Actually, you'll see the message on all your login sessions listed in the */etc/utmp* file. Some window systems won't list all your windows in the *utmp* file. Use the *who*(1) command to see where you're listed. Also, see the part of this section called "Control Your Listing in who(1)."

Maybe you don't want to be notified everywhere you're logged in. Here are a few ways to control where.

The –biff Option

On many systems, the UNIX *biff*(1) program tells your system whether or not you want to be notified about new mail. *biff* does that by setting the owner-execute bit on your terminal (the *tty* file). It's arcane, but it works.

Normally, when you aren't using your *.maildelivery* file, a daemon program called *comsat*(8) does the notification. If a terminal has its execute bit set and mail comes in for that user, *comsat* sends a notice to the terminal. You can use *.maildelivery* to do this notification instead—if if your system has the *biff* utility, that is.* If you use the *rcvtty –biff* option in your *.maildelivery* file, then *rcvtty* will only notify terminals where you've run *biff y*.

If you haven't used *biff*, here's a quick overview. To enable mail notification on your current terminal or window, type `biff y`. Typing the command `biff n` turns off notification for the terminal where you run it. Typing `biff` by itself will tell your current setting. For example:

```
% biff y
% biff
is y
%
```

The mesg Command

If you can't use *rcvtty –biff*, the *mesg*(1) command might be the answer. *mesg* uses *chmod* to allow or deny access for other users who want to send messages to your terminal. *rcvtty* will only notify sessions where you've used *mesg y*.

If you use a window system, you can pick one window to get messages; run *mesg y* there and leave the window open all the time. Use *mesg n* in other windows.

If you also get messages with the *talk*(1) program, and you're logged on more than once, this one-window access can cause trouble. Some versions (at least) of *talk* will only check for access on the first terminal you're logged in to. (Here's what I mean by "the first terminal": run the *who*(1) command, start at the top of

---

*If your system doesn't have *biff*, you could try setting the terminal's execute bit, anyway—and see if *rcvtty* will notice it:

```
% chmod u+x `tty`
```

It's probably a good idea to talk this over with your system administrator. The execute bit may be used for something else on your system.

its list, and look for the line nearest the top where you're listed. That's your first login.) If you've typed `mesg n` in your top-listed login session, *talk* may tell people that you are "refusing messages"—implying that you've shut off messages in all login sessions, when you've really only shut them off in some. So, if you use *talk*, try to make your first window or login the one that grants *mesg* access.

On systems I've tested, the *write*(1) program doesn't have the same problem as *talk*; it seems to look for any terminal with `mesg y` set.

Control Your Listing in who(1)

When *rcvtty* wants to notify you, it checks the list in the *who*(1) command. (Actually, *rcvtty* reads the system */etc/utmp* file.) It'll only try to notify you at slots where you're listed as logged in. You can use this to make *rcvtty* (and utilities like *talk*) ignore you.

For instance, in the X Window System, the terminal program *xterm* has an option to control whether a window will be listed in *who* (actually, in */etc/utmp*). If you start *xterm* with its *–ut* option, your window won't be listed and you won't get notices in it. You'll be notified in the window or windows you start with the *+ut* option.

11.5.2 How rcvtty Notifies You

rcvtty gives you some control over the notice you get. The terminal bell will ring unless you add the *–nobell* option. The cursor will move to the left-hand side of the screen first unless you use *–nonewline*. As the next two sections explain, you can control the format of the notice and what messages you're notified about.

Changing the Output Format

I don't like the default *rcvtty* format. I usually won't see the single line *rcvtty* prints, especially if it's buried in the middle of a screen while I'm editing a file. To fix that, I've used the *–form* option and written a MH format file called *rcvtty.format*. It makes a three-line output with a highlighted top line. It's explained in Section 10.2.10. With my *rcvtty.format* file, I don't need the terminal bell; the highlighted first line is enough to make me notice. The output looks like this:

```
* MAIL: 456ch @ 17:52 *
Emma H User
   Lo-cal pizza<<Do you have recipes
```

I run that setup with the following like in my *.maildelivery* file:

```
# Tell me about all new mail; use three lines and highlight:
*   -   ^   R   "/x/y/rcvtty -form rcvtty.format -nobell"
```

Because the *rcvtty.format* file is in my MH directory (the directory listed in my MH profile `Path:` line), I don't have to use its pathname.

Picking the Messages You're Notified About

Using an * (asterisk) in the field argument of *.maildelivery* lines makes *rcvtty* run for all new messages. If you don't want to be notified about all messages, use field and pattern arguments.

Of course, you can have more than one *rcvtty* line in your *.maildelivery* file. One line could notify you about all messages. Another could add an extra notice, maybe with the terminal bell, too, for important messages. For example, when you get mail from your manager, you can send a message to your terminals with from Big Boss, the size, and the subject. If you get mail about a full disk (usually from an automatic system monitor program), the bell can ring and the message DISK FULL! DISK FULL! ... can be printed across the terminal.

The *rcvtty –format* option lets you give words and an MH format (Section 10.2) without needing a form file. Here are the three lines I explained in the paragraph above. I've split each of them to fit on the page; you should join each onto its own line:

```
*,-,^,R,"/x/y/rcvtty -form rcvtty.format -nobell"
From,simmons,|,R,"/x/y/rcvtty -nobell -format
        \"*** $(size) chars. from Big Boss: %{subject}\""
Subject,"disk full",|,R,"/x/y/rcvtty -format
        \"DISK FULL! DISK FULL! DISK FULL! DISK FULL! DISK FULL!\""
```

Variables like $(size) are listed in Table 11-1. The %{subject} is an MH format component escape, covered in Section 10.2.

Section 11.9.4 shows another way to find out about mail: colored windows that pop up on an X Window screen.

11.5.3 Using a Message Preprocessor

If you give *rcvtty* the name of a command, it will run the command. *rcvtty* will give the message to the command's standard input; it will send the command's standard output to all the terminals where you're logged in. If the *–form* and *–format* command-line options don't give you enough control over the notice *rcvtty* sends—this will!

Here's a simple example. To show the first ten lines of a message, this line in your *.maildelivery* would do the job:

```
*    -    ^    R    "/x/y/rcvtty /x/y/head"
```

That uses the UNIX *head* command to read the first ten lines of the message. (If your system doesn't have *head*, use `/bin/sed 10q` instead.) A flexible program like *awk* or *perl* can do more with your message.

There are problems, though. If a terminal you're logged onto is running a full-screen application that puts the terminal in *raw mode*, the *rcvtty* output can:

```
jump down
          the screen
                    like this
```

Also, if your cursor is in the middle of a screen of text, the message from *rcvtty* can be hard to see because it's buried in the text:

```
jump downfh jlasfujarlh aelr uhgwp9t th p4yr hy49r5 y4ht wlth
sdajflfja8the screeneasjfau eworu wepr d;9f ua4 aw4; hfuha4e;
fdsa;fjw03pu 4hhertjjlike thisasdf;jasf0aura 0;o3u54t 9fh04o2
```

(Can you find the words?) The *rcvtty.fixup* shell script helps. You tell *rcvtty* to run the *rcvtty.fixup* shell script; tell *rcvtty.fixup* to run the command you really want to run. *rcvtty.fixup* will give the message from *rcvtty* to your command, and it will filter the output of your command this way:

• Add a carriage return character to the end of each line of output.

• Add a carriage return before the first line output; this makes the first line start at the left margin instead of the cursor position.

• Replace empty lines with 70 space characters. That keeps empty lines of the message from being filled with the existing text on the screen.

Here's how to run the *head* command via *rcvtty.fixup*:

```
*    -    ^    R    "/x/y/rcvtty /x/y/rcvtty.fixup /x/y/head"
```

If your system can't directly execute files that start with `#!`, as Section 12.4 explains, add `/bin/sh` before `/x/y/rcvtty.fixup`.

Here's the *rcvtty.fixup* script. If you haven't installed a shell script before, see Section 12.2, "Writing a Simple Shell Program."

```
#! /bin/sh
# $Id: rcvtty.fixup,v 1.1 92/07/31 08:09:24 jerry book2 $
### rcvtty.fixup - fix rcvtty output for raw-mode ttys
### Usage: rcvtty rcvtty.fixup command [command-args]

# MAKE CR (OCTAL 015) CHARACTER PORTABLY:
cr="`echo x | tr x '\015'`"
# WHITESPACE TO REPLACE EMPTY LINES AND MAKE THEM MORE VISIBLE:
spaces="                                                    "

# RUN COMMAND AND ARGUMENTS, PIPE TO sed FOR CLEANUP AND OUTPUT TO tty:
"$@" |
sed -e "s/^[     ]*\$/$spaces/" -e "1s/^/$cr/" -e "s/\$/$cr/"

exit    # RETURN EXIT STATUS OF COMMAND TO rcvtty
```

11.6   Storing Messages in Folders: rcvstore

The *rcvstore* program will store a message in an MH folder. (It's handy from a shell prompt, too; see below.) You can use *rcvstore* to presort some or all of your incoming messages by the person or mailing list they come from, by certain words in the Subject:, and so on. Give the folder name (only one folder at a time) on the *rcvstore* command line. For example, if you're on your system's *managers* alias and you want to save all messages sent to *managers* in your *read_now* folder:

```
to    managers    ^    A    "/x/y/rcvstore +read_now"
```

Of course, if you use an R result instead of the A, a copy of the message will be put in the folder but it won't be marked "delivered"—so the message can also be delivered by other *.maildelivery* lines.

By default, if you give *rcvstore* a folder name that doesn't exist, it will create the folder. With the *–nocreate* switch, if a folder doesn't exist, *rcvstore* will exit without storing the message.

When *rcvstore* puts a message in a folder, it can also add the message to an MH sequence (see Section 7.3). You might have all your messages dropped into *inbox* folder automatically—but added to different sequences, depending on some rules you choose. Here's an example. The first two lines below store messages sent to *managers* or from *cert* into the *inbox* folder and its *readnow* sequence. The third line stores messages with a subject that includes "status report" into *inbox* and its *reports* sequence:

```
to,managers,^,A,"/x/y/rcvstore +inbox -seq readnow"
from,cert,^,A,"/x/y/rcvstore +inbox -seq readnow"
subject,"status report",^,A,"/x/y/rcvstore +inbox -seq reports"
```

Remember that a folder can't have more than ten sequences.

The *rcvstore* command is useful for copying any message file into a MH folder quickly. Just pipe or redirect the file to *rcvstore*'s standard input. For example, USENET news articles are in the same format as mail messages. When I read a message I want to save in my *src* folder, I can do it with *rcvstore* at an *rn* prompt:

```
End of article 89 (of 99)--what next? [npq] |rcvstore +src
```

(I don't have to type the full pathname, like */usr/local/lib/mh/rcvstore* , because I've added that directory to my shell's search path. Section 12.3.4 explains search paths.)

11.7 Redistributing Messages: rcvdist

If you receive messages that should be sent to other people, use *rcvdist*. It does the same thing as the MH *dist* command (Section 6.9). *rcvdist* adds a Resent- . . . : header, with one or more new addresses, to the message—then resends the message. Here are some ways to use *rcvdist*:

- While you're out of your office, reroute some messages to other people. Or maybe you're training someone else to do your job and you'd like them to get duplicates of some of your mail. (To route *all* of your mail to someone else, put that person's address in your *forward* file—if your system supports *forward*, that is.)

- If you get messages that are sent regularly or automatically, and you'd like other people (coworkers, subordinates, or anyone) to see those messages too, use *rcvdist* to do it automatically.

- Maybe you're on a mailing list that's sent from a distant computer site, and other people in your company would like copies of the messages, too. The long-distance network might be used more efficiently if the mailing list messages are sent only to you—then you run *rcvdist* to redistribute the messages to people on other computers in your company. (If you aren't sure, your system's postmaster can help you decide.)

11.7.1   Running rcvdist from .maildelivery

To run *rcvdist* from your *.maildelivery* file, give the address or addresses as arguments. For example, to redistribute *mh-users-request* mail (see Section 11.2.1) to *lisa* and *ed@foo.com*, use:

```
source mh-users-request ^ R "/x/y/rcvdist lisa ed@foo.com"
```

Try not to use any spaces within an address. If you have to do it, remember to put escaped double quotes (\ ") around that address:

```
from root ^ R "/x/y/rcvdist \"The Guru <om@mt.top.com>\""
```

Unless you need to use the *pipe* or | action, it's much better to use the *qpipe* or ^ action. That way, if your addresses are single words with no space in them, you won't have to worry about shell quoting. For instance, the line below works fine with *qpipe* (^)—but it doesn't work with *pipe* (|) because the shell would interpret < and > as redirection characters:

```
to managers ^ R "/x/y/rcvdist <jane> <al@fbar.com>"
```

If you have to use special characters and the *pipe* or | action, protect the addresses with single quotes (') or escaped double quotes (\ "). For more information about quoting, see Section 12.6.

11.7.2   Automatic Folder Copies

By default, *rcvdist* adds the following line to the message header before resending it:

```
Resent-Fcc: outbox
```

That line drops a copy of the redistributed message into your folder named *outbox*. (See Section 6.4.1.) You don't have an *outbox* folder, you say? You will after you run *rcvdist*.

The folder copy is made by the default *rcvdistcomps* file. Your system administrator may have modified *rcvdistcomps*, so things may be different on your system. If you want folder copies to go to another folder, or no folder copies at all, you can make your own *rcvdistcomps* file. See Section 10.2.11.

Every so often, you might remove old folder copies made by *rcvdist*. One way to do that automatically is by modifying the *rm_msgs* scripts in Section 13.6.3 through Section 13.6.5. The scripts could clean up your *outbox* folder as well as the *DELETE* folders they're designed for.

Part III
Customizing MH

11.7.3 Watch Out for Mail Loops

When you redistribute a message to another address, make sure that address won't send the same message back to you. If it does, then *rcvdist* could start an infinite loop.

For example, let's say you're one of the people on the system alias called *managers*. You want to reroute all status reports to the other managers automatically. *Don't* do it this way:

```
subject "status report" ^ R "/x/y/rcvdist managers"
```

Unless your system mailer is smart enough to catch problems like this, *rcvdist* will send your message to *managers*, that alias will route the message back to you, *rcvdist* will send it to *managers* again, and so on ... (If a loop starts, you can stop it pronto by editing your *.maildelivery* file and adding a hash mark (#) at the start of the line with the *rcvdist*.)

The best fix is to replace `managers` in that *rcvdist* command line with all the managers' addresses except yours. But that can fix be tough to do if the members of *managers* change often—or if the alias is on another computer and you can't find out what addresses are on it.

A workaround: make your own *rcvdistcomps* file (you might name it *rcvdistcomps.noloop*)—see Section 10.2.11. Write the file to add a special comment header to the message *rcvdist* resends:

```
Resent-comments: noloop
```

(There's nothing special about the word `noloop`; you can use any word.) Next, in your *.maildelivery* file, on the line *before rcvdist*, add a line that will *destroy* messages with that special header. Be sure that the *rcvdist* line uses the ? (question mark) action so it won't be executed if the previous *destroy* succeeds:

```
resent-comments,noloop,destroy,A,-
subject,"status report",^,?,"/x/y/rcvdist
                    -form rcvdistcomps.noloop managers"
```

(The second line above was broken to fit across the page.) How does it work? The first time a status report comes in, *rcvdist* will add your new `Resent-comments: noloop` header and send the message to *managers*. When the message comes back from *managers* to you, though, *.maildelivery* will match that special header—and destroy the message before *rcvdist* can send it again.

A dirty fix? Maybe. But, at least, it's a good demonstration of how these *mhook* utilities can be combined.

11.8 Saving Messages in Mailbox Files: rcvpack

The *rcvpack* program isn't used very much. The *file* or > action does the same thing more efficiently. For example, both of these lines append the message to a file named *autoproc.log* in the home directory:

```
From  autoproc  >  R  autoproc.log
From  autoproc  ^  R  "/x/y/rcvpack autoproc.log"
```

rcvpack is useful on systems with the *sendmail* MTA if users want to run *msh* (Section 7.11.2) on new mail. On those systems, the *file* or > action is usually set to write mailboxes in UUCP format. But *rcvpack* always uses MMDF format; that's what *msh* needs.

11.9 Alternatives to mhook Programs

Some systems with MH can't use the *mhook* utilities because the MTA doesn't support them, because the MTA runs on another computer, and so on. You may want your mail processed in batches, late at night.

Besides, the *.maildelivery* file and *mhook* programs can't do everything:

- How about printing some or all messages automatically—especially for users (managers, maybe, or their secretaries) who want to get their messages on paper?

- Wouldn't it be nice to have UNIX regular expression matching of message headers and bodies—instead of the case-insensitive substring matches you get in *.maildelivery*?

- Maybe you need to process incoming mail quickly but interactively, so you have a choice about what's done with each message.

- Do you want to be notified about important mail with pop-up windows or big notices—not just the 80 characters that *rcvtty* sends?

- You might want to process incoming mail in a batch, automatically, once a day or once a week. That can be more efficient than running a handler for each new message. It can also let you make decisions about the whole group of messages.

I hope that gives you an idea of what's possible. You can replace part or all of the *mhook* utilities with utilities that you develop or get from someone else. This chapter explains the basic concepts and shows a few examples. For more about shell programming and using MH utilities like *scan* in your programs, see Chapter 12, *Introduction to Shell Programming for MH*, and Chapter 13, *MH Shell Programs*. With shell programming, as well as utilities like *awk** and *perl*,† you can develop your own ways of handling mail automatically.

11.9.1 Replacing All of Your .maildelivery

You may not need to use the *.maildelivery* file at all. Your system's MTA may be able to start a program of yours for each new message you get. I think it's safer (for beginners, at least) *not* to do this. If your handler fails, your mail could bounce. Instead, run your mail handler from the *.maildelivery* file, as Section 11.9.3 explains. But that's your choice, not mine!

How to Set Up

If your system uses the popular *sendmail* or *smail* MTAs, you can probably start your own mail-handling program by putting its pathname in your *.forward* file. For example, this line in my *.forward* file will start the program */u/jerry/bin/inmail*:

```
"| /u/jerry/bin/inmail"
```

If your system handles executable files that start with # ! (see Section 12.4), you can probably execute shell scripts that way by just giving the script's name. Otherwise, start scripts by giving the pathname to the interpreter—for example:

```
"| /bin/sh /u/jerry/bin/inmail"
```

The MTA will start the program and feed the incoming message to the program's standard input. When the program finishes and returns a zero exit status, the message will have been delivered.

---

*See the Nutshell Handbook *sed & awk*, by Dale Dougherty.

†See the Nutshell Handbook *Programming Perl*, by Larry Wall and Randal Schwartz.

Gotchas: UID, GID, Permissions . . .

If your mail handler is run directly by the system MTA, you can run into some tough problems making it work correctly. On our Sun with SunOS 4.1, for instance, the *sendmail* MTA will run a private mail handler in several ways:

- If I send mail to myself, the mail handler runs as me (*jerry*) with all my groups set, with all my current environment variables set, and so on.

- If another user on the same computer sends mail, the handler runs as *jerry* but with the environment of the other user. So any files the handler creates will be owned by me (*jerry*).

- If the mail comes in from the Internet or by UUCP, the handler runs as *jerry* and creates files owned by me. But the *USER* and *LOGNAME* environment variables are set to values like *uremote* or *daemon*; the home directory to, for instance, */var/spool/uucppublic*; and so on.

So, running your handler this way may mean some careful programming. You might run your handler as Section 11.9.3 shows (a safer but maybe less efficient way to do it). To find out more about the environment set in your handler, start with a Bourne shell script like the one in Example 11-2. It stores the incoming message in one temporary file. It also opens a temporary log file. The log file stores the verbose output from the shell and the output of two commands that help you see the environment while the handler runs. Both files are created in */tmp*; you can list them with *ls –l* to see what permissions and ownership your handler will give files it creates.

Example 11-2. Mail handler for debugging

```
#! /bin/sh
exec > /tmp/inmail$$.log 2>&1      # Send all output to log file
set -xv      # Make shell show debugging output
/bin/id      # On BSD systems, use "whoami" and "groups" instead
/bin/env     # On BSD systems, use "printenv" instead
/bin/cat > /tmp/inmail$$.stdin   # Grab incoming message
exit 0       # Important to set a zero status if handler succeeds
```

Part III
Customizing MH

289

11.9.2 The vacation Mail Handler

Many UNIX systems come with the Berkeley *vacation* program. It's designed to run from a *.forward* file, sending automatic replies when you're away from the office. When I run it, my *.forward* file looks like this:

```
\jerry, "| /usr/ucb/vacation jerry"
```

If you just want to acknowledge incoming mail or send a standard reply, *vacation* can be a good way to do it. The details about the format of the reply, as well as who will get replies and how often, should be in your online *vacation*(1) manual page.

11.9.3 Running Your Mail Handler from .maildelivery

Do you want to have all incoming messages processed by your own mail handler? It's probably safer to run your handler from a line in a *.maildelivery* file than to have the MTA run your handler directly as Section 11.9.1 shows. (On some systems, you don't even have a choice!) That's because, if no line in your *.maildelivery* file delivers a message, the system defaults will be used; you'll still get the message and it won't "bounce back" to the sender. Also, when your MTA delivers a message through *.maildelivery*, the environment doesn't have the inconsistencies listed at the end of Section 11.9.1.

Setting Up

To feed all of your mail to your handler, put a line in your *.maildelivery* file like one of the three below. Use the first line if your handler can be executed directly. The second line runs *awk*; the third runs a Bourne shell:

```
*   -   ^   A   /u/jerry/bin/inmail
*   -   ^   A   "/usr/bin/awk -f /u/jerry/bin/inmail"
*   -   |   A   ". /u/jerry/bin/inmail"
```

Of course, you can use fields besides * to control what messages are passed to your handler—and results besides A to control what other lines in *.maildelivery* are executed.

The exit status that your handler returns is important. If your handler returns a nonzero status, *.maildelivery* will act as if that the handler failed. Try to make your handler set a zero status when it succeeds. (Section 12.8 explains exit status. Section 12.11 shows how to set it in shell scripts.)

Printing Incoming Mail

You can print incoming mail from *.maildelivery*. For instance, the following line would print all messages sent to the *company-standards* address. As always, the R means that messages won't be marked "delivered" when they're printed:

```
to   company-standards   ^   R   "/usr/ucb/lpr -Plaser"
```

The print job may come out with a banner page that says it was printed by *daemon* or some other user you wouldn't expect. See the part of Section 11.9.1 called "Gotchas: UID, GID, Permissions . . . "

11.9.4 Replacing rcvtty with Pop-Up Windows

If you use a window system like X, *rcvtty* will tell you about new mail in a window where you're logged in. That window might be buried behind other windows, iconified, or full of other text when important mail comes in. Will you see the notice? This script, *rcvxterm*, makes sure that you will. It's designed for the X Window System, but it should be easy to adapt for other window systems.

If you don't need a pop-up window, you might look at the script. It uses a technique for running programs from *.maildelivery* that's good to know.

The script should probably be run only for important mail. It opens a red *xterm* (X terminal emulator) window in the top-right corner of an X display. The title bar will say (depending on your window manager):

Important mail. Press q to quit.

There'll be a copy of the mail message inside the window, shown by a pager program like *less* or *pg*.* The script is simple on purpose: to make it easy to customize for your window system, and to make it easy to understand. The environment inside your *.maildelivery* file has almost no information about where you're logged on. So, I hard-coded most of the information into the script. If you need help understanding the script, see Chapter 12, *Introduction to Shell Programming for MH*, or a good shell programming book. To run it, put a line like the one below in your *.maildelivery* file. (If your system can directly execute files that start with # !, as Section 12.4 explains, you can omit the /bin/sh.)

```
From  root  |  R  "/bin/cat >/tmp/m$$; /bin/sh /x/y/rcvxterm /tmp/m$$ &"
```

The script reads a file named on its command line. It could read its standard input, the message from the *.maildelivery* file. But actions in *.maildelivery* that

---

*To keep the window from closing too soon, the pager program can't exit until you select the window and type a command like *q*. The *more* pager quits at the end of the file, so it won't do.

don't finish after a reasonable amount of time are killed automatically. To be sure your window stays there, and to avoid blocking other actions in *.maildelivery*, run *rcvxterm* in the background as shown above. Use *cat* to copy the message into a temporary file.* The script is below. If you haven't installed a shell script before, there's help in Section 12.2, "Writing a Simple Shell Program."

```
#! /bin/sh
# $Id: rcvxterm,v 1.2.1.2 92/08/02 18:19:27 jerry book2 $
### rcvxterm - HACK script to notify you about new mail
### Usage in .maildelivery: "/bin/cat >/tmp/m$$; /x/y/rcvxterm /tmp/m$$ &"


trap '/bin/rm -f $1' 0 1 2 15    # REMOVE TEMP FILE BEFORE EXITING

# USE less BECAUSE IT DOESN'T QUIT UNTIL YOU TYPE q.  pg WORKS, TOO.
# USE FULL PATHS; REMEMBER THAT .maildelivery ENVIRONMENT IS LIMITED.
/usr/bin/X11/xterm -display hostname:0.0 \
    -geometry 80x24-0+0 -bg red -fg white \
    -title "important mail.  Press q to quit" \
    -ut -e /usr/local/bin/less $1
```

11.9.5 Processing with at or cron or by Hand

Instead of running your handler separately each time a new message comes in, it can be better to run a separate handler periodically. On systems where you can't run a handler for each new message, this is your only choice!

A handler can read your system mailbox file directly, usually with *inc*. I think it's easier to do that, splitting your messages into a folder—then have my handler run MH programs like *scan* and *pick* to handle the messages.

Most handlers are probably shell or *perl* scripts. A script can be run by hand when you type its name at a shell prompt, or your computer can run it automatically with *at* or *cron*. One automatic handler is the *autoinc* shell script in Section 13.14.

After you write a script like *autoinc*, add a line to your personal *crontab* file or start an *at* job to run your script whenever you want. It's probably a good idea to run it late at night, if you can. The load on the system might be less then. Also, and more important, there's less chance of the handler being executed while you're logged on and might be reading mail—it could change your current folder

---

*During *.maildelivery*, your *umask* is set at 077. That keeps other users from reading the temporary file.

and current message while you weren't expecting it.* If you haven't run *crontab* or *at* before, there are examples in Sections 13.6.3 through 13.6.5.

11.10 Practical Tips

This section has some tips and tricks to help make your *.maildelivery* setup better.

11.10.1 Finding Mail from Mailing Lists

A lot of mailing lists put one of these headers in their messages:

```
Precedence: bulk
Precedence: junk
```

You can catch that mail with lines like this:

```
precedence,bulk,|,A,"/x/y/rcvstore +later -seq bulkmail"
precedence,junk,|,A,"/x/y/rcvstore +later -seq bulkmail"
```

The messages will be automatically filed into the *later* folder and added to the *bulkmail* sequence in that folder.

11.10.2 Handing Periodic Mail

Do you get a certain message regularly or automatically that you want to be sure your *.maildelivery* file identifies correctly? The best answer, if it's possible, is to put a unique header in the message. (Section 8.9 shows how to do that in MH.) For example, if the message header has:

```
     ...
To: jerry
X-auto-m-p: monthly report
```

Your *.maildelivery* file could match that message reliably with the line:

```
x-auto-m-p  "monthly report"  ^  R  "/x/y/rcvpack reports"
```

---

*Though you can avoid that by making the handler use a different MH profile, context, and sequences file. The *rmmer* script in Section 13.6 uses most of those tricks.

If special headers are out of the question, special words or characters in the `To:` or `Subject:` header can do it. For example, this message header has a comment (in parentheses):

```
To: ajones, jerry@ora.com (Jerry-report-archiver), bsmith, ...
```

The mail will be delivered to *jerry@ora.com*. The comment will come along with the address and be matched in this *.maildelivery* line:

```
to  jerry-report-archiver  ^  R  "/x/y/rcvpack reports"
```

11.10.3 Think About cc:, Resent–To:, ...

Mail can come to you via the headers `To:`, `cc:`, `Resent-To:`, `Apparently-To:`, and more. If it's important to know exactly what address was used—for instance, if you can get mail through several system aliases (as shown in Section 11.10.4)—then you should consider testing all of those headers and more in your *.maildelivery* file:

```
# store book questions to handle later:
to          bookquestions        ^  A  "/x/y/rcvstore +bookq"
cc          bookquestions        ^  A  "/x/y/rcvstore +bookq"
resent-to   bookquestions        ^  A  "/x/y/rcvstore +bookq"
# process book-info subscriptions:
to          book-info-request    |  A  "/u/jerry/bin/book-info-proc"
cc          book-info-request    |  A  "/u/jerry/bin/book-info-proc"
resent-to   book-info-request    |  A  "/u/jerry/bin/book-info-proc"
    ...
```

If you don't care what address was used, it's much easier to use an `*` (asterisk) or `default`:

```
    ...
# put everything else in my $HOME/.mailbox file:
default   -   >   ?   .mailbox
```

11.10.4 System Aliases, the to and addr Fields

If your name is listed in the system mail alias file, people can send you mail without addressing it to your username. On most systems, that alias name stays in the message header, so you can test for it in your *.maildelivery* file.

For example, here are some of the system aliases I'm on at *ora.com*:

```
Jerry.Peek:     jerry
bookquestions: jerry, eric
authors:        ..., jerry, ...
```

If someone sends mail to *Jerry.Peek*, *bookquestions*, or *authors*, it'll be delivered to my *jerry* mailbox. I can separate that mail with *.maildelivery* lines like these:

```
to       bookquestions ^  A  "/x/y/rcvdist jerry@somewhere.ca"
default -               >  ?  /usr/spool/mail/jerry
```

The first line would resend all *bookquestions* mail to *jerry@somewhere.ca*, but leave the rest of the mail in my system mailbox.

If I wanted to resend all my mail (to *bookquestions*, *Jerry.Peek*, *authors*, or plain *jerry*), a line like this would *not* do it:

```
to    jerry ^ A  "/x/y/rcvdist jerry@somewhere.ca"
```

Instead, to match all mail sent to my mailbox, no matter what alias, I'd use the `addr` field (or just a `default` or `*`):

```
addr  jerry ^ A  "/x/y/rcvdist jerry@somewhere.ca"
```

(Of course, an easier way to forward all my mail is by putting *jerry@some-where.ca* in my *.forward* file. But this `addr` example applies to any command, not just resending with *rcvdist*.)

11.10.5 Flagging Important Mail

If you can't read all your mail for some reason—you're out of your office, unusually busy, or whatever—you can ask people who send you important messages to mark them "urgent." Your *.maildelivery* file can catch those messages and handle them specially: forward them to you on the road, use *rcvtty* to alert you, print them on your secretary's printer (the part of Section 11.9.3 called "Printing Incoming Mail"), or whatever.

For instance, tell people to put the word "urgent" somewhere in the `Subject:` of your important mail. This line in *.maildelivery* will find those messages:

```
subject  urgent  ^  R  "/x/y/rcvdist jerry@somewhere.ca"
```

11.10.6 Making Your Mail Follow You

If you're on the road, you don't have to give people a list of the e-mail addresses where they can find you on certain days. Tell them to send to your normal address; let your *.maildelivery* file send the important mail (with *rcvdist*) to wherever you are. Each time you move, you or someone in your office can edit your *.maildelivery* file to forward mail to your new location. Your *.maildelivery* file can be set to forward only some of your mail; the rest can stay in your system mailbox or be forwarded to someone else.

11.10.7 Splitting Mail to Several Places

Example 11-3 is a *.maildelivery* file that I worked out for a friend. It has a combination of ideas for splitting messages into a few places automatically. I've split the long lines onto several lines; you should type them all together.

Example 11-3. .maildelivery that routes to several places

```
# Route all mail from Jim Shankland or Laura Enz to +wordy folder;
# also tell Mark about them so he can check when he has time:
from,shank@foo.com,|,R,
    "/bin/echo \"Mail ($(size) characters!) from Jim Shankland.\" |
    /bin/mail markw"
from,shank@foo.com,^,A,"/x/y/rcvstore +wordy"
from,enz@usnd.edu,|,R,
    "/bin/echo \"Mail ($(size) characters!) from Laura Enz.\" |
    /bin/mail markw"
from,enz@usnd.edu,^,A,"/x/y/rcvstore +wordy"
# Send first 200 lines of undelivered mail to roady.
# Don't mark it delivered, so it'll also go to lines below:
default,-,|,R,
    "/x/y/mhl -form roady.mhl -nomoreproc |
    /bin/sed -e 200q |
    /x/y/rcvdist rhonda@roady.rspx.com"
# Send complete copy of all undelivered mail to my system mailbox:
default,-,>,?,/usr/mail/rhonda
```

That long *rcvdist* pipeline above is interesting. It filters mail sent to the *roady* computer (a laptop PC with dialup UUCP used to get mail from wherever she's traveling around the world) to make sure that no very long messages waste modem time on international long-distance—or fill up her disk. (All messages are copied, full length, to her system mailbox.) First in the pipe is *mhl* with a filter file that strips out headers she won't need on the road. Example 11-4 shows the *roady.mhl* file in her MH directory. Next, *sed* truncates any message more than 200 lines long. Finally, *rcvdist* sends what's left to her UUCP address.

Because the *rcvdist* pipeline uses the `default` field, it won't send messages from the long-winded people. The *rcvdist* line uses the R result, so it will always send undelivered messages to *roady*. But the last line uses the ? (question mark) result, so the only messages written to her system mailbox will be the ones that weren't already filed in the *wordy* folder.

Example 11-4. roady.mhl file filters junk before distributing mail

```
width=10000
ignores=received,mmdf-warning,x-face
Date:
From:
To:
cc:
Subject:
extras:nocomponent
:
body:nocomponent
```

11.11 Debugging Tips

If your mail-handling setup doesn't seem to work, read these sections.

The first thing to do is to look through the instructions for setting up your *.maildelivery* file (Sections 11.1 and 11.2) and executing it (Section 11.3). Look for:

- Missing arguments.

- Extra or missing double quotes (").

- Double quotes that should be escaped (\ ").

- Spaces or commas that should be inside double quotes.

Display or print a few messages. Follow them through *.maildelivery* in your mind. Make sure you understand what conditions each message should match and how each condition is related to others. Section 11.11.1 can help here; it has more about the way that *slocal* reads your *.maildelivery* file.

The debugging in *slocal* is pretty lousy. A lot can go wrong that the debugging won't tell you about; for example, *slocal* can silently skip an error without printing anything (Section 11.11.3 explains that). There are some helpful debugging tips here.

NOTE

Many of these sections below apply to the *slocal* program that runs your *.maildelivery* file on many systems. If your system doesn't use *slocal*, the tips in Section 11.11.5 should still be helpful—others may help, too.

11.11.1 slocal Documentation vs. Real Life

If I were going to write the *slocal* program from scratch, I'd try to make it work more predictably. Even after I sat down to read the source code (it's in the file *uip/slocal.c*, by the way), I still had questions about what would happen in some cases.

If you're having trouble with your *.maildelivery* file, try comparing it to the list below. It tells what *slocal* does, step by step, as it reads a line in *.maildelivery*. If that doesn't help, look at the source code yourself or call Rent-a-Guru : -) . The *usr_delivery( )* function parses the lines in *.maildelivery*.

First, when *slocal* reads a line of *.maildelivery*, it checks a list of conditions that make it skip the line. The line will be skipped if:

1. It's a comment or it has less than five arguments.

2. It has an *N* result and the previous line with a field other than * (asterisk) did not match.

3. It has a *?* result and the message has been delivered by any previous line.

4. It has the undocumented `select` arguments 6-8 and these tell *slocal* to skip the message. (See Section 11.2.6.)

5. It has a `default` field (first argument) and some previous line has delivered the message.

6. It has a field (first argument) with a message header named (but not an *, asterisk)—and no header in the message matches that field.

7. It has an invalid action argument.

If the message isn't skipped by any of the tests in the list above, *slocal* will try to perform the action. The message will be marked "delivered" if the action succeeds, unless the result was *R*.

11.11.2 Catching slocal Errors

When you run a program from your terminal—usually by typing its name at a shell prompt—the process has a "controlling tty": your terminal. The standard input, standard output, and standard error of the process usually come to your terminal unless they're redirected.

When *sendmail* runs a program like *slocal*, the process doesn't have a controlling tty. (That is, the TTY column in the *ps* output has a ? character.) Errors won't come to your terminal.

To see errors from *slocal*, you can run it by hand. Or, if you can't reproduce the errors running *slocal* by hand, grab the *stdout* and *stderr* before they're "thrown away." The following two sections show how.

Even with those tips, you still won't see any output from the individual programs in *.maildelivery*. Section 11.11.4 shows how to handle that.

Running slocal by Hand

Example 11-6, in the next section, shows a long chunk of *slocal* debugging output. It's made automatically, by a setup in the *.forward* file, for every new message that comes in.

For most *.maildelivery* debugging, that's more than you need. You want to send a test message through the *.maildelivery* file and watch what happens. Example 11-5 shows the steps. To do that, first store a test message in a file. If you use *mhl* to show your messages, give *–noshowproc* to bypass *mhl* when you store the message. You can edit the test message if you want to change some address in the header (or any other part of the header). Then, run *slocal* with its *–verbose* switch; give the message to *slocal*'s standard input:

Example 11-5. Running slocal -verbose interactively

```
% show -noshowproc > testmsg
% vi testmsg
% /usr/local/lib/mh/slocal -verbose -user jerry < testmsg
    delivering to pipe "/usr/local/lib/mh/rcvstore +DELETE", wins.
    delivering to pipe "/usr/local/lib/mh/rcvtty"
17:43:   307 Jerry Peek      testing slocal<<test test
, wins.
    delivering to file "/usr/spool/mail/jerry"
slocal: /usr/spool/mail/.jerry.map:
pointer mismatch or incomplete index (67054!=1920524), continuing...
, done.
```

That example is choppy—the output was broken up by the line from *rcvtty* and the error message near the end. The *–verbose* switch prints the lines that start with `delivering to . . . .` If I'd used *–debug*, I'd have seen *slocal* parse the message and the *.maildelivery* file (Example 11-6 shows that).

First, *slocal* delivers a copy of the message to my backup *DELETE* directory (I use it for debugging). As *slocal* starts the program, you can see the pause until `,wins.` is printed to show that the program returned a zero ("true") exit status. Next, *slocal* runs *rcvtty*; you can see the *rcvtty.format* output on my screen before *slocal* prints the verbose `,wins..` Finally, *slocal* tried to deliver to my system mailbox. I saw what I needed: an error from *slocal*, caused by a bug in MH 6.7.2.* Because of the error, *slocal* delivered the message another way (see the footnote); it printed `,done.` when it had delivered the message to the file.

Save slocal Debugging Output with Real Messages

When you run *slocal* and a *.maildelivery* file, it can be hard to see what's happening if something goes wrong in "real time" as a message is being delivered. If an individual command in your *.maildelivery* file prints error (or other) messages, you won't see them because *slocal* throws away that output. It's especially important to see "real time" output for errors that happen intermittently, that you can't reproduce by hand—like the error at the end of Example 11-5, errors when the filesystem fills up, and so on.

Here are some tricks with the Bourne shell to work around those problems. The basic idea: instead of running *slocal*, *rcvstore*, and other programs directly, run a Bourne shell. Have the shell execute *slocal* or whatever program you want to debug. Use the shell command `exec 2>>logfile` to make the shell append its standard error to a log file. To see the program's output, read the log file. I'll start with an example using *slocal*.

The usual way to start *slocal*, with debugging, is by a line like this in your *.forward* file:

```
"| /x/y/slocal -debug -verbose -user jerry"
```

---

*When the MH 6.7.2 *slocal* appends to a system maildrop in UUCP format (with the `[RPATHS]` configuration option), it can fail once in a while. Then it defaults to the MMDF format. It also leaves a file named *.yourname.map* in the */usr/spool/mail* directory. That's supposed to be fixed in the next version of MH.

Instead, use a line like the one below. This is shown broken onto two lines; you should type it on one line:

```
"| /bin/sh -c 'exec >>/tmp/sllog.jerry 2>&1;
    /x/y/slocal -debug -verbose -user jerry'"
```

That appends the standard output and standard error from *slocal* into the file */tmp/sllog.jerry*. (*/tmp* is a system temporary-file directory. */tmp* is a good place for files like these because it's world-writable, also because files in */tmp* are erased periodically and during reboots.)

Example 11-6 shows the contents of my *sllog.jerry* file after I got a message from a friend in Germany. First, here's the *.maildelivery* file I was using:

```
# toss anything from uucp (save for a few days, in case):
From    uucp  | A   "/usr/local/lib/mh/rcvstore +DELETE"
# put other stuff into mailbox
default  -    > ?  /usr/spool/mail/jerry
# always run rcvtty
*        -    | R   "/usr/local/lib/mh/rcvtty -nobell"
```

And the header of the message I got:

```
From martinek@agpsa.de  Sun Jun 28 18:32:31 1992
Delivery-Date: Sun, 28 Jun 92 10:47:00 -0400
Return-Path: <martinek@agpsa.de>
Received: from mail.Germany.EU.net by ora.com (5.65c/Spike-2.1)
     id AA08683; Sun, 28 Jun 1992 10:46:52 -0400
Received: from apgwdf
    by mail.Germany.EU.net with UUCP (5.65+/UNIDO-2.1.0.b)
    via EUnet for ora.com
    id AA08647; Sun, 28 Jun 92 16:48:00 +0200
Received: from is0001 by agpsa.de (5.52.1/APG-1.1)
    id AA21195; Sun, 28 Jun 92 15:26:58  +0100
    for ora.com!jerry
Received: from localhost by is0001 (AIX 3.1/UCB 5.61/4.03)
        id AA56358; Sun, 28 Jun 92 16:32:32 +0200
      for jerry@ora.com
Message-Id: <9206281432.AA56358@is0001>
To: Jerry Peek <jerry@ora.com>
Phone: +49 6239-000000  Home: +49 6241-000000
Subject: Re: your book
In-Reply-To: Jerry Peek's message of Fri, 26 Jun 92 14:42:35 -0400
          <13386.709584155@babble.ora.com>
Reply-To: Hans Martinek <martinek@agpsa.de>
Date: Sun, 28 Jun 92 16:32:31 +0200
From: Hans Martinek <martinek@agpsa.de>
```

In Example 11-6 any line that doesn't start with a line number is a continuation of
the line above; we split it to fit the book page.

Example 11-6. Sample slocal –debug –verbose output

```
 1> temporary file "/tmp/slocala08688" selected
 2> addr="jerry" user="jerry" info="" file="/tmp/slocala08688"
 3> sender="martinek@agpsa.de" mbox="/usr/spool/mail/jerry"
    home="/home/jerry" from="From martinek@agpsa.de  Sun Jun 28 18:32:31 1992
 4> "
 5> ddate="Delivery-Date: Sun, 28 Jun 92 10:47:00 -0400
 6> " now=10:47
 7> vec[0]: "From"
 8> vec[1]: "uucp"
 9> vec[2]: "|"
10> vec[3]: "A"
11> vec[4]: "/usr/local/lib/mh/rcvstore +DELETE"
12> vars[3]: name="reply-to" value=" Hans Martinek <martinek@agpsa.de>
13> "
14> hdrs[0]: name="source" value="martinek@agpsa.de"
15> hdrs[1]: name="addr" value="jerry"
16> hdrs[2]: name="Return-Path" value=" <martinek@agpsa.de>
17> "
18> hdrs[3]: name="Reply-To" value=" Hans Martinek <martinek@agpsa.de>
19> "
20> hdrs[4]: name="From" value=" Hans Martinek <martinek@agpsa.de>
21> "
22> hdrs[5]: name="Sender" value="(null)"
23> hdrs[6]: name="To" value=" Jerry Peek <jerry@ora.com>
24> "
25> hdrs[7]: name="cc" value="(null)"
26> hdrs[8]: name="Resent-Reply-To" value="(null)"
27> hdrs[9]: name="Resent-From" value="(null)"
28> hdrs[10]: name="Resent-Sender" value="(null)"
29> hdrs[11]: name="Resent-To" value="(null)"
30> hdrs[12]: name="Resent-cc" value="(null)"
31> hdrs[13]: name="Received" value=" from mail.Germany.EU.net by ora.com
    (5.65c/Spike-2.1)
32>     id AA08683; Sun, 28 Jun 1992 10:46:52 -0400
33>      from apgwdf
34>     by mail.Germany.EU.net with UUCP (5.65+/UNIDO-2.1.0.b)
35>     via EUnet for ora.com
36>     id AA08647; Sun, 28 Jun 92 16:48:00 +0200
37>      from is0001 by agpsa.de (5.52.1/APG-1.1)
38>     id AA21195; Sun, 28 Jun 92 15:26:58  +0100
39>     for ora.com!jerry
40>      from localhost by is0001 (AIX 3.1/UCB 5.61/4.03)
41>         id AA56358; Sun, 28 Jun 92 16:32:32 +0200
42>       for jerry@ora.com
43> "
44> hdrs[14]: name="Message-Id" value=" <9206281432.AA56358@is0001>
```

Example 11-6. Sample slocal –debug –verbose output (continued)

```
45> "
46> hdrs[15]: name="Phone" value=" +49 6239-000000  Home: +49 6241-000000
47> "
48> hdrs[16]: name="Subject" value=" Re: your book
49> "
50> hdrs[17]: name="In-Reply-To" value=" Jerry Peek's message of Fri, 26 Jun
       92 14:42:35 -0400
51>                <13386.709584155@babble.ora.com>
52> "
53> hdrs[18]: name="Date" value=" Sun, 28 Jun 92 16:32:31 +0200
54> "
55> vec[0]: "default"
56> vec[1]: "-"
57> vec[2]: ">"
58> vec[3]: "?"
59> vec[4]: "/usr/spool/mail/jerry"
60>     delivering to file "/usr/spool/mail/jerry" (uucp style), done.
61> vec[0]: "*"
62> vec[1]: "-"
63> vec[2]: "|"
64> vec[3]: "R"
65> vec[4]: "/usr/local/lib/mh/rcvtty -nobell"
66> vars[0]: name="sender" value="martinek@agpsa.de"
67> vars[1]: name="address" value="jerry"
68> vars[2]: name="size" value="1235"
69> vars[3]: name="reply-to" value=" Hans Martinek <martinek@agpsa.de>
70> "
71> vars[4]: name="info" value=""
72>     delivering to pipe "/usr/local/lib/mh/rcvtty -nobell", wins.
```

Line 1 shows the name of the temporary file where *slocal* stores the message it's processing.

Lines 2-6 list some internal variables:

- ddate= shows the header line that *slocal* will add if the message is dropped into a file with the *file* or > action.

- now= is the time used by the undocumented select argument.

Line 5 is an example of a variable holding a line of characters that ends with a newline. The closing double quote mark will be on the following line (here, line 6).

In line 7, *slocal* is starting to read and parse the *.maildelivery* lines. If you compare **lines 7-11** of the debugging output to the first uncommented line of the *.maildelivery* file above it, you can see that the five arguments in the line have been split into the array members vec[0] through vec[4]. The first *vec* array member, vec[0], always holds the field argument, vec[1] always holds the pattern argument, and so on.

Lines similar to lines 12-54 will be printed the first time *slocal* calls its internal *parse()* function. That reads the message and splits out the headers. You can use these header names (shown as name= in the debugging output) as the field argument on *.maildelivery* lines. The pattern argument in *.maildelivery* lines is compared to the value= here.

- First *slocal* shows the setting of the $(reply-to) variable (**line 12**). It contains the Reply-to: address if the message had one; otherwise it has the From: address. (This message has both, and they're both the same.)

- Then *slocal* reads all other headers in the message and assigns each to its own hdrs[] array member.

There are some headers *slocal* always looks for; these are hdrs[0] through hdrs[12] (shown in **lines 14-30**). Notice that some of those headers were missing; they're shown with value=" (null) ".

The rest of the headers in the message go into more hdrs[] array members, as many as it takes. The information from all header lines with the same name all go into the same array member. In this case, it takes all of **lines 31-43** to show all of the Received: information in the message. A *.maildelivery* file can match any part of this. For example, if you needed to catch mail that had been relayed through the host *Germany.EU.net* (see **line 34**), this *.maildelivery* entry would do it:

```
received    germany.eu.net   ...
```

The message didn't match this first *.maildelivery* line because it isn't from *uucp*. So, *slocal* checks the next *.maildelivery* line; **lines 55-59** show the five arguments on it.

It matches, so the action is performed; **line 60** shows that. By the way, this is the first line that we'd have seen if I'd only used the *slocal –verbose* option!

Lines 66-72 show the last line of the *.maildelivery* file being parsed and the pipe executed. In case you didn't notice, successful pipe actions "win" but deliveries to files (like line 60) are just "done".

11.11.3 Even –debug Doesn't Show Syntax Errors

The *slocal –debug* switch will show some problems. There are a lot of problems that *–debug* won't tell you about. For example, if a *.maildelivery* line has less than five arguments, it's skipped silently. If you have the MH source tree on your computer and you can read C programs, take a look at the *uip/slocal.c* file. Search for the expression `if (debug)` to see the six places that debugging messages are printed. In the *usr_delivery( )* function, look at the `continue` and `return` NOTOK statements that silently skip *.maildelivery* lines.

Choosing the lines that *debug* prints was a design decision. As it is, *debug* can give you an overwhelming amount of information. If you're having debugging trouble, though, you might recompile your your *slocal* code with more of `if (debug)` and `fprintf (stderr . . . )`.

11.11.4 slocal Eats .maildelivery Errors

When *slocal* runs *.maildelivery*, it throws away error messages from the commands run by *pipe*, |, *qpipe*, and ^ actions. Here's a trick that should help you see the errors. *slocal* runs the *pipe* action with a Bourne shell. You can set that shell's debugging options with *set –xv*. Also, redirect the shell's *stdout* and *stderr* to a file in your home directory with a command like:

```
exec >/home/jerry/rcvstore.debug 2>&1
```

What I mean is: change the line in your *.maildelivery* file to something like the one below (we broke this onto two lines for printing, but you should type it all on one line):

```
to    gripe | R "set -xv; exec >/home/jerry/rcvstore.debug 2>&1;
        /usr/local/lib/mh/rvcstore +gripes"
```

Send a message and look at the debugging file. The shell shows a plus sign (+) before every command it runs:

```
% cat rcvstore.debug
+ /usr/local/lib/mh/rvcstore +gripes
sh: /usr/local/lib/mh/rvcstore: not found
```

Oh! I typed *rvcstore* instead of *rcvstore* . . .

11.11.5 Most Environment Variables Hidden

Programs in *.maildelivery* are run in a different environment, not from your login shell. Environment variables, aliases, shell functions, and other things set in your *.cshrc*, *.login* or *.profile* files probably won't reach your programs in *.maildelivery*. For instance, your MH profile file has to be in the standard place, *$HOME/.mh_profile*, unless you use a trick to reset your *MH* environment variable. (*slocal* passes in the system default settings of three environment variables: *HOME, SHELL,* and *USER*.)

For example, on my workstation I keep my mail on a separate filesystem named */Mail*. But my *.maildelivery* file is read on a fileserver where */Mail* doesn't exist. I have a separate MH profile for the fileserver named *.mh_profile.server*. But unless I do something, the programs in *.maildelivery* won't know that.

Here's the trick for running programs from *.maildelivery*. Don't use the *qpipe* or ^ action. Instead, use the *pipe* or | action and give the shell the environment settings it needs. Here's my *.maildelivery* line for running *rcvtty*:

```
*    -   |  R   "MH=$HOME/.mh_profile.server /x/y/rcvtty"
```

What's that? In the Bourne shell, which runs when you use the *pipe* or | action, you can set an environment variable before a command is run. Before starting *rcvtty*, I set the MH environment variable.

12

Introduction to Shell Programming for MH

One of the great things about MH is that it's made up of individual UNIX programs, "building blocks," that you run from a shell prompt. Because MH isn't a monolithic "one program does everything" mail agent, it's easy to use MH in shell programs.

If you don't like the MH interface, you can write your own. You can make new programs that combine MH programs in your own way to do exactly what you need. (*xmh* is an example of this.)

This chapter assumes that you've written programs in some language before, and that you understand the shell file-redirection operators < (left angle bracket), > (right angle bracket), and the | symbol. Using the Bourne shell, this chapter shows you enough basics of UNIX shell programming to write programs of your own. This chapter also prepares you for the techniques used in Chapter 13, *MH Shell Programs*. If you've never written a shell program, read carefully; you may also want to pick up *UNIX Shell Programming* by Kochan and Wood for more information. Read this chapter even if if you've programmed with the C shell—when you get beyond the basics, the Bourne and C shells are quite different.

Section 12.17 introduces MH features and commands you'll use with shell programs.

A note about command versions: unfortunately, the same commands on different versions of UNIX can have different options. Some Bourne shells are a little different than others. For instance, some *test* commands have a –*x* option to test for an executable file; others don't. Some *echo* commands use a –*n* option to mean "no newline at the end of this string"; others have you put \c at the end of the string. And so on. Where there are differences, this book generally uses the commands in Berkeley 4.3 BSD UNIX. If a command doesn't seem to work on your system, check its online manual page or the *sh*(1) manual page.

12.1 Two Examples

Our first example is a shell program called *fols* that lists the names of your MH folders in columns. The program has just one line:

```
folders -fast -recurse $* | pr -l1 -4 -w78 -t
```

Here's a comparison of *fols* and the standard *folders –fast –recurse*. Besides being easier to type, *fols* uses less space on the screen.

```
% folders -fast -recurse
drafts
drafts/DELETE
inbox
inbox/DELETE
mh-users_ADD
mh-users_ADD/DELETE
mh-workers_ADD
reference
reference/DELETE
% fols
drafts                 drafts/DELETE      inbox           inbox/DELETE
mh-users_ADD           mh-users_ADD/DELET mh-workers_ADD   reference
reference/DELETE
```

You can see that the end of one of the subfolder names is cut off. There are a few ways to fix that—you'll need to add another line or two to the shell program. But this is an introduction, so let's skip that for now. (See the improved *fols* in Section 13.5.)

Our second program, *incs*, uses *inc* to incorporate new mail messages, then uses *show* to display them all. If there were no messages, it doesn't run *show*:

```
% incs
inc: no mail to incorporate
```
    ...Later, after some mail comes in...
```
% incs
Incorporating new mail into inbox...
   45+ 02/04 boris@kremvax.kgb  UNIX question<<Comrade Emma, I ha
   46  02/05 Jim Bob Smith      Re: Encapsulation destroying good
(Message inbox:45)
From: boris@kremvax.kgb.ussr
To: ehuser@mysun.xyz.edu
   ...
```

incs uses some more advanced features of the shell, but it's still pretty simple. It looks like this:

```
% cat incs

#! /bin/sh
# $Id: incs,v 2.0 92/08/02 18:45:50 jerry book2 $
### incs - incorporate messages, then show them
### Usage: incs [+folder] [-inc options]
#
#   incs DOES AN inc, THEN A show OF ALL MESSAGES inc'D.  IF YOU
#   SET THE ENVIRONMENT VARIABLE $INCSHOW TO THE NAME OF A PROGRAM
#   THEN incs WILL USE THAT PROGRAM INSTEAD OF show.

temp=/tmp/INCS$$
stat=1   # DEFAULT EXIT STATUS; RESET TO 0 ON NORMAL EXIT
trap 'rm -f $temp; exit $stat' 0 1 2 15

# ONLY SHOW MESSAGE IF inc ACTUALLY INCORPORATED ONE.
# BE SURE inc CHANGES CURRENT MESSAGE (OVERRIDE .mh_profile):
if inc -changecur $* > $temp
then
    cat $temp
    ${INCSHOW-show} cur-last
    stat=0
fi
```

I won't explain all of that here. But you can see that with only nine lines of code (and nine more lines of comments), you can write a very useful program. Whether you're interested in just writing basic one line programs like *fols* or you want to dig in and really use the shell, this chapter and the next have information and examples to help.

12.2 Writing a Simple Shell Program

Here's how to write the *fols* command from Section 12.1. You'll use these steps for longer programs, too.

1. First, at a shell prompt (%, $, or whatever), type the following command. It doesn't matter what shell *your* account uses.

   ```
   % folders -fast -recurse | pr -l1 -4 -w78 -t
   ```

   A list of your folder names should come out in columns as you saw at the start of this chapter. (The -l1 is lowercase letter "l" followed by the digit 1.)

2. Start your favorite text editor (*emacs*, *vi*, whatever) on a new file named *fols*.

3. Leave the first line blank. Put this on the second line:

   ```
   folders -fast -recurse $* | pr -l1 -4 -w78 -t
   ```

   (In Section 12.12 we'll see what the $* does.)

4. Save the file and leave the editor.

5. Next, you need to make the shell script you just wrote executable. The *chmod* (change mode) command is used to change permissions on a file. The plus sign (+) makes the file executable. Type the following command:

   ```
   % chmod +x fols
   ```

6. If your account uses the C shell, you'll need to reset its command search table. To do that, type:

   ```
   % rehash
   ```

7. Finally, try the script. Just type its name and it should run:

   ```
   % fols
   ```

   If that doesn't run, your current directory may not be in your shell's command search path. In that case, try this:

   ```
   % ./fols
   ```

   and, if you need to, read Section 12.3.4.

That's how you write a shell script. If you have any problems, you should check with a local expert.

12.3 What's a Shell, Anyway?

A *shell* is a program that interprets your command lines and runs other programs. Another name for the shell is "command interpreter." This section covers the two major UNIX shells, including discussion about how shells run, how they search for programs, and how they read shell script files.

12.3.1 How Shells Run Other Programs

For each command it runs, a shell repeats a series of steps:

1. Prints a prompt (such as a % or $) if it's reading commands from a terminal (interactively).

2. Reads a command line (like *show –noshowproc 6 > afile*).

3. Parses (breaks apart and analyzes) the command line.

4. Looks at the first word on the command line: the command name. Looks for a built-in command with that name. If there isn't one, it searches a list called the *search path*—these are directories that contain executable files (programs).

5. Passes arguments like *–noshowproc 6* to the program, runs the program, and routes its input and output.

6. Starts over at step 1.

12.3.2 Interactive Use vs. Shell Scripts

A shell can read command lines from a terminal or it can read them from a file. When you put command lines into a file, that file is called a *shell script* or shell program. The shell handles the shell script just as it handles the commands you type from a terminal (though it doesn't print the % or $ prompts). With this information, you already know how to write simple shell scripts—just put commands in a file and feed them to the shell!

In addition, though, there are a number of programming constructs that make it possible to write shell programs that are much more powerful than just a list of commands.

12.3.3 Types of Shells

There are two main kinds of shells in UNIX:

- The *C shell* (*csh*) is especially good for working on a terminal. *csh* will read shell scripts and has some useful features for programmers. Unfortunately, it has some quirks that can make more advanced shell programming tough.*

- The *Bourne shell* (*sh*), and shells like it, which are probably used more often for shell programming. (Some newer *sh*-like shells, including *ksh* and *bash*, combine handy interactive C shell-like features with Bourne shell syntax.)

12.3.4 Shell Search Paths

As Section 12.3.1 explained, if the shell is trying to run a command and the command isn't built in to the shell itself, it looks in a list of directories called a *search path*. UNIX systems have standard directories with names like */bin* and */usr/bin* which hold standard UNIX programs. Almost everyone's shell search path has these directories.

If you do much shell programming, you should make a directory on your account for executable files. Most people name theirs *bin* and put it under their home directories. See Section 9.2.1 if you'd like instructions.

12.3.5 Bourne Shell Used Here

For the rest of this chapter, it may be easier if you have a terminal close by so that you can try the examples. All the shell programs in Chapter 13 are written for the Bourne shell. Bourne shell scripts will work fine if you use a C shell interactively—but the programming examples in this chapter will be easier to try if you run a Bourne shell interactively while you read.

If your account uses the Bourne shell or one of its relatives (*ksh*, *bash*, etc.), your prompt probably has a dollar sign ($) in it. If your account isn't running the Bourne shell, start one by typing sh. Your prompt should change to a dollar sign ($). You'll be using the Bourne shell until you type CTRL-D at the start of a line:

---

*For instance, continuation lines must end with a backslash (\), which makes it hard to handle backquoted text. Some test and loop constructs are very picky about syntax. It's almost impossible to manipulate file descriptors. You can't redirect input or output of loops without an explicit subshell. Your script may run more slowly. But some people do prefer it.

```
% sh
$
$ ...Type commands...
$ CTRL-D
%
```

12.4 Testing How Your System Executes Files

Try one more thing: see whether your version of UNIX understands the # ! notation. This is a way to tell UNIX which shell should execute the commands in your
file.* If your UNIX doesn't recognize # !, you'll need to be sure that you know
how to make it read shell scripts using the Bourne shell—regardless of the shell
you use interactively—because this book only deals with the Bourne shell.

To test your system, let's make a two line file named *testing*.

NOTE

Do not make programs named *test*. There's an important system command named *test*, and your command might be used, accidentally, instead
of the system program. Name your test programs *testing*, *atest*, whatever—just not *test*.

1. First make the file named *testing* (use an editor, or just make the file by hand).

2. Put the following two lines in the file. Be sure to start on the *first* line of the
    file, and type this text just as it's shown. Be sure that the hash mark (#) char-
    acter is at the left-hand edge (column 1) of the first line:

    ```
    #! /bin/echo just
    export stuff
    ```

3. Exit the editor and save the file. Make the file executable with the
    chmod +x testing command as you did before.

Part III
Customizing MH

---

*Actually, you can use # ! to specify any interpreter program, not just a shell.

Now run the program by typing its name at a shell prompt. There are four kinds of responses:

1. If this happens, then the # ! business is working. You'll be able to tell your system which shell should run each script:

   ```
   % testing
   just testing
   %
   ```

2. If this happens, then your UNIX doesn't understand # ! , but it ran your program with the Bourne shell anyhow:

   ```
   % testing
   %
   ```

3. If this happens, then your system ran the program with an older version of the Bourne shell. You should not use comment lines starting with a hash mark (#):

   ```
   % testing
   #!: not found
   %
   ```

4. If this happens, then your UNIX doesn't understand # ! , and it ran your program with the C shell:

   ```
   % testing
   export: Command not found.
   %
   ```

Many UNIX systems, especially newer ones, will answer just testing.

If your system ran the shell script with the C shell, find a way to make it use the Bourne shell instead. It's best to ask a local expert such as your system administrator.

12.5 Using Shell and Environment Variables

Bourne shell variables hold strings of characters. There are two kinds of variables: *shell variables* and *environment variables* (called *envariables* in MH documentation). A shell variable is used to hold values within a shell script. An environment variable is passed from program to program; the shell can read and modify environment variables.

12.5.1 Shell Variables

To store a value in a variable, use the syntax:

name=value

If the value has spaces or special characters in it, use quotes (see Section 12.6 for more information).

For example, to store the string `first cur last` in a variable called *msgs*, type:

```
$ msgs="first cur last"
```

Those quotes should be double quotes ("), not a pair of single quotes (' '), and not a pair of backquotes (` `). For a list of all the shell variables that are set now, type set. You'll get a list similar to this:

```
$ set
HOME=/xxx/yyy/ehuser
IFS=

PATH=/usr/ucb:/bin:/usr/bin:/xxx/yyy/ehuser/bin:/usr/local/mh:
PS1=$
PS2=>
SHELL=/bin/csh
USER=ehuser
msgs=first cur last
```

To get the value of a single shell variable, put a $ before its name. Here are two examples. The first shows the value of the variable *msgs*. Then we add some message numbers to the variable and show its value again. The *echo* command is good for showing what's in a variable.

```
$ echo $msgs
first cur last
$ msgs="23 45 $msgs"
$ echo "The messages are: $msgs"
The messages are: 23 45 first cur last
```

Shell variables aren't passed to other shells or programs. For example, if you start a second Bourne shell (a *child shell*), the *msgs* shell variable won't be set there. But when you end the second shell, *msgs* will still be set in the first (or *parent*) shell:

```
$ echo $msgs
23 45 first cur last
$ sh
$ echo $msgs
```

```
$ CTRL-D
$ echo $msgs
23 45 first cur last
```

To empty a variable, just set its value to an empty string:

```
$ msgs=
$ echo $msgs

$
```

12.5.2 Environment Variables

Environment variables work pretty much like shell variables. But environment variables don't just stay in the shell where you create them. Environment variables are copied to child processes, that is, to programs that the shell starts running. They're a good way to pass information to a program you start.

Other programs besides shells can also pass environment variables to programs that they start. MH uses several environment variables. If your shell program is started by MH programs (as a *–editor*, for instance), your program can use those environment variables' values.

To set an environment variable, first make a shell variable with that name. One convention that I like to follow is to make shell variables with lowercase names and environment variables with uppercase names. Not everyone follows that convention, but I will in this book (except where UNIX or MH don't follow that convention, of course).

So, to make an environment variable called *MSGS*, first I execute MSGS=*value*. That makes the shell variable. The *printenv* command, which shows the values of environment variables, shows that the variable isn't in the environment yet. (On System V UNIX, use *env* instead of *printenv*.) Then, I add the shell variable to the environment with the *export* command, and *printenv* finds it.

```
$ MSGS="first:3 12-17"
$ echo $MSGS
first:3 12-17
$ printenv MSGS
$ export MSGS
$ printenv MSGS
MSGS=first:3 12-17
```

Now that *MSGS* is in the environment, another program can find its value. For instance, you could start a child shell as you did in the shell variable example in the previous section. Unlike the shell variable, the environment variable would still be set in the child shell.

You can also get the value of an environment variable by putting a dollar sign ($) before its name. For example, echo $USER would show the value of the *USER* variable, whether it's a shell variable or an environment variable.

12.6 Quoting

The Bourne shell uses quite a few characters as "special characters" which have some special meaning to the shell. For example, you should know that when you use the right angle bracket (>) in a command line like x > y, it means "redirect the standard output of the program x to the file named y." The dollar sign ($) in front of a variable's name tells the shell to replace the name with its value. And an asterisk (*) in a construct like *old causes the shell to replace it with all file (and directory) names that end in *old*.

Another character that's special to the shell is the space. The shell uses the space to separate words—that is, to separate command names from options and arguments on the command line.

Sometimes you want to keep the shell from interpreting these special characters and to treat them the same as it would treat, say, any alphanumeric character: just pass it on unchanged. To do that, you use *quoting*. Quoting tells the shell to ignore the special meaning of certain characters.

For example, compare these two *echo* commands:

```
$ echo The  files      are          myfile*
The files are myfile1 myfile2 myfile3 myfile32
$ echo "The  files      are          myfile*"
The  files      are          myfile*
```

Without the quotes, the shell turned myfile* into filenames. The shell also ignored the multiple spaces because they're just argument separators. The resulting seven separate arguments were passed to the *echo* command, which output them with spaces between. With the quotes, the shell didn't interpret the space or asterisk as special characters; it just passed the one long argument to the *echo* command, which output the argument.

Table 12-1 lists the quoting characters and what they do.

Table 12-1. Bourne Shell Quoting Characters

Quoting Character	Explanation
`'xxx'`	Disable all special characters in *xxx*.
`"xxx"`	Disable all special characters in *xxx* except $ and
`\x`	Disable special meaning of character *x*.

In general, a backslash (\) is best for turning off the meaning of a single character. Use double quotes (`"`) if you want the shell to do command substitution (explained in Section 12.7) or variable substitution inside the quoted string. Use single quotes (`'`) to turn off all special meaning.

And if it's not obvious: quotes disable other kinds of quoting. You can get a literal single quote by putting it inside double quotes or by putting a backslash before it.

Here's an example—a shell script named *vidraft*:

```
#! /bin/sh
# $Id: vidraft,v 1.1 92/07/19 09:36:09 jerry Exp $
### vidraft -- edit draft message starting at top of body

# ex command goes to top, then row of dashes; then next (if can):
exec /usr/ucb/vi +'1;/^--*$/;+'. $*
```

(There are two new things here that you'll read more about later: the $* passes command-line arguments to *vi*, as Section 12.12.1 explains. The shell's *exec* command saves a process—this is described with the *resend.fixmsg* script in Section 13.9.2.)

The important part for now is the quotes around most of the first argument to *vi*. I needed single quotes, not double quotes, to protect the $. That argument is an *ex-mode* startup command with three parts, separated by semicolons (;). (Like the shell, *ex* uses semicolons as a command separator. The quoting protects them from the shell so *ex* will see them.) The three commands move the cursor to the first line of the draft body. The first command, 1, goes to the first line of the file. The /^--*$/ is a regular expression that searches for the line of all dashes before the body. The final + moves down one more line, to the first line under the dashes, if that line exists (otherwise, *vi* prints an error that you can ignore).

vidraft is usually run by a command like *forw*; you add:

```
forw: -editor vidraft
```

to the MH profile.

12.7 Command Substitution

A pair of backquotes (` `) does *command substitution*. This is really useful—it lets you use the output from one command as arguments to another command. Here's an example. (If you have the *–sequence* switch in your MH profile, use `pick -list` below, instead of just `pick`):

```
$ pick -from yourfriend
1
2
113
227
$ scan `pick -from yourfriend`
    1  01/28 yourfriend        Test message<<Hi!>>
    2  01/28 yourfriend        Another test<<Well, this is anot
  113+ 02/14 yourfriend        The latest on my project<<It's g
  227  03/03 yourfriend        <<I can't get MH to work so I'm
$
```

The first command line runs *pick*; the output goes to the screen. The second command line has the same *pick* command on it, but the backquotes tell the shell to use the output of the *pick* command as arguments to the *scan* command. The *scan* command scans the messages that *pick* found.*

12.8 Using Exit Status

When a UNIX command runs, it can return a numeric status value to the program that started it. The status can tell the calling program whether the command succeeded or failed. Many (but not all) UNIX commands return a status of zero if everything was okay or nonzero (1, 2, etc.) if something went wrong. Almost all MH programs return a status.

---

*You might be wondering about the difference between the "vertical" output from *pick*, and the "horizontal" way that people usually type arguments on a command line. The shell handles this with no problems. Inside backquotes, both a newline and a space are argument separators.

12.8.1 Seeing Status in $?

The shell puts the exit status in a question mark (?) variable. You can get its value by preceding it with a dollar sign ($), just like any other shell variable. For example, when *inc* brings in new messages, it sets the status to 0. If there are no messages, *inc* sets the status to 1:

```
$ inc
Incorporating new mail into inbox...
   45+ 02/04 root              <<The job you submitted to at, "
   46  02/05 Jim Bob Smith     Re: Encapsulation destroying goo
$ echo $?
0
$ inc
inc: no mail to incorporate
$ echo $?
1
```

Of course, you usually don't have to display the exit status in this way, because the shell provides a couple of ways to use the exit status of one command as a condition of further execution.

12.8.2 Testing Exit Status with if

After a shell program (or a program in a higher-level language like C) runs a UNIX command, it can test the exit status to see if there was a problem. Here's a simple example: a shell script called *newmsgs*. If *inc* brings in some messages, *newmsgs* runs the *show* command to show the current message (the first new message). Otherwise, the program prints a note that there were no messages to show.

```
% cat newmsgs
#! /bin/sh
if inc
then
    show
else
    echo "Sorry; no new message to show now."
fi
```

That's a Bourne shell *if* structure. It runs a command (here, it runs *inc*). Then it tests and branches:

- If the command returns zero status, control goes to the then line (which, in this example, runs the *show* command). Then, control goes to the fi line ("if" spelled backwards), which ends the structure.

- If the command returns nonzero status and there's an `else` line, control goes there (in this example, the shell *echo*'s a message).* Control then goes to the `fi` line. The *else* section is never required but is often useful.

You can try typing in that shell script and running it—or just typing in the lines (starting with the `if`) on a terminal running the Bourne shell.

The *if* structure is often used with a command named *test*. The *test* command does a test and returns an exit status of 0 or 1. See Section 12.14.

12.9 Loops That Test Exit Status

The Bourne shell has two kinds of loops that run a command and test its exit status. An *until* loop will continue until the command returns a zero status. A *while* loop will continue until the command returns a nonzero status.

12.9.1 Looping Until a Command Succeeds

The *until* loop runs a command repeatedly until it succeeds. That is, if the command returns a nonzero status, the shell executes the body of the loop and then runs the loop control command again. The shell keeps running the command until it returns a zero status, as shown in the following example:

```
% cat wait_inc
#! /bin/sh
waittime=60
until inc
do
    echo waiting $waittime seconds...
    sleep $waittime
done
show
% wait_inc
inc: no mail to incorporate
waiting 60 seconds...
inc: no mail to incorporate
waiting 60 seconds...
Incorporating new mail into inbox...
   47+ 02/05 root          <<The job you submitted to at, "n
(Message inbox:47)
```

---

*A more UNIX-like shell script wouldn't tell you that there were no messages; the `no mail to in-corporate` message from *inc* would be enough. But this is a demonstration ...

```
From: root
To: ehuser
    ...
```

The loop runs the *inc* command. If the command returns nonzero (there were no new messages), it waits 60 seconds (here the *sleep* command pauses for waittime seconds). Then the loop repeats, and the script tries the *inc* command again. It keeps doing this until *inc* returns a zero status—then, the loop is broken and control goes past the done line. The *show* command shows the first new message from *inc*.

12.9.2 Looping Until a Command Fails

The *while* loop is the opposite of the *until* loop; it loops until the command fails (returns a nonzero status). For instance, the *next* command shows the next message and returns 0 status unless there's no next message. This program shows the next message, then asks the user if it should repeat the loop (and show the next message). The loop can end in one of two ways: if the *next* command fails (there's no next message) or if the user decides to quit.

```
% cat all_next
#! /bin/sh
while next
do
    echo "q quits, r removes, anything else shows next message: \c"
    read ans
    case "$ans" in
    q) break ;;
    r) rmm ;;
    *) echo "Current time is `date`..." ;;
    esac
done
% all_next
(Message folder:25)
To: ehuser (Emma H. User)
    ...
q quits, r removes, anything else shows next message: y
Current time is Fri Feb 23 13:15:08 EST 1990...
(Message folder:26)
To: ehuser
    ...
q quits, r removes, anything else shows next message: q
%
```

The following list describes more new shell features shown in the preceding example:

`echo` command

> Ends with \c, which tells many versions of *echo* to leave the cursor at the end of the line for a user's answer. If your version of *echo* just prints the \c, try this instead:

```
echo -n "q quits, r removes, anything else shows next message: "
```

> The −n tells some versions of *echo* not to put the automatic newline at the end of its output.

`read ans` command

> Reads the next line that the user types and stores it in the shell variable named *ans* (you can use any shell variable name).

`case` structure

> Compares the string between the words `case` and `in` to the strings at the left-hand edge of the lines ending with a) character. If it matches the first case (in this example, if it's the letter q), the command up to the ; ; is executed; here the *break* command ends the loop. The ; ; means "jump to the `esac`" (*esac* is "case" spelled backwards). You can put as many commands as you want before each ; ;, but put each command on a separate line.

> If the first case doesn't match, it compares the string to the next case—here, it's the letter r. If that matches, it runs *rmm* to remove the current message.

> The last case is a *, which matches any answer other than q or r. This echoes a message, using command substitution to show the output of the *date* command.

12.10 Pattern Matching in `case` Structures

A *case* structure is good at string pattern matching. Its "wildcard" pattern-matching metacharacters work like the filename wildcards in the shell, with a few twists. Here are some examples:

?)   Matches a string with exactly one character like a, 3, !, and so on.

?*)   Matches a string with one or more characters (a nonempty string).

[yY] | [yY] [eE] [sS])

> Matches y, Y or yes, YES, YeS, etc. The | means "or."

`/*/*[0-9])`

> Matches a file pathname like that of a message, */xxx/yyy/Mail/inbox/2* , that starts with a slash, contains at least one other slash, and ends with a digit.

`'What now?')`

> Matches the pattern `What  now?`. The quotes tell the shell to treat the string literally: not to break it at the space and not to treat the `?` as a wild-card.

`"$msgs")`

> Matches the contents of the *msgs* variable. The quotes protect the contents of the variable from the shell.

12.11   Exiting a Script

Most standard UNIX and MH commands return a status. Your shell script should too. This section shows how to set the right exit status for both normal exits and error exits. It also explains the shell's *trap* command for handling interrupts.

12.11.1 Exiting Normally with exit

To end a shell script and set its exit status, use the *exit* command. Give *exit* the exit status that your script should have. If it has no explicit status, it will exit with the status of the last command run.

Here's an example: a rewrite of the *newmsgs* script from Section 12.8.2. If there's a new message, *show* is run and the script returns the exit status from *show* (usually zero). If there's no new message, the program prints a message and exits with status 1.

```
$ cat newmsgs
#! /bin/sh
if inc
then
    show
    exit    # USE STATUS FROM show COMMAND
else
    echo "Sorry; no new message to show now."
    exit 1
fi
$ newmsgs
inc: no mail to incorporate.
Sorry; no new message to show now.
$ echo $?
1
```

The shell ignores any characters after a hash mark (#) (unless you have an old Bourne shell), so USE STATUS FROM show COMMAND is a comment. I like to put my comments in uppercase letters so that the lowercase program text in them stands out without quoting.

12.11.2 Trapping Exits Caused by Interrupts

If you're running a shell script and you press your interrupt key (like CTRL-C), the shell quits right away. That can be a problem if you use temporary files in your script because the sudden exit might leave the temporary files there. The *trap* command lets you tell the shell what to do before it exits. A *trap* can be used for a normal exit, too. See Table 12-2.

Here's a script named *scan_sort* that uses a temporary file named */tmp/ss$$* in a system temporary file directory. The shell will replace *$$* with its process ID number. Because no other process will have the same ID number, that file should have a unique name. What the script does—sorting the output of the *scan* command—isn't extremely useful. It's nice for collecting related messages spread out across a folder without using *sortm* to sort the folder. The important part of the script is how it uses two *trap*s to clean up its temporary files, even if the user presses CTRL-C.

After the shell script, there's a comparison of plain *scan* and *scan_sort*:

```
% cat scan_sort

#! /bin/sh
# scan_sort - SHOW SORTED scan LIST
# Usage: scan_sort [scan arguments]
stat=1   # DEFAULT EXIT STATUS; RESET TO 0 BEFORE NORMAL EXIT
out=$HOME/sorted_scan
temp=/tmp/ss$$
trap 'rm -f $temp; exit $stat' 0
trap 'echo Quitting early... 1>&2' 1 2 15

# SORT ON THE ADDRESS FIELD (SKIP 12 CHARACTERS TO FIND IT):
scan | sort +0.12 >$temp
more $temp

echo -n "Save that list in the '$out' file (y/n)? " 1>&2
read yn
case "$yn" in
y*) cp $temp $out ;;
esac

stat=0
exit
% scan
```

*Part III
Customizing MH*

```
    4  03/21 Alison Cosgreave    What's happening here at UMass<<
    6  04/29 To:rbq@animals.nc   What we talked about at lunch<<Jo
    9  12/14 jdpeek@rodan.acs.   I'm out of town<<I'm out of town
   10  03/23 To:ann@suxpr.mar.   Re: FTP in the background<<> Is p
   12  04/02 Alison Cosgreave    Re: What's happening at Tek<<Not
   15  02/03*To:jerryp           a test<<dfkjdf --Jerry Peek; Syra
   24  12/14 nathan@demps.vme.   I'm out of town<<I'm not here now
% scan_sort
   10  03/23 To:ann@suxpr.mar.   Re: FTP in the background<<> Is p
   15  02/03*To:jerryp           a test<<dfkjdf --Jerry Peek; Syra
    6  04/29 To:rbq@animals.nc   What we talked about at lunch<<Jo
   12  04/02 Alison Cosgreave    Re: What's happening at Tek<<Not
    4  03/21 Alison Cosgreave    What's happening here at UMass<<
    9  12/14 jdpeek@rodan.acs.   I'm out of town<<I'm out of town
   24  12/14 nathan@demps.vme.   I'm out of town<<I'm not here now
Save that list in the '/xxx/yyy/sorted_scan' file (y/n)? y
```

There are two *trap*s in the script:

- The first trap, ending with the number 0, is executed for all shell exits—normal or interrupted. It runs the command line between the single quotes. In this example, there are two commands separated with a semicolon (;). The first command removes the temporary file (using the *–f* option, so *rm* won't give an error message if the file doesn't exist yet). The second command exits with the value stored in the *stat* shell variable. Look ahead at the rest of the script—$stat will always be 1 unless the folder list was shown successfully, in which case it will be reset to 0. Therefore, this shell script will always return the right exit status—if it's interrupted before it finishes, it'll return 1; otherwise, 0.*

- The second trap has the numbers 1 2 15 at the end. These are signal numbers that correspond to different kinds of interrupts. There's a short list in Table 12-2. For a list of all signals, see your online *signal*(3) manual page.

  This trap is done on an abnormal exit (like CTRL-C). It prints a message, but it could run any list of commands.

---

* It's important to use single quotes, rather than double quotes, around the trap. That way, the value of $stat won't be used until the trap is actually executed at the end of the script.

Table 12-2. Some UNIX Signal Numbers for trap Commands

Signal Number	Signal Name	Explanation
0	Normal exit	*exit* command.
1	SIGHUP	When session disconnected.
2	SIGINT	Interrupt—often CTRL-C.
15	SIGTERM	From *kill*(1) command.

Shell scripts don't always have two *traps*. Look back at the *incs* script in Section 12.1 for another example of *trap*.

Also, notice that the *echo* commands in the script have 1>&2 at the end. That tells the shell to put the output of the *echo* command on the standard error channel instead of the standard output. This is a good idea because it helps to make sure that errors come to your screen instead of being redirected to a file or down a pipe with the other standard output text.

12.12 Handling Command-line Arguments

To write flexible shell scripts, you usually want to give them command-line arguments. The $* parameter has a list of all the command-line arguments. You can also use the Bourne shell's *for* loop to step through the arguments one by one.

12.12.1 With the $* Parameter

Until now, most shell scripts you've seen didn't accept command-line arguments. Wouldn't it be nice to tell the *scan_sort* script which messages and/or folders to scan instead of just scanning all the messages in the current folder? (Say "yes," please!)

Okay; you talked me into it. If you put $* in a script, the shell will replace that string with the script's command-line arguments. Then you can pass arguments such as a sequence name and a folder name to the script:

```
% scan_sort picked +friends
  44+ 04/29 To:jbq@animals.nc  What we talked about at lunch<<J
  23  04/02 Alison Cosgreave   Re: What's happening at Tek<<Not
   4  03/21 Alison Cosgreave   What's happening here at UMass<<
  21  04/01 Steven Dommer      Re: meeting minutes<<> A while b
Save that list in the '/xxx/yyy/sorted_scan' file (y/n)?
```

In this case, we want the arguments to be passed to the *scan* command. Let's change the *scan_sort* script (Section 12.11.2) to read:

```
scan $* | sort +0.12 >$temp
```

When the shell runs the script with the arguments `picked +friends` it will actually execute a command line like this one:

```
scan picked +friends | sort +0.12 >/tmp/ss12345
```

If there are no command-line arguments, the shell won't pass any arguments to *scan*, so the script will scan all messages in the current folder—as it should with no arguments.

12.12.2 With a for Loop

Sometimes you want a script that will step through the command-line arguments one by one. (The $* parameter gives you all of them at once.) The Bourne shell has a *for* loop that looks like this:

```
for arg in list
do
    ...Handle $arg...
done
```

If you omit the `in list`, the loop steps through the command-line arguments. It puts the first command-line argument in the *arg* shell variable, then executes the commands from do to done. Then it puts the next command-line argument in *arg*, does the loop ... and so on ... ending the loop after handling all the arguments. (To see a *for* loop used with a list, see Section 12.13.)

Example 12-1 shows how a shell script can find the options and arguments from a command line.

Example 12-1. for loop parsing a command line

```
folder= switches=
for arg
do
    case "$arg" in
    +*|@*) # IT'S A FOLDER
        case "$folder" in
        "") folder="$arg" ;;
        *) echo "`basename $0`: '$arg'?  Only one folder at a
            time." 1>&2
            exit
            ;;
        esac
        ;;
```

Example 12-1. for loop parsing a command line (continued)

```
        *) switches="$switches $arg" ;;
        esac
done
```

The loop gets and checks each command-line argument. For an example, let's say that a user typed:

```
% progname +project -nocc to
```

The first pass through the *for* loop, $arg is +project. Because the argument starts with a plus sign (+) or an at sign (@), the *case* in **line 22** treats it as a folder name. **Line 23** checks to see if there was a folder name in some earlier argument. There wasn't, so line 24 stores +project in the *folder* shell variable and control goes to line 28, then to line 31, and then the loop repeats with the next argument.

The next argument, −nocc, doesn't look like a folder name. The test in **line 30** succeeds. Now the *switches* variable is replaced by its previous contents (an empty string), a space, and −nocc.

The loop starts over once more, with to in $arg. Again, this matches line 30, so now *switches* has its previous contents followed by a space and the new $arg. Now $switches is −nocc to. Because to was the last argument, the loop ends; $folder has the folder name and $switches has all the other arguments.

You could add more tests that catch particular options; the rest of the options can be stored in the *switches* variable. The *mysend* shell script in Section 13.13 does that.

12.13 More About for Loops

The previous section showed how to step through command-line arguments with a *for* loop. You can also use a *for* loop to step through any list. Just put the word in, with values after it, at the start of the loop:

```
for folder in inbox outbox project
do
      ...Process $folder...
done
```

If you have a shell variable with one or more words in it, you can use that as the list for the loop. The list will be split at the spaces:

```
msgs="first cur last"
    ...
for msg in $msgs
do
    ...Process $msg...
done
```

12.14 Testing Files and Strings

UNIX has a command called *test* that does a lot of useful tests. For instance, it can test to see if a file is writable before your script tries to write to it. It can treat the string in a shell variable as a number and do comparisons ("is that number less than 1000?"). You can combine tests too ("if the file exists *and* it's readable *and* the message number is more than 500 . . . "). For a complete list, read your online *test*(1) manual page.

The *test* command returns a zero status if the test was true or a nonzero status otherwise. So people usually use *test* with *if*. Here's a way your program could check to see if the user has a readable MH profile:*

```
if test -r $HOME/.mh_profile
then
    ...Do whatever...
else
    echo "Can't read your '.mh_profile'.  Quitting." 1>&2
    exit 1
fi
```

The *test* command also lets you test for something that *isn't* true. Add an exclamation point (!) before the condition you're testing. For example, the following test is true if the *.mh_profile* file is *not* readable:

```
if test ! -r $HOME/.mh_profile
then
    echo "Can't read your '.mh_profile'.  Quitting." 1>&2
    exit 1
fi
```

UNIX also has a version of *test* (a link to the same program, actually) named *[*. Yes, that's a left bracket. You can use it interchangeably with the *test* command

---

*In practice, this should test the MH environment variable before it defaults to *$HOME/.mh_profile*. See Section 12.17.1.

with one exception: there has to be a matching right bracket (]) at the end of the test. The second example above could be rewritten this way:

```
if [ ! -r $HOME/.mh_profile ]
then
    echo "Can't read your '.mh_profile'.  Quitting." 1>&2
    exit 1
fi
```

Be sure to leave space between the brackets and other text.

Some other shell scripts in this and the next chapter use *test* as well. If you want examples, look at *distprompter* in Section 13.10 and *showpr* in Section 13.11.

Many Bourne shell programmers use *test* (and the left bracket ([)) whenever they can, probably because the syntax isn't as strange as the syntax of a *case* structure. Also, *test* can do many tests (on files, for instance) that *case* cannot. But there are two good reasons to use *case* instead of *test*:

1. *case* string comparisons are much more powerful (see Section 12.10).

2. All Bourne shells have *case* built in—that is, they don't have to start a UNIX process and run an external command to use *case*. Older Bourne shells don't have the *test* command built in. Shells that don't have built-in *test* will run that command more slowly than the equivalent test done with a *case*.

12.15 Finding Program Name; Multiple Program Names

A UNIX program should use its name as the first word in error messages it prints. That's important when the program is running in the background or as part of a pipeline—you need to know which program has the problem:

```
someprog: quitting: can't read file xxx
```

It's tempting to use just the program name in the *echo* commands:

```
echo "someprog: quitting: can't read file $file" 1>&2
```

but, if you ever change the program name, it's easy to forget to fix the messages. A better way is to store the program name in a shell variable at the top of the script file, and then use the variable in all messages:

```
myname=someprog
    ...
echo "$myname: quitting: can't read file $file" 1>&2
```

Even better, use the $0 parameter. The shell automatically puts the script's name there. But $0 can have the full pathname of the script, such as

/*xxx*/*yyy*/*bin*/*someprog*. The *basename* program fixes this: *basename* strips off the head of a pathname—everything but the filename.

For example, if $0 is /*u*/*ehuser*/*bin*/*sendit*, then:

```
myname="`basename $0`"
```

would put *sendit* into the *myname* shell variable.

Just as MH can use links to give messages more than one name (see Section 7.8), and just as you can make links to give MH programs several names (see Chapter 9, *New Versions of MH Commands*), you can use links to give your program several names. For instance, see the script named both *rmmer* and *rmmer.one_fdr* in Section 13.6. Use $0 to get the current name of the program.

The inset entitled "What Good is a File with 1000 Links?" shows a handy use of multiple program names.

12.16 Debugging

Depending on what version of the Bourne shell you have, the error messages it gives can be downright useless. For instance, it can just say `End of file unexpected`. Here are a few tricks to use.

12.16.1 Use –xv

If you start your script like this:

```
#! /bin/sh -xv
```

the −xv shows you what's happening as the shell reads your script. The lines of the script will be shown as the shell reads them. The shell shows each command it executes with a plus sign (+) before the command.

Note that the shell reads in an entire loop (*for*, *while*, etc.) before it executes any commands in the loop.

What Good is a File With 1000 Links?

You can take linking to extremes in a useful way by the following short shell script. It's named *README*. It's also named *1, 2, 3 ... 125 ...* and *999*. In fact, it has 1000 links (though it could have more or fewer):

```
#! /bin/sh
# This shell script has lots of hard links, and all of them are
# to this file.  When you run this program, it shows the MH
# mail message with its name.  For instance, if you type:
#    % 5
# this program will execute the command 'show 5'.
/usr/local/mh/show `basename $0` $*
```

I put that short file in a directory named *shows*. My friends and I put the *shows* directory in our shell search paths (Section 9.2.1 explains how). Then I made the *README* file executable and made 999 hard links to it with the C shell loop below. The @ is the C shell's arithmetic operator:

```
% chmod +x README
% @ num=1
% while ($num < 1000)
? ln README $num
? echo made link $num
? @ num++
? end
made link 1
    ...
made link 999
```

The result is that I can read an MH message just by typing the message number. In fact, the $* in the script lets me give arguments to the *show* command. The following line will show messages 3, 12, and 22:

```
% 3 12 22
```

(That executes show 3 12 22.) Folders like +*inbox* work, too.

Actually, to make this more efficient, I used the shell's *exec* command:

```
exec /usr/local/mh/show `basename $0` $*
```

The *exec* saves a process (this is described with the *resend.fixmsg* script in Section 13.9.2).

Check with your system administrator before you do this; it is unusual to have thousands of links. Some filesystem-handling programs might not be robust enough to cope.

12.16.2 Exit Early

If you're getting an `end of file unexpected` error, put these two lines near the top of your script:

```
echo "DEBUG: quitting early..." 1>&2
exit
```

Then run your script. If you don't get the `end of file` unexpected error anymore, you know that the problem is somewhere after the `exit` line. Move those two lines farther down and try again.

12.16.3 Quoting

If the shell says `End of file unexpected`, look for a line in your script that has an opening quote, but no closing quote. The shell is probably searching for, but never finding, the matching quote. The same goes for missing parentheses and braces ({ }).

12.16.4 Missing or Extra esac, ;;, fi, etc.

A message like `line 23: ;; unexpected` means that you have an unmatched piece of code somewhere before line 23. Look at all nested *if* and *case* constructs and constructs like them to be sure that they end in the right places.

12.16.5 Line Numbers Reset Inside Redirected Loops

The shell may give you an error that mentions "line 1" or another line number that seems way too small, when there's no error close to the top of your script. Look at any loops or other structures with redirected inputs or outputs, like:

```
scan -form xxx |
while read ...
```

or:

```
for blat
do
    ...
done > outputfile
```

Some Bourne shells start a separate shell to run these loops and lose track of the line numbers.

12.17 Techniques and Tips for Programming with MH

Before we start looking at shell scripts, here are some useful miscellaneous things to know about programming with MH.

12.17.1 A Test Mail Setup⊠

I hate to experiment when I have folders full of important mail. I've made another MH directory named *Mail_test*. It has a duplicate set of files like *replcomps*, some folders with useless messages, and so on.

Whenever I want to test commands, I edit my MH profile and change the `Path:` component to read:

```
Path: Mail_test
```

Until I change that line back, MH commands use my *Mail_test* directory.

If I *inc* some messages that I want to keep, I just refile them into my "real" MH directory with a command like:

```
% refile +$HOME/Mail/inbox
```

and read them after I change the `Path:` back.

Another way to change your MH setup is by defining the *MH* environment variable. If it's defined, MH will use it as the location of the MH profile file—otherwise, MH defaults to *.mh_profile* in your home directory. You can make an MH profile with a name like *tmpMHprofile* in your home directory and set it up however you want for testing. Then, in the C shell, type the following command:

```
% setenv MH ~/tmpMHprofile
```

or in the Bourne shell:

```
$ MH=$HOME/tmpMHprofile
$ export MH
```

and your MH commands should use the alternate MH profile until you log out or unset that environment variable.

CAUTION

Some versions of *xmh* ignore the *MH* environment variable. See Section 16.5 for a workaround.

An easy way to make test messages is by linking to one message over and over. This is easiest if you create a test folder, then change your shell's current directory to it. After that, use *cp* to copy in a test message from some other folder. For example:

```
% folder +test
Create folder "/yourMHdir/test"? y
% cd `mhpath +test`
% pwd
/yourMHdir/test
% cp `mhpath cur +inbox` 100
% scan 100
  100  04/01 Steven Dommer       Re: meeting minutes<<> A while b
```

Be sure not to link this first message to the other folder (here, *inbox*). That's because any changes you make to a link will appear in the original message too!

Now you're ready to make your links to this test message. The easiest way is with a shell loop (Section 7.4 has another example). Each shell has a different way to do this; for the C shell, see Example 12-2.

Example 12-2. C shell loop to make 100 test messages

```
% @ num=1
% while ($num < 100)
? ln 100 $num
? echo made link $num
? @ num++
? end
made link 1
    ...
made link 99
%
```

The at sign (@) operator in Example 12-2 is the C shell's way of doing arithmetic. The command line @ num=1 sets $num to 1, and @ num++ increments $num by one. The loop makes the first link, adds 1 to num, then tests to see if $num is still less than 100.

The links save filesystem space. If you want individual copies instead of links, though, use *cp* instead of *ln*.

The standard Bourne shell doesn't have built-in arithmetic. To speed things up, Example 12-3 shows a tricky way to get numbers from the Bourne shell without addition. This set of nested loops does the same thing as the C shell loop above. They're indented for clarity.

Example 12-3. Bourne shell nested loop to make 100 test messages

```
$ for t in "" 1 2 3 4 5 6 7 8 9
> do
>     for o in 0 1 2 3 4 5 6 7 8 9
>     do
>           ln 100 $t$o
>           echo made link $t$o
>     done
> done
made link 0
made link 1
    ...
made link 99
$ rm 0
```

The loop in Example 12-3 is a little messy, and the *echo* command will slow it down if your shell doesn't have *echo* built in. It has an outer loop that sets $t, the "tens" place. The inner loop sets $o, the "ones" place. The loops are messy because they create a link named *0* which MH won't like; you can remove it with rm 0.

12.17.2 Mailing Files and Command Output with mhmail

Section 6.10 had an introduction to *mhmail*. This section shows some examples of its uses in shell programming.

Here's an example of running the UNIX *make* command and sending all of its output (*stdout* and *stderr*) to the *mhmail* command. The syntax is different in the Bourne and C shells; I'll show you both:

```
$ make dist 2>&1 | mhmail janeq -cc joed\        Bourne shell
    -subject "make dist output" &
```

```
% make dist |& mhmail janeq -cc joed\            C shell
    -subject "make dist output" &
```

mhmail reads the message from its standard input (here, the pipe). The message is sent to janeq; there's a cc: to joed. The Subject: is make dist output—you need the quotes to protect the spaces from the shell. The ampersand (&) at the end puts the job into the background.

You can do the same thing from inside a Bourne or C shell script, of course. For instance, to mail a temporary file named $temp to the user who is running your script ($USER), your shell script could execute:

```
mhmail $USER -subject "XXX XXX" < $temp
```

Be sure to use a left angle bracket (<), not a right angle bracket (>).

mhmail also has a *–body* switch. For example, to mail the contents of the shell variable named *msgnums* to *carolo* and *projboss*, your shell script could use:

```
mhmail carolo,projboss -subj 'contents of $msgnums' -body "$msgnums"
```

Notice the quoting: the subject will have a literal $msgnums, but the body will have the contents of the variable.

As Section 6.3 explained, *mhmail* doesn't pay attention to mail aliases. To use an alias with *mhmail*, have the *ali* command (in Section 6.3.2) get it for you. Use backquotes to put the addresses on the *mhmail* command line:

```
mhmail `ali -list group` < msgfile
```

Watch out: without command-line arguments, *mhmail* runs *inc*.* In that example, if *ali* doesn't match your alias, *mhmail* won't do what you want. A workaround would run *mhmail* only if *ali* returns some characters:

```
addrs="`ali -list group`"
case "$addrs" in
"") echo "scriptname: 'ali' can't find 'group' alias." 1>&2 ;;
*)  mhmail $addrs < msgfile ;;
esac
```

12.17.3 The mhpath Command

Because users can change their MH directory structures completely, your shell programs shouldn't assume anything about the locations of folders or the names of their MH directories. Instead, use *mhpath* to get this information.

Here are some examples:

```
$ folder
        inbox+ has  23 messages (   2-  47); cur=  15.
$ mhpath
/u/ehuser/Mail/inbox
$ mhpath last:2
/u/ehuser/Mail/inbox/46 /u/ehuser/Mail/inbox/47
$ mhpath new
/u/ehuser/Mail/inbox/48
$ mhpath +somefolder
/u/ehuser/Mail/somefolder
```

---

*mhmail was designed to be similar the standard UNIX *mail* command. With no addresses, *mail* gets your new mail.

```
$ mhpath +
/u/ehuser/Mail
$ folder
        inbox+ has  23 messages (   2-  47); cur=  15.
```

With no arguments, *mhpath* gives the full pathname of your current folder. If you give message numbers, sequences, or ranges, you'll get the full pathname of each message. The special argument new gives you the pathname that a new message in the folder would have—useful if you're creating a new message. If you give a folder name, *mhpath* gives the full pathname of that folder but it doesn't change the current folder. The folder doesn't have to exist yet unless you want the paths of messages in the folder. Finally, an argument of just a plus sign (+) gives the path of the MH directory itself.

You'll almost always use *mhpath* with command substitution (the backquotes). For efficiency, you can run *mhpath* once at the start of the shell script to grab things like the location of the user's MH directory and store that information in a shell variable.

12.17.4 Getting Message Numbers

Does your program handle command-line arguments like *last:10* or *6 25-cur*? If your script is running only MH commands, that's no problem because MH commands can understand those message lists. If you're using a standard UNIX command like *grep* or *awk*, you'll need the message filenames.

The *mhpath* command in Section 12.17.3 will give you full pathnames. That's usually okay for short lists of messages. But pathnames aren't always what you want:

- Pathnames aren't efficient for handling lots of messages. UNIX has to traverse the same list of directories in the path to get each message. That can slow down your program and waste disk access time.

- Some programs don't need the message pathnames; they just need the individual message numbers.

Two MH commands, *pick* and *scan*, can convert a message range like *25-cur* into a list of messages. For example, if the current message is 34, the next command might store the list 6 25 26 29 31 33 34 in the variable *msgs*:

```
args="6 25-cur"
msgs="`pick -list $args`"
```

Using *pick* that way can cause trouble if you have certain *pick* switches in your MH profile. For example, using *–sequence picked* in the MH profile means that

your script will overwrite a folder's *picked* sequence every time you run *pick* to
get a message number list.* A better (but slightly ugly) answer is to use *scan*.
Give *scan* the MH format string % (cur) that prints just the message numbers.
(Section 10.2 explains MH format strings.) Here's the previous example with
scan instead of *pick*:

```
args="6 25-cur"
msgs="`scan -format '%(msg)' $args`"
```

Whether you get the list from *pick* or *scan*, though, here's how to access the individual messages in a folder. Grab any folder name from the command line (as
shown in Example 12-1) and *cd* to the folder like this:

```
cd `mhpath $folder` || exit 1
```

If *mhpath* fails or the folder name isn't valid, the || exit 1 will abort the
script. Otherwise, you can use the message numbers from *pick* or *scan* as
filenames because the messages will be files in the current directory.

12.17.5   Getting Information from the MH Profile

MH programs search for components in the MH profile—for instance, *show* uses
the show: and showproc: components. The shell script called *mhprofile*, in
Section 13.4, will let your script get its own (or other) components from the MH
profile. For instance, a script named *progname* could execute these lines to get
any MH profile switches into a shell variable named *progopts*:

```
myname="`basename $0`"
progopts="`mhprofile $myname`"
```

12.17.6   Getting Information from the Environment

When an MH command runs, it may set some environment variables to be used
by programs it calls. For example, when *repl* starts its *–editor* program, the editor
can get the value of *$editalt* from the environment; it holds the pathname of the
original message.

Table 12-3 is taken from the *mh–profile*(5) manual page. For more description of
each environment variable, see the manual page in Appendix I. The table doesn't
include MH environment variables set by parts of MH which this book doesn't

---

*There's no *pick –nosequence* switch to solve this problem.

cover, such as BBoards. In this table, a "full pathname" means a pathname starting at the root directory like */yourMHdir/inbox/4* .

Table 12-3. Environment Variables that MH Sets

Variable	Command	Description
editalt	*dist* *repl*	Full pathname of message being distributed or replied to.
mhaltmsg	*dist* *repl*	Full pathname of message being distributed or replied to.
mhannotate	*dist* *forw* *repl*	If *−annotate* is used, set to annotation string for original message header: `Forwarded:`, `Replied:`, or `Resent:`.
mhdist	*dist*	Contains 1 if draft message is being distributed (signal not to allow text in the draft body), 0 otherwise.
mhdraft	*comp* *dist* *forw* *repl*	Full pathname of the draft message.
mheditor	all	Full pathname of text editor program.
mhfolder	*dist* *forw* *repl* *show* *prev* *next*	Full pathname of folder that holds the alternate message.
mhinplace	*dist* *forw* *repl*	Set to 1 if *−annotate −inplace* used, to 0 if *−annotate* is used.
mhmessages	*dist* *forw* *repl*	List of message number(s) to annotate; for example, `23−25 34`.
mhuse	*comp*	Set to 1 during *comp −use*; 0 otherwise.
MHFD	all	File descriptor of MH profile (experimental) (only if OVERHEAD configuration option set).
MHCONTEXTFD	all	File descriptor of MH context (experimental) (only if OVERHEAD configuration option set).

Part III
Customizing MH

12.17.7 Changing the MH Environment⊠

As Sections 12.5.2 and 12.17.6 explain, some MH commands add environment
variables that are passed to environments of their child processes. MH commands
also read their own environments, set by their parent processes. For example, if
the variable *MHCONTEXT* is set, MH commands will use that pathname for the
MH context file instead of the file named *context* in the MH directory.

Table 12-4 was adapted from the *mh–profile*(5) manual page. For more description of each environment variable, see that manual page in Appendix I. This
table doesn't include environment variables used by parts of MH (like BBoards)
which this book doesn't cover.

Table 12-4. Environment Variables that MH Checks

Variable	Command	Description
HOME	all	Full pathname of your home directory.
MAILDROP	*inc*	Default maildrop (like */usr/spool/mail/ehuser*).
MH	all	Pathname of MH profile* (default: *.mh_profile* in home directory).
MHCONTEXT	all	Pathname of *context* file.
SIGNATURE	*send* *post*	Your name, for `From:` component (for example, `"Emma H. User"`).
TERM *TERMCAP*	*scan* *mhl*	Terminal information; see the *environ*(5) manual page.

12.17.8 Writing Your Own Draft Message Editor(s)

You may want to do more than an editor like *vi* or *emacs* can do to a draft message. For instance, you might want to start *prompter* on the new draft, then run a
second editor to fill in the body. Or you might want to do something automatically each time a draft message is edited, like updating a mail message log. Or
you could customize the way that a particular MH program, such as *dist*, handles
a draft message. These are all good reasons to write a special editing shell script.

---

* *xmh* Release 4, and possibly earlier versions too, ignore the *MH* environment variable at startup time.
It always reads the *.mh_profile* in your home directory to find the `Path:` of your MH directory.
There's a workaround in Section 16.5.

There are five things to know before you write your editor script:

1. Each of the four mail composition commands will make a draft message for you. If no other editor (including *prompter*) has touched it, the draft will contain:

   - For *comp*, an empty copy of the *components* file. (Exception: with *comp –use*, draft will be exactly as it was left before.)

   - For *repl*, the result of the *replcomps* file, with the original message filtered through the *–filter* file (if you used one).

   - For *forw*, a copy of the *forwcomps* file, with the forwarded message(s) (filtered through *–format* or *–filter* if you used one).

   - For *dist*, a copy of the *distcomps* file.

   For more information, see Section 6.1.1.

2. The full pathname of the draft message will be in the $1 parameter.

3. You can use the environment variables listed in Table 12-3.

4. Your editor should save the edited draft in the same file ($1) where it read the draft from.

5. If your editor exits with a zero status, *whatnow* will prompt the user What now?. If your editor exits with a nonzero status, *whatnow* will abort without sending the message, and:

   - If the *mhuse* variable is set to 1 (the *comp –use* program is being used), your draft message won't be deleted.

   - Otherwise, the draft message will be deleted.

Section 13.10 has an editor shell script that acts like *prompter* to read the message header of a message you're distributing with *dist*. When it's done reading the header components, it saves the draft and exits without giving you a chance to type the body (you can't type a body for *dist*).

Even if you don't run *distprompter*, it's a good example of what you can do with an MH draft editor. To run *distprompter* or another editor that you write, put a component like this in your MH profile:

```
dist: -editor distprompter
```

If you write a more general purpose shell script editor for all the MH message composing programs, you can use an MH profile component like this instead:

```
Editor: myeditor
```

One more note about editors: even though the *mh–profile*(5) and *whatnow*(1) manual pages have a lot of details, they don't explain an editor's environment or the effect of its exit status very thoroughly. I wrote this little test editor script that helped me learn. Maybe it'll help you:

```
#! /bin/sh
echo The environment of $0:
printenv
echo "Command line had: '$*'"
echo -n "Enter exit status for $0: "
read stat
exit $stat
```

Run it by typing, for example:

```
% comp -editor testedit
```

12.17.9   Using scan Format Strings to Get Information

Section 10.2 showed how to write format files for *scan*. Format files, or format strings, are a great way to get information about mail messages for a shell program. For instance, here's a a format string that prints the message number in a field of width 4, a space, then either the Sender: (if the message has one) or the From:. It formats the addresses with the %(friendly) function, which gives a "nice" output when it can:

```
$ scan -format \
    "%4(msg) %<{sender}%(friendly{sender})%|%(friendly{from})%>"
  46 "Don C. Meach"
  47 mh-users-request@ics.uci.edu
  48 Jerry Peek
```

You could use a *scan* format string like that to write a simple loop that processes mail messages automatically. This one uses the *(mbox)* function to get the address without the hostname:*

```
msgfrom="%(msg) %<{sender}%(mbox{sender})%|%(mbox{from})%>"
    ...
scan -format "$msgfrom" |
while read msgnum from
do
        # DON'T READ ANYTHING FROM steveq; refile ALL mh-users MAIL.
        # LEAVE OTHER MESSAGES ALONE:
        case "$from" in
```

---

*There are more efficient ways to process incoming mail—see Chapter 11, *Processing New Mail Automatically*.

```
        steveq) rmm $msgnum ;;
        mh-users) refile $msgnum +mh-users ;;
        esac
    done
```

This is using a Bourne shell *while* loop with its standard input taken from the pipe (from the *scan* command). The *read* command reads a line of input; it puts the first word (here, the message number) in a shell variable named *msgnum*, and the rest (the local part of the address) goes into the variable called *from*. Then, a *case* structure checks who sent the message and does the right thing with it.

12.17.10 Watch Out for the MH Profile

If you use MH commands in your scripts and your script depends on the format of the command's output, you could have trouble if someone edits the MH profile and changes the command's default options. It's usually safer either to give all the command-line options explicitly, right in your shell script, like this:

```
    show -showproc mhl -noheader ...
```

or to make a temporary MH profile (see the script in Section 13.6 for an example).

One special note: in UNIX, many users can share the same shell script. If a shell script uses the default *scan* output without a format file or format string, the user can change the output (in their MH profile files) and there's no way for you to stop it. In other words, *scan* doesn't have *–noform* or *–noformat* switches to override the user's format. To take care of the problem, you can make your own format file that gives the default *scan* output and run *scan* in your scripts with *–form scan.default*. The format file is in Section 10.2.4.

12.17.11 Problems with folder, inc, and refile

If you give a folder name to *folder*, *inc*, or *refile* and that folder doesn't exist, you'll be asked whether to create the folder. That's usually fine. But if you leave the shell script running unattended, your script can hang, waiting for an answer, if you accidentally give a nonexistent folder name:

```
    % somescript +inbog
```

There can be a worse problem if you put your shell script into the background (if you type an ampersand (&) at the end of the command line)—and if your shell doesn't have job control. In this case, the *folder*, *inc*, and *refile* commands will still prompt for a y or n answer. But they'll immediately assume you answered y, create the folder you didn't want, and the script will keep running.* The workaround is code like the following in shell scripts before every *refile*, *inc*, or *folder* (or, at least, before the first use of any folder name):

```
if test -d `mhpath +$folderarg`
then
      # do whatever you want to do with +$folderarg
else
      # complain that folder doesn't exist...
fi
```

The preceding example uses *mhpath* to get the pathname where the folder would be, then uses *if test -d* to see whether the folder really exists. If the folder doesn't exist, the script can print an error, abort, or whatever you want.

---

*This is because, if these three MH commands read *anything* except the character n, they assume you mean "yes." Shells without job control run background shell scripts with standard input taken from */dev/null*, the UNIX "empty file," which is always readable. Even reading a null string from */dev/null* is a "yes" to these three commands!

13

MH Shell Programs

This chapter has shell programs that I think you'll find useful. Even if you don't want to use them in your day-to-day work, each one demonstrates something new about shell programming with MH—so they're worth studying.

Shell programs let you go further with MH customization. You can use groups of MH commands to do things that MH versions (in Chapter 9, *New Versions of MH Commands*) won't let you do. Because MH is the only user agent whose commands are typed from the shell prompt, this chapter shows you another reason that MH is so useful.

The best way to find out what the programs do is to browse through the first part of each section. Each section starts with an introduction and demonstration of that shell script.

The scripts use a lot of the same techniques; I'll explain a technique in detail only in the first script that uses it. Check the Index by command name or character to find the detailed explanation. If you haven't done UNIX Bourne shell programming, you should read Chapter 12, *Introduction to Shell Programming for MH*, first. A good reference book on UNIX shell programming may help you, too—see Appendix C, *Reference List*.

13.1 Some Notes About Shell Scripts

Here's overall information that will help you use this chapter. Some of it is to answer the questions that always come up about design and programming philosophy.

These scripts don't use features of the newer Bourne shells that have more built-in commands and options. Some programs (like *distprompter* in Section 13.10) are longer because of that. The benefit is that the scripts should work on all Bourne shells. If you want to modify these for your system's shell, you might add a comment at the top warning that the script won't be portable.

Many UNIX users believe that a short shell script is better than a longer script with more error checking. "Make it short, sweet, and simple," they say. I agree, to a point. Short scripts are easier to understand—and short, elegant scripts are just plain beautiful. But they're not always robust; many short scripts can't catch the sort of mistakes that inexperienced users make. People who aren't UNIX experts need help and more complete explanation than an error message like ? or RE botch. (Helpful messages can help UNIX experts, too, when they forget what a shell script is expecting. It beats digging through the code to find out what's wrong.)

In this chapter, I've tried to include programs that use features I've found useful and are full of error checking. If you'd like shorter scripts, just chop out the parts you don't want.

The scripts in this chapter are all available over the network and by e-mail from O'Reilly & Associates archive sites. Appendix E, *Copies of Files Over the Network*, explains how.

The shell scripts printed here don't have their initial comment blocks. That's because of the limited space in this book, and also because each shell script is explained in the text. If you type in these scripts yourself from the text, you can make a respectable comment block or manual page from the explanations in the text. The archived versions of the scripts come with a full comment block at the top.

Before you run any of these scripts, do what you'd do with any unknown software: read through it and test to be sure that it'll work well in your setup. Although I use the scripts myself and have tried to write them portably, I can't be responsible for problems you have. Finally, if you find a bug or have a suggestion, please tell us about it. Our address is in the Preface. We'll update the online archives periodically. If you got your copy of a script awhile ago, you might look for an updated version online.

Enough of this. Let's get on with the scripts!

13.2 Add Files to Your Draft Messages: append

To add the contents of a file to your draft message, you can always go into an editor such as *vi* and use its read file (:r) command. But that's not very efficient, especially for attaching several files.

The paper "MH.5: How to Process 200 Messages a Day and Still Get Some Real Work Done," by Marshall T. Rose and John L. Romine, has a shell script called *append*.* Here's a version of the script that lets you type more than one filename; it also allows wildcards, environment variables, and abbreviated filenames. You call it as an editor at the What now? prompt. For example, to append a copy of your file *report* to your draft message:

```
What now? edit append report
```

After it appends the file(s), you get another What now? prompt. If you want to separate the files you append with blank lines, rows of dashes, or whatever, an easy way is to make a little file named something like *separator* with that separator in it:

```
% cat separator
-=-=-=-=-=-=-=-=-=-=-=-=-=-=-=-=-=-=-=-=-=-=-=-=-=-=-=-=
```

---

*There's also a version, with work by Bob Desinger, in the *miscellany/scripts* directory of the MH 6.7 distribution. It comes with an online manual page.

This next example shows how to append all the files from the *$HOME/proj* direc-
tory whose names end with *.out*, then your separator file, and then a file in the
current directory named *.signature*:

```
What now? e append $HOME/proj/*.out sep .signature
```

The sep above is an abbreviation for the separator file's full filename. See the
explanation in Section 13.2.2.

Section 13.13 shows a way to add files automatically: a *sendproc* script. Section 8.9.6 has a simpler way to add text (like a signature) every time you send a
message: by changing your draft message template files.

13.2.1 Listing of append

Here's the *append* program. The line numbers to the left of each line (like *12>*)
are not part of the file; they are for reference only. Like other scripts in the chapter, this is explained afterward, in Section 13.2.2.

```
1> #! /bin/sh
2> # $Id: append,v 1.12 92/07/24 17:35:58 jerry book2 $
3> ### append - append file(s) to an MH mail message
4> ### Usage:   What now? e append file [files...]
5>
6> case $# in
7> 0)   echo 1>&2 "`basename $0`: shouldn't get here!"; exit 1;;
8> 1)   echo 1>&2 "Usage: e[dit] `basename $0` file [files...]"; exit 1 ;;
9> *)   while :
10>        do
11>           case $# in
12>           1)   msg=$1; break ;;
13>           *)   # WIRE IN COMMON NAMES HERE.  COMMENT OUT IF NOT USING. -emv
14>                case "$1" in
15> #            sig)    files="$files $HOME/.signature" ;;
16> #            sep)    files="$files $HOME/Mail/separator" ;;
17>              *)      files="$files $1" ;;
18>              esac
19>              shift
20>              ;;
21>           esac
22>        done
23>        ;;
24> esac
25>
26> eval cat $files '>>' $msg  # EXPAND ENVARIABLES IN $files (PROTECT >>)
27> exit 0  # FAKE SUCCESS TO KEEP MH FROM DELETING DRAFT IF cat FAILED
```

13.2.2 Explanation of append

To install the *append* program, first create the file *append*. Then make the file executable by entering:

```
% chmod 755 append
```

Line 1 of the code tells UNIX to use the Bourne shell, and **line 2** is a marker from RCS, the UNIX *R*evision *C*ontrol *S*ystem. **Lines 3-4** are comments and usage information.

Line 6 starts a *case* that checks the number of command-line arguments. There should be at least two: the filename that the user wants to add and the draft message pathname, which the *whatnow* program adds automatically to the end of the command line. **Line 7** should never be reached if *whatnow* is working right, and **line 8** reminds you to type a filename. (The `basename $0` in **line 7** is explained in Section 12.15.)

Lines 9-22 are a *while* loop that puts a list of the filename(s) in the *files* shell variable. The colon (`:`) on **line 9** is a Bourne shell operator that returns a zero status. So, the `while  :` always tests true—and the loop keeps running until there are no more filenames, which the *case* handles. The *case* tests `$#`, the number of command-line arguments.

If there's more than one argument (and there will be the first time through the loop), **line 14** tests the first argument (`$1`) to see if it's one of your personal abbreviations for a file—or just a filename. Each line of the *case* structure adds a filename to the list in the *files* shell variable—then it *shift*s away the first argument and repeats the loop.

Lines 15-16 handle the filename abbreviations. For example, the abbreviation `sig` on the command line will be replaced by the file *.signature* in your home directory. These abbreviations keep you from appending a file that's actually named *sig* or *sep*, so lines 15 and 16 are commented out. To use them, remove the comments. Of course, you can change these abbreviations and add other abbreviation lines. When there's just one argument left, **line 12** puts the last argument in the *msg* shell variable—then it executes *break*, which ends this "endless" loop.

After the *while* loop ends, if the user had typed a command line like this:

```
What now? e append file* $HOME/end
```

then `$files` would contain exactly `file*  $HOME/end`. That's because the *whatnow* program doesn't expand wildcards or environment variables at its

What now? prompt. If you tried to append these files with a command such as the following:

```
cat $files >> $msg
```

the shell would change `file*` into filenames, but it would not expand `$HOME/end`—and *cat* would complain that it couldn't find that file. To fix that, **line 26** uses the shell's *eval* command to reinterpret the command line—in other words, to parse it twice. Table 13-1 shows the steps.

Table 13-1. Using eval, Line 26 of append

Step	Command Line
Original line	`eval cat $files '>>' $msg`
After `eval`	`cat filea fileb $HOME/end >> /yourMHdir/draft`
Command executed	`cat filea fileb /xx/yy/end >> /yourMHdir/draft`

When you use *eval*, you have to remember to quote special characters that shouldn't be interpreted until the command is executed. That's why the two right angle brackets (`'>>'`) (the shell's append-to-file operator) have quotes around them. Watch what happens to it in Table 13-1: the shell doesn't interpret the `'>>'` as a redirection operator until *eval* is done.

Finally, the `exit 0` command on **line 27** sets an exit status of 0 to be sure that *whatnow* won't delete the draft. An editor that returns nonzero status has "failed"—by default, *whatnow* will delete a failed draft and quit. Section 6.5.3, "Deleted Draft Messages," explains more.

13.3 Finish Draft Messages in Draft Folder: recomp

When you type q at a What now? prompt, it leaves the draft message without sending it. If you have a draft folder, the command line you'd type to recompose the draft is long. Also, it can be hard to remember the draft number—so you have to *scan* the draft folder, then remember to change your folder back.

The *recomp* script helps with that. If you give it a message number in the draft folder, it starts *comp −use* on that message with your favorite editor program. Without a message number, *recomp* scans the draft folder, then lets you enter the number of the message you want to recompose, and then starts *comp −use*. When you exit your editor, you get the usual What now? prompt.

13.3.1 Listing of recomp

Any line that doesn't start with a line number is a continuation of the line above; we split it to fit the book page but you should type it on one line. This program is explained in Section 13.3.2.

```
1> #! /bin/sh
2> # $Id: recomp,v 1.8 92/07/24 17:35:59 jerry book2 $
3> ### recomp - re-compose a draft mesage in MH draft folder
4> ### Usage: recomp [msgnum]
5>
6> draftf=+drafts  # NAME OF DRAFT FOLDER
7> folopts="-fast -norecurse -nolist -nototal -nopack"
8> mh=/usr/local/mh     # WHERE MH PROGRAMS LIVE
9>
10> # THIS CAN LEAVE US IN THE $draftf FOLDER.  SO, PUSH
11> # CURRENT FOLDER ON STACK AND COME BACK AFTER EDITING:
12> $mh/folder -push $folopts $draftf >/dev/null || {
13>     echo "`basename $0`: quitting: problem with draft folder '$draftf'."
    1>&2
14>     exit 1
15> }
16> stat=1   # DEFAULT EXIT STATUS; RESET TO 0 FOR NORMAL EXITS
17> trap '$mh/folder -pop $folopts >/dev/null; exit $stat' 0
18> trap 'echo "`basename $0`: Interrupt!  Cleaning up..." 1>&2' 1 2 15
19>
20> case $# in
21> 0)  # THEY DIDN'T GIVE MESSAGE NUMBER; SHOW THEM FOLDER:
22>     if $mh/scan
23>     then
24>         echo -n "Which draft message number do you want to re-edit? "
25>         read msgnum
26>     else
27>         echo "`basename $0`: quitting: no messages in your $draftf
    folder?" 1>&2
28>         exit
29>     fi
30>     ;;
31> 1)  msgnum="$1" ;;
32> *)  echo "I don't understand '$*'.
33>     I need the draft message number, if you know it... otherwise,
    nothing.
34>     Usage: `basename $0` [msgnum]" 1>&2
35>     exit
36>     ;;
37> esac
38>
39> $mh/comp -use -e ${VISUAL-${EDITOR-${EDIT-vi}}} -draftm $msgnum -draftf
    $draftf
40> stat=$?   # SAVE comp'S STATUS (IT'S USUALLY 0) FOR OUR exit
```

13.3.2 Explanation of recomp

Line 6 sets the draft folder name. If more than one person is running *recomp*, you should replace line 6 with a call to the *mhprofile* program, shown in Section 13.4. The following code will set the right draft folder for everyone—and exit if *mhprofile* has trouble:

```
draftf="+`mhprofile -b draft-folder`" || {
    echo "`basename $0`: quitting: trouble finding your draft folder." 1>&2
    exit 1
}
```

Line 7 is a list of command-line switches for *folder* that override any undesirable switches in the user's MH profile. This is important because, for instance, `folder: -pack` in the MH profile would renumber the draft messages—but the user wouldn't be expecting that here. You shouldn't always override MH profile switches this way. For example, the *scan* in line 22 can't hurt much; as a matter of fact, users would probably appreciate having the *scan* output they're used to seeing ...

Line 8 holds information that isn't *required* to be in a shell variable. It's at the start of the script so it'll be easy to see and to change if needed. A line like line 8 is especially important for programs, such as MH programs, which aren't likely to be in every user's search path.* I try to write my scripts so that any user on the system can run them without errors and without resetting their search path.

Line 12 pushes the draft folder onto the folder stack; it's popped at the end of the script.† */dev/null* is the UNIX "trash can," a place to redirect output that you don't want. The | | { . . . } after the *folder* command is like a backwards *if*. It reads "if *folder* returns a nonzero status, then do the list of commands between the braces." The | | is an OR operator that tests the exit status of the command on its left side; if it's zero, the command list on its right-hand side is skipped. The braces ({ }) are the Bourne shell's list operator; they group commands together into a unit.

Line 16 sets a default exit status of 1 that will be used in the *trap* in line 17. The only time *stat* is reset is after *comp –use* runs; if the script exits any sooner, it will exit with a nonzero status. The *trap* pops the draft folder off the stack.

---

*Some programmers like to reset the search path during a shell script by putting an explicit PATH= line at the start of the script.

†The script actually needs to push the folder only if the *scan* in line 23 is run, because this script wouldn't change the current folder otherwise. But that way, there'd have to be some sort of conditional trap, or the *trap* would have to be buried inside the *case* structure somewhere. This just seemed cleaner.

The first *trap*, **line 17**, is "sprung" when the shell script exits—it pops the draft folder off the stack and exits with the status saved in the *stat* variable. The second *trap*, **line 18**, looks almost useless—it just echoes a message to the screen on signal 1, 2, or 15 (the *hangup* signal, the signal from CTRL-C , and the signal from the *kill*(1) command, respectively).* But the second trap is doing more than just echoing a message. If signals 1, 2, and 15 weren't trapped, the trap for signal 0 would not be sprung on interrupt. If that happened, the folder stack wouldn't be popped. After this second trap is sprung, the first trap will be, too.

Line 20 starts a *case* structure that checks the number of command-line arguments. If there are no arguments, **lines 22-29** scan the draft folder and prompt for a message number to recompose. If there aren't any messages in the draft folder or there is some other problem, *scan* returns nonzero status and the script is aborted in lines 27-28. If there was one command-line argument, **line 31** stores it; we let the *comp* command check to see if it's a valid message number. If there was more than one argument, **lines 32-35** catch this.

Finally, **line 39** runs comp –use –editor *xxx* on the draft message, where *xxx* is one of several editors. In the Bourne shell, ${*varname-default*} means that if the variable *varname* is set, use its value; otherwise, use *default*. The script has four choices. First, if the *VISUAL* environment variable is defined, it's used; second, the shell tries the *EDITOR* environment variable; third, it tries *EDIT*. Finally, if none of those choices are defined, the default editor is *vi*.

Line 40 stores the exit status of *comp* in the shell variable *stat*. The *trap* exits *recomp* with the same status.

13.4 Get Information from MH Profile: mhprofile

When you're writing a shell script, you can extract information like the Draft-Folder: name or the Msg-Protect: mode number from the MH profile. You can also store default options for a shell script of yours in the MH profile.

The *mhprofile* shell script lets you do that. It reads all lines with a certain component name from the profile and writes them on its standard output. With the *–b*

---

*I don't trap signal 3 (*SIGQUIT*, often made with CTRL-\ ) because that gives me a way to abort the script without springing the traps.

option it will also strip off the component name, leaving just the value. For example:

```
% cat .mh_profile
     ...
myprog: -noverbose -sort
     ...
% mhprofile myprog
myprog: -noverbose -sort
% mhprofile -b myprog
-noverbose -sort
```

Your program could use lines such as the following to get its profile ($profswch) and command-line ($*) switches:

```
myname="`basename $0`"
# IF mhprofile FAILS, EXIT WITH ITS STATUS:
profswch="`mhprofile -b $myname`" || exit
for arg in $profswch $*
do
    ...Parse switches...
done
```

However, *mhprofile* uses *grep* to search for matching lines. Because *grep* doesn't understand MH's idea of continuation lines, *mhprofile* will only find the first line of a component as in the following example:

```
progname: -xxx 'blah blah blah' -yyy 'etc. etc. etc;'
    -zzz 'whatever else'
```

The easiest solution is to make your line long and not split it.

If you need to search for multiline components, either make *mhprofile* use something besides *grep* or put your patterns on multiple lines:

```
progname: -xxx 'blah blah blah' -yyy 'etc. etc. etc;'
progname: -zzz 'whatever else'
```

For most MH programs, that's not a problem.

13.4.1 Listing of mhprofile

This program is explained in Section 13.4.2.

```
1> #! /bin/sh
2> # $Id: mhprofile,v 1.6 92/07/24 17:36:00 jerry book2 $
3> ### mhprofile - show matching line(s) from MH profile file
4> ### Usage: mhprofile [-b] component-name
5>
6> grep=/bin/grep   # HAS -i OPTION, HANDLES REGULAR EXPRESSIONS
```

```
 7> sed=/bin/sed
 8> profile=${MH-${HOME?}/.mh_profile}  # COMPLAIN, EXIT IF $HOME NOT SET
 9>
10> # GET -b OPTION, IF ANY, AND shift IT AWAY:
11> case "$1" in
12> -b) stripname=y; shift;;
13> -*) echo "Usage: `basename $0` [-b] component-name" 1>&2; exit 2 ;;
14> esac
15>
16> # ONLY REMAINING ARGUMENT SHOULD BE A COMPONENT NAME:
17> case $# in
18> 1)  ;;
19> *)  echo "`basename $0` quitting: wrong number of args." 1>&2; exit 2 ;;
20> esac
21>
22> # IF grep FAILS, RETURN ITS STATUS (1=NO MATCH, 2=ERROR):
23> lines="`$grep -i \"^${1}:\" $profile`" || exit
24>
25> # IF -b SET, USE sed TO SEARCH AND STRIP OFF LABEL+WHITESPACE.
26> # ASSUME NO COLON IN NAME, ":" AND MAYBE WHITESPACE AFTER NAME:
27> case "$stripname" in
28> y)  echo "$lines" | $sed -n 's/^[^:]*:[    ]*//p' ;;
29> *)  echo "$lines" ;;
30> esac
31> exit 0  # A LITTLE PRESUMPTUOUS
```

13.4.2 Explanation of mhprofile

This program returns two different nonzero exit statuses—the same way that *grep*(1) does. The calling program might want to know the difference. If *mhprofile* doesn't find a matching line in the MH profile, it returns status 1. If there was some other error (like an invalid option), *mhprofile* returns 2.

Line 6 chooses one of the two *grep* programs that are available on some systems. **Line 8** chooses the profile in the *MH* environment variable, if it's set. Otherwise, it uses *$HOME/.mh_profile*. The ${HOME?} tells the shell to print an error and exit if the *HOME* variable isn't set.

Lines 10-14 check for a *–b* option. If there is one, **line 12** sets a flag (puts a y in the variable called stripname) and does a *shift*. The shell's *shift* command throws away the first command-line argument that used to be in $1, and replaces it with the second argument (that used to be $2, now renamed to $1)—and so on, with the other command-line arguments (there should be only one). **Line 13** checks for any other option (that's not *–b*) and complains about it.

Whether there was a *–b* option or not, by the time the shell gets to line 16, the component name should be in $1. **Lines 16-20** check this by testing the shell's

$# parameter, which is a count of the number of command-line arguments remaining. If there isn't exactly one, the script exits with a 2 status.

Line 23 uses *grep –i* to search for any lines that start with the component name you want, in any combination of uppercase and lowercase letters. Let's look at the quoting (the grayed section):

```
lines="`$grep -i \"^${1}:\" $profile`" || exit
```

The backslashes (\) before the quotes tell the shell to pass those quotes into the backquoted *grep* command line, thereby telling the shell not to interpret the quotes until the inner *grep* command line is executed. The braces ({ }) in ${1}: tell the shell that the colon (:) isn't part of the command-line argument $1.* The caret (^) tells *grep* to only match at the start of a line. The colon helps to make sure that *grep* only matches the exact component names, like repl:—not parts of other components, like replx:.

The end of line 23, || exit, will be executed only if *grep* returns a nonzero status. That will make this shell script exit, too. Because the exit doesn't have an explicit value to return (like 0), it returns the exit status of the previous command—in this case, the *grep* command. So if *grep* can't find a match, *mhprofile* will return exit status 1. And, if *grep* has some other error (like a missing MH profile file), *mhprofile* will return 2.

grep will probably find only one matching line—or, at most, a few lines. So the script stores the output of *grep* in a shell variable ($lines) instead of using a temporary file. This is more efficient and it means there's no temporary file to remove. The shell will keep the newline characters between lines, if there's more than one matching line.

There are also more sophisticated ways to handle quoting from inside the MH profile—for an example, see the way that the *showpr* script (in Section 13.11) uses *mhprofile*.

Lines 25-30 output the matching line(s). If there was a *–b* option, **line 28** uses *sed* to strip off the component name, colon (:), and any spaces or tabs after the colon. Otherwise, **line 29** just *echo*s the line(s).

The comment on **line 31** complains that the script doesn't test for anything to go wrong with the *sed* command. That might be too picky . . .

---

*Separating a parameter name from a colon is only required in C shell scripts—but it's not a bad idea in the Bourne shell.

13.5 List Folders in Columns with fols

Here's a new version of *fols*, the program that's shown at the start of Chapter 12, *Introduction to Shell Programming for MH*. *fols* prints the *folders –fast* output in columns. Like *folder*, the *fols* script also has a *–recurse* option for listing subfolders. This one uses two *sed* expressions to do the following:

- Shorten long folder names in the middle and put an equal sign (=) where characters were deleted.

- Put a plus sign (+) at the end of the current folder name.

Here's an example with nine folders listed. The current folder is *inbox* and the *mh–users_tosave/DELETE* folder name has been shortened:

```
% fols -r
drafts              drafts/DELETE    inbox+          inbox/DELETE
mh-users_tosave     mh-users=ve/DELETE mh-workers    reference
reference/DELETE
```

13.5.1 Listing of fols

This program is explained in Section 13.5.2.

```
1> #! /bin/sh
2> # $Id: fols,v 1.9 92/07/24 17:36:00 jerry book2 $
3> ### fols - Show list of folders, in columns, current folder marked
4> ### Usage: fols [ -recurse ]  << (just -r is enough...)
5>
6> folopts="-fast -nolist -nototal -nopack" # OVERRIDE MH PROFILE
7> rec=
8>
9> case "$#$1" in
10> 0"") ;;
11> 1-r*) rec=-recurse ;;
12> *)   echo "Usage: `basename $0` [ -recurse ]" 1>&2; exit 1 ;;
13> esac
14>
15> # USE BACKQUOTES TO "PASTE" THE CURRENT FOLDER NAME
16> # INTO THE sed EXPRESSION THAT ADDS A + TO END.
17> # THEN, IN ANY LINE WHICH HAS AT LEAST 19 CHARACTERS,
18> # SAVE FIRST 8 AND LAST 9 CHARACTERS AND REPLACE
19> # MIDDLE CHARACTER(S) WITH AN = SIGN.  FINALLY, GIVE
20> # TO pr WITH LINE LENGTH OF 1 TO MAKE INTO 4 COLUMNS:
21> folders $rec $folopts |
```

*Part III
Customizing MH*

```
22> sed -e "s@^`$mh/folder $folopts`\$@&+@" \
23>     -e 's/^\(........\)...*\(.........\)$/\1=\2/' |
24> pr -l1 -4 -w78 -t
```

13.5.2 Explanation of fols

Lines 9-13 check the command line for a –r option. The $#$1 in **line 9** is replaced by the number of command-line arguments and the contents of $1 (if any). That may look tricky, but it's really simple. Here's how it works:

- If there is one command-line argument and it's exactly −r, the string set on line 9 will be 1−r. This will match **line 11**, which stores the switch *–recurse* in the shell variable *rec*.

  The asterisk (*) means that this *case* will allow any string in $1 that starts with 1−r. That includes −rec, −recurse, and so on.

- If there are no command-line arguments, **line 10** will match. The pair of double quotes (" ") really isn't needed because $1 will always be empty if there are no command-line arguments.

- **Line 12** is where the $#$1 pattern comes in handy. If there's one command-line argument but it does not start with −r, line 11 won't match—and control will "fall through" to line 12. Also, if there's more than one command-line argument, the 2 from $# means that lines 10 and 11 cannot match.

  So line 12 catches errors in the number of arguments or the contents of $1.

Line 21 feeds *folders –fast* output, which has one folder name per line, into a pipe. (The Bourne shell lets you make multiline pipes without backslashes at the ends of lines.) Here are a few typical lines of output from the *folders* command, assuming $rec is −recurse:

```
project
project/Independent_Life
project/Retirement
```

Next is a two-line *sed* command that does the real work here.* (Because this is all part of one command line, you *do* need to continue it with a backslash.) There are two *sed* expressions (with −e before each).

---

*For help with *sed*, see *sed & awk*, a Nutshell Handbook by Dale Dougherty.

Line 22 puts a plus sign (+) after the current folder name with a *sed* expression that looks like this:

```
s@^foldername$@&+@
```

- The expression is surrounded by double quotes (") so the shell will run the command inside the backquotes. (If I had used single quotes (') instead of double quotes, command substitution would have been disabled.)

- The expression uses *folder –fast*, inside backquotes, to get the current folder (`foldername`). Because the folder name might have a slash (/) in it, I didn't use a slash as the *sed* delimiter. Instead, I used an at sign (@), which the *folder* command should never output. (In other words, people usually do substitutions with s/old/new/, but I used s@old@new@ here.)

- The *sed* expression is anchored to the start of the line with a caret (^) and the end of the line with a dollar sign ($). If the current folder is *project*, this expression would not match the folder name *project/Retirement* because of the dollar sign ($) anchor at the end of the folder name. I actually had to use a backslash followed by a dollar sign (\$), not just $—otherwise, the shell would have treated the $@ as a shell parameter because it's inside double quotes.

- The ampersand followed by a plus sign (&+) is replaced by the folder name with a plus sign (+) after it. (*sed* replaces an ampersand (&) with whatever matched on the left-hand side of the expression. In this case, the left-hand side contained the folder name.)

Ready for **line 23**?

```
's/^\(........\)...*\(.........\)$/\1=\2/'
```

- It's another *sed* substitution command. The important part is that it *only* matches lines that are longer than 18 characters (which is how wide the *pr –4 –l78* command makes its columns). Shorter lines aren't affected because they don't match the expression.

- It takes the first eight characters and the last nine characters of a folder name, ignores the middle—then outputs the two pieces with an equal sign (=) between them. This makes an 18-character-long folder name with an = replacing what's been cut out.

- It uses *tagged fields*. The \(and \) "grabs" a part of the left-hand side of the substitution command. The first tagged field grabs the first eight characters (first because it has a start-of-line anchor, a caret (^), before it). The second tagged field grabs the last nine characters (last because it has an end-of-line anchor, $, after it). The middle of the line is matched by

... *—this matches the ninth and tenth characters in the line and all the characters after it, up to the last nine.

- Then, on the replacement side, \1 puts back the first field, and \2 puts back the second field. The = is output as is.

Line 24 reads the output from *sed* (because of the pipe). Not all UNIX systems have programs especially designed to write output in columns, but all systems should have *pr*. Here, it's used to make columns by giving a page length of 1 (-l1) with no headers (-t), a line 78 characters wide (-w78), and four columns (-4). The page length of 1 with four columns means that *pr* will read four lines of input, spread them left-to-right across the line, and then output it.

13.6 A Better Way to Remove Messages: rmmer ⊠

The default *rmm* command "removes" a mail message by renaming it with a leading comma (,), hash mark (#), or other character. This hides the message from other MH commands, but it doesn't really remove the message file. A system program comes along later to actually remove the "removed" message.

That scheme lets you recover a deleted message, but it's not very easy. Also, if you delete a message and then later delete another message with the same number, the first "deleted" message will be overwritten by the second one. The *rmmer* shell script changes that. For instance, when you type, say:

```
% rmm
```

rmmer moves the deleted message to a subfolder named *DELETE*. (See Section 7.1.5, "Subfolders.") For example, let's say that you deleted a message by accident. To get it back, you look in the subfolder. Your message will be the last one in the subfolder because you just removed it. You *show* the deleted message. To recover the deleted message, move it back to the parent folder (where it was before) with *refile* and a relative folder name (explained in Section 7.1.6). After you recover it, it'll be the last message in the folder. Here's an example:

```
% rmm
% show last @DELETE
(Message inbox/DELETE:25)
    ...A message appears--this is the one you "deleted"...
% refile @..
% show last @..
(Message inbox:54)
    ...The same message appears--now it's back in the parent folder...
```

Of course, you can *scan* the deleted messages, use *pick* on them, and so forth. You run a periodic job to clean out the *DELETE* subfolders—see Sections 13.6.3 - 13.6.5 about the *rm_msgs* scripts.

If you don't want *rmmer* to use a subfolder and instead you want it to put all the messages in a central *+DELETE* folder, you can call the program with the name *rmmer_1* and that'll do it. The script checks its name (from $0) and uses that to decide where to move the messages. You use a UNIX link (see Section 2.7) to give the same script more than one name.

Like the UNIX *rm −i* command, *rmmer* can prompt to be sure you want to remove messages. *rmmer* will only ask in folders where you've created a file named *.rmmer.ask*. The best way to make this file is with the *touch* command. It creates a zero-length file which doesn't take any disk space to store. For example, to make *rmmer* prompt in your *archive* folder:

```
% touch `mhpath +archive`/.rmmer.ask
```

When you remove messages in that folder, you can type n (or just RETURN) to stop the removal* :

```
% rmm last:3
rmmer: remove 91 94 95 in +archive? [ny] (n)
```

Sometimes, *rmmer* shouldn't prompt, even with a *.rmmer.ask* file. For example, if a job is running without a terminal on its standard input, like *cron*, then *rmmer* will never prompt. If you never want *rmmer* to prompt (if you use *xmh*, for example) use one of the versions with *.noask* on the end of its name, *rmmer.noask* or *rmmer_1.noask*.

You don't actually type a name like *rmmer* or *rmmer_1* to run this script. Instead, you put one of its names in your MH profile. For example:

```
rmmproc: rmmer.noask
```

The *rmm* and *refile* commands will then run *rmmer.noask* to "delete" messages.

Because the rmmproc: might be called from a *cron* job where your shell's search path is short, it's a good idea to use the full pathname in your MH profile:

```
rmmproc: /xxx/yyy/bin/rmmer_1
```

---

*Something interesting happens when you use *refile* to move a message out of a folder, then answer *n* when *rmmer* asks you. The *refile* command will already have linked the message into the destination folder by the time it runs the *rmmproc*. You'll end up with a link between the two folders, as if you'd used *refile −link*.

13.6.1 Listing of rmmer

This program is explained in Section 13.6.2.

```
 1> #! /bin/sh
 2> # $Id: rmmer,v 4.4 92/08/03 06:03:46 jerry book2 $
 3> ### rmmer, rmmer.noask, rmmer_1, rmmer_1.noask - MH "rmmproc" SCRIPT
 4> ### rmmer AND rmmer.noask MOVE MAIL TO @DELETE FOR find TO CLEAN UP
 5> ### rmmer_1 AND rmmer_1.noask MOVE MAIL TO +DELETE FOR find TO CLEAN UP
 6> ### xmh USERS SHOULD USE A ".noask" VERSION.
 7>
 8> askfile=.rmmer.ask  # IF THIS FILE EXISTS IN FOLDER, ASK BEFORE REMOVING
 9> moveto=DELETE       # NAME OF FOLDER FOR DELETED MESSAGES
10> myname=rmmer        # NAME FOR PROMPTS, FASTER/CLEANER THAN basename $0
11>
12> mhbin=/usr/local/mh mkdir=/bin/mkdir touch=/bin/touch # SET FOR YOUR
        SYSTEM
13> profile=/tmp/RMMERp$$ context=/tmp/RMMERc$$
14> folder="`$mhbin/folder -fast`" || exit
15> mhdir="`$mhbin/mhpath +`" || exit
16>
17> # UNCOMMENT THE RIGHT LINE FOR YOUR UNIX:
18> # echo="echo -n" nnl=    # BSD
19> # echo=echo       nnl="\c"  # SYSV
20> echo="echo -n" nnl=      PATH=/usr/bin:$PATH; export PATH    # SunOS
21>
22> # PROGRAM NAME SETS DESTINATION FOLDER, WHETHER TO LOOK FOR $askfile:
23> case "$0" in
24> *rmmer)         destfol="@$moveto" ask=ok ;;
25> *rmmer.noask)   destfol="@$moveto" ask=no ;;
26> *rmmer_1)       destfol="+$moveto" ask=ok ;;
27> *rmmer_1.noask) destfol="+$moveto" ask=no ;;
28> *)  echo "$0 aborting: can't find my name." 1>&2; exit 1 ;;
29> esac
30>
31> stat=1  # DEFAULT EXIT STATUS; RESET TO 0 BEFORE NORMAL EXIT
32> trap '/bin/rm -f $profile $context; exit $stat' 0
33> trap 'echo "$0: ouch! $* may not be removed." 1>&2; exit' 1 2 15
34>
35> # TO AVOID ENDLESS LOOPS WHERE THE refile IN rmmer RUNS rmmproc,
36> # MAKE TEMPORARY MH PROFILE TO BYPASS USER'S rmmproc: rmmer.
37> # rmm SETS SHELL'S DIRECTORY TO THE FOLDER WITH THE MESSAGES.
38> # STORE $folder IN CONTEXT FILE SO refile CAN FIND FOLDER.
39> # rmm UPDATES THE SEQUENCES BEFORE THE rmmproc RUNS, SO
40> # THIS rmmproc CAN HIDE SEQUENCE FILE FROM refile.
41> /bin/cat > $profile << ENDPROF || exit
42> Path: $mhdir
43> rmmproc: /bin/rm
44> mh-sequences:
45> context: $context
46> ENDPROF
47> echo "Current-Folder: $folder" > $context || exit
```

```
48> MH=$profile MHCONTEXT=$context
49> export MH MHCONTEXT
50>
51> # IF CURRENT FOLDER ISN'T ALREADY $moveto, WE MIGHT MAKE SUB-FOLDER.
52> # OTHERWISE, DON'T BURY MESSAGE DEEPER (IT'S PROBABLY BEING UNDELETED).
53> # THANX TO David Vezie, dv@Sonoma.EDU, FOR THE SUGGESTION, 3/24/92.
54> case "$folder" in
55> ?*/$moveto)
56>     # DON'T RUN refile (BELOW) SO MESSAGE WILL STAY HERE.
57>     stat=0
58>     exit
59>     ;;
60> *)  # rmm SETS CURRENT DIRECTORY TO FOLDER, SO IT'S EASY TO MAKE
61>     # NEW SUB-FOLDER.  (LET USER MAKE THEIR OWN "+DELETE" ONCE.)
62>     if [ "$destfol" = "@$moveto" -a ! -d "$moveto" ]
63>     then $mkdir $moveto || exit
64>     fi
65>     ;;
66> esac
67>
68> # IF WE SHOULD ASK AND USER ANSWERS "NO", EXIT:
69> if [ -f $askfile -a -t 0 -a "$ask" = ok ]
70> then
71>     $echo "$myname: remove $* in +$folder? [ny](n) $nnl"
72>     read ans
73>     case "$ans" in
74>     [yY]*) ;;   # DO refile BELOW
75>     *)  exit ;;
76>     esac
77> fi
78> # rmm PUTS SINGLE MESSAGE NUMBERS INTO $* (LIKE 12 13 14).
79> # UPDATE LAST-MOD TIME SO find -mtime WON'T DELETE TOO SOON.
80> # USE refile TO "REMOVE" THE MESSAGES.  EXIT WITH refile's STATUS:
81> $touch $* >/dev/null 2>&1
82> $mhbin/refile $destfol $*
83> stat=$?
84> exit
```

13.6.2 Explanation of rmmer

To install the *rmmer* program, first create the file *rmmer*. Next, give the script its three other names. Then make the file executable (you don't need four *chmod* commands; just change any link). Here's an example:

```
% ln rmmer rmmer_1
% ln rmmer rmmer.noask
% ln rmmer rmmer_1.noask
% chmod 755 rmmer
```

Lines 8-12 store information that isn't required to be in a shell variable. This is at the start of the script so it'll be easy to see and to change if needed. Lines like these are especially important for programs that users might make local versions of. For instance, some users make a version of *mkdir* that starts an editor and creates a description of the new directory. That causes real trouble in scripts which shouldn't be asking questions. Even worse is a user's version which is broken or which is not as robust as the system version.

Line 13 sets two variables that hold the names of temporary files in the */tmp* directory, which is designed for temporary files. Making temporary files in your current directory is a bad idea because it might be read-only. */tmp* is writable by all users, so your script will always be able to write to it. You should take care that your script's temporary filenames are unique, though. The $$ in each filename is replaced with the shell's process ID number, a unique number like 12345. Using $$ and a few letters in your temp filenames helps to keep them unique.

The *rmm* or *refile* command sets the current folder before it starts this *rmmproc*, so the folder name stored at **line 14** will be correct. **Line 15** gets the full pathname of your MH directory.

Lines 17-20 take care of the unfortunate difference between the System V and Berkeley versions of *echo*. They have different conventions for telling *echo* not to print a newline. For System V, line 71 needs a \c at the end, like this:

```
echo "rmmer: remove 22 in +archive? [ny](n) \c"
```

Berkeley UNIX needs this instead:

```
echo -n "rmmer: remove 22 in +archive? [ny](n) "
```

The variables set here take care of the problem. For Berkeley, $echo is echo -n and $nnl is empty. On System V, $echo is plain echo and $nnl is \c. On systems like SunOS with an *echo* command that handles both System V and UNIX, we set a *PATH* with */usr/bin* first—this makes a Berkeley *echo*. Take the comment character (#) off the line that's right for your system.

The *case* structure in **lines 23-29** tests $0, the name of the script file. The value of $0 is usually a full pathname—for example, /*xxx*/*yyy*/bin/rmmer—so the cases all start with an asterisk (*) to match the leading part of the pathname. If users have rmmproc: rmmer in their MH profile files, they want the program to move messages into a subfolder—**lines 24-25** set the *destfol* to @$moveto, which means the script will use a subfolder name like @*DELETE*. Those two lines set different values of the *ask* variable to tell the script whether to prompt if the folder has a $askfile file in it. If the program is named *rmmer_1*, **lines 26-27** set a destination folder like +*DELETE*. There's always a chance that the script was linked to a different name; **line 28** catches this goof.

Line 31 sets a default exit status of 1. Any *exit* command from here until line 82 will exit with a status of 1. (The shell actually *exits* with the *trap* set in **line 32**. If line 83 has been executed, the exit status will be 0 if *refile* succeeds; otherwise, the exit status will default to 1.)*

Lines 41-46 create a substitute MH profile in */tmp*. If the *cat* in **line 41** returns a nonzero status, the | | exit at the end aborts the shell script. The script doesn't print its own error message because this error shouldn't happen much—besides, there should be some kind of failure message from the shell or *cat* here.

This substitute MH profile has four lines, something like these:

```
Path: /xxx/yyy/Mail
rmmproc: /bin/rm
mh-sequences:
context: /tmp/RMMERc12345
```

From here (actually, line 49) until the end of the script, MH commands ignore your default MH profile. This is how *rmmer* avoids infinite loops caused by the *refile* in line 82—otherwise, *refile* would run this *rmmproc* too. All *refile* needs from its *rmmproc* is to remove the message in the current folder; at that point, *refile* has already linked the message into the *DELETE* subfolder or folder. So, **line 43** sets */bin/rm* as the *rmmproc* for *refile*.

Line 47 creates a substitute *context* file like this:

```
Current-Folder: foldername
```

The script needs this trickery because **line 44** sets private sequences to keep the *refile* in line 82 from changing the current message number. But then *refile* could still change any private sequences stored in your normal *context* file. So we make this substitute context file that's deleted when the script finishes. It needs the Current-Folder: line so *refile* can find the messages in this folder. (Without a Current-Folder: line, *refile* would default to *inbox*.)

Lines 48-49 reset the value of the *MH* and *MHCONTEXT* environment variables to our temporary versions of those files. Because of the way UNIX environments are set, this will only reset those environment variables for the rest of the *rmmer* script (basically, during the *refile* command). See Section 12.17.7, "Changing the MH Environment."

---

*Unfortunately, MH *rmm* ignores the *rmmproc*'s exit status and doesn't give any error if the *rmmproc* fails. *rmmer* depends on the individual commands it runs to print errors—printing its own errors would take more code, which would make it run a little more slowly.

If you're removing a message from a *DELETE* folder—for instance, when you're "undeleting" a deleted message—you probably don't want *rmmer* to bury the message in yet another *DELETE/DELETE* folder. The *case* in **lines 54-55** catch this. If your current folder name ends with *DELETE*, the script doesn't need to do anything because the message has already been "deleted"; the script exits silently with a zero status. (You might want to add an *echo* here to explain what's happening.)

When you type *rmm*, MH sets its current directory to the folder where messages are being deleted before it starts the *rmmproc* running. So this shell script can work in the folder directly; it doesn't need a pathname. **Line 62** tests to see if the subfolder* named *DELETE* exists; the subfolder will be a subdirectory of the current directory. If there isn't a *DELETE* subfolder, the script creates it with *mkdir*. If the script had let *refile* create the subfolder at line 82, it would cause trouble for *xmh* users. *xmh* wouldn't display the prompt *create folder?* from *refile*, and *xmh* would hang there forever, waiting for you to answer.† The square brackets ([ ]) in line 62 are another way to run the *test* command. If your system doesn't have this, replace the [with the word `test` and delete the].

Lines 69-77 test to see if there's a *.rmmer.ask* file in the current directory (current folder), if the standard input is coming from a terminal (so you can answer the prompt), and if the *ask* variable was set to `ok` in lines 24-27. If all those are true, it prompts you (see the explanation of lines 17-20) and quits if you answer anything but upper or lower-case "y". When *rmm* starts its *rmmproc*, it has already translated sequences into message numbers—so the *rmmproc* doesn't have to. For instance, the command:

```
% rmm first:2 cur 26
```

might leave the numbers 1 3 12 26 in $*.

If the script hasn't quit at lines 58 or 75, it's time to remove the messages. **Line 81** runs the *touch* program to update the last-modification "timestamp" of the message files. That's for the *find* that cleans up the folder (see the *rm_msgs* scripts in Sections 13.6.3-13.6.5)—it should delete messages that were not modified in the last *n* days. Renaming a file doesn't change its modification time, so

---

*This is only done for subfolders because there can be a lot of them. The script should be able to make new *DELETE* subfolders because an MH user can easily add new folders that'll need their own subfolders. I think that if the program was called as *rmmer_1*, the user should create a +*DELETE* folder by hand. That one-time operation is more efficiently done by hand than to add the extra code to check for a +*DELETE* every time this program runs.

†Actually, that only causes trouble for *xmh* users who start *xmh* from a shell prompt. If *xmh* doesn't have a controlling terminal, then *refile* won't prompt for an answer and *xmh* won't hang.

the messages might be months old, and deleted the next time *find* runs, without a grace period.*

Finally, in **line 82**, the MH *refile* command moves the messages to the *DELETE* folder or subfolder. Remember the substitute MH profile with its *rmmproc* line; it keeps line 82 from starting an infinite loop of *refile*'s and *rmmproc*'s.

Lines 83-84 save the *refile* exit status and spring the *trap* to clean up and leave. If you think that seems like a lot of work just to remove messages, look at the inset entitled "Why Do All That Work?"

Why Do All That Work?

Are you wondering why *rmmer* doesn't just use the *refile* command, or *mv* and *mhpath new* commands, to move all the messages into the *DELETE* folder at once? There are three reasons:

1. The MH *refile* command calls the *rmmproc* to delete the source message after refiling it to the destination folder. If *rmmproc* used *refile*, it could get into an endless loop. As the *rmm* manual page suggests, a shell alias could run *refile* without having this problem. But as explained in the part of Section 8.2.1 called "They Won't Always Work," other MH commands (including *refile itself*) couldn't use your alias.

2. *refile* changes the current message number. The generic *rmm* command doesn't. In the commands below, an *rmmproc* that uses the generic *rmm* would work, but one that used *refile* wouldn't:

   ```
   % show
   (Message inbox:234)
       ...
   % rmm 1 5 7
   % next
   (Message inbox:235)
       ...
   ```

   An *rmmproc* that used *refile* would leave the current message set to 7 instead of 234.

3. Using plain *mv* to "move" the messages won't update the MH message sequences. (Section 7.3 and others discuss sequences.)

---

*If the *find* used the last-access time (*–atime*) instead, it might *never* delete the messages because each *scan* of the folder updates the last-access time of each message. Using the *ctime* won't work right if the message has other links which cause the file's *ctime* to be updated sometime before the link in *DELETE* is removed.

13.6.3 Removing Messages Deleted by rmmer: rm_msgs.at

Here are two versions of a small script file named *rm_msgs.at*. It deletes messages removed with *rmmer*. It's designed to be put in your MH directory and run with *at*(1) every night. Users on some versions of UNIX have their own private *crontab* files. If you have them, that's a better way to run *rm_msgs* (see Section 13.6.4).

Here are two versions of *rm_msgs.at*. If your system has the *xargs* command, use the second version; it's more efficient.

First Version

```
find `find . –type d –name DELETE –print` –type f –mtime +4 –exec rm –f {} \;
sleep 60
at 0330 rm_msgs.at
```

Second Version

```
find `find . –type d –name DELETE –print` –type f –mtime +4 –print | \
    xargs rm –f
sleep 60
at 0330 rm_msgs.at
```

Running rm_msgs.at with at(1)

Run this job from your MH directory. To start the job the first time, just type:

```
% cd `mhpath +`
% at 0330 rm_msgs.at
```

If you've never submitted an *at* job, you might want to check with a local expert for help. The basics are easy, but there may be problems in your account's *.cshrc* file or your system may not have *at* enabled.

13.6.4 Removing Messages Deleted by rmmer: rm_msgs.cron

Section 13.6.3 showed two versions of the script file named *rm_msgs.at*. Here are the same two versions, rewritten for users on versions of UNIX with private *crontab* files.

For information, type:

```
% man 1 cron
% man crontab
```

Here are two versions of *rm_msgs.cron*. If your system has the *xargs* command, use the second version; it's more efficient.

First Version

```
find=/xxx/find
cd `/xxx/mhpath +` || exit
$find `$find . -type d -name DELETE -print` -type f -mtime +4 -exec rm -f {} ;
```

Second Version

```
find=/xxxx/find xargs=/xxxx/xargs
cd `/xxxx/mhpath +` || exit
$find `$find . -type d -name DELETE -print` -type f -mtime +4 -print | \
    $xargs rm -f
```

Running rm_msgs.cron with cron(1)

First, pick a location for your *rm_msgs.cron* file (I put mine in a directory named *lib*). Because *cron* usually doesn't set a full search path, it's a good idea to use a full pathname for commands run by your *crontab*. To do that, replace each xxx with the full pathname of the directory where your system stores the commands. For instance, if *find* is in */usr/bin*, the first line should have the following:

```
find=/usr/bin/find
```

To add the job to your personal *crontab* file, use your system's command for editing the *crontab* file. Add a line like this to the file:

```
30 3 * * * /bin/sh /xxx/yyy/lib/rm_msgs.cron
```

If you've never used *cron*, you might want to check with a local expert for help.

13.6.5 Explanation of rm_msgs Scripts

Here are some notes about those scripts:

- The *find* commands use `-mtime +4` to find messages modified more than four days ago. You can change this time period if you want to. If you don't use the *rmmer* script to remove your messages, you should use *–ctime* instead of *–mtime*, because the default *rmm* command doesn't change a file's *mtime*.

- The `sleep 60` in the *at* versions makes sure that the time is 0331 (3:31 a.m.) or later before the script resubmits itself. Without this, some versions of *at* may run the script twice in the same day.

- In each script, the *find* is actually two *find*s on one line. The inner *find* finds all the directories (folders) named *DELETE*; the outer one finds all of the old messages in that folder. (If you have experience with the standard UNIX *find*(1), you might be wondering why I had to use the nested *find*s. It's because predicates like `-name 'DELETE/[1-9]*'` don't work.)

- I used `` `find -type d ...` `` to get a list of folders, instead of using `` `folders -fast -recurse` ``, because there might be some other users' folders or read-only folders in the output of the *folder* command. Because these *rm_msgs* scripts run from your MH directory, the *find* will only locate folders there.

- If several users on your system will be running this script, they shouldn't all run it at 3:30 a.m. because the system load will go up suddenly. It's better to stagger each user's time a few minutes or to have the system administrator run a system-wide script that cleans all users' *DELETE* folders.

- Before you run your *rm_msgs* script for the first time, you may want to be sure that the system administrator has a backup copy of your account. That's a safe idea the first few times you run any new program that uses *find* and *rm*.

13.7 A Better xmh Printer: xmhprint ⊠

The printer support with *xmh* isn't very good. It hands all of your message files to a printer command at once. It doesn't filter them to remove uninteresting header components. You can't use a pipe as part of the printer command because *xmh* puts the message filenames at the end of the printer command line. For more information about this, see Section 16.8.

The *xmhprint* program is a simple shell script. It takes message filenames and any options from the command line. The shell script gets the message filenames from *xmh*, and it can process them any way you want it to. The options let you change your print setup easily—instead of storing a complicated xmh*PrintCommand in the resource manager, just change the option on the command line.

By default, *xmhprint* gives your messages straight to the *lpr* command for printing. If you use its *–p1* option, *xmhprint* will give your messages straight to *pr* and pipe the result to *lpr*. With the *–p2* option, *xmhprint* puts each message's subject in the *pr* page heading before sending them to *lpr*. With what you know about shell programming, you can add your own *xmhprint* options to customize printing for your site and your needs. If you set environment variables before starting *xmh*, *xmhprint* can test its environment for them—this gives you even more flexibility. Also, on Berkeley-type UNIX systems, you can set the *PRINTER* environment variable to the printer *lpr* will use. (On System V, set *LPDEST*.)

The script handles redirection of printer errors, too, so you don't need the >/dev/null 2>/dev/null business that the *xmh* manual page recommends. In fact, for *xmh* versions after Release 3, I don't agree with the manual page. If you use 2>/dev/null to throw away errors, you won't see the dialog boxes *xmh* pops up to show messages like printer disabled. Worse, some versions of *lpr* and *lp* put their error messages on the standard *output* instead of the standard error! *xmh* doesn't put standard output messages into a dialog box. The *xmhprint* script takes care of that by rerouting all printer *stdout* to *stderr*.

Using *xmhprint*, here's how uncomplicated your printing resource entry can be:

```
xmh*PrintCommand: xmhprint –p2
```

13.7.1 Listing of xmhprint

Here's the program. It's described in Section 13.7.2.

```
 1> #! /bin/sh
 2> # $Id: xmhprint,v 1.6 92/07/25 07:12:47 jerry book2 $
 3> ### xmhprint - print command for xmh
 4> ### Usage (in X resource): xmh*PrintCommand: xmhprint [-cmd_num]
 5>
 6> errsubj="xmh*PrintCommand print ERROR" # FOR MAILED ERRORS
 7> printcmd="/usr/ucb/lpr"      # CAN ADD OPTIONS INSIDE QUOTES
 8>
 9> # IN xmh RELEASE 3, MUST REDIRECT ALL OUTPUT AWAY FROM xmh.
10> # IN RELEASE 4 AND 5, STDERR (FD 2) GOES TO ERROR DIALOG BOX.
11> # UNCOMMENT THIS TO APPEND ALL OUTPUT TO FILE:
12> #  errfile=$HOME/.xmh_printerrs
13> #  exec >> $errfile 2>&1
```

```
14>
15> # GET OPTION (xmh ALWAYS PUTS FILENAMES LAST):
16> case "$1" in
17> -p1) # JUST pr; PUTS PATHNAME IN HEADER.  NOTHING FANCY:
18>     shift
19>     pr "$@" | $printcmd 1>&2
20>     ;;
21> -p2) # SHOW SUBJECT IN pr HEADER OF EACH MESSAGE:
22>     shift
23>     for f
24>     do
25>         pr -h "`sed -n '/^[sS]ubject: / {
26>             s///p
27>             q
28>         }' $f`" $f
29>     done | $printcmd 1>&2
30>     ;;
31> "") echo "No filenames or command line arguments!?!" |
32>     mail -s "$errsubj" $USER
33>     exit 1       # xmh IGNORES THIS :-(
34>     ;;
35> *) # DEFAULT: SEND ALL OPTIONS AND FILENAMES TO lpr:
36>     $printcmd "$@" 1>&2
37>     ;;
38> esac
```

13.7.2 Explanation of xmhprint

Line 6 holds a subject line for an e-mailed error message; the program sends some errors in the mail to you. **Line 7** is where you set the printer command and any options that should always be used. For instance, with the *lp* command, you might add the *–s* option to stop messages from *lp* such as `request id is` *nnn*. **Lines 9-13** are especially for *xmh* Release 3, which can't handle error messages. If you take the comment characters off lines 12-13, they'll set up a file to hold printer and script error messages. If something goes wrong, look in the file for the error messages. (Remember to empty the file once in a while.) Line 13 is a Bourne shell command that redirects the standard output and standard error of all the following commands (lines 14 and after) to the error file. This is easier (and more efficient) than trying to put individual redirection on each command, and it guarantees that there won't be output.

The rest of the shell script is a *case* structure that checks the first command-line parameter and runs something different in each case. Because *xmh* always puts the filename(s) to print at the end of its command line, any option should be first on the command line — in the $1 parameter.

You can customize this script any way you want to—the programs that are run and the option names I chose are arbitrary. I tried to pick *xmhprint* options (numbers like −p1, −p2, etc.) that don't conflict with any *lpr* or *lp* options.

- Lines 17-20 are executed for command lines that start with the *−p1* option. **Line 18** uses the Bourne shell *shift* command to remove the option (in $1) from the command-line parameters. What's left is passed to the *pr* command at **line 19**, in "$@". If you had the following resource entry set:

    ```
    xmh*PrintCommand: xmhprint −p1 −f
    ```

    and if *xmh* was printing the messages */yourMHdir*/inbox/3 and */yourMHdir*/inbox/4, the command in **line 19** would be:

    ```
    pr −f /yourMHdir/inbox/3 /yourMHdir/inbox/4 | $printcmd
    ```

    (The −f is a *pr* option that means "separate pages with formfeeds." Your printer might need that.)

    The 1>&2 after $printcmd redirects any standard output from the printer command to the standard error; that lets *xmh* R4 and R5 show those messages in a dialog box.

- **Lines 23-29** are a *for* loop for the *−p2* option. After *shift*ing away the *−p2* in line 22, the loop steps through the command-line parameters one by one, treating each one as a file. The output of the loop is piped to the printer command—the printer command reads its standard input as long as the *pr* commands keep running. So all the files are printed in one print job instead of the individual jobs you'd get if the loop restarted the printer for each new *pr* command. (For another example and more explanation of redirected loops, see the script in Section 13.10.2 .)

    Lines 25-28 are a little complicated. There's a pr −h "*title*" command which puts the message subject at the top of each page. The *sed* command, inside backquotes, grabs the subject line and passes it to *pr*.

    The *sed −n* option tells it not to print anything without an explicit *p* command. The test on **line 25** makes sure that the *sed* script only matches a Subject: line. When it finds a Subject: line, **line 26** deletes the label ([Ss]ubject:) and then the *p* command outputs what's left. After that, **line 27** makes *sed* quit—so this script will never output more than the first Subject: component in a message (forwarded messages can have several subject components).

- **Line 31** catches the "impossible" case when the script doesn't have any options or arguments. It sends you mail to be sure that you know there was an error—maybe there's some problem in *xmh*, or somehow your script is being run accidentally.

- If none of the options match, **line 35** just passes all the command-line parameters to the printer command.

Again, you can customize this script to fit your needs. Add *mhl* to clean up the message headers, use other printers, use a PostScript filter ... go wild!

13.8 Work on Draft Folder: scandrafts

The *scandrafts* script is nice when you're wondering what's in your draft folder or you need to work in it.

- By default, *scandrafts* shows a list of the messages you've already sent (these messages are in files with a comma (,) or hash mark (#) before their names). Then, it *scan*s your draft folder for drafts you're working on and finally pops you back to your current folder.

- If you use its *–stay* option, *scandrafts* will start a shell with both the current directory and current folder set to the draft folder. That way, you can restore one of the already-sent messages (as explained in Section 7.5) and/or refile it to another folder (in case you forgot to give yourself a copy when you sent it). Or you can do extensive work on the drafts more directly than a script like *recomp* will let you.

Here's a demonstration using *–stay* (without *–stay*, there wouldn't be a `scandrafts` prompt):

```
$ scandrafts -stay
Draft message(s) you've already sent:

,1:Subject: Re: SC or GA islands
,5:Subject: Re: our previous message about banners dialups
,6:Subject: Re: Can you help?
,7:Subject: Out this morning

To get them back, use 'mv'.
=================================================================
Draft message(s) you haven't sent:

    1  03/07*To:alison@mvus.cs  Project status<<Alison, the
scan: message 2: empty
    3+ 03/07*To:kx9cq@cornell.  Scientific Visualization Dem

          You'll be in a /bin/ksh shell in the +drafts folder
          To quit, type control-d.
scandrafts> rmm 2
scandrafts> mv ,6 6
```

```
scandrafts> scan
  1  03/07*To:alison@mvus.cs  Project status<<Alison, the p
  3+ 03/07*To:kx9cq@cornell.  Scientific Visualization Demo
  6  03/04*To:"Warren Z. Von  Re: Can you help?<<Warren, yo
scandrafts> refile 6 +outbox
scandrafts> CTRL-D

[folder +inbox now current]
$
```

First, you see four messages that have already been sent. The *send* program put commas at the start of their names. Next come the messages that haven't been sent. One is empty (this can happen if you have trouble composing a message).

Then, because the *–stay* switch was used, *scandrafts* starts the default shell (this person uses the Korn shell). The shell prompt is set to `scandrafts>`. The current folder and current directory are the draft folder, so *rmm* removes the empty draft and *mv* takes the comma off message 6. A *scan* shows the cleaned-up folder. CTRL-D ends the shell and the *scandrafts* script.

13.8.1 Listing of scandrafts

This program is explained in Section 13.8.2.

```
 1> #! /bin/sh
 2> #     $Id: scandrafts,v 1.7.1.1 92/08/03 07:18:20 jerry book2 $
 3> ### scandrafts - scan MH draft folder; return to original folder if no
      -stay
 4> ### Usage: scandrafts [-stay] [scan arguments]
 5>
 6> args=    # RESET IN CASE THERE'S AN args ENVIRONMENT VARIABLE
 7> folopts="-fast -nolist -nototal -nopack"
 8> mh=/usr/local/mh
 9> mhprf=/xxxxxxxxxxxx/mhprofile    # READS MH PROFILE
10> pageprog=${PAGER-/usr/ucb/more}  # DISPLAYS SCREEN-BY-SCREEN
11> stat=1   # DEFAULT EXIT STATUS; RESET TO 0 FOR NORMAL EXITS
12> temp=/tmp/SCANDRFTS$$
13> >$temp
14> chmod 600 $temp
15> trap 'rm -f $temp; exit $stat' 0 1 2 15
16>
17> # IF -stay SWITCH IS SET, SET $stay TO y:
18> for arg
19> do
20>     case "$arg" in
21>     -stay)  stay=y ;;
22>     *)  args="$args $arg" ;;
23>     esac
24> done
```

```
25>
26> # GET DRAFT FOLDER NAME:
27> draftfold="`$mhprf -b draft-folder`" || {
28>     echo "`basename $0`: quitting: can't find your 'Draft-Folder'." 1>&2
29>     exit
30> }
31>
32> $mh/folder $folopts -push +$draftfold >/dev/null || exit
33> folpath=`$mh/mhpath +$draftfold` || exit
34> cd $folpath || exit
35>
36> # IF ANY UN-SENT DRAFTS, SHOW THEM; THEN, scan FOLDER.
37> # PIPE ALL OF IT TO PAGER SO NONE OF IT SCROLLS OFF SCREEN:
38> grep "^Subject: " [,#]*[1-9]* >$temp 2>/dev/null
39> (if test -s $temp
40> then
41>     echo "Draft message(s) you've already sent:
42>     "
43>     cat $temp
44>     echo
45>     case "$stay" in
46>     y) echo "To get them back, use 'mv'." ;;
47>     *) echo "To get them back, use 'cd $folpath' and 'mv'." ;;
48>     esac
49>     echo "==========================================================="
50>     echo "Draft message(s) you haven't sent:
51>     "
52> fi
53> $mh/scan $args 2>&1) | $pageprog
54>
55> # USE THEIR $SHELL, IF DEFINED... OTHERWISE, USE sh:
56> case "$stay" in
57> y) echo "
58>     You'll be in a ${SHELL-Bourne} shell in the +$draftfold folder.
59>     To quit, type control-d."
60>     PS1="scandrafts> " ${SHELL-sh}
61>     ;;
62> esac
63>
64> # POP FOLDER BACK; PUT NEWLINE BEFORE MESSAGE:
65> echo "
66> [folder +`$mh/folder $folopts -pop` now current]"
67> stat=0
```

13.8.2   Explanation of scandrafts

Line 10 sets a program to display what's in the folder screen by screen. If you don't have a *PAGER* environment variable set, this defaults to the *more* program. If your system doesn't have *more*, see if you have the pager called *pg* and use:

```
pageprog=${PAGER-"/xxx/yyy/pg -e"} # DISPLAYS SCREEN-BY-SCREEN
```

where /xxx/yyy is the location of *pg* on the filesystem (though you can probably omit this) and the *–e* option means that *pg* won't stop if there's less than a screenful of lines to show.

Lines 12-14 create an empty temporary file and make it private. That's done right away so that when *grep* runs (on line 38), other users won't be able to read the lines it writes to the file.

Lines 18-24 parse the command line. If the switch called *–stay* is there, *scandrafts* sets a shell variable as a flag. All other arguments are passed to *scan*.

Lines 27-30 run the *mhprofile* program (Section 13.4) to get the user's draft folder name. If *mhprofile* returns nonzero status, *scandrafts* prints a message and exits.

Line 32 pushes the current folder onto the folder stack (see Section 7.1.9) then sets the current folder to the draft folder. **Line 33** uses the *mhpath* command to get the full pathname of the draft folder, and **line 34** sets the current directory there.

Line 38 reads all the files whose names start with a comma (,) or hash mark (#), followed by a digit (the shell wildcards for this are [,#]*[1-9]*). *grep* looks in these files for lines which start with the word Subject: and puts those lines in the temporary file. Messages on the standard error (about no matching files or identifying some other problem) are thrown into the */dev/null* "trash can." All we care about is useful output—the Subject: lines.

Lines 39-53 (except the end of line 53) are run in a subshell. This is a way to collect the output of several commands and channel them all to the same place. The parentheses— (. . .) —enclose the commands to be run in the subshell. The standard output of this subshell is going to the *$pageprog* program in line 53. This shows the output of all the commands in a group; if there are more than enough lines to fill the screen, the paging program will pause until you use its "continue" command.*

---

*If the subshell wasn't here, and each individual command was fed to a paging program, the output of each program might scroll the other's output off the screen before you could see it. Collecting all the output and feeding it to one pager solves this.

The *test –s* command checks the output of *grep*. If there was output, then we print a heading before the output; otherwise we print nothing. The commands in the subshell do the following:

- **Lines 41-42** and **lines 50-51** echo headings to the screen. Because the quotes enclose more than one line, each *echo* command prints all its lines at once. In shells without a built-in *echo* command, this makes output faster than a separate *echo* for each line.

- **Lines 45-48** print one of two messages, depending on whether the *–stay* option was used.

- The part of **line 53** inside the subshell scans the draft folder. The 2>&1 tells the shell to combine *scan*'s standard error onto its standard output. This makes errors (like the error for the empty message 2 in the demonstration above) come out along with the rest of the paged lines. Without this fix, errors could mess up the paged output—overwriting parts of other lines, scrolling the display off the screen, and so on.

Lines 56-62 start a shell if the *–stay* option was used:

- The start of **line 60** uses a special feature of the Bourne shell. It puts a variable named *PS1* into the environment of the process on that line, but does not set that variable for the current shell. That's a way to temporarily set an environment variable while you run one command. In this case, the script sets the environment variable *PS1*, which is the prompt string for the Bourne and Korn shells. The shell that *scandrafts* starts will prompt with scandrafts> instead of the default dollar sign ($). Unfortunately, there's no way to set the C shell prompt like this.

- If the user has defined the *SHELL* environment variable, **line 58** will print its name and **line 60** will invoke it. Otherwise, those two lines default to the Bourne shell, *sh*.

Finally, **lines 65-67** pop the draft folder off the stack and show the name of the current folder. This is done in one operation by +`$mh/folder $folopts –pop`.*

---

*Unfortunately, though this trick saves running *folder* twice, it also prints the whole list of folders on the stack if there is more than one folder remaining. If you use folder stacks, you should move the *folder* command from line 66 to a previous line, redirect its output to */dev/null*, and use a plain +`$mh/folder $folopts`. (The *–fast* switch is in *$folopts*.)

The script doesn't need to *cd* back to the directory where it started. That's because it runs in a subshell. Its current directory of the subshell doesn't affect the current directory of its parent shell.

Line 67 sets a zero exit status for the *trap* to use.

13.9 Resend a Returned Message: resend

You've probably received a few returned mail messages like the one below. Usually, after you figure out what went wrong, you want to resend the message. The *resend* program helps you do that. It's a version of the *forw* command. It has an *–editor* shell script called *resend.fixmsg* that removes everything from the forwarded draft except the original message, then puts you into an editor to do any other cleanup.

How well does it work? I've used *resend* for about four years now, and it works quite well at the sites where I've tried it. You may have to tweak it for your site. But, when it doesn't work, *ed* (the editor it uses to clean up the draft noninteractively) usually just prints a question mark (?) and leaves the forwarded draft alone—*resend.fixmsg* pops me into *vi*, I edit the draft by hand and send it. Here is an example of *resend*:

```
% comp
        . . .
What now? push
%
        . . .Time passes . . .
You have new mail.
% inc
  45+ 12/07 MAILER-DAEMON        Returned mail: Host unknown
% show
        . . .Nasty-gram from MAILER-DAEMON . . .
% resend
        . . .My editor (vi) starts . . .
        . . .I fix the address . . .
What now? push
% rmm
%
```

13.9.1 Setup and Listing, resend and resend.fixmsg

To set this up, make a version of *forw* named *resend* (for directions, see Section 9.2). Then, put this line in your MH profile:

```
resend: -editor resend.fixmsg -nodashmunging -filter mhl.noformat
```

Section 6.8.3 explains the undocumented *–nodashmunging* switch. The *mhl.noformat* file, shown in the same section, is there because *–nodashmunging* requires either *–filter* or *–format*.

Here's the *resend.fixmsg* editor:

```
1> #! /bin/sh
2> # $Id: resend.fixmsg,v 1.6 92/07/24 18:23:58 jerry book2 $
3> ### resend.fixmsg - editor for fixing up returned mail
4> ### Usage in MH profile:  resend: -editor resend.fixmsg -nodashmunging
5> ###    MUST ALSO ADD:   -format   OR   -filter xxx
6>
7> # $1 IS PATH TO DRAFT (SET BY forw).  THEN ed SCRIPT:
8> # DELETES LINES THROUGH FIRST "To: (you)".
9> # DELETES LINES TO BUT NOT INCLUDING NEXT "To: (original)".
10> # REMOVES Date:/From:/Sender: LINES THAT MAILER PUT IN MESSAGE.
11> # REMOVES FROM BLANK LINE BEFORE "---- End of Forwarded Message"
12> #    THROUGH THE END OF THE FILE.
13> /bin/ed - $1 << "END"
14> 1,/^To: /d
15> 1,/^To: /-1d
16> 1,/^$/g/^Date: /d
17> 1,/^$/g/^From: /d
18> 1,/^$/g/^Sender: /d
19> $
20> ?^------- End of Forwarded Message?-1,$d
21> w
22> q
23> END
24>
25> # EDIT WITH $VISUAL, $EDITOR OR vi.  exec TO SAVE A PROCESS:
26> exec ${VISUAL-${EDITOR-vi}} $1
```

13.9.2 Explanation of resend and resend.fixmsg

When you type *resend*, it starts *forw*. This makes a draft message that's a copy of your *forwcomps* file with the returned message below it. (In the draft, the returned message will have lines around it that say Forwarded Message and End of Forwarded Message.) We could have used a special draft template form file and an *mhl* filter file to delete a lot of the garbage lines, but we'd still end up with some text to delete.

Here's a sample returned mail message that the *resend* version of *forw* has made into a draft. The *resend.fixmsg* editor edits this. The draft is shown with line numbers (actually, letters) to the left of each line; they are not part of the draft, but are for reference only.

```
A> To:
B> cc:
C> Subject:
D> -------
E>
F> ------- Forwarded Message
G>
H> Date: Mon, 07 Dec 92 06:57:36 EST
I> From: MAILER-DAEMON (Mail Delivery Subsystem)
J> Received: by mysun.csa.syr.edu (5.54/CSA)
K>   id AA04361; Mon, 07 Dec 92 06:57:36 EST
L> Subject: Returned mail: Host unknown
M> Message-Id: <9003071157.AA04361@mysun.csa.syr.edu>
N> To: <ehuser>
O>
P>    ----- Transcript of session follows -----
Q> 550 rtp@gxa.nsq.edu... Host unknown
R>
S>    ----- Unsent message follows -----
T> Received: by mysun.csa.syr.edu (5.54/CSA)
U>   id AA04355; Mon, 07 Dec 92 06:57:36 EST
V> Message-Id: <9003071157.AA04355@mysun.csa.syr.edu>
W> To: rtp@gxa.nsq.edu, tko@gax.nsq.edu
X> Subject: Incredibly boring seminar
Y> Date: Mon, 07 Dec 92 06:57:35 -0600
Z> From: "Emma H. User" <ehuser>
AA>
BB>    ...Body of message not shown here...
XX>
YY> ------- End of Forwarded Message
ZZ>
```

Lines 14-22 of *resend.fixmsg* are *ed* editor commands; they're fed to the standard input of *ed* by the redirection on **line 13**. Because the terminator in line 13 has quotes around it (`"END"`), none of the special characters in lines 14-20 have to be quoted to protect them from the shell.

There's not space here to explain every detail of the *ed* editor script. But here's what the lines do:

- **Line 14** deletes the empty draft header and the returned message header (lines A-N of the previous sample draft message).

- **Line 15** deletes the errors in lines O-V.

- **Line 16** searches the lines between W and AA to find the `Date:` header component line and deletes it. (MH won't let you send a draft that already has a `Date:` line in it.) For example, it would delete line Y of the previous example.

- **Line 17** deletes the header component line for `From:`. For example, it would delete line Z of the previous example.

- **Line 19** tells *ed* to go to the end of the draft message. **Line 20** searches backward for the line just before the `End of Forwarded Message` line, then deletes every line between there and the end of the draft. In this case, it deletes lines XX through ZZ.

- **Lines 21-22** save and quit *ed* (the `q` isn't required here, but I think it's a good idea).

Finally, **line 26** puts you into an editor. It starts the editor in the *VISUAL* environment variable (if there is one). Next, it tries the *EDITOR* environment variable. If neither of those variables are set, it starts *vi*. The *exec* tells the shell to replace itself with a copy of the editor program. This is a good thing to do in cases when there's nothing else to do in a shell program—no *trap* to spring—and the exit status of the command you *exec* should be the exit status of the shell script. Don't do this if your editor returns a nonzero status, though, because your draft could be deleted before the `What now?` prompt. See Section 12.17.8.

13.10 Draft Editor for dist: distprompter

distprompter is an editor designed for *dist*. It's also an example of writing your own draft message editor (Section 12.17.8 has more about that).

By default, *dist* uses *prompter* to edit the draft. *prompter* isn't a great editor for *dist* because if you accidentally type a message body after the row of dashes, the message can't be sent. Also, you always have to press CTRL-D to skip the body and get the `What now?` prompt.

Besides fixes for the two problems listed above, *distprompter* acts a lot like *prompter*:

- It reads the draft file that *dist* gives it, line by line.

- If a component is empty, *distprompter* prompts you. If you don't type anything but RETURN, the component is deleted.

- If a component is already complete, *distprompter* shows the component but doesn't prompt.

- *distprompter* won't allow header components that don't start with `Resent-`. (MH won't allow them, either.)

- When *distprompter* has read the header, it exits; you don't need CTRL-D .

To use *distprompter*, type its name on the *dist* command line or add it to your MH profile:

```
dist: -editor distprompter
```

13.10.1 Listing of distprompter

This program is explained in Section 13.10.2.

```
1> #! /bin/sh
2> # $Id: distprompter,v 1.9 92/08/03 07:31:17 jerry book2 $
3> ### distprompter - replaces "prompter" for MH "dist" command
4> ### Usage (in .mh_profile):    dist: -editor distprompter
5>
6> myname="`basename $0`"
7> err=/tmp/DISTPRe$$ header=/tmp/DISTPRd$$
8> > $header
9> chmod 600 $header
10>
11> # UNCOMMENT THE RIGHT LINE FOR YOUR UNIX:
12> # echo="echo -n" nnl=        # BSD
13> # echo=echo        nnl="\c"   # SYSV
14> echo="echo -n" nnl=      PATH=/usr/bin:$PATH; export PATH    # SunOS
15>
16> stat=1  # DEFAULT EXIT STATUS; RESET TO 0 FOR NORMAL EXITS
17> trap 'rm -f $header $err; exit $stat' 0
18> trap 'echo "$myname: Interrupt!  Cleaning up..." 1>&2; exit' 1 2 15
19>
20> if [ ! -w "$1" -o -z "$1" ]
21> then
22>     echo 1>&2 "$myname: quitting: missing or unwritable draft
23>     '$1'"
24>     exit
25> fi
26>
27> # READ DRAFT (A COPY OF distcomps FILE) LINE-BY-LINE.
28> # ACT LIKE prompter, BUT EXIT AFTER WE'VE READ DRAFT FILE
29> # (WHEN YOU USE dist, THE DRAFT FILE IS ONLY A HEADER).
30> # read AT TOP OF LOOP GETS STDIN (FD 0), SO SAVE FD 0 NOW:
31> exec 4<&0   # SAVE ORIGINAL STDIN (USUALLY TTY) AS FD 4
32> while read label line
```

```
33> do
34>     case "$label" in
35>     [Rr]esent-?*:)
36>         case "$line" in
37>         ?*) # SHOW LINE ON SCREEN AND PUT INTO HEADER FILE:
38>             echo "$label $line"
39>             echo "$label $line" 1>&3
40>             ;;
41>         *)  # FILL IT IN OURSELVES:
42>             $echo "$label $nnl"
43>             exec 5<&0   # SAVE DRAFT FILE FD; DO NOT CLOSE!
44>             exec 0<&4   # RESTORE ORIGINAL STDIN
45>             read ans
46>             exec 0<&5   # RECONNECT DRAFT FILE TO STDIN
47>             case "$ans" in
48>             "") ;;  # EMPTY; DO NOTHING
49>             *)  echo "$label $ans" 1>&3 ;;
50>             esac
51>             ;;
52>         esac
53>         ;;
54>     ""|---*) # END OF HEADER
55>         echo "-------" 1>&3
56>         break   # PROBABLY NOT NEEDED...
57>         ;;
58>     *)  echo "$myname: illegal header component
59>         '$label $line'" 1>&2
60>         break
61>         ;;
62>     esac
63> done <$1 2>$err 3>$header
64>
65> # IF THE ERROR FILE HAS SOMETHING IN IT, SHOW IT AND QUIT:
66> if [ -s $err ]
67> then
68>     /bin/cat $err 1>&2
69>     echo "$myname: quitting." 1>&2
70> else
71>     if /bin/cp $header $1
72>     then stat=0
73>     else echo "$myname: can't replace draft '$1'?" 1>&2
74>     fi
75> fi
76> exit
```

13.10.2 Explanation of distprompter

The main part of *distprompter* is the loop in **lines 32-63**. It reads the template draft file that *dist* built from $1. It writes the edited header into the $header file.

For efficiency, the script uses UNIX file descriptors to keep several files open at once. The loop reads and writes those open files, one line at a time. The Bourne shell can manipulate file descriptors with its *exec* command and operators like 2>&1 and 0<&-. There isn't room here for a complete explanation; to get that, see an advanced Bourne shell programming book. The comments in the script and the explanation here will tell you what each file descriptor redirection does.

NOTE

I thought a lot before I decided to put a script in the book that uses advanced shell concepts like file descriptor manipulation. A draft editor script doesn't have to be this complex!

I decided to do it, anyway. This script is an example of a draft editor that's fast, flexible, and robust. To write your own, you don't need to start over. You can adapt this one; follow the patterns in it—replace the tests with your own and leave the rest of the code as it is.

Let's get started. Table 13-2 lists the file descriptor numbers used in operators like 4<&0.

Table 13-2. UNIX File Descriptor Numbers

Number	Default Use
0	Standard input
1	Standard output
2	Standard error
3–9	Not assigned*

Outside the loop, in lines 1-31 and 64-77, the standard input of the commands is from your keyboard. But the loop is different because of the redirection at the

---

*If your MH was built with the [OVERHEAD] configuration option, some of the file descriptors 3-9 may already have been used. (Section 4.9 shows how to list your configuration options.) This *distprompter* script uses file descriptors 3-5. If you need to use those special [OVERHEAD] file descriptors inside *distprompter* (and that's not too likely), see Table 12-3 for an explanation of the *MHFD* and *MHCONTEXTFD* descriptors.

done line (line 63—see below). Every command in the loop reads its standard input from the template draft file, not from your terminal. It "takes over" standard input during the loop. So, the *read* command at the top of the loop (**line 32**) reads the template draft file. But the *read* command inside the loop, on **line 45**, couldn't read from your terminal.

The answer is to connect any other files you want to read to their own file descriptors. **Line 31** does that. Inside the loop, instead of reading its standard input, the *read* on **line 45** reads file descriptor 4.

Before reconnecting to the saved file descriptor 4, there's one more thing the script needs to do. **Line 43** saves the open draft file template as file descriptor 5. Because we don't close the file here (with exec 5<&-), the next *read* command at the top of the loop (line 32) will read the next line of the file. If we'd just closed the template file and reopened it, the next *read* on line 32 would read the first line of the file instead of the correct line.

Next, **line 44** changes file descriptor 0 to point to the original standard input before the loop—it was saved as file descriptor 4 in line 30. Now, the *read ans* command on **line 45** can read the original standard input and get your answer to the prompt. **Line 46** rearranges descriptors for the rest of the loop—it reconnects the draft template file from file descriptor 5 back to file descriptor 0. So, the next *read* at the top of the loop will read the template file.

Some shells can solve the problem on line 45 directly. They let you change what file descriptor the *read* command reads, instead of the default (file descriptor 0, the standard input). For instance, to read the value of the *ans* variable from file descriptor 4, line 45 could look like one of these:

```
read ans 0<&4
read -u4 ans
```

But some Bourne shells won't let you redirect the input of *read* on the same line.

That's why *distprompter* was written this way: the kind of redirection around line 45 works on all Bourne shells.

Misdirected Redirection

The version of *distprompter* in the first edition of this book handled the problem a different way. It used the Berkeley UNIX *head* command to read one line. The standard input was redirected from the terminal, */dev/tty*, and command substitution (the backquotes) copied the line into the *ans* variable:

```
# stdin IS FROM DRAFT, SO READ DIRECTLY FROM TERMINAL:
ans="`/usr/ucb/head -1 </dev/tty`"
```

That's an ugly hack. Some systems don't have *head* (or a similar command, *line*). Also, that ugly hack "hard-codes" the script to assume that you'll always distribute messages from a terminal—it prevents you from running *dist* this way:

```
% command-generator-program | dist
% dist < command-file
```

To solve that, the second edition of this script uses the file descriptor manipulation in lines 31, 43-44, and 46.

Now, about the loop: three file descriptors (*fds*) are redirected at **line 63**; these affect the input and output of every command inside the loop:

fd 0 The standard input; taken from the draft template file. Each *read* command on **line 32** will read the next line from the template file.

Any other command inside the loop that reads its standard input would read from this template file, too. That would be bad here, of course. See the explanation of lines 43-47, below.

fd 2 The standard error; goes to an error-collecting file. Line 66 handles that file.

fd 3 Written to the new message header file. Anything that is written to file descriptor 3 during the loop will be added to the new header.

The following inset entitled "The Ins and Outs of Redirected I/O Loops" points out some things to keep in mind when you write other loops like this one.

The Ins and Outs of Redirected I/O Loops

The Bourne shell usually runs a loop with redirected input or output in a sub-shell. For the *distprompter* script, this means, among other things:

- Any command inside the loop which reads its standard input will read from the pipe or file redirected to the loop's standard input. That's something you have to pay attention to, because the only command which should read from the file is the *read* command in line 32. The inputs of other commands inside the loop—like line 45—have to be redirected to read from somewhere other than the loop's standard input.

- In some Bourne shells, if you use the *exit* command inside a redirected loop, that will only terminate the subshell that's running the loop; it will *not* terminate the script. It's hard to call this a "feature"; I'd call it a bug. The script has a workaround for this; see the next paragraph. Later versions of Bourne-like shells have fixed this problem, more or less, but my fix should work in all Bourne shells.

- If there's any error inside the loop that should terminate the script, an *echo* writes an error message to file descriptor 2 (lines 58-59). Error messages from other commands that print errors to their standard error go to the same place. file descriptor 2 is redirected to an error-holding file at the subshell (loop) output (line 63). After the loop ends, if the file has anything in it (line 66), that means there was an error—and the script terminates.

- If you change the value of any shell or environment variables inside the loop, their values outside the loop (after the *done* command in line 63) will not be changed.

  Although this script doesn't need to use it, here's the usual fix for that problem. You use another file descriptor, like file descriptor 6, and write variable-setting commands to it. You redirect that file descriptor to a temporary file. Then, use the shell's dot command (.) to read the temporary file into the shell outside the loop. For example, to get the value of a variable named *varname* outside the loop:

```
while whatever
do
    ...
    echo "varname='value'" 1>&6
    ...
done 6>var_set_file
. var_set_file
```

The *read* in **line 32** reads two shell variables. The first variable, *label*, always contains the first word on the line—usually a component label like `Resent-Fcc:`. If the draft file has any other text (like the word `outbox`), that goes into the *line* variable.

The body of the loop is a big *case* structure. It tests the label and branches:

- If the label starts with `Resent-`, **lines 35-53** test to see if the rest of the component had any text.

  - A complete component is echoed to the terminal (via standard output) in **line 38** and to the new header file (by file descriptor 3) in **line 39**.

  - If the draft component was empty, **line 42** *echo*s it without a newline. This leaves the cursor to the right of the colon, ready for the user's response. The `$echo` and `$nnl` set at one of the lines 12-14 makes this work portably.

    A simple *read* command won't read what you type at the prompt because the loop's standard input comes from the draft file. As you read at the start of this section, some shells' built-in *read* command will not let you redirect their standard input to another file descriptor. A workaround that should take care of all Bourne shells starts at line 43. It's explained in detail near the start of this section (Section 13.10.2).

  - The *case* in **lines 47-50** tests the response. The component is only printed to the new header if the user typed an answer.

- The *case* in **line 54** matches an empty line or a line that starts with at least three dashes. This is the end of the header. The script *echo*s its own row of dashes to the draft file. Then it *break*s the loop—that probably isn't necessary because the next *read* in line 32 should return a nonzero status when it reads the end of the template file.

- **Line 58** matches anything else in the header. Because MH is strict about the components in the *dist* header, this test does some early enforcement of the rules and avoids those problems when you try to send the message.

Line 66 tests the error file's size. If there's something in the file, **line 68** shows the errors collected and **line 69** tells you that the draft wasn't finished. The nonzero status returned by the *trap* means that *whatnow* will print a message like the following one. Some newer versions of *whatnow* print a different message; see Section 6.5.3, "Deleted Draft Messages":

```
whatnow: problems with edit--/yourMHdir/draft deleted.
```

Otherwise, **line 71** copies the new header file on top of the original empty template. If that succeeds, **line 72** sets a zero status to tell *whatnow* that the edit went okay. Otherwise **line 73** prints an error and leaves the *stat* variable at the default value of 1, for *whatnow* to clean up.

13.11 Custom Message Printing: showpr

You can print your mail messages like this (assuming your printer program is named *lpr*), but all the messages will be run together:

```
% show 23 24 29 | lpr
```

Or you can use *pr*(1) to make simple headers (with the folder and message number), to make page numbers, and to start each message on a new page:

```
% show -showproc pr 23 24 29 | lpr
```

The *showpr* program lets you do more. It can use *mhl* to clean up each message before printing. You can customize the page heading—to include the message subject, for instance. And you can pass options to *pr* to tell it how to format your message. The script lets you store default *showpr* options in your MH profile because *showpr* reads them with the *mhprofile* script (from Section 13.4).

You can use *mh-format* strings on the *showpr* command line—like the ones you'd give to the *scan* command. (See Section 10.2.1.)

Here are some examples. Some of these might look pretty complicated to type just for printing a message. But remember that you can store any set of options as defaults in your MH profile:

- To print the current message with the message subject in each page heading (assuming that you haven't put any *showpr* options in your MH profile):

  ```
  % showpr | lpr
  ```

- To print the last three messages with the message subject in each page heading, format the messages with *mhl* and tell *pr* to use its options *–f* (separate pages with formfeeds) and *–l50* (make page length 50 lines):

  ```
  % showpr -mhl -pr '-f -l50' last:3
  ```

  (You can shorten the options to –m and –p, if you want.)

- To print the last three messages with *mhl* formatting, with the `From:` address and message date in the heading as follows:

  ```
  Dec 31 08:49 1992  From: Al Bok  Date: 12/07/92  Page 2
  ```

  Use a command line like this (split onto two lines here for readability—but don't split it yourself):

  ```
  showpr -mhl -format 'From: %(friendly{from})  \
      Date: %(mon{date})/%(mday{date})/%(year{date})' last:3 | lpr
  ```

  To make that easier, you could put the following component in your MH profile (note: although it's split onto two lines here, you should put it all on one line in your MH profile):

  ```
  showpr: -m -f 'From: %(friendly{from})
          Date: %(mon{date})/%(mday{date})/%(year{date})'
  ```

  Then get that formatting and print your messages with:

  ```
  % showpr last:3 | lpr
  ```

Finally, a note about *mhl*. You can make an *mhl* format file named *mhl.showpr* and put it in your MH directory (like /*yourMHdir*/mhl.showpr). If you do, and if you use the *–mhl* option, then *showpr* will format your messages with *mhl* *–form mhl.showpr*. Otherwise, the *–mhl* option uses the standard *mhl.format* file.

13.11.1 Listing of showpr

This program is explained in Section 13.11.2.

```
 1> #! /bin/sh
 2> # $Id: showpr,v 2.4 92/07/24 19:43:32 jerry book2 $
 3> ### showpr - show MH message(s) with pr(1), custom heading, maybe mhl(1)
 4> ### Usage: showpr [fdr] [msgs] [-mhl] [-format 'mh-format-str'] [-pr
      'pr-opts']
 5>
 6> folopts="-nolist -nototal -nopack"
 7> mh=/usr/local/mh              # WHERE MOST MH PROGRAMS LIVE
 8> mhl=/usr/local/lib/mh/mhl    # WHERE mhl LIVES
 9> mhprofile=/XXXXXXXXXXX/.bin/mhprofile   # READS MH PROFILE
10> myname="`basename $0`"
11> pr=/bin/pr
12> prwidth=55  # MAX WIDTH OF -h FIELD IN $pr + 5 FOR MSG NUM
13> scanopts="-noclear -noheader -noreverse"
14> stat=1  # DEFAULT EXIT STATUS, RESET TO 0 BEFORE NORMAL EXIT
15> usage="usage: $myname [fdr] [msgs] [-mhl] [-format 'mh-format-str'] [-pr
      'pr-opts']"
16>
```

```
17> # RESET "COMMAND LINE" PARAMETERS.  FIRST, AN x, WHICH WE
18> # shift AWAY, IN CASE THERE ARE NO OTHER PARAMETERS.
19> # THEN, MH PROFILE OPTIONS (IGNORE mhprofile RETURN STATUS).
20> # LAST, ORIGINAL COMMAND LINE ARGS (WITH SHELL BUG PATCH):
21> eval set x `$mhprofile -b $myname` '${1+"$@"}'
22> shift
23>
24> # PARSE set ARGS.  IF OPTIONS REPEATED, LAST ONES PREVAIL:
25> while :
26> do
27>     case "$1" in
28>     "") break ;;     # NO MORE ARGUMENTS
29>     [+@]*)  newfdr="$1" ;;
30>     -h*) # HELP:
31>         echo "$usage
32>         \$Revision: 2.4 $ \$Date: 92/07/24 19:43:32 $"
33>         exit
34>         ;;
35>     -m*) # SET mhlopts AS FLAG TO USE mhl.
36>         mhlopts="-nobell -noclear -nofaceproc -nomoreproc"
37>         # USE mhl.showpr FILE, IF ANY:
38>         if test -r `$mh/mhpath +`/mhl.showpr
39>         then mhlopts="$mhlopts -form mhl.showpr"
40>         fi
41>         ;;
42>     -f*)
43>         case "$2" in
44>         "") echo "$usage
45>             (Missing string after '$1')." 1>&2
46>             exit
47>             ;;
48>         *)  format="$2"; shift ;;
49>         esac
50>         ;;
51>     -p*)
52>         case "$2" in
53>         "") echo "$usage
54>             (Missing string after '$1')." 1>&2
55>             exit
56>             ;;
57>         +*|-*)  propts="$2"; shift ;;
58>         *)  echo "$usage
59>             (Bad options after '$1')." 1>&2
60>             exit
61>             ;;
62>         esac
63>         ;;
64>     *)  msgs="$msgs $1" ;;
65>     esac
66>
67>     shift
68> done
69>
```

```
70> # SET FORMAT OF pr HEADER.  IF NO -format OPTION, AND IF NO
71> # "showpr:" LINE IN MH PROFILE, DEFAULT TO MESSAGE SUBJECT:
72> : ${format='%{subject}'}
73>
74> # CHANGE FOLDER (IF USER GAVE ONE), GET NAME.
75> folder="`$mh/folder $folopts -fast $newfdr`"
76> cd `$mh/mhpath +` || exit    # cd TO MH DIRECTORY
77>
78> # scan ALL MESSAGES; FEED TO LOOP.  IF NONE, DEFAULT TO cur:
79> scan -width $prwidth $scanopts -format "%(msg) $format" ${msgs-cur} |
80> while read msgnum heading
81> do
82>     # IF MESSAGE UNREADABLE, MH 6.6 scan PRINTS (TO stdout!)
83>     # LIKE THIS, WITH LEADING BLANKS UNLESS msgnum > 999:
84>     #   <msgnum>  unreadable
85>     # IF THERE ARE LEADING BLANKS, SOME sh'S WILL COPY BOTH
86>     # MESSAGE NUMBER AND unreadable INTO $heading, AND LEAVE
87>     # $msgnum EMPTY.  TRY TO CATCH BOTH CASES:
88>     case "$msgnum" in
89>     "") echo "$myname: skipping, message $msgnum $heading" 1>&2;
    continue ;;
90>     esac
91>     case "$heading" in
92>     unreadable) echo "$myname: skipping unreadable message '$msgnum'."
    1>&2; continue ;;
93>     esac
94>
95>     msgpath=$folder/$msgnum
96>     case "$mhlopts" in
97>     "")  $pr $propts -h "$heading" $msgpath || break ;;
98>     *) $mhl $mhlopts $msgpath | $pr $propts -h "$heading" || break ;;
99>     esac
100> done
101>
102> stat=0
103> exit
```

13.11.2 Explanation of showpr

Line 11 sets the location of the *pr* program (for systems that have a second version of *pr* with different features).

Line 12 sets the width passed to *scan* (in line 79). This is the maximum width of the heading that is given to *pr*, not including the first five characters of the *scan* output (namely, the message number). Because our version of *pr* can take headings that are about 50 characters wide without making the output line more than 80 characters wide, I've set `prwidth=55` here (50 + 5 = 55). You might need to adjust it for your version of *pr*.

Lines 21-22 combine options from your MH profile with the options typed on the command line. We use the script in Section 13.4. To understand line 21 completely, you'll need to know shell quoting pretty well. Here's some information you'll need to know about shell quoting:

- The *set* command stores its arguments "in the command line"—in other words, in $1, $2, etc. Line 21 will replace the original command-line arguments you typed to *showpr*.

- The first new command-line argument is an x. This is a standard trick in Bourne shell programming. I do this because the *set* command must have at least one argument. If the rest of this line happens to be empty (if there are no options in the MH profile or on the command line)—then *set* would have no arguments. In that case, *set* would print a list of all shell variables currently set—and we don't want that! The x makes sure that *set* doesn't print a variable list.

    The *shift* in **line 22** removes this "dummy" first parameter, x.

- The `` `$mhprofile -b $myname` `` pulls *showpr* ($myname) options from the MH profile. Any quotes from the MH profile are copied as is. That's why line 21 uses *eval*—to interpret any quotes from the MH profile.

- The `'${1+"$@"}'` has single quotes around it, which *eval* strips off—without touching the inner part, `${1+"$@"}`.

    This inner part gives a quoted set of all shell command-line arguments. On some shells, you can do the same thing with just `"$@"`. But some Bourne shells have a bug that makes this workaround necessary.

    Without the workaround, when there are no command-line arguments, those buggy shells will substitute a single *empty* argument for `"$@"`. In English, the workaround says:

    > If the *first* command-line argument exists,
    >> then replace `${1+"$@"}` with a quoted set of
    >> *all* command-line arguments.
    >
    > Otherwise,
    >> replace it with a null string (nothing).

Table 13-3 shows what happens inside the shell as it interprets **line 21**. It assumes that the MH profile line looks like this:

```
showpr: -format 'Message %(msg)' -mhl
```

And the command line is:

```
% showpr -pr -f
```

Table 13-3. Shell Evaluating Line 21 of showpr

Step	Command Line
Original line	eval set x `$mhprofile -b $myname` '${1+"$@"}'
Before eval	eval set x -format 'Message %(msg)' -mhl ${1+"$@"}
After eval*	set x -format Message %(msg) -mhl -pr -f

Notice that some of those arguments—like Message %(msg)—have embedded spaces. The shell doesn't have any problem with that. Here are a few debugging lines you can add to *showpr* that show the command-line arguments one by one, with a count of how many:

```
echo "DEBUG: $# arguments now.   They are:"
for arg
do echo "$arg"
done
```

For example, with the command line above, putting that code after line 21 would print:

```
DEBUG: 6 arguments now.   They are:
x
-format
Message %(msg)
-mhl
-pr
-f
```

Another way to look at this is by setting the shell's *–xv* flags. See Section 12.16.

Lines 25-68 parse the command line that was set in lines 21-22. The loop keeps reading arguments, and *shift*ing them away (at line 67), until **line 28** sees that $1 is empty; then it *break*s the loop. **Line 32** has revision information for the help message. The revision number and date are filled in by the *co* command of the Revision Control System, RCS, with its $Revision$ and $Date$ keywords. The backslash (\) before each dollar sign ($) stops the shell from trying to expand $Revision and $Date as shell variables.

---

*Arguments are grayed.

If there was an *–mhl* (or just an *–m*) option, **lines 35-40** would set the *mhlopts* shell variable as a flag. **Line 96** tests for this variable; if *mhlopts* is set, then it uses *mhl* formatting.

Line 42 starts a test for the format string (the *–format* option). It tests to be sure that there's really a string (`$2`) after the switch itself (which will be in `$1`); after the subject is stored in `$format`, there's a *shift* command. This *shift* gets rid of the current `$1`; the *shift* at the end of the loop (line 67) takes care of what was `$2`.

Line 52 tests the start of the string after the *–pr* option. All valid *pr* options start with a minus sign (–) or a plus sign (+). If the string doesn't start with – or +, then *showpr* prints an error.

Line 72 uses the Bourne shell's colon (`:`) operator. Some people call colon a "do-nothing" operator—in fact, it was used to put comments in old Bourne shells that didn't have a # comment character. But the colon evaluates its arguments, so a lot of programmers use it in places like this. The shell's `${var=default}` means "if the variable named `var` is not set, set it to `default`. Then use whatever value was set." Here, it's testing the value of `$format`—if `$format` didn't get a value from the MH profile or the command line, it is set to the literal string `%{subject}`, which is a *scan* format string that puts the subject on the printout. See line 79.

Line 75 gets the current folder name—and changes it to `$newfdr` if there was a new folder name set. **Line 76** changes the current directory to the MH directory.

Line 79 runs *scan* with a format made from the message number and the `$format` set above. The output width is set to a maximum of `$prwidth` so that *pr*'s headings don't go past the printer's right margin. (See the explanation of line 12.) If there were no messages given on the command line, we just scan *cur* (without this, *scan* would scan—and the script would print—all the messages in the folder). About error handling: if *scan* has complaints about its command-line arguments, it writes a message to standard error and aborts—then, the pipe would be empty, so the *while* loop quits and the script aborts.

In **line 80**, the *while* loop reads *scan*'s standard output. The message number goes into the *msgnum* shell variable; the heading (the rest of *scan*'s output, including spaces and whatever) goes in the *heading* variable.

Lines 82-93 watch for unreadable messages that *scan* complains about (it complains on the standard output channel, unfortunately, so the error messages go down the pipe and into the loop!). This problem was fixed in MH 6.7. When versions of *scan* before MH 6.7 can't read a message, they will print a line of output that starts with several spaces (when it's printing this error, *scan* puts the message number in columns 1-4, padded with spaces on the left):

```
27 unreadable
```

When the input starts with a space, some Bourne shell *read* commands don't split the input; they put the whole line into the *subjnow* shell variable and leave *msg* empty. Lines 88-93 try to catch both behaviors.

The new MH 6.7 *scan* prints a much more useful message. Even better, the message goes to the standard error:

```
scan: can't open message 12: Permission denied, continuing...
```

That message on *stderr* never reaches *stdout*—so the *read* gets the next line of *scan*'s standard output, and the loop continues right away.

Lines 97-98 print the message—either formatting it first with *mhl* or piping the file directly into *pr*. Nonzero statuses are caught by the | | break at the end of lines 97 and 98; these terminate the *while* loop.

Because the loop keeps running until it's read all the messages, and because *pr* prints out complete pages, the user running *showpr* can't tell how many times the loop is executed. To the user (or the program reading from *showpr*), the output looks like a constant stream of pages to print.

13.12 Configure MH Programs for xmh: edprofile ⊠

xmh does a lot of its work by running MH commands. People who use MH commands at a shell prompt can add switches on the command line to control the way MH commands work—to set the way that a folder is sorted, for example, or how *scan* formats its output. *xmh* users can edit the MH profile to change command options, but there isn't an easy way to change the way a command works "on the fly."

The *edprofile* script helps there. It lets you edit lines in the MH profile while you're running *xmh*. You can set buttons that run *edprofile* commands. For example, the *edprofile* command could change the *sortm* options. Then your next Sort Folder will sort the folder that new way.

NOTE

edprofile only works with *xmh* Release 5 and its new *xmhShellCommand( )* action.

The command-line syntax of *edprofile* is:

```
edprofile [-v] component [new-value] --
```

Brackets, like [-v], mean that part isn't required. The parts are:

- If there isn't an error, *edprofile* edits silently. The *-v* switch tells *edprofile* to open a dialog box that shows the edited line in your MH profile.

- The `component` is the command name (from the start of a line in the MH profile, like `sortm:`) that you want to edit. Don't use the colon (`:`).

- The `new-value` is the list of options you want to appear after the command name. Put spaces between them.

  If you don't give a value, *edprofile* leaves an empty component (just the name) in the MH profile. Then *xmh* will use the MH default action of the MH command.

- The last argument must be two dashes (`--`), with no space between. This separates the *edprofile* arguments you type from the message filenames that *xmh* adds when it executes *XmhShellCommand( )*. *edprofile* ignores those filenames.

Section 16.4.6 shows how to use *edprofile* in *xmh* buttons.

One last note: if you've defined the *MH* environment variable, *edprofile* will edit the file it points to. The default file is *$HOME/.mh_profile*.

13.12.1 Listing of edprofile

This program is explained in Section 13.12.2.

```
1> #! /bin/sh
2> # $Id: edprofile,v 1.0 92/08/03 08:30:09 jerry book2 $
3> ### edprofile - edit line in $MH file (default: $HOME/.xmh_profile)
4> ### Usage: edprofile [-v] component [new-value] --
5>
6> # ON ERROR, XmhShellCommand SHOWS ALL ARGUMENTS IN NOTICE BOX; WE DON'T
     HAVE TO.
7>
8> grep=/bin/grep
9>
```

```
10> : ${MH=${HOME?}/.mh_profile}     # THE PROFILE FILE WE EDIT
11>
12> case "$1" in
13> -v) verbose=yes; shift;;
14> esac
15> # COMPONENT WE SEARCH FOR IS IN $1; REST OF ARGS HANDLED IN for LOOP:
16> case $# in
17> 0) echo "`basename $0` quitting: not enough arguments." 1>&2; exit 1 ;;
18> *)  cmd="$1"; shift;;
19> esac
20>
21> ended= newargs=
22> for arg
23> do
24>     case "$arg" in
25>     --) ended=yes; break ;;
26>     *)  newargs="$newargs $arg" ;;
27>     esac
28> done
29>
30> if [ "$ended" != yes ]; then
31>     echo "`basename $0` quitting: missing '--' after argument list."
    1>&2
32>     exit 1
33> fi
34>
35> if [ ! -r "$MH" -o ! -w "$MH" ]; then
36>     echo "`basename $0` quitting: can't read and/or write profile
37>     '$MH'" 1>&2
38>     exit 1
39> elif $grep "^$cmd:" "$MH" >/dev/null; then
40>     # DO THE EDIT.  SAVE ed OUTPUT AND STATUS FOR TESTING:
41>     errs=`/bin/ed - "$MH" << ENDEDIT 2>&1
42>     /^$cmd:[    ]*/s/:.*/: $newargs/
43>     w
44> ENDEDIT`
45>     status=$?
46>     if [ -n "$errs" -o $status != 0 ]; then
47>         echo "`basename $0`: edit bombed?  ed status=$status, messages:
48>         $errs" 1>&2
49>         exit 1
50>     elif [ "$verbose" = yes ]; then
51>         case "$newargs" in
52>         "") echo "$cmd set to default (no parameters)" 1>&2 ;;
53>         *)  echo "$cmd set to: $newargs" 1>&2 ;;
54>         esac
55>     fi
56>     exit 0
57> else
58>     echo "`basename $0` quitting: can't find '$cmd:' in profile
59>     '$MH'" 1>&2
60>     exit 1
61> fi
```

13.12.2 Explanation of edprofile

First, the script parses the command line. **Lines 12-14** find any −*v* switch, set `$verbose` as a flag, and *shift* the argument away. **Lines 16-19** do the same thing for the next argument, which must be the component name (at the start of the MH profile line) to be edited. The loop in **lines 22-28** parses the rest of the command line. It stores all arguments for the MH profile component in the *newargs* shell variable. When the loop finds the double dashes, it quits. The rest of the arguments will be message pathnames that *xmh* adds to all commands run with *XmhShellCommand( )*—*edprofile* doesn't need these pathnames, so the script ignores them.

The *if* structure in **lines 35-61** tests the MH profile to be sure it's readable and writable and contains the component name to be edited. **Lines 41-44** run the *ed* editor on the MH profile. The tricky part is that *ed* doesn't return a nonzero status if something goes wrong; it just prints a short error message. The 2>&1 merges *ed*'s standard error (file descriptor 2) onto its standard output (file descriptor 1). Then backquotes (`` ` ``) are used to grab any messages *ed* outputs from the standard output into the *errs* shell variable. That way, the shell variable will also get what's written to *stderr*.

Because of the `ed −`, the editor won't display any lines (except errors); it just does the editing commands.

Line 42 finds the component (in `$cmd`). It changes the rest of the line, including any leading spaces and tabs, to the new arguments from `$newargs`.

Line 43 writes the file. When the *ed* script ends (at line 43), the end of the redirected input signals *ed* to quit. The ENDEDIT terminator must be at the left margin or the shell won't see it. (Some Bourne shells have <<− here-document operators that let you indent the terminator, but not all do.)

If `$errs` isn't empty or the *ed* exit status saved at **line 45** is not 0, an error is printed and the script quits. Otherwise, verbose information is printed if the −*v* switch was used.

13.13 Add Signature (or Anything) to Drafts: mysend

Section 8.9.6 shows how to edit your draft template files to add a standard signature to the end of many (but not all) of your messages. Section 13.2 has the *append* shell script, an editor you run from the What Now? prompt to add files to the end of a draft before you send it. This section has a third way: a shell script that edits your draft message when you execute:

```
What now? send
```

(It also works when you use *push*.) The script is written to append a copy of the file *.signature* from your home directory, with a line of two dashes before it. That's easy to change by editing the script.

By default, the script does not add your signature unless you type:

```
What now? send -signature
```

(Abbreviate that −sig if you'd like.) You can change a shell variable to make the opposite the default: a signature unless you type −nosig. No matter what, the script won't add a signature if the draft you're composing is from the *dist* command (see Section 6.9).

Any other arguments you type at What now? are passed to the standard MH *send* command. *mysend* runs it after editing the draft.

Of course, *mysend* can do more to a draft than add a signature. Whatever you do, of course, remember that the script processes all of your mail; make sure it's reliable and does what you want. A test mail setup like the one in Section 12.17.1 is a good place for debugging a script this important.

To install the script, add this line to your MH profile:

```
sendproc: /xxx/yyy/mysend
```

where /xxx/yyy is the location of *mysend* on the filesystem.

NOTE

At press time, this script wouldn't work with the *dist* command. There seemed to be a bug in MH Version 6.7.2 (at least) that won't tell the *post* command to allow a message to be redistributed. The bug only happens when you add your own *sendproc* program; it had nothing to do with this *mysend* script. The result is errors like these during the *dist* command:

```
What now? send
post: illegal header line -- Resent-To:
post: illegal header line -- Resent-cc:
```

If you use *dist* and your MH version has that bug, you should also use the *mydist* script in Section 13.13.3.

13.13.1 Listing of mysend

This program is explained in Section 13.13.2.

```
 1> #! /bin/sh
 2> # $Id: mysend,v 1.0 92/08/03 08:38:13 jerry book2 $
 3> ### mysend -- sendproc that adds signature (or anything) to mail
 4> ### Usage (in MH profile):     sendproc: /xxx/yyy/mysend
 5>
 6> mh=/usr/local/mh              # WHERE MH COMMANDS LIKE send LIVE
 7> dosig=n                       # DEFAULT: NO SIGNATURE
 8> signature=$HOME/.signature  # SIGNATURE FILE TO READ
 9>
10> # PARSE COMMAND LINE, GRAB OUR OPTIONS.
11> # FIRST ARGS ARE OPTIONS; LAST IS DRAFT FILENAME:
12> while :
13> do
14>     case "$1" in
15>     "")         break ;;             # ALL DONE
16>     -sig*)      dosig=y ;;
17>     -nosig*)    dosig=n ;;
18>     *)          args="$args $1" ;;   # FOR send
19>     esac
20>     draft="$1"  # EVENTUALLY THIS GETS DRAFT PATHNAME
21>     shift
22> done
23>
24> # NO SIGNATURE IF $mhdist ENVARIABLE IS 1 (DRAFT IS A dist HEADER):
25> case "${mhdist}${dosig}" in
26> 1*) ;;
27> *y) if [ -w "$draft" -a -r "$signature" ]
28>     then
29>         # SOME echoS CHOKE ON DASHES, SO DO IT THIS WAY:
30>         /bin/cat - "$signature" << \ENDPRESIG >> $draft || exit 1
31> --
32> ENDPRESIG
33>     else
34>         echo "$0 quitting: unreadable '$signature' or unwritable
    '$draft'" 1>&2
35>         exit 1
36>     fi
37>     ;;
38> esac
39> exec $mh/send $args
```

13.13.2 Explanation of mysend

The script is simple. The variable set on **line 7** determines whether the script adds a signature or not by default.

Line 26 tests the string that combines the setting of the *mhdist* environment variable (shown in Table 12-3) with the setting of the *dosig* shell variable. If *mhdist* is 1, then the script was called from the *dist* command (via *whatnow*). You shouldn't add text to the body of a redistributed message. So, line 26 will branch straight to the *send* command.

Otherwise, if the draft file is writable and your *.signature* file is readable, **lines 30-32** append a row of dashes and your signature file to the draft message. The *cat* command has two command-line arguments, in the following order:

1. The dash (–) tells *cat* to read its standard input. This comes from the here-document lines between the *cat* command and the ENDPRESIG terminator on line 32. Right now, this "presignature" is just a line of two dashes. You can change it to anything you want.

2. The next *cat* argument is your signature file.

Line 37 runs the MH *send* command. The $args passes all arguments you typed at What now? except *–nosig* or *–sig*. Note that any send: arguments from the MH profile are *not* passed to *sendproc* scripts like *mysend*. If you want to set mysend: defaults in your MH profile, see the *mhprofile* script in Section 13.4.

One last note: as the *whatnow* manual page mentions, if you rename this script to something besides *mysend*, don't call it *send* because *whatnow* won't use it.

13.13.3 Workaround for MH sendproc Bug with dist: mydist

The NOTE in Section 13.13 explains a problem with *mysend* that keeps the script from working with the MH *dist* command. The *mydist* script works around that problem. It disables the *mysend* script while you *dist* a message. *mydist* makes a temporary copy of your MH profile without the sendproc: line that runs *mysend*. Then it runs the real *dist*.

There are two ways to install *mydist*:

1. Make a shell alias or function named *dist* that actually runs *mydist*. (If you haven't used aliases or functions, see Section 8.2.1.)

2. Rename the *mydist* script to *dist*. Put it in a directory that's listed before the MH binary directory in your shell search path. That way, the shell will find your version before it finds the real *dist*. The NOTE: at the start of the script will remind you what *dist* you're really using.

Here's the script:

```
 1> #! /bin/sh
 2> # $Id: mydist,v 1.2 92/08/03 08:45:38 jerry book2 $
 3> ### mydist - workaround for dist/sendproc problem in "mysend"
 4> ### Usage: use as shell alias or function, or rename to "dist"
 5>
 6> echo "NOTE: using workaround $0" 1>&2
 7> stat=1   # DEFAULT EXIT STATUS; RESET BY dist
 8> tempprfl=/tmp/MYDIST$$
 9> trap 'rm -f $tempprfl; exit $stat' 0 1 2 15
10> sed '/^[Ss]endproc:/d' ${MH-$HOME/.mh_profile} >$tempprfl ||
       exit
11> MH=$tempprfl /usr/local/mh/dist $*
12> stat=$?     # SAVE STATUS FROM dist FOR exit IN trap
13> exit
```

Line 10 does the real work. The *sed* command copies all lines from your current MH profile, except the `sendproc:` line, to a temporary MH profile. That filename is temporarily stored in the *MH* environment variable before the real *dist* command runs on **line 11**. You may need to correct the *dist* pathname.

13.14 Process New Mail in a Batch: autoinc ⊠

Chapter 11, *Processing New Mail Automatically*, shows the *mhook* features for processing each new message automatically as it comes in. Some systems won't allow users to run "mail hook" programs as mail comes in. Some users might want to process mail in a batch, to have a program (or themselves) make decisions about what to do with the mail as a group.

You can probably adapt the *autoinc* script for that kind of mail processing. It's designed to be run automatically from a *cron* or *at* job but you can also type its name at a shell prompt. First, *autoinc* compares the amount of incoming mail you have to your disk quota. If you don't have enough room, it sends mail to some address (probably not yours!) to complain. You can hack *autoinc* to tell you in some other way. If your system doesn't have disk quotas—or even if it does—you might also want to have *autoinc* run *df* to see if there's enough disk space left on your filesystem before it incorporates all your mail.* Next, *autoinc*

---

*This test isn't completely accurate. Once the mail has been incorporated, each message will take at

incorporates your new mail and starts a loop to *scan* the messages one by one. A MH format string lets *scan* pull out just the information you need. The script *refile*s messages it knows what to do with. It leaves the rest of the mail in your *inbox* for you to look at.

With the techniques in Chapter 12, *Introduction to Shell Programming for MH*, the power of all the MH commands, as well as all the other utilities on your UNIX system, you can probably make *autoinc* do just what you need.

While you're debugging *autoinc*, remember the *inc* –*notruncate* switch. It incorporates your new mail but doesn't remove the messages from your system mailbox. That way, you can incorporate and test the same messages over and over.

13.14.1   Listing of autoinc

This program is explained in Section 13.14.2.

```
 1> #! /bin/sh
 2> # $Id: autoinc,v 1.4 92/10/19 21:00:48 jerry book2+ $
 3> ### autoinc - Incorporate new mail; refile from inbox automatically
 4> ### Usage: autoinc
 5>
 6> df=/bin/df  expr=/bin/expr  grep=/bin/grep  mailer=/usr/ucb/mail
 7> quota=/usr/ucb/quota        sed=/bin/sed    tr=/bin/tr
 8> error=xxx@yyy,aaa@bbb   # WHERE TO MAIL ERRORS
 9> margin=300             # HOW MANY EXTRA KBYTES WE NEED
10> mh=/usr/local/mh       # WHERE MH PROGRAMS LIVE
11>
12> # GET NAME OF FILESYSTEM WITH HOME DIRECTORY FROM LINES LIKE
13> # THIS.  TAKE LAST WORD STARTING WITH A SLASH ON SECOND LINE:
14> # Filesystem          kbytes    used    avail capacity  Mounted on
15> # hostname:/u1        842171   442588   315365    58%      /u1
16> homedir="`$df ${HOME?} | $sed -n '2s@.*\(/[^/]*\)$@\1@p'`"
17>
18> # GET QUOTA VALUES.  USE sed TO GRAB LINE THAT STARTS WITH ${homedir}:
19> #     Disk quotas for yourname (uid 1234):
20> #     Filesystem  usage  quota  limit  timeleft  files  quota  limit
21> #     /u1         18451  20000  20000            1474    0      0
22> # AND PUT THE FIRST TWO NUMBERS ON THE LINE INTO SHELL VARIABLES:
23> eval `$quota -v |
24> $sed -n "s@^${homedir} *\([0-9][0-9]*\) *\([0-9][0-9]*\).*@used=\1
       total=\2@p"`
25>
26> # PUT x IN $1, NUMBER OF KBYTES IN $2, MAILBOX FILENAME IN $3.
```

---

least one disk block—but the test doesn't account for that extra disk usage. The *margin* shell variable can work around that problem.

```
27>  # (NOTE: SOME ls -s OUTPUT IS IN 512-BYTE BLOCKS; NEED TO DOUBLE THOSE.)
28>  set x `/bin/ls -s /usr/spool/mail/$USER`
29>  wouldbe="`$expr $used + $2 + $margin`"
30>  if [ $wouldbe -ge $total ]
31>  then
32>      echo "used $used kytes, incoming mail $2 kbytes, quota is $total." |
33>      $mailer -s "ERROR -- no room to 'inc' mail!  Clean up now!" $error
34>      exit
35>  fi
36>
37>  # FILTER inc OUTPUT THROUGH grep, PUT LEFTOVERS BACK ONTO STDERR.
38>  # IF inc RETURNS NON-ZERO, EXIT.
39>  $mh/inc 2>&1 | $grep -v '^inc: no mail to incorporate' 1>&2  || exit
40>
41>  set -e  # IF ANY ERRORS FROM NOW ON, EXIT
42>
43>  # SCAN inbox MESSAGES.  GET MSG. NUMBER, From: AND Sender: ADDRESS.
44>  # TURN UPPER TO LOWER CASE.  THEN FEED TO STANDARD INPUT OF LOOP.
45>  # INSIDE LOOP, refile MESSAGES WE KNOW HOW TO HANDLE; LEAVE OTHERS:
46>  $mh/scan +inbox -format '%(msg) %(mbox{from}) %(mbox{sender})' |
47>  $tr '[A-Z]' '[a-z]' |
48>  while read msg from sender
49>  do
50>      # FOR MOST, MATCH From: COMPONENT AND PUT INTO THAT FOLDER:
51>      case "$from" in
52>      aaaa|bbbbb|ccccc|ddddd|eeeeeee|fffffff|ggggggg|hhhhhh)
53>          $mh/refile $msg +$from
54>          continue
55>          ;;
56>      iiiiii|jjjjj|kkkkkkkk|lllllllll|mmmmmmm|nnnnnn|ooooooo)
57>          $mh/refile $msg +$from
58>          continue
59>          ;;
60>      # ... AND SO ON ...
61>      esac
62>      # THIS ONE IS BETTER TO MATCH ON Sender: COMPONENT:
63>      case "$sender" in
64>      ppppppp)
65>          $mh/refile $msg +ppppppp
66>          continue
67>          ;;
68>      esac
69>  done
```

13.14.2 Explanation of autoinc

Overall, **lines 6-7** set full pathnames of commands. This is important because *cron* jobs run in an environment with a different search path than yours. **Lines 12-35** check to be see whether the script will be able to incorporate all your new mail. That's a good idea if you get a lot of mail and if your disks run close to full (especially late at night, when the system administrator isn't there to clean them up). **Lines 37-69** incorporate the new mail and loop through the messages one by one. You'll probably want to make a lot of changes to *autoinc*. Still, a few lines of this version are worth explaining more:

- **Lines 16 and 24** use *sed* "tagged fields" to grab certain fields from the output of *df* and *quota –v*. Some people use *awk* to do this, but *sed* usually runs faster.

- **Lines 23-24** use the shell's *eval* command to read a line like the following that *sed* outputs:

      used=1345 total=2048

  That sets two variables, $used and $total, from the output of *quota –v*.

- **Line 28** stores the mailbox size, from *ls –s*, in $2. (The set x trick is explained in Section 13.11.2.) If you're using *inc* with POP, that won't work, of course. But you can parse the output of *msgchk*—use another *sed* expression to find the number *nnn* in the string (*nnn* bytes).

- **Line 39** uses *grep* to filter out the typical *inc* message when there's no mail—but to write any other messages to the standard error. Some fancy trickery with file descriptors could have used *grep* on just the *stderr*, but combining *stdout* and *stderr* was easier. Besides, you're going to hack this script and make it perfect, aren't you? :-)

- Instead of checking for errors at every line, **line 41** makes the shell quit if any command returns a nonzero status. If there's a problem, just fix it and rerun *autoinc* by hand. When you rerun *autoinc*, it will look through all the leftover mail in *inbox* as well as any new mail.

- Inside the redirected-input *while* loop are *case* structures that check the output of the special *scan* command (Section 12.17.9, "Using scan Format Strings to Get Information," explains more). If course, your loop can use any tests it needs to.

  Or, you might not want to use a loop at all. Depending on what you need, a few commands like the one below could be more efficient:

      $pick --sender a -or --sender b ... -seq temp && $refile temp +x

Part IV:

Using and
Customizing
xmh

*Part IV covers the xmh client from X11 Release 5. xmh with
Release 5 is similar to Release 4, although the windows look a
little different. Part IV will help Release 3 users, too.*

*Part IV starts with a tour that will let you use xmh for everyday
work. By the end of Part IV, you'll be able to customize xmh for
your needs.*

14

Tour Through xmh ⊠

This chapter takes you on a tour through *xmh* for the X Window System Version 11 Release 5. Although the examples show the *twm* window manager, any X window manager is fine.

You'll learn how to use basic functions to send and receive mail, organize it, and do most of the basic things you'd want to do with electronic mail. Along the way are some brief looks at advanced features that are covered in the next two chapters.

If your site doesn't have Release 5, try the tour anyhow. The *xmh* basics are similar in Version 11 Release 3 and almost identical in Release 4.

After you do the tutorial in this section, you'll have enough experience to handle your day-to-day mail with *xmh*.

14.1 Getting Started

You'll probably want to start with this *xmh* tour first. Then, if you're curious, open an *xterm* window and try the MH tour in Chapter 4. You can use both *xmh* and MH, though running both at the same moment can get confusing if you aren't careful.

Before you start the tour, be sure that you've read Chapter 3, *Setting Up for MH and xmh*.

Ask someone to send you two or three short mail messages. The messages don't have to be sent with *xmh*. Almost any mail agent will work, although it should be able to put a Subject: on the message. You'll use these as test messages later in the tour. They don't have to make sense—any old garbage will do.

By now, you should have a *.mh_profile* file in your home directory—whether MH created it or the file was already there. As you saw in Section 1.4, the file customizes your MH setup. Make a mental note of the words at the start of each line (words like scan: and repl:). As you do the tour, if your commands seem to work differently than the book shows, remember that the settings in your MH profile may have changed how MH works by default. Because *xmh* runs MH commands for you, changes in your MH profile can change the way that *xmh* works.

X setup files like *.xsession* and *.Xdefaults*, as well as the version of X you're running, can also make *xmh* look and/or work differently than the examples here. If you have questions, ask a local X-pert or check a reference like Volume Three, *X Window System User's Guide*, by Valerie Quercia and Tim O'Reilly.

14.2 Running xmh

The command to start *xmh* looks something like this:

```
% xmh -display foobar:0.0 -geometry 660x460+200+5 &
```

That command opens a 660x460-pixel *xmh* window close to the top of the 0 display on screen 0 of the host *foobar*. If you have both monochrome and color screens, the monochrome screen may give you a faster response. The *–geometry* setting makes a different *xmh* window size than the default. I've made it that size in this book. If you want the default size, leave out the 660x460 in that command line. If you want the window in a different place, change the +200+5. Your window manager probably lets you place the window yourself—in that case, you can omit the position completely.

To start *xmh* now, you can type the command line in an *xterm* window. If you want an *xmh* window to open automatically whenever you start X, add that line to your startup file (like *.xsession*). If your window manager has a menu and *xmh* isn't on the menu, you might add it.

14.3 What's in the xmh Window

Here's a description of the parts of the *xmh* window and what they're for. Your window should look something like Figure 14-1, but your window will be emptier unless you've used MH before.

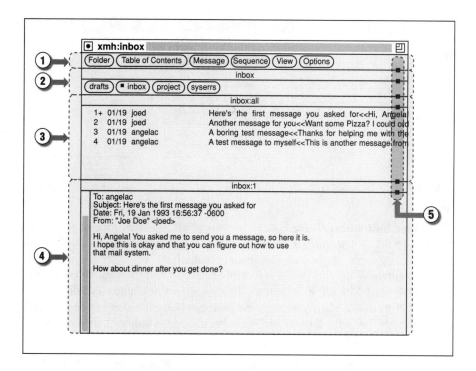

Figure 14-1. xmh first master window

The window is split into four areas. (Or, if *xmh* has been customized, there may be five areas—see Figure 16-7 in Section 16.4.3.) Let's take a look at them. (For more detail, see Figure 15-1; it has every area of the master window labeled.)

1. **Command menu bar.** The top pane has buttons that give commands to *xmh*. These buttons have drop-down menus.

   For example, when you point to the Sequence button and hold down the first mouse button, a menu will drop down. As you slide the pointer down, different commands on this Sequence menu are highlighted. Commands that aren't available use gray letters; you can't highlight them. In Figure 14-2, I've highlighted the Pick command for finding messages and sequences. Because the folder doesn't have any sequences, most commands are grayed. Try it yourself with your folder.

   If you release the mouse button while that command is highlighted, the command will be executed. But, if you slide the pointer off that menu item (say, to the right) before you release the button, the command won't be executed.

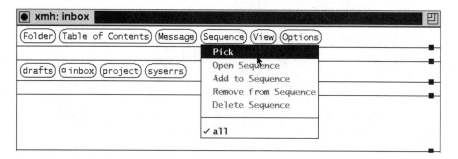

Figure 14-2. Selecting a command

2. **Folder buttonbox.** These buttons let you select a folder of messages. (Section 15.6.3 explains how to select another folder.) There's one button for each folder. X users call this set of buttons a *buttonbox*. You'll start with at least two buttons—for your *inbox* and *drafts* folders—and there might be more if you've used MH (or *xmh*) before. If a folder has subfolders, a folder menu will drop down when you click the button—but most *xmh* beginners don't need to bother with subfolders. The label above the buttons tells the name of your selected folder.

3. **Table of Contents.** The third area shows the folder name followed by a colon (:) and the *sequence name*. In Figure 14-1, the folder is named inbox and the sequence is all. Under the titlebar is a summary list of the messages in your *inbox* folder (empty if you're a new user). If the list of messages in your Table of Contents is longer than the window, an *xterm*-like scrollbar will let you control your view of the list. (Section 15.2 has more.) There's no scrollbar now because there are just a few messages.

4. **Viewed message.** The top pane of this area is a titlebar that shows the folder name (here, `inbox`) and message number (here, `1`). The message is shown under the titlebar. There's a scrollbar at the left-hand edge.

5. **Grips**. The squares close to the right-hand side of the window are for adjusting the size of each area.

Your window may have round or rectangular buttons. Section 16.3.9 explains how to control that.

14.4 Sending Mail

Let's get started by sending a message to yourself (you can send it to someone else, as well, but you'll need the message, too). Here are the steps you'll need to follow:

1. Go to the command menu bar and pull down the `Message` menu. Select the `Compose Message` command. A new window such as the one in Figure 14-3 will open. (Figure 14-4 shows the filled-in draft.)

   If you've used the GNU *emacs* editor before, the commands in this window are a subset of those familiar commands.

   In this window, a text caret (ʌ) shows where the text you type will be placed. When you first open the composition window, the caret will usually be to the right of the `To:` component in the header—ready for you to type the address where you want to send the message. If the caret (ʌ) isn't there, move it there. An easy way to move the text caret is by pointing with the mouse and clicking the first mouse button. You can also move it by pressing the arrow keys, if your keyboard has them. The GNU *emacs*-like commands CTRL-F, CTRL-B, CTRL-P, and CTRL-N work too. For a complete list, see Table 15-2.

   Type your username (login name) after the `To:`. This will address the message to you. If you want to add someone else to the end of the `To:` line, type a comma (`,`) and the other person's username. Section 1.3, "Addressing E-mail," has more information.

   People listed on the `cc:` line will get a "courtesy" (or "carbon") copy of your message. By convention, the message is especially meant for the people in the `To:` component, and people in the `cc:` component are getting the message "for information." In this exercise, please leave `cc:` empty.

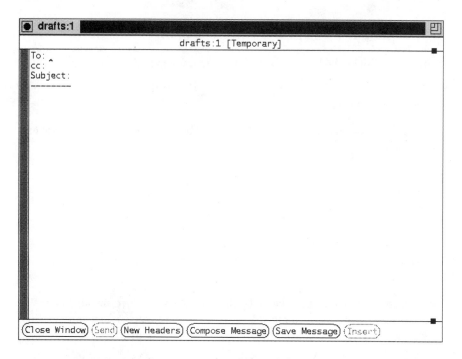

Figure 14-3. xmh message composition window

2. Press the "next-line" command, CTRL-N , twice to go to the right-hand side of the Subject: line. If you need to move to the end of the line, use CTRL-E or the arrow keys.

   Type a subject for the message. The people who receive your message can get a quick idea about its contents from the subject, so it's a good idea to spend a moment to think of a descriptive one. For this message, you might type something like Test message from Judy and the xmh system. Or, for now, type anything you feel like.

3. Before you go on, be sure that you didn't leave any empty lines in the header. (By empty, I don't mean a line with just a label, like Cc:. I mean a *completely* empty line, with no text on it—these confuse MH.) If you did, move the cursor back to it (CTRL-P goes to the previous line) and delete it by pressing the DELETE key until the cursor moves back to the end of the previous line.

4. After you type the Subject:, use the next-line command twice (type CTRL-N twice) to move to the start of the message body. Notice that the cursor won't move past the end of a line where you haven't typed anything. (In

other words, you can't create spaces at the end of a line just by moving the cursor there. If you want to move past the end of a line, use the space bar.)

Now you can type your message. To move backward and forward along a line, use CTRL-B and CTRL-F (or the arrow keys). As you type, when the cursor gets to the right-hand side of a line, it'll "word wrap"—move automatically to the start of the next line. To leave a blank line (at the end of a paragraph), press RETURN (or ENTER).

Your window should look approximately like Figure 14-4.

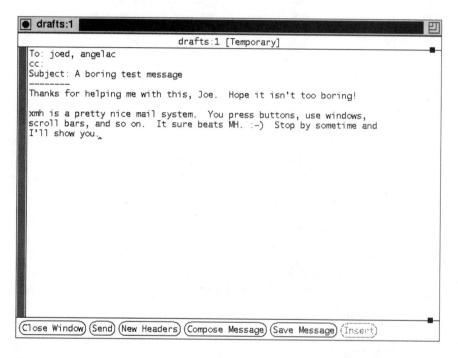

Figure 14-4. Composition window with finished message

5. If you're happy with the message, you can send it by pointing to the Send button at the bottom of the window and clicking the first mouse button. When the message has been sent, the Send button will turn gray. Use the Close Window button to get back to the master *xmh* window.

   Or, if you're not happy with the message, just click the Close Window button without first clicking Send. After *xmh* asks for confirmation, as in Figure 14-5, you'll be back at the master *xmh* window without saving or sending.

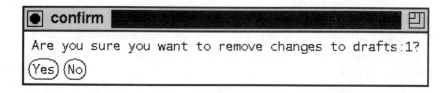

Figure 14-5. Closing composition window without saving or sending

Practice sending yourself another few messages. Make one fairly long—30 lines or so. You might type a few lines—then use your mouse to copy the lines and paste them in again a few times.

NOTE

If you make your composition wider than 80 characters (in the font you're using), the lines in the message you send can be too long. Resize your window to 80 characters or less (Figure 14-9 shows an easy way to check the width). Then use the META-Q command to rewrap your paragraphs. Section 15.3 has more about line wrapping in *xmh*.

14.5 Getting New Mail

By now, your friend should have sent you mail and you'll have the messages you sent yourself. The master *xmh* window should be on your screen. The black square inside the inbox folder button should be solid black—a sign that new mail is waiting.

Select the Incorporate New Mail command on the Table of Contents menu.* The Table of Contents will show a list of the new messages you've received. There's a plus sign (+) next to the message number of the first new message—this marks the *current message*. You'll see the current message in the message viewing area (which has been empty until now). If the first message doesn't appear, select View Next Message on the Message menu. Your window will look like Figure 14-6 (with different messages, of course).

---

*If Incorporate New Mail is "grayed," you're probably not viewing the *inbox* folder. Click the inbox button in the folder buttonbox, then select Open Folder from the Folder menu.

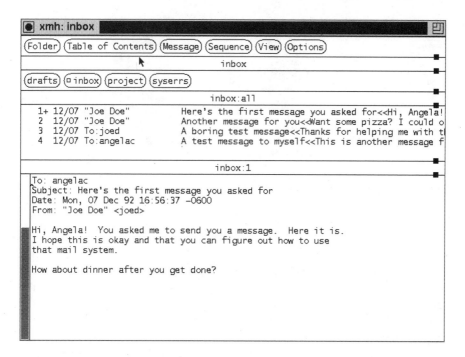

Figure 14-6. After incorporating new messages

The first part of the message, the *header*, has lines of information ("components") that aren't all important. Your message may have more, fewer, or different header components than the ones shown here. If your *xmh* has not been set to *HideBoringHeaders* (see Section 16.3.1), you may see more components.

There are two ways to see the next message. You can select the View Next Message command from its menu. Or you can use the accelerator key, META-N. To use META-N, look for a key on your keyboard marked "Meta." (Old Sun keyboards label the Meta keys "Left" and "Right"; newer ones use a diamond symbol. Others label them things like "Alt" or "Compose." The key is almost always next to the space bar.) Making a meta-character is like making a control character. To make META-N, for instance, hold down the META key and tap the "n" key. As soon as you enter META-N, you should see the next message.

Logically enough, the View Previous command will show you the previous message. The accelerator is META-P.

If you want to read another message out of order, first select the message by clicking the mouse pointer on it. Choose a message and click on the message line in the Table of Contents (with your left button). Then, to read the selected message, use View Next Message (or META-N). Figure 14-7 shows how this looks.

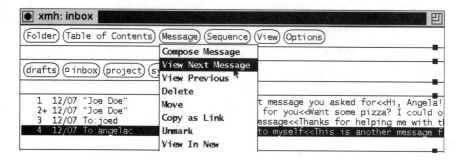

Figure 14-7. Selecting a message to view

The accelerator for viewing a message is pointing to its line in the Table of Contents and clicking with the second mouse button. This is quick—try it!

Now, about the scrollbar: Your friend (or you) should have sent at least one long message. When you read it, use the viewing area's thumb (the gray part of the scrollbar) to see the message. To move the viewed message, put the pointer in the scrollbar. Then, you have about a zillion and two choices. I'll explain a couple of them here; see Section 15.2 for the other zillion.

To jump ahead to the next screenful, put the pointer at the bottom of the scrollbar and click the first button. If you put the pointer in the thumb, hold down the second button, then slide the mouse up and down, the message will move up and down with you. So you can move to the top of the message by holding down the middle button and sliding off the top of the scrollbar.

There are accelerators for reading, too. CTRL-V scrolls the message view forward and META-V scrolls it backward. These accelerators also work while you're editing.

14.6 Replying to Mail

Now that you've seen the messages, pick one from your friend that you'd like to answer. Select it (in the Table of Contents) and select Reply from the Message menu—or use the META-R accelerator. A composition window like Figure 14-8 will open.

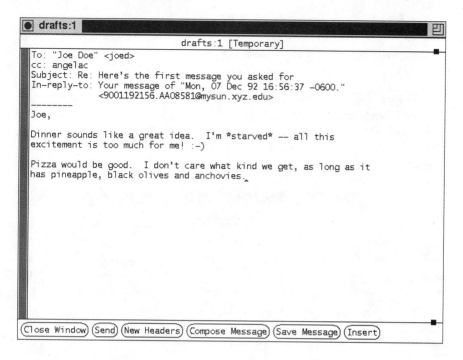

```
● drafts:1                                                    ⊞
                    drafts:1 [Temporary]
To: "Joe Doe" <joed>                                          ■
cc: angelac
Subject: Re: Here's the first message you asked for
In-reply-to: Your message of "Mon, 07 Dec 92 16:56:37 -0600."
             <9001192156.AA08581@mysun.xyz.edu>
--------
Joe,

Dinner sounds like a great idea.  I'm *starved* -- all this
excitement is too much for me!  :-)

Pizza would be good.  I don't care what kind we get, as long as it
has pineapple, black olives and anchovies.




                                                              ■
(Close Window) (Send) (New Headers) (Compose Message) (Save Message) (Insert)
```

Figure 14-8. Composition window with reply

The message header is already filled in—that's why the Reply button is so useful. Be sure that your username is listed in the Cc: component; if it isn't, use
the editor and add your username so you'll get a copy of the reply.*

Move the cursor into the body area, the way you did when you sent the messages
a few minutes ago. Fill in a reply. As you did before, click Send to send the
reply, then use Close Window—or just click Close Window to skip the
reply.

In a minute (unless your computer is very busy) you should have a copy of your
reply. Select Incorporate New Mail on the Table of Contents menu
to get it; read it the way you did before. (The accelerator is META-↑I.)

---

*Your MH may have been set up to send you a copy of replies automatically. Section 6.7.2 explains
how to set your default choice.

14.7 Changing Sizes of Each Area

In most *xmh* windows, close to the right-hand side of each border (horizontal line), there's a small solid square, a *grip*. A grip moves a border and changes the size of one or more areas without changing the size of the whole *xmh* window. This is useful if, say, you want to stretch the Table of Contents to see a lot of messages. How about some practice? See Figure 14-9.

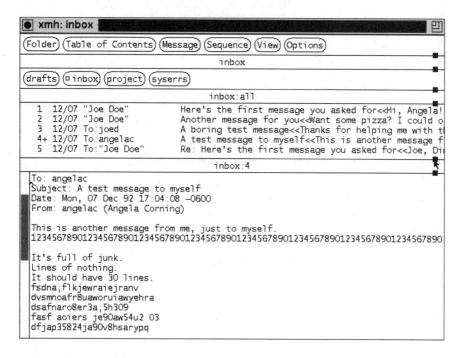

Figure 14-9. Master xmh window before using grips to change sizes

Here's a list of what the mouse buttons do when you point to a grip:

Button 1   Adjusts the size of the area above the border. *xmh* will adjust the areas below the border to compensate.

Button 2   Moves only the border that the grip is on. Because *xmh* won't let you make areas larger or smaller than a certain size, this button usually doesn't help much.

Button 3   Adjusts the size of the area below the border. *xmh* will change areas above the border to compensate.

In Figure 14-9, the Table of Contents could be shortened a little to show more of the viewed message area. Point to the grip on the border between the Table of Contents and the message. (In Figure 14-9, this is the border just above the title `inbox:4`.) Hold down Button 1 on your mouse and drag the border up. See how the message window gets bigger, while the areas above the border adjust to make up for it? Because the Table of Contents area got too small to show all of its lines, it has a scrollbar now, too. After you've adjusted that grip, your window should look something like Figure 14-10.

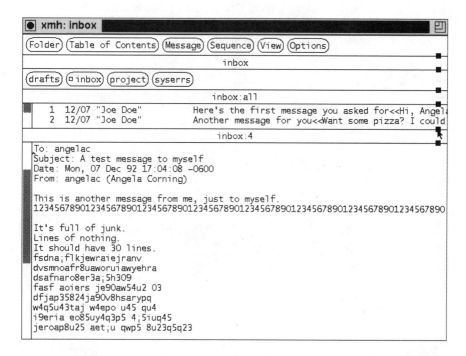

Figure 14-10. Master xmh window after increasing viewed message area

When you adjust a grip, *xmh* will try to adjust all of the areas in the window but it won't let you make any area too small. In this case, the area it shrank was the Table of Contents. Try adjusting other grips, too, if you'd like.

14.8 Searching for Messages

Here's a look at a great feature for people who have lots of e-mail. You can
search for messages that are from a certain user, that have certain words in the
subject or body, and so on. You can also combine searches, like "show me any
messages from *ellaby* sent before May 15 containing the word *expenses*."

To get started, set the folder you want to search if it isn't already set (see Section 15.6.3). Then select Pick from the Sequence menu. A new pick window
like the one in Figure 14-11 will open. The top half of the window lets you select
what to search for. The bottom half has a sequence name and other settings
(leave all of these for now; we'll use them later).

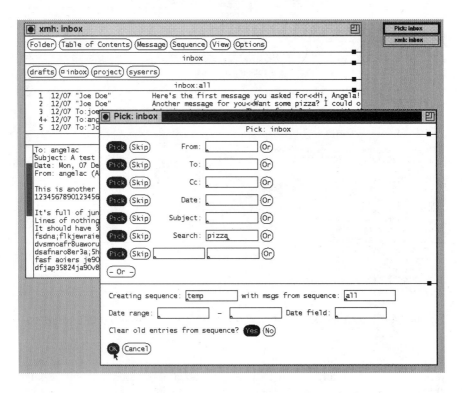

Figure 14-11. Pick window

Let's pick the messages that have the word pizza in them. (If your messages
don't have that word, pick a word that a few of the messages—but not all—contain.) Use the mouse to move the insertion point into the Search: area. Then,

fill in the word. Click the OK button. The original window, like Figure 14-12, will come back when the search is finished.

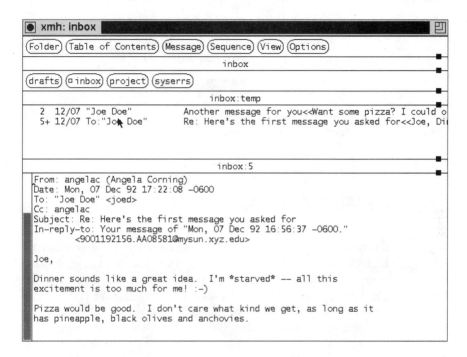

Figure 14-12. After picking messages containing pizza

Look at the Table of Contents—it should have only the messages with the word you searched for. You can read the messages, reply to them, and so on, the way you have before. In Figure 14-12, notice that `Pick` found the word `Pizza` (with an uppercase "P") in message 5. Searches for lowercase letters match both uppercase and lowercase letters. (If you type an uppercase letter, though, it will only match uppercase letters.) The title above the Table of Contents shows that it's listing the messages in the `temp` sequence. If you pull down the `Sequence` menu, you'll see that you've selected the `temp` sequence—it has a check mark next to its name. (Actually, the `Pick` command created and selected the `temp` sequence for you. `Pick` automatically puts a list of all the picked messages in the `temp` sequence unless you tell it to use another name. More on that later.)

When you're done with the picked messages and want to get back a list of all the messages in your *inbox*, select the `all` sequence from the `Sequence` menu (as shown in Figure 14-13) and then select `Open Sequence`. Or, use the accelerator: use the second mouse button to select the `all` sequence, and the sequence will open right away.

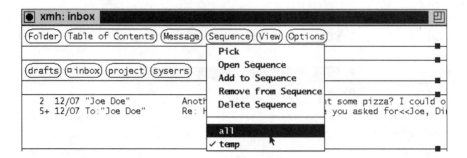

Figure 14-13. Selecting the all sequence

14.9 Forwarding Messages

If you want to send a copy of a message or messages to someone, select the message(s) in the Table of Contents. There are two ways to select more than one message (though the messages must be next to each other). You can click on the first line in the Table of Contents with your first button, release the button, move to the last line, and click with the third button. That should select all the message lines (they'll be shown in reverse video). Or you can click on the first message you want to forward with the first button—then, hold down the first button and drag the pointer across the other messages—release the first button when you've selected all the message lines you want. The selected message(s) should be in reverse video—see Figure 14-14.

Next, select `Forward` from the `Message` menu—or use the accelerator, META-F. A composition window will open. (If you already moved your second window, as in the `Pick` example, the new composition window will automatically open in that place. Otherwise, the composition window will open on top of the master window.)

Fill in the header. You can add a note of your own above or below the forwarded messages. You can edit the forwarded message(s), too, if you want. Send or abort the messages in the usual way.

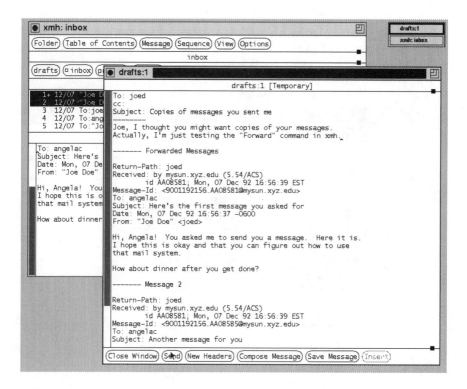

Figure 14-14. Forwarding two messages

14.10 Removing Messages

When you're done with messages, you might want to remove them to save disk space and cut down clutter. *xmh* uses two steps to remove messages. First, you mark the messages you want to delete. Then, you tell *xmh* to delete them.

For example, delete a message or two that you sent yourself. You can do this with or without accelerators:

*   With the mouse, select the message(s)—they will display in reverse video. To delete the current message (the message with a plus sign (+) by it in the Table of Contents), you don't need to select it. Then choose Delete from the Message menu. The messages you want to delete will have a D next to them in the Table of Contents. If you're viewing one of the messages to be deleted, the titlebar will have -> *Delete* in it. See Figure 14-15.

If you're sure that you want to delete the messages you marked, use `Commit Changes` on the `Table of Contents` menu. If you change your mind, select the message(s) you've decided not to delete and use the `UnMark` command on the `Message` menu.

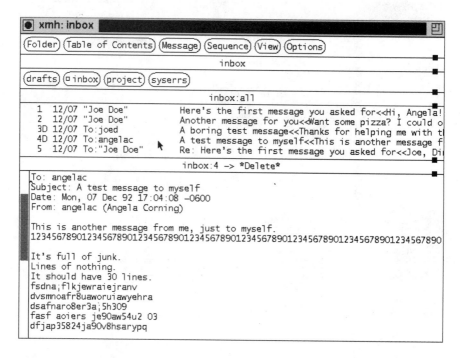

Figure 14-15. Master xmh window with two messages marked for deletion

- The accelerator that you should use to mark the current message for deletion is META-D . If there's another message after the current message, it will automatically be viewed. (This is an easy way to scan through your messages; use META-D to delete the current message and see the next one or use META-N to see the next one without deleting.)

To mark other message(s) for deletion, use the mouse to select them in the Table of Contents. When you press META-D , they'll be marked for deletion.

Next, to actually delete the marked messages (to commit the changes in the Table of Contents), use the accelerator META-↑C . If you want to unmark one or more messages, select the message(s) in the Table of Contents with your mouse. Use META-U to unmark the messages.

14.11 Leaving xmh

To quit *xmh*, use the `Close Window` command on the `Folder` menu.

14.12 More About xmh

If you think *xmh* will do everything you want an electronic mail system to do, go ahead and read Chapter 15, *Using xmh*. Chapter 15 explains more about *sequences*, which provide a way to organize and keep track of your messages, and also covers other *xmh* features such as folders. You can customize *xmh*, too—Chapter 16 explains how.

Here's a list commonly-used features of *xmh*—and a few others that are good to know, anyway.

- Organize messages into folders and subfolders; "link" messages into multiple folders without taking more disk space. (Section 15.6.)

- If you accidentally remove a message, get it back. (Section 15.6.6.)

- Reorder messages in a folder many different ways. (Section 15.6.10, Section 16.4.6.)

- Print your messages flexibly. (Section 16.8.)

- Store long mail address(es) in an alias. (Section 15.1.6, Section 6.3.)

- Handle many draft messages at a time with a draft folder. (Section 15.1.1.)

- Add your standard "signature" text to the ends of messages automatically. (Section 13.13.)

- Customize and change the headers of mail you send. (Section 16.6.)

- All about editing. (Section 15.3.)

- Reformat the Table of Contents. (Section 16.7.)

- Search for messages, store the lists automatically for reuse any time later. (Section 15.8.)

- Handle incoming mail automatically. (Section 15.4.1, Chapter 11.)

- Insert original message into your reply with custom formatting. (Section 16.3.3.)

- Change and add buttons and accelerators. (Section 16.4.)
- Set colors. (Section 16.4.4.)

Remember that you can also use MH commands while there's no *xmh* window open. If you're interested, read about MH in Parts II and III.

15

Using xmh ⊠

Chapter 14, *Tour Through xmh*, had an overview of *xmh*. This chapter explains more about those features and covers others, too. You'll learn how to save draft messages and come back to them later, how to reply to and forward messages, and how to read and organize your mail with folders and subfolders. One section describes scrollbars in detail, and another section gives you the basics of text editing in *xmh*.

There's also an introduction to MH sequences, which *xmh* uses more than MH does. Finally, there's an explanation of the powerful Pick window. This is one *xmh* feature that even MH users will appreciate.

Figure 15-1 shows an *xmh* main window with its parts labeled. (Your window probably won't be this cluttered-looking most of the time.)

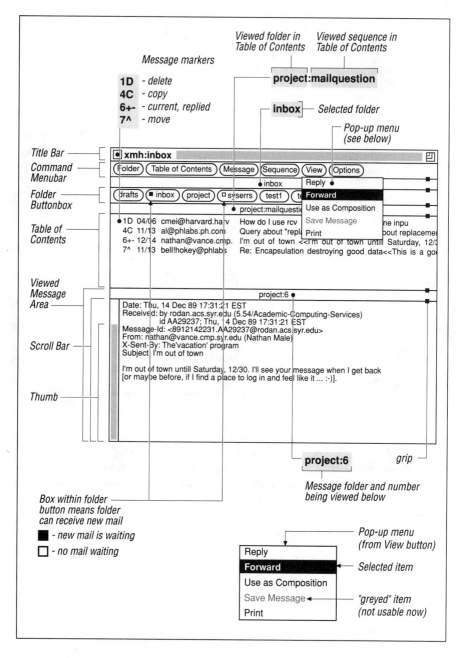

Figure 15-1. xmh main window with parts labeled

15.1   Sending Mail

This section explains *xmh* features you'll use to compose and send mail. The drafts can be composed in a main window or a composition window. You can work on more than one draft at the same time, store them, and come back some time later or make a "form letter" draft that you use over and over.

15.1.1   Working with Draft Messages; The drafts Folder

xmh automatically makes a folder named *drafts*. Like the draft folder in MH, the draft messages you compose are stored here. For more about folders, see Section 15.6.

Making a New Draft with Compose Message

If you're using the master *xmh* window or other main windows like it, you can select Compose Message on the Message menu—a composition window will open for your new draft message. Or, if you're already working in a composition window and you click the Compose Message button at the bottom, it will make another composition window. You can work on several different drafts at once. For instance, in Figure 15-2 I have two composition windows open. I'm clicking the Compose Message button on the drafts:1 window to open a third composition window.

Each time you use Compose Message, *xmh* automatically creates an empty draft file in the *drafts* folder. If your draft folder is empty, the first draft you create will be message number 1 in the folder. A message-composition window will open onto that draft; the titlebar will say drafts:1. You can click the Send button to send that draft message right away or you can click Save Message and then Close Window. If you save without sending, the draft file stays in the *drafts* folder for you to finish later.

If you start a second draft before you've sent the first, that draft will be number 2 (unless there's already a message 2 in the draft folder). An editor window will open onto that draft; the titlebar will say drafts:2. From here, as you did before, you can send or save the message.

Figure 15-2. Working on several drafts at once

A composition window's titlebar will be marked [Temporary] unless the message has been saved at least once. See Figure 15-2.

Re-editing an Existing Draft

There are at least two ways you can work on a draft that you saved a while ago:

1. Open a new main window onto the *drafts* folder. To do that, select the drafts folder button, then select Open Folder in New Window on the Folder menu. A new *xmh* main window will open. The new window will be on top of the first one unless you've set the *compGeometry* resource to open the window in a particular place. (See Section 16.3, "Changing How Commands Work," and the *xmh* manual page in Appendix I.)

   Then, select a draft message from the list of messages: either click on it in the Table of Contents or make it the current message by displaying it. Finally, select Use as Composition on the Message menu—and be sure to use the Message menu on the window that's showing the *drafts* folder.

After you move this composition window (if you want to), your screen will look something like Figure 15-3.

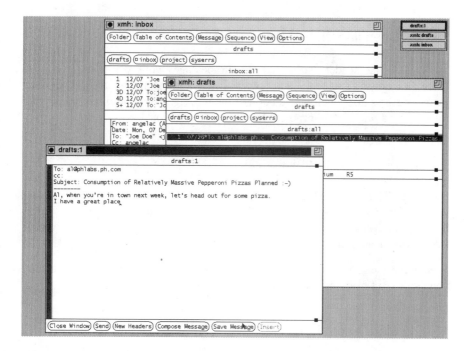

Figure 15-3. Recomposing a draft from a second main window

2. If you don't want to open a new main window on your *drafts* folder, just view the *drafts* folder in any main window. You can select a message, and then open a composition window with `Use as Composition` on the `Message` menu.

If you are viewing the draft message in a view window, you can also click `Use as Composition` in the buttonbox at the bottom of the window. (See Section 15.4.2.)

If you're typing a long message, remember to click the `Save Message` button every so often. This saves your work (so that you won't lose it if the system goes down) then lets you keep editing.

After you save a draft once, it will stay in the *drafts* folder even after you send it. This is a nice way to make "form letters" that you send every so often—you can change a few details of the draft, send it . . . then come back later, change some parts, send it again . . .

If you've saved the draft at least once, remember to delete it when you're done. Section 15.6.6 explains how.

15.1.2 Changing Draft Message Headers

You can edit the header (`To:`, etc.) of your messages while you're in the composition window. You can add other header components then, too—like `Fcc: project`, which puts a copy of the message you send directly into your folder named *project*.* For more information, see Section 16.6.

15.1.3 More About Forwarding

Section 14.9 has an introduction to forwarding copies of messages. There are two ways to forward messages in *xmh*. The `Forward` button on the view window forwards the message you're viewing there. The `Forward` command on the `Message` menu of the main window forwards all of the selected messages.

Section 6.8.1 explains how to reformat the messages you forward—delete lines you don't want from the header, fold long lines in the body, and so on.

15.1.4 More About Replying

You can set an entry in your resource file that will let you include a copy of the original message in your reply when you press the `Insert` button at the bottom of the composition window. See Section 16.3.3.

Because *xmh* runs the MH *repl* command to build the draft message before it opens the composition window, some `repl:` switches in your MH profile will affect the draft you get. For example, a component such as the following:

```
repl: -filter replfilt
```

includes the original message in your reply, formatted through the *replfilt* filter file. See Section 6.7.5.

Some switches can cause trouble. For example, using the *repl –query* switch in your MH profile will "freeze" *xmh*. The best answer is probably to use a separate MH profile for *xmh*. Section 16.5 explains how.

---

*If this is the first time you've used a particular folder, such as the *project* folder shown here, the folder will be silently created when you send the message. But a button for the new folder won't appear in the master window until you restart *xmh*. Also note that if you `Fcc:` a message to a folder, *xmh* will have to rescan the folder the next time you look at it.

MH profile switches that aren't used to build the draft message won't affect *xmh* replies, though. For example, the *–annotate* switch, which asks the MH *repl* command to annotate the original message with a `Replied:` component in the header, won't work under *xmh*.

15.1.5 Resending a Message with Use As Composition

When you're viewing a message, you can copy it into your *drafts* folder and start editing the copy. This is handy for resending a "bounced" mail message that was returned to you with some problems. (Usually, the problem is in the message's header.)

To do this, use the `Use as Composition` command on the `Message` or `View` menus. (Or click the `Use as Composition` button at the bottom of a view window.) It copies the message into the *drafts* folder* and opens a composition window.

For example, in Figure 15-4 the bad headings from a bounced mail message are being deleted by selecting the region (shown in inverse video) and pressing CTRL-W to kill the region. The `To:` address component has been fixed (the hostname was wrong). Don't forget to delete the `End of Unsent Draft` line at the end. Clicking the `Send` button will send the fixed-up draft.

15.1.6 Aliases

Because *xmh* uses the MH *send*(1) command, you can use MH mail aliases. These let you replace long lists of mail addresses with one short alias name. For example, instead of typing all of the addresses below:

```
To: alissa@ketneg.com, uunet!abo!pxu341i, abd@mvus.bitnet
```

you could type the name of your alias that stands for those addresses:

```
To: project
```

You have to maintain the aliases from a shell window or editor window instead of an *xmh* window. But once you're set up, you can use aliases from an *xmh* composition window just as you'd use any other address. For details, see Section 6.3.

---

*Messages already in the *drafts* folder aren't copied to it.

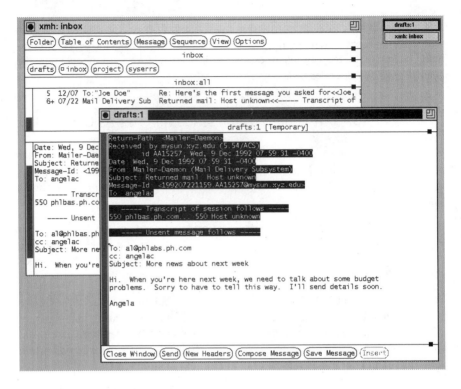

Figure 15-4. Resending a returned message with Use As Composition

15.2 Scrollbars

Here's more than you ever wanted to know about scrollbars. When will you have a scrollbar? What's a thumb and how do you move one? There are some handy hints for moving through your messages.

15.2.1 When They Appear

Whenever an area gets too short (vertically or horizontally) to show everything inside, a scrollbar pops up. This goes for buttonboxes, too—you can scroll through the buttons! If you want to experiment, try using the grips to make a buttonbox smaller (Section 14.7 has instructions for grips).

15.2.2 Length and Position of the Thumb

The thumb (the gray part of the scrollbar) tells you about the text you're viewing. The thumb's length shows what percentage of the text you're seeing. The length of the thumb is inversely proportional to the length of the text—the shorter the thumb, the longer the text. The thumb's position shows what part of the text you're seeing. If the thumb is at the top of the scrollbar, you're seeing the top of the message. If the top of the thumb is about three-fourths of the way down the scrollbar, you're about three-fourths of the way through the message. And so on.

15.2.3 Moving the Thumb

To see different parts of the message, move the thumb. Do that by clicking one of the mouse buttons and, sometimes, sliding the mouse:

Button 2   The second button relates the position of the message in the window to where you move the pointer. Button 2 is probably the most flexible and is the one I usually use:

- Clicking it at any place in the scrollbar moves the top of the thumb there. To see the top of the message, point to the top of the scrollbar and click the second mouse button. To see the bottom of the message, click button 2 at the bottom of the scrollbar. And so on . . .

- You can also point to any place in the thumb, hold down the second button, and then slide the mouse button up and down. The message will move with you. If you have a slow network or a jumpy display, though, this can be frustrating.

Button 1   The first button moves the line of text at the right of the pointer to the top of the area. I like to use this for scrolling forward through the text:

- Put the pointer at the bottom of the scrollbar and click the first button to see the next page forward (with about a line of the previous page at the top).

- Put the pointer near the top of the scrollbar and click the first button to move down line by line. Point a little farther from the top and you'll jump several lines at a time.

Button 3   The third button moves the line at the top of the window down to the pointer's location. Think of it as the opposite of the first button. I use it for scrolling backward through text:

- Put the pointer at the bottom of the scrollbar and click the third button to see the previous page (with about a line of overlap).

- Or put the pointer near the top of the scrollbar and click the third button to move up line by line. Point a little farther from the top and you'll jump several lines at a time.

15.3   Editing in xmh

xmh lets you edit draft messages and other messages too. Here are some tips about editing in *xmh*. The following sections describe common editing commands, using buttons in a composition window, line wrapping, and copying and pasting text between windows.

15.3.1   Text Editing Commands

The composition window uses a set of editing commands that are a subset of GNU *emacs* editor commands. All of the text editing commands actually come from the Athena Text widget. Most of the commands are control characters and meta-characters. Tables 15-1 and 15-2 list editing commands. The tables are adapted from the X Toolkit Athena Text widget manual page. There's a summary of these commands in the *xmh Reference Guide* in the table "xmh Text Editing Commands."

Table 15-1. xmh Text Editing Commands: Modifying

Key	What It Does
CTRL-D CTRL-H Delete Backspace	Remove the character immediately after or before the insertion point. If a carriage return is removed, the next line is appended to the end of the current line.
META-D META-H META-Delete META-Backspace	Remove all characters between the insertion point location and the next word boundary. A word boundary is defined as a space, a tab, or a carriage return.
META-↑-D META-↑-H META-↑-Delete META-↑-Backspace	These actions act exactly like the un-shifted actions in the previous cell of this table, but they store the word that was killed into the kill buffer.
CTRL-W	Delete the current selection and store the deleted text into the kill buffer.
CTRL-K	Delete the entire line to the right of the insertion point, and store the deleted text into the kill buffer.
META-K	Delete everything between the current insertion point and the next paragraph boundary, and put the deleted text into the kill buffer.
CTRL-J Linefeed	Insert a newline into the text and add spaces to that line to indent it to match the previous line. (Note: this action still has a few bugs.)
CTRL-O	Insert a newline into the text *after* the insertion point.
CTRL-M Return	Insert a newline into the text *before* the insertion point.
META-I	Activate the insert-file pop up. The filename is empty at startup.
META-Q	Remove all the carriage returns from the current paragraph and reinsert them so that each line is as long as possible, while still fitting on the current screen. Lines are broken at word boundaries if at all possible.

Table 15-1. xmh Text Editing Commands: Modifying (continued)

Key	What It Does
CTRL-T	Switch the positions of the character to the left of the insertion point and the character to the right of the insertion point. The insertion point will then be advanced one character.
CTRL-L	Recompute the location of all the text lines on the display, scroll the text to center vertically the line containing the insertion point on the screen, clear the entire screen, and then redisplay it.

Table 15-2. xmh Text Editing Commands: Moving

Key	What It Does
CTRL-F Right Arrow CTRL-B Left Arrow	Move the insertion point forward or backward one character in the buffer. If the insertion point is at the end (or beginning) of a line, this action moves the insertion point to the next (or previous) line.
META-F META-B	Move the insertion point to the next or previous word boundary. A word boundary is defined as a space, a tab, or a carriage return.
META-] META-[	Move the insertion point to the next or previous paragraph boundary. A paragraph boundary is defined as two carriage returns in a row with only spaces or tabs between them.
CTRL-A CTRL-E	Move to the beginning or end of the current line. If the insertion point is already at the end or beginning of the line, no action is taken.
CTRL-V META-V	Move the insertion point up or down one page in the file. One page is defined as the current height of the text widget. These actions always place the insertion point at the first character of the top line.

Table 15-2. xmh Text Editing Commands: Moving (continued)

Key	What It Does
META-< META->	Place the insertion point at the beginning or end of the current text buffer. The text widget is then scrolled the minimum amount necessary to make the new insertion point location visible.
CTRL-P Up Arrow CTRL-N Down Arrow	Move the insertion point up or down one line. If the insert point is currently n characters from the beginning of the line then it will be n characters from the beginning of the next or previous line. If n is past the end of the line, the insertion point is placed at the end of the line.
CTRL-Z META-Z	Scroll the current text field up or down by one line. These do not move the insertion point. Other than the scrollbars, this is the only way that the insertion point may be moved off of the visible text area. The widget will be scrolled so that the insertion point is back on the screen as soon as some other action is executed.

15.3.2 Search and Replace

Pressing CTRL-S in an editable window pops up a search-and-replace window like the one in Figure 15-5.

If the text in the window can't be edited (for example, it's displaying a message), you can search but you can't replace. The search moves forward—that is, from the top of the file toward the end. To move backward, start with CTRL-R or click the Backward button.

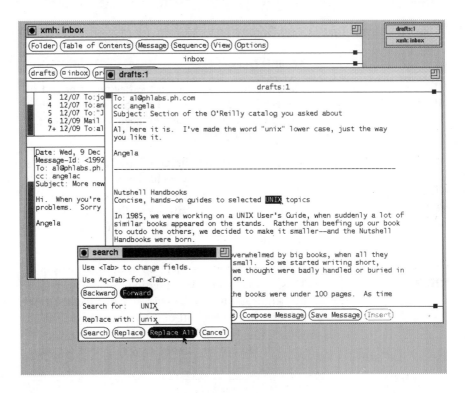

Figure 15-5. Search and replace pop-up window

15.3.3 Composition Window Buttons

When you compose, forward, or reply to a message, a composition window opens. The functions of buttons at the bottom of the window may seem obvious, but three of them could use more explanation:

- The `New Headers` button is misleading. It doesn't just make new headers. It replaces *everything* in the message, like starting from scratch. A confirmation box comes up to be sure that you're sure.

- The `Close Window` button does just that. If you've made changes, you should have saved them with the `Save Message` button first (though you'll be asked for confirmation if you haven't saved).*

---

xmh Release 4 has a bug here: if you click the `Close Window` button twice, you'll get two copies of the confirmation window. If you click `Yes` in both of them, *xmh* will crash.

Closing the window leaves the draft message in your *drafts* folder—if you've saved the draft at least once before. You can come back to it later by opening the *drafts* folder in a main window, selecting the draft message that you want to work on, and selecting `Use as Composition` or `Edit Message`.

- The `Insert` button is grayed (which means you can't use it) unless you're replying to a message. When you're replying, if you click the button, a copy of the message you're replying to will be inserted at the text caret (⌃). See Section 16.3.3 for more information.

15.3.4 Reformatting Paragraphs

To neaten the lines in a paragraph you're editing, press META-Q. The lines will fill neatly, broken at the spaces between words closest to the right margin. To me, this makes the lines a little too wide for people to include them neatly in their replies. If I'll be reformatting paragraphs, I resize my window to a 65-character width first.

There's one "gotcha" with META-Q. If you press it in the first paragraph of a message, just under the header, it will reformat the header, too. Figure 15-6 shows the mess you'll get.

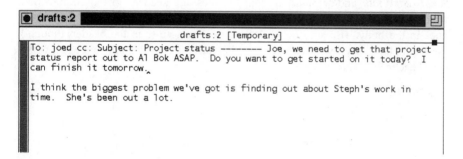

Figure 15-6. META-Q Reformatting Mistake

An easy fix is to put a blank line before the paragraph before typing META-Q. I couldn't teach myself to do that. So, instead, I changed my *components* draft file (see Section 16.6) and replaced the row of dashes with a blank line. I start typing at the end of the draft, as always, but now there's no row of dashes that joins the header to the paragraph.

15.3.5 Line Wrapping

When you're typing an original mail message or adding text to an existing one, each line you type will *wrap* automatically. That is, until you press RETURN, the words on all the lines will be adjusted to fit neatly between margins. To start a new paragraph, simply press RETURN. When you send the message, text in each paragraph is broken into lines—it's not necessarily broken the way it looks in your window. You can make two settings that affect the way lines are broken. Here's what the two of them do:

SendBreakWidth   A "high-water mark" for line length. No line will be broken unless it's wider than *SendBreakWidth*.

SendWidth   The maximum width for lines that have been broken.

You can set these on lines in your message header (as explained later in this section) or in your resource manager (see Section 16.3.4 and Section 16.3.5, respectively). For example, with the *SendBreakWidth* set to 2000 (that's the default in *xmh* Release 5), it's a good bet that no lines will be broken—no matter what setting of *SendWidth* you use—because no line will be longer than *SendBreakWidth*.

You can tell *xmh* to cut the line width for you by putting new values of *SendBreakWidth* and/or *SendWidth* in the message header. In the composition window, add the new line(s) to the header the same way that you'd insert new lines in the body. (Be sure not to leave any empty lines in the header, though.) For example, to set *SendBreakWidth* and *SendWidth* at 60 characters each, make your header look something like this:

```
SendWidth: 60
SendBreakWidth: 60
To: joed
Cc: angelac
Subject: Section of xmh(1) manual page you asked for
```

xmh takes those special lines out of the header before sending the message.

15.3.6 Copy and Paste

You can copy text from one window into another or within a window. For instance, let's say that you have an *xterm* window open and it's showing an error message. You can mail a copy of that error to the software maintainers by copying it into an *xmh* composition window.

Here are the steps to use for copying text from one window to another:

1. Open the composition window and start to compose your message. Move the text cursor (the caret (˄)) to the place where you want to insert the copied text.

2. In the window you want to copy from, select the text to copy. There are two ways to select the text. You can click on the first character in the text you want to copy (with your first mouse button), release the button, move to the last character, and click with the third button. That should select all the text in between (it'll be shown in reverse video).

   Or you can point to the first character—then, hold down the first button and drag the pointer across the other text you want—release the first button when you've selected all the text. Again, the selected text should be in reverse video.

   If you can't get it to work, be sure that your pointer is inside the window border. Also, you can't copy text from every window on your screen—some won't let you copy.

3. You should have a highlighted area in the window now. Click the second mouse button in the composition window, and the text should be copied in.

   If you accidentally click the first mouse button before you copy the text, you'll need to reselect the text and try again.

15.3.7 Use Another Editor

If you'd like to try a different text editor with *xmh* and you have access to the X Release 5 source code from MIT, look in the directory *contrib/clients/xmh.editor*. This contains patches to the *xmh* code that allow, among other things, you to choose your own editor.

For example, the patch would let you add a line like one of the two below to your resource file. The first one chooses the *gnu* editor; the second opens an *xterm* window running *vi*:

```
Xmh.editorCommand: gnu -i -w 80x35+100+20 %s
Xmh.editorCommand: xterm -e vi %s
```

If you haven't patched X source code, ask your system administrator. There's not room in this book to explain how . . .

If you can't patch the source code, there's another way to use an external editor—though it's clumsy. The new *XmhShellCommand( )* action can start an external editor. Section 16.4.7 shows how.

15.4 Reading Your Mail

As you've seen, it's easy to read mail with *xmh*. Here are some fine points that might be helpful to you, though.

15.4.1 Incorporate New Mail

If your viewed folder is able to receive new mail (like *inbox* can, by default), then the `Incorporate New Mail` command will be sensitive (the words will be made with a solid line); you can select it to get your new mail. If you're viewing some other folder, then the `Incorporate New Mail` command will be grayed.

Section 5.4 covers MH options for incorporating mail.

A handy *xmh* feature that wasn't documented until Release 5 is the *.xmhcheck* file. It works with the MH *mhook* automatic mail-handling features (explained in Chapter 11, *Processing New Mail Automatically*) to let you automatically incorporate mail into several folders. In fact, this works with any system where you have more than one incoming mailbox (and write permission to modify the mailbox when you incorporate new mail from it). Figure 15-7 shows the changes in the folder buttons when another folder besides *inbox* can incorporate new mail.

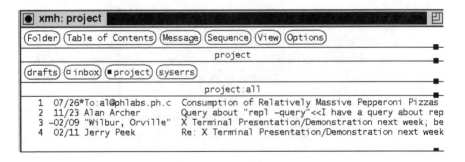

Figure 15-7. Two folders that can incorporate mail

The `inbox` button has an empty square; there's no mail waiting for your inbox. The `project` button has a filled black square; there's mail waiting for it. If you view a folder with a filled black square (as I've done for `project` here), use `Incorporate New Mail` (on the `Table of Contents` menu) to bring in the mail waiting. Only the viewed folder will get new messages; the other folders wait.

To set this up, make a file named *.xmhcheck* in your home directory. Each line in the file has two entries: the name of a folder and the mailbox that should be checked (and read) for that folder. See Example 15-1.

Example 15-1. A simple .xmhcheck file

```
inbox      /usr/spool/mail/jerry
project    /home/jerry/.project_mail
```

From the filled black square in Figure 15-7, you can see that there's mail waiting in */home/jerry/.project_mail*. My system mailbox, */usr/spool/mail/jerry*, is empty.

15.4.2 View Window

Here is another mail-reading feature that wasn't covered in Chapter 14, *Tour Through xmh*. If you've selected a message, the View In New command on the Message menu will open a new full-size message viewing window. Figure 15-8 shows one. In Release 5, *xmh* added a new Delete button to mark the viewed message for deletion.

15.4.3 Line Folding

When you read a message, lines that are too wide for the window will have a black blob at the right-hand side. The black blob means "there's more here." If you have a narrow window or a large font, the lines in your messages may be cut off. To fix that, resize your window—use the window manager's resizing command or change the window geometry. See Section 16.3.7 and Section 15.3.5.

Part IV
xmh

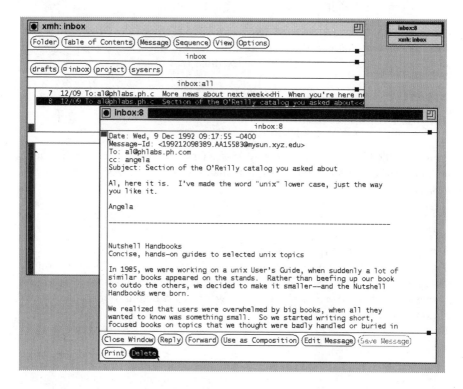

Figure 15-8. A view window

15.5 Printing Your Mail

If you've selected one or more messages in a main window, you can print them by selecting `Print` from the `Message` menu. Or, if you're in a view window, you can use its `Print` button to print the message from that window.

Message printing with *xmh* isn't very flexible. For instance, it just hands the message file to the print command, without preformatting it to remove semi-useless header components, fold long lines, and so on. By default, *xmh* uses the *enscript* command to turn messages into PostScript files and send them to a Post-Script printer. See Section 16.8.

15.6 Organizing Your Mail with Folders

When you first start *xmh*, you will have folders named *inbox* and *drafts*. Folders are like the folders you'd find in an office file cabinet: they group related messages. If you don't have many messages, you may not want new folders. People who get a lot of mail, though, will. Here's how to make new folders and move or copy messages into them.

15.6.1 Making a New Folder

The `Create Folder` command on the `Folder` menu will make a small window and prompt you for a folder name. After you type in the name, the folder and a new folder button will be created.

The folder name should be all one word—don't use spaces. You can use a character like an underscore (_) to join two words into one. Long names are okay, but remember that they make the buttons bigger than short names. This is demonstrated in Figure 15-9.*

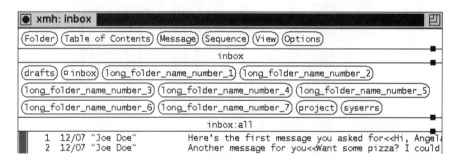

Figure 15-9. Folder buttonbox with some long folder names

xmh Release 5 supports a single level of subfolders. (Section 15.6.2 has more information.) Make a subfolder like a top-level folder—but put a slash (/) and the subfolder name after the top-level folder name. For example, to make a *cheese* subfolder in the existing *project* folder, type `project/cheese` in the `Create Folder` box.

---

*If you have a lot of buttons, or buttons with long names, you can always shorten the folder buttonbox so that it has a scrollbar—and scroll through the folder buttons.

15.6.2 Folders and Subfolders

xmh Release 4 introduced limited support for MH subfolders. A subfolder is a folder within a folder, as Figure 15-10 shows.

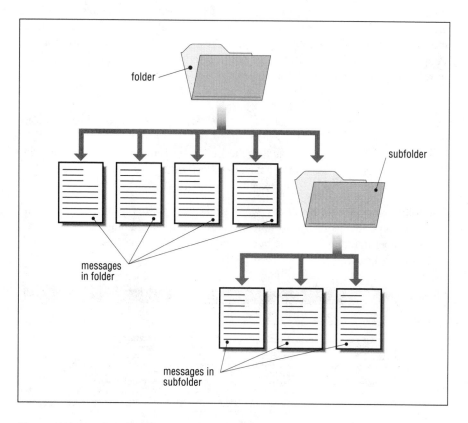

Figure 15-10. A folder with one subfolder

MH can have folders inside subfolders, many levels deep. *xmh* supports just one level—but that's plenty for most users.

If a folder has a subfolder, a list box will drop down when you select the button. The first entry in the list is always for the top-level folder. The other entries are for its subfolders. Figure 15-11 shows how to select the *system_b* subfolder of the *syserrs* folder.

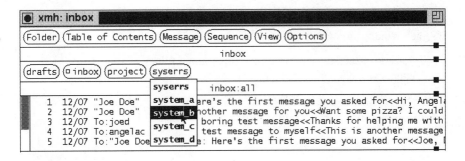

Figure 15-11. A folder with four subfolders

All *xmh* operations work as well on subfolders as they do on top-level folders.

15.6.3 Selecting Another Folder

To see another folder, you have two choices: either change the folder you're viewing now in the main window or open a new main window for the folder.

- To change the folder you're viewing in a main window, select the new folder by clicking the button named for the folder. Then select `Open Folder` on the `Folder` menu. The Table of Contents will display the first few messages in the folder—if there are more messages, there'll be a scrollbar. Select, view, or delete messages the same way you did for *inbox*.

  The accelerator for opening a new folder is handy and fast. Click on the folder button with your second mouse button. That selects and opens the folder in one step.

  If a folder has a subfolder, slide down the subfolder list to the folder you want, as Figure 15-11 shows.

- One advantage of *xmh* over standard (uncustomized) MH is that you can have windows open onto several different folders—*xmh* won't get confused. To open a separate folder window, use your first mouse button to select the button named for the folder you want. Then, select `Open Folder in New Window` from the `Folder` menu. A new main window will open with a view of that folder.

  Notice that the first main window is still displaying the original folder. That's possible because *xmh* keeps the *selected folder* separate from the *viewed folder*. You can select a different folder by clicking its folder button, but *xmh* does not view that folder until you have selected `Open Folder` or `Open Folder in New Window`.

Once you have the new window open, you can compose new messages from each window, move messages to other folders, and so on.

If you move messages between two open main folder windows, the Tables of Contents will change automatically.

If you try to view the same folder from two windows, things can get confusing. It's probably best to stick with one window per folder.

NOTE

If you make a new folder and you don't move or copy any messages into it—then, when you open it for the first time, you'll get an error message like `scan: no messages in` *folderpath*.

This isn't really an error—it's just the MH *scan* command telling you that the folder is empty. If you move or link a message into the folder before you open it for the first time, you won't see the error.

15.6.4 Moving Messages Between Folders

Here are the steps for moving messages to another folder, with and without an accelerator. First, make sure that the Table of Contents shows the folder you want to take messages from (the folder you want to move messages out of):

1. Here's how to move messages without an accelerator:

    a. Select the message(s) you want to move by highlighting the message line(s) in the Table of Contents: use the first mouse button, as you did before.

    b. Next, select the destination folder (this is called the *selected folder*). To do this, just click the first mouse button on the destination folder-name button in the folder-name buttonbox. Do *not* use the `Open Folder` command, though!

    The viewed folder (in the Table of Contents) won't change. (If it does change, you probably used the second mouse button accidentally.)

    c. Pull down the `Message` menu and choose `Move`. This doesn't actually move the messages; it just marks them for moving. The scan lines of the messages to be moved will get a caret (∧) next to the message numbers. (If the viewed and destination folders are the same, *xmh* will just ring the bell.)

d. Repeat the steps above to mark more messages, if you want to. It's okay to have different destination folders for different messages. After you highlight the message(s), you can choose any destination folder.

e. You can use UnMark on the Message menu to clear the mark from a selected message. When you're done, you can scroll the Table of Contents up and down to be sure that the messages you want to move are marked.

f. When you use the Commit Changes command, the messages will move to their destination folders. The accelerator for Commit Changes is META-↑C.

2. Here's how to move messages with an accelerator. Using accelerators saves you time and steps:

a. In the Table of Contents, use the first mouse button to select the message(s) you want to move.

b. To unmark message(s) so they won't be moved, select the messages (put in reverse video) with the first mouse button. Then, press META-U.

c. To move the marked messages, select the destination folder with the third mouse button.

Here are some miscellaneous facts about moving messages:

• If you're viewing one of the messages before you move it, you will see -> *foldername* in the titlebar, as shown in Figure 15-12. In fact, if you changed destination folders while you were marking, this is a good way to find out where a message is going.

• The messages you move will be renumbered starting after the last message in the destination folder.

• Accelerators for viewing the next and previous message (META-N and META-P, respectively) will skip over messages that have been marked for moving, copying, or deleting—that's the default. To change it, you can set the *SkipMoved*, *SkipDeleted*, and *SkipCopied* resources to false. See Section 16.3.6.

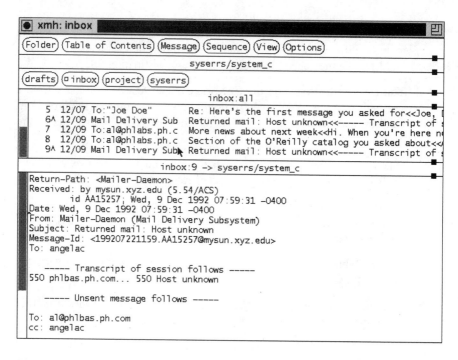

Figure 15-12. Two messages marked for moving

15.6.5 Linking (not Copying) Messages Between Folders

xmh Release 4 has a `Copy` command (on the `Message` menu) for "copying" messages between folders. This isn't really what *xmh* does with the messages—instead, it links the messages to the new folder. In *xmh* Release 5, the command name was changed to `Copy as Link`—but it does the same thing it did before. For more details about what linking means, see Section 7.8 and Section 2.7. Basically, linking saves disk space.

CAUTION

If you edit one of the "copied" (linked) messages by displaying it in the view window and choosing `Edit Message`, all the "copies" of the messages in all folders will show the same edit!

A link isn't a true copy. In this book I'll call it a link, not a copy.

Linking a message to another folder takes the same steps as moving. (The steps are in Section 15.6.4.) The difference is that when the message is marked for copying, *xmh* puts a C in the Table of Contents next to the message number and `-> foldername` (Copy) in the titlebar above the message view. Be sure to use `Commit Changes` when you're ready.

The accelerator for marking to copy is META-C. The accelerator for committing the changes is META-↑C.

15.6.6 Deleting (and Restoring) Messages

To delete messages, use the steps in Section 15.6.4 for selecting the messages, but use the `Delete` command on the `Message` menu. The accelerator for marking to delete is META-D. The accelerator for committing the changes is META-↑C.

If you accidentally delete a message, you can probably get it back (though you may have to exit *xmh*). See Section 7.5.

Also see the *rmmer* shell script in Section 13.6, which makes it easy to recover your deleted messages. If you install *rmmer* on your account, you still use the `Delete` and `Commit Changes` commands (or the accelerators), as always. But *rmmer* puts your deleted messages into a subfolder named *DELETE* where it's easy to recover them if you need to. (A system program removes the "deleted" messages later.)

This is a real win for *xmh* users because you don't have to open an *xterm* window or use MH commands to recover deleted messages anymore.*

The first time you delete a message in a folder, *rmmer* will create the *DELETE* subfolder for you. But the new subfolder won't appear on a menu until the next time you start *xmh*.

To recover a deleted message, go to the folder where it was deleted. Then go to the *DELETE* subfolder (see Figure 15-13) and move the message to its parent folder. (You can actually move the message to any folder, not just its parent.)

---

*Remember that because *xmh* can't deal with sub-subfolders (yet), you'll need to use MH commands to recover messages you delete from subfolders—see Section 7.5.2 for help. Or use the *rmmer_1.noask* script in Section 13.6 instead—it puts all deleted messages in one top-level folder (not a subfolder) named *DELETE*. If you have to recover a deleted message with MH, you should use the *xmh* `Rescan Folder` command so *xmh* will update its folder list. This is a good thing to do any time after you use an MH command.

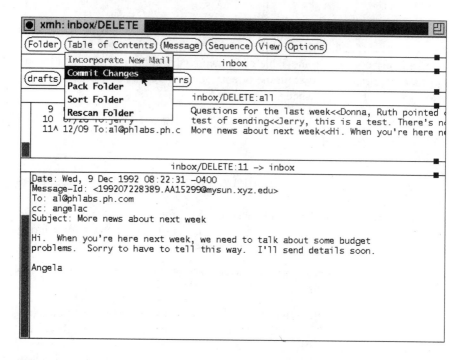

Figure 15-13. Recovering a message deleted by rmmer

15.6.7 Rescan Folder

Unlike MH, where you can always find out what's in your folder with *scan*, *xmh* only rescans your folder every so often (depending on the *CheckFrequency* setting)—see the *xmh* manual page in Appendix I.

If you think *xmh* doesn't have the latest view of the folder, use the `Rescan Folder` command on the `Table of Contents` menu. (The accelerator is `META-↑R`.) This is good to do after you've used some MH commands from, say, an *xterm* window.

15.6.8 Viewed Message vs. Viewed Folder

The viewed message area of the main window will hold a view of one message. It can even be a message from a different folder than the viewed folder. Figure 15-14 is viewing a message from the *drafts* folder, but with a different folder and sequence selected in the Table of Contents. You might want to do this if your screen is already full of windows and you don't want to open a separate window on a separate folder.

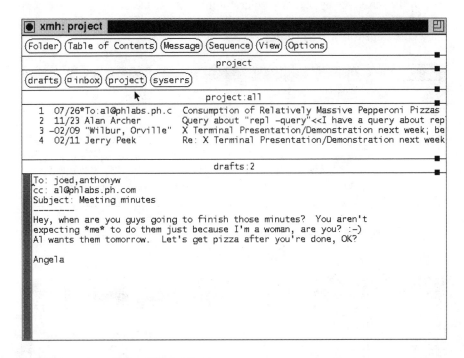

Figure 15-14. Message and Table of Contents from different folders

15.6.9 Packing a Folder

If you use the `Pack Folder` command on the `Table of Contents` menu, messages in the folder will be renumbered as 1, 2, 3, and so on. This closes gaps caused by removing messages (if you don't pack the folder, the messages aren't renumbered). MH and *xmh* don't care much what numbers your messages have, although *xmh* isn't happy with message numbers larger than 9999.

15.6.10 Sorting a Folder

To sort the messages by date from oldest to newest use the Sort Folder command.* Figure 15-15 is an example of a folder before sorting. Figure 15-16 shows the same folder after sorting.

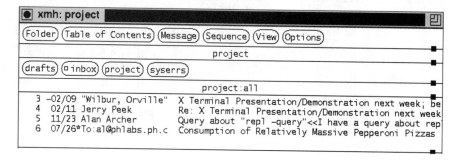

Figure 15-15. Folder before sorting

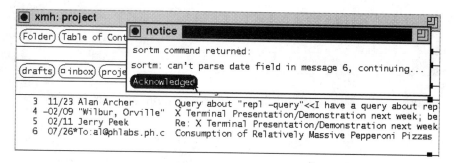

Figure 15-16. Folder after sorting

Notice that one of the messages has an asterisk (*) by the number. This means that there's no acceptable Date: component in the header—so *xmh* shows the date that the message file itself was modified. The message from the MH *sortm* command pops up in a dialog box.

After sorting, the messages don't seem to be in date order (message 3 was sent on November 23, but message 4 was sent on February 9?). But the dates *are* in order—the date sort pays attention to the year. For instance, message 3 was sent

---

*Depending on the version of MH you're running, this may also renumber the messages starting from 1 (like packing the folder). Check your online *sortm*(1) manual page.

in 1989. If a message doesn't have an acceptable date, the sort tries to keep the message in about the same relative position it was before—but, as you can see, this doesn't always work.

If you have the MH 6.7 or later version of *sortm*, you can change it to sort by other components. For instance, it can sort by subject. Section 7.4 explains sorting switches.

You can set default *sortm* switches in your MH profile, so you always get one kind of sort. You can also set up *xmh* buttons that run the *edprofile* shell script—to change the sorting order at any time while you're running *xmh*. See Section 13.12 and Section 16.4.6 for more about *edprofile*.

15.6.11   Deleting a Folder

The `Delete Folder` command on the `Folder` menu deletes the selected folder and all messages in it. Before it deletes the folder, *xmh* will list it in the Table of Contents. Then, it will will ask for confirmation in a dialog box.

NOTE

`Delete Folder` deletes the *selected* folder, not the viewed folder.

Even though the dialog box is up, you should be able to browse through the Table of Contents, view messages, and so on. When you're sure, click `Yes`.

CAUTION

When you delete a folder, there's no going back. Be careful ...

15.7   Introduction to Sequences

Chapter 14 and this one have mentioned sequences more than once. Let's summarize that information here—and add to it.

A sequence is a list of message numbers, just like an MH sequence (described in Section 7.3). It's used for grouping messages temporarily or permanently. When you view the sequence in your Table of Contents, you'll only see those particular messages from the folder. The other messages are still in the folder; they're just not shown. Note the following:

- Every folder and subfolder has its own sequence named all. Naturally enough, this sequence has all messages in the folder.

- Each folder can have up to ten sequences (not counting the all sequence). When you make a sequence, it stays with the folder until you delete it.

- Each sequence in a folder has its own entry on the Sequence menu. The selected sequence has a check mark by it. Figure 15-17 shows that mailquestions is currently selected, but I'm about to select all (the sequence will be selected after I let go of the mouse button).

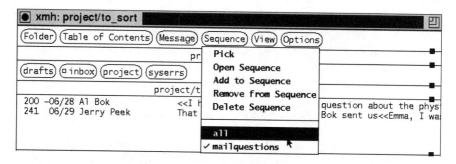

Figure 15-17. Selecting a sequence (all)

There are two ways to select a sequence:

1. If you select the sequence with the first mouse button, that changes the selected sequence but doesn't view it in the Table of Contents.

   When you use Open Sequence, a listing of the messages opens in the Table of Contents. If you're adding a message to a sequence, though, you won't want to open it.

2. The accelerator is selecting the sequence with the second mouse button. That selects the sequence and views it in the Table of Contents.

To make a sequence, use the Pick command—then, if you want, you can use the Add to Sequence and Remove from Sequence commands to move messages into or out of the sequence. First, let's take a look at the way to make sequences: Pick.

15.8 Using Pick

Let's look at the `Pick` command on the `Sequence` menu. It lets you search for messages by any component in the header, any word(s) in the body, or a combination of these. It's a flexible and powerful way to find messages.

15.8.1 A Pick Example

When you use `Pick`, a window like Figure 15-18 opens (by default, it's on top of the main *xmh* window; I've moved it to the side so you can see both).

To select messages, point to one of the boxes by a component name and type what you want to search for. For example, to find messages from *nathan*, point to the `From:` box and type `nathan`.

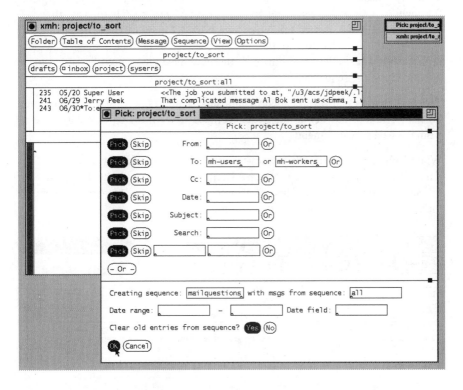

Figure 15-18. Main and Pick windows

In Figure 15-18, I want to find messages which were sent to either *mh–users* or *mh–workers* mailing lists (see Appendix A, *Where Can You Go from Here?*, for information on these lists). I point to the To: box and type mh-users. Then, I click the Or button next to the window; another box opens, where I type mh-workers. Because I leave the other boxes blank, Pick will ignore those fields. If I had filled in one (or more) of them, Pick would have found only messages that fit *all* the criteria—for instance, if I had also put the word bug in the Search: box, Pick would have selected only messages to *mh–users* or *mh–workers* which contained the word "bug."

Remember that, in some cases, messages may be sent to an address via the To: header or the cc: header. You wouldn't want to type those addresses in the Cc: boxes of Figure 15-18, though, because the address would have to be listed in *both* the To: and cc: headers to be matched. In this case, you want the "big -Or-" button—see Section 15.8.2.

By default, the Pick window creates a sequence named temp. That sequence is normally reused each time you use Pick. Because I want to keep this sequence for awhile, I changed its name to mailquestions. There was already a sequence with that name; the Yes button at Clear old entries from sequence? is selected, so the old message list in that sequence will be replaced. If I had clicked No instead, the new messages would be added to the list already in the sequence.

Sequence names can be alphabetic characters (letters) only—if you use an invalid name, *xmh* won't define the sequence; you'll see a dialog box with an error from the MH *pick* command.

When I click OK, the Pick window closes. The main window's Table of Contents title changes to project:mailquestions, and the list shows the messages in the sequence. There'll also be an entry on the Sequence menu for the mailquestions sequence. See Figure 15-19.

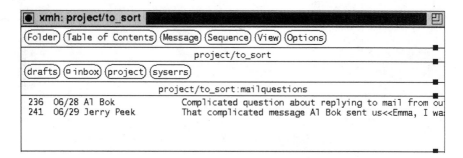

Figure 15-19. Main window after picking mailquestions sequence

When you're done looking at the sequence, you can select another existing sequence by selecting the name on the Sequence menu, then using Open Sequence. The mailquestions sequence entry will remain, and MH will "remember" the messages in the sequence. Or, you can add and delete messages from a sequence—see Section 15.9.

15.8.2 Using the Big -Or- Button

Pick lets you make much more complicated searches. For example, to find messages from *john* to *alison* or from *mona* to *zelda* (but not from *john* to *zelda* or *mona* to *alison*), you would use the big -Or- button at the lower-left corner of the Pick area. This makes a duplicate of all the From:, To:, etc. boxes below the first set and puts scrollbars on the area. I've filled in the names. Figure 15-20 shows this (I've dragged down the grip to show the important parts).

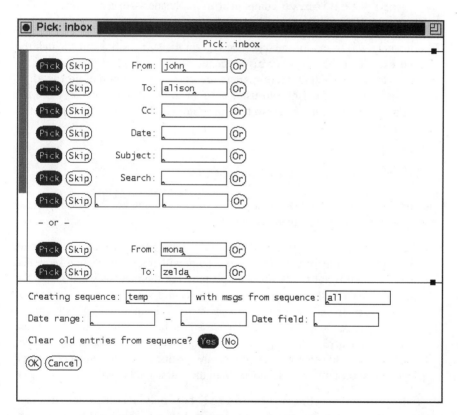

Figure 15-20. Pick window after big –Or– clicked in top area

15.8.3 Finding Other Components, Skipping a Component

The `Pick` and `Skip` buttons choose whether messages should or should not match the search string you type. All the examples so far have used the `Pick` buttons. But if you click the `Skip` button next to a field, it tells *xmh* to find messages which do *not* match that field.

The box with a blank field name lets you specify another header component besides `From:`, `To:`, and so on. For instance, to search for all messages which had the following component:

```
Reply-To: jerryu
```

in the header, you'd fill in the blank field-name box as shown in Figure 15-21. (These messages might be ones that *jerryu* sent from *angelac*'s account.) The window in Figure 15-21 would match all messages from the *angelac* account that have a `Reply-to: jerryu` component in the header—except messages sent on January 24, 1993.

Unfortunately, the format of the date you type in the `Date:` box must match the message exactly. (The `Date range:` boxes don't have this problem.) As we get closer to the year 2000, more mailers are converting from the old two-digit year format (like `93` for 1993) to using all four digits. So, if you can't use the `Date range:` boxes, it's safest to type the date with both formats. I did that in Figure 15-21.

15.8.4 Bottom Area of the Pick Window

The bottom area of the `Pick` window isn't used too often, but it's good to know about. Here are some of its features:

- The `Creating sequence:` box lets you choose the sequence name `Pick` should write. It defaults to *temp*. *xmh* will empty an existing sequence unless you tell it not to. If you want to preserve the messages that are in the sequence and add the new messages to it, be sure you've clicked `No` next to `Clear old entries from sequence?`. It's not a good idea to choose a new sequence name each time you use `Pick` because you can't have more than ten sequences defined per folder. Sequence names must be alphabetic; uppercase and lowercase case letters are distinct, so the sequence named *Temp* would be a different sequence than the one named *temp*.

- The `with msgs from sequence:` box tells `Pick` which message sequence to search for the messages you're picking. This is set automatically to the same sequence that was selected in the main window before you started `Pick`. Usually, you'll set this to search `all` messages, but a name besides all can make the search go faster because there'll be fewer messages to search.

- The Date range: boxes take a starting and ending date to search. Pick ignores messages not sent between these two dates. Unfortunately, filling in dates doesn't make the search more efficient, because Pick still has to search all the messages to find what date each one was sent. If the Date field: is empty, Pick gets the date from the Date: component in each message header. That's usually what you want. But you can change it to use, say, Delivery-Date:, if your mail is processed through the MH *slocal* program (see Chapter 11, *Processing New Mail Automatically*).

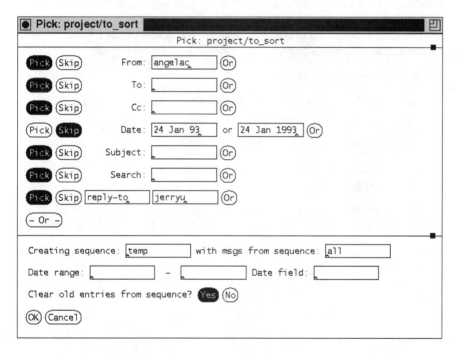

Figure 15-21. Example of Pick skip button

xmh will put a horizontal scrollbar above this area if it's too wide to fit in the window.

15.9 Modifying Sequences

Let's go back to the main window now.

Once you have defined a sequence with Pick, you'll be able to use the Add to Sequence and Remove from Sequence commands to move messages into or out of the sequence.

To remove a message from a sequence, be sure that you're viewing the sequence in the Table of Contents (if you aren't, select that sequence on the menu, then select Open Sequence). Then, highlight the message(s) in the Table of Contents and use Remove from Sequence. This doesn't delete the message! It just takes the message out of the sequence. If you remove all the messages from a sequence, the sequence is deleted.

To add a message to a sequence:

1. Find a sequence that the message is in now (usually, all). View that sequence in the Table of Contents.

2. Select the message(s) in the viewed sequence by highlighting them.

3. Select the destination sequence (the sequence you want to add the messages to) with the first mouse button.

   The accelerator uses the third mouse button instead of the first. It selects the sequence and adds the selected message(s) to it—if you do that, you can skip step 4.

4. At this point, your window might look like Figure 15-22; we're adding message 8, from the displayed sequence all, into the mailquestions sequence. Notice that the check mark in the Sequence menu is next to the selected sequence mailquestions.

   Use the Add to Sequence command.

5. If you want to open the selected sequence (here, mailquestions), choose Open Sequence.

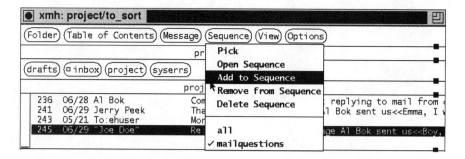

Figure 15-22. Adding a message to the mailquestions sequence

15.10 The Master xmh Window

When you start *xmh* running, it opens a main window. I call this first main window the *master window*. There are two important differences between master windows and other main windows:

1. Geometry settings affect it differently from all other windows. See Section 16.1 and Section 16.3.7.

2. Using the Close Window command (on the Folder menu) in the first master window terminates *xmh*. But *xmh* won't terminate if you have other main windows open—you have to close them first.

If you have another main window open and use its Close Window command, only that window will close.

16

Customizing xmh [X]

Setting Command-line Options and
    Resources
Command-line Options
Changing How Commands Work
Changing Buttons; Accelerators
Conflicts Between xmh and MH
    Customization
Using Template Draft Files for Headers
Changing Table of Contents Format
Changing the Print Command
Snooping on xmh

When using MH or *xmh*, you'll notice that they may not work exactly the way you want them to. It's easy to customize *xmh*, add new commands and features, and more. For a lot of the work, you don't have to be a programmer.

This chapter shows you how to change *xmh* under X11 Release 5. (A lot of this doesn't apply to Release 3, but many of the techniques work the same way. You can use almost all of this with the *xmh* in Release 4.) I'll explain how to change the way that buttons work, add or modify accelerators, add new buttons with your own commands, change the size of windows and areas, modify the way replies look, and modify the way the Table of Contents looks. Finally, you'll learn some techniques for "snooping" on *xmh*, to see which MH commands it uses and (with some experience) change the way it uses MH.

16.1 Setting Command-line Options and Resources

Most X users can store can store command-line options in an X startup file like
.xsession or *.xinitrc*. For example, here is the section of my *.xsession* file used for
this book:

```
#
# Start xmh mail system on monochrome screen:
#
xmh -display :0.1 -geometry 660x460+200+5 &
```

The −display and −geometry options are standard X Toolkit options; see
the *X*(1) manual page. Command-line options might be most useful when you
start *xmh* from an *xterm* window or a shell script, or when you want to override
resource settings. See Section 16.3, "Changing How Commands Work."

You can customize *xmh* with entries in a resource file like *.Xdefaults*, instead of,
or in addition to, setting command-line options. These override any existing
defaults—though you'll first have to restart *xmh*, restart X, or give a command
such as the following:

```
% xrdb $HOME/.Xdefaults
```

For more information, see O'Reilly & Associates' Volume Three, *X Window System User's Guide*, by Valerie Quercia and Tim O'Reilly.

16.2 Command-line Options

You'll make most changes to *xmh* with resource entries; Section 16.3 explains
that. This section explains *xmh* command-line options.

16.2.1 MH Directory Path

As Chapter 2, *MH and the UNIX Filesystem*, explains, MH keeps messages, folders, and other files in a directory. By default, *xmh* looks for a subdirectory named
Mail in your home directory. You can change that by changing the Path: component in your MH profile, as shown in Section 8.4. Or, you can use the *−path*
option to *xmh*.* For example, to use a directory named *.Mail* (the dot at the start

---

*See the Caution in Section 16.5.

of the directory name hides the directory from the *ls* command), you might start *xmh* this way:

```
xmh -path /xxx/yyy/.Mail &
```

where */xxx/yyy* is your home directory.

NOTE

As explained in Section 8.7, everyone in a group can share an MH directory if they have UNIX filesystem permission to read and write to the directory. But this might not be a good idea with *xmh*, because *xmh* keeps a "snapshot" of each folder in a hidden file named *.xmhcache*. If one *xmh* user changes the contents of a folder (packing it, moving messages, and so on) the other user won't see the changes until *xmh* rebuilds its *.xmhcache* file—or the user selects `Rescan Folder`.

Worse, if a folder isn't writable, you can mark messages for deletion, copying, and so on—when you use `Commit Changes`, *xmh* gives you an error but can also update the table of contents to show that the changes have been made!

The `Rescan Folder` command will usually get you back to reality. But, if you need to use unwritable folders, think about using MH instead.

16.2.2 Initial Folder

Normally, *xmh* begins with a view of your *inbox* folder. You can change that with the *-initial* command-line option. For instance, to start with your *project* folder, use a line such as:

```
xmh -initial project &
```

16.2.3 Toolkit Options

Because *xmh* is built with the X Toolkit, it recognizes standard toolkit command-line options. For a complete list, see your online *X*(1) manual page.

Here are a few of the options:

–iconic   Starts *xmh* as an icon instead of an open window. The icon will have the folder name (like *inbox*) in it. See the *–flag* option, too.

–flag   Tries to change the *xmh* icon into a mailbox. The icon can look different if there's new mail. The new icon with *xmh* Release 5 is neatly drawn. I like the older one, shown in Figure 16-1.

Figure 16-1. Old-fashioned xmh –flag mailbox icons

–bw   Sets the border width in pixels. For example:

```
xmh -bw 15 &
```

sets a 15-pixel-wide border.

–fg, –bg   Set the foreground and background colors, respectively. *–bd* is the border color. For instance, the following command would make red text on a dark blue background, with a yellow border and lines (don't tell my art teacher that I said you could do this!):

```
xmh -fg red -bg navyblue -bd yellow &
```

–xrm   Lets you use other resource entries without typing them in your resource file. For a partial list of these, see Section 16.3. Here are a couple of useful examples:

1. To make a *pick* window that's wider than it is tall (you might do this to get room for lots of Or buttons), type:

    ```
    xmh -xrm '*PickGeometry:600x450' &
    ```

2. You can use more than one *–xrm* switch. For instance, to set the *PickGeometry* (as in the previous example) and also disable the default *HideBoringHeaders* feature (which scrolls off header components like Received:), use:

```
xmh -display :0.1 -xrm '*PickGeometry:600x450'\
    -xrm '*HideBoringHeaders:off' &
```

16.3 Changing How Commands Work

As with all standard X applications, *xmh* may be customized through entries in a resource file. Section 16.1 gives an overview. The *xmh*(1) manual page in Appendix I has a complete list of resources. (The section is called "Application-Specific Resources.") Most of them are pretty straightforward. A few resource file entries that change the way commands work are explained in this section.

16.3.1 HideBoringHeaders

If *HideBoringHeaders* is *on*, then *xmh* will attempt to skip uninteresting header components within messages by scrolling them off. The line at the top of the window will be the first "interesting" component (`Date:`, `To:`, `From:`, or `Subject:`) in the message. You can use the scrollbar to see the hidden headers. (The default is *on*.)

16.3.2 PrintCommand

PrintCommand is the *sh* (Bourne shell) command to execute to print a message. You have to specifically redirect standard output (and standard error, in *xmh* Release 3). When the print command is run, the full file path of each message file is appended to the specified print command. (The default is `enscript >/dev/null 2>/dev/null`.)

For more information and examples, see Section 16.8.

16.3.3 ReplyInsertFilter

ReplyInsertFilter is a shell command to be executed when you click the `Insert` button in a composition window. The full path and filename of the source message is added to the end of the command before being passed to *sh*(1). The default filter is *cat*, which puts a copy of the message header and body into the composition. This section shows two other interesting filters. The first filter uses the *sed* stream editor to include a copy of the original message, without the header, with a right angle bracket and a space at the start of each line, as in Figure 16-2:

```
xmh*ReplyInsertFilter: sed -e "1,/^$/d" -e "s/^/> /"
```

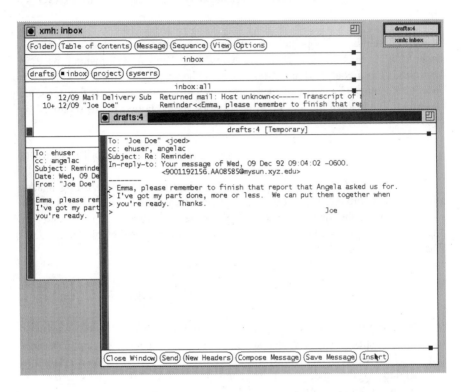

Figure 16-2. Original message and reply with special ReplyInsertFilter

Another useful filter is:

```
xmh*ReplyInsertFilter: /xxx/yyy/mhl -form mhl.body
```

(You'll need to replace the /*xxx*/*yyy* with the pathname of the MH library directory on your system, where the *mhl* program is stored.) The *mhl* program is for message formatting, and its standard *mhl.body* format file extracts the body of a mail message. For help, read Section 10.1.

NOTE

There's a bug in some *xmh app–defaults* files. If your filter doesn't seem to work, try using xmh.ReplyInsertFilter instead of xmh*ReplyInsertFilter in your resource file.

16.3.4 SendBreakWidth

Lines in a draft message that have more characters than the *SendBreakWidth* will be broken when the draft is sent. The default is 2000 in *xmh* Release 5—but only 85 in Release 4, which means that lines longer than 85 characters wide will be broken in *xmh* R4. Setting a very large *SendBreakWidth*, such as 2000, is a good idea when you're mailing source code or other text that should never be broken. For a more detailed explanation, see Section 15.3.5.

16.3.5 SendWidth

After lines (longer than the *SendBreakWidth*, see the previous section) in a draft message are broken, the longest resulting line will be no longer than *SendWidth*. (The default is lines 72 characters wide.) For a more detailed explanation, see Section 15.3.5.

16.3.6 SkipCopied, SkipDeleted, SkipMoved

By default, when you mark a message for deleting, moving, or copying (actually, linking), the View Next Message and View Previous Message commands skip over the message. For instance, they'll skip over a message to be deleted if the *SkipDeleted* value is true. (By default, all three of these are true.)

If you want the View Next Message and the View Previous Message commands to let you view messages marked for copying (linking), set this line in your resource file:

```
xmh*SkipCopied: false
```

Messages marked for deleting and moving would still be skipped because the *SkipDeleted* and *SkipMoved* would default to *true*.

16.3.7 TocGeometry

TocGeometry is the initial geometry for new main *xmh* windows. This geometry setting doesn't include the master window that opens when you first start *xmh* (see Section 16.1, "Setting Command-line Options and Resources"). For example, if you start *xmh* this way:

```
xmh -geometry 830x250+50+5 -xrm '*TocGeometry:475x440' \
    -xrm '*CompGeometry: 660x460' &
```

you'll get a short, wide master window at the top of the screen (830 pixels wide and 250 pixels high). Each time you click on Open Folder in New Window, you'll get a 475x440-pixel table of contents window. It's important to make an entry for *CompGeometry* to make sure that the composition windows are no more than the normal 72 (or 80) characters wide—this keeps lines the right length in messages you send. These geometries let you use setups like the one in Figure 16-3, with windows onto several folders at the same time.

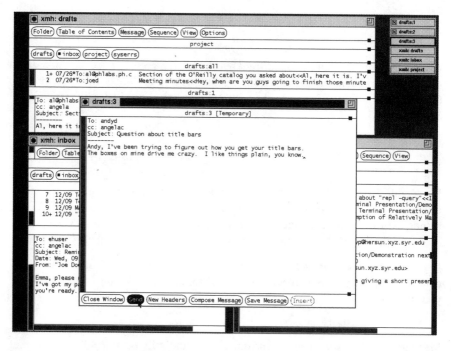

Figure 16-3. Screen with new geometry settings

Otherwise, the messages you send could have lines that are too wide or too narrow for most peoples' terminals.

16.3.8 TocWidth

TocWidth sets the number of characters to generate for each message in a folder's Table of Contents (which is stored in the *.xmhcache* file). (The default is 100.)

If your folders have thousands of messages, you can speed up *xmh* by setting *TocWidth* to a smaller number than 100—just enough to fill your Table of Contents window. Try a setting of 80 instead.

For more information see Section 16.7.

16.3.9 ShapeStyle

If your X setup can do it, *xmh* R5 will use rounded buttons. (The figures in this book do.) Using rectangular buttons can speed up your display, though. To do that, use the entry:

```
xmh*ShapeStyle: Rectangle
```

16.4 Changing Buttons; Accelerators

xmh has a long list of *action procedures* that it runs when you click a mouse button, select a command from a menu, or click a button in a window. These are set in a resource file named (usually) */usr/lib/X11/app–defaults/Xmh*. There's a copy of the default file in Appendix G. You can change the way *xmh* works by adding entries to your own resource file (like *.Xdefaults*).

Table 16-1 is an alphabetical list of *xmh* actions. For a list grouped by function, with longer descriptions, see the section called PROCESSING YOUR MAIL in the *xmh*(1) manual page (Appendix I).

Table 16-1. xmh Release 5 Actions

Action	Description
XmhAddToSequence( )	Add selected messages to selected sequence.
XmhClose( )	Close main window.
XmhCloseView( )	Close view window or composition window.
XmhCommitChanges( )	Execute all deletions, moves and links.
XmhComposeMessage( )	Compose new message.
XmhCreateFolder( )	Create folder or subfolder.

Table 16-1. xmh Release 5 Actions (continued)

Action	Description
XmhDeleteFolder( )	Delete selected folder (with confirmation).
XmhDeleteSequence( )	Remove selected sequence.
XmhEditView( )	Edit viewed message.
XmhForceRescan( )	Rebuild Table of Contents.
XmhCheckForNewMail( )	Check all mail drops.
XmhForward( )	Forward selected or current message(s).
XmhIncorporateNewMail( )	Incorporate new mail.
XmhInsert( )	Insert message you're replying to.
XmhLeaveFolderButton( )	Update menu button when pointer moves out.
XmhMarkCopy( )	Mark message(s) to link.
XmhMarkDelete( )	Mark message(s) to delete.
XmhMarkMove( )	Mark message(s) to move.
XmhOpenFolder([foldername])	Open *foldername* or selected folder.
XmhOpenFolderInNewWindow( )	Open selected folder in new window.
XmhOpenSequence( )	View selected sequence.
XmhPackFolder( )	Renumber messages as 1, 2, ...
XmhPickMessages( )	Open Pick window to define new sequence.
XmhPopFolder( )	Pop folder off stack, set selected folder.
XmhPopSequence( )	Pop sequence off stack of sequence names.
XmhPopupFolderMenu( )	Build folder button menu if any; open it.
XmhPrint( )	Print selected or current message(s).
XmhPrintView( )	Print the viewed message.
XmhPromptOkayAction( )	"Click OK" for *XmhCreateFolder( )*.
XmhPushFolder ([foldername, . . .])	Push argument or selected folder(s) on stack.
XmhPushSequence ([sequencename, . . .])	Push argument or selected sequences(s) on stack.
XmhReloadSeqLists( )	Update sequence menu from public MH sequences in current folder.
XmhRemoveFromSequence( )	Remove selected messages from selected sequence.
XmhReply( )	Reply to selected or current message.
XmhResetCompose( )	New Headers button.
XmhSave( )	Save composition in drafts folder.
XmhSaveView( )	Save message in view window.
XmhSend( )	Send composition.
XmhSetCurrentFolder( )	Set selected folder. (Menu widget buttons only.)

Table 16-1. xmh Release 5 Actions (continued)

Action	Description
XmhShellCommand (parameter[, parameter])	Give *parameters* with full pathname of selected or current message(s) to UNIX shell.
XmhSortFolder( )	Sort folder.
XmhUnmark( )	Remove link/delete/move marks from selected or current message(s).
XmhUseAsComposition( )	Create composition window from selected or current message(s).
XmhViewForward( )	Forward viewed message.
XmhViewInNewWindow( )	View first selected or current message in new window.
XmhViewMarkDelete( )	Mark viewed message for deletion.
XmhViewNextMessage( )	View first selected message or first message after current.
XmhViewPrevious( )	View last selected message or first message before current.
XmhViewReply( )	Reply to viewed message.
XmhViewUseAsComposition( )	Use message in view window as composition.
XmhWMProtocols ([wm_delete_window] [wm_save_yourself])	For window manager communication protocols. See *xmh*(1) manual page.

16.4.1 New Accelerator for Compose Message

This section shows how to add and change resource entries for accelerators.

Let's add an accelerator for `Compose Message`.

Example 16-1 shows the section of the *app–defaults/Xmh* file (see Appendix G.3) that sets accelerators for commands on the `Message` menu:

Example 16-1. Default message menu accelerators

```
*messageMenu.Accelerators: #override\n\
      Meta<Key>space: XmhViewNextMessage()\n\
    :Meta<Key>c:    XmhMarkCopy()\n\
    :Meta<Key>d:    XmhMarkDelete()\n\
    :Meta<Key>f:    XmhForward()\n\
    :Meta<Key>m:    XmhMarkMove()\n\
    :Meta<Key>n:    XmhViewNextMessage()\n\
```

Example 16-1. Default message menu accelerators (continued)

```
:Meta<Key>p:    XmhViewPreviousMessage()\n\
:Meta<Key>r:    XmhReply()\n\
:Meta<Key>u:    XmhUnmark()\n
```

The first line has the name of the resource, *messageMenu.Accelerators*. The other lines have entries in pairs, one pair per accelerator. Because each line except the last one ends with a backslash (\) (which is the line continuation character), all of these are part of the same resource entry.

For example, the third line defines the META-C accelerator. When you type META-C, that executes the *XmhMarkCopy()* action, which marks the selected messages for copying.

As Table 16-1 shows, the action for composing a new message is *XmhComposeMessage()*. You'll want to pick an accelerator key that's not already used. Look through the list in the *xmh* manual page. Let's say that you choose META-↑M. You'll need to add a new accelerator/action pair to the resource list.

The order of the accelerators in a resource list doesn't matter. Let's add it to the end. Copy all ten lines of the entry into your resource file (like *.Xdefaults*) and add a new pair for your new accelerator. I added a continuation character (a backslash (\)) to the end of the last existing line in Example 16-1. Then I added the new META-↑M accelerator on a new line below it. The new lines in the resource file look like Example 16-2:

Example 16-2. Message menu accelerators with new ComposeMessage()

```
*messageMenu.Accelerators: #override\n\
        Meta<Key>space: XmhViewNextMessage()\n\
    :Meta<Key>c:    XmhMarkCopy()\n\
    :Meta<Key>d:    XmhMarkDelete()\n\
    :Meta<Key>f:    XmhForward()\n\
    :Meta<Key>m:    XmhMarkMove()\n\
    :Meta<Key>n:    XmhViewNextMessage()\n\
    :Meta<Key>p:    XmhViewPreviousMessage()\n\
    :Meta<Key>r:    XmhReply()\n\
    :Meta<Key>u:    XmhUnmark()\n\
    :Meta<Key>M:    XmhComposeMessage()\n
```

Restarting *xmh* will bring in this new accelerator. Try it—type META-↑M and a composition window should open.

16.4.2   Redefining Composition Window Buttons

These examples show how to change the labels and actions of two buttons on the composition window buttonbox. They also add a new accelerator.

Accelerator to Send Draft and Close Window

This one defines META-S to send the draft and close the window. It uses two *xmh* actions. Add the following to your resource file:

```
Xmh*comp.translations: #override\n\
        :Meta<Key>s:              XmhSend()XmhCloseView()\n
```

As you can see, to get more than one action from an accelerator, just list the actions one after the other. This was taken from the file in Appendix G.2—see that file for many more examples.

Redefine New Headers Button to be Send and Close

The new META-S accelerator in the previous section speeds up a common thing you do from a composition window: send the draft and close the window. Next, let's see how to redefine a much less used button, New Headers, and make the button Send and Close instead.

Here are the two new resource entries for your resource file:

```
xmh*compButtons.reset.Translations: #override\n\
        <Btn1Down>,<Btn1Up>: XmhSend()XmhCloseView()unset()\n
xmh*compButtons.reset.label: Send and Close
```

Those entries do two things:

1. When you point to the third composition window button (.reset), then press (<Btn1Down>) and release (<Btn1Up>) the first mouse button, *xmh* should perform the XmhSend() and XmhCloseView() actions, then unset() to finish.

2. The resource entries change the label of the button from the default (New Headers) to Send and Close.

Figure 16-4 and Figure 16-5, respectively, are before-and-after pictures of the composition window buttonbox.

Figure 16-4. Default composition window buttonbox

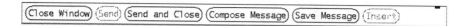

Figure 16-5. Composition window New Headers changed to Send and Close

If you still would like the New Headers button, you can replace the Compose Message button with a New Headers button. I've always thought that New Headers was a misleading name because it removes *all* changes, not just the headers. So I'll also rename New Headers to Start Over. Here are the new resource file entries (they work the same as the button redefinitions above, but they redefine the fourth button, .compose):

```
xmh*compButtons.compose.Translations: #override\n\
    <Btn1Down>,<Btn1Up>: XmhResetCompose()unset()\n
xmh*compButtons.compose.label: Start Over
```

After that redefinition, the composition window buttonbox looks like Figure 16-6.

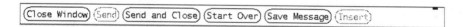

Figure 16-6. Composition window with two buttons redefined

16.4.3 A New Buttonbox for the Main Windows

You can set a resource called *CommandButtonCount* that lets you make completely new buttons on the main window. *CommandButtonCount* is the number of command buttons to create in a new buttonbox between the Table of Contents and the view areas of the main window. *xmh* will create these buttons with the names button1, button2, and so on, in a box with the name commandBox. You can specify labels and actions for the buttons in a private resource file.

Figure 16-7 is an example of an uncustomized display. It's made with this single resource file entry:

```
Xmh*CommandButtonCount:5
```

The default *CommandButtonCount* is 0, which gives no buttonbox. Now let's fill in the buttonbox. If you're an MH user, too, you may want buttons labeled with the MH command equivalents. If you know those names, this is a good way to get a lot of use out of a small area on the main window. (I like these buttons because I forget the accelerators sometimes.)

After you add entries for the buttons to your resource file, your main windows will look like Figure 16-8.

Once you see the pattern, the buttons are easy to figure out yourself. Example 16-3 shows the parts of the resource file entries for the first and fourth buttons. Putting an exclamation point (!) at the start of a line makes it a comment.

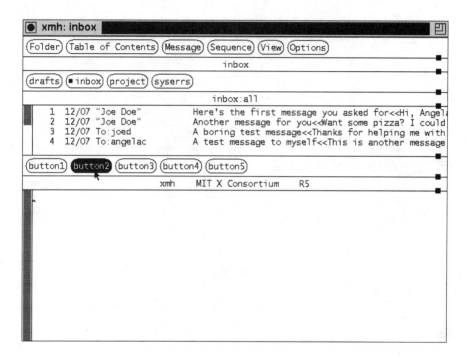

Figure 16-7. Display (not customized yet) with *CommandButtonCount:5

Example 16-3. Defining two of the new command buttons

```
!
!# define the number of buttons in the buttonbox
!
Xmh*CommandButtonCount: 12
!
!# 1: left mouse button:                "inc" MH command
!
Xmh*commandBox.button1.label:    inc
Xmh*commandBox.button1.translations:    #override\n\
     <Btn1Down>,<Btn1Up>: XmhIncorporateNewMail()unset()
     ...
!
```

Example 16-3. Defining two of the new command buttons (continued)

```
!# 4: left or right mouse buttons:        "rmm" MH command
!
Xmh*commandBox.button4.label:     rmm
Xmh*commandBox.button4.translations:       #override\n\
     <Btn1Down>,<Btn1Up>: XmhMarkDelete()unset()\n\
     <Btn3Down>,<Btn3Up>: XmhMarkDelete()unset()
```

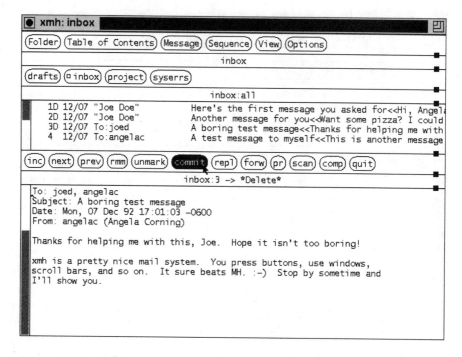

Figure 16-8. Main window with new buttonbox

Notice that the fourth button in the buttonbox can be activated with either the first or the third mouse button.

16.4.4 Adding Color

You can change foreground and background color of new buttons just the way you can change the color of other resources. For example, the following lines would change the colors of the first and last buttons (inc and quit) in the new buttonbox on the main window:

```
xmh*commandBox.button1.foreground: yellow
xmh*commandBox.button1.background: navy
xmh*commandBox.button12.foreground: navy
xmh*commandBox.button12.background: red
```

Using color is a nice way to group related buttons.

16.4.5 Moving a Message to a Specific Folder

Here's how to add a button that marks a message for moving directly to a specific folder or subfolder. The folder here is named *todo/June* (you can use another name, of course).

```
xmh*commandButtonCount: 1
xmh*commandBox.button1.label: Move to todo/June
xmh*commandBox.button1.translations: #override\n\
    <Btn1Down>,<Btn1Up>: set() XmhPushFolder()\
    XmhPushFolder(todo/June) XmhPopFolder()\
    XmhMarkMove() XmhPopFolder() unset()
```

16.4.6 Changing Command Options with edprofile

xmh does some of its work, such as displaying messages, with internal programs. It calls MH commands to do everything else.* Those MH commands read options from your MH profile file. Some MH profile options are overridden by *xmh*; you can set the others in your MH profile. For example, you can change the options that *scan* uses to build the Table of Contents.

Before *xmh* introduced the *XmhShellCommand()* action in Release 5, the only way to change MH profile options was with a text editor. Now you can define buttons that call a shell script named *edprofile* (in Section 13.12)—and edit your MH profile from a main *xmh* window.

The details of setting up *edprofile* are in Section 13.12. Section 16.4.3 shows how to add new buttons to the main window. Example 16-4 has the lines to put in your resource file for making two buttons that change *scan*.

---

*According to the *xmh* Revision 5 manual page, *xmh* uses at least the following *MH* commands: *inc*, *msgchk*, *comp*, *send*, *repl*, *forw*, *refile*, *rmm*, *pick*, *pack*, *sort*, and *scan*.

Example 16-4. Changing sort order with edprofile

```
Xmh*CommandButtonCount: 2
Xmh*commandBox.button3.label: size toc
Xmh*commandBox.button3.translations: #override\
    <Btn1Down>,<Btn1Up>: XmhShellCommand(edprofile scan -form scan.size --) unset()
Xmh*commandBox.button1.label: default toc
Xmh*commandBox.button1.translations: #override\
    <Btn1Down>,<Btn1Up>: XmhShellCommand(edprofile -v scan --) unset()
```

The first button, labeled `size toc`, adds the size of each message to the Table of Contents the next time the folder is rescanned. (Section 5.2.1 explains and shows examples of this.) The button runs the command:

```
edprofile scan -form scan.size --
```

that changes the MH profile *scan* entry to look like this:

```
scan: -form scan.size
```

Any switches on that MH profile `scan` line before *edprofile* runs are deleted.

The second button, labeled `default toc`, will run the command:

```
edprofile -v scan
```

the `scan` line in the MH profile will be changed to this:

```
scan:
```

The next time a folder is rescanned, it will have the default format.

Unfortunately, there must be a current or selected message before you run *XmhShellComand()*. If there's not a message selected, choose any one before you click the button that runs *edprofile*.

16.4.7 Use an External Editor

If you don't want to use the standard *xmh* editor on your drafts, and you can't use the patches for an external editor explained in Section 15.3.7, here's another way. Add the lines shown in Example 16-5 to your resource file. (If you haven't added buttons before, there's help in Section 16.4.3.)

Example 16-5. Button to edit a message with vi

```
Xmh*commandBox.button1.label: edit vi
Xmh*commandBox.button1.translations: #override\
    <Btn1Down>,<Btn1Up>: XmhShellCommand(xterm -e vi) unset()
```

The button runs *vi* in an *xterm* window; it gives *vi* the full pathname of the message(s) you select. When you exit *vi*, the window will close. It's clumsy, but it works. The steps to use the button are:

1. Start a draft message and Save it.

2. Open the *drafts* folder in a main window.

3. Select the draft message to edit.

4. Click your vi editor button. An *xterm* window with the editor pops up.

5. Do your edits. Save and quit *vi*.

6. Select Use as Composition to bring up the draft again. Click Send to send the message.

If you use this a lot, you could bind more of the actions to the button. The list of *xmh* actions is in Table 16-1.

You can use this same technique to run spell-checking programs or any other UNIX program to help you edit.

16.5 Conflicts Between xmh and MH Customization

Because *xmh* runs MH commands for you, many of the things that you change in MH will affect *xmh*, too. Unless you look at the *xmh* source code, it's not always easy to know exactly what changes will affect *xmh*.

If you only use *xmh*, and never use MH, you don't need to worry. Otherwise, read on . . .

As you saw in previous chapters, you can change MH dramatically, adding new commands and changing the way existing commands work. You can change a lot about *xmh*, too, but it's hard to change the way that *xmh* uses MH commands. If you're good at UNIX shell programming, though, check Section 16.9 for ideas.

xmh doesn't use MH commands for everything, though. Here's a list of some things that *xmh* does for itself. Customizing MH will not affect these *xmh* functions:

• Displaying messages in a main window or view window.

• Editing messages in a composition window.

- Selecting a sequence or folder.

- Printing messages (unless you customize *xmh* to use MH commands for printing).

By now you know that each MH command looks for default switches in the MH profile. If you use *xmh*, you should understand how defaults like these affect it.

If you run both MH and *xmh*, life can get confusing. Changing command options for MH can affect *xmh* in weird ways.

The best answer I've found is to make a separate MH profile file for *xmh* named *.xmh_profile*. Keep only basic components in there, like the `Path:` component. Customize MH in your *.mh_profile* file.

To make *xmh* use your *.xmh_profile* file, store its full pathname in the environment variable named *MH*. Make sure that the environment variable is only set while you're using *xmh*—otherwise, it will affect your MH use, too. The easiest way to do this is by setting the environment variable in your startup file (like *.xsession*). If your startup file is read by the Bourne shell, use the following line:

```
MH=$HOME/.xmh_profile xmh other_xmh_stuff &
```

If yours uses the C shell, there isn't a direct way—but this one is easy to understand:

```
(setenv MH ~/.xmh_profile; xmh other_xmh_stuff)&
```

For more information, see Section 16.9.

NOTE

xmh Release 4 ignores the *MH* environment variable at startup time and also when you use the `Reply` command. It looks for the `Path:` component directly in your *.mh_profile* file, no matter where your *MH* environment variable points it.

16.6 Using Template Draft Files for Headers

You can change the default header of your mail messages. That's a handy way to put in changes that you want made to the headers of all (or most) of the messages you send.

The first time you click the Compose Message button, *xmh* runs the MH *comp* command and reads a copy of the header that *comp* makes.* It does the same kind of thing with Reply and Forward commands.

By default, those MH commands read the template draft component files named *components*, *replcomps*, and *forwcomps*. To change the *xmh* draft headers, you can change those template draft files. For detailed information, see Section 8.9.

For instance, if you make a *components* file like this:

```
To:
Reply-to: ehuser@asun.xxx.yyy.zzz
cc:
Fcc: outbox
Subject:
---------
```

that's what the default headers in your composition window will look like when you use Compose Message.

Note that *xmh* only runs *comp* once per *xmh* session and saves the result. Therefore, if you change your *components* file, you'll need to restart *xmh* for the changes to take effect there. But *xmh* has to run the MH *repl* and *forw* commands before each message that you reply to or forward. Your changes to *replcomps* and *forwcomps* take effect right away.

16.7 Changing Table of Contents Format

You can change the appearance of the Table of Contents. This section shows how to use MH *scan* format files such as *scan.timely*. It also gives an example of creating your own format with a custom format file. There's more information about this in Section 5.2.1 and Section 10.2.

16.7.1 Introduction

xmh makes its Table of Contents by running the MH *scan* command. It stores *scan* output in a *.xmhcache* file in each folder. *xmh* displays the *.xmhcache* file in its Table of Contents area. Before displaying the file, *xmh* "edits" the file (in effect) to add characters like the plus sign (+) (for the current message), D (for messages marked to be deleted), and so on.

---

*It actually runs comp −file *tempfile* −nowhatnowproc −nodraftfolder and gets a copy of *tempfile*.

Whenever *xmh* rescans a folder, it remakes the *.xmhcache* file. If you'd like to see the file for yourself, you can read the *inbox* file with *more*(1) by using commands like:

```
% ls -l `mhpath +inbox`/.xmhcache
-rw-r--r--  1 ehuser  400 Jul 14 04:47 /u/ehuser/Mail/inbox/.xmhcache
% more `mhpath +inbox`/.xmhcache
   1  12/07 "Joe Doe"          Here's the first message you asked
for<<Hi, Angela! You asked me to
   2+ 12/07 "Joe Doe"          Another message for you<<Want some
pizza? I could order and they'd b
      ...
```

That *.xmhcache* file is actually 100 characters wide (see Section 16.3.8). I've shown the lines folded here, but each message is actually all on one line—just like the output of *scan*(1) in its standard format.

If you follow some simple rules, you can change what's shown by the Table of Contents. Those rules are:

1. The message number goes in the first four columns, right justified (just like the standard *scan*(1) output). If your format file tries to make the message number wider or left-justify it, *xmh* can get unhappy.

2. Column 5 is reserved for *xmh* to write the plus sign (+), D, and so on.

3. The rest of the line—columns 6 to the column width set by the *TocWidth* resource—are yours to play with.

4. Each message summary must fit on one line; there are no multiline scans in *xmh*.

A good overall rule for changing things is: don't try to edit the *.xmhcache* file yourself. Instead, change the output of the *scan*(1) command. You do that by changing the *scan* switches in your MH profile.* If you change the *scan* format, remember that old *.xmhcache* files won't be updated automatically. It's a good idea to do a Rescan Folder in any folders you use much. In the same way, if you stop using a format file, you'll need to Rescan again for the same reason.

---

*Don't try to set *–width* in MH profile, though. Instead, use the *TocWidth* resource (in your *.Xdefaults* file).

16.7.2 Using a Standard scan Format File

For example, to make *scan* use its standard *scan.timely* format file in its Table of Contents, use this component in your MH profile:

```
scan: -form scan.timely
```

Then, use the `Rescan Folder` command to rebuild *.xmhcache*. Your Table of Contents will change from the default, in Figure 16-9, to the new version with *scan.timely* in Figure 16-10. (If you haven't seen *scan.timely* before, look at the date column in Figure 16-10 and see Section 5.2.1.)

```
                        project/reports:all
1   12/01 "Joe Doe"     Status Report, November 1991<<It was a busy month.
2   03/01 "Joe Doe"     Status Report, February 1992<<We fixed all the prob
3   06/03 "Joe Doe"     Status Report, May 1992<<It was a quiet month. Four
4   07/27 "Joe Doe"     Status Report, June 1992<<Fireworks is a good word
5   08/01 "Joe Doe"     Status Report, July 1992<<The oven problems from la
```

Figure 16-9. Table of Contents with default scan(1) format

```
                        project/reports:all
1   Dec91 "Joe Doe"     Status Report, November 1991<<It was a busy month.
2   01Mar "Joe Doe"     Status Report, February 1992<<We fixed all the prob
3   03Jun "Joe Doe"     Status Report, May 1992<<It was a quiet month. Four
4    Mon  "Joe Doe"     Status Report, June 1992<<Fireworks is a good word
5   09:09 "Joe Doe"     Status Report, July 1992<<The oven problems from la
```

Figure 16-10. Table of Contents with scan.timely format file

In the next few sections, we'll be adapting the format file called *scan.default*. It's explained in Section 10.2.4. By the way, if you haven't read Chapter 10, *MH Formatting*, yet, this is a good time. You won't need to understand it to make the changes shown in the next few sections. Reading it will help you understand what's happening, though—and go on to make your own changes. Example 16-6 has a copy of *scan.default*.

Example 16-6. scan.default format file

```
%4(msg)%<(cur)+%| %>%<{replied}-%|%<{encrypted}E%| %>%>\
%02(mon{date})/%02(mday{date})%<{date} %|*%>\
%<(mymbox{from})To:%14(friendly{to})%|%17(friendly{from})%> \
%{subject}%<{body}<<%{body}>>%>
```

16.7.3 A Wider Table of Contents

If your *xmh* window usually doesn't come close to filling your screen's width, and you'd like more information across the screen, this section shows how.

Figure 16-11 is an example of what the wide Table of Contents looks like. (Yours doesn't have to look just like this.) The date is spelled out. The time is shown (on a 24-hour clock). Next comes the size of the message, in characters. The space for the sender's (or the addressee's) address is wider—in most cases, you can see the whole address instead of just the first part. The leftover room goes to the subject and body.

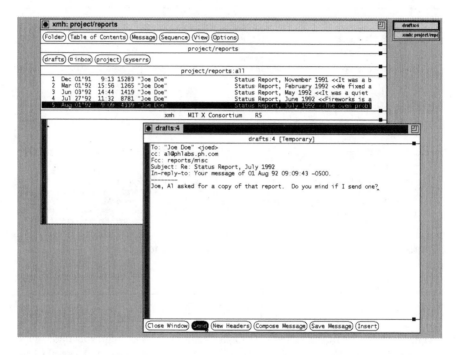

Figure 16-11. Wide main window (and normal composition window)

That took just a few changes to the *scan.default* format file (shown previously in Example 16-6). Compare it to the edited *scan.xmhwide* format file in Example 16-7.

Example 16-7. scan.xmhwide format file

```
%4(msg)%<(cur)+%| %>%<{replied}-%| %>\
%(month{date}) %02(mday{date})'%02(year{date})\
```

Example 16-7. scan.xmhwide format file (continued)

```
%<{date} %|*%> \
%2(hour{date}):%02(min{date}) \
%5(size) \
%<(mymbox{from})To:%24(friendly{to})\
%|%27(friendly{from})%>\
  %{subject}%<{body} <<%{body}>>%>
```

If you haven't read Section 10.2, you can just copy the text from Example 16-7 into your MH directory, in a file named *scan.xmhwide*, ... and try it. See Appendix E, *Copies of Files Over the Network*.

You'll need to set a wider *TocWidth* so that the standard *scan*(1) command will make enough output to fill the window. A resource entry of **TocWidth:133* is right in this example, but yours may be different. Also, because you'll be setting a wide master window (in the *xmh –geometry* command below), you should explicitly make your composition windows normal size.

Tell *scan* to read this new format file. Do that by editing a *scan* component in your MH profile:

```
scan: -form scan.xmhwide
```

Finally, start *xmh*. To set the master window size, I like to use the *–geometry* option on the command line (but your resource file might be a better place for it after you get a setting you like):

```
xmh -geometry 830x450+50+5 -xrm '*CompGeometry: 660x460' &
```

When you understand *scan* format files and the way that *xmh* uses them, you can use almost any format that will fit on a line.

16.8 Changing the Print Command

The resource entry *xmh*PrintCommand* controls the way that *xmh* prints messages. This entry is the command line that you'd type at a Bourne shell prompt to print a file. When you select one or more messages and then select Print, *xmh* will start the print command and append the full pathnames of the messages. The following default print command:

```
enscript >/dev/null 2>/dev/null
```

prints files on a PostScript printer (assuming you've installed Adobe System's *enscript* command).

For instance, let's say your MH directory is `/xxx/yyy/Mail`, your current folder is _inbox,_ and you select messages 25 and 26 to print. When you choose `Print`, _xmh_ will execute:

```
enscript >/dev/null 2>/dev/null /xxx/yyy/Mail/inbox/25 /xxx/yyy/Mail/inbox/26
```

The command line above has the following problems:

1. You might want to use some of the _enscript_ options.

2. You might not have the _enscript_ command.

3. You might not have, or want to use, a PostScript printer.

4. Error messages are thrown away (into _/dev/null,_ the UNIX "trash can").

16.8.1 Grabbing Error Output

The default printer command doesn't let you see printer errors; it just throws them away. If you don't get your output, it's nice to be able to see the error messages (if any). In _xmh_ Release 5, printer messages on the standard error are put into a small window that pops up when there's a message. But the standard output of printer commands is thrown away unless you redirect it. (For some reason, on my version of UNIX, the _lpr_ and _lp_ commands write their errors to the standard output!) I've merged the standard output of my printer command onto the standard error so that any kind of printer message will be shown in the pop-up window. Here's what that looks like with the default _enscript_ command:

```
Xmh*PrintCommand: enscript 1>&2
```

For _xmh_ Release 3 (or any release, actually), you can set your print command so that any output it makes goes to a file named _.xmh_printerrs_ in your home directory. If you want to do that, here's a line to use in your _.Xdefaults_ file (replace the `/xxx/yyy` with the pathname of your home directory):

```
xmh*PrintCommand: enscript >>/xxx/yyy/.xmh_printerrs 2>&1
```

The two right angle brackets (`>>`) mean that each new error is appended to the file. If you get a lot of printer errors, you'll want to clean out the file occasionally. Or, you can use one right angle bracket (`>`) instead—that means that each time you use `Print`, any old errors will be overwritten (which could be good or bad). The `2>&1` means that all messages, from both the standard output and standard error, will go into the file (by itself, `>>` would only redirect standard output).

16.8.2 Printing with lpr and lp

To print on a line printer (which only handles text, not PostScript), try a command such as this on Berkeley-compatible systems which have the *lpr*(1) command:

```
xmh*PrintCommand: lpr -p 1>&2
```

The −p formats your mail messages with the *pr*(1) command.

If your system has the System V *lp* command, which doesn't have a −p option, you should use this instead:

```
xmh*PrintCommand: lp -s 1>&2
```

The −s option stops messages like `request id is . . .` But that command won't format your output with *pr*.

16.8.3 Other Printer Commands, Including a Shell Script

If the printer you'll be using is different from the previous examples, you'll basically need to put everything but the filename into your *xmh*PrintCommand*. For example, if you type this command to print a file when you're not using *xmh*:

```
% tcprint -Pwest -nolog filename
```

you'd put this line in your *.Xdefaults* file:

```
xmh*PrintCommand: tcprint -Pwest -nolog 1>&2
```

Unfortunately, you can't use a UNIX pipe (|) to print your files, such as `pr myfile | lp`. That's because *xmh* puts the filenames to print at the *end* of the command line, after the last command in the pipe.

To solve this, or to do other fancy things with mail printing, you'll need to write a little program that handles *xmh* printing. The program in Section 13.7 is a good starting place.

16.9 Snooping on xmh

If you're trying to find out how *xmh* uses MH commands so that you can change the way commands work without causing problems, try the techniques in this section.

16.9.1 Use the debug Resource

If you set the *xmh*debug* resource, *xmh* will write debugging information to its standard error. The easiest way to do that is by starting *xmh* from an *xterm* window (probably with a scrollbar). For example:

```
% xmh -xrm '*debug:1'
# 4 : /u/ehuser/.mh_profile
# 4 : <Closed>
# 4 : /u/ehuser/.xmhcheck
# 4 : <Closed>
Making screen ... Realizing... done.
 setting toc ... # 4 : /u/ehuser/Mail/inbox/.xmhcache
# 4 : <Closed>
# 4 : /u/ehuser/Mail/inbox/.mh_sequences
# 4 : <Closed>
done.
(Checking for new mail... done)
(Checking for new mail... done)
      ...etc....
[magic toc check ... done]
      ...etc....
(Checking for new mail... done)
[magic toc check ...# 4 : /u/ehuser/Mail/inbox/.xmhcache
# 4 : <Closed>
Executing scan ... pid=13898 blocking.
unblocked; child not done.
reading alternate input...read.
blocking.
unblocked; child not done.
reading alternate input...read.
done
# 4 : /u/ehuser/Mail/inbox/.xmhcache
# 4 : <Closed>
# 4 : /u/ehuser/Mail/inbox/.mh_sequences
# 4 : <Closed>
 done]
```

Here's some brief explanation:

* Messages like # 4 : /u/ehuser/.mh_profile show *xmh* opening the MH profile file; the 4 means *xmh* is using UNIX file descriptor 4. The # 4 : <Closed> lines is printed when it's done.

* As *xmh* builds the master window, it prints Making screen . . . Realizing . . . done.

* The lines between setting toc . . . and the next done. show the steps in building the Table of Contents.

- A message (Checking for new mail . . . done) is printed every time *xmh* checks your system mailbox—and other mail drops listed in your *.xmhcheck* file (Section 15.4.1).

- The [magic toc check . . . done] shows *xmh* checking the Table of Contents to see if it's out of date for some reason. For instance, maybe an Fcc: message was dropped into the folder. If the TOC needs updating, you'll see the message Rescanning *foldername* above the Table of Contents; *xmh* will run *scan*.

- Executing scan . . . pid=13898 shows the MH command name and the UNIX process ID number. While the process runs, *xmh* waits for it and prints blocking.. Every second or so, *xmh* prints unblocked; child not done.; then it reads output from the process and says reading alternate input . . . read. until the process finishes.

To learn more, start *xmh*, try things, and watch the messages in your *xterm* window. You might want to browse through the source code (Section 16.9.4) to find out exactly what's happening as each debugging message is printed. Search the code for the string DEBUG.

16.9.2 Use Accounting Information

Many UNIX systems keep accounting data about the processes that each user runs. When *xmh* runs a standard UNIX command, it starts a process to do that. Therefore, to find out whether *xmh* used an MH command, run the *xmh* command, then check the accounting data. Many UNIX systems show that data with the *lastcomm*(1) program. For example, after I used the *xmh* Sort Folder command, *lastcomm* showed that the *sortm* and *scan* commands had been run:

```
% lastcomm ehuser
scan          ehuser    ??      0.23 secs Wed Jul 18 09:10
sortm         ehuser    ??      0.48 secs Wed Jul 18 09:10
xwud          ehuser    ttyp1   0.45 secs Wed Jul 18 08:48
    . . .
```

Unfortunately, *lastcomm* doesn't show what command-line switches were used or what was in the command's environment as it ran. The next section can help with that.

16.9.3 Make a Front End Shell Script

A much more flexible way to snoop on *xmh* is by replacing MH commands with shell scripts. In fact, this method doesn't just work for snooping—you can also use it to change the way that *xmh* runs MH commands.

The idea is to make a directory full of symbolic links to all the MH programs. Tell *xmh* to use that directory by adding it to your path or setting the *MhPath* resource. Then, when you want to see or change how *xmh* uses an MH command, replace the symbolic link with a shell script. The shell script can write log messages to a file, display command-line options that *xmh* called it with, and execute the MH command. The steps are explained in the next section.

CAUTION

With a radical change like this, there's always the chance of making a mistake that loses or corrupts your mail. If you use *xmh* for reading important e-mail, I don't recommend this method unless you're very comfortable with UNIX and shell programming.

Making the MhPath Directory, Making xmh Use It

Here are the steps you need to follow to set up the *MHPath* directory. You only need to do this once.

1. First, make a directory on your account with symbolic links to the executable MH commands. You could name it *xmhbin*. (To make the directory, use the command `mkdir $HOME/xmhbin`.)

2. Next, link the MH commands. I use symbolic links because they're easy to list (with *ls –l*) and see where the links "point." But you may also be able to use UNIX "hard" links if the MH executables are on the same filesystem as your home directory.

   - For instance, if your MH commands (*comp*, *inc*, etc.) are all stored in the directory */usr/local/mh*, you could link them into your new directory this way:

```
% ln -s /usr/local/mh/* $HOME/xmhbin
% cd $HOME/xmhbin
% ls -l
lrwxrwxrwx  1 ehuser   17 Jul 15 09:37 ali -> /usr/local/mh/ali
lrwxrwxrwx  1 ehuser   18 Jul 15 09:37 anno -> /usr/local/mh/anno
   ...
```

xmh doesn't actually use all of the MH commands, so you could probably omit some of those links. There's a list of MH commands used at the end of the *xmh* manual page in Appendix I.

- If your system's MH commands are mixed in a directory with other executables, you usually won't want to link in the other programs. Use a shell loop (I use *csh* here) to make the links you want. Start from your *xmhbin* directory.

  ```
  % foreach prog (ali anno burst ...)
  ? ln -s /usr/local/bin/$prog
  ? end
  ```

  Section 7.4 and Section 12.17.1 have more information on shell loops.

3. Then start *xmh* using the new executables and be sure it still works. Type one of the following commands.

   - For *xmh* Release 3 or 4:

     ```
     % xmh -xrm "*MhPath:$HOME/xmhbin" &
     ```

     The double quotes (") around the −xrm string let the shell replace $HOME with its value. If you put the *MhPath* entry in a resource file such as *.Xdefaults* which isn't read by a shell, you'll need to use the full pathname of the directory (like */xxx/you/xmhbin*).

   - *xmh* Release 5 looks in the search path for commands before it uses the **MhPath* resource. Set your search path temporarily before you start *xmh*. If you want to make the change permanent, edit your *.cshrc* or *.profile* file later. Put your *$HOME/xmhbin* directory somewhere before the MH binary directory (like */usr/local/mh*). Here's an example for the C shell:

     ```
     % set path=($HOME/xmhbin $path)
     % xmh &
     ```

4. Try a couple of *xmh* commands that run MH commands, such as `Incorporate New Mail` or `Sort Folder`. Then use *ls −lut* to show the last access time of the symbolic links in your *xmhbin*; when *xmh* uses them, their last access time (*atime*) will be updated, and you can see that in the *ls −l* output.

Replace a Link with a Shell Script

The next step is to replace a link with a front-end shell script. First, rename the link (or remove it):

```
% pwd
/xxx/yyy/xmhbin
% mv sortm sortm.orig
```

Here's a simple shell script for *sortm*. It writes a lot of information to a log file in your home directory, and then executes the MH command:

```
#! /bin/sh
# sortm - front end to MH sortm command, run from xmh
# appends logging information to $HOME/sortm.log first
# use subshell to gather all command output, stdout and stderr:
(date
echo "args are: $0 $*"
echo "environment has:"
printenv) >> $HOME/sortm.log 2>&1

# run the real command with exec, so this script
# (and the shell that runs it) can exit now:
exec /usr/local/mh/sortm $*
```

After you've installed the script, try it (in this case, use the `Sort Folder` command). The *sortm.log* file in your home directory should look something like this:

```
% cat $HOME/sortm.log
Wed Jul 18 10:12:46 EDT 1990
args are: /xxx/you/xmhbin/sortm +/xxx/you/Mail/inbox -noverbose
environment has:
DISPLAY=unix:0.0
EDITOR=/usr/ucb/vi
HOME=/xxx/you
        ...
```

and, of course, your current folder should have been sorted.

Standard Output vs. Standard Error

If your shell script writes any messages to the standard output, *xmh* may ignore them. Or, in cases where *xmh* is expecting to read useful information on the standard output, *xmh* could accidentally include what your script writes to the standard output. For example, when you `Rescan Folder`, *xmh* runs *scan* and puts the *scan* standard output into the *.xmhcache* file.

xmh Release 4 added a nice new feature: if a command writes a message to the standard error, the message is displayed in a notice box. Your script can use this feature to send you messages. As a semi-useless but easy to understand example, here's a version of *pick* that shows the command-line options *xmh* uses:

```
#! /bin/sh
echo "pick arguments are: $*" | fmt -50 1>&2
exec /usr/local/mh/pick ${1+"$@"}
```

The ${1+"$@"} is explained in Section 13.11.2.) I ran that *pick* front-end with search shown in Figure 15-21. The window I got after *pick* finishes is shown in Figure 16-12. (It makes me glad I did that with an *xmh* Pick window instead of typing the MH *pick* command myself.)

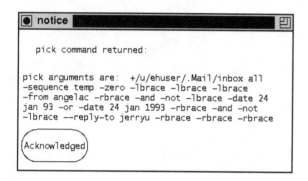

Figure 16-12. Making a notice box

I don't recommend using *xmh* notice boxes for commands that make a lot of output. I'd bet that they weren't really designed for this sort of abuse . . . .

NOTE

xmh Release 3 isn't happy about unexpected output and doesn't make the nice notice boxes. Use a log file instead.

16.9.4 Read the Source Code

Here's one last idea: if your computer has the *xmh* source code online and you feel like digging into it, that's the best way to find out exactly what's happening. Look at the C programs (the **.c* files) in the subdirectory *mit/clients/xmh*.

Part V:

Appendices

Part V contains appendices with copies of programs and configuration files, a reference list, and other information about MH and xmh.

The last appendix has selected MH reference pages from the standard MH 6.7.2 distribution, as well as the xmh *manual page from Release 5.*

A

Where Can You Go from Here?

MH BBoards
More Information About MH⌧

This book has only covered a part of MH. If you'd like to learn more, here are some suggestions.

A.1 MH BBoards

This book doesn't cover the MH BBoards (Bulletin Boards) programs. They're quite useful, especially if your site reads bulletin boards and/or digests that are sent in mail messages. The commands include *bbaka*, *bbc*, *msh*, and *vmh*. If your version of MH has been configured for BBoards, you can see your online manual pages for more information; also, check the reference list in Appendix C.

A.2 More Information About MH ⊠

Amazingly, not a lot has been written about MH. This book is the first work of this depth that I know of. Here are some ways to find out more about MH.

A.2.1 Documents Distributed with MH

The MH distribution has a directory called *papers* with tutorials, detailed descriptions of applications, and related programs. MH also comes with an Administrator's Guide, a good place to learn about installing MH and to discover some of its inner workings.

A.2.2 The MH Source Code

MH is written in the C programming language. One way to find out what it does is in classic UNIX hackers' style: read the code. Most of the code is clean and modular.

A.2.3 USENET Newsgroup, Mailing Lists ⊠

If you read the USENET "netnews," the *comp.mail.mh* newsgroup is a good place to read about MH—and post questions, if you have them.

If you can't read USENET, you can subscribe to the *mh–users* mailing list. It carries the same articles as the *comp.mail.mh* newsgroup. To subscribe, send a mail message to *mh–users–request@ics.uci.edu*.

As of this printing, old *mh–users* articles since 1986 or so were archived on *ftp.ics.uci.edu*. They're available by anonymous *ftp* and *ftpmail* from the *mh/mh–users* directory. For help, see Appendix E, *Copies of Files Over the Network*.

Finally, if you're interested in nitty-gritty details of MH, at the level of MH developers, the *mh–workers* mailing list is the place to look. To subscribe, send a mail message to *mh–workers–request@ics.uci.edu*.

B

Early History of MH
From Bruce Borden
From Stockton Gaines

Section 1.6.1 has an overview of the development of MH since the late 1970s. The first section of this appendix was written by Bruce S. Borden, the person responsible for much of the early MH programming. The second section was written by R. Stockton Gaines after he read the section that Bruce wrote. Stock, along with Norman Z. Shapiro, wrote a memo that laid out some of the design principles for MH.

Both sections are interesting reading.

B.1 From Bruce Borden

I joined the Rand Corporation in 1978. My first assignment was to "improve" the MS mail system, which had been developed over the previous two years by Dave Crocker and others at Rand. MS was synthesized from the various mail packages the authors had used and researched on other systems, most notably, Tenex. It was the ultimate in monolithic mail packages, attempting to provide every feature provided by all other packages. It was terrible. It was so unlike common UNIX programs that I found it totally unusable. It was also huge and slow. (We were running on a PDP-11/70!) I was supposed to speed it up and make it more robust. After about a month, I gave up. I went to my management and recommended that MS be discarded, and a much simpler package built from the ground up. MS was developed on government contract, and Rand was committed to delivering a product.

At that point, I started talking with Stockton Gaines and Norm Shapiro about a memo they had written, in which they had proposed that standard UNIX files and directories be used for mail messages, along with standard UNIX commands like *ls* and *cat* to list and display messages. They also proposed that UNIX environments be used to hold things like current message number. Finally, they suggested that the user *chdir* into a working folder to operate on it. They had proposed these ideas at the start of the MS project, but they were not able to convince anyone that such a system would be fast enough to be usable. I proposed a very short project to prove the basic concepts, and my management agreed.

Looking back, I realize that I had been very lucky with my first design. Without nearly enough design work, I built a working environment and some header files with key structures and wrote the first few MH commands: *inc, show/next/prev,* and *comp. show/next/prev* were one command—it looked at its name to determine which flavor to be. With these three, I was able to convince people that the structure was viable. This took about three weeks.

About this time, I also came up with the name MH—Mail Handler; I needed a name, and I couldn't think of anything better. I've never liked the name!

Over the next six months, I completed the basic MH commands: *inc, show, next, prev, comp, repl, forw,* (Steve Tepper wrote *dist*), *rmm, rmf, folder(s), scan, refile,* and *pick.* I then wrote *mhmail, anno, ali,* and *prompter* (because I was tired of using *vi* to do simple composes).

There were so many "small" decisions made during this process, it is amazing how consistent MH turned out to be. For example, I needed a way to name a folder as an argument to the MH commands, and I didn't want the user to have to type `-folder foo`. Even with abbreviations (a very non-UNIX design decision), this was too cumbersome. So, I introduced the `+folder` syntax. This also simplified the syntax when two folders could be specified (*refile,* for example). Because everything was modularized, I was able to add message names, like `first` and `last` without changing anything but a library routine. Many initial users wanted shorter names for commands—even the mostly four-letter lengths were too long for most users. Rather than rename the basic commands, I designed MH for use with shell aliases. Most users preferred *n* and *p* for *next* and *prev,* for example. Another common request was to combine *rmm* and *next,* which was commonly aliased as *rn,* or, for me, as `,` (that's right, a comma).

There are a few other design decisions which have been very successful. Default switches and global settings in the *.mh_profile* file worked very well. Pulling files out of the user's mail drop into an MH folder with *inc* provided a clean interface between the external mail delivery environment and MH.

Some early decisions have been changed by later developers of MH. For example, I felt that the backquote conventions of the shell were too clumsy for most users, so I didn't provide an *mhl* program, and *pick* had *scan* and *file* switches to make it useful. I also kept most changeable information in the *.mh_profile* file in an attempt to speed up MH operations. Most of these variables have been moved into other context files within the MH tree.

I think MH worked and has survived for many reasons. First, it is very UNIX-like. There isn't much to learn to use it. Second, it keeps its own context, which is almost completely independent from anything else the user is doing. A user can run *inc* or *comp* anywhere and any time without affecting his current context. Mail isn't something you stop to do—mail processing is interwoven into the fabric of a user's daily activities. You're running a program and discover a bug, you send a quick mail message, perhaps piping the output of the program into mail. No other package that I know of makes this type of interwoven mail handling so easy and intuitive. Finally, the structure of the source tree and the implementation of a comprehensive support library have made MH command development and support very easy. Any good UNIX programmer can modify an MH command, fix a bug, or add a new command with a few hours of source tree review.

I have a few regrets with MH. After using MH for a few years, I decided that some fundamental functionality of e-mail communication was missing. For example, I'd send a message to someone asking some simple question, and when I finally got a "yes" message back, I had no idea what the original question was, and no easy way to find it with MH. The bigger requirement here is for conversation support. Embedding replied-to messages in the body of a reply message is insanity. E-mail packages should provide automatic retrieval of the replied-to message. The In-reply-to: component is sufficient for this. Imagine being able to walk down a multi-branching tree of messages which represent a long-running conversation on some topic and its related topics. This is still missing from MH and other mail packages.

For many years, MH was limited to 999 messages in a folder. I made this decision consciously—anyone with that many messages in one folder needed to divide it up into subfolders. I'm not sure I should have imposed my own views this way.

It was many years from the time MH was completed until it was put in the public domain. I developed MH on Rand's own money (the MS development contract had been completed), and Rand worried about legal ramifications of releasing MH to the world. I'm very glad that MH has become public domain and that it is so widely used. Although I've done many exciting things in my career, I get the most satisfaction from MH, knowing how widely it is used and how well it has aged. I am also thankful to all the people who have worked on MH and enhanced it over the years. MH still has the same flavor, and when I look at the source tree, it is still familiar after 14 years!

Bruce Borden, July 1992

B.2 From Stockton Gaines

It is now 15 years since the beginning of MH, and inevitably there are some differences in what we all remember about those days. Herewith I include some of my own recollections ...

The memo from Norm and me speaks for itself. After the memo, there was a meeting to discuss it, at which almost everyone present (who shall remain nameless) opposed it. Arguments were given about inefficiencies, etc. Bruce arrived at Rand a month or so after this.

When he discovered our memo in the late spring of 1977, he came to talk to me and told me that he thought it would be pretty straightforward to create a mail system such as Norm and I had described. At that time, I headed a project funded by the Air Force, and I thought that this work would be appropriate, so I provided the support for Bruce.

My recollection is that six days after our conversation, Bruce showed us an initial version with about six commands working! I was extremely impressed with what Bruce was able to do, and naturally pleased that the ideas from the memo were validated. Bruce suggests that there was an initial working version in about three weeks, so probably what he demonstrated earlier wasn't complete enough to use.

The next several months were quite exciting. It is a prime example of experimental computer science, and it is impossible to imagine that MH would have evolved to what it became with more formal software engineering practices. To have begun with a full requirements specification and a top-level design would have been to rob the whole project of its creative energy.

During the initial period of development, all of the work and most of the ideas came from Bruce. However, others did contribute, including Norm and me, and also Bob Anderson.

Bruce made one significant invention that I found particularly impressive. The various commands for handling messages (for example, *forw*) needed to be able to work on subsets of the messages in a directory. Specifying a range was easy, but specifying by date or other contents of a message or header was not. We appeared to be in danger of ending up with an extremely complex command format for MH.

Bruce's elegant solution was to define a separate function, *pick*, to do the selection. The initial implementation simply linked all selected messages into a subfolder, from which the desired activities could be carried out (also an elegant idea). Subsequently, other ways of using the results of the *pick* command have been devised, but the insight of making *pick* a separate function was profound and has contributed greatly to the success of MH.

Stock Gaines, July 1992

C

Reference List X

Standard for the Format of ARPA Internet Text Messages (RFC822). Is presently available by *anonymous ftp* from many sites, including (at this writing) *nic.ddn.mil* in the directory *rfc*, *wuarchive.wustl.edu* in *rfc* (compressed files), and *src.doc.ic.ac.uk* in *rfc* (compressed files).

Proposed Standard for Message Encapsulation (RFC934). To get this, see RFC822 above.

Anderson, Robert H., Norman Z. Shapiro, Tora K. Bikson, and Phyllis H. Kantar, *The Design of the MH Mail System*, The RAND Corporation, Santa Monica (CA), December 1989. (N–3017–IRIS)

Borden, Bruce S., R. Stockton Gaines, and Norman Z. Shapiro, *The MH Message Handling System: User's Manual*, The RAND Corporation, Santa Monica (CA), November 1979. (R–2367–AF)

Dougherty, Dale, *sed & awk*, O'Reilly & Associates, Inc., Sebastopol (CA), November 1990.

Frey, Donnalyn, and Rick Adams, *!%@:: A Directory of Electronic Mail Addressing and Networks*, 2nd Edition, O'Reilly & Associates, Inc., Sebastopol (CA), May 1990.

Kernighan, Brian, and Rob Pike, *The UNIX Programming Environment*, Prentice-Hall, Inc., Englewood Cliffs (NJ), 1984.

Kochan, Stephen G., and Patrick H. Wood, *UNIX Shell Programming*, Hayden Books, Indianapolis (IN), 1985. (A revised edition is out, but it unfortunately doesn't cover the C Shell.)

Quercia, Valerie, and Tim O'Reilly, *Volume Three: X Window System User's Guide for X11 R3 and R4*, 3rd Edition, O'Reilly & Associates, Inc., Sebastopol (CA), May 1990.

Rose, M. T., E. A. Stefferud, and J. N. Sweet, "MH: A Multifarious User Agent," *Computer Networks*, Vol. 10, No. 2, September 1985, pp. 65–80. (This paper is distributed with MH.)

Rose, M. T., and John L. Romine, "MH.5: How to Process 200 Messages a Day and Still Get Some Real Work Done," Proceedings, Summer USENIX Conference and Exhibition, Portland, OR, June 1985, pp. 455-487. (This paper is distributed with MH.)

Rose, M. T., "The RAND MH Message Handling System: Administrator's Guide, UCI Version." (This paper is distributed with MH.)

Rose, M. T., "The RAND MH Message Handling System: The UCI BBoards Facility." (This paper is distributed with MH.)

Waite, Mitchell, D. Martin, and S. Prata, *UNIX Primer Plus*, H. W. Sams and Company (Indianapolis, IN).

D

Converting Messages to MH x

System Mailbox and Other Mail Files
Converting from UNIX mail Program
Converting from VMS Mail
Converting from GNU-emacs Rmail
Converting from Other Mail Systems

If you've never used any mail agent besides MH, you don't need to read this appendix. This is for people who've been using a different e-mail system on UNIX or another operating system and want to use MH instead. It explains the ways that other mail agents store messages, and it lists ways to convert those messages to MH. If you're moving from another operating system to UNIX and you'll be using MH on UNIX, you can probably convert your mail messages from the other system to MH.

This appendix has procedures for using MH and UNIX commands to convert your mail. It also has two shell scripts, which you can type in yourself or copy from the archive on the *uunet* computer (see Appendix E, *Copies of Files Over the Network*).

These procedures and shell scripts aren't guaranteed to work with every mail message you have, with every version of the mail systems, and so on. They also may not convert your mail messages perfectly. But they should get you close—and, because MH stores its messages in individual UNIX files, you can always use a text editor to do final cleanup on the messages. Finally, if you find a bug or have a suggestion, please tell us about it. Our address is in the Preface. We'll update the online archives periodically. If you got your copy of a script awhile ago, you might look for an updated version online.

D.1 System Mailbox and Other Mail Files

When someone sends you new mail, your computer's mail transport agent adds the new message to the end of your system mailbox file. The system mailbox has a name something like */usr/spool/mail/johndoe*. It's usually not stored in or under your home directory.

Some mail agents store all of your messages, both old and new, in the system mailbox. If you use one of these mail agents, converting to MH is easy. When you run the *inc* command, it automatically moves all messages—old and new—from the system mailbox into your *inbox* folder.

Other user mail agents—programs like *elm* and GNU *emacs rmail*—will store old messages as a group, in one or more special mail files. Because MH stores your mail messages differently, each message is kept in a separate file on the disk—you'll want to convert your old mail files to MH.

D.2 Converting from UNIX mail Program

The UNIX program called *mail* keeps messages in two places:

- Existing messages are saved in a file named *mbox* in your account's home directory. You can make a backup copy, then read them into your MH *inbox* automatically with these commands:

  ```
  % cd
  % cp mbox mbox.backup
  % inc -file mbox
  ```

  If you see the usual `Incorporating new mail into inbox . . .` message and a scan listing, the messages probably were converted. Read some or all of them (with the *show* command) and be sure. Then you can remove your *mbox* (and the backup copy you made with *cp*) by typing:

  ```
  % rm mbox mbox.backup
  ```

- New messages go to the same system mailbox file that MH uses. To bring them into your MH folder, you just have to type:

  ```
  % inc
  ```

D.3 Converting from VMS Mail

The VMS Mail utility stores mail in an indexed file. If you use its *EXTRACT/ALL* command, you can extract all the messages from a VMS mail folder into a text file. Then use file transfer software such as *ftp* to move the extracted messages to a UNIX system. Finally, run the shell script called *vmsmail2mh* in Section D.3.1. It will split the VMS messages into separate MH files. If you haven't done much work on UNIX or with shell programming, you should probably read Chapter 12, *Introduction to Shell Programming for MH*, first.

D.3.1 The vmsmail2mh Shell Script

```
 1> #! /bin/sh
 2> # $Id: vmsmail2mh,v 1.2 90/03/22 06:53:59 jdpeek Exp $
 3> ### vmsmail2mh - split VMS mail messages from EXTRACT/ALL into MH folder
 4> ### Usage: vmsmail2mh [+folder] [...vmsmsg-files]
 5> ##
 6> ##   AN EASY WAY TO TRANSFER VMS MAIL MESSAGES TO UNIX IS BY EXTRACTING
 7> ##   ALL THE MESSAGES FROM A VMS MAIL FOLDER INTO A FILE... USE:
 8> ##       MAIL> EXTRACT/ALL
 9> ##       _file: FILENAME
10> ##   THEN, YOU CAN TRANSFER THEM TO THE SYSTEM RUNNING MH.
11> ##
12> ##   WHEN YOU GET THEM TO THE MH SYSTEM, vmsmail2mh WILL READ THROUGH
13> ##   THE FILE (OR STANDARD INPUT, IF YOU DON'T GIVE A FILENAME):
14> ##       - THE MESSAGES ARE SEPARATED BY FORMFEEDS (CONTROL-L).
15> ##         vmsmail2mh WILL CUT THEM INTO SEPARATE MH MESSAGES
16> ##         IN THE CURRENT FOLDER (OR +folder IF YOU GIVE ONE).
17> ##       - THE FORMAT OF THE VMS MAIL MESSAGE IS DIFFERENT.
18> ##         * Subj: LINES ARE CONVERTED TO Subject: LINES.
19> ##         * From: LINES ARE SPLIT INTO From: AND Date: LINES.
20> ##         ONLY THE FIRST Subj: AND From: IN EACH MESSAGE IS CONVERTED.
21> ##
22> ##   BUG: VMS ADDRESSES LIKE:
23> ##       SMTP%"user@host"
24> ##       HOST::USER
25> ##   AREN'T CONVERTED.  IN FACT, *NO* ADDRESSES ARE CONVERTED.
26>
27> #    NOTE: PROGRAM HASN'T BEEN TESTED THOROUGHLY.
28> #    CHECK THE MESSAGES!
```

```
29> #    Placed in the public domain.  Use at your own risk.
30> #         --Jerry Peek, 22 March 1990
31>
32> dfltprot=600    # DEFAULT MESSAGE PROTECTION (IF NONE IN MH PROFILE)
33> folopts="-fast -nolist -nototal -nopack -norecurse"
34> mh=/usr/local/mh
35> mhprofile=/xxx/yyy/mhprofile # READS MH PROFILE
36> scanopts="-noclear -noheader -noreverse"
37>
38> case "$1" in
39> [@+]?*)
40>     # IF $1 DOESN'T EXIST, folder WILL CREATE IT (SIGH).
41>     # THAT'S BECAUSE stdout IS REDIRECTED AWAY FROM TERMINAL.
42>     if $mh/folder $folopts "$1" >/dev/null
43>     then
44>         # GET PATHNAME OF FOLDER, LAST MESSAGE NUMBER:
45>         folpath="`$mh/mhpath`" || exit
46>         firstmsg="`$mh/scan -format '%(msg)' last`" || exit
47>     else
48>         echo "`basename $0`: no folder.  quitting." 1>&2
49>         exit 1
50>     fi
51>     ;;
52> *)  echo "Usage: `basename $0` +folder|@folder [file]
53>     ('$1' doesn't start with + or @.)" 1>&2
54>     exit 1
55>     ;;
56> esac
57>
58> if [ -n "$2" -a \( ! -r "$2" \) ]
59> then
60>     echo "`basename $0`: quitting: can't read VMS file '$2'." 1>&2
61>     exit 1
62> fi
63>
64> # GET PROTECTION MODE FROM MH PROFILE (IF NONE, USE $dfltprot):
65> msgprot="`$mhprofile -b msg-protect`" || msgprot=$dfltprot
66>
67> # MAKE SHELL ARCHIVE FILE ON awk'S STANDARD OUTPUT.
68> # PIPE IT INTO sh TO CREATE THE MESSAGE FILES...
69> awk "BEGIN {
70>     folpath=\"$folpath\" # STORE AS STRING, WITH QUOTES
71>     msgprot=$msgprot     # STORE AS NUMBER (NO QUOTES)
72>     msgnum=$firstmsg'    # CHANGE FROM DOUBLE TO SINGLE QUOTES
73>     inmsg = 0
74> }
75> # PROCESS MESSAGES.  EACH MESSAGE STARTS WITH CONTROL-L.
76> # HOPE THERE ARE NO LINES WITH JUST A CONTROL-L IN MESSAGES!
77> {
78>     # MESSAGE STARTS WITH CTRL-L ON A LINE BY ITSELF.
79>     # PRINT SHELL COMMANDS AND RESET FLAGS:
80>     if ($0 ~ /^\014$/ && inmsg == 1) {
81>         printf "END-OF-%s/%d\n", folpath, msgnum
```

```
 82>        # SET PROTECTION (INEFFICIENT; SHOULD DO ALL MSGS. AT ONCE)
 83>        printf "chmod %d %s/%d\n\n", msgprot, folpath, msgnum
 84>        inmsg = 0
 85>    }
 86>    # AT START OF MESSAGE, PRINT START OF ARCHIVE AND SET FLAGS:
 87>    if (inmsg == 0) {
 88>        inmsg = 1
 89>        msgnum += 1
 90>        printf "/bin/cat > %s/%d << \\END-OF-%s/%d\n", \
 91>            folpath, msgnum, folpath, msgnum
 92>        didsubj = 0
 93>        didfrom = 0
 94>        next
 95>    }
 96>    # TURN Subj: INTO Subject: AND SET FLAG TO MAKE SURE WE DO NOT
 97>    # TRASH ANY OTHER Subj: LINES (LIKE IN FORWARDED MESSAGES).
 98>    # STRIP DATE (14-MAR-1990 15:31:12.02) OFF END OF THE From: LINE
 99>    # AND MOVE IT TO LINE OF ITS OWN, THEN SET FLAG LIKE ABOVE:
100>    if ($1 ~ /^Subj:/ && didsubj == 0) {
101>        $1 = "Subject:"
102>        didsubj = 1
103>        print
104>    }
105>    else if ($1 ~ /^From:/ && didfrom == 0) {
106>        for (i = 1; i <= NF - 3; i++)
107>            printf "%s ", $i
108>        printf "%s\n", $(NF - 2)
109>        printf "Date: %s %s\n", $(NF - 1), $NF
110>        didfrom = 1
111>    }
112>    else
113>        print
114> }' $2 |     # IF NO $2, WILL READ STANDARD INPUT...
115> /bin/sh -e  # EXIT ON ANY ERROR
116>
117> exit # RETURN STATUS FROM PIPE ABOVE
```

D.3.2   Explanation of vmsmail2mh Script

(Note: This explanation assumes that you've read Chapter 12, *Introduction to Shell Programming for MH*, and have followed the sample programs in Chapter 13, *MH Shell Programs*.)

The script converts a VMS-style message file, which looks something like this:

```
^L
From:   NODE::USERNAME   "Personal Information"   DATE   TIME
To:     NODE::USERNAME
CC:     NODE::USERNAME
SUBJ:   SUBJECT
```

```
BODY
^L
From:   NODE::USERNAME    "Personal Information"  DATE   TIME
To:     NODE::USERNAME
CC:     NODE::USERNAME
SUBJ:   SUBJECT

BODY
```

to an intermediate shell archive format, which looks like this:

```
/bin/cat > /yourMHdir/inbox/23 << \END-OF-/yourMHdir/inbox/23
From: NODE::USERNAME    "Personal Information"
Date: DATE   TIME
To:     NODE::USERNAME
CC:     NODE::USERNAME
SUBJ:   SUBJECT

BODY
END-OF-/yourMHdir/inbox/23
chmod 600 /yourMHdir/inbox/23

/bin/cat > /yourMHdir/inbox/24 << \END-OF-/yourMHdir/inbox/24
From: NODE::USERNAME    "Personal Information"
Date: DATE   TIME
To:     NODE::USERNAME
CC:     NODE::USERNAME
SUBJ:   SUBJECT

BODY
END-OF-/yourMHdir/inbox/24
chmod 600 /yourMHdir/inbox/24
```

From there, a Bourne shell creates the actual files in one pass.

About the program:

Line 46 gets the last message number in the folder with a simple *scan* format string; the last argument means that *scan* will only scan the last message. This number is incremented in the loop to get numbers for the new messages that the script makes.

The test in **line 58** first checks (with −n) to see if $2 is set at all, before it tests for readability. Some versions of *test*(1) will return unreliable answers unless the test checks for a nonempty string.

Line 69 starts an *awk* script. It starts with a doublequote ("). The matching double quote is on **line 72**. This lets us pass in the shell variables $msgprot and $firstmsg. In line 72, because we open a singlequote, the rest of this script can use the *awk* $ without worrying about the shell interpreting it.

Lines 80-85 are invoked at the start of every message *except* the first one. They make a terminator for a here-document and a *chmod* command to set the message protection (part of the shell archive format that this *awk* script generates on its standard output).

Lines 87-95 start a new message file in the shell archive. They increment the msgnum variable so that the archive file has the next highest message number in the folder.

Lines 100-104 change the first Subj: line in every message so that they read Subject:, and then set a flag to be sure that any other Subj: lines are not converted.

Lines 105-111 split the VMS Mail From: line, which has both the sender's address and the date, into separate From: and Date: lines—again, it sets a flag to be sure this is only done once per message. If the text isn't the first Subj: or From: line, then the text is printed as is in **line 113**.

Line 114 starts a pipe that sends the standard output of the *awk* script, which is in shell archive format now, to the standard input of a Bourne Shell. The shell creates the files. The −e flag means the shell will abort right away if it has trouble creating any of the message files.

D.4 Converting from GNU-emacs Rmail

The GNU-*emacs* editor has a mail handler called *Rmail*. (This isn't the same as GNU *emacs MH-Rmail*, which is a front end to MH.) *Rmail* stores mail in files with names like *RMAIL* in a format called *babyl*.

Babyl format is nothing like the standard UNIX *mail* format; you can't just *inc* the *Rmail* file. Instead, a shell script named *babyl2mh* in Appendix D, *Converting Messages to MH*, can help you convert your files. If you haven't done much work on UNIX or with shell programming, look into Chapter 12, *Introduction to Shell Programming for MH*, first.

D.4.1 The babyl2mh Shell Script

```
1> #! /bin/sh
2> # $Id: babyl2mh,v 1.1 90/03/22 03:57:05 jdpeek Exp $
3> ### babyl2mh - slow way to convert GNU emacs Rmail files to MH
4> ### Usage: babyl2mh +mh-folder [RMAIL-FILE]
5>
6> #    NOTE: PROGRAM HASN'T BEEN TESTED THOROUGHLY.
7> #    CHECK THE MESSAGES!
```

```
 8> #    Placed in the public domain.  Use at your own risk.
 9> #         --Jerry Peek, 22 March 1990
10>
11> dfltprot=600     # DEFAULT MESSAGE PROTECTION (IF NONE IN MH PROFILE)
12> folopts="-fast -nolist -nototal -nopack -norecurse"
13> mh=/usr/local/mh
14> mhprofile=/xxx/yyy/mhprofile # READS MH PROFILE
15> scanopts="-noclear -noheader -noreverse"
16>
17> case "$1" in
18> [@+]?*)
19>     # IF $1 DOESN'T EXIST, folder WILL CREATE IT (SIGH).
20>     # THAT'S BECAUSE stdout IS REDIRECTED AWAY FROM TERMINAL.
21>     if $mh/folder $folopts "$1" >/dev/null
22>     then
23>         # GET PATHNAME OF FOLDER, LAST MESSAGE NUMBER:
24>         folpath="`$mh/mhpath`" || exit
25>         firstmsg="`$mh/scan -format '%(msg)' last`" || exit
26>     else
27>         echo "`basename $0`: no folder.  quitting." 1>&2
28>         exit 1
29>     fi
30>     ;;
31> *)  echo "Usage: `basename $0` +folder|@folder [file]
32>     ('$1' doesn't start with + or @.)" 1>&2
33>     exit 1
34>     ;;
35> esac
36>
37> if [ -n "$2" -a \( ! -r "$2" \) ]
38> then
39>     echo "`basename $0`: quitting: can't read Rmail file '$2'." 1>&2
40>     exit 1
41> fi
42>
43> # GET PROTECTION MODE FROM MH PROFILE (IF NONE, USE $dfltprot):
44> msgprot="`$mhprofile -b msg-protect`" || msgprot=$dfltprot
45>
46> # MAKE SHELL ARCHIVE FILE ON awk'S STANDARD OUTPUT.
47> # PIPE IT INTO sh TO CREATE THE MESSAGE FILES...
48> awk "BEGIN {
49>     folpath=\"$folpath\" # STORE AS STRING, WITH QUOTES
50>     msgprot=$msgprot     # STORE AS NUMBER (NO QUOTES)
51>     msgnum=$firstmsg"'   # CHANGE FROM DOUBLE- TO SINGLE-QUOTES
52>     gotflags=0
53>     gotgoodhdr=0
54>     gotbadhdr=0
55> }
56> # SKIP BABYL HEADER:
57> NR==1, /\037\014/ {
58>     next
59> }
60> # PROCESS MESSAGES.  USE gotflags, ETC. TO "REMEMBER"
```

```
 61>  # WHEN WE HAVE PASSED EACH PART OF EACH MESSAGE.
 62>  {
 63>      # MESSAGE ENDS WITH CTRL-UNDERSCORE AT START OF A LINE.
 64>      # PRINT SHELL COMMANDS AND RESET FLAGS:
 65>      if ($0 ~ /^\037/) {
 66>          printf "END-OF-%s/%d\n\n", folpath, msgnum
 67>          # SET PROTECTION (INEFFICIENT; SHOULD DO ALL MSGS. AT ONCE)
 68>          printf "chmod %d %s/%d\n", msgprot, folpath, msgnum
 69>          gotflags = 0
 70>          gotgoodhdr = 0
 71>          gotbadhdr = 0
 72>          next
 73>      }
 74>      # INSTEAD OF FLAGS LINE (LIKE "1,,"), PRINT START OF ARCHIVE:
 75>      if (gotflags == 0) {
 76>          gotflags = 1
 77>          msgnum += 1
 78>          printf "/bin/cat > %s/%d << \\END-OF-%s/%d\n", \
 79>              folpath, msgnum, folpath, msgnum
 80>          next
 81>      }
 82>      # PRINT THE FULL HEADER (UP TO FIRST BLANK LINE):
 83>      if (gotgoodhdr == 0) {
 84>          if ($0 !~ /^$/) {
 85>              print
 86>              next
 87>          }
 88>          else {
 89>              gotgoodhdr = 1
 90>              next
 91>          }
 92>      }
 93>      # SKIP THE SHORT HEADER (UP TO NEXT BLANK LINE):
 94>      if (gotbadhdr == 0 && $0 !~ /^$/)
 95>          next
 96>      gotbadhdr = 1
 97>      # PRINT THE MESSAGE (UP TO ^_):
 98>      print
 99>      next
100>  }' $2 |
101>  /bin/sh -e   # EXIT ON ANY ERROR
102>
103>  exit # RETURN STATUS FROM PIPE ABOVE
```

D.4.2   Explanation of babyl2mh Script

The script converts a GNU-emacs *babyl* mail file, which looks something like this:

```
BABYL OPTIONS:
Version: 5
Labels:
Note:    This is the header of an rmail file.
Note:    If you are seeing it in rmail,
Note:     it means the file has no messages in it.
^_^L
1,,
Date: Mon, 07 Dec 92 08:16:20 EST
From: ehuser (Emma H. User)
Received: by bigsun.ncs.syr.edu (5.54/ACS)
        id AA02012; Mon, 07 Dec 92 08:16:20 EST
Message-Id: <9003191316.AA02012@bigsun.ncs.syr.edu>
To: ehuser
Subject: test of GNU emacs rmail sending

*** EOOH ***
Date: Mon, 07 Dec 92 08:16:20 EST
From: ehuser (Emma H. User)
To: ehuser
Subject: test of GNU emacs rmail sending

This is a test.  What will happen?

We'll see..

^_^L
1,,
Date: Mon, 07 Dec 92 08:18:31 EST
From: ehuser (Emma H. User)
Received: by bigsun.ncs.syr.edu (5.54/ACS)
        id AA02048; Mon, 07 Dec 92 08:18:31 EST
Message-Id: <9003191318.AA02048@bigsun.ncs.syr.edu>
To: ehuser
Subject: test from 'mail' program

*** EOOH ***
Date: Mon, 07 Dec 92 08:18:31 EST
From: ehuser (Emma H. User)
To: ehuser
Subject: test from 'mail' program

I'm sending this test from the standard UNIX "mail"
program.

^_
```

The file is converted to the same shell archive format as shown above for *vmsmail2mh*.

About the script:

Lines 57-58 skip the *babyl* header.

Lines 65-81 do the same thing as their counterparts in the *vmsmail2mh* script: they make the shell archive start and end.

Lines 93-96 skip the second header, which starts with the * * * EOOH * * * line, because the same information is in the first header.

D.5 Converting from Other Mail Systems

If you're using e-mail on another computer and can get the messages into one or more files on your UNIX computer, you can probably convert them to MH.

If one of the shell programs in this appendix isn't exactly what you need, you might be able to adapt it.

Otherwise, here are the basic things you'll need to do:

1. Get your messages from the other system into text files. The easiest way is to have one message per file. But you can also pack a lot of messages into a single file, as long as every message starts with a recognizable pattern.

2. Transfer the text file to the UNIX system with a program like *ftp*, *rcp*, *kermit*, etc. Or put it on magnetic tape. You might also be able to use a personal computer for intermediate file storage.

3. Reformat the messages to have a header, followed by a blank line, followed by the message body. Look at typical MH messages throughout this book, or start up MH and create a few messages to see what they're like.

   If there are just a few messages, it might be easier to use a text editor to re-format each message by hand. If there are lots of messages, a shell program can help.

4. When you have a single converted message in a single file, use a command similar to:

   ```
   % cp message `mhpath new +somefolder`
   ```

This command uses *mhpath* to find a new message number and copies the message into the MH folder. Or write a shell loop that puts the messages into a new folder in files called *1*, *2*, *3*, and so on.

Good luck. Even if converting is kind of tough, MH will be worth the work!

E

Copies of Files Over the Network $\boxed{X}$

Obtaining the Example Programs
MH
MH Scripts and Examples

Most of the complicated files in this book—like *scan* format files and the shell scripts from Chapter 13, *MH Shell Programs*—are available electronically. You can also get the latest copies of MH itself, as well as other programs and archives of the *mh-users* mailing list.

E.1 Obtaining the Example Programs

The example programs in this book are available electronically in a number of ways: by ftp, ftpmail, bitftp, and uucp. The cheapest, fastest, and easiest ways are listed first. If you read from the top down, the first one that works for you is probably the best. Use *ftp* if you are directly on the Internet. Use ftpmail if you are not on the Internet but can send and receive electronic mail to internet sites (this includes CompuServe users). Use BITFTP if you send electronic mail via BIT-NET. Use UUCP if none of the above works.

E.1.1 FTP

To use FTP, you need a machine with direct access to the Internet. A sample session is shown, with what you should type in boldface.

```
% ftp ftp.uu.net
Connected to ftp.uu.net.
220 FTP server (Version 6.21 Tue Mar 10 22:09:55 EST 1992) ready.
Name (ftp.uu.net:ambar): anonymous
331 Guest login ok, send domain style e-mail address as password.
Password: ambar@ora.com (use your user name and host here)
230 Guest login ok, access restrictions apply.
ftp> cd /published/oreilly/nutshell/MHxmh
250 CWD command successful.
ftp> binary (Very important! You must specify binary transfer for compressed files.)
200 Type set to I.
ftp> get MHxmh2.tar.Z
200 PORT command successful.
150 Opening BINARY mode data connection for MHxmh2.tar.Z.
226 Transfer complete.
ftp> quit
221 Goodbye.
%
```

The file is a compressed tar archive. Extract the files from the archive by typing:

```
% zcat MHxmh2.tar.Z | tar xf -
```

System V systems require the following tar command instead:

```
% zcat MHxmh2.tar.Z | tar xof -
```

If *zcat* is not available on your system, use separate *uncompress* and *tar* commands.

E.1.2 FTPMAIL

FTPMAIL is a mail server available to anyone who can send and receive electronic mail to and from Internet sites. This includes most workstations that have an e-mail connection to the outside world, and CompuServe users. You do not need to be directly on the Internet. Here's how to do it.

You send mail to *ftpmail@decwrl.dec.com*. In the message body, give the name of the anonymous ftp host and the ftp commands you want to run. The server will run anonymous ftp for you and mail the files back to you. To get a complete help file, send a message with no subject and the single word *help* in the body. The following is an example mail session that should get you the examples. This command sends you a listing of the files in the selected directory, and the requested examples file. The listing is useful in case there's a later version of the examples you're interested in.

```
% comp
To: ftpmail@decwrl.dec.com
Cc:
Subject:
------
reply alan@ora.com                    (where you want files mailed)
connect ftp.uu.net
chdir /published/oreilly/nutshell/MHxmh
dir
binary
uuencode                              (or btoa if you have it)
get MHxmh2.tar.Z
quit
CTRL-D
--------
What now? send
```

A signature at the end of the message is acceptable as long as it appears after "quit."

All retrieved files will be split into 60KB chunks and mailed to you. You then remove the mail headers and concatenate them into one file, and then *uudecode* or *btoa* it. Once you've got the desired file, follow the directions under FTP to extract the files from the archive.

VMS, DOS, and Mac versions of *uudecode*, *btoa*, *uncompress*, and *tar* are available. The VMS versions are on *gatekeeper.dec.com* in */archive/pub/VMS*.

E.1.3 BITFTP

BITFTP is a mail server for BITNET users. You send it electronic mail messages requesting files, and it sends you back the files by electronic mail. BITFTP currently serves only users who send it mail from nodes that are directly on BITNET, EARN, or NetNorth. BITFTP is a public service of Princeton University. Here's how it works.

To use BITFTP, send mail containing your ftp commands to *BITFTP@PUCC*. For a complete help file, send HELP as the message body.

The following is the message body you should send to BITFTP:

```
FTP  ftp.uu.net  NETDATA
USER  anonymous
PASS your Internet e-mail address (not your BITNET address)
CD  /published/oreilly/nutshell/MHxmh
```

```
DIR
BINARY
GET  MHxmh2.tar.Z
QUIT
```

Once you've got the desired file, follow the directions under FTP to extract the files from the archive. Since you are probably not on a UNIX system, you may need to get versions of *uudecode*, *uncompress*, *btoa*, and *tar* for your system. VMS, DOS, and Mac versions are available. The VMS versions are on *gatekeeper.dec.com* in */archive/pub/VMS*.

Questions about BITFTP can be directed to Melinda Varian, *MAINT@PUCC* on BITNET.

E.1.4 UUCP

UUCP is standard on virtually all UNIX systems, and is available for IBM-compatible PCs and Apple Macintoshes. The examples are available by UUCP via modem from UUNET; UUNET's connect-time charges apply.

You can get the examples from UUNET whether you have an account or not. If you or your company has an account with UUNET, you will have a system with a direct UUCP connection to UUNET. Find that system, and type:

```
uucp uunet\!~/published/oreilly/nutshell/MHxmh/MHxmh2.tar.Z yourhost\!~/yourname/
```

The backslashes can be omitted if you use the Bourne shell (*sh*) instead of *csh*. The file should appear some time later (up to a day or more) in the directory */usr/spool/uucppublic/yourname*. If you don't have an account but would like one so that you can get electronic mail, then contact UUNET at 703-204-8000.

If you don't have a UUNET account, you can set up a UUCP connection to UUNET using the phone number 1-900-468-7727. As of this writing, the cost is 50 cents per minute. The charges will appear on your next telephone bill. The login name is "uucp" with no password. For example, an *L.sys/Systems* entry might look like:

```
uunet Any ACU 19200 1-900-468-7727 ogin:--ogin: uucp
```

Your entry may vary depending on your UUCP configuration. If you have a PEP-capable modem, make sure s50=255s111=30 is set before calling.

It's a good idea to get the file */published/oreilly/nutshell/ls-lR.Z* as a short test file containing the filenames and sizes of all the files in the directory.

Once you've got the desired file, follow the directions under FTP to extract the files from the archive.

E.2 MH

You can use the commands in Section E.1 to get the latest version of MH from the hosts *ftp.ics.uci.edu* and *louie.udel.edu*. Other sites may have older versions (the version on *ftp.uu.net* usually seems to be up to date). In Europe, you can get a copy of MH via e-mail from the mail server at *mail–server@nluug.nl*. Start by sending a message with *help* in the body. After you've read the server's help message, ask for the file *mail/mh/MH.6.7.2.Z*. Outside North America and Europe, check with your network or system administrator for best route to get MH on your continent—the MH file is big; getting it from a site on another continent can be expensive and slow.

Depending on the site you're copying MH from, there can be several directories and files. There might be an update directory with copies of the latest enhancements and bug fixes. Look for a file named *mh–6.7.tar.Z*—that's the MH 6.7.2 (or MH 6.7!) archive file. Copy it and any update files to your host. (The MH file is big: about 1.5 Megabytes compressed. As a courtesy to other network users, you should probably transfer it in the evening or overnight.)

E.3 MH Scripts and Examples

The anonymous ftp site *ftp.ics.uci.edu* has a directory named *pub/mh/contrib* with assorted shell programs and MH examples. You can access it by any of the methods in Section E.1 above, except *uucp*.

F

The execit Programs

How execit Works
Getting the Program Files
The Program Files

This is the *execit* program that lets you make multiple versions of MH commands. It's written in the C programming language. For an introduction, see Section 9.2.

F.1 How execit Works

The purpose of the *execit* program is to run an MH command but give the command a different name as it runs. That new name is put in *argv[0]*, where the command can read it. Because each MH command reads a component with its name in your *.mh_profile* file, you can set different options from those for the command's normal name.

Before you compile *execit*, you define a table of command names and pathnames called *execit.include*. There's a short table in Section F.3.2.

After you compile *execit*, you make one link to it with the name of each new command from the left-hand column of the *execit.include* file. Because these are links (sometimes called "hard links"), they take practically no disk space. You can make as many as you want. You generally do this in a directory like your *bin*, a central place for executable files. The shell script in Section F.3.3 will make the links automatically.

This program is named *execit* because it uses the UNIX *exec()* system call to run the command directly. First, *execit* checks *argv[0]* to find out what name you ran it with. Then it finds the pathname of the real MH command you want to run from the (compiled-in) *execit.include* table. Finally, *execit* overlays its running image with the MH program you want to run.

The comment block of the C program source (in Section F.3.1) has more information.

F.2   Getting the Program Files

You can create each file by hand by typing in the code below. If you don't type all of the long *execit.c* comment block, this won't take too long. You can also get the files electronically from the *MHxmh2.tar.Z* file. There are instructions in Appendix E, *Copies of Files Over the Network*.

F.3   The Program Files

F.3.1   execit.c

This should compile with a standard UNIX C compiler. The code is very simple—most of the file consists of comments!

```
#ifndef lint
static char *rcsid = "$Id: execit.c,v 1.3 90/02/17 07:18:39 jdpeek Exp $";
#endif

/* execit - run a program; use a different name
 *
 *   Usage: progname [arguments]
 *
 *   Some programs, especially MH programs, check the name they're
 *   invoked with (from their argv[0]) and change the way they work.
 *   The easiest way to do this with system programs is to make a new
 *   link (symbolic or "hard") to the program's executable code, like this:
 *   % ln /usr/local/bin/folder /usr/myhome/bin/folders
 *   Then, you can run "folder" with the name "folders".
 *
 *   The problems with that are:  you can only make hard links (ln) if
 *   you have access to a directory on the same filesystem as the system
```

```
 *   executables.  And some systems don't have symbolic links (ln -s).
 *   That's when you need "execit".  This "execit" program lets you
 *   define a table of system commands and the names you want to run them
 *   with.  Then, you make a link to "execit" with the name of the program
 *   you want to run.  It invokes the system program with the name you use.
 *   This way, you get fast execution of a system program with your own name.
 *   And, if you make new hard links to "execit", defining new program names
 *   doesn't take any more filesystem space.
 *
 *   Here's an example of how to set up "execit" so it will run the program
 *   "/usr/local/mh/repl", but make "repl" think its name is "replx":
 *
 *   1) Edit the file "execit.include" and add a new line like this:
 *           "replx", "/usr/local/mh/repl",
 *       (the second string should be where repl is located on your system!)
 *       Be sure to make the line look just like that -- quotes and commas.
 *       This file is read into the xref structure at compile time.
 *
 *   2) Recompile this program, something like this:
 *           % cc -o execit execit.c
 *
 *   3) If there were no errors, make a link to "execit" named "replx":
 *           % ln execit replx
 *       Then, use "ls -li" to be sure previous links to "execit" still exist:
 *           % ls -li execit replx tscan
 *           2379 -rwx------ 3 jdpeek 35982 Feb 10 22:14 execit
 *           2379 -rwx------ 3 jdpeek 35982 Feb 10 22:14 replx
 *           2379 -rwx------ 3 jdpeek 35982 Feb 10 22:14 tscan
 *           ^^^^             ^      ^^^^^^^^^^^^
 *           SAME            SAME                TODAY'S
 *           i-NUMS          LINK COUNT          DATE AND TIME
 *
 *       (Delete any old links and re-link to the new "execit" with "ln".)
 *
 *   4) Now, assuming the directory is in your shell's search path,
 *       (and, for MH programs, you may want a line in .mh_profile like this:
 *           replx: -switches -go -here
 *       ) you can run "replx" and pass the switch "-query" to it this way:
 *               % replx -query
 *
 *   Placed in the public domain by its author, Jerry Peek, 12 February 1990.
 *   (jdpeek@rodan.acs.syr.edu)  Use at your own risk.  Suggestions welcome!
 */
#include <stdio.h>

/* Table of command name user wants to run as,
 * and full pathname of actual system program to run.
 * Edit the "execit.include" file to add more entries to the structure below;
 * then recompile and re-link this code with the new name.
 */
struct xref {
    char *runas, *torun;
} xrefs[] = {
```

```
      "EDIT_ME", "/YOUR/PATH/NAME/HERE",
#include "execit.include"
      "tscan", "/usr/local/mh/scan"
};

main(argc, argv, envp)
int argc;
char **argv, **envp;
{
    char *myname, *p;
    int ret, index, bogus;
    int numcmds = sizeof(xrefs) / sizeof(struct xref);

    /* Get basename of this program by stepping past final '/': */
    myname = p = *argv;
    while (*p)
        if (*p++ == '/')
            myname = p;

    /* Find program to run (xrefs[index].torun) from lookup table: */
    bogus = 1;
    for (index = 0; index < numcmds; index++) {
        if (strcmp(myname, xrefs[index].runas) == 0) {
            bogus = 0;  /* found it */
            break;
        }
    }
    if (bogus) {
        fprintf(stderr,
        "%s: Can't run myself!  Fix execit.include and/or run execit.link.\n",
        argv[0]);
        exit(1);
    }

    /* Set fake program name in argv[0], then try to run real program.
     * If exec succeeds, return program's exit status.
     * Otherwise, print errno message and return -1.
     */
    argv[0] = xrefs[index].runas;
    if ((ret = execve(xrefs[index].torun, argv, envp)) != -1)
        exit(ret);
    else {
        perror(xrefs[index].torun);
        exit(-1);
    }
}
```

F.3.2 execit.include

This is the file that is compiled into *execit.c*. When you add lines to it, be sure to use the same format. See instructions in the *execit.c* comment block.

This file has two sample lines in it. They're not required; they're just here as an example:

```
"thanks", "/usr/local/mh/repl",
"replx", "/usr/local/mh/repl",
```

F.3.3 execit.link

This little shell script reads the *execit.include* file and automatically builds the links. Run it after you've recompiled *execit.c*.

```
#! /bin/sh
incfile=execit.include
dest=/xxx/yyy/bin # WHERE YOUR LINKS SHOULD GO
if [ ! -r $incfile ]
then
        echo "`basename $0`: can't read '$incfile'; quitting." 1>&2
        exit 1
fi

# EACH LINE OF $incfile HAS LINK NAME AND PROGRAM, LIKE THIS:
#       "thanks", "/usr/local/mh/repl",
# USE sed TO GRAB FIRST WORD ON EACH LINE, WITHOUT THE QUOTES.
for link in `sed 's/^[^"]*"\([^"][^"]*\)".*/\1/' $incfile`
do
        rm -f $dest/$link
        ln ./execit $dest/$link
done
exit 0
```

G

Customizing xmh: Configuration Files

Overview
clients/xmh/Xmh.sample File
app-defaults/Xmh File

G.1 Overview

The files in this appendix show examples of customizing *xmh*. Look through the files and pick customizations that you like; you don't have to use the whole file. Add the entries to your resource manager file (like *.Xdefaults*).

These files come with the distribution of the X Window System, Version 11 Release 5—from the */usr/lib/X11* directory. They're a supplement to the information in Chapter 16, *Customizing xmh*.

G.2 clients/xmh/Xmh.sample File

```
!       Examples of customizing xmh with resource specifications.
!       These can be copied to your private X resource file or to
!       a private Xmh application defaults file.

!       To create command buttons in the middle of the main window:

Xmh*CommandButtonCount:        8

Xmh*commandBox.button1.label:    inc
Xmh*commandBox.button1.translations: #override\
     <Btn1Down>,<Btn1Up>: XmhIncorporateNewMail() unset()

Xmh*commandBox.button2.label:    compose
Xmh*commandBox.button2.translations: #override\
     <Btn1Down>,<Btn1Up>: XmhComposeMessage() unset()

Xmh*commandBox.button3.label:    next
Xmh*commandBox.button3.translations: #override\
     <Btn1Down>,<Btn1Up>: XmhViewNextMessage() unset()

Xmh*commandBox.button4.label:    prev
Xmh*commandBox.button4.translations: #override\
     <Btn1Down>,<Btn1Up>: XmhViewPreviousMessage() unset()

Xmh*commandBox.button5.label:    commit
Xmh*commandBox.button5.translations: #override\
     <Btn1Down>,<Btn1Up>: XmhCommitChanges() unset()

Xmh*commandBox.button6.label:    delete
Xmh*commandBox.button6.translations: #override\
     <Btn1Down>,<Btn1Up>: XmhMarkDelete() unset()

Xmh*commandBox.button7.label:    move
Xmh*commandBox.button7.translations: #override\
     <Btn1Down>,<Btn1Up>: XmhMarkMove() unset()

Xmh*commandBox.button8.label:    reply to viewed msg
Xmh*commandBox.button8.translations: #override\
     <Btn1Down>,<Btn1Up>: XmhViewReply() unset()


!       To use popup menus on the title bars of the main window,
!       have them popup with the pointer over the previously selected item,
!       and not be clipped by the screen boundary:

Xmh*stickyMenu: True
Xmh*messageMenu.MenuOnScreen: True
```

```
Xmh*folderTitlebar.translations: #override\n\
<BtnDown>: XawPositionSimpleMenu(folderMenu)MenuPopup(folderMenu)\n
Xmh*tocTitlebar.translations: #override\n\
<Btn2Down>: XawPositionSimpleMenu(messageMenu)MenuPopup(messageMenu)\n\
<BtnDown>: XawPositionSimpleMenu(tocMenu)MenuPopup(tocMenu)\n

Xmh.Paned.viewTitlebar.translations: #override\n\
<Btn2Down>: XawPositionSimpleMenu(sequenceMenu)MenuPopup(sequenceMenu)\n\
<BtnDown>: XawPositionSimpleMenu(viewMenu)MenuPopup(viewMenu)\n


! To redefine the accelerator bindings to exclude modifier keys,
! and add a translation for Compose Message:

Xmh*tocMenu.accelerators: #override\n\
        !:<Key>I:        XmhIncorporateNewMail()\n\
        !:<Key>C:        XmhCommitChanges()\n\
        !:<Key>R:        XmhForceRescan()\n\
        !:<Key>P:        XmhPackFolder()\n\
        !:<Key>S:        XmhSortFolder()\n
Xmh*messageMenu.accelerators: #override\n\
        !:<Key>M:        XmhComposeMessage()\n\
        !<Key>space:     XmhViewNextMessage()\n\
        !:<Key>c:        XmhMarkCopy()\n\
        !:<Key>d:        XmhMarkDelete()\n\
        !:<Key>f:        XmhForward()\n\
        !:<Key>m:        XmhMarkMove()\n\
        !:<Key>n:        XmhViewNextMessage()\n\
        !:<Key>p:        XmhViewPreviousMessage()\n\
        !:<Key>r:        XmhReply()\n\
        !:<Key>u:        XmhUnmark()\n


!       Here is an example of some miscellaneous accelerators:
!       ("clients/xmh" is a subfolder; it must be existing.)

Xmh*toc.accelerators: #override\n\
        <Key>F1:        XmhOpenFolder(inbox)XmhOpenSequence(all)\n\
        <Key>F2:        XmhOpenFolder(drafts)\n\
        <Key>F3:        XmhOpenFolder(clients/xmh)\n\
        <Key>F4:        XmhViewInNewWindow()\n\
        <Key>F5:        XmhPickMessages()\n


!       Define Meta-S in the Compose window to do a send and close.

Xmh*comp.translations: #override\n\
        !:Meta<Key>S:   XmhSend()XmhCloseView()
```

G.3 app-defaults/Xmh File

Lines with a backslash (\) at the right-hand edge of the page were broken at that point for printing.

```
! AppDefaultsVersion should only be defined in the site-wide file
Xmh.AppDefaultsVersion:          1

Xmh.Geometry:                    508x750
Xmh.ReplyInsertFilter:           cat
Xmh.SendBreakWidth:              2000
*ShapeStyle:                     Oval
*Command.BorderWidth:    1
*MenuButton.BorderWidth:         1
*toc*cursor:                     left_ptr

*menuBox.folderButton.Label:     Folder
*menuBox.tocButton.Label:        Table of Contents
*menuBox.messageButton.Label:    Message
*menuBox.sequenceButton.Label:   Sequence
*menuBox.viewButton.Label:       View
*menuBox.optionButton.Label:     Options
*SimpleMenu*SmeLine.Height:      20

*close.Label:                    Close Window
*compose.Label:                  Compose Message
*open.Label:                     Open Folder
*openInNew.Label:                Open Folder in New Window
*create.Label:                   Create Folder
*folderMenu*delete.Label:        Delete Folder
*inc.Label:                      Incorporate New Mail
*next.Label:                     View Next Message
*prev.Label:                     View Previous
*delete.Label:                   Delete
*move.Label:                     Move
*copy.Label:                     Copy as Link
*unmark.Label:                   Unmark
*viewNew.Label:                  View In New
*reply.Label:                    Reply
*forward.Label:                  Forward
*useAsComp.Label:                Use as Composition
*commit.Label:                   Commit Changes
*print.Label:                    Print
*pack.Label:                     Pack Folder
*sort.Label:                     Sort Folder
*rescan.Label:                   Rescan Folder
*pick.Label:                     Pick
*openSeq.Label:                  Open Sequence
*addToSeq.Label:                 Add to Sequence
```

```
*removeFromSeq.Label:           Remove from Sequence
*deleteSeq.Label:               Delete Sequence
*edit.Label:                    Edit Message
*save.Label:                    Save Message
*send.Label:                    Send
*reset.Label:                   New Headers
*insert.Label:                  Insert
*optionMenu*reverse.Label:      Read in Reverse

Xmh.notice.Dialog.Text.BorderWidth: 0
Xmh.notice.Dialog.Text.TextSink.Font:
-*-courier-bold-r-*--*-120-*-*-*-*-iso8859-1
Xmh.notice.Dialog.confirm.Label:Acknowledged
Xmh.notice.BorderWidth:         2
Xmh.confirm.Dialog.yes.Label:   Yes
Xmh.confirm.Dialog.no.Label:    No
Xmh.prompt.Dialog.okay.Label:   Okay
Xmh.prompt.Dialog.cancel.Label: Cancel
Xmh.error.Dialog.OK.Label:      Acknowledged

*toc.rightMargin:               0
*toc.scrollVertical:            WhenNeeded
*view.scrollVertical:           Always
*view.scrollHorizontal:         WhenNeeded
*view.autoFill:                 True
*comp.scrollVertical:           Always
*comp.scrollHorizontal:         WhenNeeded
*comp.autoFill:                 True

*sequenceMenu.Translations: #override\n\
<Btn2Up>:XtMenuPopdown()notify()XmhOpenSequence()unhighlight()\n\
<Btn3Up>:XtMenuPopdown()XmhPushSequence()notify()XmhAddToSequence()           \
XmhPopSequence()unhighlight()\n\
<BtnUp>:XtMenuPopdown()notify()unhighlight()\n

*sequenceMenu.baseTranslations: #override\n\
<Btn2Up>:XtMenuPopdown()notify()XmhOpenSequence()unhighlight()\n\
<Btn3Up>:XtMenuPopdown()XmhPushSequence()notify()XmhAddToSequence()           \
XmhPopSequence()unhighlight()\n\
<BtnUp>:XtMenuPopdown()notify()unhighlight()\n

*folders*MenuButton.Translations:#override\n\
<BtnDown>:set()XmhPopupFolderMenu()\n\
<Btn2Up>:XmhSetCurrentFolder()XmhOpenFolder()reset()\n\
<Btn3Up>:XmhPushFolder()XmhSetCurrentFolder()XmhMarkMove()               \
XmhPopFolder()reset()\n\
<BtnUp>:XmhSetCurrentFolder()reset()\n\
<LeaveWindow>:reset()XmhLeaveFolderButton()\n

*folders*MenuButton.baseTranslations:#override\n\
<BtnDown>:set()XmhPopupFolderMenu()\n\
<Btn2Up>:XmhSetCurrentFolder()XmhOpenFolder()reset()\n\
<Btn3Up>:XmhPushFolder()XmhSetCurrentFolder()XmhMarkMove()               \
```

```
XmhPopFolder()reset()\n\
<BtnUp>:XmhSetCurrentFolder()reset()\n\
<LeaveWindow>:reset()XmhLeaveFolderButton()\n

*folders*SimpleMenu.Translations:#override\n\
<Btn2Up>:XtMenuPopdown()notify()XmhOpenFolder()unhighlight()\n\
<Btn3Up>:XtMenuPopdown()XmhPushFolder()notify()XmhMarkMove()                \
XmhPopFolder()unhighlight()\n\
<BtnUp>:XtMenuPopdown()notify()unhighlight()\n

*folders*SimpleMenu.baseTranslations:#override\n\
<Btn2Up>:XtMenuPopdown()notify()XmhOpenFolder()unhighlight()\n\
<Btn3Up>:XtMenuPopdown()XmhPushFolder()notify()XmhMarkMove()                \
XmhPopFolder()unhighlight()\n\
<BtnUp>:XtMenuPopdown()notify()unhighlight()\n

*toc.Translations: #override\n\
    <Btn2Down>: select-start()\n\
    <Btn2Up>:select-end(PRIMARY)XmhViewNextMessage()\n\
    Ctrl<Key>R:      no-op(RingBell)\n\
    Ctrl<Key>S:      no-op(RingBell)\n

*toc.baseTranslations: #override\n\
    <Btn2Down>: select-start()\n\
    <Btn2Up>:select-end(PRIMARY)XmhViewNextMessage()\n\
    Ctrl<Key>R:      no-op(RingBell)\n\
    Ctrl<Key>S:      no-op(RingBell)\n

*toc.Accelerators: #override\n\
    :Ctrl<Key>V:     next-page()\n\
    :Meta<Key>V:     previous-page()\n
*view.Accelerators: #override\n\
    :Ctrl<Key>v:     next-page()\n\
    :Meta<Key>v:     previous-page()\n

*tocMenu.Accelerators: #override\n\
    :Meta<Key>I:     XmhIncorporateNewMail()\n\
    :Meta<Key>C:     XmhCommitChanges()\n\
    :Meta<Key>R:     XmhForceRescan()\n\
    :Meta<Key>P:     XmhPackFolder()\n\
    :Meta<Key>S:     XmhSortFolder()\n

*messageMenu.Accelerators: #override\n\
    Meta<Key>space: XmhViewNextMessage()\n\
    :Meta<Key>c:     XmhMarkCopy()\n\
    :Meta<Key>d:     XmhMarkDelete()\n\
    :Meta<Key>f:     XmhForward()\n\
    :Meta<Key>m:     XmhMarkMove()\n\
    :Meta<Key>n:     XmhViewNextMessage()\n\
    :Meta<Key>p:     XmhViewPreviousMessage()\n\
    :Meta<Key>r:     XmhReply()\n\
    :Meta<Key>u:     XmhUnmark()\n
```

```
*viewButtons.close.Translations:#override\n\
    <Btn1Down>,<Btn1Up>:    XmhCloseView()unset()\n
*viewButtons.reply.Translations:#override\n\
    <Btn1Down>,<Btn1Up>:    XmhViewReply()unset()\n
*viewButtons.forward.Translations:#override\n\
    <Btn1Down>,<Btn1Up>:    XmhViewForward()unset()\n
*viewButtons.useAsComp.Translations:#override\n\
    <Btn1Down>,<Btn1Up>:    XmhViewUseAsComposition()unset()\n
*viewButtons.edit.Translations:#override\n\
    <Btn1Down>,<Btn1Up>:    XmhEditView()unset()\n
*viewButtons.save.Translations:#override\n\
    <Btn1Down>,<Btn1Up>:    XmhSaveView()unset()\n
*viewButtons.print.Translations:#override\n\
    <Btn1Down>,<Btn1Up>:    XmhPrintView()unset()\n
*viewButtons.delete.Translations:#override\n\
    <Btn1Down>,<Btn1Up>:    XmhViewMarkDelete()unset()\n

*compButtons.close.Translations:#override\n\
    <Btn1Down>,<Btn1Up>:    XmhCloseView()unset()\n
*compButtons.send.Translations:#override\n\
    <Btn1Down>,<Btn1Up>:    XmhSend()unset()\n
*compButtons.reset.Translations:#override\n\
    <Btn1Down>,<Btn1Up>:    XmhResetCompose()unset()\n
*compButtons.compose.Translations:#override\n\
    <Btn1Down>,<Btn1Up>:    XmhComposeMessage()unset()\n
*compButtons.save.Translations:#override\n\
    <Btn1Down>,<Btn1Up>:    XmhSave()unset()\n
*compButtons.insert.Translations:#override\n\
    <Btn1Down>,<Btn1Up>:    XmhInsert()unset()\n
```

H

Glossary

alias

In electronic mail, a single word or name that stands for one or more electronic mail addresses.

anonymous ftp

Anonymous ftp uses a special restricted account on the remote computer. It's usually used for transferring public domain files and programs like MH from central sites to users at many other computers. *See also* ftp.

backquote

The ` character (sometimes called a *grave accent*). The backquote is used to mark a command substitution (running a command, replacing the command with its output) on the UNIX command line.

backslash

The character \. In UNIX, it changes the interpretation of the next character in some way. See the inset "When is a Backslash not a Backslash?" in Section 6.1.2.

BBoards

Software for reading electronic mail digest files. BBoards were created by, and are also read and managed with, the MH software from the University of California, Irvine.

bin directory

A directory for storing executable programs.

body *See* message body.

button

A small area of an X window. Pointing to it with a mouse and clicking a mouse button (usually, the first button), runs a command.

buttonbox

A group of buttons in an X window. A buttonbox is usually enclosed in a frame or box.

command line

The text you type at a shell prompt. A UNIX shell reads the command line, parses it to find the command name (which is the first word on the command line), and executes the command. You type MH commands on a command line.

component

Entry in a message header—for example:

```
Subject: Important message.
```

Most components fit on a single line, but they can continue on other lines if the second and following lines start with a space or tab. *See also* empty component.

composition window

An *xmh* window used for composing (writing/editing) draft messages.

control character

A character you make by holding down the keyboard CTRL (Control) key while pressing a letter or another character key.

CTRL-X

The character called "control *x*," where *x* is a key on the keyboard. *See also* control character.

current message

If you don't tell an MH command which message to act on, most will use the current message. The current message is set by most MH commands when you give them a specific message number.

For example, if you type show 23 to read message number 23, that makes message 23 the current message. Then, if you don't give a message number to the folowing *show* command (or most other MH commands), they will use message 23.

.cshrc file
> *See* dot files.

default
> In a program that gives you more than one choice, the default choice is the one you get by not choosing. The default is usually the most common choice.

> As an example, the default editor for the MH programs is named *prompter*. If you don't choose another editor, MH programs will run *prompter*.

directory
> *See* bin directory, MH directory, MH library directory, subdirectory.

Dot (.) files (.cshrc, .login, .profile ...)
> Files that are read when you log in. These set up your environment and run any other UNIX commands (for instance, *inc*). If your account uses the C shell, it will read *.cshrc* and *.login*. Accounts that use the Bourne shell and shells like it use *.profile*.

doublequote
> The " character. This isn't the same as two singlequotes (' ') together. The " is used around a part of a UNIX command line where the shell should do variable and command substitution (and, on the C shell, history substitution), but no other interpretation.

draft file
> A text file that holds an MH message to be sent. The draft is created by *comp*, *repl*, *forw*, and *dist* and edited by programs such as *prompter*.

draft message
> An MH mail message that's ready to send or being prepared to send.

elm
> An electronic mail user agent.

emacs
> *See* GNU emacs.

empty component
> A line of a message header with no information—Subject:, for example. MH usually deletes empty components.

exit status

A program that runs under UNIX sets an integer value when it exits. By convention, a zero value means that the program ran without errors; a nonzero value means there was some problem. Not all UNIX programs return an exit status, though.

file *See* dot files, draft file, filter file, format file, MH profile file, template draft file.

filter file

A file that the *repl* and *forw* commands can use to change the formatting of messages. Filter files are written in *mhl*(1) syntax.

folder

See parent folder, subfolder, top-level folder.

format file

A file with formatting instructions for *scan* and *mhl*. Format files are written in *mh-format*(5) format.

front end

In this book, a program that runs MH commands for you. For instance, when you use its `Incorporate New Mail` command, the *xmh* front end runs the MH *inc* command.

ftp A way to transfer files between your computer and another computer with TCP/IP, often over the Internet network. *ftp* requires a username and password on the remote computer. *See also* anonymous ftp.

GNU emacs

A full screen text editor which runs on UNIX and other operating systems.

grip

A small solid box near the edge of the boundary between each area of an *xmh* window. A grip is used to change the size of one or more areas.

header

See message header.

i-number

A UNIX file has a name (for people to identify it with) and an i-number (for UNIX to identify it with). Each file's i-number is stored in a directory, along with the filename, to let UNIX find the file that you name.

link

A name given to a file. Also called a *hard link*. Any UNIX file can actually have more than one link—that is, more than one name. See Section 2.7; *see also* **symbolic link**.

.login file

See dot files.

mailbox

See system mailbox.

MAILER–DAEMON

A system program (as opposed to a user program) that handles electronic mail. A MAILER–DAEMON is a *transport agent*.

main window

An *xmh* window that has overall control buttons, a Table of Contents, and an area for viewing a message.

master window

The main window that opens when you start *xmh*.

message

See current message, draft message, message body.

message body

An e-mail message has two parts. The body is the text of a message and includes everything after the last header line. *See also* message header.

message header

A mail message header consists of a series of components such as To: joe@xyz.com and Subject: Important meeting. There's a blank line between the header and the body. The header can't have any blank lines in it.

metacharacter

A character you make by holding down the keyboard $\boxed{\text{META}}$ key while pressing an uppercase or lowercase letter or another character key. The Meta key isn't always labeled "Meta". The key is usually near the space bar.

Some keyboards don't have Meta keys. In that case, you'll have to use another command to do what you need. If you're using a telecommunications program like Kermit or a window system like X, though, you can probably map (redefine) another set of keys to make metacharacters. See the manual for your software.

MH directory

Each MH user has a directory where his or her MH folders and files are kept. By default, the directory is named *Mail* and is stored in the user's home directory.

mhe

Brian Reid's GNU *emacs* front end for MH.

MH library directory

A directory on your computer's filesystem which holds auxiliary MH files (like *replcomps*) and programs (such as *mhl*). Typically, the directory is */usr/local/lib/mh*.

MH profile file

A configuration file that each MH user must have. It locates the MH directory and configures MH commands. By default, it is called *.mh_profile* and is kept in the user's home directory.

mode

In UNIX, an octal number that describes what access a file's owner, group, and others have to the file.

MTA

See transport agent.

mush

The *M*ail *U*ser's *Sh*ell—a user agent.

option switch

Typed on a command line to modify the way that a UNIX command works. Usually starts with a dash (–). These terms are more or less interchangeable. An option may have several settings, but a switch usually has two settings: on and off (enabled and disabled), yes or no, etc. Switches usually have a default setting, which is what happens if you don't type anything on the command line. For instance, you can type the commands:

```
% refile -link 1 3 5 +folder
% refile -nolink 1 3 5 +folder
```

The first command uses the *–link* switch ... in other words, it "turns on the *link* switch." The second one, with *–nolink*, "turns off the *link* switch." If you don't use either *–link* or *–nolink*, you get the default:

```
% refile 1 3 5 +folder
```

which, for *refile*, is *–nolink*.

parent folder

The folder which contains a particular subfolder. For instance, if you have a subfolder named *+project/January*, its parent folder is *+project*. Also, a subfolder named *+a/b/c* would have a parent folder named *+a/b*.

parse

To split into pieces and interpret.

path, search

See **search path**.

perl

The Practical Extraction and Report Language, or the Pathologically Eclectic Rubbish Lister, or ...

A language for manipulating text, files, and processes that many people use with MH. See the Nutshell Handbook *Programming Perl* by Larry Wall and Randal Schwartz.

pick window

An *xmh* window that lets you select messages by one or more characteristics.

pipe

A part of UNIX that connects the output of one command to the input of another command. The commands can run at the same time. Shells use the | character to make a pipe.

POP, POP daemon

*P*ost *O*ffice *P*rotocol and the program that provides that service. POP lets users get their mail over a network from a remote machine without logging on to it.

postmaster

This is an address (an account, or a mail alias) on each computer. It's a place to send problem reports and questions. Each computer should have a person who acts as the postmaster. That person configures the mail system and answers questions.

.profile file

See dot files.

prompt

See shell prompt.

pseudo-code

A way to write out program text, structured like a program, without using the actual programming language. Pseudo-code is usually used to explain a program.

quote

See backquote, doublequote, singlequote.

reverse video

On a video display, reversed foreground and background colors or tones. Reverse video is used to highlight an area or to identify text to be used or modified.

For instance, if text is usually shown with black letters on a white background, reverse video would have white letters on a black background.

scrollbar

A long thin box at the edge of a window area that lets you position the window's contents.

search path

A list of directories that the shell searches to find the program file you want to execute.

sequence

In MH, a list of message numbers in a folder. The sequence has a name. When you type the sequence name, MH uses the messages in the sequence.

shell

A program that reads and interprets command lines and also runs those programs.

shell prompt

A signal from a shell (when it's used interactively) that the shell is ready to read a command line. By default, the percent sign (%) is the C shell prompt and the dollar sign ($) is the Bourne shell prompt.

singlequote

The ' character. This isn't the same as a backquote (`). The singlequote is used around a part of a UNIX command line where the shell should do no interpretation (except history substitution in the C shell).

string

A sequence of characters.

subdirectory

A directory within a directory.

subfolder

A folder within a folder.

switch

See option switch.

symbolic link

A part of the filesystem on many newer versions of UNIX. Also called a *soft link*. It holds the pathname of another object (file, directory, etc.) on the filesystem. It can give the object a new name.

system mailbox

The file where mail messages wait for you to incorporate them. Usually a file with your username in the directory */usr/spool/mail* or */usr/mail*.

template draft file

File read by *comp* and other MH mail-sending commands. It sets the default format for mail messages sent by that command.

termcap

Stands for *term*inal *cap*abilities, an early (and still common) way to describe terminals to UNIX. *See also* **terminfo**.

terminfo

A newer way to describe terminal capabilities to UNIX. See also **termcap**.

text widget

A collection of X Window System code that handles text display and editing in a consistent way, as part of many different X clients.

thumb

The part of a scrollbar that moves along with the current text position in a window. The thumb can be "grabbed" with the mouse to change the position.

top-level folder

A mail folder that's stored in the *MH* directory, with no parent folder. Its name is written starting with a + (plus sign); there is no / (backslash) in its name. For example, *+inbox* is a top-level folder; *+project/January* is not.

transport agent

A program that runs "behind the scenes" to deliver mail. Often abbreviated MTA ("mail transport agent"). Some common transport agents are *sendmail* and *MMDF*. *See also* **user agent**.

UNIX group

A UNIX group is a set of one or more users. The group has a name such as *support*, *adm*, *staff*, etc. Often everyone in an organization, department, or job category will be a member of the same UNIX group. The system administrator defines the groups, and adds and removes users from them.

user agent

A program that users read and send mail with. MH is a user agent. *See also* **transport agent**.

view window

An *xmh* window for reading a message.

widget

See text widget.

window

See composition window, main window, master window, pick window, view window.

xmh

An MH front end that runs under the X Window System.

Manual Pages X

This section has copies of selected online manual pages. Most are taken directly from the MH 6.7.2 distribution.

The *xmh*(1) manual page isn't distributed with standard MH.

The manual pages use some system-dependent parameters. Those are listed in Table I-1, along with a typical value and explanation. The parameter names start and end with angle brackets (< >).

Table I-1. Manual Page Parameters and Explanation

Abbreviation	Typical Value	Explanation
<EOT>	`CTRL-D`	End-of-input character.
<INTERRUPT>	`CTRL-C`	INTERRUPT character.
<mh–dir>	`$HOME/Mail`	Your MH directory.
<MHBINPATH>	`/usr/local/mh`	Directory with MH commands.
<MHDROPLOC>	`/usr/spool/mail/username`	Path to maildrop file.

Table I-1. Manual Page Parameters and Explanation (continued)

Abbreviation	Typical Value	Explanation
<MHEDITOR>	prompter	Editor for *comp*, etc.
<MHETCPATH>	/usr/local/lib/mh	MH library directory.
<QUIT>	CTRL-\	QUIT character.
<RETURN>	RETURN	Press the RETURN key.

Name

maildelivery*

Synopsis

User delivery specification file

Description

The delivery of mail by the local channel can run through various courses, including using a user tailorable file. The delivery follows the following strategy, giving up at any point it considers the message delivered.

1)   If the address indicates a pipe or file default then that is carried out.

2)   The file *.maildelivery* (or something similar) in the home directory is read if it exists and the actions in it are followed.

3)   A system-wide file is consulted next, such as */usr/lib/maildelivery* and the actions are similar to 2.

4)   If the message still hasn't been delivered, then it is put into the user's normal mailbox or *mailbox*) depending on the system.

The format of the *.maildelivery* file is

field *<FS>* **pattern** *<FS>* **action** *<FS>* **result** *<FS>* **string**

where

field   is name of a field that is to be searched for a pattern. This is any header field that you might find in a message. The most commonly used headers are usually From, to, cc, subject and sender. As well as the standard headers, there are some psuedo-headers that are can also be used. These are :-

                 source   The out of band sender information. This is the address MMDF would use for reporting delivery problems with the message.

                 addr   the address that was used to mail to you, normally 'yourname' or 'yourname=string' (see below).

---

*This manual page title was changed at O'Reilly & Associates. If you have an online copy, it is proba-bly named *maildelivery*(5).

default   if the message hasn't been delivered yet, this field is matched.

*   this case is always true regardless of any other action.

pattern   is some sequence of characters that may be matched in the above *field*. Case is not significant.

action   is one of the mail delivery actions supported by the local channel. Currently the supported actions are **file** or >, which appends the message to the given file, with delimiters; **pipe** or |, which starts up a process with the message as the standard input; and **destroy** which throws the message away. There is also **qpipe** or ^, which fakes a pipe command and is quicker than the standard pipe, but does not do header reformatting.

For piped commands, the exit status of the command is significant. An exit status of 0 implies that the command succeeded and everything went well. An exit status of octal 0300-0377 indicates that a permanent failure occured and the message should be rejected, these error codes are given in mmdf.h. Any other exit status indicates a temporary failure and the delivery attempt will be aborted and restarted at a later time.

result   is one of the letters A, R or ? which stand for Accept, Reject and "Accept if not delivered yet". They have the following effects:

A   If the result of this line's action is OK, then the message can be considered delivered.

R   The message is not to be considered delivered by this action.

?   This is equivalent to A except that the action is not carried out if the message has already been accepted.

The file is always read completely so that several matches can be made, and several actions taken. As a security check, the *.maildelivery* file must be owned by either the user or root, and must not have group or general write permission. In addition the system delivery file has the above restrictions but must also be owned by root. If the field specified does not need a pattern a dash (–) or similar symbol is usually inserted to show that the field is present but not used. The field separator character can be either a tab, space or comma (,). These characters can be included in a string by quoting them with double quotes (") (double quotes can be included with a backslash '\').

MMDF treats local addresses which contain an equals sign ('=') in a special manner. Everything in a local address from an equals sign to the '@' is ignored and passed on to the local channel. The local channel will make the entire string available for matching against the *addr* string of the *.maildelivery* file. For example, if you were to subscribe to a digest as "foo=digest@bar.NET", **submit** and the local channel will verify that it is legal to deliver to "foo", but then the entire string "foo=digest" will be available for string matching against the *.maildelivery* file for the **addr** field.

Environment

The environment in which piped programs are run contains a few standard features, specifically:

HOME is set to the user's home directory.
USER is set to the user's login name.
SHELL is set to the user's login shell (defaults to /bin/sh).

The default umask is set up to 077, this gives a very protective creation mask. Initgroups is called if 4.2 version of UNIX is running. If further requirements are needed, then a shell script can be run first to set up more complex environments.

There are certain built-in variables that you can give to a piped program. These are *$(sender)*, *$(address)*, *$(size)*, *$(reply-to)* and *$(info)*. *$(sender)* is set to the return address for the message. *$(address)* is set to the address that was used to mail to you, normally 'yourname' or 'yourname=string'. *$(size)* is set to the size in bytes of this message. *$(reply-to)* is set to the Reply-To: field (or the From: field if the former is missing) and so can be used for automatic replies. *$(info)* is the info field from the internal mail header and is probably only of interest to the system maintainers.

Example

Here is a rough idea of what a *.maildelivery* file looks like:

```
# lines starting with a '#' are ignored.
# as are blank lines
# file mail with mmdf2 in the "To:" line into file mmdf2.log
To    mmdf2    file    A    mmdf2.log
# Messages from mmdf pipe to the program err-message-archive
```

```
From    mmdf    pipe    A    err-message-archive
# Anything with the "Sender:" address "uk-mmdf-workers"
# file in mmdf2.log if not filed already
Sender   uk-mmdf-workers    file    ?    mmdf2.log
# "To:" unix - put in file unix-news
To    Unix    >    A    unix-news
# if the address is jpo=mmdf - pipe into mmdf-redist
Addr    jpo=mmdf    |    A    mmdf-redist
# if the address is jpo=ack - send an acknowledgement copy back
Addr    jpo=ack    |    R    resend  -r  $(reply-to)
# anything from steve - destroy!
from    steve    destroy    A    -
# anything not matched yet - put into mailbox
default    -    >    ?    mailbox
# always run rcvalert
*    -    |    R    rcvalert
```

Files

$HOME/.maildelivery - the files normal location.

/usr/lib/maildelivery - the system file. This should be protected against attack. It may contain contents such as:

```
default    -    pipe    A    stdreceive
*    -    |    R    ttynotify
```

This allows interfacing to non-standard mail systems, ones that don't believe in delimiter-separated mailboxes.

See Also

rcvtrip(1)

Bugs

And why not?

NAME

maildelivery*

Synopsis

User delivery specification file

Description

The format of each line in the *.maildelivery* file is

field pattern action result string

where

field:

The name of a field that is to be searched for a pattern. This is any field in the headers of the message that might be present. In addition, the following special fields are also defined:

source: the out–of–band sender information

addr: the address that was used to cause delivery to the recipient

default: this matches *only* if the message hasn't been delivered yet

*: this always matches

pattern:

The sequence of characters to match in the specified field. Matching is case–insensitive but not RE–based.

action:

The action to take to deliver the message. This is one of

file or >:

Append the message to the file named by **string**. The standard maildrop delivery process is used. If the message can be appended to the file, then this action succeeds.

---

*This manual page was created by O'Reilly & Associates from a section of the *mhook*(1) manual page. (Your online copy is probably named *mhook*(1).)

When writing to the file, a new field is added:

Delivery–Date: date

which indicates the date and time that message was appended to the file.

pipe or | :

Pipe the message as the standard input to the command named by **string**, using the Bourne shell *sh* (1) to interpret the string. Prior to giving the string to the shell, it is expanded with the following built–in variables:

$(sender): the return address for the message
$(address): the address that was used to cause delivery to the recipient
$(size): the size of the message in bytes
$(reply–to): either the "Reply–To:" or "From:" field of the message
$(info): miscellaneous out–of–band information

When a process is invoked, its environment is: the user/group id:s are set to recipient's id:s; the working directory is the recipient's directory; the umask is 0077; the process has no /dev/tty; the standard input is set to the message; the standard output and diagnostic output are set to /dev/null; all other file–descriptors are closed; the envariables **$USER, $HOME, $SHELL** are set appropriately, and no other envariables exist.

The process is given a certain amount of time to execute. If the process does not exit within this limit, the process will be terminated with extreme prejudice. The amount of time is calculated as ((size x 60) + 300) seconds, where size is the number of bytes in the message.

The exit status of the process is consulted in determining the success of the action. An exit status of zero means that the action succeeded. Any other exit status (or ₍abnormal termination) means that the action failed.

In order to avoid any time limitations, you might implement a process that began by *forking*. The parent would return the appropriate value immediately, and the child could continue on, doing whatever it wanted for as long as it wanted. This approach is somewhat risky if the parent is going to return an exit status of zero. If the parent is going to return a non–zero exit status, then this approach can lead to quicker delivery into your maildrop.

qpipe or *<caret>*:

Similar to *pipe*, but executes the command directly, after built–in variable expansion, without assistance from the shell.

destroy:

This action always succeeds.

result:

Indicates how the action should be performed:

A:

Perform the action. If the action succeeds, then the message is considered delivered.

R:

Perform the action. Regardless of the outcome of the action, the message is not considered delivered.

?:

Perform the action only if the message has not been delivered. If the action succeeds, then the message is considered delivered.

N:

Perform the action only if the message has not been delivered and the previous action succeeded. If this action succeeds, then the message is considered delivered.

The file is always read completely, so that several matches can be made and several actions can be taken. The *.maildelivery* file must be owned either by the user or by root, and must be writable only by the owner. If the *.maildelivery* file can not be found, or does not perform an action which delivers the message, then the file <MHETCPATH>/maildelivery is read according to the same rules. This file must be owned by the root and must be writable only by the root. If this file can not be found or does not perform an action which delivers the message, then standard delivery to the user's maildrop, <MHDROPLOC>, is performed.

Arguments in the *.maildelivery* file are separated by white–space or comma. Since double–quotes are honored, these characters may be included in a single argument by enclosing the entire argument in double–quotes. A double–quote can be included by preceeding it with a backslash.

To summarize, here's an example:

```
#field    pattern              action result string
# lines starting with a '#' are ignored, as are blank lines
#
# file mail with mmdf2 in the "To:" line into file mmdf2.log
To      mmdf2              file  A    mmdf2.log
# Messages from mmdf pipe to the program err-message-archive
From    mmdf               pipe  A    err-message-archive
# Anything with the "Sender:" address "uk-mmdf-workers"
# file in mmdf2.log if not filed already
Sender  uk-mmdf-workers file  ?    mmdf2.log
# "To:" unix – put in file unix-news
To      Unix               >     A    unix-news
# if the address is jpo=mmdf – pipe into mmdf-redist
addr    jpo=mmdf           |     A    mmdf-redist
# if the address is jpo=ack – send an acknowledgement copy back
addr    jpo=ack            |     R    "resend –r $(reply-to)"
# anything from steve – destroy!
From    steve              destroy  A–
# anything not matched yet – put into mailbox
default –                  >     ?    mailbox
# always run rcvalert
*       –                  |     R    rcvalert
```

See Also

mhook(1)

Part V
Manual Pages

Name

mh–format – format file for MH message system

Synopsis

some *MH* commands

Description

Several *MH* commands utilize either a *format* string or a *format* file during their execution. For example, *scan* (1) uses a format string which directs it how to generate the scan listing for each message; *repl* (1) uses a format file which directs it how to generate the reply to a message, and so on.

Format strings are designed to be efficiently parsed by *MH* which means they are not necessarily simple to write and understand. This means that novice, casual, or even advanced users of *MH* should not have to deal with them. Some canned scan listing formats are in <MHETCPATH>/scan.time, <MHETCPATH>/scan.size, and <MHETCPATH>/scan.timely. Look in <MHETCPATH> for other *scan* and *repl* format files which may have been written at your site.

It suffices to have your local *MH* expert actually write new format commands or modify existing ones. This manual section explains how to do that. Note: familiarity with the C *printf* routine is assumed.

A format string consists of ordinary text, and special multi-character *escape* sequences which begin with '%'. When specifying a format string, the usual C backslash characters are honored: '\b', '\f', '\n', '\r', and '\t'. Continuation lines in format files end with '\' followed by the newline character. There are three types of *escape* sequences: header *components*, built-in *functions*, and, flow *control*.

A *component* escape is specified as '%{*component*}', and exists for each header found in the message being processed. For example '%{date}' refers to the "Date:" field of the appropriate message. All component escapes have a string value. Normally, component values are compressed by converting any control characters (tab and newline included) to spaces, then eliding any leading or multiple spaces. However, commands may give different interpretations to some component escapes; be sure to refer to each command's manual entry for complete details.

A *function* escape is specified as '%(*function*)'. All functions are built-in, and most have a string or numeric value.

Control-flow escapes

A *control* escape is one of: '%<', '%?', '%|', or '%>'. These are combined into the conditional execution construct:

```
%<condition
        format text 1
%?condition2
        format text 2
%?condition3
        format text 3
...
%|
        format text N
%>
```

Extra white space is shown here only for clarity. These constructs may be nested without ambiguity. They form a general **if–elseif–else–endif** block where only one of the *format text* segments is interpreted.

The '%<' and '%?' control escapes causes a condition to be evaluated. This condition may be either a *component* or a *function*. The four constructs have the following syntax:

```
%<{component}
%<(function)
%?{component}
%?(function)
```

These control escapes test whether the function or component value is non-zero (for integer-valued escapes), or non-empty (for string-valued escapes).

If this test evaulates true, then the format text up to the next corresponding control escape (one of '%|', '%?', or '%>') is interpreted normally. Next, all format text up to the corresponding '%>' control escape (if any) is skipped. The '%>' control escape is not interpreted; normal interpretation resumes after the '%>' escape.

*Part V
Manual Pages*

If the test evaluates false, however, then the format text up to the next corresponding control escape (again, one of '%|', '%?', or '%>') is skipped, instead of being interpreted. If the control escape encountered was '%?', then the condition associated with that control escape is evaluated, and interpretation proceeds after that test as described in the previous paragraph. If the control escape encountered was '%|', then the format text up to the corresponding '%>' escape is interpreted normally. As above, the '%>' escape is not interpreted and normal interpretation resumes after the '%>' escape.

The '%?' control escape and its following format text is optional, and may be included zero or more times. The '%|' control escape and its following format text is also optional, and may be included zero or one times.

Function escapes

Most functions expect an argument of a particular type:

Argument	*Description*	*Example Syntax*
literal	A literal number,	%(*func* 1234)
	or string	%(*func* text string)
comp	Any header component	%(*func* {*in-reply-to* })
date	A date component	%(*func* {*date* })
addr	An address component	%(*func* {*from* })
expr	An optional component,	%(*func* (*func2*))
	function or control,	%(*func* %<{*reply-to* }%|%{*from*}%>)
	perhaps nested	%(*func* (*func2* {*comp* }))

The types *date* and *addr* have the same syntax as *comp*, but require that the header component be a date string, or address string, respectively.

All arguments except those of type *expr* are required. For the *expr* argument type, the leading '%' must be omitted for component and function escape arguments, and must be present (with a leading space) for control escape arguments.

The evaluation of format strings is based on a simple machine with an integer register *num*, and a text string register *str*. When a function escape is processed, if it accepts an optional *expr* argument which is not present, it reads the current value of either *num* or *str* as appropriate.

Return values

Component escapes write the value of their message header in *str*. Function escapes write their return value in *num* for functions returning *integer* or *boolean* values, and in *str* for functions returning string values. (The *boolean* type is a subset of integers with usual values 0=false and 1=true.)

All component escapes, and those function escapes which return an *integer* or *string* value, pass this value back to their caller in addition to setting *str* or *num*. These escapes will print out this value unless called as part of an argument to another escape sequence. Function escapes which return a *boolean* value do pass this value back to their caller, but will never print out the value.

Function	*Argument*	*Return*	*Description*
msg		integer	message number
cur		integer	message is current
size		integer	size of message
strlen		integer	length of *str*
width		integer	output buffer size in bytes
charleft		integer	bytes left in output buffer
timenow		integer	seconds since the UNIX epoch
me		string	the user's mailbox
eq	literal	boolean	*num* == *arg*
ne	literal	boolean	*num* != *arg*
gt	literal	boolean	*num* > *arg*
match	literal	boolean	*str* contains *arg*
amatch	literal	boolean	*str* starts with *arg*
plus	literal	integer	*arg* plus *num*
minus	literal	integer	*arg* minus *num*
divide	literal	integer	*num* divided by *arg*
num	literal	integer	Set *num* to *arg*
lit	literal	string	Set *str* to *arg*
getenv	literal	string	Set *str* to environment value of *arg*
nonzero	expr	boolean	*num* is non-zero
zero	expr	boolean	*num* is zero
null	expr	boolean	*str* is empty
nonnull	expr	boolean	*str* is non-empty
void	expr		Set *str* or *num*
comp	comp	string	Set *str* to component text
compval	comp	integer	*num* set to "**atoi**(*str*)"
trim	expr		trim trailing white-space from *str*

*Part V
Manual Pages*

putstr	expr	print *str*
putstrf	expr	print *str* in a fixed width
putnum	expr	print *num*
putnumf	expr	print *num* in a fixed width

These functions require a date component as an argument:

Function	Argument	Return	Description
sec	date	integer	seconds of the minute
min	date	integer	minutes of the hour
hour	date	integer	hours of the day (0-23)
wday	date	integer	day of the week (Sun=0)
day	date	string	day of the week (abbrev.)
weekday	date	string	day of the week
sday	date	integer	day of the week known? (0=implicit,−1=unknown)
mday	date	integer	day of the month
yday	date	integer	day of the year
mon	date	integer	month of the year
month	date	string	month of the year (abbrev.)
lmonth	date	string	month of the year
year	date	integer	year of the century
zone	date	integer	timezone in hours
tzone	date	string	timezone string
szone	date	integer	timezone explicit? (0=implicit,−1=unknown)
date2local	date		coerce date to local timezone
date2gmt	date		coerce date to GMT
dst	date	integer	daylight savings in effect?
clock	date	integer	seconds since the UNIX epoch
rclock	date	integer	seconds prior to current time
tws	date	string	official 822 rendering
pretty	date	string	user-friendly rendering
nodate	date	integer	*str* not a date string

These functions require an address component as an argument. The return value of functions noted with '*' pertain only to the first address present in the header component.

Function	Argument	Return	Description
proper	addr	string	official 822 rendering
friendly	addr	string	user-friendly rendering
addr	addr	string	mbox@host or host!mbox rendering*
pers	addr	string	the personal name*
note	addr	string	commentary text*
mbox	addr	string	the local mailbox*
mymbox	addr	integer	the user's addresses? (0=no,1=yes)
host	addr	string	the host domain*
nohost	addr	integer	no host was present*
type	addr	integer	host type* (0=local,1=network, −1=uucp,2=unknown)
path	addr	string	any leading host route*
ingrp	addr	integer	address was inside a group*
gname	addr	string	name of group*
formataddr	expr		append *arg* to *str* as a (comma separated) address list
putaddr	literal		print *str* address list with *arg* as optional label; get line width from *num*

When escapes are nested, evaluation is done from inner-most to outer-most. The outer-most escape must begin with '%'; the inner escapes must not. For example,

        %<(mymbox{from}) To: %{to}%>

writes the value of the header component "From:" to *str*; then (*mymbox*) reads *str* and writes its result to *num*; then the control escape evaluates *num*. If *num* is non-zero, the string "To: " is printed followed by the value of the header component "To:".

A minor explanation of (*mymbox*{*comp*}) is in order. In general, it checks each of the addresses in the header component "*comp*" against the user's mailbox name and any *Alternate-Mailboxes*. It returns true if any address matches, however, it also returns true if the "*comp*" header is not present in the message. If needed, the (*null*) function can be used to explicitly test for this condition.

When a function or component escape is interpreted and the result will be immediately printed, an optional field width can be specified to print the field in exactly a given number of characters. For example, a numeric escape like %4(*size*) will print at most 4 digits of the message size; overflow will be indicated by a '?' in the first position (like '?234'). A string escape like %4(*me*) will print the first 4 characters and truncate at the end. Short fields are padded at the right with the fill character (normally, a blank). If the field width argument begins with a leading zero, then the fill character is set to a zero.

As above, the functions (*putnumf*) and (*putstrf*) print their result in exactly the number of characters specified by their leading field width argument. For example, %06(*putnumf*(*size*)) will print the message size in a field six characters wide filled with leading zeros; %14(*putstrf*{*from*}) will print the "From:" header component in fourteen characters with trailing spaces added as needed. For *putstrf*, using a negative value for the field width causes right-justification of the string within the field, with padding on the left up to the field width. The functions (*putnum*) and (*putstr*) print their result in the minimum number of characters required, and ignore any leading field width argument.

The available output width is kept in an internal register; any output past this width will be truncated.

With all this in mind, here's the default format string for *scan*. It's been divided into several pieces for readability. The first part is:

    %4(msg)%<(cur)+%| %>%<{replied}-%| %>

which says that the message number should be printed in four digits, if the message is the current message then a '+' else a space should be printed, and if a "Replied:" field is present then a '−' else a space should be printed. Next:

    %02(mon{date})/%02(mday{date})

the month and date are printed in two digits (zero filled) separated by a slash. Next,

    %<{date} %|*>

If a "Date:" field was present, then a space is printed, otherwise a '*'. Next,

> %<(mymbox{from})To:%14(friendly{to})

if the message is from me, print 'To:' followed by a "user-friendly" rendering of the first address in the "To:" field. Continuing,

> %|%17(friendly{from})%>

if the message isn't from me, then the print the "From:" address is printed. And finally,

> %{subject}%<{body}<<%{body}%>

the subject and initial body (if any) are printed.

For a more complicated example, next consider the default *replcomps* format file.

> %(lit)%(formataddr %<{reply-to}%|

This clears *str* and formats the "Reply-To:" header if present. If not present, the else clause is executed:

> %<{from}%|%<{sender}%|%<{return-path}%>%>%>%>)\

This formats the "From:", "Sender:" and "Return-Path:" headers, stopping as soon as one of them is present. Next:

> %<(nonnull)%(void(width))%(putaddr To:)\n%>\

If the *formataddr* result is non-null, it is printed as an address (with line folding if needed) in a field *width* wide with a leading label of "To: ".

> %(lit)%(formataddr{to})%(formataddr{cc})%(formataddr(me))\

str is cleared, and the "To:" and "Cc:" headers, along with the user's address (depending on what was specified with the "–cc" switch to *repl*) are formatted.

> %<(nonnull)%(void(width))%(putaddr cc:)\n%>\

If the result is non-null, it is printed as above with a leading label of "cc: ".

```
%<{fcc}Fcc: %{fcc}\n%>\
```

If a "–fcc folder" switch was given to *repl* (see *repl* (1) for more details about %{*fcc*}), an "Fcc:" header is output.

```
%<{subject}Subject: Re: %{subject}\n%>\
```

If a subject component was present, a suitable reply subject is output.

```
%<{date}In-reply-to: Your message of "\
%<(nodate{date})%{date}% | %(pretty{date})%>."%<{message-id}
     %{message-id}%>\n%>\
```

_____

If a date component was present, an "In-Reply-To:" header is output with the preface "Your message of ". If the date was parseable, it is output in a "pretty" format, otherwise it is output as-is. The message-id is included if present. As with all plain-text, the row of dashes are output as-is.

This last part is a good example for a little more elaboration. Here's that part again in pseudo-code:

```
if (comp_exists(date))  then
        print ("In-reply-to: Your message of \"")
        if (not_date_string(date.value) then
                print (date.value)
        else
                print (rfc822(date.value))
        endif
        print ("\"")
        if (comp_exists(message-id)) then
                print ("\n\t")
                print (message-id.value)
        endif
        print ("\n")
endif
```

Although this seems complicated, in point of fact, this method is flexible enough to extract individual fields and print them in any format the user desires.

Files

None

Profile Components

None

See Also

scan(1), repl(1), ap(8), dp(8)

Defaults

None

Context

None

History

This software was contributed for MH 6.3. Prior to this, output format specifications were much easier to write, but considerably less flexible.

Bugs

On hosts where *MH* was configured with the BERK option, address parsing is not enabled.

Name

mh–mail – message format for MH message system

Synopsis

any *MH* command

Description

MH processes messages in a particular format. It should be noted that although neither Bell nor Berkeley mailers produce message files in the format that *MH* prefers, *MH* can read message files in that antiquated format.

Each user possesses a mail drop box which initially receives all messages processed by *post* (8). *Inc* (1) will read from that drop box and incorporate the new messages found there into the user's own mail folders (typically '+inbox'). The mail drop box consists of one or more messages. To facilitate the separation of messages [only on systems configured for the MMDF or MH mail transport agents —JP], each message begins and ends with a line consisting of nothing but four CTRL–A (octal 001) characters.

Messages are expected to consist of lines of text. Graphics and binary data are not handled. No data compression is accepted. All text is clear ASCII 7-bit data.

The general "memo" framework of RFC–822 is used. A message consists of a block of information in a rigid format, followed by general text with no specified format. The rigidly formatted first part of a message is called the header, and the free-format portion is called the body. The header must always exist, but the body is optional. These parts are separated by an empty line, i.e., two consecutive newline characters. Within *MH*, the header and body may be separated by a line consisting of dashes:

```
To:
cc:
Subject:
--------
```

The header is composed of one or more header items. Each header item can be viewed as a single logical line of ASCII characters. If the text of a header item extends across several real lines, the continuation lines are indicated by leading spaces or tabs.

Each header item is called a component and is composed of a keyword or name, along with associated text. The keyword begins at the left margin, may NOT contain spaces or tabs, may not exceed 63 characters (as specified by RFC–822), and is terminated by a colon (':'). Certain components (as identified by their keywords) must follow rigidly defined formats in their text portions.

The text for most formatted components (e.g., "Date:" and "Message–Id:") is produced automatically. The only ones entered by the user are address fields such as "To:", "cc:", etc. Internet addresses are assigned mailbox names and host computer specifications. The rough format is "local@domain", such as "MH@UCI", or "MH@UCI–ICSA.ARPA". Multiple addresses are separated by commas. A missing host/domain is assumed to be the local host/domain.

As mentioned above, a blank line (or a line of dashes) signals that all following text up to the end of the file is the body. No formatting is expected or enforced within the body.

Following is a list of header components that are considered meaningful to various MH programs.

Date:

> Added by *post* (8), contains date and time of the message's entry into the transport system.

From:
>   Added by *post* (8), contains the address of the author or authors (may be more than one if a "Sender:" field is present). Replies are typically directed to addresses in the "Reply–To:" or "From:" field (the former has precedence if present).

Sender:
>   Added by *post* (8) in the event that the message already has a "From:" line. This line contains the address of the actual sender. Replies are never sent to addresses in the "Sender:" field.

To:
>   Contains addresses of primary recipients.

cc:
>   Contains addresses of secondary recipients.

Bcc:
>   Still more recipients. However, the "Bcc:" line is not copied onto the message as delivered, so these recipients are not listed. *MH* uses an encapsulation method for blind copies, see *send* (1).

Fcc:
>   Causes *post* (8) to copy the message into the specified folder for the sender, if the message was successfully given to the transport system.

Message–ID:
>   A unique message identifier added by *post* (8) if the '–msgid' flag is set.

Subject:
>   Sender's commentary. It is displayed by *scan* (1).

In–Reply–To:
>   A commentary line added by *repl* (1) when replying to a message.

Resent–Date:
>   Added when redistributing a message by *post* (8).

Resent–From:
>   Added when redistributing a message by *post* (8).

Resent–To:
> New recipients for a message resent by *dist* (1).

Resent–cc:
> Still more recipients. See "cc:" and "Resent–To:".

Resent–Bcc:
> Even more recipients. See "Bcc:" and "Resent–To:".

Resent–Fcc:
> Copy resent message into a folder. See "Fcc:" and "Resent–To:".

Resent–Message–Id:
> A unique identifier glued on by *post* (8) if the '–msgid' flag is set. See "Message–Id:" and "Resent–To:".

Resent:
> Annotation for *dist* (1) under the '–annotate' option.

Forwarded:
> Annotation for *forw* (1) under the '–annotate' option.

Replied:
> Annotation for *repl* (1) under the '–annotate' option.

Files

<MHDROPLOC>   Location of mail drop

Profile Components

None

See Also

Standard for the Format of ARPA Internet Text Messages (aka RFC–822)

Defaults

None

Context

None

Name

.mh_profile – user customization for MH message system

Synopsis

any *MH* command

Description

Each user of *MH* is expected to have a file named *.mh_profile* in his or her home directory. This file contains a set of user parameters used by some or all of the *MH* family of programs. Each line of the file is of the format

profile–component: *value*

The possible profile components are exemplified below. Only 'Path:' is mandatory. The others are optional; some have default values if they are not present. In the notation used below, (profile, default) indicates whether the information is kept in the user's *MH* profile or *MH* context, and indicates what the default value is.

Path: Mail

> Locates *MH* transactions in directory "Mail". (profile, no default)

context: context

> Declares the location of the *MH* context file, see the **HISTORY** section below. (profile, default: <mh–dir>/context)

Current–Folder: inbox

> Keeps track of the current open folder. (context, default: +inbox)

Previous–Sequence: pseq

> Names the sequences which should be defined as the 'msgs' or 'msg' argument given to the program. If not present, or empty, no sequences are defined. Otherwise, for each name given, the sequence is first zero'd and then each message is added to the sequence. (profile, no default)

Sequence–Negation: not

> Defines the string which, when prefixed to a sequence name, negates that sequence. Hence, "notseen" means all those messages that are not a member of the sequence "seen". (profile, no default)

Unseen–Sequence: unseen

> Names the sequences which should be defined as those messages recently incorporated by *inc*. *Show* knows to remove messages from this sequence once it thinks they have been seen. If not present, or empty, no sequences are defined. Otherwise, for each name given, the sequence is first zero'd and then each message is added to the sequence. (profile, no default)

mh–sequences: .mh_sequences

> The name of the file in each folder which defines public sequences. To disable the use of public sequences, leave the value portion of this entry blank. (profile, default: .mh_sequences)

atr–*seq–folder*: 172 178–181 212

> Keeps track of the private sequence called *seq* in the specified folder. (context, no default)

Editor: /usr/ucb/ex

> Defines editor to be used by *comp* (1), *dist* (1), *forw* (1), and *repl* (1). (profile, default: <MHEDITOR>)

Msg–Protect: 644

> Defines octal protection bits for message files. See *chmod* (1) for an explanation of the octal number. (profile, default: 0644)

Folder–Protect: 711

> Defines protection bits for folder directories. (profile, default: 0711)

program: default switches

> Sets default switches to be used whenever the mh program *program* is invoked. For example, one could

override the *Editor*: profile component when replying to messages by adding a component such as:

> repl: –editor /bin/ed

(profile, no defaults)

lasteditor–next: nexteditor

Names "nexteditor" to be the default editor after using "lasteditor". This takes effect at "What now?" level in *comp*, *dist*, *forw*, and *repl*. After editing the draft with "lasteditor", the default editor is set to be "nexteditor". If the user types "edit" without any arguments to "What now?", then "nexteditor" is used. (profile, no default)

bboards: system

Tells *bbc* which BBoards you are interested in. (profile, default: system)

Folder–Stack: *folders*

The contents of the folder–stack for the *folder* command. (context, no default)

mhe:

If present, tells *inc* to compose an *MHE* auditfile in addition to its other tasks. *MHE* is Brian Reid's *Emacs* front–end for *MH*. An early version is supplied with the *mh.6* distribution. (profile, no default)

Alternate–Mailboxes: mh@uci–750a, bug-mh*

Tells *repl* and *scan* which addresses are really yours. In this way, *repl* knows which addresses should be included in the reply, and *scan* knows if the message really originated from you. Addresses must be separated by a comma, and the hostnames listed should be the "official" hostnames for the mailboxes you indicate, as local nicknames for hosts are not replaced with their official site names. For each address, if a host is not given, then that address on any host is considered to be you. In addition, an asterisk ('*') may appear at either or both ends of the mailbox and host to indicate wild–card matching. (profile, default: your user-id)

Aliasfile: aliases

>Indicates a default aliases file for *ali*, *whom*, and *send*. This may be used instead of the '–alias file' switch. (profile, no default)

Draft–Folder: drafts

>Indicates a default draft folder for *comp*, *dist*, *forw*, and *repl*. (profile, no default)

digest–issue–*list*: 1

>Tells *forw* the last issue of the last volume sent for the digest *list*. (context, no default)

digest–volume–*list*: 1

>Tells *forw* the last volume sent for the digest *list*. (context, no default)

MailDrop: .mail

>Tells *inc* your maildrop, if different from the default. This is superceded by the **$MAILDROP** envariable. (profile, default: <MHDROPLOC>)

Signature: RAND MH System (agent: Marshall Rose)

>Tells *send* your mail signature. This is superceded by the **$SIGNATURE** envariable. On hosts where *MH* was configured with the UCI option, if **$SIGNATURE** is not set and this profile entry is not present, the file $HOME/.signature is consulted. Your signature will be added to the address *send* puts in the "From:" header; do not include an address in the signature text. (profile, no default)

The following profile elements are used whenever an *MH* program invokes some other program such as *more* (1). The *.mh_profile* can be used to select alternate programs if the user wishes. The default values are given in the examples.

fileproc:	<MHBINPATH>/refile
incproc:	<MHBINPATH>/inc
installproc:	<MHETCPATH>/install–mh
lproc:	/usr/ucb/more
mailproc:	<MHBINPATH>/mhmail

mhlproc:	<MHETCPATH>/mhl
moreproc:	/usr/ucb/more
mshproc:	<MHBINPATH>/msh
packproc:	<MHBINPATH>/packf
postproc:	<MHETCPATH>/post
rmmproc:	none
rmfproc:	<MHBINPATH>/rmf
sendproc:	<MHBINPATH>/send
showproc:	/usr/ucb/more
whatnowproc:	<MHBINPATH>/whatnow
whomproc:	<MHBINPATH>/whom

If you define the envariable **$MH**, you can specify a profile other than
.mh_profile to be read by the *MH* programs that you invoke. If the value of
$MH is not absolute, (i.e., does not begin with a /), it will be presumed to
start from the current working directory. This is one of the very few excep-
tions in *MH* where non–absolute pathnames are not considered relative to
the user's *MH* directory.

Similarly, if you define the envariable **$MHCONTEXT**, you can specify a
context other than the normal context file (as specified in the *MH* profile).
As always, unless the value of **$MHCONTEXT** is absolute, it will be
presumed to start from your *MH* directory.

MH programs also support other envariables:

$MAILDROP : tells *inc* the default maildrop
> This supercedes the "MailDrop:" profile entry.

$SIGNATURE : tells *send* and *post* your mail signature
> This supercedes the "Signature:" profile entry.

$HOME : tells all *MH* programs your home directory

$SHELL : tells *bbl* the default shell to run

$TERM : tells *MH* your terminal type
> The **$TERMCAP** envariable is also consulted. In particular, these
> tells *scan* and *mhl* how to clear your terminal, and how many col-
> umns wide your terminal is. They also tell *mhl* how many lines
> long your terminal screen is.

$editalt : the alternate message

> This is set by *dist* and *repl* during edit sessions so you can peruse the message being distributed or replied-to. The message is also available through a link called "@" in the current directory if your current working directory and the folder the message lives in are on the same UNIX filesystem.

$mhdraft : the path to the working draft

> This is set by *comp*, *dist*, *forw*, and *repl* to tell the *whatnowproc* which file to ask "What now?" questions about. In addition, *dist*, *forw*, and *repl* set **$mhfolder** if appropriate. Further, *dist* and *repl* set **$mhaltmsg** to tell the *whatnowproc* about an alternate message associated with the draft (the message being distributed or replied–to), and *dist* sets **$mhdist** to tell the *whatnowproc* that message re–distribution is occurring. Also, **$mheditor** is set to tell the *whatnowproc* the user's choice of editor (unless overridden by '–noedit'). Similarly, **$mhuse** may be set by *comp*. Finally, **$mhmessages** is set by *dist*, *forw*, and *repl* if annotations are to occur (along with **$mhannotate**, and **$mhinplace**). It's amazing all the information that has to get passed via envariables to make the "What now?" interface look squeaky clean to the *MH* user, isn't it? The reason for all this is that the *MH* user can select *any* program as the *whatnowproc*, including one of the standard shells. As a result, it's not possible to pass information via an argument list.
>
> If the WHATNOW option was set during *MH* configuration (type '–help' to an *MH* command to find out), and if this envariable is set, if the commands *refile*, *send*, *show*, or *whom* are not given any 'msgs' arguments, then they will default to using the file indicated by **$mhdraft**. This is useful for getting the default behavior supplied by the default *whatnowproc*.

$mhfolder : the folder containing the alternate message

> This is set by *dist* and *repl* during edit sessions so you can peruse other messages in the current folder besides the one being distributed or replied-to. The **$mhfolder** envariable is also set by *show*, *prev*, and *next* for use by *mhl*.

$MHBBRC :

> If you define the envariable **$MHBBRC**, you can specify a BBoards information file other than *.bbrc* to be read by *bbc*. If the

value of **$MHBBRC** is not absolute, (i.e., does not begin with a
/), it will be presumed to start from the current working directory.

$MHFD :

If the OVERHEAD option was set during *MH* configuration (type
'–help' to an *MH* command to find out), then if this envariable is
set, *MH* considers it to be the number of a file–descriptor which is
opened, read–only to the *MH* profile. Similarly, if the envariable
$MHCONTEXTFD is set, this is the number of a file–descriptor
which is opened read–only to the *MH* context. This feature of *MH*
is experimental, and is used to examine possible speed improve-
ments for *MH* startup. Note that these envariables must be set and
non–empty to enable this feature. However, if OVERHEAD is
enabled during *MH* configuration, then when *MH* programs call
other *MH* programs, this scheme is used. These file–descriptors
are not closed throughout the execution of the *MH* program, so
children may take advantage of this. This approach is thought to
be completely safe and does result in some performance enhancements.

Files

$HOME/.mh_profile	The user profile
or $MH	Rather than the standard profile
<mh–dir>/context	The user context
or $CONTEXT	Rather than the standard context
<folder>/.mh_sequences	Public sequences for <folder>

Profile Components

All

See Also

mh(1), environ(5)

Defaults

None

Context

All

History

In previous versions of *MH*, the current–message value of a writable folder was kept in a file called "cur" in the folder itself. In *mh.3*, the *.mh_profile* contained the current–message values for all folders, regardless of their writability.

In all versions of *MH* since *mh.4*, the *.mh_profile* contains only static information, which *MH* programs will **NOT** update. Changes in context are made to the *context* file kept in the users MH *directory*. This includes, but is not limited to: the "Current–Folder" entry and all private sequence information. Public sequence information is kept in a file called *.mh_sequences* in each folder.

To convert from the format used in releases of *MH* prior to the format used in the *mh.4* release, *install–mh* should be invoked with the '–compat' switch. This generally happens automatically on *MH* systems generated with the "COMPAT" option during *MH* configuration.

The *.mh_profile* may override the path of the *context* file, by specifying a "context" entry (this must be in lower-case). If the entry is not absolute (does not start with a /), then it is interpreted relative to the user's *MH* directory. As a result, you can actually have more than one set of private sequences by using different context files.

Bugs

The shell quoting conventions are not available in the .mh_profile. Each token is separated by whitespace.

There is some question as to what kind of arguments should be placed in the profile as options. In order to provide a clear answer, recall command line semantics of all *MH* programs: conflicting switches (e.g., '–header and '–noheader') may occur more than one time on the command line, with the last switch taking effect. Other arguments, such as message sequences, filenames and folders, are always remembered on the invocation line and are not superseded by following arguments of the same type. Hence, it is safe to place only switches (and their arguments) in the profile.

If one finds that an *MH* program is being invoked again and again with the same arguments, and those arguments aren't switches, then there are a few possible solutions to this problem. The first is to create a (soft) link in your *$HOME/bin* directory to the *MH* program of your choice. By giving this link a different name, you can create a new entry in your profile and use an alternate set of defaults for the *MH* command. Similarly, you could create a small shell script which called the *MH* program of your choice with an alternate set of invocation line switches (using links and an alternate profile entry is preferable to this solution).

Finally, the *csh* user could create an alias for the command of the form:

    alias cmd 'cmd arg1 arg2 ...'

In this way, the user can avoid lengthy type–in to the shell, and still give *MH* commands safely. (Recall that some *MH* commands invoke others, and that in all cases, the profile is read, meaning that aliases are disregarded beyond an initial command invocation)

Part V
Manual Pages

Name

mh–sequence – sequence specification for MH message system

Synopsis

most *MH* commands

Description

Most *MH* commands accept a 'msg' or 'msgs' specification, where 'msg' indicates one message and 'msgs' indicates one or more messages. To designate a message, you may use either its number (e.g., 1, 10, 234) or one of these "reserved" message names:

Name	*Description*
first	the first message in the folder
last	the last message in the folder
cur	the most recently accessed message
prev	the message numerically preceding "cur"
next	the message numerically following "cur"

In commands that take a 'msg' argument, the default is "cur". As a shorthand, "." is equivalent to "cur".

For example: In a folder containing five messages numbered 5, 10, 94, 177 and 325, "first" is 5 and "last" is 325. If "cur" is 94, then "prev" is 10 and "next" is 177.

The word 'msgs' indicates that one or more messages may be specified. Such a specification consists of one message designation or of several message designations separated by spaces. A message designation consists either of a message name as defined above, or a message range.

A message range is specified as "name1–name2" or "name:n", where 'name', 'name1' and 'name2' are message names, and 'n' is an integer.

The specification "name1–name2" designates all currently-existing messages from 'name1' to 'name2' inclusive. The message name "all" is a shorthand for the message range "first–last".

The specification "name:n" designates up to 'n' messages. These messages start with 'name' if 'name' is a message number or one of the reserved names "first" "cur", or "next", The messages end with 'name' if 'name' is "prev" or "last". The interpretation of 'n' may be overridden by preceding 'n' with a plus or minus sign; '+n' always means up to 'n' messages starting with 'name', and '–n' always means up to 'n' messages ending with 'name'.

In commands which accept a 'msgs' argument, the default is either "cur" or "all", depending on which makes more sense for each command (see the individual man pages for details). Repeated specifications of the same message have the same effect as a single specification of the message.

User–Defined Message Sequences

In addition to the "reserved" (pre-defined) message names given above, *MH* supports user-defined sequence names. User-defined sequences allow the *MH* user a tremendous amount of power in dealing with groups of messages in the same folder by allowing the user to bind a group of messages to a meaningful symbolic name.

The name used to denote a message sequence must consist of an alphabetic character followed by zero or more alphanumeric characters, and can not be one of the "reserved" message names above. After defining a sequence, it can be used wherever an *MH* command expects a 'msg' or 'msgs' argument.

Some forms of message ranges are allowed with user-defined sequences. The specification "name:n" may be used, and it designates up to the first 'n' messages (or last 'n' messages for '–n') which are elements of the user-defined sequence 'name'.

The specifications "name:next" and "name:prev" may also be used, and they designate the next or previous message (relative to the current message) which is an element of the user-defined sequence 'name'. The specificaitions "name:first" and "name:last" are equivalent to "name:1" and "name:–1", respectively. The specification "name:cur" is not allowed (use just "cur" instead). The syntax of these message range specifcations is subject to change in the future.

User-defined sequence names are specific to each folder. They are defined using the *pick* and *mark* commands.

Part V
Manual Pages

Public and Private User-Defined Sequences

There are two varieties of sequences: *public* sequences and *private* sequences. *Public* sequences of a folder are accessible to any *MH* user that can read that folder and are kept in the .mh_sequences file in the folder. *Private* sequences are accessible only to the *MH* user that defined those sequences and are kept in the user's *MH* context file. By default, *pick* and *mark* create *public* sequences if the folder for which the sequences are being defined is writable by the *MH* user. Otherwise, *private* sequences are created. This can be overridden with the '–public' and '–private' switches to *mark*.

Sequence Negation

MH provides the ability to select all messages not elements of a user-defined sequence. To do this, the user should define the entry "Sequence–Negation" in the *MH* profile file; its value may be any string. This string is then used to preface an existing user-defined sequence name. This specification then refers to those messages not elements of the specified sequence name. For example, if the profile entry is:

Sequence–Negation: not

then anytime an *MH* command is given "notfoo" as a 'msg' or 'msgs' argument, it would substitute all messages that are not elements of the sequence "foo".

Obviously, the user should beware of defining sequences with names that begin with the value of the "Sequence–Negation" profile entry.

The Previous Sequence

MH provides the ability to remember the 'msgs' or 'msg' argument last given to an *MH* command. The entry "Previous–Sequence" should be defined in the *MH* profile; its value should be a sequence name or multiple sequence names separated by spaces. If this entry is defined, when when an *MH* command finishes, it will define the sequence(s) named in the value of this entry to be those messages that were specified to the command. Hence, a profile entry of

Previous–Sequence: pseq

directs any *MH* command that accepts a 'msg' or 'msgs' argument to define the sequence "pseq" as those messages when it finishes.

Note: there can be a performance penalty in using the "Previous–Sequence" facility. If it is used, **all** *MH* programs have to write the sequence information to the .mh_sequences file for the folder each time they run. If the "Previous–Sequence" profile entry is not included, only *pick* and *mark* will write to the .mh_sequences file.

The Unseen Sequence

Finally, some users like to indicate messages which have not been previously seen by them. Both *inc* and *show* honor the profile entry "Unseen–Sequence" to support this activity. This entry in the .mh_profile should be defined as one or more sequence names separated by spaces. If there is a value for "Unseen–Sequence" in the profile, then whenever *inc* places new messages in a folder, the new messages will also be added to the sequence(s) named in the value of this entry. Hence, a profile entry of

Unseen–Sequence: unseen

directs *inc* to add new messages to the sequence "unseen". Unlike the behavior of the "Previous–Sequence" entry in the profile, however, the sequence(s) will **not** be zeroed by *inc*.

Similarly, whenever *show* (or *next* or *prev*) displays a message, that message will be removed from any sequences named by the "Unseen–Sequence" entry in the profile.

Files

$HOME/.mh_profile	The user profile
<mh–dir>/context	The user context
<folder>/.mh_sequences	Public sequences for <folder>

Profile Components

Sequence–Negation:	To designate messages not in a sequence
Previous–Sequence:	The last message specification given
Unseen–Sequence:	Those messages not yet seen by the user

See Also

mh(1), mark(1), pick(1), mh-profile(5)

Defaults

None

Context

All

Bugs

User-defined sequences are stored in the .mh_sequences file as a series of message specifications separated by spaces. If a user-defined sequence contains too many individual message specifications, that line in the file may become too long for *MH* to handle. This will generate the error message ".mh_sequences is poorly formatted". You'll have to edit the file by hand to remove the offending line.

This can happen to users who define the "Previous–Sequence" entry in the *MH* profile and have a folder containing many messages with gaps in the numbering. A workaround for large folders is to minimize numbering gaps by using "folder –pack" often.

Name

mh – Message Handler

Synopsis

any *MH* command

Description

MH is the name of a powerful message handling system. Rather then being a single comprehensive program, *MH* consists of a collection of fairly simple single-purpose programs to send, receive, save, and retrieve messages. The user should refer to the *MH User's Manual* and the pages for the *MH* programs in the Unix Programmers Manual.

Unlike *mail*, the standard UNIX mail user interface program, *MH* is not a closed system which must be explicitly run, then exited when you wish to return to the shell. You may freely intersperse *MH* commands with other shell commands, allowing you to read and answer your mail while you have (for example) a compilation running, or search for a file or run programs as needed to find the answer to someone's question before answering their mail.

The rest of this manual entry is a quick tutorial which will teach you the basics of *MH*. You should read the manual entries for the individual programs for complete documentation.

To get started using *MH*, put the directory **<MHBINPATH>** on your **$PATH**. This is best done in one of the files: **.profile**, **.login**, or **.cshrc** in your home directory. (Check the manual entry for the shell you use, in case you don't know how to do this.) Run the *inc* command. If you've never used *MH* before, it will create the necessary default files and directories after asking you if you wish it to do so.

inc moves mail from your system maildrop into your *MH* '+inbox' folder, breaking it up into separate files and converting it to *MH* format as it goes. It prints one line for each message it processes, containing the from field, the subject field and as much of the first line of the message as will fit. It leaves the first message it processes as your current message. You'll need to run *inc* each time you wish to incorporate new mail into your *MH* file.

scan prints a list of the messages in your current folder.

The commands: *show*, *next*, and *prev* are used to read specific messages from the current folder. *show* displays the current message, or a specific message, which may be specified by its number, which you pass as an argument to *show*. *next* and *prev* display, respectively, the message numerically after or before the current message. In all cases, the message displayed becomes the current message. If there is no current message, *show* may be called with an argument, or *next* may be used to advance to the first message.

rmm (remove message) deletes the current message. It may be called with message numbers passed as arguments, to delete specific messages.

repl is used to respond to the current message (by default). It places you in the editor with a prototype response form. While you're in the editor, you may peruse the item you're responding to by reading the file **@**. After completing your response, type **l** to review it, or **s** to send it.

comp allows you to compose a message by putting you in the editor on a prototype message form, and then lets you send it.

All the *MH* commands may be run with the single argument: '–help', which causes them to print a list of the arguments they may be invoked with.

Commands which take a message number as an argument (*scan*, *show*, *repl*, ...) also take one of the words: *first*, *prev*, *cur*, *next*, or *last* to indicate (respectively) the first, previous, current, next, or last message in the current folder (assuming they are defined).

Commands which take a range of message numbers (*rmm*, *scan*, *show*, ...) also take any of the abbreviations:

> *<num1>-<num2>* - Indicates all messages in the range <num1> to <num2>, inclusive. The range **must** be nonempty.

> *<num>:+N*
> *<num>:-N* - Up to *N* messages beginning with (or ending with) message *num*. *Num* may be any of the pre-defined symbols: *first,* prev, or *last*.

first:N
prev:N
next:N
last:N - The first, previous, next or last *N* messages, if they exist.

There are many other possibilities such as creating multiple folders for different topics, and automatically refiling messages according to subject, source, destination, or content. These are beyond the scope of this manual entry.

Following is a list of all the *MH* commands:

ali (1)	– list mail aliases
anno (1)	– annotate messages
burst (1)	– explode digests into messages
comp (1)	– compose a message
dist (1)	– redistribute a message to additional addresses
folder (1)	– set/list current folder/message
folders (1)	– list all folders
forw (1)	– forward messages
inc (1)	– incorporate new mail
mark (1)	– mark messages
mhl (1)	– produce formatted listings of MH messages
mhmail (1)	– send or read mail
mhook (1)	– MH receive–mail hooks
mhpath (1)	– print full pathnames of MH messages and folders
msgchk (1)	– check for messages
msh (1)	– MH shell (and BBoard reader)
next (1)	– show the next message
packf (1)	– compress a folder into a single file
pick (1)	– select messages by content
prev (1)	– show the previous message
prompter (1)	– prompting editor front end
rcvstore (1)	– incorporate new mail asynchronously
refile (1)	– file messages in other folders
repl (1)	– reply to a message
rmf (1)	– remove folder
rmm (1)	– remove messages
scan (1)	– produce a one line per message scan listing
send (1)	– send a message
show (1)	– show (list) messages
sortm (1)	– sort messages

Part V
Manual Pages

vmh (1)	– visual front–end to MH
whatnow (1)	– prompting front–end for send
whom (1)	– report to whom a message would go
mh–alias (5)	– alias file for MH message system
mh–format (5)	– format file for MH message system
mh–mail (5)	– message format for MH message system
mh–profile (5)	– user customization for MH message system
mh–sequence (5)	– sequence specification for MH message system
ap (8)	– parse addresses 822–style
conflict (8)	– search for alias/password conflicts
dp (8)	– parse dates 822–style
fmtdump (8)	– decode MH format files
install–mh (8)	– initialize the MH environment
post (8)	– deliver a message

Files

| <MHBINPATH> | directory containing *MH* commands |
| <MHETCPATH> | *MH* library |

See Also

The RAND MH Message Handling System: User's Manual,
The RAND MH Message Handling System: Tutorial,
The RAND MH Message Handling System: The UCI BBoards Facility,
MH.5: How to process 200 messages a day and still get some real work done

Bugs

If problems are encountered with an *MH* program, the problems should be reported to the local maintainers of *MH*. When doing this, the name of the program should be reported, along with the version information for the program.

To find out what version of an *MH* program is being run, invoke the program with the '–help' switch. In addition to listing the syntax of the command, the program will list information pertaining to its version. This information includes the version of *MH*, the host it was generated on, and the date the program was loaded. A second line of information, found on versions of *MH* after #5.380 include *MH* configuration options. For example,

version: MH 6.1 #1[UCI] (glacier) of Wed Nov 6 01:13:53 PST 1985
options: [BSD42] [MHE] [NETWORK] [SENDMTS] [MMDFII] [SMTP] [POP]

The '6.1 #1[UCI]' indicates that the program is from the UCI *MH.6.1* version of *MH*. The program was generated on the host 'glacier' on 'Wed Nov 6 01:13:53 PST 1985'. It's usually a good idea to send the output of the '–help' switch along with your report.

If there is no local *MH* maintainer, try the address **Bug-MH**. If that fails, use the Internet mailbox **Bug-MH@ICS.UCI.EDU**.

Files

$HOME/.mh_profile   The user profile

Profile Components

Path: To determine the user's MH directory

Name

mhl – produce formatted listings of MH messages

Synopsis

<MHETCPATH>/mhl   [–bell]   [–nobell]   [–clear]   [–noclear]
[–folder +folder]   [–form formfile]   [–length lines]   [–width col-
umns] [–moreproc program] [–nomoreproc] [files ...] [–help]

Description

Mhl is a formatted message listing program. It can be used as a replacement for *more* (1) (the default *showproc*). As with *more*, each of the
messages specified as arguments (or the standard input) will be output. If
more than one message file is specified, the user will be prompted prior to
each one, and a <RETURN> or <EOT> will begin the output, with
<RETURN> clearing the screen (if appropriate), and <EOT> (usually
CTRL–D) suppressing the screen clear. An <INTERRUPT> (usually
CTRL–C) will abort the current message output, prompting for the next
message (if there is one), and a <QUIT> (usually CTRL-\) will terminate
the program (without core dump).

The '–bell' option tells *mhl* to ring the terminal's bell at the end of each
page, while the '–clear' option tells *mhl* to clear the scree at the end of each
page (or output a formfeed after each message). Both of these switches
(and their inverse counterparts) take effect only if the profile entry
moreproc is defined but empty, and *mhl* is outputting to a terminal. If the
moreproc entry is defined and non-empty, and *mhl* is outputting to a terminal, then *mhl* will cause the *moreproc* to be placed between the terminal
and *mhl* and the switches are ignored. Furthermore, if the '–clear' switch is
used and *mhl's* output is directed to a terminal, then *mhl* will consult the
$TERM and **$TERMCAP** envariables to determine the user's terminal
type in order to find out how to clear the screen. If the '–clear' switch is
used and *mhl's* output is not directed to a terminal (e.g., a pipe or a file),
then *mhl* will send a formfeed after each message.

To override the default *moreproc* and the profile entry, use the
'–moreproc program' switch. Note that *mhl* will never start a *moreproc* if
invoked on a hardcopy terminal.

The '–length length' and '–width width' switches set the screen length and width, respectively. These default to the values indicated by **$TERMCAP**, if appropriate, otherwise they default to 40 and 80, respectively.

The default format file used by *mhl* is called *mhl.format* (which is first searched for in the user's *MH* directory, and then sought in the *<MHETCPATH>* directory), this can be changed by using the '–form formatfile' switch.

Finally, the '–folder +folder' switch sets the *MH* folder name, which is used for the "messagename:" field described below. The envariable **$mhfolder** is consulted for the default value, which *show*, *next*, and *prev* initialize appropriately.

Mhl operates in two phases: 1) read and parse the format file, and 2) process each message (file). During phase 1, an internal description of the format is produced as a structured list. In phase 2, this list is walked for each message, outputting message information under the format constraints from the format file.

The "mhl.format" form file contains information controlling screen clearing, screen size, wrap–around control, transparent text, component ordering, and component formatting. Also, a list of components to ignore may be specified, and a couple of "special" components are defined to provide added functionality. Message output will be in the order specified by the order in the format file.

Each line of mhl.format has one of the formats:

```
;comment
:cleartext
variable[,variable ... ]
component:[variable, ... ]
```

A line beginning with a ';' is a comment, and is ignored. A line beginning with a ':' is clear text, and is output exactly as is. A line containing only a ':' produces a blank line in the output. A line beginning with "component:" defines the format for the specified component, and finally, remaining lines define the global environment.

For example, the line:

width=80,length=40,clearscreen,overflowtext="***",overflowoffset=5

defines the screen size to be 80 columns by 40 rows, specifies that the screen should be cleared prior to each page, that the overflow indentation is 5, and that overflow text should be flagged with "***".

Following are all of the current variables and their arguments. If they follow a component, they apply only to that component, otherwise, their affect is global. Since the whole format is parsed before any output processing, the last global switch setting for a variable applies to the whole message if that variable is used in a global context (i.e., bell, clearscreen, width, length).

variable	*type*	*semantics*
width	integer	screen width or component width
length	integer	screen length or component length
offset	integer	positions to indent "component: "
overflowtext	string	text to use at the beginning of an overflow line
overflowoffset	integer	positions to indent overflow lines
compwidth	integer	positions to indent component text after the first line is output
uppercase	flag	output text of this component in all upper case
nouppercase	flag	don't uppercase
clearscreen	flag/G	clear the screen prior to each page
noclearscreen	flag/G	don't clearscreen
bell	flag/G	ring the bell at the end of each page
nobell	flag/G	don't bell
component	string/L	name to use instead of "component" for this component
nocomponent	flag	don't output "component: " for this component
center	flag	center component on line (works for one–line components only)
nocenter	flag	don't center
leftadjust	flag	strip off leading whitespace on each line of text
noleftadjust	flag	don't leftadjust
compress	flag	change newlines in text to spaces

nocompress	flag	don't compress
split	flag	don't combine multiple fields into a single field
nosplit	flag	combine multiple fields into a single field
formatfield	string	format string for this component (see below)
addrfield	flag	field contains addresses
datefield	flag	field contains dates

To specify the value of integer–valued and string–valued variables, follow their name with an equals–sign and the value. Integer–valued variables are given decimal values, while string–valued variables are given arbitrary text bracketed by double–quotes. If a value is suffixed by "/G" or "/L", then its value is useful in a global–only or local–only context (respectively).

A line of the form:

    ignores=component, . . .

specifies a list of components which are never output.

The component "MessageName" (case–insensitive) will output the actual message name (file name) preceded by the folder name if one is specified or found in the environment. The format is identical to that produced by the '–header' option to *show*.

The component "Extras" will output all of the components of the message which were not matched by explicit components, or included in the ignore list. If this component is not specified, an ignore list is not needed since all non–specified components will be ignored.

If "nocomponent" is NOT specified, then the component name will be output as it appears in the format file.

The default format is:

```
: -- using template mhl.format --
overflowtext="***",overflowoffset=5
leftadjust,compwidth=9
ignores=msgid,message-id,received
Date:formatfield="%<(nodate{text})%{text}% |%(pretty{text})%>"
To:
cc:
:
From:
Subject:
:
extras:nocomponent
:
body:nocomponent,overflowtext=,overflowoffset=0,noleftadjust
```

The variable "formatfield" specifies a format string (see *mh–format* (5)). The flag variables "addrfield" and "datefield" (which are mutually exclusive), tell *mhl* to interpret the escapes in the format string as either addresses or dates, respectively.

By default, *mhl* does not apply any formatting string to fields containing address or dates (see *mh–mail* (5) for a list of these fields). Note that this results in faster operation since *mhl* must parse both addresses and dates in order to apply a format string to them. If desired, *mhl* can be given a default format string for either address or date fields (but not both). To do this, on a global line specify: either the flag addrfield or datefield, along with the apropriate formatfield variable string.

Files

<MHETCPATH>/mhl.format	The message template
or <mh–dir>/mhl.format	Rather than the standard template
$HOME/.mh_profile	The user profile

Profile Components

moreproc: Program to use as interactive front–end

See Also

show(1), ap(8), dp(8)

Defaults

'–bell'
'–noclear'
'–length 40'
'–width 80'

Context

None

Bugs

There should be some way to pass 'bell' and 'clear' information to the front–end.

On hosts where *MH* was configured with the BERK option, address parsing is not enabled.

Name

mhook – MH receive–mail hooks*

Synopsis

$HOME/.maildelivery

<MHETCPATH>/rcvdist   [–form formfile]   [switches for *postproc*]
      address ... [–help]

<MHETCPATH>/rcvpack file [–help]

<MHETCPATH>/rcvtty [command] [–form formatfile] [–format string]
      [–bell] [–nobell] [–newline] [–nonewline] [–biff] [–help]

Description

A receive–mail hook is a program that is run whenever you receive a mail
message. You do **NOT** invoke the hook yourself. The hook is invoked by
your transport agent:

- On MMDF hosts, hook is invoked on your behalf by *MMDF* when you
  (symbolically) link <MHETCPATH>/slocal to the file bin/rcvmail in
  your home directory.

- On MMDFII hosts, the hook is invoked on your behalf by *MMDF*.

- On *SendMail* hosts, the hook is invoked on your behalf by *SendMail*,
  when you include the line
        "| <MHETCPATH>/slocal -user $USER"
  in your .forward file in your home directory.

- On hosts running the MH transport agent, the hook is invoked on your
  behalf by *MH*.

The *.maildelivery* file, which is an ordinary ASCII file, controls how local
delivery is performed. This file is read by *slocal* on hosts configured for the
MMDF and *SendMail* transport agents, by the local channel on MMDFII
hosts, and by *post* on hosts that use the MH transport agent.

---

*This manual page has been split into parts. See the NOTE section below.

NOTE

The next part of this manual page is automatically configured for your system when MH is built. To avoid confusion, O'Reilly & Associates split out the section of text that describes the *.mail-delivery* file.

- If your host is configured for the mail transport agent *SendMail*, MMDFI, or MH, read the *maildelivery-slocal* manual page. Your online copy of this "manual page" is actually part of the *mhook*(1) manual page.

- If your host is configured for MMDFII, read the *maildelivery-mmdfII* manual page. Your online version of this manual page is named *maildelivery*(5).

Four programs are currently standardly available, *rcvdist* (redistribute incoming messages to additional recipients), *rcvpack* (save incoming messages in a *packf*'d file), and *rcvtty* (notify user of incoming messages). The fourth program, *rcvstore* (1) is described separately. They all reside in the *<MHETCPATH>/* directory.

The *rcvdist* program will resend a copy of the message to all of the addresses listed on its command line. It uses the format string facility described in *mh–format* (5).

The *rcvpack* program will append a copy of the message to the file listed on its command line. Its use is obsoleted by the *.maildelivery*.

The *rcvtty* program executes the named file with the message as its standard input, and writes the resulting output on your terminal.

If no file is specified, or is bogus, etc., then *rcvtty* will instead write a one–line scan listing. Either the '–form formatfile' or '–format string' option may be used to override the default output format (see *mh–format* (5)). A newline is output before the message output, and the terminal bell is rung after the output. The '–nonewline' and '–nobell' options will inhibit these functions.

Normally, *rcvtty* obeys write permission as granted by *mesg* (1). With the '–biff' option, *rcvtty* will obey the notification status set by *biff* (1). If the terminal access daemon (TTYD) is available on your system, then *rcvtty* will give its output to the daemon for output instead of writing on the user's terminal.

Part V Manual Pages

Files

<MHETCPATH>/mtstailor   tailor file
$HOME/.maildelivery   The file controlling local delivery
<MHETCPATH>/maildelivery   Rather than the standard file

See Also

rcvstore (1), mh–format(5)

Context

None

History

On *slocal* hosts: For compatibility with older versions of *MH*, if *slocal* can't find the user's *.maildelivery* file, it will attempt to execute an old–style rcvmail hook in the user's $HOME directory. In particular, it will first attempt to execute:

.mh_receive file maildrop directory user

failing that it will attempt to execute:

$HOME/bin/rcvmail user file sender

before giving up and writing to the user's maildrop. In addition, whenever a hook or process is invoked, file–descriptor three (3) is set to the message in addition to the standard input.

On *MMDF* hosts: In addition to an exit status of zero, the *MMDF* values *RP_MOK* (32) and *RP_OK* (9) mean that the message has been fully delivered. All other non–zero exit status, including abnormal termination, is interpreted as the *MMDF* value *RP_MECH* (200), which means "use an alternate route" (deliver the message to the maildrop).

Bugs

Only two return codes are meaningful, others should be.

Versions of *MMDF* with the *maildelivery* mechanism aren't entirely back-wards–compatible with earlier versions. If you have an old–style hook, the best you can do is to have a one–line *.maildelivery* file:

default – pipe A "bin/rcvmail $(address) $(info) $(sender)"

Name

rcvstore – incorporate new mail asynchronously

Synopsis

<MHETCPATH>/rcvstore   [+folder]   [–create]   [–nocreate]
[–sequence name ...] [–public] [–nopublic] [–zero] [–nozero]
[–help]

Description

Rcvstore incorporates a message from the standard input into an *MH* folder.
If '+folder' isn't specified, the folder named "inbox" in the user's *MH*
directory will be used instead. The new message being incorporated is
assigned the next highest number in the folder. If the specified (or default)
folder doesn't exist, then it will be created if the '–create' option is specified, otherwise *rcvstore* will exit.

If the user's profile contains a "Msg–Protect: nnn" entry, it will be used as
the protection on the newly created messages, otherwise the *MH* default of
0644 will be used. During all operations on messages, this initially
assigned protection will be preserved for each message, so *chmod*(1) may
be used to set a protection on an individual message, and its protection will
be preserved thereafter.

Rcvstore will incorporate anything except zero length messages into the
user's MH folder.

If the profile entry "Unseen–Sequence" is present and non–empty, then
rcvstore will add the newly incorporated message to each sequence named
by the profile entry. This is similar to the "Previous–Sequence" profile
entry supported by all *MH* commands which take 'msgs' or 'msg' arguments. Note that *rcvstore* will not zero each sequence prior to adding
messages.

Furthermore, the incoming messages may be added to user-defined
sequences as they arrive by appropriate use of the '–sequence' option. As
with *pick*, use of the '–zero' and '–nozero' switches can also be used to
zero old sequences or not. Similarly, use of the '–public' and '–nopublic'
switches may be used to force additions to public and private sequences.

Files

$HOME/.mh_profile   The user profile

Profile Components

Path:	To determine the user's MH directory
Folder–Protect:	To set mode when creating a new folder
Msg–Protect:	To set mode when creating a new message
Unseen–Sequence:	To name sequences denoting unseen messages

See Also

inc(1), pick(1), mh–mail(5)

Defaults

'+folder' defaults to "inbox"
'–create'
'–nopublic' if the folder is read–only, '–public' otherwise
'–nozero'

Context

No context changes will be attempted, with the exception of sequence manipulation.

Name

xmh – send and read mail with an X interface to MH

Synopsis

xmh [–path *mailpath*] [–initial *foldername*] [–flag] [*–toolkitoption* ...]

Description

The *xmh* program provides a graphical user interface to the *MH* Message Handling System. To actually do things with your mail, it makes calls to the *MH* package. Electronic mail messages may be composed, sent, received, replied to, forwarded, sorted, and stored in folders. *xmh* provides extensive mechanism for customization of the user interface.

This document introduces many aspects of the Athena Widget Set.

Options

–path *directory*
This option specifies an alternate collection of mail folders in which to process mail. The directory is specified as an absolute pathname. The default mail path is the value of the Path component in the *MH* profile, which is determined by the **MH** environment variable and defaults to $HOME/.mh_profile. $HOME/Mail will be used as the path if the *MH* Path is not given in the profile.

–initial *folder*
This option specifies an alternate folder which may receive new mail and is initially opened by *xmh*. The default initial folder is ''inbox''.

–flag
This option will cause *xmh* to change the appearance of appropriate folder buttons and to request the window manager to change the appearance of the *xmh* icon when new mail has arrived. By default, *xmh* will change the appearance of the ''inbox'' folder button when new mail is waiting. The application-specific resource **checkNewMail** can be used to turn off this notification, and the **–flag** option will still override it.

These three options have corresponding application-specific resources, **MailPath**, **InitialFolder**, and **MailWaitingFlag**, which can be specified in a resource file.

The standard toolkit command line options are given in *X(1)*.

Installation

xmh requires that the user is already set up to use *MH*, version 6. To do so, see if there is a file called .mh_profile in your home directory. If it exists, check to see if it contains a line that starts with "Current-Folder". If it does, you've been using version 4 or earlier of *MH*; to convert to version 6, you must remove that line. (Failure to do so causes spurious output to stderr, which can hang *xmh* depending on your setup.)

If you do not already have a .mh_profile, you can create one (and everything else you need) by typing "inc" to the shell. You should do this before using *xmh* to incorporate new mail.

For more information, refer to the *mh(1)* documentation.

Much of the user interface of *xmh* is configured in the *Xmh* application class defaults file; if this file was not installed properly a warning message will appear when *xmh* is used. *xmh* is backwards compatible with the R4 application class defaults file.

The default value of the SendBreakWidth resource has changed since R4.

Basic Screen Layout

xmh starts out with a single window, divided into four major areas:

- Six buttons with pull-down command menus.

- A collection of buttons, one for each top level folder. New users of *MH* will have two folders, "drafts" and "inbox".

- A listing, or Table of Contents, of the messages in the open folder. Initially, this will show the messages in "inbox".

- A view of one of your messages. Initially this is blank.

XMH and the Athena Widget Set

xmh uses the X Toolkit Intrinsics and the Athena Widget Set. Many of the features described below (scrollbars, buttonboxes, etc.) are actually part of the Athena Widget Set, and are described here only for completeness. For more information, see the Athena Widget Set documentation.

Scrollbars

Some parts of the main window will have a vertical area on the left containing a grey bar. This area is a *scrollbar*. They are used whenever the data in a window takes up more space than can be displayed. The grey bar indicates what portion of your data is visible. Thus, if the entire length of the area is grey, then you are looking at all your data. If only the first half is grey, then you are looking at the top half of your data. The message viewing area will have a horizontal scrollbar if the text of the message is wider than the viewing area.

You can use the pointer in the scrollbar to change what part of the data is visible. If you click with pointer button 2, the top of the grey area will move to where the pointer is, and the corresponding portion of data will be displayed. If you hold down pointer button 2, you can drag around the grey area. This makes it easy to get to the top of the data: just press with button 2, drag off the top of the scrollbar, and release.

If you click with button 1, then the data to the right of the pointer will scroll to the top of the window. If you click with pointer button 3, then the data at the top of the window will scroll down to where the pointer is.

Buttonboxes, Buttons, and Menus

Any area containing many words or short phrases, each enclosed in a rectangular or rounded boundary, is called a *buttonbox*. Each rectangle or rounded area is actually a button that you can press by moving the pointer onto it and pressing pointer button 1. If a given buttonbox has more buttons in it than can fit, it will be displayed with a scrollbar, so you can always scroll to the button you want.

Some buttons have pull-down menus. Pressing the pointer button while the pointer is over one of these buttons will pull down a menu. Continuing to hold the button down while moving the pointer over the menu, called dragging the pointer, will highlight each selectable item on the menu as the pointer passes over it. To select an item in the menu, release the pointer button while the item is highlighted.

Adjusting the Relative Sizes of Areas

If you're not satisfied with the sizes of the various areas of the main window, they can easily be changed. Near the right edge of the border between each region is a black box, called a *grip*. Simply point to that grip with the pointer, press a pointer button, drag up or down, and release. Exactly what happens depends on which pointer button you press.

If you drag with the pointer button 2, then only that border will move. This mode is simplest to understand, but is the least useful.

If you drag with pointer button 1, then you are adjusting the size of the window above. *xmh* will attempt to compensate by adjusting some window below it.

If you drag with pointer button 3, then you are adjusting the size of the window below. *xmh* will attempt to compensate by adjusting some window above it.

All windows have a minimum and maximum size; you will never be allowed to move a border past the point where it would make a window have an invalid size.

Processing Your Mail

This section will define the concepts of the selected folder, current folder, selected message(s), current message, selected sequence, and current sequence. Each *xmh* command is introduced.

For use in customization, action procedures corresponding to each command are given; these action procedures can be used to customize the user interface, particularly the keyboard accelerators and the functionality of the buttons in the optional button box created by the application resource **CommandButtonCount**.

Folders and Sequences

A folder contains a collection of mail messages, or is empty. *xmh* supports folders with one level of subfolders.

The selected folder is whichever foldername appears in the bar above the folder buttons. Note that this is not necessarily the same folder that is currently being viewed. To change the selected folder, just press on the desired folder button with pointer button 1; if that folder has subfolders, select a folder from the pull-down menu.

The Table of Contents, or toc, lists the messages in the viewed folder. The title bar above the Table of Contents displays the name of the viewed folder.

The toc title bar also displays the name of the viewed sequence of messages within the viewed folder. Every folder has an implicit "all" sequence, which contains all the messages in the folder, and initially the toc title bar will show "inbox:all".

Folder Commands

The *Folder* command menu contains commands of a global nature:

Open Folder
Display the data in the selected folder. Thus, the selected folder also becomes the viewed folder. The action procedure corresponding to this command is **XmhOpenFolder**(*[foldername]*). It takes an optional argument as the name of a folder to select and open; if no folder is specified, the selected folder is opened. It may be specified as part of an event translation from a folder menu button or from a folder menu, or as a binding of a keyboard accelerator to any widget other than the folder menu buttons or the folder menus.

Open Folder in New Window
Displays the selected folder in an additional main window. Note, however, that you cannot reliably display the same folder in more than one window at a time, although *xmh* will not prevent you from trying. The corresponding action is **XmhOpenFolderInNewWindow**().

Create Folder
Create a new folder. You will be prompted for a name for the new folder; to enter the name, move the pointer to the blank box provided and type. Subfolders are created by specifying the parent folder, a slash, and the subfolder name. For example, to create a folder named "xmh" which is a subfolder of an existing folder named "clients", type "clients/xmh". Click on the Okay button when finished, or just type Return; click on Cancel to cancel this operation. The action corresponding to Create Folder is **XmhCreateFolder**().

Delete Folder
Destroy the selected folder. You will be asked to confirm this action (see CONFIRMATION WINDOWS). Destroying a folder will also destroy any subfolders of that folder. The corresponding action is **XmhDeleteFolder**().

Close Window

Exits *xmh*, after first confirming that you won't lose any changes; or, if selected from any additional *xmh* window, simply closes that window. The corresponding action is **XmhClose()**.

Highlighted Messages, Selected Messages and the Current Message

It is possible to highlight a set of adjacent messages in the area of the Table of Contents. To highlight a message, click on it with pointer button 1. To highlight a range of messages, click on the first one with pointer button 1 and on the last one with pointer button 3; or press pointer button 1, drag, and release. To extend a range of selected messages, use pointer button 3. To highlight all messages in the table of contents, click rapidly three times with pointer button 1. To cancel any selection in the table of contents, click rapidly twice. The selected messages are the same as the highlighted messages, if any. If no messages are highlighted, then the selected messages are considered the same as the current message. The current message is indicated by a '+' next to the message number. It usually corresponds to the message currently being viewed. Upon opening a new folder, for example, the current message will be different from the viewed message. When a message is viewed, the title bar above the view will identify the message.

Table of Contents Commands

The *Table of Contents* command menu contains commands which operate on the open, or viewed, folder.

Incorporate New Mail

Add any new mail received to viewed folder, and set the current message to be the first new message. This command is selectable in the menu and will execute only if the viewed folder is allowed to receive new mail. By default, only "inbox" is allowed to incorporate new mail. The corresponding action is **XmhIncorporateNewMail()**.

Commit Changes

Execute all deletions, moves, and copies that have been marked in this folder. The corresponding action is **XmhCommitChanges()**.

Pack Folder

Renumber the messages in this folder so they start with 1 and increment by 1. The corresponding action is **XmhPackFolder()**.

Sort Folder

Sort the messages in this folder in chronological order. (As a side effect, this may also pack the folder.) The corresponding action is **XmhSort-Folder()**.

Rescan Folder

Rebuild the list of messages. This can be used whenever you suspect that *xmh*'s idea of what messages you have is wrong. (In particular, this is necessary if you change things using straight *MH* commands without using *xmh*.) The corresponding action is **XmhForceRescan()**.

Message Commands

The *Message* command menu contains commands which operate on the selected message(s), or if there are no selected messages, the current message.

Compose Message

Composes a new message. A new window will be brought up for composition; a description of it is given in the COMPOSITION WINDOWS section below. This command does not affect the current message. The corresponding action is **XmhComposeMessage()**.

View Next Message

View the first selected message. If no messages are highlighted, view the current message. If current message is already being viewed, view the first unmarked message after the current message. The corresponding action is **XmhViewNextMessage()**.

View Previous

View the last selected message. If no messages are highlighted, view the current message. If current message is already being viewed, view the first unmarked message before the current message. The corresponding action is **XmhViewPrevious()**.

Delete

Mark the selected messages for deletion. If no messages are highlighted, mark the current message for deletion and automatically display the next unmarked message. The corresponding action is **XmhMarkDelete()**.

Move

Mark the selected messages to be moved into the currently selected folder. (If the selected folder is the same as the viewed folder, this command will just beep.) If no messages are highlighted, mark the current message to be moved and display the next unmarked message. The corresponding action is **XmhMarkMove()**.

Copy as Link

Mark the selected messages to be copied into the selected folder. (If the selected folder is the same as the viewed folder, this command will just beep.) If no messages are highlighted, mark the current message to be copied. Note that messages are actually linked, not copied; editing a message copied by *xmh* will affect all copies of the message. The corresponding action is **XmhMarkCopy()**.

Unmark

Remove any of the above three marks from the selected messages, or the current message, if none are highlighted. The corresponding action is **XmhUnmark()**.

View in New

Create a new window containing only a view of the first selected message, or the current message, if none are highlighted. The corresponding action is **XmhViewInNewWindow()**.

Reply

Create a composition window in reply to the first selected message, or the current message, if none are highlighted. The corresponding action is **XmhReply()**.

Forward

Create a composition window whose body is initialized to contain an encapsulation of of the selected messages, or the current message if none are highlighted. The corresponding action is **XmhForward()**.

Use as Composition

Create a composition window whose body is initialized to be the contents of the first selected message, or the current message if none are selected. Any changes you make in the composition will be saved in a new message in the "drafts" folder, and will not change the original message. However, there is an exception to this rule. If the message to be used as composition was selected from the "drafts" folder, (see BUGS), the changes will be reflected in the original message (see COMPOSITION WINDOWS). The action procedure corresponding to this command is **XmhUseAs-Composition()**.

Print
Print the selected messages, or the current message if none are selected. *xmh* normally prints by invoking the *enscript*(1) command, but this can be customized with the *xmh* application-specific resource **PrintCommand**. The corresponding action is **XmhPrint()**.

Sequence Commands

The *Sequence* command menu contains commands pertaining to message sequences (See MESSAGE-SEQUENCES), and a list of the message-sequences defined for the currently viewed folder. The selected message-sequence is indicated by a check mark in its entry in the margin of the menu. To change the selected message-sequence, select a new message-sequence from the sequence menu.

Pick Messages
Define a new message-sequence. The corresponding action is **XmhPick-Messages()**.

The following menu entries will be sensitive only if the current folder has any message-sequences other than the ''all'' message-sequence.

Open Sequence
Change the viewed sequence to be the same as the selected sequence. The corresponding action is **XmhOpenSequence()**.

Add to Sequence
Add the selected messages to the selected sequence. The corresponding action is **XmhAddToSequence()**.

Remove from Sequence
Remove the selected messages from the selected sequence. The corresponding action is **XmhRemoveFromSequence()**.

Delete Sequence
Remove the selected sequence entirely. The messages themselves are not affected; they simply are no longer grouped together to define a message-sequence. The corresponding action is **XmhDeleteSequence()**.

View Commands

Commands in the *View* menu and in the buttonboxes of view windows (which result from the *Message* menu command **View In New**) correspond in functionality to commands of the same name in the *Message* menu, but they operate on the viewed message rather than the selected messages or current message.

Close Window
When the viewed message is in a separate view window, this command will close the view, after confirming the status of any unsaved edits. The corresponding action procedure is **XmhCloseView()**.

Reply
Create a composition window in reply to the viewed message. The related action procedure is **XmhViewReply()**.

Forward
Create a composition window whose body is initialized contain an encapsulation of the viewed message. The corresponding action is **XmhViewForward()**.

Use As Composition
Create a composition window whose body is initialized to be the contents of the viewed message. Any changes made in the composition window will be saved in a new message in the ''drafts'' folder, and will not change the original message. An exception: if the viewed message was selected from the ''drafts'' folder, (see BUGS) the original message is edited. The action procedure corresponding to this command is **XmhViewUseAsComposition()**.

Edit Message
This command enables the direct editing of the viewed message. The action procedure is **XmhEditView()**.

Save Message
This command is insensitive until the message has been edited; when activated, edits will be saved to the original message in the view. The corresponding action is **XmhSaveView()**.

Print
Print the viewed message. *xmh* prints by invoking the *enscript*(1) command, but this can be customized with the application-specific resource **PrintCommand**. The corresponding action procedure is **XmhPrintView()**.

Delete

Marks the viewed message for deletion. The corresponding action procedure is **XmhViewMarkDelete()**.

Options

The *Options* menu contains one entry.

Read in Reverse

When selected, a check mark appears in the margin of this menu entry.
Read in Reverse will switch the meaning of the next and previous
messages, and will increment to the current message marker in the opposite
direction. This is useful if you want to read your messages in the order of
most recent first. The option acts as a toggle; select it from the menu a second time to undo the effect. The check mark appears when the option is
selected.

Composition Windows

Composition windows are created by selecting **Compose Message** from the
Message command menu, or by selecting **Reply** or **Forward** or **Use as
Composition** from the *Message* or *View* command menu. These are used
to compose mail messages. Aside from the normal text editing functions,
there are six command buttons associated with composition windows:

Close Window

Close this composition window. If changes have been made since the most
recent Save or Send, you will be asked to confirm losing them. The corresponding action is **XmhCloseView()**.

Send

Send this composition. The corresponding action is **XmhSend()**.

New Headers

Replace the current composition with an empty message. If changes have
been made since the most recent Send or Save, you will be asked to confirm
losing them. The corresponding action is **XmhResetCompose()**.

Compose Message

Bring up another new composition window. The corresponding action is
XmhComposeMessage().

Save Message

Save this composition in your drafts folder. Then you can safely close the
composition. At some future date, you can continue working on the composition by opening the drafts folder, selecting the message, and using the

"Use as Composition" command. The corresponding action is **XmhSave()**.

Insert

Insert a related message into the composition. If the composition window was created with a "Reply" command, the related message is the message being replied to, otherwise no related message is defined and this button is insensitive. The message may be filtered before being inserted; see **ReplyInsertFilter** under APPLICATION RESOURCES for more information. The corresponding action is **XmhInsert()**.

Accelerators

Accelerators are shortcuts. They allow you to invoke commands without using the menus, either from the keyboard or by using the pointer.

xmh defines pointer accelerators for common actions: To select and view a message with a single click, use pointer button 2 on the message's entry in the table of contents. To select and open a folder or a sequence in a single action, make the folder or sequence selection with pointer button 2. To mark the highlighted messages, or current message if none have been highlighted, to be moved to a folder in a single action, use pointer button 3 to select the target folder and simultaneously mark the messages. Similarly, selecting a sequence with pointer button 3 will add the highlighted or current message(s) to that sequence. In both of these operations, the selected folder or sequence and the viewed folder or sequence are not changed. *xmh* defines the following keyboard accelerators over the surface of the main window, except in the view area while editing a message:

Meta-I	Incorporate New Mail
Meta-C	Commit Changes
Meta-R	Rescan Folder
Meta-P	Pack Folder
Meta-S	Sort Folder
Meta-space	View Next Message
Meta-c	Mark Copy
Meta-d	Mark Deleted
Meta-f	Forward the selected or current message
Meta-m	Mark Move
Meta-n	View Next Message
Meta-p	View Previous Message

| Meta-r | Reply to the selected or current message |
| Meta-u | Unmark |

Ctrl-V	Scroll the table of contents forward
Meta-V	Scroll the table of contents backward
Ctrl-v	Scroll the view forward
Meta-v	Scroll the view backward

Text Editing Commands

All of the text editing commands are actually defined by the Text widget in the Athena Widget Set. The commands may be bound to different keys than the defaults described below through the X Toolkit Intrinsics key re-binding mechanisms. See the X Toolkit Intrinsics and the Athena Widget Set documentation for more details. Whenever you are asked to enter any text, you will be using a standard text editing interface. Various control and meta keystroke combinations are bound to a somewhat Emacs-like set of commands. In addition, the pointer buttons may be used to select a portion of text or to move the insertion point in the text. Pressing pointer button 1 causes the insertion point to move to the pointer. Double-clicking button 1 selects a word, triple-clicking selects a line, quadruple-clicking selects a paragraph, and clicking rapidly five times selects every-thing. Any selection may be extended in either direction by using pointer button 3. In the following, a *line* refers to one displayed row of characters in the window. A *paragraph* refers to the text between carriage returns. Text within a paragraph is broken into lines for display based on the current width of the window. When a message is sent, text is broken into lines based upon the values of the **SendBreakWidth** and **SendWidth** application-specific resources. The following keystroke combinations are defined:

Ctrl-a	Beginning Of Line
Ctrl-b	Backward Character
Ctrl-d	Delete Next Character
Ctrl-e	End Of Line
Ctrl-f	Forward Character
Ctrl-g	Multiply Reset
Ctrl-h	Delete Previous Character
Ctrl-j	Newline And Indent
Ctrl-k	Kill To End Of Line
Ctrl-l	Redraw Display
Ctrl-m	Newline
Ctrl-n	Next Line

Ctrl-o	Newline And Backup
Ctrl-p	Previous Line
Ctrl-r	Search/Replace Backward
Ctrl-s	Search/Replace Forward
Ctrl-t	Transpose Characters
Ctrl-u	Multiply by 4
Ctrl-v	Next Page
Ctrl-w	Kill Selection
Ctrl-y	Unkill
Ctrl-z	Scroll One Line Up
Meta-b	Backward Word
Meta-f	Forward Word
Meta-i	Insert File
Meta-k	Kill To End Of Paragraph
Meta-q	Form Paragraph
Meta-v	Previous Page
Meta-y	Insert Current Selection
Meta-z	Scroll One Line Down
Meta-d	Delete Next Word
Meta-D	Kill Word
Meta-h	Delete Previous Word
Meta-H	Backward Kill Word
Meta-<	Beginning Of File
Meta->	End Of File
Meta-]	Forward Paragraph
Meta-[	Backward Paragraph

Meta-Delete	Delete Previous Word
Meta-Shift Delete	Kill Previous Word
Meta-Backspace	Delete Previous Word
Meta-Shift Backspace	Kill Previous Word

In addition, the pointer may be used to copy and paste text:

Button 1 Down	Start Selection
Button 1 Motion	Adjust Selection
Button 1 Up	End Selection (copy)
Button 2 Down	Insert Current Selection (paste)

Button 3 Down	Extend Current Selection
Button 3 Motion	Adjust Selection
Button 3 Up	End Selection (copy)

Confirmation Dialog Boxes

Whenever you press a button that may cause you to lose some work or is otherwise dangerous, a popup dialog box will appear asking you to confirm the action. This window will contain an ''Abort'' or ''No'' button and a ''Confirm'' or ''Yes'' button. Pressing the ''No'' button cancels the operation, and pressing the ''Yes'' will proceed with the operation. Some dialog boxes contain messages from *MH*. Occasionally when the message is more than one line long, not all of the text will be visible. Clicking on the message field will cause the dialog box to resize so that you can read the entire message.

Message-Sequences

An *MH* message sequence is just a set of messages associated with some name. They are local to a particular folder; two different folders can have sequences with the same name. The sequence named ''all'' is predefined in every folder; it consists of the set of all messages in that folder. As many as nine sequences may be defined for each folder, including the predefined ''all'' sequence. (The sequence ''cur'' is also usually defined for every folder; it consists of only the current message. *xmh* hides ''cur'' from the user, instead placing a ''+'' by the current message. Also, *xmh* does not support *MH*'s''unseen'' sequence, so that one is also hidden from the user.) The message sequences for a folder (including one for ''all'') are displayed in the ''Sequence'' menu, below the sequence commands. The table of contents (also known as the ''toc'') is at any one time displaying one message sequence. This is called the ''viewed sequence'', and its name will be displayed in the toc title bar after the folder name. Also, at any time one of the sequences in the menu will have a check mark next to it. This is called the ''selected sequence''. Note that the viewed sequence and the selected sequence are not necessarily the same. (This all pretty much corresponds to the way folders work.) The **Open Sequence**, **Add to Sequence**, **Remove from Sequence**, and **Delete Sequence** commands are active only if the viewed folder contains message-sequences other than ''all'' sequence.

Note that none of the above actually affect whether a message is in the folder. Remember that a sequence is a set of messages within the folder; the above operations just affect what messages are in that set. To create a new sequence, select the "Pick" menu entry. A new window will appear, with lots of places to enter text. Basically, you can describe the sequence's initial set of messages based on characteristics of the message. Thus, you can define a sequence to be all the messages that were from a particular person, or with a particular subject, and so on. You can also connect things up with boolean operators, so you can select all things from "weissman" with a subject containing "xmh". The layout should be fairly obvious. The simplest cases are the easiest: just point to the proper field and type. If you enter in more than one field, it will only select messages which match all non-empty fields.

The more complicated cases arise when you want things that match one field or another one, but not necessarily both. That's what all the "or" buttons are for. If you want all things with subjects that include "xmh" or "xterm", just press the "or" button next to the "Subject:" field. Another box will appear where you can enter another subject. If you want all things either from "weissman" or with subject "xmh", but not necessarily both, select the "–Or–" button. This will essentially double the size of the form. You can then enter "weissman" in a from: box on the top half, and "xmh" in a subject: box on the lower part. If you select the "Skip" button, then only those messages that *don't* match the fields on that row are included. Finally, in the bottom part of the window will appear several more boxes. One is the name of the sequence you're defining. (It defaults to the name of the selected sequence when "Pick" was pressed, or to "temp" if "all" was the selected sequence.) Another box defines which sequence to look through for potential members of this sequence; it defaults to the viewed sequence when "Pick" was pressed.

Two more boxes define a date range; only messages within that date range will be considered. These dates must be entered in RFC 822-style format: each date is of the form "dd mmm yy hh:mm:ss zzz", where dd is a one or two digit day of the month, mmm is the three-letter abbreviation for a month, and yy is a year. The remaining fields are optional: hh, mm, and ss specify a time of day, and zzz selects a time zone. Note that if the time is left out, it defaults to midnight; thus if you select a range of "7 nov 86" – "8 nov 86", you will only get messages from the 7th, as all messages on the 8th will have arrived after midnight. "Date field" specifies which field in the header to look at for this date range; it defaults to "Date". If the sequence you're defining already exists, you can optionally merge the old set with the new; that's what the "Yes" and "No" buttons are all about.

Finally, you can "OK" the whole thing, or "Cancel" it. In general, most people will rarely use these features. However, it's nice to occasionally use "Pick" to find some messages, look through them, and then hit "Delete Sequence" to put things back in their original state.

Widget Hierarchy

In order to specify resources, it is useful to know the hierarchy of widgets which compose *xmh*. In the notation below, indentation indicates hierarchical structure. The widget class name is given first, followed by the widget instance name. The application class name is Xmh.

The hierarchy of the main toc and view window is identical for additional toc and view windows, except that a TopLevelShell widget is inserted in the hierarchy between the application shell and the Paned widget.

```
Xmh xmh
      Paned xmh
            SimpleMenu  folderMenu
                  SmeBSB  open
                  SmeBSB  openInNew
                  SmeBSB  create
                  SmeBSB  delete
                  SmeLine  line
                  SmeBSB  close
            SimpleMenu  tocMenu
                  SmeBSB  inc
                  SmeBSB  commit
                  SmeBSB  pack
                  SmeBSB  sort
                  SmeBSB  rescan
            SimpleMenu  messageMenu
                  SmeBSB  compose
                  SmeBSB  next
                  SmeBSB  prev
                  SmeBSB  delete
                  SmeBSB  move
                  SmeBSB  copy
                  SmeBSB  unmark
                  SmeBSB  viewNew
                  SmeBSB  reply
                  SmeBSB  forward
```

```
                    SmeBSB  useAsComp
                    SmeBSB  print
          SimpleMenu  sequenceMenu
                    SmeBSB  pick
                    SmeBSB  openSeq
                    SmeBSB  addToSeq
                    SmeBSB  removeFromSeq
                    SmeBSB  deleteSeq
                    SmeLine  line
                    SmeBSB  all
          SimpleMenu  viewMenu
                    SmeBSB  reply
                    SmeBSB  forward
                    SmeBSB  useAsComp
                    SmeBSB  edit
                    SmeBSB  save
                    SmeBSB  print
          SimpleMenu  optionMenu
                    SmeBSB  reverse
          Viewport.Core  menuBox.clip
                    Box  menuBox
                              MenuButton  folderButton
                              MenuButton  tocButton
                              MenuButton  messageButton
                              MenuButton  sequenceButton
                              MenuButton  viewButton
                              MenuButton  optionButton
      Grip  grip
      Label folderTitlebar
      Grip  grip
      Viewport.Core  folders.clip
                    Box  folders
                              MenuButton  inbox
                              MenuButton  drafts
                                   SimpleMenu  menu
                                        SmeBSB  <folder_name>
                                            .
                                            .
                                            .
```

```
Grip  grip
Label  tocTitlebar
Grip  grip
Text toc
        Scrollbar  vScrollbar
Grip  grip
Label  viewTitlebar
Grip  grip
Text  view
        Scrollbar  vScrollbar
        Scrollbar  hScrollbar
```

The hierarchy of the Create Folder popup dialog box:

```
TransientShell  prompt
        Dialog  dialog
                Label  label
                Text  value
                Command  okay
                Command  cancel
```

The hierarchy of the Notice dialog box, which reports messages from MH:

```
TransientShell  notice
        Dialog  dialog
                Label  label
                Text  value
                Command  confirm
```

The hierarchy of the Confirmation dialog box:

```
TransientShell  confirm
        Dialog  dialog
                Label  label
                Command  yes
                Command  no
```

The hierarchy of the dialog box which reports errors:

```
TransientShell  error
        Dialog  dialog
                Label  label
                Command  OK
```

The hierarchy of the composition window:

```
TopLevelShell  xmh
        Paned  xmh
                Label  composeTitlebar
                Text  comp
                Viewport.Core  compButtons.clip
                        Box  compButtons
                                Command  close
                                Command  send
                                Command  reset
                                Command  compose
                                Command  save
                                Command  insert
```

The hierarchy of the view window:

```
TopLevelShell  xmh
        Paned  xmh
                Label  viewTitlebar
                Text  view
                Viewport.Core  viewButtons.clip
                        Box  viewButtons
                                Command  close
                                Command  reply
                                Command  forward
                                Command  useAsComp
                                Command  edit
                                Command  save
                                Command  print
                                Command  delete
```

The hierarchy of the pick window:
(Unnamed widgets have no name.)

```
         TopLevelShell  xmh
               Paned  xmh
                       Label  pickTitlebar
                       Viewport.Core  pick.clip
                              Form  form
                                      Form  groupform
```
The first 6 rows of the pick window have identical structure:
```
                                              Form  rowform
                                                      Toggle
                                                      Toggle
                                                      Label
                                                      Text
                                                      Command


                                              Form  rowform
                                                      Toggle
                                                      Toggle
                                                      Text
                                                      Text
                                                      Command
                                              Form  rowform
                                                      Command
                       Viewport.core  pick.clip
                              Form  form
                                      From  groupform
                                              Form  rowform
                                                      Label
                                                      Text
                                                      Label
                                                      Text
                                              Form  rowform
                                                      Label
                                                      Text
                                                      Label
                                                      Text
                                                      Label
                                                      Text
```

                                    Form rowform
                                            Label
                                            Toggle
                                            Toggle
                                    Form rowform
                                            Command
                                            Command

Application-Specific Resources

The application class name is **Xmh**. Application-specific resources are listed below by name. Application-specific resource class names always begin with an upper case character, but unless noted, are otherwise identical to the instance names given below.

Any of these options may also be specified on the command line by using the X Toolkit Intrinsics resource specification mechanism. Thus, to run *xmh* showing all message headers,

    % xmh –xrm '*HideBoringHeaders:off'

If **TocGeometry**, **ViewGeometry**, **CompGeometry**, or **PickGeometry** are not specified, then the value of **Geometry** is used instead. If the resulting height is not specified (e.g., "", "=500", "+0-0"), then the default height of windows is calculated from fonts and line counts. If the width is not specified (e.g., "", "=x300", "-0+0"), then half of the display width is used. If unspecified, the height of a pick window defaults to half the height of the display.

The following resources are defined:

banner
A short string that is the default label of the folder, Table of Contents, and view. The default is "xmh   MIT X Consortium   R5".

blockEventsOnBusy
Whether to disallow user input and show a busy cursor while *xmh* is busy processing a command. Default is true.

busyCursor
The name of the symbol used to represent the position of the pointer, displayed if **blockEventsOnBusy** is true, when *xmh* is processing a time-consuming command. The default is "watch".

busyPointerColor
The foreground color of the busy cursor. Default is XtDefaultForeground.

checkFrequency
How often to check for new mail, make checkpoints, and rescan the Table of Contents, in minutes. If **checkNewMail** is true, *xmh* checks to see if you have new mail each interval. If **makeCheckpoints** is true, checkpoints are made every fifth interval. Also every fifth interval, the Table of Contents is checked for inconsistencies with the file system, and rescanned if out of date. To prevent all of these checks from occurring, set **CheckFrequency** to 0. The default is 1. This resource is retained for backward compatibility with user resource files; see also **checkpointInterval**, **mailInterval**, and **rescanInterval**.

checkNewMail
If true, *xmh* will check at regular intervals to see if new mail has arrived for any of the top level folders and any opened subfolders. A visual indication will be given if new mail is waiting to be incorporated into a top level folder. Default is true. The interval can be adjusted with **mailInterval**.

checkpointInterval (class **Interval**)
Specifies in minutes how often to make checkpoints of volatile state, if **makeCheckpoints** is true. The default is 5 times the value of **checkFrequency**.

checkpointNameFormat
Specifies how checkpointed files are to be named. The value of this resource will be used to compose a file name by inserting the message number as a string in place of the required single occurance of '%d'. If the value of the resource is the empty string, or if no '%d' occurs in the string, or if "%d" is the value of the resource, the default will be used instead. The default is "%d.CKP". Checkpointing is done in the folder of origin unless an absolute pathname is given. *xmh* does not assist the user in recovering checkpoints, nor does it provide for removal of the checkpoint files.

commandButtonCount
The number of command buttons to create in a button box in between the toc and the view areas of the main window. *xmh* will create these buttons with the names *button1, button2* and so on, in a box with the name *commandBox*. The default is 0. *xmh* users can specify labels and actions for the buttons in a private resource file; see the section ACTIONS AND INTERFACE CUSTOMIZATION.

compGeometry
Initial geometry for windows containing compositions.

cursor

The name of the symbol used to represent the pointer. Default is "left_ptr".

debug

Whether or not to print information to stderr as *xmh* runs. Default is false.

draftsFolder

The folder used for message drafts. Default is "drafts".

geometry

Default geometry to use. Default is none.

hideBoringHeaders

If "on", then *xmh* will attempt to skip uninteresting header lines within messages by scrolling them off the top of the view. Default is "on".

initialFolder

Which folder to display on startup. May also be set with the command-line option **–initial**. Default is "inbox".

initialIncFile

The absolute path name of your incoming mail drop file. In some installations, for example those using the Post Office Protocol, no file is appropriate. In this case, **initialIncFile** should not be specified, or may be specified as the empty string, and *inc* will be invoked without a –file argument. By default, this resource has no value. This resource is ignored if *xmh* finds an *.xmhcheck* file; see the section on multiple mail drops.

mailInterval (class **Interval**)

Specifies the interval in minutes at which the mail should be checked, if **mailWaitingFlag** or **checkNewMail** is true. The default is the value of **checkFrequency**.

mailPath

The full path prefix for locating your mail folders. May also be set with the command line option, **–path**. The default is the Path component in the *MH* profile, or "$HOME/Mail" if none.

mailWaitingFlag

If true, *xmh* will attempt to set an indication in its icon when new mail is waiting to be retrieved. If **mailWaitingFlag** is true, then **checkNewMail** is assumed to be true as well. The **–flag** command line option is a quick way to turn on this resource.

makeCheckpoints
If true, *xmh* will attempt to save checkpoints of volatile edits. The default
is false. The frequency of checkpointing is controlled by the resource
checkpointInterval. For the location of checkpointing, see **checkpointNameFormat**.

mhPath
What directory in which to find the *MH* commands. If a command isn't
found in the user's path, then the path specified here is used. Default is
''/usr/local/mh6''.

newMailBitmap (class **NewMailBitmap**)
The bitmap to show in the folder button when a folder has new mail. The
default is ''black6''.

newMailIconBitmap (class **NewMailBitmap**)
The bitmap suggested to the window manager for the icon when any folder
has new mail. The default is ''flagup''.

noMailBitmap (class **NoMailBitmap**)
The bitmap to show in the folder button when a folder has no new mail.
The default is ''box6''.

noMailIconBitmap (class **NoMailBitmap**)
The bitmap suggested to the window manager for the icon when no folders
have new mail. The default is ''flagdown''.

pickGeometry
Initial geometry for pick windows.

pointerColor
The foreground color of the pointer. Default is XtDefaultForeground.

prefixWmAndIconName
Whether to prefix the window and icon name with "xmh: ". Default is true.

printCommand
An *sh* command to execute to print a message. Note that stdout and stderr
must be specifically redirected. If a message or range of messages is
selected for printing, the full file paths of each message file are appended to
the specified print command. The default is ''enscript >/dev/null
2>/dev/null''.

replyInsertFilter
An *sh* command to be executed when the *Insert* button is activated in a
composition window. The full path and filename of the source message is
appended to the command before being passed to *sh*(1). The default filter

is *cat*; i.e. it inserts the entire message into the composition. Interesting filters are: *sed 's//> /'* or *awk -e '{print "   " $0}'* or *<mh directory>/lib/mhl –form mhl.body*.

rescanInterval (class **Interval**)
How often to check the Table of Contents of currently viewed folders and of folders with messages currently being viewed, and to update the Table of Contents if *xmh* sees inconsistencies with the file system in these folders. The default is 5 times the value of **checkFrequency**.

reverseReadOrder
When true, the next message will be the message prior to the current message in the table of contents, and the previous message will be the message after the current message in the table of contents. The default is false.

sendBreakWidth
When a message is sent from *xmh*, lines longer than this value will be split into multiple lines, each of which is no longer than **SendWidth**. This value may be overridden for a single message by inserting an additional line in the message header of the form *SendBreakWidth: value*. This line will be removed from the header before the message is sent. The default is 2000 (to allow for sending mail containing source patches).

sendWidth
When a message is sent from *xmh*, lines longer than **SendBreakWidth** characters will be split into multiple lines, each of which is no longer than this value. This value may be overridden for a single message by inserting an additional line in the message header of the form *SendWidth: value*. This line will be removed from the header before the message is sent. The default is 72.

showOnInc
Whether to automatically show the current message after incorporating new mail. Default is true.

skipCopied
Whether to skip over messages marked for copying when using "View Next Message" and "View Previous Message". Default is true.

skipDeleted
Whether to skip over messages marked for deletion when using "View Next Message" and "View Previous Message". Default is true.

skipMoved

Whether to skip over messages marked for moving to other folders when using ''View Next Message'' and ''View Previous Message''. Default is true.

stickyMenu

If true, when popup command menus are used, the most recently selected entry will be under the cursor when the menu pops up. Default is false. See the file *clients/xmh/Xmh.sample* for an example of how to specify resources for popup command menus.

tempDir

Directory for *xmh* to store temporary files. For privacy, a user might want to change this to a private directory. Default is ''/tmp''.

tocGeometry

Initial geometry for main *xmh* toc and view windows.

tocPercentage

The percentage of the main window that is used to display the Table of Contents. Default is 33.

tocWidth

How many characters to generate for each message in a folder's table of contents. Default is 100. Use less if the geometry of the main *xmh* window results in the listing being clipped at the right hand boundary, or if you plan to use *mhl* a lot, because it will be faster, and the extra characters may not be useful.

viewGeometry

Initial geometry for windows showing a view of a message.

Multiple Mail Drops

Users may need to incorporate mail from multiple spool files or mail drops. If incoming mail is forwarded to the *MH slocal* program, it can be sorted as specified by the user into multiple incoming mail drops. Refer to the *MH* man page for *slocal* to learn how to specify fowarding and the automatic sorting of incoming mail in a *.maildelivery* file.

To inform *xmh* about the various mail drops, create a file in your home directory called *.xmhcheck*. In this file, a mapping between existing folder names and mail drops is created by giving a folder name followed by the absolute pathname of the mail drop site, with some white space separating them, one mapping per line. *xmh* will read this file whether or not resources are set for notification of new mail arrival, and will allow incorporation of new mail into any folder with a mail drop. *xmh* will invoke *inc* with the *–file* argument, and if *xmh* has been requested to check for new mail, it will check directly, instead of using *msgchk*.

An example of *.xmhcheck* file format, for the folders "inbox" and "xpert":

> inbox /usr/spool/mail/converse
> xpert /users/converse/maildrops/xpert

Actions and Interface Customization

Because *xmh* provides action procedures which correspond to command functionality and installs accelerators, users can customize accelerators and new button functionality in a private resource file. For examples of specifying customized resources, see the file *mit/clients/xmh/Xmh.sample*. To understand the syntax, see the Appendix of the *X Toolkit Intrinsics* specification on *Translation Table Syntax*, and any general explanation of using and specifying *X* resources. Unpredictable results can occur if actions are bound to events or widgets for which they were not designed.

Here's an example of how to bind actions to your own *xmh* buttons, and how to redefine the default accelerators so that the Meta key is not required, in case you don't have access to the sample file mentioned above.

! To create buttons in the middle of the main window and give them semantics:

Xmh*CommandButtonCount: 5

Xmh*commandBox.button1.label: Inc
Xmh*commandBox.button1.translations: #override\
    <Btn1Down>,<Btn1Up>: XmhIncorporateNewMail() unset()

Xmh*commandBox.button2.label: Compose
Xmh*commandBox.button2.translations: #override\
    <Btn1Down>,<Btn1Up>: XmhComposeMessage() unset()

Xmh*commandBox.button3.label: Next
Xmh*commandBox.button3.translations: #override\
    <Btn1Down>,<Btn1Up>: XmhViewNextMessage() unset()

```
Xmh*commandBox.button4.label:    Delete
Xmh*commandBox.button4.translations: #override\
    <Btn1Down>,<Btn1Up>: XmhMarkDelete() unset()

Xmh*commandBox.button5.label:    Commit
Xmh*commandBox.button5.translations: #override\
    <Btn1Down>,<Btn1Up>: XmhCommitChanges() unset()
```

! To redefine the accelerator bindings to exclude modifier keys,
! and add your own keyboard accelerator for Compose Message:

```
Xmh*tocMenu.accelerators: #override\n\
    !:<Key>I:   XmhIncorporateNewMail()\n\
    !:<Key>C:   XmhCommitChanges()\n\
    !:<Key>R:   XmhForceRescan()\n\
    !:<Key>P:   XmhPackFolder()\n\
    !:<Key>S:   XmhSortFolder()\n
Xmh*messageMenu.accelerators: #override\n\
    !:<Key>E:   XmhComposeMessage()\n\
    !<Key>space:   XmhViewNextMessage()\n\
    !:<Key>c:   XmhMarkCopy()\n\
    !:<Key>d:   XmhMarkDelete()\n\
    !:<Key>f:   XmhForward()\n\
    !:<Key>m:   XmhMarkMove()\n\
    !:<Key>n:   XmhViewNextMessage()\n\
    !:<Key>p:   XmhViewPreviousMessage()\n\
    !:<Key>r:   XmhReply()\n\
    !:<Key>u:   XmhUnmark()\n
```

xmh provides action procedures which correspond to entries in the command menus; these are given in the sections describing menu commmands, not here. In addition to the actions corresponding to commands in the menus, these action routines are defined:

XmhPushFolder([*foldername, ...*])
This action pushes each of its argument(s) onto a stack of foldernames. If no arguments are given, the selected folder is pushed onto the stack.

XmhPopFolder()
This action pops one foldername from the stack and sets the selected folder.

XmhPopupFolderMenu()
This action should always be taken when the user selects a folder button. A folder button represents a folder and zero or more subfolders. The menu of

Part V
Manual Pages

subfolders is built upon the first reference, by this routine. If there are no subfolders, this routine will mark the folder as having no subfolders, and no menu will be built. In that case the menu button emulates a toggle button. When subfolders exist, the menu will popup, using the menu button action PopupMenu().

XmhSetCurrentFolder()
This action allows menu buttons to emulate toggle buttons in the function of selecting a folder. This action is for menu button widgets only, and sets the selected folder.

XmhLeaveFolderButton()
This action ensures that the menu button behaves properly when the user moves the pointer out of the menu button window.

XmhPushSequence([*sequencename,* ...])
This action pushes each of its arguments onto the stack of sequence names. If no arguments are given, the selected sequence is pushed onto the stack.

XmhPopSequence()
This action pops one sequence name from the stack of sequence names, which then becomes the selected sequence.

XmhPromptOkayAction()
This action is equivalent to pressing the okay button in the Create Folder popup.

XmhReloadSeqLists()
This action rescans the contents of the public *MH* sequences for the currently opened folder and updates the sequence menu if necessary.

XmhShellCommand(*parameter* [*, parameter*])
At least one parameter must be specified. The parameters will be concatenated with a space character separator, into a single string, and the list of selected messsages, or if no messages are selected, the current message, will be appended to the string of parameters. The string will be executed as a shell command. The messages are always given as absolute pathnames. It is an error to cause this action to execute when there are no selected messages and no current message.

XmhCheckForNewMail()
This action will check all mail drops known to xmh. If no mail drops have been specified by the user either through the *.xmhcheck* file or by the **initialIncFile** resource, the *MH* command *msgchk* is used to check for new mail, otherwise, *xmh* checks directly.

XmhWMProtocols([wm_delete_window] [wm_save_yourself])
This action is responsible for participation in window manager communication protocols. It responds to delete window and save yourself messages. The user can cause *xmh* to respond to one or both of these protocols, exactly as if the window manager had made the request, by invoking the action with the appropriate parameters. The action is insensitive to the case of the string parameters. If the event received is a ClientMessage event and parameters are present, at least one of the parameters must correspond to the protocol requested by the event for the request to be honored by *xmh*.

Customization Using *MH*

The initial text displayed in a composition window is generated by executing the corresponding *MH* command; i.e. *comp*, *repl*, or *forw*, and therefore message components may be customized as specified for those commands. *comp* is executed only once per invocation of *xmh* and the message template is re-used for every successive new composition.

xmh uses *MH* commands, including *inc*, *msgchk*, *comp*, *send*, *repl*, *forw*, *refile*, *rmm*, *pick*, *pack*, *sort*, and *scan*. Some flags for these commands can be specified in the *MH* profile; *xmh* may override them. The application resource **debug** can be set to true to see how *xmh* uses *MH* commands.

Environment

HOME - users's home directory
MH - to get the location of the *MH* profile file

Files

~/.mh_profile - *MH* profile, used if the MH environment variable is not set
~/Mail - directory of folders, used if the *MH* profile cannot be found
~/.xmhcheck - optional, for multiple mail drops in cooperation with *slocal*.
/usr/local/mh6 - *MH* commands, as a last resort, see **mhPath**.
~/Mail/<folder>/.xmhcache - *scan* output in each folder
~/Mail/<folder>/.mh_sequences - sequence definitions, in each folder
/tmp - temporary files, see **tempDir**.

See Also

X(1), xrdb(1), X Toolkit Intrinsics, Athena Widget Set, mh(1), enscript(1)
At least one book has been published about *MH* and *xmh*.

Bugs

- When the user closes a window, all windows which are transient for that window should also be closed by *xmh*.
- When **XmhUseAsComposition** and **XmhViewUseAsComposition** operate on messages in the **DraftsFolder**, *xmh* disallows editing of the composition if the same message is also being viewed in another window.
- Occasionally after committing changes, the table of contents will appear to be completely blank when there are actually messages present. When this happens, refreshing the display, or typing Control-L in the table of contents, will often cause the correct listing to appear. If this doesn't work, force a rescan of the folder.
- Should recognize and use the "unseen" message-sequence.
- Should determine by itself if the user hasn't used *MH* before, and offer to create the .mh_profile, instead of hanging on inc.
- A few commands are missing (rename folder, resend message).
- WM_DELETE_WINDOW protocol doesn't work right when requesting deletion of the first toc and view, while trying to keep other *xmh* windows around.
- Doesn't support annotations when replying to messages.
- Doesn't allow folders to be shared without write permission.
- Doesn't recognize private sequences.
- *MH* will report that the *.mh_sequences* file is poorly formatted if any sequence definition in a particular folder contains more than *BUFSIZ* characters. *xmh* tries to capture these messages and display them when they occur, but it cannot correct the problem.

Copyright

Author

Terry Weissman, formerly of Digital Western Research Laboratory
Donna Converse, MIT X Consortium

Index

Index

Reference Guide

This section has two parts. The first part is a chart of the MH commands covered in this book. It lists each command's switches and parameters, refers you to the book section about each one, and gives a brief explanation. It's an easy way to find examples and description of specific MH commands.

The second part lists *xmh* menus, buttonboxes and text editing commands.

Remember, you can type *–help* to any MH command. See Section 4.9.

	Switch or Parameter	See Book Section	Short Description
ali list MH mail aliases	−alias *aliasfile* . . . −noalias	6.3.1 6.3.2	Name personal alias files Don't read system alias file
	−list **−nolist**	6.3.2 6.3.2	Print each address on new line Separate addresses with commas
	−normalize **−nonormalize**	— —	Try to get official hostname Don't get official hostname
	−user **−nouser**	6.3.2 6.3.2	List aliases that contain this address List addresses that this alias contains
	alias/address . . . †	6.3.2	Aliases to list (with −nouser) or addresses to list (with −user); if no aliases given with −nouser, lists all aliases and addresses in alias file(s)
anno annotate messages	+*folder* *msgs*	7.1 4.7	Folder name (default: current folder) Message(s) to annotate (default: current)
	−component *field*	7.7	Component name (will prompt you if missing)
	−inplace **−noinplace**	7.7 7.7	Annotate in place (don't break any links) Break any links before annotating
	−date −nodate	7.7 7.7	Include '*field: the-date-now*' annotation Only annotate with *body*
	−text *body*	7.7	Text (if any) to annotate message with
burst explode digests into messages	+*folder* *msgs*	7.1 4.7	Folder name (default: current folder) Message(s) to burst (default: current)
	−inplace **−noinplace**	— 7.9	Replace digest with Table of Contents; insert digest messages next, renumber others Put burst messages at end of folder
	−quiet **−noquiet**	— —	Don't complain about nondigest messages Complain
	−verbose **−noverbose**	7.9 —	Explain what's happening Only report errors
comp compose a message	+*folder* *msg*	9.4.3 9.4.3	Folder with message form (default: current) Message to use as form (default: current)
	−draftfolder +*folder* −draftmessage *msg* **−nodraftfolder**	6.5.2 6.5.2 6.5.1	Name of draft folder Draft message number (default: current) Don't use draft folder
	−editor *editor* −noedit	6.2.2 —	Draft editor instead of **prompter** Don't edit draft
	−file *file*	—	Use *file* as message draft
	−form *formfile*	8.9.2	Draft message template (default: components)
	−use **−nouse**	6.5 —	Edit existing draft Make new draft
	−whatnowproc *program* −nowhatnowproc	6.1.3, 9.8 —	Program to replace **whatnow** Create draft and quit

bold face means it's the default.   . . . stands for other parameters or switches.   † means it's required.

	Switch or Parameter	See Book Section	Short Description
dist redistribute a message to more addresses	+*folder* *msg*	7.1 6.9	Folder name (default: current folder) Message to redistribute (default: current)
	−annotate **−noannotate**	6.9.2 —	Add Resent: header to original message Don't add Resent: header
	−draftfolder +*folder* −draftmessage *msg* **−nodraftfolder**	6.5.2 6.5.2 6.5.1	Name of draft folder Draft message number (default: current) Don't use draft folder
	−editor *editor* −noedit	6.2.2, 13.10 —	Draft editor instead of **prompter** Don't edit draft
	−form *formfile*	6.9.1, 8.9.5	Draft message template (default: distcomps)
	−inplace **−noinplace**	— —	Annotate in place (don't break any links) Break any links before annotating
	−whatnowproc *program* −nowhatnowproc	6.1.3, 9.8 —	Program to replace **whatnow** Create draft and quit
folder set/list current folder/message	+*folder* *msg*	7.1 —	Folder name (default: current folder) Message to make current
	−all	7.1.8	List top-level folders (see −recurse, **folders**)
	−fast **−nofast**	7.1.7 —	Don't summarize folder contents Summarize each folder
	−header **−noheader**	7.1.1 —	Print explanatory heading (default if -all) Don't print heading
	−pack **−nopack**	7.1.10 —	Renumber messages to remove gaps Don't renumber messages
	−recurse **−norecurse**	7.1.5 —	List subfolders Don't list subfolders
	−total **−nototal**	7.1.8 —	Count messages and folders (default if -all) Don't total messages and folders
	−print −noprint	7.1.9 —	May set current message during -push, -pop Can't set current message during -push, -pop
	−list **−nolist**	7.1.9 —	Print folder stack Don't print folder stack
	−push	7.1.9	Make +*folder* current, push current folder on stack; if no +*folder*, swap current folder and top of stack
	−pop	7.1.9	Pop folder from top of stack, make it current
folders do *folder −all*	*switches for* **folder**	7.1.8	See **folder**

	Switch or Parameter	See Book Section	Short Description
forw forward messages	+*folder*	7.1	Folder name (default: current folder)
	msgs	4.7	Message(s) to forward (default: current)
	−annotate	6.8.6	Add Forwarded: header to original message
	−noannotate	—	Don't add Forwarded: header
	−dashmunging	6.8.3	Format messages for **burst**ing
	−nodashmunging	—	Don't prepend "−" to dashes in column 1
	−draftfolder +*folder*	6.5.2	Name of draft folder
	−draftmessage *msg*	6.5.2	Draft message number (default: current)
	−nodraftfolder	6.5.1	Don't use draft folder
	−editor *editor*	6.2.2	Draft editor instead of **prompter**
	−noedit		Don't edit draft
	−filter *filterfile*	6.8.1, 10.1.4	Filter message(s) through **mhl** *filterfile*
	−format	6.8.1	Use −filter mhl.forward
	−noformat	6.8.1	Forward message exactly, don't filter.
	−form *formfile*	6.8.5, 8.9.4	Draft message template (default: forwcomps, or digestcomps with −digest)
	−inplace	—	Annotate in place (don't break any links)
	−noinplace	—	Break any links before annotating
	−whatnowproc *program*	6.1.3, 9.8	Program to replace **whatnow**
	−nowhatnowproc	—	Create draft and quit
	−digest *list*	6.8.7	Digest name
	−issue *number*	6.8.7	Issue number (default: last issue plus 1)
	−volume *number*	6.8.7	Volume number (default: last volume)
inc incorporate new mail	+*folder*	7.1	Folder name (default: inbox)
	−audit *audit-file*	5.4.1	Write **scan** lines to *audit-file*
	−noaudit	—	Don't audit
	−changecur	—	Make first new message the current message
	−nochangecur	5.4.2	Don't change current message
	−file *file*	D.2	Read messages from *file*, not system mailbox
	−form *formatfile*	5.4.1, 10.2	**scan** format file for message display
	−format *string*	10.2	**scan** format string for message display
	−width *columns*	10.2.6	**scan** output width (default: screen width)
	−silent	5.4.2	Don't **scan** to screen or *audit-file*
	−nosilent	—	Write **scan** lines to screen, and *audit-file* if given
	−truncate	—	Empty system mailbox after incorporating messages
	−notruncate	13.14	Don't empty mailbox (default if −file)
(continued)	−host *host*	5.4.3	(POP only) POP server host
	−user *user*	5.4.3	(POP only) Username on POP server host

bold face means it's the default.   ... stands for other parameters or switches.   † means it's required.

	Switch or Parameter	See Book Section	Short Description
inc (continued)	−pack *file*	—	(POP only) Write all messages to *file* instead of splitting into folder
	−nopack	—	(POP only) Put POP'ed messages into folder
	−rpop	—	(POP only) User authentication via trusted connection
	−norpop	5.4.3	(POP only) Prompt for user's POP server host password
mark mark messages	+*folder*	7.1	Folder name (default: current folder)
	msgs	4.7	Message(s) to use (default: current)
	−sequence *name* ...	7.3	Sequence(s) to use
	−add	7.3.1	Add message(s) to sequence (default if −sequence)
	−delete	7.3.2	Remove message(s) from sequence
	−list	7.3.3	List messages in sequence (default if no −sequence)
	−public	—	Store sequence in folder (default for your folders)
	−nopublic	7.3.7	Store sequence in user's MH context (default for read-only folders)
	−zero	7.3.1	Remove previous contents of sequence (with −delete, add all messages except *msgs*)
	−nozero	7.3.1	Merge into existing sequence, if any
mhl produce formatted listing of MH messages	−bell	10.1.5	Ring bell after each page (only with −nomoreproc)
	−nobell	10.1.5	Don't ring bell (only with −nomoreproc)
	−clear	10.1.5	Clear screen before each page (only with −nomoreproc)
	−noclear	10.1.5	Don't clear screen (only with −nomoreproc)
	−folder +*folder*	—	Folder name to display with Messagename: component: (Message *folder*:files) NOT name of folder to read message from!
	−form *formfile*	10.1.1	Name of format file (default: mhl.format)
	−length *lines*	10.1.5	Number of lines to display (only with −nomoreproc; default: screen length, else 40)
	−width *columns*	10.1.5	Number of columns to display (only with −nomoreproc; default: screen width, else 80)
	−moreproc *program*	10.1.5	Text paging program (default: **more**)
	−nomoreproc	10.1.5	Use internal paging routine
	files ...	—	UNIX relative or absolute pathname of message file(s)

bold face means it's the default.   ... stands for other parameters or switches.   † means it's required.

	Switch or Parameter	See Book Section	Short Description
mhmail send or read mail	addresses ...	6.10, 12.17.2	To: addresses
	−body text	6.10, 12.17.2	Text for body (default: standard input)
	−cc addresses ...	6.10, 12.17.2	cc: addresses
	−from address	6.10	From: address (default: you)
	−subject subject	6.10, 12.17.2	"Subject:" component
mhpath full pathnames of folder or messages	+folder	12.17.3	Folder name (if only +, list MH directory)
	msgs	4.7	Message(s) to list (if none, list folder)
msgchk check for messages	−date	—	Print last date mail was read, if possible
	−nodate	—	Don't print last date mail was read
	−notify all/mail/nomail	—	What to tell you about maildrop(s)
	−nonotify all/mail/nomail	—	What not to tell you about maildrop(s)
	−host host	5.3.2	(POP only) POP server host
	−user user	5.3.2	(POP only) Username on POP server host
	−rpop	—	(POP only) User authentication via trusted connection
	−norpop	5.3.2	(POP only) Prompt for user's POP server host password
	users ...	—	Maildrop name(s) to check (note: different than −user)
msh MH shell	−scan	—	Do scan unseen at startup
	−noscan	—	Don't scan unseen at startup
	−topcur	—	Current message at top of vmh scan window
	−notopcur	—	Current message at middle of vmh scan window
	−prompt string	—	User prompt (default: (msh))
	file	7.11	File to process, in mailbox/packf format (default: msgbox in current directory)
next show the next message	+folder	7.1	Folder name (default: current folder)
	−header	5.1.5	Print folder name and message number before displaying message
	−noheader	5.1.5	Don't print header
	−showproc program	5.1.5	Program to display message with
	−noshowproc	5.1.7	Display message with **cat**
	switches for showproc	10.1	Other command-line switches for showproc
packf compress a folder into a single file	+folder	7.1	Folder name (default: current folder)
	msgs	4.7	Message(s) to pack (default: all)

676   **bold face** means it's the default.   ... stands for other parameters or switches.   † means it's required.

	Switch or Parameter	See Book Section	Short Description
pick	+*folder*	7.1	Folder name (default: current folder)
select messages by content	*msgs*	4.7	Message(s) to search (default: all)
	... −and ...	7.2.5	Require both of two conditions
	... −or ...	7.2.5	Allow either of two conditions
	−not ...	7.2.5	Require opposite of condition
	−lbrace ... −rbrace	7.2.5	For grouping: "left brace" ... "right brace"
	−to *pattern*	7.2.1	Messages with *pattern* in To:
	−cc *pattern*	7.2.6	Messages with *pattern* in cc:
	−from *pattern*	7.2.1	Messages with *pattern* in From:
	−subject *pattern*	7.2.1	Messages with *pattern* in Subject:
	−date *pattern*	7.2.1	Messages with *pattern* in Date:
	−−*component pattern*	7.2.6	Match *pattern* in miscellaneous header *component*
	−search *pattern*	7.2	Messages with *pattern* anywhere
	−after *date*	7.2.1	Messages on or after this Date:
	−before *date*	7.2.1	Messages before this Date:
	−datefield *field*	7.7	Date field to use instead of Date:
	−sequence *name* ...	4.8, 7.3	Store message numbers in sequence *name*
	−public	—	Store sequence in folder (default for your folders)
	−nopublic	7.3.7	Store sequence in user's MH context (default for read-only folders)
	−zero	—	Remove previous contents of sequence
	−nozero	7.2.3	Merge into existing sequence, if any
	−list	7.2.3	Print message numbers on standard output
	−nolist	—	Don't print message numbers (default if −sequence)
prev	+*folder*	7.1	Folder name (default: current folder)
show the previous message	**−header**	—	Print folder name and message number before displaying message
	−noheader	5.1.5	Don't print header
	−showproc *program*	5.1.5	Program to display message with
	−noshowproc	5.1.7	Display message with **cat**
	switches for showproc	10.1	Other command-line switches for showproc program
prompter	−erase *character*	—	Character that erases previous character (default: system value)
prompting editor front-end	−kill *character*	—	Character that erases line (default: system value)
	−prepend	8.9.1	Insert new message text before existing message body
(continued)	−noprepend	8.9.1, 9.7	Add new message text at end of message

	Switch or Parameter	See Book Section	Short Description
prompter (continued)	–rapid	6.1.2, 9.7	Don't display message body
	–norapid	—	Display message body
	–doteof	6.1.2	Exit with dot at start of empty line or end-of-input
	–nodoteof	—	Only exit with end-of-input character (usually CTRL-D)
	file †	—	Relative or absolute pathname of draft file
rcvdist redistribute mail from std. input	*address ...* †	1.3	Address(es) to resend to
	–form *formfile*	11.7	MH-format file for header (default: rcvdistcomps)
rcvpack store message from std. input to file	*file* †	11.8	Relative or absolute pathname of mailbox-format file
rcvstore store message from std. input to folder	+*folder*	7.1	Folder name (default: inbox)
	–create	—	Create folder if it doesn't exist
	–nocreate	11.6	Abort if folder doesn't exist
	–sequence *name ...*	4.8, 7.3	Store message number in sequence *name*
	–public	7.3.7	Add message to public sequence (default in writable folders)
	–nopublic	7.3.7	Add message to private sequence (default in a read-only folder)
	–zero	7.3.1	Remove old messages from sequence
	–nozero	7.3.1	Add to sequence
rcvtty notify user about message from std. input	*command*	11.5.3	UNIX command to read message and format for tty (default: **scan**-like listing)
	–form *formatfile*	11.5.2, 10.2.10	**scan**-like format file for message display
	–biff	11.5.1	Notify if **biff y** used (default: **mesg y** permission)
	–newline	11.5.2	Output a newline character before notice
	–nonewline	11.5.2	Don't output newline before notice
	–bell	11.5.2	Ring terminal bell before notice
	–nobell	11.5.2	Don't ring bell
refile file messages in other folders (continued)	*msgs*	4.7	Message(s) to refile (default: current)
	–draft	6.1.3	Refile draft message
	–link	7.1.4	Link message into destination folder
	–nolink	—	Move message

bold face means it's the default.   ... stands for other parameters or switches.   † means it's required.

	Switch or Parameter	See Book Section	Short Description
refile (continued)	−preserve **−nopreserve**	7.1.4 —	Keep same number in destination folder Add message to end of destination folder
	−src +*folder* −file *file*	7.8.2 —	Move message(s) from *folder* Refile message from this UNIX pathname
	+*folder* ... †	7.1.4	Folder(s) to refile message into
repl reply to a message	+*folder* *msg*	7.1 4.6	Folder name (default: current folder) Message to reply to (default: current)
	−annotate **−noannotate**	4.6, 6.7.7 —	Add Replied: header to original message Don't add Replied: header
	−cc all/to/cc/me −nocc all/to/cc/me	6.7.1 6.7.1	Send copy to addresses in these components Don't copy to addresses in these components
	−draftfolder +*folder* −draftmessage *msg* **−nodraftfolder**	6.5.2 6.5.2 6.5.1	Name of draft folder Draft message number (default: current) Don't use draft folder
	−editor *editor* −noedit	4.6, 6.2.2 —	Draft editor instead of **prompter** Don't edit draft
	−fcc +*folder*	8.9.3	Copy to *folder* (via template file)
	−filter *filterfile* −form *formfile*	6.7.5 6.7.3, 8.9.3	Include messsage formatted with **mhl** *filterfile* Draft message template (default: replcomps)
	−inplace **−noinplace**	— —	Annotate in place (don't break any links) Break any links before annotating
	−query **−noquery**	6.7.1 6.7.1	Ask about each recipient Send to all recipients
	−whatnowproc *program* −nowhatnowproc	6.1.3, 9.8 —	Program to replace **whatnow** Create draft and quit
	−width *columns*	—	Width of To:, cc:, Bcc: fields (default: 72)
rmf remove folder	+*folder*	7.1	Folder name (default: current folder)
	−interactive	7.6	Ask for confirmation (default if +*folder* not given)
	−nointeractive	7.6	Don't ask (default if +*folder* given)
rmm remove messages	+*folder* *msgs*	7.1 4.7, 4.8	Folder name (default: current folder) Message(s) to remove (default: current)
scan produce a one-line- per-message listing	+*folder* *msgs*	7.1 4.7, 4.8	Folder name (default: current folder) Message(s) to list (default: all)
	−clear −noclear	— —	Clear screen or print form feed Don't clear screen or print form feed
	−form *formatfile* −format *string*	5.2.1, 10.2 10.2	Format file for message display Format string for message display
(continued)	−header **−noheader**	8.1 8.1	Print one-line header above listing Don't print header

---

bold face means it's the default.　... stands for other parameters or switches.　† means it's required.　679

	Switch or Parameter	See Book Section	Short Description
scan (continued)	–width *columns*	10.2.6	Output width (default: terminal width)
	–reverse	5.2.2	Scan from highest to lowest message number
	–noreverse	—	Scan from lowest to highest message number
	–file *file*	**5.2.3**	UNIX relative or absolute pathname of mailbox-format file to scan
send send a message	–alias *aliasfile*	6.3.1	Name of alias file
	–draft	9.8	Send draft message without asking
	–draftfolder +*folder*	6.5.2, 9.8	Name of draft folder
	–draftmessage *msg*	6.5.2, 9.8	Draft message number (default: current)
	–nodraftfolder	—	Don't use draft folder
	–filter *filterfile*	—	**mhl** format file for Bcc: (blind) copies
	–nofilter	—	Don't reformat Bcc:'s
	–format	—	Reformat headers to Internet standards
	–noformat	—	Leave message headers as they are
	–forward	—	Mail unsendable draft back to you (only with –push)
	–noforward	—	Don't return unsendable draft (only with –push)
	–msgid	—	Add Message–ID: field to draft
	–nomsgid	—	Don't add Message–ID
	–push	6.1.3, 9.8	Detach from terminal, send in background
	–nopush	—	Don't push
	–verbose	6.1.3	Show interactions with transport agent
	–noverbose	—	Don't show transport agent interactions
	–watch	6.1.3	Monitor delivery of local and network mail
	–nowatch	—	Don't monitor delivery
	–width *columns*	—	Width of header addresses in columns (default: 72)
	file ...	—	UNIX relative or absolute pathname of draft files to send (default: draft in MH directory)
show show (list) messages	+*folder*	7.1	Folder name (default: current folder)
	msgs	4.7	Message(s) to show (default: current)
	–draft	—	Show draft message
	–header	5.1.5	Print folder name and message number before displaying message
	–noheader	5.1.5	Don't print header
	–showproc *program*	5.1.5	Program to display message with
	–noshowproc	5.1.7	Display message with **cat**
	switches for showproc	10.1	Other command-line switches for showproc

	Switch or Parameter	See Book Section	Short Description
slocal process .maildelivery on non-MMDF systems	−addr *address*	11.10.4, Table 11-1	Address to use for addr field
	−user *username*	11.3, 11.2.6	User name for mailbox, home directory, and undocumented select argument
	−file *pathname*	—	Pathname of temporary file
	−sender *address*	11.2.1, Table 11-1	addr field and $(sender) variable
	−mailbox *pathname*	—	pathname of mailbox file
	−home *pathname*	—	pathname of home directory
	−maildelivery *pathname*	—	pathname of .maildelivery file
	−verbose	11.11.2	List each delivery action
	−noverbose	—	Be quiet
	−debug	11.11.2	Show .maildelivery parsing and variables
	address info sender	11.10.4, 11.2.1, Table 11-1	In .maildelivery file: − Available in $(address), $(info), and $(sender) variables, respectively. − *address* is tested as addr field and *sender* is tested as source field.
sortm sort messages	+*folder*	7.1	Folder name (default: current folder)
	msgs	4.7	Message(s) to sort (default: all)
	−datefield *field*	7.4.1	Field to use for date sorts (default: Date:)
	−textfield *field*	7.4	Field to use for text sorts
	−notextfield	—	Don't sort on text field
	−limit *days*	7.4.2	On −textfield sort, group messages sent within *days* days of each other
	−nolimit	7.4.2	On −textfield sort, group all messages with same textfield
	−verbose	—	Explain actions before and during sort
	−noverbose	—	Be quiet
whatnow prompting front-end for **send**	−draftfolder +*folder*	6.5.2	Name of draft folder
	−draftmessage *msg*	6.5.2	Draft message number (default: current)
	−nodraftfolder	—	Don't use draft folder
	−editor *editor*	6.2.2	Draft editor instead of **prompter**
	−noedit	—	Don't edit draft
	−prompt *string*	—	Prompt string (default: "What now? ")
	file	—	Relative or absolute pathname of draft file
whom report to whom a message would go	−alias *aliasfile*	6.3.1	Alias filename (default: MhAliases in MH library)
	−check	6.1.3	Try to verify address
	−nocheck	—	Don't verify address
	−draftfolder +*folder*	6.5.2	Name of draft folder
	−draftmessage *msg*	6.5.2	Draft message number (default: current)
	−nodraftfolder	—	Don't use draft folder
	file	—	UNIX relative or absolute pathname of draft file (default: draft in MH directory)

---

bold face means it's the default.   ... stands for other parameters or switches.   † means it's required.   681

Folder Menu of global commands

Command	Accelerator	See Book Section	Short Description
Open Folder	Choose folder name with button 2	15.6.3	View the selected folder
Open Folder In New Window	—	15.6.3	Open selected folder in new main window
Create Folder	—	15.6.1	Make a new folder
Delete Folder	—	15.6.11	Delete folder and any subfolders
Close Window	—	15.10	Close this main window

Table of Contents Menu for handling viewed folder

Command	Accelerator	See Book Section	Short Description
Incorporate New Mail	META-↑I	14.5, 15.4.1	Bring new mail into folder(s)
Commit Changes	META-↑C	15.6.4	Process all marked messages (delete, link, move)
Pack Folder	META-↑P	15.6.9	Renumber messages as 1, 2, ...
Sort Folder	META-↑S	15.6.10	Order messages by date sent
Rescan Folder	META-↑R	15.6.7	Force Table of Contents update

Message Menu for handling current or selected message

Command	Accelerator	See Book Section	Short Description
Compose	—	14.4, 15.1.1	Start a new message
View Next Message	META-Space, META-N	14.5	View just-selected or next message
View Previous	META-P	14.5	View just-selected or previous message
Delete	META-D	14.10	Mark message(s) for deletion
Move	Choose folder name with button 3	15.6.4	Mark message(s) for moving to selected folder
Copy as Link	META-C	15.6.5	Mark message(s) for linking to selected folder
Unmark	META-U	15.6.4	Un-do the move, delete, and link mark on selected message(s)
View in New	—	15.4.2	Show message in separate view window
Reply	META-R	14.6, 15.1.4	Reply to message
Forward	META-F	14.9, 15.1.3	Forward copy of message(s)

Message Menu for handling current or selected message (continued)

Command	Accelerator	See Book Section	Short Description
Use as Composition	—	15.1.5	Open message (usually from drafts folder) in composition window
Print	—	15.5, 16.8	Print message(s)

Sequence Menu for message sequences and searching

Command	Accelerator	See Book Section	Short Description
Pick	—	15.8	Search for messages
Open Sequence	—	15.7, 15.8	View the selected sequence
Add to Sequence	—	15.9	Add selected messages to the selected sequence
Remove from Sequence	—	15.9	Remove selected messages from the selected sequence
Delete Sequence	—	—	Remove selected sequence (the list of messages numbers, not the messages themselves).

View Menu for handling viewed message

Command	Accelerator	See Book Section	Short Description
Reply	—	14.6, 15.1.4	Reply to viewed message
Forward	—	14.9, 15.1.3	Forward copy of viewed message
Use as Composition	—	15.1.5	Open message (usually from drafts folder) in composition window
Edit Message	—	—	Edit viewed message
Save Message	—	—	Save message during Edit Message
Print	—	15.5, 16.8	Print viewed message

Options Menu that may be longer some day

Command	Accelerator	See Book Section	Short Description
Read in Reverse	—	—	Swap meaning of "next" and "previous" message

Composition window Buttonbox for handling drafts

Command	Accelerator	See Book Section	Short Description
Close Window	—	14.4, 15.1.1	Close composition window
Send	—	14.4, 15.1.1	Send composition
New Headers	—	15.3.3	Replace composition with empty message
Compose Message	—	15.1.1	Open another composition window
Save Message	—	15.1.1	Save this composition
Insert	—	16.3.3	Insert copy of message being replied to

xmh Text Editing Commands*

Command	Function	Command	Function
CTRL-A	Beginning Of Line	META-B	Backward Word
CTRL-B	Backward Character	META-D	Delete Next Word
CTRL-D	Delete Next Character	META-↑-D	Kill Word
CTRL-E	End Of Line	META-F	Forward Word
CTRL-F	Forward Character	META-H	Delete Previous Word
CTRL-G	Multiply Reset	META-↑-H	Backward Kill Word
CTRL-H	Delete Previous Character	META-I	Insert File
CTRL-J	Newline And Indent	META-K	Kill to End of Paragraph
CTRL-K	Kill To End Of Line	META-Q	Form Paragraph
CTRL-L	Redraw Display	META-V	Previous Page
CTRL-M	Newline	META-Y	Insert Current Selection
CTRL-N	Next Line	META-Z	Scroll One Line Down
CTRL-O	Newline And Backup	META-<	Beginning of File
CTRL-P	Previous Line	META->	End of File
CTRL-R	Search/Replace Backward	META-]	Forward Paragraph
CTRL-S	Search/Replace Forward	META-[	Backward Paragraph
CTRL-T	Transpose Characters	META-Delete	Delete Previous Word
CTRL-U	Multiply by 4	META-↑-Delete	Kill Previous Word
CTRL-V	Next Page	META-Backspace	Delete Previous Word
CTRL-W	Kill Selection	META-↑-Backspace	Kill Previous Word
CTRL-Y	Unkill		
CTRL-Z	Scroll One Line Up		

* Adapted from *xmh*(1) manual page.

How to Order by E-mail

E-mail ordering promises to be quick and easy. Because we don't want you sending credit card information over a non-secure network, we ask that you set up an account with us before ordering by e-mail.
To find out more about setting up an e-mail account, you can either call us at (800) 998-9938 or select `Ordering Information` from the Gopher root menu.

O'Reilly & Associates Inc.
103A Morris Street, Sebastopol, CA 95472

(800) 998-9938 • (707) 829-0515 • FAX (707) 829-0104 • order@ora.com

How to get information about O'Reilly books online

• If you have a local gopher client, then you can launch gopher and connect to our server:
`gopher gopher.ora.com`
• If you want to use the Xgopher client, then enter:
`xgopher -xrm "xgopher.rootServer: gopher.ora.com"`
• If you want to use telnet, then enter:
`telnet gopher.ora.com  login: gopher  [no password]`
• If you use a World Wide Web browser, you can access the gopher server
by typing the following http address:
`gopher://gopher.ora.com`

WE'D LIKE TO HEAR FROM YOU

Company Name

Name

Address

City/State

Zip/Country

Telephone

FAX

Internet or *Uunet* e-mail address

Which O'Reilly book did this card come from? _____

Is your job: ❑ SysAdmin? ❑ Programmer?

❑ Other? What?_____

Do you use other computer systems besides UNIX? If so, which one(s)?

_____

Please send me the following:

❑　A free catalog of titles

❑　A list of bookstores in my area
　　that carry O'Reilly books

❑　A list of distributors outside of
　　the U.S. and Canada

❑　Information about bundling
　　O'Reilly books with my product

O'Reilly & Associates Inc.

How to order books by e-mail:

1. Address your e-mail to: order@ora.com
2. Include in your message:
   - The title of each book you want to order
     (an ISBN number is helpful but not necessary)
   - The quantity of each book
   - Your account number and name
   - Anything special you'd like us to know about your order

_____

O'Reilly Online Account Number

Use our online catalog to find out more about our books (see reverse).

BUSINESS REPLY MAIL
FIRST CLASS MAIL   PERMIT NO. 80   SEBASTOPOL, CA

Postage will be paid by addressee

O'Reilly & Associates, Inc.
103A Morris Street
Sebastopol, CA 95472-9902

About the Author

Jerry Peek has used UNIX and MH since the early 1980's. He has a B.S. in Electronic Engineering Technology from California Polytechnic State University, San Luis Obispo. At Syracuse University, Jerry was a user consultant for UNIX and VMS. At Tektronix, Inc., he was a UNIX course developer and trainer; a System Administrator of a VAX 11/780 running BSD UNIX; and a Bourne Shell and C language job-shop programmer. Jerry is currently a user consultant and writer for O'Reilly & Associates, Inc.

Colophon

Our look is the result of reader comments, our own experimentation, and distribution channels.

Distinctive covers complement our distinctive approach to technical topics, breathing personality and life into potentially dry subjects. UNIX and its attendant programs can be unruly beasts. Nutshell Handbooks help you tame them.

The animal featured on the cover of *MH & xmh: E-mail for Users & Programmers* is an octopus, an eight-armed marine mollusk. An invertebrate with no shell or fins, the octopus moves by crawling across rocks and sand, using the double row of suckers on the underside of its tentacles to pull itself along, or by swimming—ejecting spurts of water from a siphon near the base of its head which propel it forward. Found throughout the world, both in shallow water and deep, the octopus comes in a variety of sizes, from two inches across to monsters with arms 16 feet long.

Octopus can change color quickly to blend in with their surroundings. When threatened they can eject a brown or black inky fluid which will block an enemy's vision and anesthetize its olfactory senses. Though very shy animals, octopus are also very curious. Divers frequently lure them out of hiding by blowing bubbles at them or showing them shiny objects.

Edie Freedman designed this cover and the entire UNIX bestiary that appears on other Nutshell Handbooks. The beasts themselves are adapted from 19th-century engravings from the Dover Pictorial Archive.

The text of this book is set in Times Roman and Courier. The text pages are formatted in troff. Figures were created by Chris Reilley in Aldus Freehand. The cover was produced in QuarkXPress.

UNIX

From the best-selling The Whole Internet *to our Nutshell Handbooks, there's something here for everyone. Whether you're a novice or expert UNIX user, these books will give you just what you're looking for: user-friendly, definitive information on a range of UNIX topics.*

Using UNIX

Connecting to the Internet: An O'Reilly Buyer's Guide — NEW

By Susan Estrada
1st Edition August 1993
188 pages
ISBN 1-56592-061-9

More and more people are interested in exploring the Internet, and this book is the fastest way for you to learn how to get started. This book provides practical advice on how to determine the level of Internet service right for you, and how to find a local access provider and evaluate the services they offer.

!%@:: A Directory of Electronic Mail Addressing & Networks — NEW

By Donnalyn Frey & Rick Adams
3rd Edition August 1993
458 pages, ISBN 1-56592-031-7

The only up-to-date directory that charts the networks that make up the Internet, provides contact names and addresses, and describes the services each network provides. It includes all of the major Internet-based networks, as well as various commercial networks such as CompuServe, Delphi, and America Online that are "gatewayed" to the Internet for transfer of electronic mail and other services. If you are someone who wants to connect to the Internet, or someone who already is connected but wants concise, up-to-date information on many of the world's networks, check out this book.

Learning the UNIX Operating System — NEW

By Grace Todino, John Strang & Jerry Peek
3rd Edition August 1993
108 pages, ISBN 1-56592-060-0

If you are new to UNIX, this concise introduction will tell you just what you need to get started and no more. Why wade through a six-hundred-page book when you can begin working productively in a matter of minutes? This book is the most effective introduction to UNIX in print. This new edition has been updated and expanded to provide increased coverage of window systems and networking. It's a handy book for someone just starting with UNIX, as well as someone who encounters a UNIX system as a visitor via remote login over the Internet.

The Whole Internet User's Guide & Catalog

By Ed Krol
1st Edition September 1992
400 pages, ISBN 1-56592-025-2

A comprehensive—and best-selling—introduction to the Internet, the international network that includes virtually every major computer site in the world. The Internet is a resource of almost unimaginable wealth. In addition to electronic mail and news services, thousands of public archives, databases, and other special services are available: everything from space flight announcements to ski reports. This book is a comprehensive introduction to what's available and how to find it. In addition to electronic mail, file transfer, remote login, and network news, *The Whole Internet* pays special attention to some new tools for helping you find information. Whether you're a researcher, a student, or just someone who likes electronic mail, this book will help you to explore what's possible.

Smileys

By David W. Sanderson, 1st Edition March 1993
93 pages, ISBN 1-56592-041-4

Originally used to convey some kind of emotion in an e-mail message, smileys are some combination of typographic characters that depict sideways a happy or sad face. Now there are hundreds of variations, including smileys that depict presidents, animals, and cartoon characters. Not everyone likes to read mail messages littered with smileys, but almost everyone finds them humorous. The smileys in this book have been collected by David Sanderson, whom the *Wall Street Journal* called the "Noah Webster of Smileys."

UNIX Power Tools

By Jerry Peek, Mike Loukides, Tim O'Reilly, et al.
1st Edition March 1993
1162 pages
(Bantam ISBN)
0-553-35402-7

Ideal for UNIX users who hunger for technical—yet accessible—information, *UNIX Power Tools* consists of tips, tricks, concepts, and freely-available software. Covers add-on utilities and how to take advantage of clever features in the most popular UNIX utilities. CD-ROM included.

Learning the Korn Shell

By Bill Rosenblatt
1st Edition June 1993
363 pages, ISBN 1-56592-054-6

This new Nutshell Handbook is a thorough introduction to the Korn shell, both as a user interface and as a programming language. Provides a clear explanation of the Korn shell's features, including *ksh* string operations, co-processes, signals and signal handling, and command-line interpretation. Also includes real-life programming examples and a Korn shell debugger *(kshdb)*.

Learning perl

By Randal L. Schwartz, 1st Edition November 1993 (est.)
220 pages (est.), ISBN 1-56592-042-2

Perl is rapidly becoming the "universal scripting language". Combining capabilities of the UNIX shell, the C programming language, *sed*, *awk*, and various other utilities, it has proved its use for tasks ranging from system administration to text processing and distributed computing. *Learning perl* is a step-by-step, hands-on tutorial designed to get you writing useful perl scripts as quickly as possible. In addition to countless code examples, there are numerous programming exercises, with full answers. For a comprehensive and detailed guide to programming with Perl, read O'Reilly's companion book *Programming perl*.

Programming perl

By Larry Wall & Randal L. Schwartz
1st Edition January 1991, 428 pages, ISBN 0-937175-64-1

Authoritative guide to the hottest new UNIX utility in years, co-authored by its creator. Perl is a language for easily manipulating text, files, and processes.

Learning GNU Emacs

By Deb Cameron & Bill Rosenblatt
1st Edition October 1991
442 pages, ISBN 0-937175-84-6

An introduction to the GNU Emacs editor, one of the most widely used and powerful editors available under UNIX. Provides a solid introduction to basic editing, a look at several important "editing modes" (special Emacs features for editing specific types of documents), and a brief introduction to customization and Emacs LISP programming. The book is aimed at new Emacs users, whether or not they are programmers.

sed & awk

By Dale Dougherty, 1st Edition November 1990
414 pages, ISBN 0-937175-59-5

For people who create and modify text files, *sed* and *awk* are power tools for editing. Most of the things that you can do with these programs can be done interactively with a text editor. However, using *sed* and *awk* can save many hours of repetitive work in achieving the same result.

MH & xmh: E-mail for Users & Programmers

By Jerry Peek, 2nd Edition September 1992
728 pages, ISBN 1-56592-027-9

Customize your e-mail environment to save time and make communicating more enjoyable. *MH & xmh: E-mail for Users & Programmers* explains how to use, customize, and program with the MH electronic mail commands available on virtually any UNIX system. The handbook also covers *xmh*, an X Window System client that runs MH programs. The new second edition has been updated for X Release 5 and MH 6.7.2. We've added a chapter on *mhook*, new sections explaining under-appreciated small commands and features, and more examples showing how to use MH to handle common situations.

Learning the vi Editor

By Linda Lamb, 5th Edition October 1990
192 pages, ISBN 0-937175-67-6

A complete guide to text editing with *vi*, the editor available on nearly every UNIX system. Early chapters cover the basics; later chapters explain more advanced editing tools, such as *ex* commands and global search and replacement.

UNIX in a Nutshell:
For System V & Solaris 2.0

By Daniel Gilly and the staff of O'Reilly & Associates
2nd Edition June 1992, 444 pages, ISBN 1-56592-001-5

You may have seen UNIX quick reference guides, but you've never seen anything like *UNIX in a Nutshell*. Not a scaled-down quick-reference of common commands, *UNIX in a Nutshell* is a complete reference containing all commands and options, along with generous descriptions and examples that put the commands in context. For all but the thorniest UNIX problems this one reference should be all the documentation you need. Covers System V Releases 3 and 4 and Solaris 2.0.

An alternate version of this quick-reference is available for Berkeley UNIX.
Berkeley Edition, December 1986
(latest update October 1990)
272 pages, ISBN 0-937175-20-X

Using UUCP and Usenet

By Grace Todino & Dale Dougherty
1st Edition December 1986 (latest update October 1991)
210 pages, ISBN 0-937175-10-2

Shows users how to communicate with both UNIX and non-UNIX systems using UUCP and *cu* or *tip*, and how to read news and post articles. This handbook assumes that UUCP is already running at your site.

System Administration

Managing UUCP and Usenet

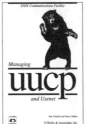

By Tim O'Reilly & Grace Todino
10th Edition January 1992
368 pages, ISBN 0-937175-93-5

For all its widespread use, UUCP is one of the most difficult UNIX utilities to master. This book is for system administrators who want to install and manage UUCP and Usenet software. "Don't even TRY to install UUCP without it!"—Usenet message 456@nitrex.UUCP

sendmail   NEW

By Bryan Costales, with Eric Allman & Neil Rickert
1st Edition October 1993 (est.)
600 pages (est.), ISBN 0-937175-056-2

This new Nutshell Handbook is far and away the most comprehensive book ever written on *sendmail*, a program that acts like a traffic cop in routing and delivering mail on UNIX-based networks. Although *sendmail* is the most widespread of all mail programs, it's also one of the last great uncharted territories—and most difficult utilities to learn—in UNIX system administration. The book covers both major versions of *sendmail*: the standard version available on most systems, and IDA *sendmail*, a version from Europe.

termcap & terminfo

By John Strang, Linda Mui & Tim O'Reilly
3rd Edition July 1992
270 pages, ISBN 0-937175-22-6

For UNIX system administrators and programmers. This handbook provides information on writing and debugging terminal descriptions, as well as terminal initialization, for the two UNIX terminal databases.

DNS and BIND

By Cricket Liu & Paul Albitz, 1st Edition October 1992
418 pages, ISBN 1-56592-010-4

DNS and BIND contains all you need to know about the Domain Name System (DNS) and BIND, its UNIX implementation. The Domain Name System (DNS) is the Internet's "phone book"; it's a database that tracks important information (in particular, names and addresses) for every computer on the Internet. If you're a system administrator, this book will show you how to set up and maintain the DNS software on your network.

Essential System Administration

By Æleen Frisch, 1st Edition October 1991
466 pages, ISBN 0-937175-80-3

Provides a compact, manageable introduction to the tasks faced by everyone responsible for a UNIX system. This guide is for those who use a stand-alone UNIX system, those who routinely provide administrative support for a larger shared system, or those who want an understanding of basic administrative functions. Covers all major versions of UNIX.

X Window System Administrator's Guide

By Linda Mui & Eric Pearce
1st Edition October 1992
372 pages, With CD-ROM: ISBN 1-56592-052-X
Without CD-ROM: ISBN 0-937175-83-8

This book is the first and only book devoted to the issues of system administration for X and X-based networks, written not just for UNIX system administrators but for anyone faced with the job of administering X (including those running X on stand-alone workstations). The *X Window System Administrator's Guide* is available either alone or packaged with the XCD. The CD provides X source code and binaries to complement the book's instructions for installing the software. It contains over 600 megabytes of X11 source code and binaries stored in ISO9660 and RockRidge formats. This will allow several types of UNIX workstations to mount the CD-ROM as a filesystem, browse through the source code and install pre-built software.

Practical UNIX Security

By Simson Garfinkel & Gene Spafford
1st Edition June 1991
512 pages, ISBN 0-937175-72-2

Tells system administrators how to make their UNIX system—either System V or BSD—as secure as it possibly can be without going to trusted system technology. The book describes UNIX concepts and how they enforce security, tells how to defend against and handle security breaches, and explains network security (including UUCP, NFS, Kerberos, and firewall machines) in detail.

Managing NFS and NIS

By Hal Stern
1st Edition June 1991
436 pages, ISBN 0-937175-75-7

Managing NFS and NIS is for system administrators who need to set up or manage a network filesystem installation. NFS (Network Filesystem) is probably running at any site that has two or more UNIX systems. NIS (Network Information System) is a distributed database used to manage a network of computers. The only practical book devoted entirely to these subjects, this guide is a must-have for anyone interested in UNIX networking.

TCP/IP Network Administration

By Craig Hunt
1st Edition July 1992
502 pages, ISBN 0-937175-82-X

A complete guide to setting up and running a TCP/IP network for practicing system administrators. Covers how to set up your network, how to configure important network applications including *send-mail*, and discusses troubleshooting and security. Covers BSD and System V TCP/IP implementations.

System Performance Tuning

By Mike Loukides, 1st Edition November 1990
336 pages, ISBN 0-937175-60-9

System Performance Tuning answers the fundamental question, "How can I get my computer to do more work without buying more hardware?" Some performance problems do require you to buy a bigger or faster computer, but many can be solved simply by making better use of the resources you already have.

Computer Security Basics

By Deborah Russell & G.T. Gangemi Sr.
1st Edition July 1991
464 pages, ISBN 0-937175-71-4

Provides a broad introduction to the many areas of computer security and a detailed description of current security standards. This handbook describes complicated concepts like trusted systems, encryption, and mandatory access control in simple terms, and contains a thorough, readable introduction to the "Orange Book."

UNIX Programming

Understanding Japanese Information Processing **NEW**

By Ken Lunde
1st Edition September 1993 (est.)
450 pages (est.), ISBN 1-56592-043-0

Understanding Japanese Information Processing provides detailed information on all aspects of handling Japanese text on computer systems. It tries to bring all of the relevant information together in a single book. It covers everything from the origins of modern-day Japanese to the latest information on specific emerging computer encoding standards. There are over 15 appendices which provide additional reference material, such as a code conversion table, character set tables, mapping tables, an extensive list of software sources, a glossary, and much more.

lex & yacc

By John Levine, Tony Mason & Doug Brown
2nd Edition October 1992
366 pages, ISBN 1-56592-000-7

Shows programmers how to use two UNIX utilities, *lex* and *yacc*, in program development. The second edition of *lex & yacc* contains completely revised tutorial sections for novice users and reference sections for advanced users. The new edition is twice the size of the original book, has an expanded index, and now covers Bison and Flex.

High Performance Computing **NEW**

By Kevin Dowd, 1st Edition June 1993
398 pages, ISBN 1-56592-032-5

High Performance Computing makes sense of the newest generation of workstations for application programmers and purchasing managers. It covers everything, from the basics of modern workstation architecture, to structuring benchmarks, to squeezing more performance out of critical applications. It also explains what a good compiler can do—and what you have to do yourself. The book closes with a look at the high-performance future: parallel computers and the more "garden variety" shared memory processors that are appearing on people's desktops.

ORACLE Performance Tuning **NEW**

By Peter Corrigan & Mark Gurry
1st Edition September 1993 (est.)
650 pages (est.), ISBN 1-56592-048-1

The ORACLE relational database management system is the most popular database system in use today. With more organizations downsizing and adopting client/server and distributed database approaches, system performance tuning has become vital. This book shows you the many things you can do to dramatically increase the performance of your existing ORACLE system. You may find that this book can save you the cost of a new machine; at the very least, it will save you a lot of headaches.

POSIX Programmer's Guide

By Donald Lewine, 1st Edition April 1991
640 pages, ISBN 0-937175-73-0

Most UNIX systems today are POSIX-compliant because the Federal government requires it for its purchases. However, given the manufacturer's documentation, it can be difficult to distinguish system-specific features from those features defined by POSIX. The *POSIX Programmer's Guide*, intended as an explanation of the POSIX standard and as a reference for the POSIX.1 programming library, helps you write more portable programs.

Understanding DCE

By Ward Rosenberry, David Kenney & Gerry Fisher
1st Edition October 1992
266 pages, ISBN 1-56592-005-8

A technical and conceptual overview of OSF's Distributed Computing Environment (DCE) for programmers and technical managers, marketing and sales people. Unlike many O'Reilly & Associates books, *Understanding DCE* has no hands-on programming elements. Instead, the book focuses on how DCE can be used to accomplish typical programming tasks and provides explanations to help the reader understand all the parts of DCE.

Guide to Writing DCE Applications

By John Shirley
1st Edition July 1992
282 pages, ISBN 1-56592-004-X

A hands-on programming guide to OSF's Distributed Computing Environment (DCE) for first-time DCE application programmers. This book is designed to help new DCE users make the transition from conventional, nondistributed applications programming to distributed DCE programming. Covers the IDL and ACF files, essential RPC calls, binding methods and the name service, server initialization, memory management, and selected advanced topics. Includes practical programming examples.

Power Programming with RPC

By John Bloomer
1st Edition February 1992
522 pages, ISBN 0-937175-77-3

RPC, or remote procedure calling, is the ability to distribute the execution of functions on remote computers. Written from a programmer's perspective, this book shows what you can do with RPC's, like Sun RPC, the de facto standard on UNIX systems. It covers related programming topics for Sun and other UNIX systems and teaches through examples.

Managing Projects with make

By Andrew Oram & Steve Talbott
2nd Edition October 1991
152 pages, ISBN 0-937175-90-0

make is one of UNIX's greatest contributions to software development, and this book is the clearest description of *make* ever written. This revised second edition includes guidelines on meeting the needs of large projects.

Software Portability with imake   NEW

By Paul DuBois
1st Edition July 1993
390 pages, 1-56592-055-4

imake is a utility that works with *make* to enable code to be complied and installed on different UNIX machines. This new Nutshell Handbook—the only book available on *imake*—is ideal for X and UNIX programmers who want their software to be portable. It includes a general explanation of *imake*, how to write and debug an *Imakefile*, and how to write configuration files. Several sample sets of configuration files are described and are available free over the Net.

UNIX for FORTRAN Programmers

By Mike Loukides
1st Edition August 1990
264 pages, ISBN 0-937175-51-X

This book provides the serious scientific programmer with an introduction to the UNIX operating system and its tools. The intent of the book is to minimize the UNIX entry barrier and to familiarize readers with the most important tools so they can be productive as quickly as possible. *UNIX for FORTRAN Programmers* shows readers how to do things they're interested in: not just how to use a tool such as *make* or *rcs*, but how to use it in program development and how it fits into the toolset as a whole. "An excellent book describing the features of the UNIX FORTRAN compiler *f77* and related software. This book is extremely well written." — American Mathematical Monthly, February 1991

Practical C Programming

By Steve Oualline
2nd Edition January 1993
396 pages, ISBN 1-56592-035-X

C programming is more than just getting the syntax right. Style and debugging also play a tremendous part in creating programs that run well. *Practical C Programming* teaches you not only the mechanics of programming, but also how to create programs that are easy to read, maintain, and debug. There are lots of introductory C books, but this is the Nutshell Handbook! In the second edition, programs now conform to ANSI C.

Checking C Programs with lint

By Ian F. Darwin
1st Edition October 1988
84 pages, ISBN 0-937175-30-7

The *lint* program is one of the best tools for finding portability problems and certain types of coding errors in C programs. This handbook introduces you to *lint*, guides you through running it on your programs, and helps you interpret *lint's* output.

Using C on the UNIX System

By Dave Curry
1st Edition January 1989
250 pages, ISBN 0-937175-23-4

Using C on the UNIX System provides a thorough introduction to the UNIX system call libraries. It is aimed at programmers who already know C but who want to take full advantage of the UNIX programming environment. If you want to learn how to work with the operating system and to write programs that can interact with directories, terminals, and networks at the lowest level you will find this book essential. It is impossible to write UNIX utilities of any sophistication without understanding the material in this book. "A gem of a book. The author's aim is to provide a guide to system programming, and he succeeds admirably. His balance is steady between System V and BSD-based systems, so readers come away knowing both." — SUN Expert, November 1989

Guide to OSF/1

By the staff of O'Reilly & Associates
1st Edition June 1991
304 pages, ISBN 0-937175-78-1

This technically competent introduction to OSF/1 is based on OSF technical seminars. In addition to its description of OSF/1, it includes the differences between OSF/1 and System V Release 4 and a look ahead at DCE.

Understanding and Using COFF

By Gintaras R. Gircys
1st Edition November 1988
196 pages, ISBN 0-937175-31-5

COFF—Common Object File Format—is the formal definition for the structure of machine code files in the UNIX System V environment. All machine-code files are COFF files. This handbook explains COFF data structure and its manipulation.

Career

Love Your Job!　　　　　　　**NEW**

By Dr. Paul Powers, with Deborah Russell
1st Edition August 1993
210 pages, ISBN 1-56592-036-8

Do you love your job? Too few people do. In fact, surveys show that 80 to 95 percent of Americans are dissatisfied with their jobs. Considering that most of us will work nearly 100,000 hours during our lifetimes (half the waking hours of our entire adult lives!), it's sad that our work doesn't bring us the rewards—both financial and emotional—that we deserve. *Love Your Job!* is an inspirational guide to loving your work. It consists of a series of one-page reflections, anecdotes, and exercises aimed at helping readers think more deeply about what they want out of their jobs. Each can be read individually (anyplace, anytime, whenever you need to lift your spirits), or the book can be read and treated as a whole. *Love Your Job!* informs you, inspires you, and challenges you, not only to look outside at the world of work, but also to look inside yourself at what work means to you.

How to Get Information about O'Reilly & Associates

The online O'Reilly Information Resource is a Gopher server that provides you with information on our books, how to download code examples, and how to order from us. There is also a UNIX bibliography you can use to get information on current books by subject area.

Connecting to the O'Reilly Information Resource

Gopher is an interactive tool that organizes the resources found on the Internet as a sequence of menus. If you don't know how Gopher works, see the chapter "Tunneling through the Internet: Gopher" in *The Whole Internet User's Guide and Catalog* by Ed Krol.

An easy way to use Gopher is to download a Gopher client, either the tty Gopher that uses curses or the Xgopher.

Once you have a local Gopher client, you can launch Gopher with:

```
gopher gopher.ora.com
```

To use the Xgopher client, enter:

```
xgopher -xrm "xgopher.rootServer:
gopher.ora.com"
```

If you have no client, log in on our machine via telnet and run Gopher from there, with:

```
telnet gopher.ora.com
login: gopher  (no password)
```

Another option is to use a World Wide Web browser, and enter the http address:

```
gopher://gopher.ora.com
```

Once the connection is made, you should see a root menu similar to this:

```
Internet Gopher Information Client v1.12
   Root gopher server: gopher.ora.com

->1. News Flash! -- New Products and
     Projects of ORA/.
  2.About O'Reilly & Associates.
  3.Book Descriptions and Information/
  4.Complete Listing of Book Titles.
  5.FTP Archive and E-Mail Information/
  6.Ordering Information/
  7.UNIX Bibliography/

Press ? for Help, q to Quit, u to go up a
menu                        Page: 1/1
```

From the root menu you can begin exploring the information that we have available. If you don't know much about O'Reilly & Associates, choose About O'Reilly & Associates from the menu. You'll see an article by Tim O'Reilly that gives an overview of who we are—and a little background on the books we publish.

Getting Information About Our Books

The Gopher server makes available online the same information that we provide in our print catalog, often in more detail.

Choose Complete Listing of Book Titles from the root menu to view a list of all our titles. This is a useful summary to have when you want to place an order.

To find out more about a particular book, choose Book Descriptions and Information; you will see the screen below:

```
Internet Gopher Information Client v1.12
    Book Descriptions and Information

->1.New Books and Editions/
  2.Computer Security/
  3.Distributed Computing Environment
    (DCE)/
  4.Non-Technical Books/
  5.System Administration/
  6.UNIX & C Programming/
  7.Using UNIX/
  8.X Resource/
  9.X Window System/
  10.CD-Rom Book Companions/
  11.Errata and Updates/
  12.Keyword Search on all Book
     Descriptions <?>
  13.Keyword Search on all Tables of
     Content <?>
```

All of our new books are listed in a single category. The rest of our books are grouped by subject. Select a subject to see a list of book titles in that category. When you select a specific book, you'll find a full description and table of contents.

For example, if you wanted to look at what books we had on administration, you would choose selection 5, System Administration, resulting in the following screen:

```
           System Administration

  1.DNS and BIND/
  2.Essential System Administration/
  3.Managing NFS and NIS/
  4.Managing UUCP and Usenet/
  5.sendmail/
  6.System Performance Tuning/
  7.TCP/IP Network Administration/
```

If you then choose `Essential System Administration`, you will be given the choice of looking at either the book description or the table of contents.

```
        Essential System Administration

->1.Book Description and Information.
  2.Book Table of Contents.
```

Selecting either of these options will display the contents of a file. Gopher then provides instructions for you to navigate elsewhere or quit the program.

Searching For the Book You Want

Gopher also allows you to locate book descriptions or tables of contents by using a word search. (We have compiled a full-text index WAIS.)

If you choose `Book Descriptions and Information` from the root menu, the last two selections on that menu allow you to do keyword searches.

Choose `Keyword Search on all Book Descriptions` and you will be prompted with:

`Index word(s) to search for:`

Once you enter a keyword, the server returns a list of the book descriptions that match the keyword. For example, if you enter the keyword DCE, you will see:

```
Keyword Search on all Book Descriptions:
                    DCE

-> 1.Understanding DCE.
   2.Guide to Writing DCE Applications.
   3.Distributed Applications Across DCE
     and Windows NT.
   4.DCE Administration Guide.
   5.Power Programming with RPC.
   6.Guide to OSF/1.
```

Choose one of these selections to view the book description.

Using the keyword search option can be a faster and less tedious way to locate a book than moving through a lot of menus.

You can also use a WAIS client to access the full-text index or book descriptions. The name of the database is

`O'Reilly_Book_Descriptions.src`

and you can find it in the WAIS directory of servers.

Note: We are always adding functions and listings to the O'Reilly Information Resource. By the time you read this article, the actual screens may very well have changed.

E-mail Accounts

E-mail ordering promises to be quick and easy, even faster than using our 800 number. Because we don't want you to send credit card information over a non-secure network, we ask that you set up an account with us in advance. To do so, either call us at 1-800-998-9938 or use the application provided in `Ordering Information` on the Gopher root menu. You will then be provided with a confidential account number.

Your account number allows us to retrieve your billing information when you place an order by e-mail, so you only need to send us your account number and what you want to order.

For your security, we use the credit card information and shipping address that we have on file. We also verify that the name of the person sending us the e-mail order matches the name on the account. If any of this information needs to change, we ask that you contact order@ora.com or call our Customer Service department.

Ordering by E-mail

Once you have an account with us, you can send us your orders by e-mail. Remember that you can use our online catalog to find out more about the books you want. Here's what we need when you send us an order:

1. Address your e-mail to: order@ora.com
2. Include in your message:
   - The title of each book you want to order (including ISBN number, if you know it)
   - The quantity of each book
   - Method of delivery: UPS Standard, Fed Ex Priority...
   - Your name and account number
   - Anything special you'd like to tell us about the order

When we receive your e-mail message, our Customer Service representative will verify your order before we ship it, and give you a total cost. If you would like to change your order after confirmation, or if there are ever any problems, please use the phone and give us a call—e-mail has its limitations.

This program is an experiment for us. We appreciate getting your feedback so we can continue improving our service.